BASIC MARKETING RESEARCH

7th edition

Gilbert A. Churchill, Jr.
University of Wisconsin – Madison

Tom J. Brown
Oklahoma State University

Tracy A. Suter
Oklahoma State University

SOUTH-WESTERN
CENGAGE Learning™

Australia • Brazil • Japan • Korea • Mexico • Singapore • Spain • United Kingdom • United States

Basic Marketing Research, Seventh Edition

Gilbert A. Churchill, Jr., Tom J. Brown, Tracy A. Suter

Vice President of Editorial, Business: Jack W. Calhoun

Editor-in-Chief: Melissa Acuña

Executive Editor: Mike Roche

Developmental Editor: Elizabeth Lowry

Marketing Communications Manager: Sarah Greber

Senior Marketing Coordinator: Sarah Rose

Executive Marketing Manager: Kimberly Kanakes

Content Project Manager: Diane Bowdler

Production Technology Analyst: Starratt Alexander

Media Editor: John Rich

Frontlist Buyer, Manufacturing: Miranda Klapper

Production Service: LEAP Publishing Services, Inc.

Copyeditor: Rachel Morris

Compositor: Knowledgeworks Global Limited

Sr. Art Director: Stacy Jenkins Shirley

Cover and Internal Design: Grannan Graphic Design

Cover Illustration: Grannan Graphic Design

Photography Manager: John Hill

Photo Researcher: Rose Alcorn

Text Permissions Acquisitions Manager: Bob Kauser

Exam*View*® is a registered trademark of eInstruction Corp. Windows is a registered trademark of the Microsoft Corporation used herein under license. Macintosh and Power Macintosh are registered trademarks of Apple Computer, Inc. used herein under license.

© 2008 Cengage Learning. All Rights Reserved.

Cengage Learning WebTutor™ is a trademark of Cengage Learning.

Library of Congress Control Number: 2009922268
Student Edition ISBN 13: 978-0-324-59934-3
Student Edition ISBN 10: 0-324-59934-X
Student Edition pkg ISBN 13: 978-1-4390-4139-0
Student Edition pkg ISBN 10: 1-4390-4139-3

South-Western Cengage Learning
5191 Natorp Boulevard
Mason, OH 45040
USA

Cengage Learning products are represented in Canada by Nelson Education, Ltd.

For your course and learning solutions, visit **www.cengage.com**
Purchase any of our products at your local college store or at our preferred online store **www.ichapters.com**

Printed in the United States of America
1 2 3 4 5 6 7 13 12 11 10 09

To our grandchildren
Kayla Marie
Johnathan Winston
Kelsey Lynn
Sean Jeffrey
Ethan Thomas
Averie Mae
(Gilbert A. Churchill, Jr.)

To *DiAnn, Drew, Taylor, Avery, and Brady*
(Tom J. Brown)

To *Kristen, Camille, and Emma—my joy, hope, and grace*
(Tracy A. Suter)

BRIEF CONTENTS

CONTENTS

Basic Marketing Research, 7th edition, provides an introductory look at marketing research for undergraduate students, managerially oriented graduate students, or anyone who wants an appreciation of the marketing research process. Our goal was to produce a readable book that overviews the information-gathering function from the perspective of both researchers who gather the information and marketing managers who use the information.

Marketing research can be a complex topic. It involves a number of questions that need to be answered and a number of decisions that need to be made in order to develop valid, usable information. *Basic Marketing Research* provides a framework for the choices and decisions that must be made. This is important, because decisions made in one stage of the research process have consequences for other stages. Both managers and marketing researchers need to appreciate the interactions among the parts of the research process so they can have confidence in a particular research result.

ORGANIZATION

Basic Marketing Research, 7th edition, is intended to serve both aspiring managers and aspiring researchers by breaking the research process down into the basic stages that must be followed when answering a research question. These stages are as follows:

1. Formulate the problem.

2. Determine the research design.

3. Determine the data collection method.

4. Design the data collection forms.

5. Design the sample and collect data.

6. Analyze and interpret the data.

7. Prepare the research report.

Organizing the material in this book around the stages in the research process has several significant benefits. First, it allows the subject of marketing research to be broken into very digestible bites. Second, it demonstrates and continually reinforces how the individual bits and pieces of research technique fit into a larger whole. Readers can easily see, for example, the relationship between problem definition and an appropriate research design, or between the type of research design and the different data collection forms that might be used. Third, the organization permits the instructor some flexibility with respect to the order in which the parts of the marketing research process may be covered.

KEY FEATURES

Basic Marketing Research has several special features to enhance the teaching and learning experience. The general approach used to discuss topics is to provide readers with the pros and cons of the various methods used to address a research problem and then to develop an appreciation of why these advantages and disadvantages arise. Our hope is that managers and researchers will be able to creatively apply and critically evaluate the procedures of marketing research. Other important features include the following.

Part Openers. Each part of the book is introduced by a short opening example from the business world that relates to the material presented in the chapters within that part. This is a new feature of this 7th edition. Examples include "CRM and the Mobile Sales Force" (Part 1), "NASCAR: Driving toward the Hispanic Market" (Part 5), and "Are iTunes Sales Collapsing?" (Part 7).

Learning Objectives. A set of learning objectives in each chapter highlights the most important topics covered in the chapter. The learning objectives are repeated in the margins in the chapter where the topics are discussed, and are then reinforced point by point in the chapter summary.

Manager's Focus. These short features provide insights into how the information in that particular chapter is relevant to marketing managers. The goal is to emphasize the role of marketing managers in the research process and to offer guidelines for achieving the most usable results. Some examples include how to determine if a focus group is useful (Chapter 5), understanding different levels of measurement (Chapter 12), and how nonsampling errors enter a study (Chapter 17).

Jon Austin, who teaches marketing research at Cedarville University and has a strong background working with clients in industry, provided the inspiration—and most of the writing—for the "Manager's Focus" entries.

Key Terms with Definitions. A running glossary appears throughout the text. Key terms in each chapter are boldfaced, and their definitions appear in the margin where the terms are discussed. A complete **Glossary** is also included at the end of the text.

Research Windows. The Research Windows provide a view of what is happening in the world of marketing research, describe what is happening at specific companies, and offer some specific how-to tips. They serve to engage the readers' interest in the chapter topic and to provide further depth of information. Some examples include "*Super Crunchers* Are Thinking-by-Numbers" (how some of today's companies use data mining, Chapter 2), "VISA: Using Strategy-Oriented Research to Select a New Brand Mark" (Visa, Chapter 4), "New-Vehicle Buyers and Psychographics" (J. D. Power and Associates and Mediamark Research Inc., Chapter 9), "The Naked Truth about Shower Heads" (Moen Inc., Chapter 9), and "Me, Doctor Mullet, and a Market-Research Mess" (professional marketer completes a survey, Chapter 10).

Technically Speaking Features. These are placed where appropriate to provide readers with additional detailed information about some of the technical topics presented, such as "Converting Continuous Measures into Categorical Measures for Use in Cross Tabulations" and "Adding Variables to an Analysis," both from Chapter 20.

Photos and Cartoons. Visual reinforcement serves to stimulate interest and to illustrate concepts. Throughout the book, photos provide readers with a look at how various aspects of the research process are conducted.

End-of-Chapter Reinforcements. Discussion questions, problems, and/or projects are found at the end of each chapter. These features provide the opportunity to apply the chapter topics to focused situations, thereby honing readers' analytical skills and developing firsthand knowledge of the strengths and weaknesses of various research techniques. New to the 7th edition are problems specific to the "real-world" example used throughout the data analysis chapters. These problems allow the student to probe a little deeper into an engaging research situation confronting a real company.

Cases. A number of business case analyses appear near the end of the book. These cases assist readers in developing their own evaluation and analytical skills. They are also useful in demonstrating the universal application of marketing research techniques. Marketing research methods can be used not only by manufacturers and distributors of products, as is commonly assumed, but also by the private and public sectors to address other issues. Cases include diverse entities and issues, and many represent real-life situations, though some of them have been disguised to protect the proprietary nature of the information.

Data. Data are provided for several of the cases to allow readers to perform analyses needed to answer case questions. We also provide the data file used for the analyses in the data analysis chapters. These data are available to adopters on the text Web site (see www.cengage.com/marketing/churchill).

CHANGES TO THE 7TH EDITION

This 7th edition of *Basic Marketing Research* brings with it several changes. The most important one is the addition of a new coauthor, Tracy Suter, who is a marketing professor at Oklahoma State University. He has taught marketing research to hundreds of undergraduate students, each of whom would vouch for his incredible skill at communicating the marketing research process. We are blessed that he agreed to lend these skills to this edition. Readers will find evidence of his work throughout the book and the accompanying supplemental materials.

The structure of the book remains the same as in previous editions; however, we have continued the process of streamlining the material where appropriate to make it more accessible and appealing to our readers. At the same time, we maintain the scholarly standards the book has created throughout previous editions. We have focused our efforts on the practical aspects of conducting marketing research—the general "how-to," including key issues and possible problems and their solutions. Through extensive examples, we demonstrate how the concepts and techniques presented are put into practice.

Existing examples, exhibits, figures, and so on, have been revised and updated throughout the book—and many new ones have been added. In addition, we'd like to highlight the following three key changes in the book and its supporting materials for the latest edition:

- The data analysis part of the book (Chapters 18–20) now features an ongoing example drawn from a real-life marketing research project for a fitness center. This allows students to participate in an experiential learning process with real data, warts and all, while seeing how answers to research problems can be obtained easily using the techniques taught in the book. In addition, the data are available to instructors for use in teaching the material or to make available to students for the analyses required to complete the associated end-of-chapter problems in Chapters 19 and 20.

- As noted earlier, we have developed new examples to open each of the seven parts of the book. These short examples, drawn from the business world, are designed to engage students' interest in the materials presented in the chapters of a particular part. For instance, the example for Part 7, which deals with communicating the results of a research project, concerns a marketing research report on iTunes' music sales that was badly misinterpreted by the media.

- The supplemental materials available to instructors have been retooled, from teaching tips to test bank questions to classroom-ready presentation slides. Our goal is to make the learning experience for students—and the teaching experience for instructors—as complete, efficient, and effective as possible. Instructors can completely customize the classroom presentation by including (or excluding) material from the presentation slides we provide or by using the presentation template and adding their own material.

COMPREHENSIVE INSTRUCTOR RESOURCES

It is important for any text to develop comprehensive supplemental materials to support instructors in their vital teaching function. Because of this pedagogical philosophy, the extensive learning package provided with *Basic Marketing Research* includes a

Test Bank, a computerized Test Bank (ExamView Testing Software), a comprehensive Instructor's Manual, PowerPoint presentation slides, data sets, and online marketing resources (available on the Web at www.cengage.com/marketing/churchill).

Instructor's Research CD-Rom (IRCD)

The Instructor's Resource CD-ROM (0-324-78544-5) includes everything instructors need for teaching the marketing research course. On the IRCD, you will find complete files for the Instructor's Manual (including solutions to the end-of-chapter material and cases, lecture outlines/teaching notes, and a class project), the Test Bank in Microsoft Word, the ExamView testing software, the PowerPoint presentation slides, and the data sets. In addition, all supplements are available on the book's Web site.

Web Resources

Web Resources at www.cengage.com/marketing/churchill provide the latest information in basic marketing research. The Instructor's Manual, Test Bank, PowerPoint slides, data sets, videos, and class project can also be found here. The site also features links to other research-related sites and access to Qualtrics.

Qualtrics

On the Instructor's side of the Churchill Web site, you will find access to the Qualtrics Research Suite. Qualtrics allows students to create and deploy surveys and provides data for analysis. Each new copy of *Basic Marketing Research* is packaged with a one-semester length access code that will provide them with access to the Qualtrics Web site at http://www.qualtrics.com/basic. Qualtrics is also a perfect solution for instructors who have students conduct a survey project as part of a term project.

WebTutor ToolBox

Preloaded with content and available free via PIN code when packaged with selected texts, WebTutor ToolBox pairs all the content of the text's rich Book Companion Web site with all the sophisticated course management functionality of a Blackboard or WebCT product. Instructors can assign materials (including online quizzes) and have the results flow automatically to their gradebooks.

ToolBox is ready to use as soon as users log on—or, instructors can customize its preloaded content by uploading images and other resources, adding Web links, or creating their own practice materials. Students only have access to student resources on the Web site. Instructors can enter a PIN code for access to password-protected instructor resources.

RESOURCES FOR STUDENTS

To promote learning and competency, it is also important to provide students with well-crafted resources. In addition to covering the latest information technology (described above), the 7th edition includes the following student resources:

Text Web Site

The dedicated text Web site, www.cengage.com/marketing/churchill, includes chapter quizzes that allow students to test and retest their knowledge of chapter concepts. Each chapter has a quiz to encourage retesting. In addition, the Web site features downloadable learning objectives, data files in Excel and SPSS, a glossary, the very best online marketing research resources available, and much more.

Qualtrics

Each new copy of *Basic Marketing Research* is packaged with a one-semester length access code that will provide them with access to the Qualtrics Web site at http://www.qualtrics.com/basic. Qualtrics is also a perfect solution for a survey project that your instructor may assign as part of your marketing research course.

ACKNOWLEDGMENTS

This book has benefited immensely from the many helpful comments received along the way from interested colleagues. We especially wish to acknowledge the following people who reviewed the manuscript for this or one of the earlier editions. While much of the credit for the strength of this book is theirs, the blame for any weaknesses is strictly ours. Thank you, one and all, for your most perceptive and helpful comments.

David Andrus	Vince Howe	Sangkil Moon
Joseph Ballenger	Glen Jarboe	Thomas Noordewier
Stephen Batory	Leonard Jensen	Astrid Proboll
Edward Bond	Deborah Roedder John	Pradeep A. Rau
Donald Bradley	Roland Jones	Debra Ringold
Terry Childers	Wesley H. Jones	Abhijit Roy
James S. Chow	Marcia Kasieta	Bruce Stern
C. Anthony Di Benedetto	Ram Kesavan	R. Sukumar
Elizabeth Ferrell	Richard H. Kolbe	John H. Summey
David Gourley	Elizabeth K. La Fleur	Michael Tsiros
Dhruv Grewal	Subhash Lonial	David Urban
Thomas S. Gruca	Daulatram Lund	Gerrit H. van Bruggen
D. S. Halfhill	Douglas Mac Lachlan	Joe Welch
James E. Hansz	Tridib Mazumdar	
Doug Hausknecht	Donald J. Messmer	

My colleagues at the University of Wisconsin have my thanks for the intellectual stimulation and psychological support they have always provided.

I also wish to thank Janet Christopher, who did most of the typing as well as many other things on earlier editions of this book. She was efficient in her efforts and patient with mine. I also wish to thank students Beth Bubon, Joseph Kuester, Jayashree Mahajan, Jennifer Markkanen, Kay Powers, and David Szymanski for their help with many of the tasks involved in completing this book. I would like to thank the editorial and production staff of Cengage Learning for their professional efforts on my behalf. I am also grateful to the Literary Executor of the late Sir Ronald A. Fisher, F.R.S; to Dr. Frank Yates, F.R.S; and to Longman Group UKLtd., for permission to reprint Table III from their book *Statistical Tables for Biological, Agricultural, and Medical Research* (6th Edition, 1974).

Finally, I once again owe a special debt of thanks to my wife, Helen, and our children. Their unyielding support and generous love not only made this book possible but also worth doing in the first place.

Gilbert A. Churchill, Jr.

Madison, Wisconsin

I want to thank my colleagues and students at Oklahoma State University, as well as my various research colleagues, for their continuing support and friendship. Many people have helped in various ways over the past several years, including Darrell Bartholomew, Tyler Bell, Janet Christopher, Steve Locy, John Phillips, and Amy Sallee; thank you! I especially want to thank Jon Austin, of Cedarville University, for his stellar contributions, in particular, the "Manager's Focus" features and several cases. Thanks also to the editorial and production staffs at Cengage Learning for their efforts on the book: Elizabeth Lowry, Susan Smart, Diane Bowdler, Mike Roche, Shanna Shelton, and Kimberly Kanakes.

To my fine colleague and even better friend, Tracy Suter: Welcome aboard! Your insights and wisdom are demonstrated throughout the book and supplemental materials. I am truly excited that you have joined us on this adventure. Thousands of students and instructors will benefit from your efforts.

As always, I am grateful to Gil Churchill for everything he's taught me over the years, and the opportunity to work with him in this endeavor. Watching him for a few years at the University of Wisconsin was a privilege, and I learned a great deal from his example. Thanks, Gil; I'll try to pass it on to my students.

Projects like this require lots of time and effort, and my family has graciously allowed me the space to work on it. My wife, DiAnn, has always been a lovely source of inspiration; DiAnn, you continue to thrill me. I also thank our children, Drew, Taylor, Avery, and Brady, for their love and for the wonderful way they help keep my attention where it really needs to be. Finally, I thank God for His blessings and the joy of knowing Him.

Tom J. Brown

Stillwater, Oklahoma

I want to begin by thanking Oklahoma State University alumnus Dean (it's a name not a title) Headley. It was Dean's Marketing Research course as an undergraduate student that provided the initial spark of interest in this topic for me. That spark carried through graduate school, the early stages of my career, and now an opportunity to join this fantastic book. While he will likely be very surprised to read this, for multiple reasons, it was that initial opportunity to conduct marketing research that motivated me to share that opportunity with others.

Second, I want to thank a variety of people in the academic community both at Oklahoma State and other institutions for their advice, friendship, guidance, and support over the years, including David Bednar, Scot Burton, O. C. Ferrell, Charles Futrell, Dan Goebel, David Hardesty, Tom Jensen, Steve Kopp, Dave Kurtz, James Lumpkin, John Mowen, Josh Wiener, and Alvin Williams. Your experience, insight, and willingness to listen have always been, and will always be, greatly valued. The same is true of Elizabeth Lowry, Mike Roche, and Susan Smart at Cengage Learning. Your patience and perseverance with the "new guy" was incredible.

Third, my friends, colleagues, and students from Oklahoma State—you are why I work and push so hard every day. Clearly, one of these colleagues is my dear friend, Tom Brown. My respect for you grows with each passing year. I cannot tell you how thankful I am that you and Gil Churchill asked me to join this book. I will do my best not to disappoint.

Finally, you don't have to know me very well or talk with me very long before you realize the joy in my life comes from a handful of critically important relationships. To my Lord and Savior, I am blessed beyond measure and thankful beyond belief. To my beautiful bride, Kristen, you are still the most giving person I know. There is no way I would have taken up this challenge without your support. To our terrific daughters, Camille and Emma, I am still in anxious anticipation of the future. I love, cherish, and appreciate all of you. You are the best!

Tracy A. Suter
Tulsa, Oklahoma

Gilbert A. Churchill, Jr., received his D.B.A. from Indiana University in 1966 and joined the University of Wisconsin faculty upon graduation. Professor Churchill was named Distinguished Marketing Educator by the American Marketing Association in 1986, the second individual so honored. This lifetime achievement award recognizes and honors a living marketing educator for distinguished service and outstanding contributions in the field of marketing education. Professor Churchill was also awarded the Academy of Marketing Science's lifetime achievement award in 1993 for his significant scholarly contributions. In 1996, he received the Paul D. Converse Award, which is given to the most influential marketing scholars, as judged by a national jury drawn from universities, businesses, and government. Also in 1996, the Marketing Research Group of the American Marketing Association established the Gilbert A. Churchill, Jr., lifetime achievement award, which is to be given each year to a person judged to have made significant lifetime contributions to marketing research. In 2002, he received the Charles Coolidge Parlin lifetime achievement award from the American Marketing Association for his substantial contributions to the ongoing advancement of marketing research practice.

Professor Churchill is a past recipient of the William O'Dell Award for his outstanding article appearing in the *Journal of Marketing Research* during the year. He has also been a finalist for the award five other times. He is a coauthor of the most and third-most influential articles of the past century in sales management as judged by a panel of experts in the field. He has served as consultant to a number of companies including Oscar Mayer, Western Publishing Company, and Parker Pen.

Professor Churchill's articles have appeared in such publications as the *Journal of Marketing Research, Journal of Marketing, Journal of Consumer Research, Journal of Retailing, Journal of Business Research, Decision Sciences, Technometrics,* and *Organizational Behavior and Human Performance,* among others.

In addition to *Basic Marketing Research,* Professor Churchill is the coauthor of several other books, including *Marketing Research: Methodological Foundations,* 9th ed. (Mason, OH: Southwestern, 2005); *Marketing: Creating Value for Customers,* 2nd ed. (Burr Ridge, IL: Irwin/McGraw-Hill, 1998); *Sales Force Management: Planning, Implementation, and Control,* 6th ed. (Burr Ridge, IL: Irwin/McGraw-Hill, 2000); and *Salesforce Performance* (Lexington, MA: Lexington Books, 1984). He is a former editor of the *Journal of Marketing Research* and has served on the editorial boards of the *Journal of Marketing Research* and *Journal of Marketing,* among others. Professor Churchill is a past recipient of the Lawrence J. Larson Excellence in Teaching Award.

Tom J. Brown received his Ph.D. from the University of Wisconsin-Madison in 1994. Prior to joining the marketing faculty at Oklahoma State University, he served on the faculty at Southern Methodist University. Professor Brown teaches marketing research and has supervised dozens of student research projects for industry clients ranging from not-for-profit service organizations to Fortune 500 companies.

Professor Brown is a past recipient of the Sheth Foundation Best Paper Award in the *Journal of the Academy of Marketing Science.* In addition, he received a Richard D. Irwin Foundation Doctoral Dissertation Fellowship while at the University of Wisconsin, the Kenneth D. and Leitner Greiner Teaching Award, and the Regents Distinguished Research Award, both at Oklahoma State University.

Professor Brown's articles have appeared in such publications as the *Journal of Marketing Research, Journal of Marketing, Journal of Consumer Research, Journal of the Academy of Marketing Science, Journal of Retailing, Cornell Hotel and Restaurant Administration Quarterly,* and *Journal of Service Research,* among others. His research interests include services marketing and corporate branding and reputation. He has served on the editorial review boards of the *Journal of the Academy of Marketing Science* and *Corporate Reputation Review* and is cofounder of the Corporate Associations/Identity Research Group. He is currently a member of the Academic Council of the American Marketing Association.

Tracy A. Suter received his Ph.D. from the University of Arkansas in 1997. Prior to joining the marketing faculty at Oklahoma State University, he served as a full-time faculty member at the University of Southern Mississippi. Professor Suter teaches a wide range of courses with emphasis on marketing research.

Professor Suter's research interests include public policy, the use of new technologies in marketing, and integrated marketing communications. He has published in journals such as the *Journal of Business Research*, *Journal of Public Policy & Marketing*, and *Journal of Retailing*. He also serves on two editorial review boards of academic journals and is a frequent reviewer for other journals and conferences.

Professor Suter has received numerous awards for both research and teaching activities including the University of Arkansas Award for Excellence in Teaching, the Sherwin-Williams Distinguished Teaching Competition Award given by the Society for Marketing Advances, and the President's Outstanding Faculty Award at Oklahoma State University. Tracy is frequently asked to speak to doctoral students about teaching excellence and transitioning to becoming university faculty members.

PART 1

INTRODUCTION TO MARKETING RESEARCH AND PROBLEM DEFINITION

CRM and the Mobile Sales Force

DASHBOARD GRAPHIC © SALESFORCE.COM, INC.;
SMART PHONE IMAGE © MANLEY620/ISTOCKPHOTO, INC.

What do 24 Hour Fitness, the Chicago Housing Authority, and Motorola have in common? Give up? Each of these companies and dozens more in various industries use a Web-based customer relationship management (CRM) tool known as Salesforce.com. If you have not heard of Salesforce.com, you might be familiar with mobile smartphone devices like the Blackberry or iPhone that run Salesforce applications.

Part 1 of the text introduces marketing research and the problem definition stage of a marketing research project. One of the central aspects of marketing research is the gathering of marketing intelligence. Intelligence gathering is a strength of Salesforce.com's business. Here's an example of how it works.

If a salesperson is out meeting with potential clients, it is often difficult to remember all the details of the meeting once the salesperson returns to her office. These details could be critical to the success of the sales team (e.g., total units orders, agreed-upon price points) or simply nice bits of insight to forge a bond between two individuals (e.g., favorite style of music, breed of a family 'pet). Either way, these details could be significant pieces of marketing intelligence. In this era of building relationships between clients and salespeople, details become increasingly important.

More portable than a laptop computer, smartphones can make a wireless connection to the Web and make the newly entered detail available instantly to other members of the sales team or managers at corporate headquarters. During the next time this same salesperson, or even another member of the sales team, visits this potential client, asking about these details could be a nice touch to enhance the conversation and aid in building the relationship between the representatives of the two companies.

With consistent access to new data, and with Salesforce.com's portability and customization, research truly is in motion. The most up-to-date marketing intelligence is available to anyone, anytime, anywhere. Marketing intelligence, whether collected in a mobile fashion or as a part of a larger project, is a vital component of quality marketing research.

Source: Salesforce.com

The Role of Marketing Research

Learning Objectives

1. Define marketing research.
2. Discuss different kinds of firms that conduct marketing research.
3. List some of the skills that are important for careers in marketing research.
4. List three reasons for studying marketing research.

Introduction

Marketing research is a much broader and more common activity than most people realize. Most of us have completed surveys on paper, online, or over the telephone, but there is much more to marketing research than just asking consumers how they think or feel about a product or an ad. This chapter introduces the broad role of marketing research within a company or an organization. In addition, we identify different types of companies that conduct marketing research and discuss three important reasons that business students should develop a working knowledge of marketing research.

In the 1940s, marketing began to be recognized and gradually accepted as an important unifying business perspective. For decades, the emergence of the profession was justified and based on what was called the "marketing concept." When organizations implement the marketing concept effectively, they are said to have a *market orientation*.[1] But what does it mean to be market oriented?

To answer this question, a team of marketing researchers interviewed many managers representing different business functional areas, levels of authority, and industries. The researchers asked a variety of open-ended questions designed to uncover different views of what market orientation is, how an organization develops this orientation, and the consequences of being market oriented. The researchers discovered that companies that followed a market orientation had three key characteristics:

- Employees at all levels of the organization *generate* market intelligence pertaining to current and future customer needs.

- They *share* that intelligence across departments.

- They *develop organizational strategy* based on this intelligence.

So, genuine marketing success hinges first on continually gathering appropriate information and second on effectively communicating that information throughout the organization. Both of these things can be accomplished systematically with a CRM system like the one discussed at the beginning of this section. That's one approach. Another approach is for a designated marketing researcher to actively collect information and share it with other departments within the company. This is what most people think of when the words "marketing research" are used. The third characteristic of marketing success is making and implementing sound decisions on the basis of that information. Managers in the various areas of marketing are responsible for directing this process and researchers are responsible for completing much of it. *Marketing managers and marketing researchers work together in close partnerships that are most successful when managers understand research processes and researchers understand management processes.* While managers are internal to the firm, researchers can be internal but usually represent external marketing research firms.

As you will learn while reading this book, many events can occur during the research process that affect the quality of the market information generated. *After projects are completed, managers must ultimately decide how to factor the market intelligence into their decision-making processes.* They need to have a sufficient understanding of research methods to assess the strengths and limitations of the information—the inability to do so can jeopardize managers' careers. Managers may rely too heavily on information of poor quality, or they may disregard information that is of higher quality than they realize. Making these types of mistakes can limit organizational success and may very well shorten the manager's tenure at the organization. As you work your way through this book, you will discover several key questions you should ask about research projects. You will need to find answers to those questions to help you determine whether to incorporate particular research information in your decision-making processes.

The primary purpose of this book, then, is to provide an understanding of marketing research methods to individuals who are planning a marketing-related career. For students pursuing a management-oriented career, the text is intended to develop a level of research competency that will enable them to interact intelligently with marketing research providers (internal or external) when requesting information, assessing proposed research projects, and evaluating and using information from completed research. For students pursuing a career in marketing research, the book is intended to lay a foundation on which more advanced marketing research courses will build.

THE PROBLEM: MARKETERS NEED INFORMATION

Learning Objective

1. Define marketing research.

Regardless of the types of products or services offered, all businesses or organizations share a common problem: They need information in order to target their audience appropriately. Consider the following examples.

Blue Smoke wanted to walk the talk and provide its northeastern customers authentic barbecue, and it did so by traveling to cities known for barbecue and digging in to the local cuisine to garner what makes true barbecue.

Example Microsoft has a team of 300 researchers who personally observe and videotape computer users at home and at work. The idea is to move beyond surveys and focus groups to get personal-level research in the context of the product's use. Recently, 50 families in seven countries allowed Microsoft into their homes to test the company's next operating system. The families tested seven software versions and found more than 1,000 problems, about 800 of which were not found by company testers. This level of detailed access and personal conversation allowed the company to eliminate many software bugs before the product was available for purchase.

Example Iams, a Procter & Gamble brand that makes pet food, noticed that some consumers were supplementing dry pet food with some form of treat, particularly to get older pets with dental problems to eat it. Iams then conducted quantitative research to determine if this practice was common among consumers. The research indicated that 40% of pet owners use such methods. In response, Iams launched Savory Sauce, a more convenient and nutritious alternative to table scraps. The product has been so successful that Iams has since extended this line to include eight varieties, including sauces for use with puppies.

Example When Danny Meyer, a successful New York City restaurant owner, decided to open a new barbecue restaurant in Manhattan, he and his team traveled across the country to cities like Memphis, Kansas City, and Austin to gather information about how to prepare *real* barbecue. After numerous stops at barbecue joints to sample the local fare, Meyer and his team took what they learned (along with a few extra pounds) back to Manhattan and opened the Blue Smoke, to great acclaim.

Example **Example** ING Direct became the largest Internet-based bank with more than 17 million customers worldwide by using marketing research to better understand its target market: comfortable—but not wealthy—time-pressed city dwellers ages 30 to 50, often with children, who use the Internet to buy products and services. The company routinely performs statistical analyses that link customer profitability to key variables such as account balances and recent activity to develop a profile of its ideal target customer.

Example The Girl Scouts use research to better understand young girls and their interests and concerns. The Girl Scout Research Institute was founded to study the "healthy development of girls." A recent study noted that girls aspire to a different kind of leadership than they currently see exhibited by women in leadership positions. The study, entitled "Change It Up! What Girls Say About Redefining Leadership," is the basis for the Girl Scout Leadership Experience program. An important finding from the study was that 68% of survey respondents said they want to be leaders who stand up for their beliefs and values.

Example When Kroger opens new Signature food stores, the shelf selection for each store is based largely on information obtained from surveys sent to residents in surrounding neighborhoods before the new store is opened. A new store opened in the

Dallas area with 860 varieties of produce, many of which were requested by the nearby Asian-American population. By paying attention to such details, the chain hopes to be able to compete effectively against price-oriented competitors like Walmart.[2]

As these examples illustrate, different companies need different kinds of information, and the information they need can be gathered in many different ways. Salespeople use the results of marketing research studies to sell their products better. Politicians use marketing research in the form of polling data to plan campaign strategies. Even churches use marketing research to determine when to hold services! The point is that marketing research is an essential activity that can take many forms, but its basic function is to gather information needed to help managers make better decisions.

Girl Scouts' aspiration to a different kind of leadership than they currently see exhibited by women is exemplified by their participation in the "Pervasive Power Charge 10-Mile and 1-Mile Fun Run."

IMAGE COURTESY PRNEWSFOTO

The task of marketing is to create exchanges with customers that satisfy the needs of both the customer and the marketer. In their attempts to create satisfying exchanges with customers, marketing managers generally focus their efforts on the four P's—namely, the *product* or service, its *price*, its *placement* or the channels in which it is distributed, and its *promotion* or communications mix. The goal is to develop a marketing strategy that combines the marketing mix elements in such a way that they complement each other and positively influence customers' value perceptions and behaviors. This task would be much simpler if all the elements that affect customers' perceptions of value were under the manager's control and if customer reaction to any contemplated change could be predicted.

Many factors in the marketing environment, however, affect the success of the marketing effort. These factors include other social actors (competitors, suppliers, governmental agencies, customers themselves, and so on) and societal trends in the external environment (economic, political and legal, social, natural, technological, and competitive trends; see Figure 1.1). Unfortunately for managers, most of these things are beyond their direct control. As a result, the marketing manager has an urgent need for information—and marketing research is traditionally responsible for providing it. Marketing research is the firm's formal communication link with the environment. Through marketing research, the firm gathers and interprets data from the environment for use in developing, implementing, and monitoring the firm's marketing plans.

The formal definition of **marketing research** emphasizes its information-linkage role.

> Marketing research is the function that links the consumer, customer, and public to the marketer through information—information used to identify and define marketing opportunities and problems; generate, refine, and evaluate marketing actions; monitor marketing performance; and improve understanding of marketing as a process.[3]

Marketing research is involved with all phases of the information-management process, including (1) the specification of what information is needed, (2) the

marketing research
The function that links the consumer to the marketer through information—information used to identify and define marketing problems; generate, refine, and evaluate marketing actions; monitor marketing performance; and improve understanding of marketing as a process.

FIGURE 1.1   The Environments Affecting Marketing

collection and analysis of the information, and (3) the interpretation of that information with respect to the objectives that motivated the study in the first place.

Another way of looking at the function of marketing research is to consider how management uses it. Some marketing research is used for planning, some for problem solving, and some for control. When used for planning, it deals largely with determining which marketing opportunities are viable and which are not promising for the firm. Also, when viable opportunities are uncovered, marketing research provides estimates of their size and scope, so that marketing management can better assess the resources needed to develop them. Problem-solving marketing research focuses on the short- or long-term decisions that the firm must make with respect to the elements of the marketing mix. Control-oriented marketing research helps management isolate trouble spots and keep abreast of current operations. The kinds of questions marketing research can address with regard to planning, problem solving, and control decisions are listed in Exhibit 1.1. The relationship between each of these questions and a marketing manager's area of responsibility is easy to see.

Solid marketing research is becoming increasingly important as the world moves to a global economy. A marketing mix that works in one environment does not necessarily work in another, as the examples in Research Window 1.1 (on page 8) illustrate. Firms operating in the international arena can use marketing research to get a perspective on what it is like to do business in specific countries. For example, marketing research helped McDonald's adjust its positioning as attitudes toward the company changed in the United Kingdom. When the company first crossed the Atlantic in the mid-1970s, customers were drawn in by its American origins and the novelty of fast food. Reflecting this appeal, McDonald's first U.K. ad slogan announced, "There's a difference at McDonald's you'll enjoy."

The fast-food giant used consumer research to keep tabs on opinions as the market matured. Fifteen years after McDonald's began serving the U.K. market, consumers were describing McDonald's as inflexible and arrogant—a negative take on the efficiency that consumers associated with the company's American heritage.

Exhibit 1.1   **Kinds of Questions Marketing Research Can Help Answer**

I. Planning
  A. What kinds of people buy our products? Where do they live? How much do they earn? How many of them are there?
  B. Are the markets for our products increasing or decreasing? Are there promising markets that we have not yet reached?
  C. Are the channels of distribution for our products changing? Are new types of marketing institutions likely to evolve?

II. Problem Solving
  A. Product
    1. Which of various product designs is likely to be the most successful?
    2. What kind of packaging should we use?
  B. Price
    1. What price should we charge for our products?
    2. As production costs decline, should we lower our prices or try to develop higher-quality products?
  C. Place
    1. Where, and by whom, should our products be sold?
    2. What kinds of incentives should we offer the trade to push our products?
  D. Promotion
    1. How much should we spend on promotion? How should it be allocated to products and to geographic areas?
    2. What combination of media—newspapers, radio, television, magazines, the Internet—should we use?

III. Control
  A. What is our market share overall? In each geographic area? By each customer type?
  B. Are customers satisfied with our products? How is our record for service? Are there many returns?
  C. How does the public perceive our company? What is our reputation with the trade?

McDonald's therefore adjusted its ad campaigns to use softer messages depicting McDonald's at the center of U.K. family life. Despite more recent concerns about the nutritional value of its meals, more than 2.5 million people in the United Kingdom visit the company's restaurants each day.[4]

WHO DOES MARKETING RESEARCH?

Learning Objective

2. Discuss different kinds of firms that conduct marketing research.

Although individuals and organizations have practiced marketing research for centuries—the need for information has always existed—the formal practice of marketing research can be traced to the nineteenth century.

More by accident than foresight, N. W. Ayer & Son applied marketing research to marketing and advertising problems. In 1879, in attempting to fit a proposed advertising schedule to the needs of the Nichols-Shepard Company, manufacturers of agricultural machinery, the agency wired state officials and publishers throughout the country requesting information on expected grain production. As a result, the agency was able to construct a crude but formal market survey by states and counties. This attempt to construct a market survey is probably the first real instance of marketing research in the United States.[5]

research window 1.1

International Missteps Caused by Environmental Differences

Example Unilever was forced to withdraw temporarily from one of its foreign markets when it learned the hard way that the French were not interested in frozen foods.

Example An American manufacturer of cornflakes tried to introduce its product in Japan but failed miserably. Because the Japanese were not interested in the general concept of breakfast cereals, how could the manufacturer expect them to purchase cornflakes?

Example When Coca-Cola re-entered India's soft drink market in 1993, the company struck a deal with Parle, the market leader at the time, to take over the company's soft drink brands. This angered many Indian consumers who viewed the deal as a destruction of the local brands. Consumers were even more upset when Coca-Cola began phasing out Thums Up, which was Parle's leading cola brand before the acquisition. Because the Coca-Cola soft drink did not catch on as quickly as the company had hoped, it was forced to begin promoting Thums Up again. Even though Thums Up went on to become the largest carbonated soft drink in India, the initial missteps caused Coca-Cola to lose $347 million over the first 10 years in the country.

Example A print advertisement available in northern Africa for men's cologne pictured a man and his dog in a rural American setting. The ad was well accepted in the United States but not in Africa. The advertiser simply assumed that the "man's best friend" depiction of dogs in America was true worldwide. However, Muslims usually consider dogs to be either signs of bad luck or symbols of uncleanliness. Neither interpretation enhances the perception of cologne.

Example CPC International met some resistance when it first tried to sell its Knorr soups in the United States. The company had test-marketed the product by serving passersby a small portion of its already prepared warm soup. After the taste test, the individuals were questioned about buying the product. The research revealed U.S. interest, but sales were very low once the packages were placed on grocery store shelves. Further investigation uncovered that the market tests had not taken into account the American tendency to avoid dry soups. During the testing, those individuals interviewed were unaware that they were tasting a dried soup. Finding the taste quite acceptable, the interviewees indicated they would be willing to buy the product. Had they known that the soup was sold in a dry form and that the preparation required 15 to 20 minutes of occasional stirring, they would have lost interest in the product. In this case, the soup's method of preparation was extremely important to the consumer, and the company's failure to test for this unique product difference resulted in an unpredicted sluggish market.

Example Warner encountered difficulties when it tried to sell cinnamon-flavored Freshen-Up gum in Chile. Because the gum's taste was unacceptable there, the product fared poorly in the marketplace. Coca-Cola also had little success in marketing a product in Chile. When the company attempted to introduce a new grape-flavored drink, it soon discovered that the Chileans were not interested. Apparently, the Chileans prefer wine as their grape drink.

Example Chase and Sanborn met resistance when it tried to introduce its instant coffee in France. In the French home, the consumption of coffee plays a more significant role than in the English home. Because the preparation of "real" coffee is a ritual in the life of the French consumer, he or she will generally reject instant coffee because of its impromptu characteristics.

Source: "India Company: Coca-Cola's Long Road to Profit," *EIU ViewsWire*, March 12, 2003 and David A. Ricks, *Blunders in International Business*, 4th edition (Cambridge, Mass.: Blackwell Publishers, 2006).

The Curtis Publishing Company is generally given credit for forming the first formal marketing research department back in 1911; The Nielsen Company (formerly ACNielsen), still a world leader in the marketing research industry, began operation in 1923. The notion of marketing research as an important business function really took off around the end of World War II as competition for customers heightened.

MANAGER'S FOCUS

No matter what type of organization completes a marketing research project—internal researchers of a product/service producer or external researchers at an advertising agency or a research company—they are always seeking to meet the information needs of marketing managers. The quality of their work will have a direct effect on the integrity of the marketing intelligence available to managers. Managers sometimes fail to realize how they play roles that significantly influence the quality of the work researchers perform on their behalf.

As a future marketing manager, how will your behavior affect the quality of marketing researchers' work? Think carefully about that question for a moment. What could you do for researchers to enhance their efforts? What behaviors on your part might limit or hinder the performance of quality marketing research?

One key role is informational in nature. To serve your needs well, researchers will need to fully understand your marketing situation. Put simply, they need to know what you already know. Who are your target customers? What is your marketing strategy? What are your competitors doing? What has been learned through prior marketing research studies or other market intelligence-gathering activities? What decisions are being considered now? What issues are unclear to you now? Under what political constraints are you operating within your organization? What failures and successes have occurred in the past?

Managers are often reluctant to admit what they don't know or how their efforts have failed in the past, but disclosure of these various types of information can have a profound impact on researchers' abilities to tailor their work to address managers' unique needs. In other words, successful marketing research depends on a series of information exchanges between researchers and managers (many other such exchanges will be discussed in subsequent sections). For this to occur, managers and researchers must develop relationships based on trust and mutual respect. By developing expertise in marketing research in this course, you will be better prepared to develop and nurture these essential relationships in your future career as a manager.

The three major categories of firms that conduct marketing research are (1) the producers of products and services, (2) advertising agencies, and (3) marketing research companies.

Producers of Products and Services

Marketing research really began to grow when firms found they could no longer sell all they could produce but instead had to gauge market needs and produce accordingly. Marketing research was called on to estimate these needs. As consumers began to have more choices in the marketplace, marketing began to assume a more dominant role and production a less important one. The marketing concept emerged, and along with it a reorganization of the marketing effort. Many marketing research departments were born in these reorganizations.

Although the growth in the number of new marketing research departments has slowed recently, most large firms (and many smaller ones, too) have one or more people assigned specifically to the marketing research activity. Marketing research departments are common among industrial and consumer manufacturing companies. These companies conduct research designed to develop and market the products they manufacture. For example, producers such as Goodyear, Pillsbury, Kraft, and Oscar Meyer either have or have had their own marketing research departments.

Marketing research departments also exist in other types of companies. Publishers and broadcasters, for example, do a good deal of research. They attempt to measure the size of the market reached by their message and construct a demographic profile

© JOHN S. STEWART/ASSOCIATED PRESS

Marketing researchers at Silver Dollar City, Inc., use marketing research to profile guests, measure satisfaction, analyze markets, and much more for their entertainment properties around the United States.

of this audience. These data are then used to sell advertising space or time. Large retailers such as Sears and JC Penney have operated marketing research departments to gather information about consumer preferences, store image, and so forth. Financial institutions such as banks and brokerage houses do research involving forecasting, measurement of market potentials, determination of market characteristics, market share analyses, sales analyses, location analyses, and product-mix studies. For example, one major home mortgage lender wanted to understand how to best serve first-time home buyers. The research team conducted one-on-one interviews followed by concept tests that allowed the company to better understand the needs of these buyers.

Many companies use marketing research to regularly track customer satisfaction and customer usage patterns. For example, the marketing research department at Silver Dollar City, a popular theme park located in Branson, Missouri, routinely surveys guests to determine their demographics, behavior, and levels of satisfaction. Researchers found that visitors from over 301 miles away (outer market) took three times longer to plan their trips to Silver Dollar City than did guests who lived less than 100 miles away (core market). Based on these findings, the marketing department altered its promotions strategy and started advertising in outer markets several weeks before beginning those same ads in the core market. This resulted in more efficient advertising purchasing, and the message was presented to those visitors at the time they were making plans to visit. Research Window 1.2 presents an overview of the various kinds of research conducted or used by Silver Dollar City.

Advertising Agencies

As you might imagine, advertising agencies often conduct research designed to help create effective advertising campaigns. This may involve testing alternative approaches to the wording or art used in the ad or investigating the effectiveness of various celebrity spokespersons. Many agencies also do marketing research for their clients, however, to determine the market potential of a proposed new product or the client's market share.

Ad agencies sometimes do research to better understand consumers, their interests, and behaviors in order to serve their corporate clients. For instance, Dentsu Inc., one of the world's largest agencies, in conjunction with Keio University, is conducting research on the virtual economic mechanisms, consumer behavior, and legal and ethical issues in the Second Life 3-D virtual community. Residents of Second Life create and build homes, vehicles, stores, and other important aspects of life in a virtual space. Dentsu and Keio want to jointly analyze the use of the Linden Dollar, the virtual currency of Second Life.[6]

A few years ago, McCann-Erickson WorldGroup conducted extensive research on attitudes about soccer, collecting data from men and women in 39 countries around the world. U.S. respondents indicated that they did not follow soccer as closely as other sports, although the majority knew that the United States was competing in the World Cup and about half knew where the games were being held that year. Non-Hispanic respondents who were interested in the games seemed to

research window 1.2

Marketing Research at Silver Dollar City

Silver Dollar City (SDC), along with the other entertainment properties owned or managed by Herschend Family Entertainment Corporation, utilizes one of the most comprehensive databases of primary and secondary entertainment-related research in the entertainment industry. This library of guest, theme park, tourism, and consumer information is largely the foundation of the company's long-term strategic plans and marketing strategies.

Guest Research, Profiling, and Analysis SDC has an ongoing (in-house) guest survey program designed to gather customer demographics, geographic origin, behavior, and level of satisfaction. These surveys are conducted in person, by telephone, or over the Internet.

SDC processes, analyzes, and produces reports on the resulting database of guest information seasonally and by customer segment. In addition to measuring each customer segment's size and attendance trends, the company also uses this information to analyze the impact of capital additions and the economic impact by customer segment.

Market Area Research, Profiling, and Analysis SDC also regularly conducts research designed to provide insights about the geographic area in which it is located. Among other things, such research identifies destination trends as well as a better understanding of the type of tourists who are visiting the area but *not* visiting SDC. The information gathered includes general tourist demographic profiles, visitor counts, resident market size and demographics, market performance, and census data.

Research and Analysis Designed to Address a Specific Issue In addition to these regularly scheduled research activities, SDC frequently invests in research and analysis designed to answer specific marketing or management questions. For example, these efforts have produced reports with titles such as "Estimates of Market Potential," "How Area Visitors Use Their Leisure Time at Home and in Our Markets," "Feasibility Studies," "Analysis of Synergy between Branson Properties," and "Guest Psychographic Profiles Assessed Using PRIZM."

The result of such studies lead to the introduction of The Grand Exposition section of the theme park. According to Brad Thomas, SDC general manager, "In conducting extensive research with moms, they told us they want more rides they can ride together as a family. So instead of adding one new major ride, we decided to add 10 new family rides that bring the park's ride capacity up more than 50 percent."

Competitive Research Competitive research is another avenue of research for SDC. The company monitors both local competition and competitive destinations and has developed a large database of top-50 theme park information. This database includes theme park attendance history, pricing history, history of capital additions and estimated capital investments, overnight domestic leisure visitors to each park's home market, resident population, resident income, resident age, year the park opened, size of the park, number of coasters installed, and other variables. The information is used to estimate the influence of these types of factors on park attendance. For example, SDC might want to determine the relationship between length of roller coaster, or number of roller coasters at a park, or overall size of the park on theme park attendance. Using such information can help SDC make better decisions about the design and layout of its own park.

Other Research and Statistical Analysis Other research and analysis activities that are frequently used include lifetime value analysis, season pass holder decay probability/retention studies, commonality analysis, and regression forecasting models. Such statistical analyses help in the understanding of the potential value (or lack thereof) of specific customer segments or market programs being considered.

Tracking Consumer and Leisure Trends

SDC closely monitors trends from a variety of industries in an effort to evolve with their customers' changing needs, wants, and behaviors. The company tracks such things as demographic and behavioral trends of guests, guests' ages, party composition, last visit, incomes, and attendance at other Herschend Family Entertainment properties. Such changes influence the creation of future strategic decisions and marketing plans.

Consumer trends are also of great concern. SDC tracks changes in social, demographic, technological, economic, and commerce trends by reviewing books, periodicals, and syndicated research studies and by attending conferences on these topics.

The company also pays attention to trends in the theme park industry. In addition to attendance, pricing, and capital trends mentioned above, SDC researches stock prices of publicly traded theme parks, consolidation

(Continued)

in the industry, new theme park queue line technologies being introduced, new types of ride technologies, and marketing promotions.

SDC follows tourism trends by gathering secondary research from the Travel Industry Association's Outlook Forum, *Yankelovich National Leisure Monitor*, Plog's *American Traveler Survey*, and other tourism-related resources.

These are just a few of the categories of trends being followed by the SDC research department. Literally hundreds of resources are evaluated and analyzed every year for the purpose of determining how such trends might impact the company.

Source: Adapted from "Corporate Research Activity Brief," Silver Dollar City, Inc., (undated) and "The Grand Exposition," Silver Dollar City's biggest expansion ever for kids, Branson Tourism Center, February 24, 2006.

focus more on the athletic ability of the participants; Hispanic respondents were also interested in athletic prowess but indicated an important social dimension as well—the enjoyment of watching the games with family and friends. Overall, U.S. respondents believed the World Cup to be much less commercial than U.S. sporting events such as the Super Bowl. The group best able to correctly identify World Cup sponsors included younger (mostly in their teens) Hispanic consumers.[7] Basic research such as that conducted by Dentsu and McCann-Erickson and other agencies is important to the process of carrying out effective advertising campaigns for clients.

Marketing Research Companies

Many companies specialize in conducting marketing research. In the United States, marketing research is an $8.6 billion industry—that's almost $30 spent on research each year for every man, woman, and child in the United States.[8] Worldwide, total revenues for the marketing research industry exceed $20 billion.[9] (And don't forget that these numbers don't reflect the research done by producers and advertising agencies.)

Exhibit 1.2 **The World's 10 Largest Marketing Research Firms**

Rank/Organization	Parent Country	Worldwide Research Revenue (U.S. $, in millions)
1. The Nielsen Co.	U.S.	$4,220.0
2. IMS Health Inc.	U.S.	2,192.6
3. Taylor Nelson Sofres plc	U.K.	2,137.2
4. GfK AG	Germany	1,593.2
5. Kantar Group	U.K.	1,551.4
6. Ipsos Group SA	France	1,270.3
7. Synovate	U.K.	867.0
8. IRI	U.S.	702.0
9. Westat Inc.	U.S.	467.8
10. Arbitron Inc.	U.S.	352.1

Source: Developed from information in "2008 Honomichl Global Top 25," *Marketing News* (August 15, 2008), pp. H1–H50. This report describes the services provided by the 25 largest global research organizations.

Although most specialized marketing research firms are small, a few are sizable enterprises. Exhibit 1.2 shows the names, home countries, and revenues of the 10 largest marketing research firms in the world. Some firms provide syndicated research; they collect certain information on a regular basis, which they then sell to interested clients. The syndicated services include such operations as The Nielsen Company, which provides product-movement data for grocery stores and drugstores, and Arbitron, which measures U.S. radio audiences. Such services are distinguished by the fact that their research is not custom designed except in the limited sense that the firm will perform special analyses for a client from the data it regularly collects. Other firms, though, specialize in custom-designed research. Some of these provide only a field service; they collect data and return the data-collection instruments directly to the research sponsor. Some are limited-service firms, which not only collect the data but also analyze them for the client. And some are full-service research suppliers, which help the client in the design of the research as well as in collecting and analyzing data. For example, GfK AG USA provides full-service customized research services for numerous *Fortune* 500 clients. GfK can conduct large-scale qualitative or quantitative studies from start to finish, utilizing a range of traditional techniques as well as online data collection.

Other organizations that provide or conduct marketing research include government agencies, trade associations, and universities. Government agencies provide much marketing information in the form of published statistics. In fact, the federal government is the largest producer of marketing facts through its various censuses and other publications. Trade associations often collect and share data gathered from members. Much university-sponsored research of interest to marketers is produced by the marketing faculty or by the bureaus of business research found in many schools of business. Faculty research is often reported in marketing journals, while research bureaus often publish monographs on various topics of interest.

JOB OPPORTUNITIES IN MARKETING RESEARCH

Learning Objective

3. List some of the skills that are important for careers in marketing research.

Employment opportunities for those interested in a career in marketing research continue to be good. Employment is expected to grow faster than the average for all occupations through the year 2012. Why is this? The demand for information continues to grow—and so will the demand for individuals who can collect, analyze, and interpret this information. In general, however, opportunities will be stronger for those with graduate degrees than for those with only undergraduate degrees. Competition is usually stiff for the relatively limited number of entry-level positions available for which those without graduate degrees will qualify.[10]

Types of Jobs in Marketing Research

There are many different kinds of tasks that a marketing researcher—whether internal or external to the firm—might perform. Depending on whether one works for a producer, an advertising agency, a marketing research firm, or some other type of organization, the type and scope of jobs available can vary greatly. In smaller companies, researchers are likely to be exposed to a greater variety of tasks, simply out of necessity. In larger firms, the work may tend to be more specialized for each employee. The responsibilities of a marketing researcher could range from simple analyses of questionnaire responses to the management of a large research department. Research Window 1.3 lists some common job titles and the functions typically performed by persons in these positions.

research window 1.3

Marketing Research Job Titles and Responsibilities

1. **Market Research Director** This is the senior position in research. The director is responsible for directing and overseeing the entire research program of the company. Accepts assignments from superiors, from clients, or may, on own initiative, develop and propose research undertakings to company executives. Employs personnel and executes general supervision of research department. Presents research findings to clients or to company executives.

2. **Marketing Research Manager** This position directs and coordinates activities concerned with market research. The manager spends time planning and formulating aspects of research and developing proposals, such as objective or purpose of the project, applications that can be utilized from findings, costs of project, and equipment and manpower requirements. They may develop and implement methods and procedures for monitoring projects, such as preparation of records of expenditures and research findings, progress reports, and staff conferences in order to inform management of current status of each project.

3. **Statistician/Data Processing Specialist** Duties are usually those of an expert consultant on theory and applications of statistical technique to specific research problems. Usually responsible for experimental design and data processing.

4. **Senior Analyst** Participates with superiors in initial planning of research projects and directs execution of projects assigned. Operates with minimum supervision. Prepares or works with analysts in preparing questionnaires. Selects research techniques, makes analyses, and writes final report. Budgetary control over projects and primary responsibility for meeting time schedules rests with the senior analyst.

5. **Analyst** The analyst usually handles the bulk of the work required for execution of research projects. Often works under senior analyst's supervision. The analyst assists in questionnaire preparation, pretests them, and makes preliminary analyses of results. Most of the library research or work with company data is handled by the analyst.

6. **Junior Analyst** Working under rather close supervision, junior analysts handle routine assignments. Editing and coding of questionnaires, statistical calculations above the clerical level, and simpler forms of library research are among the duties. A large portion of the junior analyst's time is spent on tasks assigned by superiors.

7. **Field Work Director** Usually only larger departments have a field work director, who hires, trains, and supervises field interviewers.

8. **Full-Time Interviewer** Interviewers conduct personal or telephone interviews and work under direct supervision of the field work director.

As shown in these job descriptions, there are opportunities in marketing research for people with a variety of skills. There is room for technical specialists, such as statisticians, as well as for research generalists, whose skills are relevant to managing the people and resources needed for a research project rather than the mathematical detail any study may involve. The skills required to perform each job satisfactorily will vary.

In consumer goods companies, the typical entry-level position is research analyst, often for a specific brand. While learning the characteristics and details of the industry, the analyst will receive on-the-job training from a research manager. The usual career path for an analyst is to advance to senior analyst, then research supervisor, and on to research manager for a specific brand. At that time, the researcher's responsibilities often broaden to include a group of brands.

At marketing research companies, the typical entry-level position is research trainee, a position in which the person will be exposed to the types of studies in which the supplier specializes and to the procedures required for completing them. Quite often, trainees will spend some time actually conducting interviews, coding completed data-collection forms, or assisting with the analysis. The goal is to expose trainees to the processes the firm follows so that when they become account representatives, they will be familiar enough with the firm's capabilities to respond intelligently to clients' needs for research information.

The requirements for entering the marketing research field include human-relations, communication, conceptual, and analytical skills. Marketing researchers need to be able to interact effectively with others and they need to be good communicators, both orally and in writing. They need to understand business in general and marketing processes in particular. When dealing with brand, advertising, sales, or other types of managers, they need to have some understanding of the issues with which these managers contend and the types of mental models the managers use to make sense of situations. Marketing researchers also should have basic numerical and statistical skills, or at least they should have the capacity to develop those skills. They must be comfortable with numbers and with the techniques of marketing research. Their growth as professionals and their advancement within their organization will depend on their use of these skills and acquiring other technical, management, and financial skills.

For marketing researchers working for producers, it is not uncommon to switch from research to product or brand management at some point in the career path. One advantage these people possess is that after working so closely with marketing intelligence, they often know more about the customers, the industry, and the competitors than anyone in the company with the same years of experience. Note, though, that researchers desiring such a switch need to develop more knowledge about marketing and business in general than those who plan to stay in marketing research, although all researchers need a good foundation of business and marketing knowledge if they are going to succeed.

Successful marketing researchers tend to be proactive rather than reactive. That is, they tend to identify and lead the direction in which the individual studies and overall programs go rather than simply respond to explicit requests for information. Successful marketing researchers realize that marketing research is conducted for one primary reason—to help make better marketing decisions. Unfortunately, too many marketing researchers may have accepted the role of passive order-taker, at least according to one prominent industry observer.

WHY STUDY MARKETING RESEARCH?

Learning Objective

4. List three reasons for studying marketing research.

Almost all business schools offer courses in marketing research, and many require students who are completing majors in marketing to take a marketing research course. Why is this the case?

There are at least three important reasons for a business student to be exposed to marketing research training. First, some students will discover that marketing research can be rewarding and fun. For these students, initial training in how to be an "information detective" may lead to further study and a career in marketing research. These students usually develop an immediate appreciation for the power and responsibility involved in taking preexisting or new data and converting them into information that can be used by marketing managers to make important decisions. Thus, for some students at least, the study of marketing research will be directly relevant to their careers.

Most students will not go on to careers in marketing research; why should they study marketing research? We are all consumers of marketing and public opinion research, almost on a daily basis. The second important reason for studying marketing research, therefore, is to learn to be a *smart* consumer of marketing research results. Businesspeople are often exposed to research results, usually by someone trying to convince them to do something. Suppliers use research to promote the virtues of their particular products and services; advertising agencies use research to encourage a company to promote a product in particular media vehicles; product managers inside a firm use research to demonstrate the likely demand for the products they are developing to get further funding. Effective managers, however, do not take research results at face value but instead ask the right questions to determine the likely validity of the results.

A third key reason for studying marketing research is to gain an appreciation of the process, what it can and cannot do. As a manager, you will need to know what to expect marketing research to be able to deliver. The process of gathering data and generating information is full of opportunities for error to slip into the results. Thus, no research is perfect, and managers must take this into account when making decisions. Managers also need to understand what they are asking of researchers when requesting marketing research. The process is detailed, is time consuming, and requires great amounts of thought and effort. As a result, marketing research is costly to an organization and should *not* be undertaken on trivial issues or to support decisions that have already been made.

SUMMARY

Learning Objective 1

Define marketing research.
Marketing research is the function that links the consumer to the marketer through information. The information is used to identify and define marketing problems; generate, refine, and evaluate marketing actions; monitor marketing performance; and improve understanding of marketing as a process.

Learning Objective 2

Discuss different kinds of firms that conduct marketing research.
Producers of products and services often have marketing research departments and gather information relevant to the particular products and services they produce and the industry in which they operate. Advertising agencies often conduct research, primarily to test advertising and measure its effectiveness. Marketing research companies are in business to conduct research; some focus on very specific topics or aspects of the research process, while others are more general in focus.

Learning Objective 3

List some of the skills that are important for careers in marketing research.
Most positions in marketing research require analytical, communication, and human-relations skills. In addition, marketing researchers must be comfortable working with numbers and statistical techniques, and they must be familiar with a great variety of marketing research methods.

Learning Objective 4

List three reasons for studying marketing research.
(1) Some students pursue careers in marketing research; (2) almost everyone is a consumer of marketing research in one way or another and needs to be able to know how to evaluate the likely validity of the research; and (3) managers must understand what marketing research can and cannot do, as well as what is involved in the process of conducting research.

KEY TERM

marketing research (page 5)

REVIEW QUESTIONS

1. What is marketing management? What is the task of marketing research? Is there any relation between these two?

2. How is marketing research defined? What are the key elements of this definition?

3. Who does marketing research? What are the primary kinds of research done by each enterprise?

4. Why did marketing research begin to experience real growth after World War II?

5. In a large research department, who would be responsible for specifying the objective of a research project? For deciding on specific procedures to be followed? For designing the questionnaire? For analyzing the results? For reporting the results to top management?

6. What are the necessary skills for employment in a junior or entry-level marketing research position? Do the skills change as one changes job levels? If so, what new skills are necessary at the higher levels?

7. Why is it important to study marketing research?

DISCUSSION QUESTIONS, PROBLEMS, AND PROJECTS

1. Indicate whether marketing research is relevant to each of the following organizations and, if so, how each might use it.

    a. Pepsico, Inc.

    b. Your university

    c. CitiBank

    d. The American Cancer Society

    e. A small dry cleaner

2. Specify some useful sources of marketing research information for the following situation. Ethan Moore has worked for several years as the head chef in a restaurant specializing in ethnic cuisine. Dissatisfied with his income, he has decided to start his own business. Based on his experiences in the restaurant, he recognizes a need for a local wholesale distributor specializing in hard-to-find ethnic foodstuffs. He envisions starting a firm that will handle items commonly used in Asian and African recipes.

    With the help of a local accountant, Moore prepared a financial proposal that revealed the need for $150,000 in start-up capital for Ethan's Ethnic Foods. The proposal was presented to a local bank for review by its commercial loan committee, and Moore subsequently received the following letter from the bank:

    Mr. Moore:
    We have received and considered your request for start-up financing for your proposed business. While the basic idea seems sound, we find that your sales projections are based solely on your own experience and do not include any hard documentation concerning the market potential for the products you propose to carry. Until such information is made available for our consideration, we must reject your loan application.

    Bitten hard by the entrepreneurial bug, Moore views this rejection as a minor setback. Given his extremely limited financial resources, where and how might he obtain the needed information? (*Hint:* First determine what types of information would be useful.)

3. What do the following two research situations have in common?

Situation I: The Bugs-Away Company marketed successful insect repellents. The products were effective and leaders in the market. They were available in blue aerosol cans with red caps. The instructions, in addition to a warning to keep the product away from children, were clearly specified on the container. Most competitors produced similar products in similar containers. The CEO of Bugs-Away was worried because of declining sales and shrinking profit margins. Another issue of concern was that companies such as hers were being severely criticized by government and consumer groups for their use of aerosol cans. The CEO contacted the company's advertising agency and requested that it do the necessary research to find out what was happening.

Situation II: In early 2008, the directors of Adams University were considering an expansion of the business school due to increasing enrollments over the past 10 years. Their plans included constructing a new wing, hiring five new faculty members, and increasing the number of scholarships from 100 to 120. The funding for this ambitious project was to be provided by some private sources, internally generated funds, and the state and federal governments. A previous research study (completed in 1998), using a sophisticated forecasting methodology, indicated that student enrollment would peak in 2006. Another study, conducted in November 2002, indicated that universities could expect gradual declining enrollments until roughly the year 2013. The directors were concerned about the results of the later study and the talk it stimulated about budget cuts by the government. A decision was made to conduct a third and final study to determine likely student enrollment.

4. What do the following two research situations have in common?

Situation I: The sales manager of Al-Can, an aluminum can manufacturing company, was delighted with the increase in sales over the past few months. He wondered whether the company's new cans, which would be on the market in two months, should be priced higher than the traditional products. He confidently commented to the vice president of marketing, "Nobody in the market is selling aluminum cans with screw-on tops. We can get a small portion of the market and yet make substantial profits." The product manager disagreed with this strategy. In fact, she was opposed to marketing these new cans. The cans might present problems in preserving the contents. She thought to herself, "Aluminum cans are recycled, so nobody is going to keep them as containers." There was little she could do formally because these cans were the president's own idea. She strongly recommended to the vice president of marketing that the cans should be priced in line with the other products. The vice president thought a marketing research study would resolve this issue.

Situation II: A large toy manufacturer was in the process of developing a tool kit for children in the 5- to 10-year age group. The tool kit included a small saw, screwdriver, hammer, chisel, and drill. This tool kit was different from the competitors', as it included an instruction manual with "101 things to do." The product manager was concerned about the safety of the kit and recommended the inclusion of a separate booklet for parents. The sales manager recommended that the tool kit be made available in a small case, as this would increase its marketability. The advertising manager recommended that a special promotional campaign be launched in order to distinguish it from the competitors' products. The vice president thought that all the recommendations were worthwhile, but that the costs would increase drastically. He consulted the marketing research manager, who further recommended that a study be conducted.

5. List the key attributes that an individual occupying the following positions must possess. Why are these attributes essential?

    a. Senior analyst

    b. Full-time interviewer

    c. Market research director

6. Suppose that you have decided to pursue a career in the field of marketing research. In general, what types of courses should you take in order to help yourself achieve your goal? Why? What types of part-time jobs and/or volunteer work would look good on your resume? Why?

Gathering Marketing Intelligence: The Systems Approach

Learning Objectives

1. Explain the difference between a project emphasis in research and a systems emphasis.
2. Define what is meant by a marketing information system (MIS) and a decision support system (DSS).
3. Identify the components of a decision support system.
4. Discuss trends in the gathering of marketing intelligence.

Introduction

A fundamental purpose of marketing research is to help managers make decisions they face each day in their various areas of responsibility. Marketing managers need information, or marketing intelligence, as they carry out the firm's marketing activities. Intelligence could take the form of customer purchasing patterns, assessment of demand for a firm's products, or preferences among product design alternatives just to name a few.

Broadly speaking, there are two ways marketing research can gather marketing intelligence: (1) by conducting projects to address specific problems (i.e., the project approach) or (2) by putting systems in place that provide marketing intelligence on an ongoing basis (i.e., the systems approach). Each approach has its merits; rarely is either approach undertaken at the expense, or absence, of the other. Each helps managers to have much needed information to support their decision-making responsibilities. Each plays a valuable, yet slightly different, role in the firm.

Most of this book describes the project approach. In this chapter, however, we discuss the systems approach: how it differs from the project approach and the kinds of systems marketers use for obtaining information and making decisions.

THE PROJECT AND SYSTEMS APPROACHES

Learning Objective

1. Explain the difference between a project emphasis in research and a systems emphasis.

Both the project approach and the systems approach are beneficial. The differences between the approaches have been described this way: Both sources of marketing intelligence illuminate the darkness, but the project approach is like a flashbulb, and the systems approach is like a candle.[1] A marketing research project can shed intense, focused light on a particular issue at a particular time. In contrast, a marketing information system rarely shows all the details of a particular situation, but its glow is broad and continuous, even as conditions change.

The great advantage of the project approach is its ability to generate detailed information that is customized to a specific situation. The information generated, however, often comes at great cost and is likely only useful for a limited period of time, until conditions change. The project approach is thus most useful for unusual situations in which the marketing intelligence that is needed is not readily available as part of the normal process of doing business for a company. Much of the information that marketing managers need to make decisions is more predictable and can be organized inside a company's database systems and made readily available to managers on an ongoing basis. This is the big advantage of the systems approach: Current information needed for normal operations is available when managers need it. The disadvantage to the systems approach? Managers are limited to the information that is available in the database.

The Evolution and Design of Information Systems

The earliest attempts at providing a steady flow of information input (that is, candlelight) were **marketing information systems (MISs)**. An MIS is "a set of procedures and methods for the regular, planned collection, analysis, and presentation of information for use in making marketing decisions."[2] The key word in this definition is *regular*, because the emphasis in an MIS is to produce information on a steady basis. An example of visual output of an MIS is a dashboard. Meant to approximate an automobile's dashboard, a marketing dashboard is designed to provide interactive visualization of a company's key summary measures. Figure 2.1 presents a static example of different types of data that might be part of a company's information system. In practice, selecting a different tab provides different updates on marketing performance.

The next generation of information system offered managers greater access to the information held in a company's database. In contrast to an MIS, which emphasizes real-time reporting, a **decision support system (DSS)** includes software that allows managers to more fully utilize the available information to assist in making decisions. A DSS is "a coordinated collection of data, systems, tools, and techniques with supporting software and hardware, by which an organization gathers and interprets relevant information from business and the environment and turns it into a basis for marketing decisions."[3] Thus, besides storing information and producing standardized reports, the DSS allows managers to access the database and produce customized reports whenever they are needed. The DSS includes models for analyzing the data in the system—for example, creating tables or graphs of key data and seeing how a forecast changes if assumptions are changed.

Good information systems thus have two key outputs: (a) the standardized, up-to-the-minute reports needed for day-to-day operations and (b) custom reports that can easily be produced by managers when needed. In addition, the information system should incorporate features that make it easy to use in an interactive mode by non-computer people. These features include graphical interfaces and menu-driven procedures for doing analysis of the results.

Ideally, the information system will provide the intelligence marketers need for making decisions. To accomplish this, system designers start with a detailed

marketing information system (MIS)
A set of procedures and methods for the regular, planned collection, analysis, and presentation of information for use in making marketing decisions.

Learning Objective

2. Define what is meant by a marketing information system (MIS) and a decision support system (DSS).

decision support system (DSS)
A coordinated collection of data, systems, tools, and techniques with supporting software and hardware, by which an organization gathers and interprets relevant information from business and the environment and turns it into a basis for marketing decisions.

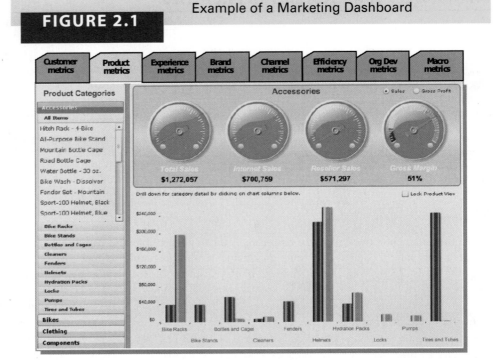

FIGURE 2.1 Example of a Marketing Dashboard

Source: Pat LaPointe, "Keys to an Effective Marketing Dashboard," downloaded from Chief Marketer Web site, http://chiefmarketer.com/crm_loop/roi/marketing_dashboard/?cid=dashboard, August 1, 2008.

MANAGER'S FOCUS

Having a superior marketing information system can be instrumental to the success of an organization. Whether or not your future organization develops and implements an exceptional MIS will be as dependent on your actions as a marketing administrator as it will be on the efforts of the information technology staff. Specifically, *you* and the other marketing managers will need to (1) make the MIS a strategic priority and (2) authorize the financial resources necessary to support a truly effective MIS.

Most businesses are relatively small, so you may become a manager in a smaller company with limited financial resources. If this is the case, will the principles presented in this chapter be applicable to you? We believe the answer is an emphatic "Yes!" Managers in smaller companies often view the establishment of an MIS to be beyond their reach. Consequently, they make many decisions based on limited information, and many smaller businesses ultimately fail due to poorly conceived marketing strategies. Small business managers would be well advised to do what they can to establish an MIS, even if it is does not rival the sophistication of those developed by large corporations. At a minimum, they should have one employee dedicated to systematically gathering relevant market intelligence and making it available in a useable format to the decision makers within the company.

analysis of each decision maker who might use the system. They attempt to understand each manager's decision-making responsibilities, capabilities, and style. They identify the types of decisions each decision maker routinely makes, the types of information needed to make those decisions, the types of information the individual receives regularly, and the special studies that are needed periodically. The analysis also considers the improvements decision makers would like in the current information system, not only in the types of information they receive, but also in the form in which they receive it. Next, systems designers specify the data to be input into the system, how to secure and store the data, how to access and combine the data, and what the report formats will look like. Only after these analysis and design steps are completed can the system be constructed. Programmers write and document the programs, making data retrieval as efficient as possible in terms of computer time and memory. When all the procedures are debugged, it is put online, so managers with authorized access can view the dashboards or request reports.

COMPONENTS OF DECISION SUPPORT SYSTEMS

Learning Objective

As noted above, MIS and DSS have evolved into useful tools for the marketing decision maker. Let's focus a bit more attention now on the various parts of a DSS. According to information systems experts, an enterprise- or firm-wide DSS has three primary components based on the mode of assistance the system provides to a manager: (1) data-driven, (2) model-driven, and (3) dialog-driven. All three components can be seen in Figure 2.2; using these three components yields managerial information as shown to the right of the figure. Further explanation of the components themselves is provided in the following sections.

3.   Identify the components of a decision support system.

Data-Driven Decision Support System: The Database

The data-driven decision support system in a DSS includes the processes used to capture and store data coming from marketing, finance, and manufacturing, as well as information coming from any number of external or internal sources. The typical data system has modules containing customer information, general economic and demographic information, competitor information, and industry information, including market trends. Where do the data in a DSS originate? One survey of *Fortune* 500 companies indicated that 62% of the data come from internal accounting and data

data-driven decision support system
The part of a decision support system that includes the processes used to capture and the methods used to store data coming from a number of external and internal sources. It is the creation of a database.

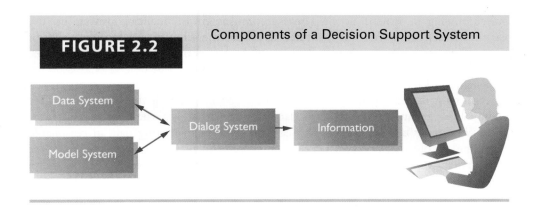

FIGURE 2.2   Components of a Decision Support System

Data System

Model System

Dialog System

Information

MANAGER'S FOCUS

Market orientation is an organizational culture of generating and disseminating market intelligence and responding appropriately to that intelligence. The key to success, however, is performing these processes on an organization-wide basis. One of your responsibilities as a marketing manager is to create a culture in which all key personnel recognize and fulfill their responsibilities of continually gathering relevant market intelligence and entering it into the organization's system. Many boundary-spanning employees obtain a wealth of valuable information through regular interaction with current or prospective customers, but all too often they are not given adequate incentives to make this information available to others in the organization. We recently observed a large company, for example, that commissioned a marketing research study to reproduce some essential market intelligence that its sales representatives already possessed but were not disseminating to decision makers. Conducting marketing research is both expensive and time consuming and should be avoided when the needed information can be obtained more quickly and at a fraction of the cost from existing sources within the organization.

processing sources, with the remainder coming from marketing research and intelligence.[4]

The growth in computing power and the emergence of increasingly sophisticated data processing capabilities have led to the development of huge databases within companies. In the past, a business's databases were limited to relatively current information; many new ones contain historical information as well. These "data warehouses" literally dwarf those available even a few years ago. For example, Wal-Mart has a data warehouse storing transaction information about each of Wal-Mart's over 7,200 stores in 15 countries. Wal-Mart uses the information to select products that need replenishment, analyze seasonal buying patterns, examine customer buying trends, select markdowns, and react to merchandise volume and movement. The data warehouse also "serves as the base for Wal-Mart's Retail Link decision support system between Wal-Mart and its suppliers. Retail Link allows suppliers to access large amounts of online, real-time, item-level data to help those suppliers improve operations." Containing over 500 terabytes of data and still growing, Wal-Mart's data warehouse is the largest in the world.[5]

As the number of commercial databases and corporate information systems has expanded, so too has public concern with the issue of privacy and if, and how, people's right to privacy is being violated in the generation and sharing of these databases. Research Window 2.1 describes recent cases in which private information was either missing or stolen. To help reassure consumers of financial institutions, the Gramm-Leach-Bliley Act was instituted to ensure the security and confidentiality of personal information collected.[6] Because of highly publicized cases such as those noted in Research Window 2.1, data security will continue to be a critical issue for information system managers.

Assuming that the privacy of the database can be assured, the key criterion for adding a particular piece of data to a database is whether it is useful for making decisions. The basic task of a DSS is to capture relevant marketing data in reasonable detail and to put those data in a truly accessible form. It is crucial that the database management capabilities built into the system can organize the data in the way that a particular manager needs it.

research window 2.1

Data Security Issues Heating Up

Well-documented privacy breaches illustrate the risks involved with storing valuable personal information. However, as breaking into company database records gets tougher from the outside, thefts and hackers are relying more on internal company employees. While external data breaches fell from 14.1% to 11.7%, internal breaches rose from 6% to 15.8% according to a recent report by the Identity Theft Resource Center (ITRC). Even more troubling, the largest percentage of security breaches—23%—remains unexplained.

Linda Foley, founder of ITRC, explained, "It's the path of least resistance. As in retail, it's much easier for a cashier to steal money out of the till than for a robber to come in with a mask and a gun."

To reinforce Foley's point, consider that mortgage broker LendingTree has several former employees who allegedly used company passwords to access and sell data from as many as 56,000 customers to home loan lenders. A similar case was brought against a former employee of Tenet Healthcare for having stolen the identity of 37,000 patients via their patient records.

The ITRC says its year-over-year increase in corporate data breach cases is 69%. This number, according to Foley, is in part due to new reporting laws in several states regarding lost or missing consumer data. Regardless of the reasons, Gartner Research has seen a 20% increase in security software spending to a total of just over $10 billion.

Source: Andy Greenberg, "Rotting at the Core," *Forbes*, June 30, 2008, downloaded from http://www.forbes.com/technology/2008/06/30/security-hackers-inside-tech-security-cx_ag_0630security.html, July 31, 2008.

Model-Driven Decision Support System: The Analytical Tools

The **model-driven decision support system** in a DSS includes all the computerized routines that allow the user to do the analyses that she or he wants. Whenever managers look at data, they have a preconceived idea of how something works and, therefore, what is interesting and worthwhile in the data. Most managers also want to manipulate data to gain a better understanding of a marketing issue. Routines for manipulating the data can range from summing a set of numbers, to conducting a complex statistical analysis, to finding an optimization strategy using some kind of nonlinear programming routine. Still, the most common procedures are the simple ones: counting the cases that fall into different groups, summing, averaging, computing ratios, building tables, and so on.

The BayCare Health System, an alliance of not-for-profit community hospitals in west central Florida, developed a DSS designed to provide managers (corporate and medical) with key information for making decisions about specific healthcare programs for the communities it served. The system tracks a large number of indicators, ranging from community socioeconomic indicators to behavioral risk factors and has been used to identify specific problem areas among the communities covered by the program. For example, several communities with unusually high levels of deaths due to stroke were identified. When follow-up research indicated the problem of lack of transportation among the elderly, minority, and low-income populations in these areas, a mobile medical unit was developed to deliver medical services and prevention/education services to the affected groups.[7]

model-driven decision support system
The part of a decision support system that includes all the routines that allow the user to manipulate the data so as to conduct the kind of analysis the individual desires. It is the collection of analytical tools to interpret the database.

© DAVE PILIBOSIAN/ISTOCKPHOTO

The ITRC believes that both consumers and businesses are victims of identity theft and fraud. As part of its mission statement, ITRC strives to educate consumers, corporations, government agencies, and other organizations on best practices for fraud and identity theft detection, reduction, and mitigation.

expert system

A computer-based, artificial intelligence system that attempts to model how experts in the area process information to solve the problem at hand.

dialog-driven decision support system

The part of a decision support system that permits users to explore the databases by employing the system models to produce reports that satisfy their particular information needs. It is the user interface of the decision support system, which is also called a language system.

More sophisticated models for manipulating data are being developed all the time, often for relatively specific purposes. For example, DSSs have been developed to enable brand managers to make better marketing mix decisions for their brands; to help bankers make stronger credit management decisions; to guide managers when they make new product development decisions; and to assess alternative marketing plans for motion pictures before they are released.[8]

The explosion in recent years in the number of databases available and the size of some of them has triggered greater need for ways to analyze them efficiently. For example, store scanners provide massive amounts of data to marketing managers. The huge amounts of data require a great amount of time for even a well-trained analyst to come up with simple summaries that show the major trends. In response, a number of firms have developed **expert systems**—computer-based, artificial intelligence systems that attempt to model how experts in the area process information to solve the problem at hand.[9]

Dialog-Driven Decision Support System: The User Interface

The element of a DSS that clearly separates it from an MIS is its **dialog-driven decision support system**, also called a language system. Dialog systems provide managers who are not programmers themselves with the user interface to explore the databases by using the analytical tools to produce reports that satisfy their own particular information needs. The reports might include tables or figures; the format can be specified by individual managers. The dialog systems are sometimes menu driven, requiring only a few clicks of a computer mouse or a few simple keystrokes. Regardless of how the manager interacts with the system, the point is that managers can do it themselves without relying on others to prepare the particular report that they need. This allows them to target the information they want and not be overwhelmed with irrelevant data. They can ask a question and, on the basis of the answer, ask a subsequent question, and then another, and another, and so on.

As the availability of online databases and sophisticated model systems has increased, so too has the need for better dialog systems. The dialog systems put data at the decision maker's fingertips. While that sounds simple enough, it is actually a difficult task because of the large amount of data available, the speed with which they hit a company, and the variety of sources from which they come.

One way to handle these problems is distributed network computing. Such systems make use of a common interface or server. Through that server, the analyst can do data entry, data query, spreadsheet analysis, plots, statistical analysis, or even report preparation, all using simple commands (see Figure 2.3). The technical term

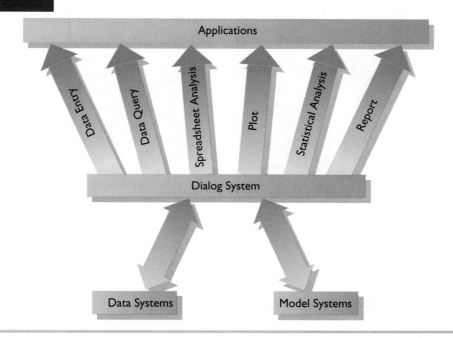

FIGURE 2.3

Use of Dialog Systems with Common Server or Interface Using Simplified, Standardized Instructions to Perform Multiple Tasks

---

for this capability is **data mining**, which has been defined as the use of "powerful analytic technologies to quickly and thoroughly explore mountains of data, isolating the valuable, useful information—the domain intelligence—that the user needs."[10] Businesses hope data mining will allow them to boost sales and profits by better understanding their customers.

A typical approach to data mining uses a supercomputer to link a number of personal computers. Decision makers at their PCs pose their questions, and the supercomputer tackles them with parallel processing, which breaks down questions into smaller computational tasks to perform simultaneously. A computer using parallel processing can readily work through trillions of pieces of data, dramatically slashing problem-solving time.

For example, coaches in the National Basketball Association (NBA) have used data mining to sort through game statistics to determine their most productive combinations of players and measure the effectiveness of individual players.[11] Fingerhut Companies, a Minnetonka, Minnesota, catalog retailer, used data mining to target a promotional effort. The company's computer sorted through 6 trillion characters of data to learn which of its 25 million customers had recently purchased outdoor furniture and thus might also be interested in a new gas grill.[12] Research Window 2.2 (on page 29) discusses how data mining is being revolutionized by *Super Crunchers*.

data mining
The use of powerful analytic technologies to quickly and thoroughly explore mountains of data to obtain useful information.

TRENDS IN OBTAINING MARKETING INTELLIGENCE

Learning Objective

4. Discuss trends in the gathering of marketing intelligence.

There is no question that the explosion in databases, computer hardware and software for accessing those databases, and not to mention the Internet are all changing the way marketing intelligence is obtained. Not only are more companies building DSSs,

© DONNA MCWILLIAM/ASSOCIATED PRESS

The process of data mining from game stats can enable professional sports coaches to tap into and use ideal player combinations.

knowledge management
The systematic collection of employee knowledge about customers, products, and the marketplace.

but those that have them are also becoming more sophisticated in using them for general business and competitive intelligence.

Knowledge Management

The sophistication in the design and uses of decision support systems opens up access to so much data that higher level management of information becomes critical. An executive in charge of information can ensure that it is used in support of strategic thinking. In many organizations, this function is now the responsibility of a chief information officer, or CIO.

The CIO's major role is to run the company's information and computer systems like a business. The CIO serves as the liaison between the firm's top management and its information systems department. He or she is responsible for planning, coordinating, and controlling the use of the firm's information resources and is much more concerned with the firm's outlook than with the daily activities of the department. CIOs typically know more about the business in general than the managers of the information system departments, who are often stronger technically. In many cases, the managers of the information system department report directly to the CIO.

A growing number of companies are extending the idea of information systems management to include management of the knowledge that resides inside its employees' heads. One of an organization's greatest assets can be what its people know about customers, its products, and its marketplace. However, few companies yet have a way to make that information widely available to those who can use it. Knowledge management is an effort to systematically collect that information and make it accessible to others.

When Arjan van Unnik, head of knowledge management and virtual team working at Shell E&P, wanted to boost knowledge management, he sought the natural early adopters within the organization to help convince the others. He began promoting knowledge to employees, and about 20% really bought into the idea. "That gave us fertile ground to kick off the community," says van Unnik. Over the first seven years of the knowledge management program, the proportion of employees participating in the system grew exponentially; over half the company's 30,000 employees had registered on the company's knowledge portal. In one recent year, company employees viewed the knowledge management site 1.7 million times.[13]

Chicago-based insurance giant CNA had 35 strategic business units spread across 175 branch offices supported by over 15,000 niche market-focused employees when it decided to build a knowledge network around three major areas. According to Gordon Larson, chief knowledge officer, "Moving from a decentralized culture to a collaborative one is a major change-management challenge." How big was the challenge? CNA covered 900 industry segments with hundreds of products. Its employees had to cede narrow product and market expertise to become well-versed in the company's portfolio at a general knowledge level. Like Shell, CNA started small by transitioning 500 employees. That number quickly grew to 4,000. Now the knowledge network stretches across the company, and it has become the underwriting company it sought to be.[14]

research window 2.2

Super Crunchers Are Thinking-by-Numbers

Can a credit card company examine a customer's charge history and determine if he or she will get divorced? Can a hospital predict physician cleanliness based on infection rates? Ian Ayres, econometrician and attorney at Yale University, says the answer to both questions is yes in his book *Super Crunchers: Why Thinking-by-Numbers Is the New Way to Be Smart*.

Ayres details his own work, as well as recounting other studies, where large databases were analyzed to find relationships between seemingly unrelated things. For example, do race and gender have a role to play in such diverse areas as interest rates on car loans and the number of citations an academic article will receive? Well, yes again. Ayres and colleague Mark Cohen from Vanderbilt University found that African-American borrowers pay about $700 in markups compared to $300 in markups by Caucasians. Moreover, over half of Caucasian borrowers paid no markups, while African-American borrowers paid 19.9% of the markup profits. In a separate study, Ayres and Fred Vars of Yale found that Caucasian women were cited in law review articles 57% more than Caucasian men while minority women were cited more than twice as often.

Other data-driven discoveries from *Super Crunchers* include: Netflix customers liking the movies the service recommends better than the ones they choose on their own, airlines predicting which customers are most vulnerable to being lured away by a competitor after a cancelled flight and giving them priority booking over the airline's own best customers, and baseball managers assessing prospects on quantifiable statistics instead of the seasoned observation of groups of scouts.

With the reams and reams of data that can be collected in a variety of industries, all it takes is a little mining to find business gold. So, with all this thinking-by-numbers success, are you ready to sign up with eHarmony.com? Its founder is a super cruncher, too.

Sources: Melissa Lafsky, "Attack of the *Super Crunchers*: Adventures in Data Mining," *New York Times*, August 23, 2007, downloaded from http://freakonomics.blogs.nytimes.com/2007/08/23/attack-of-the-super-crunchers-ian-ayres-on-data-mining/, August 2, 2008 and Jerry Adler, "Era of the Super Cruncher," *Newsweek*, September 3, 2007, downloaded from http://www.newsweek.com/id/40909, August 2, 2008.

The usefulness of a knowledge management system depends on the willingness of company employees to share information. One means of promoting such sharing of information is to simply make the process as simple as possible. At Halliburton, employees can jot down insights using pencil and paper and pass them along to the knowledge management staff to be entered in the system. "This lowers the barrier of entry," says Michael Behounek, Halliburton's director of knowledge management.[15]

Linking Marketing Intelligence to Other Business Intelligence

Another way in which powerful information systems are influencing the direction of marketing intelligence is in the blurring of distinctions between types of information management. When an organization's computer could handle only enough data for a single function's decision support system, each function needed a separate system with a separate database. However, today more and more companies are enjoying the benefits of sharing data among the various functions and levels of the organization.

For example, an enterprise resource planning (ERP) system monitors and controls all of an organization's resource requirements, such as inventory, human resources,

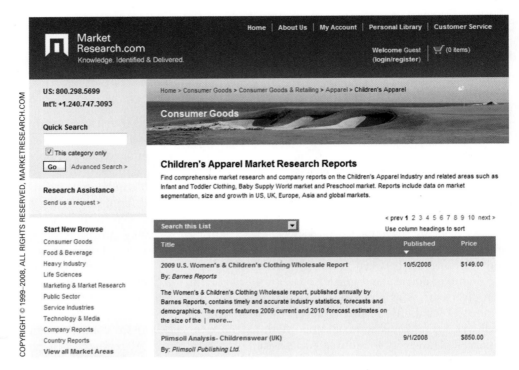

One of many marketing research companies, MarketResearch.com, an aggregator of global business intelligence, continuously updates research from the leading research firms and consultancies worldwide.

and production capacity. This sophisticated software system tracks financial data, schedules, inventory levels, and more, all in an effort to ensure that the organization has just the resources it needs to meet anticipated demand as efficiently as possible. Marketing intelligence can support ERP by helping managers prepare accurate sales forecasts. In addition, a promotional effort or new-product launch will affect all of an organization's functions and many of its resource needs. ERP can support marketing efforts by providing information about a marketing decision's impact on the entire organization.

Another meaningful development in the cross-functional use of information stored in a company's databases is customer relationship management (CRM). As detailed in Research Window 2.3, CRM attempts to gather all relevant information about a company's customers—everything from demographic data to sales data to service records and more. The goal is to better understand customers' needs and behaviors and to put this information in the hands of those who interact with customers.

Limitations of the Systems Approach

At first, the systems approach was regarded as the solution for information problems inside the firm. The reality, however, often fell short of the promise. Effective MIS or DSS systems are often difficult to implement, for several reasons. People tend to resist change, and adding an information system can lead to lots of changes. Also, many decision makers don't want to tell others what factors they use and how they combine them to make decisions; without such disclosure, it is next to impossible to design systems that will give them the information they need.

Even when managers are willing to disclose their decision-making process and information needs, there are problems. Different managers often pay attention to

research window 2.3

What Is CRM?

CRM: Gauging the Pulse of Customer Relationship Management

CRM stands for customer relationship management. It is a strategy used to learn more about customers' needs and behaviors in order to develop stronger relationships with them. After all, good customer relationships are at the heart of business success. There are many technological components to CRM, but thinking about CRM in primarily technological terms is a mistake. The more useful way to think about CRM is as a process that will help bring together lots of pieces of information about customers, sales, marketing effectiveness, responsiveness, and market trends.

What is the goal of CRM? The idea of CRM is that it helps businesses use technology and human resources to gain insight into the behavior of customers and the value of those customers. If it works as hoped, a business can

- provide better customer service
- make call centers more efficient
- cross sell products more effectively
- help sales staff close deals faster
- simplify marketing and sales processes
- discover new customers
- increase customer revenues

That sounds rosy. How does it happen? It doesn't happen by simply buying software and installing it. For CRM to be truly effective, an organization must first decide what kind of customer information it is looking for and it must decide what it intends to do with that information. For example, many financial institutions keep track of customers' life stages in order to market appropriate banking products like mortgages or IRAs to them at the right time to fit their needs.

Next, the organization must look into all of the different ways information about customers comes into a business, where and how these data are stored, and how they are currently used. One company, for instance, may interact with customers in a myriad of different ways including mail campaigns, Web sites, brick-and-mortar stores, call centers, mobile sales force staff, and

marketing and advertising efforts. *Solid CRM systems link up each of these points.* The data flow between operational systems (like sales and inventory systems) and analytical systems that can help sort through these records for patterns. Company analysts can then comb through the data to obtain a holistic view of each customer and pinpoint areas where better services are needed. For example, if someone has a mortgage, a business loan, an IRA, and a large commercial checking account with one bank, it behooves the bank to treat this person well each time it has any contact with him or her.

Are there any indications of the need for a CRM project? Not really. But one way to assess the need for a CRM project is to count the channels a customer can use to access the company. The more channels you have, the greater need there is for the type of single centralized customer view a CRM system can provide.

How long will it take to get CRM in place? A bit longer than many software salespeople will lead you to think. Some vendors even claim their CRM "solutions" can be installed and working in less than a week. Packages like those are not very helpful in the long run because they don't provide the cross-divisional and holistic customer view needed. The time it takes to put together a well-conceived CRM project depends on the complexity of the project and its components.

What are some examples of the types of data CRM projects should be collecting?

- Responses to campaigns
- Shipping and fulfillment dates
- Sales and purchase data
- Account information
- Web registration data
- Service and support records
- Demographic data
- Web sales data

What are the keys to successful CRM implementation?

- Break your CRM project down into manageable pieces by setting up pilot programs and short-term

(Continued)

milestones. Start with a pilot project that incorporates all the necessary departments and groups that gets projects rolling quickly but is small enough and flexible enough to allow tinkering along the way.

- Make sure your CRM plans include a scalable architecture framework.

- Don't underestimate how much data you might collect (there will be *lots*) and make sure that if you need to expand systems you'll be able to.

- Be thoughtful about what data are collected and stored. The impulse will be to grab and then store *every* piece of data you can, but there is often no reason to store data. Storing useless data wastes time and money.

- Recognize the individuality of customers and respond appropriately. A CRM system should, for example, have built-in pricing flexibility.

Which division should run the CRM project? The biggest returns come from aligning business, CRM, and IT strategies across all departments and not just leaving it for one group to run.

What causes CRM projects to fail? Many things. From the beginning, lack of communication between everyone in the customer relationship chain can lead to an incomplete picture of the customer. Poor communication can lead to technology being implemented without proper support or buy-in from users. For example, if the sales force isn't completely sold on the system's benefits, they may not input the kind of demographic data that are essential to the program's success. One *Fortune* 500 company is on its fourth try at a CRM implementation, primarily because its sale force resisted all the previous efforts to share customer data.

---

different things and, thus, have different data needs. Very few formats are optimal for a variety of users. Either the developers have to design with "compromises" that are satisfactory for most users, but not really best for anyone, or they have to customize the system to meet each manager's needs, one at a time.

The costs and time required to build information systems are often underestimated, because managers fail to grasp the size of the task, changes in organizational structure, key personnel, and electronic data-processing systems that are required. By the time the information systems can be developed, the managers for whom they are designed have often moved on to other jobs or organizations, or the economic and competitive environments around which they are designed have changed. As a result, they are sometimes out of date soon after implementation. In some cases, the whole process has to start all over again.

There is one final problem with the systems approach, and it's a big one: Managers are limited to the data available in the system. No matter how colorful the dashboard is or how easy the system is to use, if the right kinds of data are not collected in the first place, the system will be ineffective for guiding a current marketing decision. To some extent, this problem is unavoidable; managers are constantly learning new things and applying them to their businesses. Before we know the value of various kinds of information, it is unlikely that we will include them in our databases. Sometimes, however, limited data availability indicates that information systems managers may not have done a thorough job of identifying the kinds of data that managers need to make good decisions.

Intelligence Gathering in the Organization of the Future

Although one might expect they would, the explosion in databases and the emergence of DSSs have not eliminated traditional marketing research projects for gathering marketing intelligence. This is because the two activities are not competitive mechanisms for marketing intelligence but, rather, complementary ones. For one thing, many of the project-oriented techniques discussed in this book are used to generate the information that goes into the databases that businesses use in their DSSs. Thus, the value of the insights gained from these databases depends directly on the quality of the underlying data, and users need to be able to assess their quality. For another, while DSSs provide valuable input for broad strategic decisions, allow managers to stay in tune with what is happening in their external environments, and serve as excellent early-warning systems, they sometimes do not provide enough information as to what to do in specific instances, such as when the firm is faced with introducing a new product, changing distribution channels, evaluating a promotional campaign, and so on. When actionable information is required to address specific marketing problems or opportunities, the research project will likely continue to play a major role.

In sum, both traditional, or project-based, and systems-based approaches to marketing intelligence can be expected to remain important. In an increasingly competitive world, information is vital, and a company's ability to obtain and analyze information will largely determine its future. The light from both flashbulbs and candles offers illumination.

SUMMARY

Learning Objective 1

Explain the difference between a project emphasis in research and a systems emphasis.

The difference between the project and the systems emphases to research is that the systems approach relies on the continual monitoring of the firm's activities, competitors, and environment; the project emphasis focuses on the in-depth, but nonrecurring, study of some specific problem or environmental condition.

Learning Objective 2

Define what is meant by a marketing information system (MIS) and a decision support system (DSS).

A marketing information system is a set of procedures and methods for the regular, planned collection, analysis, and presentation of information for use in making marketing decisions. A decision support system expands the capabilities of an MIS by including tools that allow users to interact with the system to produce customized information, as opposed to the standardized reports produced by an MIS.

Learning Objective 3

Identify the components of a decision support system.

A decision support system has three major components: a data-driven system, a model-driven system, and a dialog-driven system. The data system collects and stores data from internal and external sources. It creates the database. The model system consists of routines that allow the user to manipulate data in order to analyze them as desired. It is the analytical component. The dialog system serves as the user interface permitting marketers to use the system models to produce reports based on criteria they specify themselves.

Learning Objective 4

Discuss trends in the gathering of marketing intelligence.

So much information is readily available from modern information systems that managing it has become a strategic challenge. Many organizations have placed a chief information officer in charge of how the organization gathers data and makes them available to support decision making. This process is generally known as knowledge management. In addition, many organizations are creating information systems that serve entire organizations, linking the various functions. Customer relationship management attempts to gather all relevant information about a company's customer into a system that can put this information into the hands of those who interact with customers.

KEY TERMS

marketing information system (MIS)
(page 21)
decision support system (DSS) (page 21)
data-driven decision support system (page 23)
model-driven decision support system
(page 25)

expert system (page 26)
dialog-driven decision support system
(page 26)
data mining (page 27)
knowledge management (page 28)

REVIEW QUESTIONS

1. How does a project emphasis in marketing research differ from a systems emphasis?

2. What are the steps in developing an information system?

3. What are the main differences between a marketing information system and a decision support system?

4. In a decision support system, what is a data system? A model system? A dialog system? Which of these is most important? Why?

5. How does knowledge management expand the concept of an information system? What additional kinds of marketing intelligence can it provide?

DISCUSSION QUESTIONS, PROBLEMS, AND PROJECTS

1. How is the growth in the Internet and the Web changing the way researchers use management information systems and decision support systems? Consider opportunities and challenges of researching on the Internet, as opposed to using a traditional marketing information system.

2. You have been requested to design a DSS for a manufacturer of automotive parts.

    a. What data should be included in the system (e.g., sales by sales area or by product line, age, and type of automobile driven)?

    b. What data sources might be used to create the information system?

    c. How will you structure the system conceptually, including the elements you will build into each of the subsystems?

3. In each of the following situations, which of the general approaches to gathering marketing intelligence, the project approach or the systems approach, would be most applicable? Why?

    a. The makers of Kool Aid sugar-free flavored drink mixes need information about sales trends in different regions of the United States.

    b. The makers of Kool Aid sugar-free flavored drink mixes need information about potential market demand for a new type of plastic container.

    c. The manufacturer of Mercury-Marine outboard motors wants to determine the profitability of its different product lines.

    d. A company wants to identify the amount of time spent on hold by consumers on a toll-free, customer-service assistance telephone line.

    e. A company that has installed a new telephone system wants to determine the influence of time spent on hold on customer satisfaction.

4. Arrange an interview with a manager of a local business to discuss a DSS.

    a. Complete the following:

    Name of the company: _____

    Name and title of the manager you interviewed: _____

    b. Briefly describe the system that the company is currently using, emphasizing especially the functions that are served by it (e.g., production, sales management).

    c. Write a brief assessment of the manager's familiarity with the concept. Is the manager more concerned with the technical questions (e.g., how information is stored) or with the overall concept and its impact on the organization's decision-making capabilities?

    d. Briefly describe the company's use of the system, including how it determines who gets what access to what data and how, its experience with the system, and so on.

5. Your company is in the process of installing its first DSS. The system has been designed and the hardware installed, and it is due to be up and running in two weeks. Your task is to provide system users with orientation and training. It is your feeling that the company's people will initially resist using the DSS. To help overcome this resistance, what specific capabilities of the DSS will you emphasize in your initial orientation presentations?

Gathering Marketing Intelligence: The Project Approach

Learning Objectives

1. Explain the difference between a program strategy and a project strategy in marketing research.
2. Outline the steps in the research process and show how the steps are interrelated.
3. Cite the most critical error in marketing research.
4. Highlight the main differences between the utility, justice, and rights approaches to ethical reasoning.

Introduction

Chapter 1 highlighted the many kinds of problems that marketing research can be used to solve. It emphasized that marketing research is a firm's communication link with the environment and can help the marketing manager in planning, problem solving, and control. Every company has its own way of using marketing research. As noted in Chapter 2, researchers can gather information on a continuous basis and use it as input to an information system. Sometimes, however, companies need specific, customized information that is not contained in the company's information system. These situations call for the project approach to gathering the necessary information.

A company's **program strategy** for marketing research is its overall philosophy of how marketing research projects fit into its marketing plan. A program strategy specifies the types of studies that are to be conducted and for what purposes. It might even specify how often these studies are to take place. Program strategy typically answers such questions as "Should we do marketing research?" and "How often?" and "What kind?"

How the individual studies are designed is the basis of a firm's **project strategy**. Project strategy addresses the issue of "Now that we've decided to go ahead with marketing research in a particular area, how should we proceed? Should we use in-store surveys, mail questionnaires, or a Web-based survey? Should we question more people or fewer?" In sum, project strategy deals with how a specific study should be conducted, whereas program strategy addresses the question of what type of studies the firm should conduct.

All research projects require their own special emphases and approaches, because the problems or opportunities they address are different. As a result, research procedures are custom tailored to the situation. Even so, there is a general sequence of steps—the **research process** (see Figure 3.1)—that can be followed when designing the research project. This chapter overviews the research process, and the remaining chapters discuss the stages in the process in more detail. In addition, because unethical practices can be found at each stage of the research process, we'll introduce some basic notions of marketing research ethics at the end of the chapter.

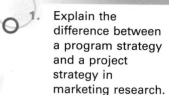

Learning Objective

1. Explain the difference between a program strategy and a project strategy in marketing research.

program strategy
A company's philosophy of how marketing research fits into its marketing plan.

project strategy
The design of individual marketing research studies that are to be conducted.

research process
The sequence of steps in the design and implementation of a research study.

SEQUENCE OF STEPS IN MARKETING RESEARCH

Learning Objective

2. Outline the steps in the research process and show how the steps are interrelated.

Formulate Problem (Chapter 4)

The first—and most important—step in the marketing research process is to define the marketing problem to be solved. Only when the problem is precisely defined can research be designed to provide the needed information. Part of the process of problem definition includes specifying the manager's *decision problem* and one or more *research problems* to be addressed. Each project to be undertaken should tie back directly to the decision problem. No further steps in the research process should be taken until the decision problem and the research problem(s) can be stated explicitly. This is the main purpose of the *research request agreement*, a document that clearly states the research problem(s) to be addressed in a research project.

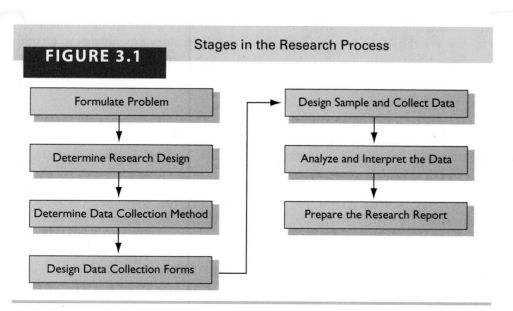

FIGURE 3.1   Stages in the Research Process

- Formulate Problem
- Determine Research Design
- Determine Data Collection Method
- Design Data Collection Forms
- Design Sample and Collect Data
- Analyze and Interpret the Data
- Prepare the Research Report

MANAGER'S FOCUS

In this chapter, we are providing a road map of what you will be studying throughout the remainder of this book. Later chapters will place much emphasis on issues that should be considered when designing projects and the steps researchers must complete to perform quality research. At this point, we simply want to remind you of why it is essential for you as a marketing manager to have a strong background in these areas. Without this knowledge, you will be completely dependent on the recommendations of others as you attempt to evaluate proposed research projects and the quality of the information produced by completed studies. *In other words,*

you will be placing your career in the hands of others—a risky proposition at best. Armed with research expertise, however, you will be a formidable force in the marketing efforts of your organization. You will be an effective independent consumer of research services and an invaluable sounding board as research providers seek feedback on the methods they propose using on your behalf. In an information-driven marketplace, managers who comprehend the role of marketing research and the limitations and strengths of the information generated by different techniques are indispensable to an organization.

Determine Research Design (Chapters 5–6)

The choice of research design depends on how much is known about the problem. If relatively little is known about the phenomenon to be investigated, *exploratory research* is needed. Typically, exploratory research is used when the problem to be solved is broad or vague. It may involve reviewing published data, interviewing knowledgeable people, conducting focus groups, or investigating trade literature that discusses similar cases. In any event, one of the most important characteristics of exploratory research is its flexibility. Because researchers know little about the problem at this point, they must be ready to follow their intuition about possible areas and tactics of investigation. Some researchers apply the label "qualitative research" to this kind of research.

If, instead of being broad or vague, a problem is well-defined and clearly stated, *descriptive* or *causal research* is needed. In these research designs, data collection is not flexible but rigidly specified, both with respect to the data collection forms and the sample design. The descriptive design focuses on describing a population, often emphasizing the frequency with which something occurs or the extent to which two variables are related to one another. The causal design uses experiments to identify cause-and-effect relationships between variables. Sometimes descriptive or causal research is referred to as "quantitative research."

Determine Data Collection Method (Chapters 7–11)

Sometimes the information that a firm needs to solve its problem already exists in the form of *secondary data,* or data that have already been collected for some purpose other than the question at hand. Such data may exist in the firm's own internal information system as feedback on warranty cards, call reports from the sales force, or orders from wholesalers. If the firm itself does not have the necessary information, it may be readily available in the form of government statistics, trade association reports, or data from a commercial research supplier. Although the firm must pay for commercial research, the fee is usually less than the cost of an original study. In any case, for reasons of both cost and time, researchers should always look first at existing sources of data before launching a research project.

If the information needed is not readily available, or if it is available only in a form that won't work for the problem at hand, then the researcher will collect *primary data*, which are data collected specifically for the study. There are lots of questions to be answered when collecting primary data, including: Should the data be collected by observation or questionnaire? How should these observations be made—personally or electronically? How should the questions be administered—in person, over the telephone, through the mail, or perhaps by e-mail?

Design Data Collection Forms (Chapters 12–14)

Once the researchers have settled on the method to be used for the study, they must design the actual observation form or questionnaire to be used on the project. Suppose a questionnaire is being used. Should it include a fixed set of questions and alternative answers, or should the responses be open-ended, to allow respondents to reply in their own words? Should the purpose be made clear to the respondents, or should the study objectives be disguised? Should some kind of rating scale be used? What type?

For a study of attitudes among residents of a particular city toward hybrid automobiles, passing out a survey on a street corner or during meetings of environmental groups would produce a nonprobablistic sample—and potentially misleading results.

Design Sample and Collect Data (Chapters 15–17)

After determining how the needed information will be collected, the researchers must decide what group will be observed or questioned. Depending on the study, the *population* might be homemakers, preschoolers, sports car drivers, Pennsylvanians, or tennis players. The particular subset of the population chosen for study is known as a *sample*.

In designing the sample, researchers must specify (1) the *sampling frame*, which is the list of population elements from which the sample will be drawn; (2) the type of sampling plan to be used; and (3) the size of the sample. There are two basic types of sampling plans. In a *probability sample*, which is the preferred category, each member of the population has a known, nonzero chance of being selected, which allows us to determine, at a certain margin of sampling error, what would have been true for the whole population if we had information from or about all elements. With a *nonprobability sample*, however, the researchers choose, in one way or another, which individuals or groups will be part of the study.

Sample size addresses the issue of how many institutions or subjects it is necessary to use in the project in order to get reliable answers without exceeding the time and money budgeted for it.

Once the dimensions of the sample design are specified, data collection can begin. Data collection often requires the use of field workers. Using field workers to collect data raises a host of questions about the selection, training, and control of the field staff. For example, what kind of background should interviewers have in order to glean the most information from respondents? What specific training is necessary to ensure that interviewers administer the questionnaires accurately? How often, and in what way, should the accuracy of the answers on the questionnaires be checked by validation studies? These are the sorts of questions to think about when designing the research.

Analyze and Interpret the Data (Chapters 18–20)

Researchers may gather a mountain of data, but data are useless unless the findings are analyzed and the results interpreted in light of the problem at hand. Data analysis generally involves several steps. First, the data collection forms must be scanned to be sure that they are complete and consistent and that the instructions were followed. This process is called *editing*. After being edited, the forms must be *coded*, which involves assigning numbers to each of the answers so that they can be analyzed by a computer. Once the data have been edited and coded, they are ready to be analyzed.

Most analysis is quite straightforward, involving frequency counts (usually, how many people answered a question a particular way) or simple descriptive statistics (for example, means and standard deviations). Sometimes the research calls for cross-tabulation, which allows a deeper look at the data by looking for differences or relationships across groups. Suppose, for instance, that researchers asked women if they have purchased a certain new cosmetic. The responses (i.e., percentage who have purchased) may be cross-classified by age group, income level, and so forth.

The editing, coding, and basic analysis functions are common to most research studies. Any additional statistical tests applied to the data are generally unique to the particular situation. These tests should be anticipated before data collection is begun, if possible, to ensure that the data and analyses will be appropriate for the problem as specified.

Prepare the Research Report (Chapter 21)

The research report is the document submitted to management that summarizes the research results and conclusions. It is all that many executives will see of the research effort, and it becomes the standard by which that research is judged. Thus, the research report must be clear and accurate, because no matter how well you've performed all the previous steps in the research, the project will be no more successful than the research report. In addition, many research reports are presented orally as well. Simply put, the written research report and oral presentation are often the most important factors affecting whether the research will be useful for its intended purposes.

Additional Comments on Marketing Research Steps

Here are some additional things to consider about the research process we've outlined. First, while each step in the process is straightforward, there are many issues to be dealt with at each stage. Exhibit 3.1 lists some of the typical questions that need to be resolved.

Second, although we've presented the stages in a particular order (see Figure 3.1), some of the steps can be carried out at about the same time—and decisions about later steps will influence what should happen at earlier stages. Figure 3.1 could be drawn with a number of feedback loops suggesting the likely need to rethink, redraft, or revise the various elements in the process as the study proceeds.

The process would begin with problem formulation and could then take any direction. The problem may not be specified explicitly enough to allow the development of the research design, in which case the researchers would need to return to

Learning Objective

3. Cite the most critical error in marketing research.

Exhibit 3.1	Questions Typically Addressed at the Various Stages of the Research Process

Stage in the Process	Typical Questions
Formulate problem	What is the purpose of the study—to solve a problem? Identify an opportunity? Is additional background information necessary? What is the source of the problem (planned change or unplanned change)? Is the research intended to provide information (discovery oriented) or to make a decision (strategy oriented)? What information is needed to make the decision at hand? How will the information be utilized? Should research be conducted?
Determine research design	How much is already known? Can a hypothesis be formulated? What types of questions need to be answered? What type of study will best address the research questions?
Determine data collection method	Can existing data be used to advantage? What is to be measured? How? What is the source of the data to be collected? Are there any cultural factors that need to be taken into account in designing the data collection method? What are they? Are there any legal restrictions on data collection methods? What are they? Can objective answers be obtained by asking people? How should people be questioned? Should the questionnaires be administered in person, over the phone, through the mail, on the Internet, or through e-mail? Should electronic or mechanical means be used to make the observations?
Design data collection forms	Should structured or unstructured items be used to collect the data? Should the purpose of the study be made known to the respondents? Should rating scales be used in the questionnaires? What specific behaviors should the observers record?
Design sample and collect data	What criteria define the target population? Is a list of population elements available? Is a sample necessary? Is a probability sample desirable? How large should the sample be? How should the sample be selected? Who will gather the data? How long will the data gathering take? How much supervision is needed? What operational procedures will be followed? What methods will be used to ensure the quality of the data collected?
Analyze and interpret the data	Who will handle the editing of the data? How will the data be coded? Who will supervise the coding? Will computer or hand tabulation be used? What tabulations are called for? What analysis techniques will be used?
Prepare the research report	Who will read the report? What is their technical level of sophistication? What is their involvement with the project? Are managerial recommendations called for? What will be the format of the written report? Is an oral report necessary? How should the oral report be structured?

© GRANTPIX/INDEX STOCK IMAGERY

The American public has become more protective of its privacy, making it increasingly difficult for marketing researchers to find consumers willing to participate in surveys and studies. Following strict ethical guidelines in research can help gain the trust of the public.

stage one to define the research problem(s) more clearly. Alternatively, the process may go smoothly all the way through the design of the data collection forms—and then the pretest of the survey may identify problems with the forms, methods used, research design, or even problem definition. The sample necessary to answer the problem as specified may be prohibitively costly, again requiring a revision of the earlier steps.

Keep in mind also that the steps in the research process are highly interrelated. A decision made at one stage will affect decisions at each of the other stages, and a revision of the procedure at any stage often requires modifications of procedures at each of the other stages.

Once the data are collected, it's too late to go back and redo the earlier steps. This is an important point: It pays to think ahead about the information needed to solve the manager's decision problem, the specific data that will be required, and the kinds of analysis necessary to get to the answers.

Finally, recognize from the beginning that no one has ever conducted a perfect marketing research project. Even the best projects contain error of one kind or another. Error is likely to enter the project at each stage of the process. The goal is to minimize total error in the project, not any particular kind of error. All the steps are necessary and vital, and it is dangerous to emphasize one to the exclusion of one or more others. Again, total error, rather than errors incurred in any single stage, is the important error in research work. Questions such as those in Exhibit 3.1 must be addressed so that total error can be minimized.

MARKETING RESEARCH ETHICS

Marketing researchers must make many decisions over the course of a single research project. Throughout the process, researchers must consider the ethics involved in the choices they make.

ethics
Moral principles and values that govern the way an individual or a group conducts its activities.

marketing ethics
The principles, values, and standards of conduct followed by marketers.

Ethics are the moral principles and values that govern the way an individual or a group conducts its activities. Ethics apply to all situations in which there can be actual or potential harm of any kind (e.g., economic, physical, or mental) to an individual or a group. **Marketing ethics** are the principles, values, and standards of conduct followed by marketers. Exhibit 3.2 provides several examples of instances in which companies demonstrated questionable (at best) ethical decision making with respect to marketing research.

Many researchers (and managers as well) often fail to think about whether it is morally acceptable to proceed in a particular way. Many think that if an action is legal, it is ethical. It's not that simple, however. There can be differences between what is ethical and what is legal. Even among those who understand this, many don't seem to evaluate the ethical implications of their decisions. Some researchers probably don't care; others may find it easier to ignore such considerations because doing the right thing isn't always easy.

| **Exhibit 3.2** | **Questionable Ethical Decision Making in Marketing Research** |

- A promotions company hired by an automobile dealership sent letters to local residents inviting them to a special "market test" at the dealership the following weekend. Recipients of the letters were led to believe that their help was needed for research purposes. Inquiries with the dealership and the promotions company eventually revealed that the only "research" being conducted involved how many people they could get into the dealership to take a test drive and—they hoped—buy a car. An employee of the promotions company admitted that they do this because it works.

- A large company conducted a series of focus groups to gather consumers' feedback on a new wireless telephone service the company was developing. In the first focus group, consumers seemed very positive until a demonstration of the new services. At that point, the focus group participants indicated that the service seemed "too difficult to use" and "too complicated." After a quick meeting, company representatives insisted that the service demonstration be eliminated from the remaining focus groups. Not surprisingly, the results of the next focus groups were quite positive and the new services were introduced. The wireless services failed in the marketplace.

- Marketing research provider Forrester Research Inc. came under fire a few years ago for conducting and publishing product comparison studies in which (a) Microsoft was favored over a competing product, and (b) PeopleSoft was judged to have higher satisfaction levels than products from several competing companies. The research may have been conducted properly, but the company's credibility was called into question when it initially failed to disclose that Microsoft and PeopleSoft had funded the research.

- Back in 2000, The Coca-Cola Company was feeling pressure to increase sales. Coke managers decided to focus on sales through the Burger King restaurant chain. Managers at Burger King were willing to sponsor a multimillion-dollar promotion for Frozen Coke if a two-week market test indicated that a sales promotion effort (a Frozen Coke coupon) was effective at increasing sales of value meals in the Richmond, Virginia, market compared with sales in Tampa, Florida. Results for the first week were not good. "It was clear that unless test results improved, the national Frozen Coke promotion was not going to happen," said the Coke marketing manager overseeing the test. Coke representatives proceeded to give $9,000 in cash to kids clubs and other nonprofits in Richmond to be used to buy hundreds of value meals. Coke's behind-the-scenes effort only added 700 value meals to the total consumed in Richmond during the test, but it helped convince Burger King to go forward with the national Frozen Coke promotion. The national promotion was deemed a disappointment.

Sources: George J. Boggs, "Listen to Customers But Don't Let Credibility Falter," *Marketing News*, April 14, 2003, p. 18, downloaded via ProQuest, June 13, 2005; Thomas Hoffman, "Market Research Providers Confront Credibility Concerns," *Computerworld*, October 13, 2003, p. 4, downloaded via ProQuest, June 12, 2005; and Chad Terhune, "Into the Fryer: How Coke Officials Beefed Up Results of Marketing Test; Consultant Gave Kids' Clubs Cash to Buy Value Meals in Burger King Promotion; Wiring $9,000 for Whoppers," *The Wall Street Journal*, August 20, 2003, p. A1, downloaded via ProQuest, June 14, 2005.

Marketing researchers must recognize that their jobs depend a great deal on the goodwill of the public. "Bad" research that violates the trust of study participants will only make it more difficult and costly to approach, recruit, and survey participants. Even researchers who don't care about whether their actions are right or wrong ought to be concerned about such issues from a business perspective. The fact that good ethics is good business is one reason that marketing and public opinion research associations have developed codes of ethics to guide the behaviors of their members. Research Window 3.1 contains the marketing research code of ethics for the Marketing Research Association. The scope and depth of this document should convince you that a discussion of ethics is very relevant to marketing research.

THREE METHODS OF ETHICAL REASONING

Learning Objective

In judging whether a proposed action is ethical or not, it is necessary to adopt one or more moral reasoning frameworks. In this section, we'll briefly overview three of these frameworks: the utility, justice, and rights approaches.[1]

4. Highlight the main differences between the utility, justice, and rights approaches to ethical reasoning.

research window 3.1

The Code of Marketing Research Standards (Marketing Research Association, Inc.)

SECTION A:

All Marketing Research Association Members agree that they:

1. Will ensure that each study is conducted according to the agreement with the Client.

2. Will never falsify or omit data for any reason at any phase of a research study or project.

   a. All marketing and opinion research released for public consumption (e.g., p-r release research) will comply with prevailing research standards specified in this Code and include statements disclosing (1) the method of data collection, (2) the date(s) of data collection, (3) the sampling frame, (4) the sampling method, (5) the sample size, and (6) the calculated margin of error for quantitative studies.

3. Will protect and preserve the confidentiality of all research techniques and/or methodologies and of information considered confidential or proprietary.

   a. Information will not be revealed that could be used to identify respondents without proper authorization, the exceptions being:
      - Customer Satisfaction Research where the express, expected result of all parties is that the client or client's agent will receive the information for follow-up.

- Compliance with a court order or other legal demand (e.g., discovery phase of a pending legal case).

4. Will report research results accurately and honestly.

5. Will protect the rights and privacy of respondents.

6. Will treat respondents in a professional manner.

7. Will take all reasonable precautions that respondents are in no way directly harmed or adversely affected as a result of their participation in a marketing research project.

8. Will not abuse public confidence in opinion and marketing research.

9. Will not misrepresent themselves as having qualifications, experience, skills, resources or other facility locations that they do not possess.

10. Will not refer to membership in the Marketing Research Association as proof of competence.

11. Will not ask our members who subcontract research to engage in any activity that is not acceptable as defined in the Code or that is prohibited under any applicable federal, state or local laws, regulations and/or ordinances.

12. Will protect the confidentiality of anything learned about a client's business as a result of access to proprietary information.

13. Will, when conducting secondary research, make the End User aware of the source of the secondary research. At no time will secondary research be presented to the End User as primary data.

14. Will inform the client if:
    - their work is to be combined or syndicated with other clients' work
    - all or part of their work will be subcontracted outside the researcher's organization

15. Will avoid all conflicts of interest in the carrying out of work for multiple clients, particularly those in the same or similar businesses.

16. When having responsibility for creating products and services for respondent use, will be responsible for providing products and services that:

- are safe and fit for their intended use
- are labeled in accordance with all laws and regulations
- will provide means to make the respondent whole should problems arise
- will provide emergency contact information

17. Will provide detailed written or verbal study instructions to those engaged in the data collection process.

18. Will not represent a non-research activity to be opinion and marketing research, such as, but not limited to:

    - questions whose sole objective is to obtain personal information about respondents whether for legal, political, commercial, private or other purposes
    - the compilation of lists, registers or databanks of names and addresses for any non-research purposes (e.g., canvassing or fund raising)
    - industrial, commercial or any other form of espionage that could cause harm to an individual or organization
    - the acquisition of information for use by credit rating services or similar organizations
    - sales or promotional approaches to the respondent
    - the collection of debts

19. Will identify surveys and other methods of data collection as such and not attempt to collect data through casual or conversational means other than for bona fide mystery shopping assignments.

20. Will not use research information to identify respondents without the permission of the respondent. The following are exceptions:

    a. Respondent identification information may be used in processing the data and merging data files.

    b. Respondent identification information may be used to append client or third-party data to a survey-based data file.

    c. Respondent identification information may be revealed in compliance with a court order or

other legal demand from a competent and recognized legal authority (e.g., discovery phase of a pending legal case).

If such permission is given, the interviewer must record it, or a respondent must do so during all surveys not involving an interviewer, at the time the permission is secured. If such permission is given, the data may only be used for the purpose to which the respondent agreed. Additionally, members will ensure that all respondent identification information is safeguarded against unauthorized access.

21. Will respect the respondent's right to withdraw or to refuse to cooperate at any stage of the study and will not use any procedure or technique to coerce or imply that cooperation is obligatory.

22. Will ensure that respondents are informed at the outset if the interview/discussion is being audio or video recorded by any means and will, if required, obtain written consent if the recorded interview/discussion will be

    - viewed by a third party
    - reproduced for outside use

23. Will give respondents the opportunity to refuse to participate in the research when there is a possibility they may be identifiable even without the use of their name or address (e.g., because of the size of the population being sampled).

24. Will adhere to the Children's Online Privacy Protection Act and will obtain permission and document consent of a parent, legal guardian or responsible guardian before interviewing children under 13 years of age. Prior to obtaining permission, the interviewer should divulge the subject matter, length of the interview and other special tasks that may be required of the respondent.

25. Will ensure that the results of the research are the sole property of the End User(s). At no time will results be shared with other clients.

26. Will treat the respondent with respect and not influence a respondent's opinion or attitude on any issue through direct or indirect attempts, including the framing of questions.

(Continued)

27. Will ensure that all formulas used during bidding and reporting during the data collection process conform with the MRA Incidence Guidelines or with an incidence calculation formula agreed upon between the client and research provider(s).

28. Will make factually correct statements, whether verbal or written, to secure cooperation and will honor promises made during the interview to respondents.

29. Will ensure that all interviewers comply with any laws or regulations that may be applicable when contacting or communicating to any minor (under 18 years of age) regardless of the technology or methodology utilized.

30. Will not reveal any information that could be used to identify clients without their written authorization.

31. Will ensure that companies, their employees and subcontractors involved in the data collection process adhere to reasonable precautions so that multiple surveys are not conducted at the same time with a specific respondent without explicit permission from the sponsoring company or companies.

32. Will consider all research materials provided by the client or generated as a result of materials provided by the client to be the property of the client. These materials will be retained or disposed of as agreed upon with the client at the time of the study.

33. Will, as time and availability permit, give their client the opportunity to monitor studies in progress to ensure research quality.

34. Will ensure that information collected during any study will not be used for any sales, solicitations or Push Polling.

35. Will respect that all information contained in a facility database or held by an independent recruiter is the sole property of these entities.

36. Will follow all use restrictions imposed by the facility in order to ensure confidentiality for all parties.

37. Will not permit use of respondent contact information for re-contacting a respondent unless the respondent has been informed of this possibility at the time of the original research, and given their consent to be contacted.

38. For Internet research, will follow all federal, state and local laws regarding Internet/online communications. This takes into account all opt-in/opt-out requests.

39. For Internet research, will be familiar with the already established guidelines from MRA, IMRO and ESOMAR, which include the definition of unsolicited emails.

40. For Internet research, will ensure that the Researcher's identity is disclosed to respondents.

41. For Internet research, will post privacy policy statements online.

42. For Internet research, will not use any data in any way contrary to the provider's published privacy statement without permission from the respondent.

43. For Internet research, will not send unsolicited email to those who have opted out.

SECTION B: Sampling

Those who provide sample must adhere to all prior standards and in addition:

44. Must be prepared to comply with requirements and limitations placed on data usage by data owners, including list brokers and database compilers. These requirements and limitations include but are not limited to:

    • required submission of questionnaire documents when requested

    • limitations on use of sensitive material including data on children, medical conditions, financial information and other areas deemed as sensitive by the list provider or owner

    • not using samples or lists for any purpose other than legitimate research purposes

    • holding household and personal data contained in sample information in the same strict confidence as collected survey data and using it only for the purposes of stratification, selection or control of survey samples or in tabulation of aggregate results

- ensuring that information derived from the sample will not be used for individual marketing efforts. It is understood that no marketing action can be taken toward an individual respondent as a result of his/her survey information and/or participation as a survey respondent

45. Will not misrepresent the impact of sample methodology and its impact on survey data.

46. Will, upon request, disclose practices and methods used for generating, stratifying and selecting specific samples.

47. Will, upon request, identify the appropriateness of the sample methodology itself and its ability to accomplish research objectives.

48. Will protect the identity and confidentiality of research organizations and will not disclose information without consent except in compliance with a court order or other legal demand (e.g., discovery phase of a pending legal case).

49. Will compile, maintain and utilize Internet samples of only those individuals who have provided their permission to be contacted (opt-in) and who have a reasonable expectation that they will receive Internet invitations for opinion and marketing research purposes.

50. Will not employ any deceptive methods in obtaining sample. Sample Providers will not employ any techniques or technologies, actively or passively, to collect e-mail addresses without a respondent's awareness or permission.

51. Will provide access to their privacy policy, which will be prominently displayed, for public review on each survey administered online.

52. Will offer respondents the choice with each survey to be removed (opt-out) from future Internet invitations.

Those Using Sample . . . .

53. Will, to the fullest extent possible on each project, counsel End Users as to the appropriateness of the sample methodology being employed. Ultimately, communication of critical information resides with the Research Provider working with the End User.

54. Will be prepared to disclose to the Sample Provider the research objectives including the nature of such decision making and data uses, and will not knowingly misrepresent or mislead intent to any entity involved in the research process.

55. Will adhere to policies and/or contracts set forth by sample providers governing the use of purchased and/or licensed sample resources or files.

56. Will offer respondents the choice with each survey to be removed (opt-out) from future Internet invitations.

SECTION C: Tabulation and Data Processing

Those who are engaged in Tabulation and Data Processing must adhere to all prior standards and in addition:

57. Will inform Clients, at their request, of the quality control procedures the Data Processing Company has in place.

58. Will provide Client, at their request, with a clear statement in writing of the work involved with regard to the scope of the project, timing, and associated costs.

59. Will inform Clients, at their request, of the archiving and storage procedures the Data Processing Company has in place.

60. Will inform clients, at their request, of the software (name, producer and version) that is being utilized for their work.

Source: Marketing Research Association, Inc., "The Code of Marketing Research Standards," downloaded from www.mra-net.org, July 1, 2008.

utility approach
A method of ethical or moral reasoning that focuses on society and the net consequences that an action may have. If the net result of benefits minus costs is positive, the act is considered ethical; if the net result is negative, the act is considered unethical.

The first method of ethical reasoning is termed the **utility approach**. This method focuses on society as the unit of analysis and stresses the consequences of an act on all those directly or indirectly affected by it. The utility approach holds that the correct course of action is the one that promotes "the greatest good for the greatest number." As a result, a researcher would need to take into account all benefits and costs to all persons affected by the proposed action—in effect, to society as a whole. If the benefits outweigh the costs, then the act is considered to be ethical and morally acceptable. Determining all the relevant costs and benefits can be extremely difficult, however. And because society is the unit of analysis, it is entirely possible that one or more individuals or groups may bear most of the costs, while other individuals or groups enjoy most of the benefits.

Take a look at Exhibit 3.3 and imagine that you are the researcher that has been hired to conduct research on how consumers shop for vegetables and other produce in a grocery store. Was the decision to use video cameras to record consumers' behaviors in the store—without their knowledge—an ethical decision? Using the utility approach, we attempt to add up the benefits (e.g., knowing how consumers *really* behave when it comes to reading nutrition labels as a starting point for developing better ways of communicating this important information; better understanding the purchase process so that the company can ultimately sell more produce, thereby employing more workers and putting more money into the economy) and the costs (e.g., violation of shoppers' privacy and ability to choose whether or not to participate in the research; the costs of doing the research). Considering only these potential costs and benefits, most people would probably say that the action was ethical from a utility perspective: the potential benefits to the company and society from the information gained seem to outweigh the costs borne by the consumers who participated in the study without their knowledge, as well as the cost of the actual research.

justice approach
A method of ethical or moral reasoning that focuses on the degree to which benefits and costs are fairly distributed across individuals and groups. If the benefits and costs of a proposed action are fairly distributed, an action is considered to be ethical.

The **justice approach** to ethical reasoning considers whether or not the costs and benefits of a proposed action are distributed fairly among individuals and groups. Who decides what amounts to a "fair" distribution of benefits or costs? Essentially, it boils down to societal consensus—what is generally accepted by most people in a society—about what is equitable. If the benefits and costs of an action are fairly distributed, then the action would be considered morally acceptable under the justice approach.

Exhibit 3.3   **Applying the Ethical Frameworks in Practice**

You have been hired to help a large producer of leafy vegetables understand how consumers shop for produce in grocery stores. The company is considering different methods of packaging its produce, especially with respect to how best to display nutritional content. Company managers believe that if more people understand the nutritional value of their products (as well as those of other producers) consumers will begin to make better decisions about the foods that they and their children eat. To accomplish this, however, they need to fully understand how consumers actually behave within the grocery store environment (e.g., how much time they spend reading nutritional information, comparing different types of vegetables, selecting particular vegetables for purchase). Because you suspect that shoppers will change their shopping behaviors if they know that they are being observed, you have decided to place small cameras in strategic locations in the produce sections of four participating grocery stores and record consumer behaviors over a two-week period.

- Is this decision ethical using the utility approach to ethical reasoning?

- Is this decision ethical using the justice approach to ethical reasoning?

- Is this decision ethical using the rights approach to ethical reasoning?

© JENNIFER GRIMES/EAST VALLEY TRIBUNE/ASSOCIATED PRESS

The utility approach would likely result in regarding hidden cameras placed strategically in grocery stores to be ethical, as the proposed benefits (such as selling more product and thus employing more workers to handle increased sales) outweigh the costs (possibly infringing on consumers' right to privacy).

Now, back to the grocery store. To the extent that the knowledge gained from the research has the potential to benefit most people in the society—including those shoppers that participated in the study along with the company that paid for the research—through improved eating habits (for consumers) and improved profits (for the firm), we could probably argue that the benefits were more or less fairly distributed. (By the way, we should note that a "fair" distribution is not necessarily an "equal" distribution. In this situation, the company itself and its workers may enjoy a greater share of the benefits, but they also took on a greater share of the costs and risks.) On the other hand, suppose that the company conducted the research for the sole purpose of figuring out how to sell more stuff without regard for its customers or their needs. If the people who pay important costs (e.g., loss of privacy, knowledge of their participation) see none of the benefits, then the action would likely be judged as unethical from the justice approach.

Finally, let's consider the **rights approach** to ethical decision making. Both the utility and justice approaches focus on the consequences of behaviors. Under the rights approach, a proposed action is right or wrong, in and of itself; there is less concern about the consequences of the action. Researchers following the rights method of ethical reasoning focus on the welfare of the individual and individuals' rights. They believe that every individual has a right to be treated in ways that ensure the person's dignity, respect, and autonomy. Probably most people in the United States would argue, for example, that every person has a right to be safe, to be informed, to choose, and to be heard.

What about the research with grocery store customers? When we focus on the rights of the individuals who are being studied without their knowledge or permission, it seems fairly easy to judge the research to be unethical under the rights approach. And this highlights one of the difficulties of applying the rights approach: In general, it is more difficult to judge an action as ethical under this approach because it is nearly impossible to ensure that every right of every relevant individual or group has not been violated.

As a practical matter, applying these models to a marketing research decision can be difficult. Each individual researcher ultimately must decide, however, whether or not a particular action is ethical and whether or not to proceed. For many people, there is a natural tendency towards the rights approach with its focus on individual

rights approach
A method of ethical or moral reasoning that focuses on the welfare of the individual and that uses means, intentions, and features of an act itself in judging its ethicality. If any individual's rights are violated, the act is considered unethical.

Problem Formulation

Introduction

A business executive once remarked that he had spent his entire career climbing the ladder of success only to discover when he got to the top that the ladder was leaning on the wrong building. He regretted that he hadn't devoted more of his time to the things that really mattered. If we aren't careful, the same thing can happen with marketing research: We can take all the necessary steps and get perfectly valid answers—only to discover that we've been asking the wrong questions.

PROBLEM FORMULATION

The Coca-Cola Company's experience with New Coke in the 1980s is a classic example of how defining the problem incorrectly can lead to disastrous results.[1] Coca-Cola's market share had shrunk from 60% in the mid-1940s to less than 24% in 1983. At the same time, Pepsi, the product's chief rival, had continued to gain market share. It was easy for Coca-Cola's managers to see that a problem existed. Stung by Pepsi-Cola's "Pepsi Challenge" promotional campaign, which showed consumers consistently preferring the taste of Pepsi to Coke in blind taste tests, company researchers, managers, and executives became convinced that Coca-Cola had a "taste problem."[2]

Coca-Cola Company researchers proceeded to conduct extensive marketing research—including 190,000 blind taste tests with consumers, costing $4 million—to compare the taste of a new version of Coca-Cola with that of Pepsi and regular Coke. The new formulation was preferred by a majority of consumers. Further research demonstrated that the results held—in fact, were stronger—when consumers were allowed to glimpse the labels to see what they were tasting. Managers were confident that they had developed a product that would successfully solve the taste problem. On the basis of the research, the company introduced New Coke to the world in April 1984, replacing the original formula.

The decision to replace the original product with New Coke is recognized as one of the biggest marketing blunders in history.[3] The company reversed course less than three months later with the reintroduction of the original Coca-Cola product. What happened? The research was technically sound; it is quite likely that people actually preferred the sweeter taste of New Coke. A far greater issue than taste for many consumers, however, was the idea that the original Coca-Cola—with a century's worth of history and imagery—was being tampered with, discontinued. Although Coca-Cola managers recognized in advance that some consumers would probably not accept a change in the brand, they continued to focus on the "taste problem." Other classic examples of poor problem definition are included in Exhibit 4.1.

| **Exhibit 4.1** | **Classic Examples of Poor Problem Definition** |

- The first Lite beer was developed by Meister Bräu. Initial taste tests indicated that people liked the newly developed beer, but it failed miserably when Meister Bräu introduced it to the marketplace. The frustrated company in turn sold it to Miller Brewing Company, who defined the marketing research problem more broadly than simply consumer taste preferences. Miller's research addressed consumer perceptions of the new type of beer and found that the very concept of a diet beer connoted "wimp"— and big beer drinkers tried to project macho images. Based on its research, Miller's emphasis became one of changing the image of the brand through its use of famous sports personalities.

- After much hard work to develop a cigarette with an acceptable taste but no visible smoke, RJR Nabisco launched Eclipse. Unfortunately, smokers didn't care to buy the product; they liked the smoke of a cigarette. Cigarette smoke was a problem only for nonsmokers—and they, by definition, were not the company's target market. The company's $100 million development effort went to correct something its customers didn't view as a problem by developing a product they didn't want.

Sources: Wayne A. Lemburg, "Past AMA President Hardin, Head of Market Facts, Looks Back at the Early Days of Marketing Research," *Marketing News 20*, December 19, 1986, p. 9 and Cliff Edwards, "A Look at the Century's Hyped Products," *Chicago Tribune*, June 13, 1999, Sec. 5, p. 12.

Problems versus Opportunities

When we talk about "defining the problem" or "problem formulation," we simply mean a process of trying to identify specific areas where additional information is needed about the marketing environment. A manager might face a situation that has obvious negative ramifications for the organization (for example, sharply reduced revenues compared with earlier periods for a retailer, chronic shortage of volunteers to support an ongoing civic organization, or lack of evidence of market demand to persuade investors to "buy in" to an entrepreneur's idea for a new kind of product). These kinds of situations are normally thought of as "problems."

On the other hand, a manager might face a situation with potentially positive results for the organization (e.g., the organization's research department has invented a new chemical compound that promises to revolutionize the product category; brand managers think they have identified a market segment of consumers whose needs are not being met adequately by competitors). Managers must often decide how to exploit these "opportunities," if at all.

Although it is sometimes useful to distinguish between problems and opportunities, it is often better to think of problems and opportunities as two sides of the same coin. Regardless of perspective, both situations require good information about the marketing environment before managers make important decisions. And today's opportunity is tomorrow's problem if a company fails to take advantage of the opportunity while its competitors do. Similarly, a company that successfully deals with a problem before its competitors do has created an opportunity to move ahead in the industry. For these reasons, we usually refer to a "problem" as something that needs information regardless of whether the organization originally viewed the situation as a problem or an opportunity.

Learning Objective

1. Specify the key steps in problem formulation.

THE PROBLEM FORMULATION PROCESS

How can a company avoid the trap of researching the wrong problem? The best way is to delay research until the problem is properly defined. Too often, the researcher's initial step is to write a proposal describing the methods that will be used to conduct the research. Instead, the researcher—in cooperation with managers—must take the time necessary to fully understand the situation. Even well-designed and executed research can't rescue a project (and the resulting business decisions and consequences) if researchers have failed to define the problem correctly.

Exhibit 4.2 presents the six key steps in problem formulation. Defining the problem is among the most difficult—and certainly most important—aspects of the entire marketing research process. The difficulty is primarily due to the uniqueness of every situation a manager may encounter. Although we provide some fairly specific directions, problem formulation involves more art than science and must be approached with great care.

Step One: Meet with Client

The first step toward defining the problem correctly is to meet with the manager(s) requesting marketing research. This should be done at the earliest stages of the project for two important reasons. First, it is essential that managers and researchers are able to communicate openly with one another, and this likely won't happen unless the parties develop an initial rapport and a relationship built on mutual trust. To the extent possible, researchers need to keep the client engaged and actively participating in the process, especially during problem formulation, but also at later stages.

Exhibit 4.2	**Key Steps in Problem Formulation**

Meet with client to obtain (a) management statement of problem/opportunity, (b) background information, (c) management objectives for research, and (d) possible managerial actions to result from research.

Clarify the problem/opportunity by questioning managerial assumptions and gathering additional information from managers and/or others as needed. Perform exploratory research as necessary.

State the manager's decision problem, including source (planned change or unplanned change in environment) and type (discovery- or strategy-oriented).

Develop full range of possible research problems that would address the manager's decision problem.

Select research problem(s) that best address the manager's decision problem, based on an evaluation of likely costs and benefits of each possible research problem.

Prepare and submit research request agreement to client. Revise in consultation with client.

The second reason to meet with the client is straightforward. The researcher must get as much information as possible from the manager with respect to the problem/opportunity at hand. In particular, the researcher needs to obtain a clear understanding of the problem from the manager's viewpoint, along with all relevant background information. Here are some questions that are appropriate at this point.

Learning Objective

2. Discuss two objectives of the initial meeting with the research client.

- What caused you to notice the problem?

- What factors do you think have created this situation?

- What is likely to happen if nothing changes in the next 12 months?

- What do you hope to accomplish using marketing research?

- What actions will you take depending upon the answers?

Planned Change versus Unplanned Change   In general, there are only two basic sources of marketing problems: (1) unplanned changes in the marketing environment and (2) planned changes in the marketing environment. Understanding the basic source of the problem will provide clues about the nature of the problem and the type of research that is needed.

Learning Objective

3. Discuss the two general sources of marketing problems/ opportunities.

Sometimes problems/opportunities show up unexpectedly due to changes in the external environment. How the firm responds to new technology or a new product introduced by a competitor or a change in demographics or lifestyles largely determines whether the change turns out to be a problem or an opportunity. For example, John Zapp operates two car dealerships—a Buick-Pontiac-GMC dealership and a Dodge-Chrysler-Jeep outlet—located next to Honda and Toyota dealerships. Changes in consumer preferences led to fewer shoppers at his dealerships and many more shoppers at competing stores, a development that Zapp didn't plan or want to have happen. How did he respond? He focused on selling used vehicles, which have profit margins that are seven times higher than for new cars.[4]

A slightly different form of unplanned change involves serendipity, or chance ideas. An unexpected new idea might come from a customer in a complaint letter. Rubbermaid has encouraged its executives to read customer letters to find out how people like the company's products, sometimes leading to new product ideas. Sometimes companies learn that customers are "misusing" products, such as when

© ROSE ALCORN

Avon's Skin So Soft product has long been recognized as a good insect repellent, but the company has never marketed it as an insect repellent and claims it has never investigated why the product wards off insects, though the idea led to its development of a new product: Skin So Soft Bug Guard Plus Insect Repellent.

consumers began to believe that Avon's Skin So Soft lotion served as an effective insect repellent. And sometimes companies experience an "Aha!" moment and discover new uses for their technologies. Research Window 4.1 tells the story of how the ingredients for 3M Company's famous Post-it Notes® came together in a church choir.

Not all change is unanticipated. Much of it is planned. Most firms want to increase their business, and they devise various marketing actions for doing so. These actions include the development and introduction of new products, improved distribution, more effective pricing, and promotion. Planned change is oriented more toward the future and is proactive; unplanned change tends to be oriented more toward the past and is often reactive. Planned change is change that the firm wishes to bring about—the basic issue is how. Often, the role of marketing research here is to investigate the feasibility of the alternatives being considered.

Step Two: Clarify the Problem/Opportunity

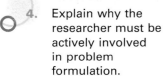

4. Explain why the researcher must be actively involved in problem formulation.

During the first step in problem formulation, the primary task of the researcher is to listen carefully as managers provide their perspective of the problem, its background and source (planned vs. unplanned change), and what they hope to learn through marketing research. Step 2 involves helping managers get precisely to the heart of the problem. This may seem odd at first—after all, shouldn't managers have a better understanding of the problem than the researcher? If you conduct the research based on the client's definition of the problem, however, and the results cannot be used, who do you think will be blamed? More often than not, you will

research window 4.1

A NOTE-able Achievement

They're little and they stick—but not too hard. That's why everyone loves Post-it Notes! Yet the unique adhesive that makes these little notes so indispensable waited more than a decade for its chance to change the world.

Dr. Spencer Silver, a 3M scientist, discovered the formula for the sticky stuff back in 1968. But it was Silver's colleague, Art Fry, who finally came up with a practical use for it. The idea for repositionable notes struck Fry while singing in the church choir. His bookmark kept falling out of his hymnal, causing him to lose his page. So, taking advantage of a 3M policy known as the bootlegging policy, Fry used a portion of his working hours to develop a solution to his problem. Now the world is singing the praises of this pet project: Post-it Notes.

After years of product development, 3M introduced the concept of Post-it Notes in four major markets in 1977. But, without actual samples in hand to try, consumers didn't catch on. A year later, 3M blanketed the Boise, Idaho, market with samples upon samples of Post-it® Notes. After trying the notes, more than 90% of users said they'd buy the product themselves. The test was a success! By 1980, Post-it Notes were being sold nationally. Today, they're used and enjoyed throughout the world.

Source: Downloaded from http://www.mmm.com/us/office/postit/pastpresent/history_ws.html, July 3, 2008.

MANAGER'S FOCUS

One of the most common criticisms managers have of marketing research studies is that the findings are not "actionable." By this, they mean that it is not clear what step(s) should be taken in response to the research. While this may be a fair assessment of many research studies, managers often share more responsibility for this outcome than they realize. There are several ways managers might "short circuit" the problem definition process and thereby limit the usefulness of research findings.

For example, managers at times believe the marketing problem was adequately defined in the request-for-proposal (RFP) they issued. Before granting a contract for a project, however, managers are understandably protective of confidential information, so they may not have revealed issues that would have led the marketing research firm to define the problem differently and possibly propose different methods. After a research firm's proposal has been accepted, managers too commonly consider the process to have been completed so they delegate subsequent interaction with the research firm to the internal marketing research staff or lower-level managers who may not be as knowledgeable about the marketing issues confronting the organization. Behaviors such as these can result in a decision problem that may not reflect all of the complexities of the actual marketing situation.

As you will see in this chapter and the next one, it is often necessary to complete some preliminary (or exploratory) research before the marketing problem can be fully or adequately defined. This means that at the time a research provider has been selected, the problem formulation stage may be only partially completed. Even though the research proposal has been accepted, you should realize that the final research methods may need to be adjusted based on what is learned from the exploratory research, and the corresponding re-specification of the decision problem. Therefore, as a marketing manager, it is essential that you stay engaged in the problem formulation process until you and the research provider agree that it has been properly finalized. By doing this, you will dramatically increase the odds that the completed project will give you the guidance you need (that is, be actionable).

Here's something else: if your research provider is willing to proceed on the basis of the marketing problem as specified in the RFP, you should consider replacing that provider with one that recognizes its responsibility to guide you through the problem formulation stage. Helping you properly formulate the problem is one of the most important services provided by a research firm because research based on a poorly defined problem will likely lead you down the wrong path.

get the blame. Even worse, the actual problem still won't have been defined, much less solved. Don't let a manager perform his or her own diagnosis and prescribe the treatment as well.

Sometimes it is necessary to challenge managers on their preexisting assumptions. For example, in the case of a new service that hasn't lived up to revenue expectations, maybe consumers never really needed that type of service. Sometimes it also helps to probe managers as to why the problem is important: "Why do you want to measure customer satisfaction? Have you seen signs that customers may not be satisfied? Are you concerned about a new competitor that has entered the market? Are you planning to upgrade service and want a baseline level of satisfaction?" The point isn't to put a manager on the spot; the point is to help the manager understand the true nature of the problem. Asking hard questions is much easier if you have demonstrated your professionalism and have begun to develop a rapport with the client.

It is often advisable to conduct exploratory research at this stage, particularly when managers have seen evidence of a problem (e.g., falling sales revenue, increasing complaints from customers) but don't know the underlying causes. As we discuss in the following chapter, exploratory research can be used to help pinpoint the problem.

One of the most important things a researcher can do for a manager is to provide a different perspective of the problem/opportunity. Many managers, particularly those who have been with a company for a long time, are afflicted with "normal thinking." That is, they have developed a routine way of looking at the business and responding to different situations. In many ways, this is a good thing; the presence of normal operating procedures allows great efficiency through the development of standards and routines. As we have seen, some forms of marketing research (e.g., marketing information system) are by nature routine and standardized.

Normal thinking often can get in the way of understanding the true nature of a problem, however. It is your job as a researcher to provide a new perspective, even though the client may not appreciate it at first. Exhibit 4.3 offers an example to help you begin thinking creatively. The security guard was guilty of normal thinking—he failed to consider alternative perspectives. Similarly, if you ask 100 people which way a clock's hands move, 99 or more of them will say "clockwise." This is true, unless you take the clock's perspective; then, the hands move counterclockwise. At this stage of the project, one of the researcher's primary tasks is to ensure that managers are focused on the true problem.

Bringing a new perspective to a problem may sound like a good idea, but how is it actually done? How could The Coca-Cola Company have known to define its problem a bit more broadly than as simply one of taste? To be honest, it's tough. Because the researcher doesn't deal with the manager's issues on a daily basis, he or she is automatically less likely to fall victim to normal thinking. Until the problem/opportunity is properly formulated, researchers must be asking key questions, listening carefully to the answers to those questions, asking more questions to clarify the situation further, and at all times carefully thinking about, or analyzing, the situation.

Step Three: State the Manager's Decision Problem

Learning Objective

5. Distinguish between two types of decision problems.

decision problem
The problem facing the decision maker for which the research is intended to provide answers.

At this point, the researcher should be able to state the manager's **decision problem**, which is simply the basic problem/opportunity facing the manager for which marketing research is intended to provide answers. A well-stated decision problem takes the manager's perspective, is as simple as possible, and takes the form of a question. For example, consider a new coffee shop near a university campus that has been open for six months but has yet to make a profit. Costs have been held as low as possible; sales revenue simply hasn't materialized as quickly as expected. While the owner no doubt has many questions about her business, its lack of success, and how to move forward successfully, her initial decision problem might best take the form, "Why are store revenues so low?" This situation was certainly unanticipated, so the problem has originated from unplanned change.

E x h i b i t 4 . 3	The Problem with "Normal Thinking"

There is an old story of a factory worker who left the factory each night pushing a wheelbarrow piled high with scrap materials. At the factory gate, the security guard would tip his hat, say "good evening," and wonder to himself why anybody would want to take that stuff home. But because the scraps held no value to the company, the guard let him pass each night. Years later, after both the security guard and the factory worker had left the company, the former guard happened to meet the worker. After they exchanged greetings, the guard leaned over to the worker and said, "Say, now that we're both retired, there's something I've just got to know. What did you want with all that trash you took home every night?" The worker looked at him and smiled. "I didn't want the trash," he said. "I was stealing wheelbarrows!"

The decision problem facing the coffee shop owner is an example of a **discovery-oriented decision problem**. Discovery-oriented problems are common with unplanned changes in the marketing environment. In these situations, managers often simply need basic information about "what is going on?" and "why is it going on?" and the researcher is asked primarily to provide facts that decision makers can use in formulating strategies in dealing with the unanticipated situation. For example, researchers could provide information about customer satisfaction (perhaps the shop doesn't consistently offer a quality product), or the overall awareness level among the target market (maybe most people don't know about the shop), or consumer perceptions of competing coffee shops (perhaps a nearby coffee shop is perceived as a better value for the money). In each case, the researcher can offer facts and figures that help shed light on the basic problem. Note, however, that discovery-oriented research rarely solves a problem in the sense of providing actionable results. This form of research simply aims to provide some of the insights and the building blocks necessary for managers to make better decisions.

Discovery-oriented decision problems may also apply to situations of planned change, particularly in early stages of planning when the issue is to identify possible courses of action (as opposed to choosing a preferred course of action). In this situation, key questions are likely to include "what options are available?" or "why might this option be effective?"

A second form of manager's decision problem, the **strategy-oriented decision problem**, aims more directly at making decisions. This type of decision problem is commonly used with planned change, with an emphasis on how the planned change should be implemented. It is also appropriate for problems originating from unplanned change, provided that enough is known about the situation (perhaps through discovery-oriented research) so that strategic decisions are warranted. Suppose that initial research for the coffee shop indicated that only 38% of the customers in its target market were aware that the coffee shop existed. An appropriate decision problem at this point might be "How do we increase awareness?" and researchers might determine the effectiveness of two proposed advertising campaigns at generating awareness. Notice that the output from the research process in this situation will be a recommendation about which of two specific alternatives to choose. The key distinction between discovery-oriented and strategy-oriented decision problems is the latter's focus on actionable results. Research Window 4.2 discusses Visa's use of strategy-oriented research to select a new brand logo.

If possible, researchers should attempt to conduct strategy-oriented research. Providing additional "facts" through discovery research doesn't necessarily get managers much closer to a good decision. And many companies place a preference on strategy-oriented research. At General Mills, for example, the emphasis is on research that evaluates alternatives. Thus, instead of asking the question, "What proportion of potato chips is eaten at meals?" General Mills would ask, "How can we advertise our potato chips for meal consumption?" or "Will a 'meal commercial' sell more chips than our present commercial?" (both strategy-oriented questions). Still, there are times when discovery-oriented research is absolutely essential, particularly when managers are confronted with unplanned changes in the environment.

ETHICAL DILEMMA

The president of a small bank approaches you with plans to launch a special program of financial counseling and support for women and asks you to establish whether there is sufficient public interest to justify starting the program. No other bank in the city caters specifically to women, and you think that professional women, in particular, might be enthusiastic. The president believes that if news of the plan leaks out, competitors may try to preempt her, so she asks you to keep the bank's identity secret from respondents and to inquire only into general levels of interest in increased financial services for women. However, as you read through the literature she has left with you, you notice that the bank is located in the most depressed area of the city, where women might be harassed and feel unsafe.

- Would it be unethical to research how much demand exists for a women's banking program, when the bank in question will interpret the demand as encouragement to launch such a program?
- What might be the costs to the researcher in voicing misgivings about the suitability of this particular bank launching this program? Would you voice your misgivings?
- Does it violate respondents' rights if you do not reveal the identity of the research sponsor? If so, is it a serious violation in this case? Is there a conflict of interest here with respect to respondents' right to be informed versus the client's right to confidentiality?

discovery-oriented decision problem
A decision problem that typically seeks to answer "what" or "why" questions about a problem/opportunity. The focus is generally on generating useful information.

strategy-oriented decision problem
A decision problem that typically seeks to answer "how" questions about a problem/opportunity. The focus is generally on selecting alternative courses of action.

research window 4.2

VISA: Using Strategy-Oriented Research to Select a New Brand Mark

Visa, headquartered in San Francisco, is one of the world's most powerful and successful brands. The company partners with 16,600 financial institution customers, and its services can be utilized at over 29 million retail locations around the world, as well as at 1.2 million automatic teller machines. The company processes over 136 million transactions per day, with $3.8 trillion in annual volume. Its market share is twice that of its nearest competitor. Back in 2003, however, managers were concerned as they thought about the future.

The Problem/Opportunity

Despite the obvious global success of the company, there was a sense among managers that the existing brand needed to be revitalized to be able to successfully carry Visa's growing business portfolio and address changing marketplace dynamics. When the existing logo was developed in the 1970s, the company featured just one basic offering: the classic Visa credit card. By 2003, more than 75 different products and services were associated with the brand—and this doesn't count the many thousands of different payment cards offered by Visa's member institutions, each of which carries the Visa brand. There were also a number of other business considerations that together reinforced the need for a new brand approach. For one thing, the industry was more mature; partner institutions now wanted more card design "real estate" (space on the front of the card) for presenting and differentiating their own brands. Industry dynamics, including merchant requirements, advances in technology, and consumer tastes also required Visa managers to take a hard look at their brand requirements for a Visa card.

Although global qualitative research with consumers indicated a great number of positive attributes of the existing brand (trusted, safe, reliable, local and global, accepted everywhere), consumers also provided comments such as "a little old-fashioned;" "it doesn't communicate what I want to do in the future;" and "this is in the steam age—not the electronic age." In addition, the research indicated that the image of Visa was tied closely to plastic cards and might be difficult to extend to some of the new services the company was developing. As a result, managers within the organization became increasingly convinced that the Visa brand could easily become anchored in the past, preventing the company from fully developing and capitalizing on the brand's potential equity as payment products and lines of businesses broadened.

Exploratory Research

In November 2003, the company set out to develop and test a new brand mark that could be used as part of an expanded brand architecture framework, developed to address its current and anticipated portfolio of services. The company's success and the wide recognition of the existing brand mark, however, meant that the core brand equities had to be retained while allowing new equities to be developed, a tall order.

Working with outside brand identity consultants, managers selected an initial set of four possible logos, ranging from small to dramatic changes in the design. The goal in this initial phase of research was to determine just how far consumers would allow the brand to stretch while still maintaining the essential meanings associated with the well-known Visa brand. Researchers conducted focus groups in seven global markets (United States, Brazil, Russia, France, Japan, United Kingdom, and Korea). Four focus groups were held in each of these markets: Two groups held primary Visa users (one female group, one male group), and two groups held nonprimary Visa users (one female group, one male group). The results confirmed that consumers were open to the idea of a change, taking the Visa brand to a more contemporary, open expression, but that the differences could not be too dramatic or trendy. Exhibit A presents the logos tested—the circle represents the approximate degree to which consumers were willing to allow a change in the logo. The results were remarkably similar across the global markets.

Armed with these results, Visa managers commissioned more design work. The resulting options were screened using two more focus groups in each of the seven global markets. In each market, one female group and one male group was held, each group comprised of both primary and nonprimary users of Visa products. There was also an effort to ensure that 25% of the participants in each group were early adopters, those considered most open to the adoption of new products and technologies. This time, participants considered only three logos. The second round of focus groups confirmed for Visa managers that the endeavor was justified; the market was willing to accept a revitalized Visa brand mark and the design solutions were moving in the right direction. Importantly,

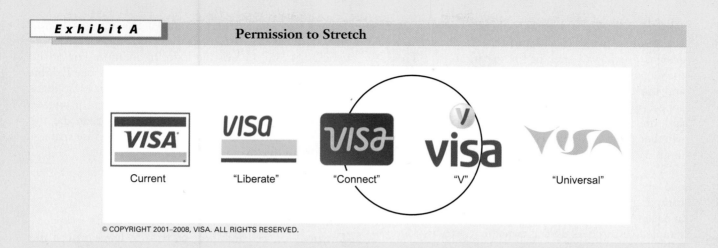

Current   "Liberate"   "Connect"   "V"   "Universal"

there were no signs that the proposed change would impact the favorability of Visa in the marketplace, obviously an important consideration to managers.

After additional design work, using a design consultant and in-house designers, three designs (plus the current logo) were screened via 16 more focus groups held in four U.S. cities. Once again, the results were encouraging. Two final options, one considered very "close-in" to the current design, and one that was more evolutionary, were selected for the quantitative phase of the research (see Exhibit B).

Descriptive Research

The qualitative research was useful for obtaining consumers' "permission" to change the long-standing Visa brand and had provided critical feedback for narrowing down the possible logo designs. Now the company needed to make a key decision: *Which brand mark should we choose?*

To help address this question, the company conducted quantitative research with consumers in 16 countries to compare the existing brand logo with the two candidate logos. The managers understood, based on numerous image and design studies, that new identities rarely portray the same core equities at the same levels as the existing identities. This is largely due to the fact that the new image is not yet fully associated (due to lack of consumer experience) with the brand. An image only inherits brand strength after significant communication activities and exposure. As such, the Visa team was intent on not using the research as a beauty contest between the contenders but as a quantitative tool to better understand the relative merits and risks of each proposed approach. The final decision would be based on business considerations informed by the quantitative design research.

The goal was to understand the relative benefits of each logo corresponding to the five objectives of the

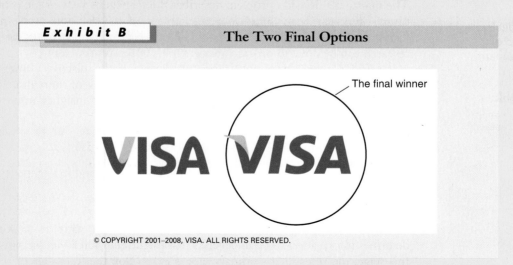

The final winner

(Continued)

research: (1) To understand whether opinion of Visa changes negatively; (2) To understand whether the new designs provide a better fit for the future; (3) To assess the degree of market confusion between the new designs and the current design; (4) To assess the strength and appeal of the new design in relation to the current design and the competition; and (5) To quantitatively assess whether the new design communicates and supports the desired attributes.

The 20-minute questionnaire was administered in one of two ways, either as an online Web survey or via computerized, face-to-face personal interviews conducted in a central facility in each of the cities represented in the sample. Researchers used a monadic research structure—each respondent saw and responded to only one brand mark (the current logo or one of the two proposed logos) until the end of the questionnaire when they were asked for a direct choice between the marks. A total of 7,084 consumers completed the questionnaire.

As an example of the researchers' creativity, to assess competitive standout, one of the three Visa logos (current brand, plus the two proposed designs identified during the exploratory research) was placed with competing logos and shown on-screen for one second. Participants then responded to the following instruction: "Please list the logo(s) that you have just seen." Recall rates for both of the new designs were higher than for the current mark or for the other competing products. The new

designs also seemed to communicate better the desired attributes "up to date," "forward looking," and "energetic" than did the existing logo. In addition, one of the new logos, known as the "winged V" design (see Exhibit B) seemed to perform better at communicating these attributes, suffered less market confusion, and produced stronger change in opinion of Visa scores than did the other option. On the basis of the research, Visa managers selected the "winged V" logo.

The Outcome

The branding research project, with 58 focus groups and over 7,000 survey respondents, bolstered Visa managers' confidence in the proposed brand revitalization effort. Most importantly, the research identified no significant business risks associated with altering a brand that had been known and accepted by consumers since 1977. In March 2005, the company's International Board of Directors approved the proposal to begin phasing in the new logo.

Sources: "Visa Inc. Corporate Overview," downloaded from the Visa Web site, http://www.visa.com, July 2, 2008 and Karen Gullett, "Visa Brand Revitalization," presented at the *Brand Architecture and Corporate Reputation* conference sponsored by the Marketing Science Institute, March 17, 2005.

Learning Objective

6. Distinguish between a decision problem and a research problem.

research problem
A restatement of the decision problem in research terms.

Step Four: Develop Possible Research Problems

The manager's decision problem describes the manager's view of the problem/opportunity. A research problem is a restatement of the decision problem in research terms, from the researcher's perspective. A research problem states specifically what research can be done to provide answers to the decision problem.

Consider again the coffee shop owner facing the discovery-oriented decision problem of "Why are store revenues so low?" As is true of most discovery-oriented problems, several avenues of research might provide insights into the problem, including:

- Investigate current customer satisfaction.

- Assess target market perceptions of the coffee shop and its competitors.

- Determine target market awareness.

Each of these possible research problems begins with an action word and describes information to be uncovered that might help solve the decision problem. At this stage, the researcher's primary task is to develop the full range of research problems for a given decision problem. Exhibit 4.4 provides examples of the relationship between decision problems and research problems.

Exhibit 4.4	Examples of the Relationship between Decision Problems and Research Problems

Decision Problems	**Possible Research Problems**
Discovery-Oriented (What? Why?)	
Why are store revenues so low?	Investigate current customer satisfaction. Assess target market perceptions of store and competitors. Determine target market awareness.
What needs do our customers have that currently are not being met?	Investigate customer lifestyles. Determine customer problems with existing products. Measure customer satisfaction.
Strategy-Oriented (How?)	
How do we increase store traffic?	Investigate effectiveness of different sales promotions. Determine consumer response to two proposed ad campaigns. Measure consumer preferences for new store layouts.
How should we introduce a new product?	Run test market to determine consumer preferences for different package sizes. Determine if at least 80% of test market purchasers are satisfied with product. Determine if product sampling promotion leads to 15% initial purchase rate.

With strategy-oriented decision problems, there are typically fewer possible research problems, because the focus has shifted onto making a choice among selected alternatives. At least, that's the way it's supposed to work. When the coffee shop owner shifted to the strategy-oriented decision problem "How do we increase awareness?" there were still several strategic options available including improved signage, increased levels of sales promotion, the introduction of an advertising campaign, and so on. Research problems might have included "determine which style of lettering is most readable on outdoor signage," "investigate the effectiveness of alternative coupon designs," or "determine consumer response to two proposed advertising campaigns." Presumably, the manager's experience, available budget, and/or discovery-oriented research led her to decide that advertising was the best area to consider for further research. (Don't forget that defining the problem is often more art than science.) At that point, the manager's decision problem might well have shifted to "Which advertising campaign should I select?" with a single associated research problem.

Where does the researcher get ideas about possible research problems? Usually, they come from the client during the process of clarifying the problem. Sometimes, however, new ideas will be uncovered through exploratory research or as a result of the researcher's experience. In any case, the key point at this stage of problem formulation is to specify the full range of potential research problems.

Step Five: Select Research Problem(s) to Be Addressed

There are often many possible research problems that would provide useful information, especially with discovery-oriented decision problems. Even strategy-oriented problems will sometimes have many associated research problems. The trick is to figure out which research problem(s) to pursue given the normal resource constraints facing managers. Only in rare cases will decision makers fund research on all possible research problems. As a result, the researcher must carefully review each identified research problem in terms of the trade-off between the information to be obtained versus the costs of obtaining that information. The costs may include money, time, and effort.

For example, we noted three of the possible research problems for the coffee shop owner facing the discovery-oriented decision problem, "Why are store revenues so low?" Investigating customer satisfaction will require gathering information from current customers. Assessing target market perceptions of the store and its competitors, as well as determining the target market's overall awareness of the store require collecting data from the target market, many of whom are not current customers. To address all three research problems adequately would be costly. In this situation, the researcher would work closely with the coffee shop owner to determine the most likely problem area(s) and, in turn, the most profitable areas of research. (Again, more art than science.) If the researcher has done a thorough job at previous stages in the problem definition process, the selection of research problems should be relatively straightforward.

It is important to note at this point that it is better to address one or two research problems fully than to try to tackle multiple issues and do a half-baked job on each. Our experience is that novice researchers, in their enthusiasm to do a good job, tend to believe that they can accomplish much more in a single project than is actually possible. The researcher cannot usually do all the research she or he would like to do because of budget considerations, which makes the choice of research problem(s) so critical.

Step Six: Prepare Research Request Agreement

Learning Objective

7. Describe the research request agreement.

research request agreement
A document prepared by the researcher after meeting with the decision maker that summarizes the problem and the information that is needed to address it.

One useful mechanism for making sure that the client and the researcher are in agreement with respect to problem definition is the written **research request agreement**. The research request agreement summarizes the problem formulation process and should include the following items:

1. **Background:** The events that led to the manager's decision problem. While the events may not directly affect the research that is conducted, they help the researcher understand the nature of the problem more deeply.

2. **Decision problem:** The underlying question confronting the manager. A brief discussion of the source of the problem (i.e., planned vs. unplanned change) should be included, along with a discussion of whether the problem is discovery oriented or strategy oriented.

3. **Research problem(s):** The range of research problems that would provide input to the decision problem. An overview of costs and benefits of each research problem should be included. The final choice of research problem(s) to be addressed must be indicated and justified.

4. **Use:** The way each piece of information will be used. For discovery-oriented decision problems, indicate key information to be obtained and how managers will use the information. For strategy-oriented decision problems, indicate the way the information will be used to help make the action decision. Supplying logical reasons for each piece of the research ensures that the research problem(s) make sense in light of the decision problem.

5. **Population and subgroups:** The groups from whom the information must be gathered. Specifying these groups helps the researcher design an appropriate sample for the research project.

6. **Logistics:** Approximate estimates of the time and money available to conduct the research. Both of these factors will affect the techniques finally chosen.

The research request agreement should be submitted to the decision maker for his or her approval. If possible, it is best to get that approval in writing with a signature directly on the agreement. Exhibit 4.5 presents the research request agreement between a research group and a nonprofit organization seeking research on the topic of domestic violence.

| **E x h i b i t   4 . 5** | **Research Request Agreement presented to Stillwater Domestic Violence Services, Inc. by Research Partners, Ltd.** |

Background

Stillwater Domestic Violence Services, Inc. (SDVS) was formed in 1979 as a nonprofit agency to offer services to individuals in the Stillwater, Oklahoma, area. Funded by the United Way, the Oklahoma Office of Attorney General, the Federal Office for Victims of Crime, the Elite Repeat Resale Shop, and by private donations from groups and individuals, the organization states its goal as follows:

> Our goal is to provide comprehensive and confidential services to individuals and families experiencing domestic violence, sexual assault, stalking and child abuse or neglect. We also seek social change through community awareness and client advocacy.

SDVS offers various services to the community, including sheltering for victims of domestic violence, a help line, counseling and consultation, a relief nursery, parenting education, community education on domestic violence, and a sexual assault response team. All services are offered to victims without consideration of individuals' ability to pay.

Despite the fact that university students make up about half of Stillwater's population, Dr. Ralph Lindsey, the SDVS director, has noted that the services offered by the organization are seriously underutilized by students at Oklahoma State University, which is located in Stillwater. This is unfortunate, because national statistics suggest that a significant number of college students are affected by domestic violence at some point during their college career. Dr. Lindsey is concerned that most students may not even know that SDVS exists and that its services are available to them when needed. In addition, SDVS relies upon volunteers in delivering many of its client support services. Perhaps more university students would volunteer their services if they knew of the existence of SDVS and the services it provides. SDVS has done no prior formal marketing research.

Decision Problem

"Why aren't more students utilizing the services of SDVS?" Dr. Lindsey desires to fulfill the organization's goals for all residents of Stillwater, including university students. This is a discovery-oriented decision problem that has arisen from an unplanned change in the marketing environment, an unexpectedly low number of university student clients.

Research Problems

There are several different research problems that might be addressed; each would offer insights into the general decision problem. This section discusses the most promising of these research problems and provides the rationale for selecting two of them for further attention.

(Research Problem 1) Investigate student awareness of the services offered by SDVS. Dr. Lindsey has already noted that he believes that lack of awareness is the likely reason that so few university students utilize the services of SDVS. Awareness is relatively straightforward to measure, student respondents can be readily accessed, and costs would probably be low.

(Research Problem 2) Determine the incidence level of domestic violence among university students in Stillwater. Another possibility is that domestic violence is simply not very common in the Stillwater area among students. This seems unlikely to be true, but establishing that the problem exists might be a good first step. One difficulty is likely to be establishing a common understanding of what constitutes "domestic violence," but researchers should be able to offer a relatively clear definition of the concept before assessing the incidence level. A more difficult hurdle is the sensitivity of the issue to respondents who have experienced domestic violence or to those who will simply consider the questions to be "too personal."

(Research Problem 3) Determine student satisfaction with the services provided by SDVS. If students have turned to SDVS for help in the past, but have been disappointed in the services offered, they likely will not return—and they'll probably share their experiences with others. Given Dr. Lindsey's belief that few students have sought help and the difficulty of finding prior student clients due to confidentiality requirements, the costs of pursuing this research problem would likely be quite high.

(Research Problem 4) Determine student awareness for any organization providing services to victims of domestic violence. It is conceivable that student need for assistance with domestic violence issues is being met by other organizations, either on campus, in the community, or in students' home towns. If this is the case, Dr. Lindsey's fears that students don't know where to go for help may be unfounded. This research problem might be easily combined with Research Problem 1 or 2 because it would require the same general population of university students. As with these research problems, the costs would be relatively low.

(Research Problem 5) Investigate student perceptions of the SDVS office location. Even if students are aware of the services offered by the organization, perhaps its location makes it less likely that students would go to SDVS for help. Although this could be an important issue, the research team believes that this is secondary to the basic awareness issue. In addition, unless the researchers can effectively describe the location to respondents, the sample would need to be drawn from among students who have actually visited the office. According to Dr. Lindsey, there just aren't many of these.

(Continued)

(Research Problem 6) Determine which media outlets university students are most likely to utilize. If an awareness problem exists among students, SDVS may need to rethink its promotion strategy. Knowing which media vehicles (newspapers, radio stations, television stations, etc.) are routinely used by students could inform future decisions about advertising and other forms of promotion. Given the number of options available, collecting this information could take significant time with each student respondent, and the accuracy of the information would be questionable. It is difficult for individuals to communicate perceptual processes such as attention to all the different media they encounter in their daily lives. Plus, it is possible that awareness is not the issue at all, which would make the information obtained from pursuing this research problem less valuable.

Research Problems Selected After reviewing these research problems (and others), the research team has concluded that Research Problems 1 and 4 offer the greatest value in terms of providing information that is likely to address the decision problem. Each involves collecting information from the same population (see below); including both issues should not make the data collection forms too long.

Use

The key information to be obtained will include (a) unaided awareness and recognition of SDVS as an entity providing services for victims of domestic violence, (b) unaided awareness for any other organizations providing similar services. Dr. Lindsey plans to use the results to determine the degree to which a problem exists in terms of student awareness and to help in making decisions about increasing communications with students.

Population and Subgroups

Although the population will be formally defined in the Research Proposal, the researchers intend to collect data from Oklahoma State University students based in Stillwater. SDVS clients have primarily been women; most respondents should be women, but a small proportion of men (say, 20% of the sample) should be included. Because Research Partners, Ltd. is donating its services (see next), the sample size will be limited to 200–250 individuals.

Logistics

The project should be completed in approximately three months. As a nonprofit organization, SDVS has limited funds available that can be dedicated to marketing research. Research Partners, Ltd. has agreed to donate its services, although Dr. Lindsey has agreed to cover out-of-pocket expenses.

Source: The contributions of student researchers Jeff Blood, Trey Curtis, Kelsey Gillen, Amie Kreger, David Pittman, and Matt Smith are gratefully acknowledged.

---

8. Outline the various elements of the research proposal.

research proposal

A written statement that describes the marketing problem, the purpose of the study, and a detailed outline of the research methodology.

THE RESEARCH PROPOSAL

Once the problem has been defined and research problem(s) agreed upon, researchers can turn their attention to the techniques that will be used to conduct the research. Notice that in the research request agreement, we paid little attention to research methods, other than a general specification of the population to be studied. That all changes with the preparation of the formal **research proposal**, which lays out the proposed method of conducting the research. The research proposal also gives the researcher another opportunity to make sure the research will provide information needed to address the decision maker's problem.

Some research proposals are very long and detailed, running 20 pages or more. Others are much shorter. Regardless of their length, however, most proposals should contain the following elements.

A. Problem Definition and Background

This section presents a short summary of the information contained in the research request agreement, including the background of the problem, the manager's decision problem, and the specific research problem(s) to be addressed by the project. It is often a good idea to include a few words justifying the particular research problem(s) under study.

B. Research Design and Data Sources

Type of research design (exploratory, descriptive, causal) and type of data to be sought (primary, secondary) along with the proposed sources of those data are discussed in this section. A brief explanation of how the necessary information or data will be gathered (e.g., surveys, experiments, library sources) is given. Sources refer to where the information is located, whether in government publications, company records, actual people, and so forth. The relevance of all techniques (qualitative and quantitative) should be discussed. The nature of the problem will probably indicate the types of techniques to be employed, such as Web surveys, in-depth interviews, or focus groups.

C. Sampling Plan

The sampling plan starts with a detailed description of the population to be studied. The researcher specifies the population, states the desired sample size (including the rationale or calculations used for obtaining the sample size), discusses sampling method, identifies the sampling frame, and discusses how item nonresponse and missing data are to be handled. The reason for using the type of sample proposed must be justified.

D. Data Collection Forms

The forms to be employed in gathering the data are discussed here. For surveys, this involves either a questionnaire or an interview schedule. For other research, the forms could include inventory forms, guidebooks for focus groups, observation checklists, and so forth. The researcher should state how these instruments have been or will be validated and provide any available evidence of their reliability and validity. The data collection form itself, in its proposed final format, will be included in an appendix (see Section H).

E. Analysis

This is a discussion of editing and proofreading of questionnaires, coding instructions, and the type of data analysis, including any specialized statistical techniques. Most importantly, the researcher should include an outline of the tables and figures that will appear in the report (i.e., dummy tables). These tables and figures will likely be included in an appendix (see Section H).

F. Time Schedule

This is a detailed outline of the plan to complete the study. The study should be divided into workable pieces. Then, considering the persons involved in each phase, their qualifications and experience, and so forth, the time for the job is estimated. Some jobs may overlap. This plan will help in estimating the time required.

	Timeline
1. Preliminary investigation	Jan. 10–Jan. 22
2. Final test of questionnaire	Jan. 24–Jan. 29
3. Sample selection	Jan. 31–Feb. 5
4. Mail questionnaires and field follow-up	Feb. 7–Apr. 2
5. Analysis and preparation of final report	Apr. 4–May 2

G. Personnel Requirements and Cost Estimate

This provides a complete list of all personnel who will be required, indicating exact jobs, time duration, and expected rate of pay. Assignments should be made indicating each person's responsibility and authority. Personnel requirements are combined with time on different phases to estimate total personnel costs. Estimates on travel, materials, supplies, drafting, computer charges, and printing and mailing costs must also be included. If an overhead charge is required, it should be calculated and added to the subtotal of the above items.

H. Appendices

This section will include data collection forms (including script for telephone interviewers and cover letter for written formats), any technical information or statistical information that would have interrupted the flow of the text, and dummy tables or figures included in the analysis plan.

Once the decision maker has read and approved the proposal, he or she should formalize acceptance of it by signing and dating the document.

Learning Objective

9. Describe types of research that should be avoided.

RESEARCH TO AVOID

Although there are many benefits of marketing research, it is not a perfect process, even when used appropriately. It is worse when researchers know that their actions are inappropriate or even unethical. Stealing competitors' documents in the name of competitive intelligence, falsifying data or results to please a client or manager, conducting advocacy research in which the goal is to support a particular position with pseudoscientific results rather than to search for the truth, and attempting to sell products or services or ideas after telling respondents you are conducting marketing research (a process known as "sugging") are all blatantly unethical uses of marketing research. Unfortunately, these offenses and many others occur all too often. Several organizations offer guidelines or codes of ethics prohibiting unethical practices. (See Research Window 3.1 in Chapter 3 for an example.)

Besides unethical research, there are other types of research that should be avoided. Sometimes a decision maker will have preset ideas about a particular situation, and his or her position may not change, regardless of what is found by the researcher. Research merely represents "conscience money" in these cases. The results are readily accepted when they are consistent with the decision the individual wants to make, or with the person's perceptions of the environment or the consequences of alternative actions. Otherwise, the results are questioned at best,

MANAGER'S FOCUS

Research has discovered important differences in orientation between managers and research providers. Managers tend to prefer research that confirms what they already believe to be true about the marketing situation. Researchers, in contrast, often value unexpected research findings that may be suggestive of new environmental opportunities or threats. When research disconfirms a manager's expectations, the tendency is to not believe the results or to blame the unexpected results on

flawed research. As a marketing manager, it is important for you to recognize the possible confirmation bias you might bring to the research process. By developing a strong understanding of the methods presented in this book, you will be in a much better position to decide whether particular unexpected results are likely based on errors in the research or might reflect true results that you simply hadn't expected. This ability will make you a valuable asset to your marketing team.

or discarded as being inaccurate at worst. The reason, of course, is that the decision maker's view of the situation is so strongly held that the research will do little to change it. When this is the case, research would be a waste of the firm's resources.

The manager in the previous situation might be described as closed minded, although his or her motives may be pure. Unfortunately, some managers take it a step further to "suggest" what the results should be when the project is completed, another form of advocacy research. In this case, however, the manager is probably setting up an alibi in case the advertising campaign fails or the new product never catches on (e.g., "But the research results were all positive..."). This is a manager to avoid if possible.

Research should also be avoided when resources such as time and budget are lacking to do the research appropriately. This may seem strange, in that some research ought to be better than none at all, but this isn't always the case. The danger is that managers will use preliminary or exploratory research as justification for important decisions. Not all research has to be expensive or take a lot of time, but important decisions should be supported by adequate research. Too often, managers are willing to take shortcuts.

Feeling pressed for time, these managers typically ask researchers to run a few focus groups, make 100 telephone calls to test a concept, or undertake one of the many other popular conventional techniques we refer to as "death wish" research. These techniques seem reasonable to the time-challenged because they're quick, low-cost, and often corroborate what the marketer already thought. They may take less time and cost less money, but death wish research techniques offer little in the way of value. What companies usually get is more misinformation than information, which then contributes to the failure of marketing programs. As a result, not surprisingly, executives' confidence in marketing research has declined.[5]

Even when done correctly, there are situations in which marketing research either cannot provide the answers a company seeks or poses disadvantages that outweigh its possible advantages. For example, the benefits of marketing research must always be weighed against the risks of tipping off a competitor, who can then rush into the market with a similar product at perhaps a better price or with an added product advantage. And when a product is truly innovative, it may be difficult for consumers to assess accurately how they would ultimately use it. For example, the telephone answering machine and computer mouse were both panned by the consumers who were first exposed to them.[6] Some companies will forgo test marketing if there is little financial risk associated with a new product introduction. The best strategy is to examine the potential benefits from the research and to make sure they exceed the anticipated costs, both financial and otherwise.

CHOOSING A RESEARCH SUPPLIER

Learning Objective

10. Describe the purpose of a request-for-proposal (RFP).

In Chapter 1, we noted that many companies have formal marketing research departments. Some companies do not, however, instead preferring to hire marketing research companies to provide the information that they need. Even companies with an internal marketing research department sometimes need the services of outside companies.

There are many advantages to using research suppliers. If the research work load tends to vary over the course of the year, the firm may find it less expensive to hire suppliers to conduct specific projects when needed than to staff an entire in-house department. Also, the skills required for various projects may differ. By hiring outside

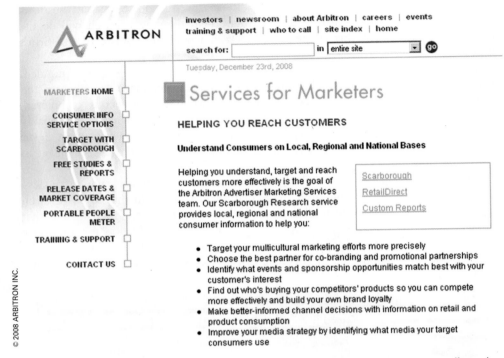

Some companies resort to marketing research companies, such as Arbitron, a media and marketing research firm serving the media—radio, television, cable, online radio, and out-of-home—as well as advertisers and advertising agencies in the United States.

suppliers, the firm can match the project to the vendor with the greatest expertise in the particular area under investigation. Another important advantage is the degree of objectivity that an outside research supplier can bring to a project.

Although it has become increasingly common to buy marketing research, many managers are uncertain as to how to select a research supplier. The first step is to decide when research is really necessary. Although there is no simple formula for assessing this need, most managers turn to research when they are unsure about their own judgment and other information sources seem inadequate. Before contacting research suppliers, it is important for the manager to identify the most critical areas of uncertainty and the issues that would benefit most from research.

Once a manager has determined the most critical area for research, he or she is ready to seek the right supplier for the job. If the company has a particular research provider in mind, perhaps because of prior relationships or recommendations from others, it would be normal to move on to discussions with that provider, leading to a research request agreement and later the research proposal. If the company does not have a particular provider in mind or by policy must receive proposals from multiple research vendors, a request-for-proposal will often be issued to a number of research providers who might be interested in taking on the project.

request-for-proposal (RFP)
A document that describes, as specifically as possible, the nature of the problem for which research is sought and that asks providers to offer proposals, including cost estimates, about how they would perform the job.

A **request-for-proposal (RFP)** is simply a document that describes, as specifically as possible, the nature of the problem for which research is sought and that asks providers to offer proposals, including cost estimates, about how they would perform the job. The RFP should be structured in such a way that it will be easy to compare the proposals from different providers. Asking for specific information about each step of the research process is a good way to accomplish this, particularly when the company issuing the RFP has been thorough in describing the kind of information and project it is seeking.

Experts suggest that managers seek proposals from at least three companies. In general, the most important asset of a research firm is the qualifications of the research professional(s) who will be involved in the design, day-to-day supervision,

MANAGER'S FOCUS

Academic researchers have examined various factors that influence whether or not managers utilize specific marketing research information when making decisions. One significant factor is the extent to which the manager trusts the research provider. The effect of trust on information utilization is particularly strong when managers lack the research expertise necessary to evaluate the actual quality of the marketing research information. This may seem like a reasonable response. There is some evidence, however, which suggests that research providers sometimes get complacent about how they conduct their research when they are in a long-term relationship with a client. Because they believe it is unlikely that they will be replaced, research providers may lack the drive to ensure that the project is conducted, analyzed, and interpreted carefully. As a result, a manager's trust in an existing research provider can blind the manager to quality issues. It is in your own best interest to learn how to determine the quality of a proposed or completed research project rather than to rely on a general (and possibly unwarranted) belief about the trustworthiness of the researcher who provided it. As we've said before, helping you develop this ability is a central objective of this book.

and interpretation of the research. It pays to talk with these people before selecting a vendor.

After reading the proposals and meeting key personnel, the manager should perform a comparative analysis. She should use the proposals to evaluate each vendor's understanding of the problem, how each will address it, and the cost and time estimates of each.

An increasingly popular way for firms to work with marketing research suppliers is to form long-term partnering relationships with a few select firms. In such arrangements, the client and research firms work together on an ongoing basis on those projects for which the research firm has the necessary expertise, instead of the client relying on project-by-project bids to select suppliers for specific projects.

SUMMARY

Learning Objective 1

Specify the key steps in problem formulation.
The six key steps are (1) meet with client, (2) clarify the problem/opportunity, (3) state the manager's decision problem, (4) develop full range of possible research problems, (5) select research problem(s), and (6) prepare and submit a research request agreement.

Learning Objective 2

Discuss two objectives of the initial meeting with the research client.
The two goals are (1) to develop rapport and open communication lines, and (2) to obtain as much information as possible about the problem/opportunity.

Learning Objective 3

Discuss the two general sources of marketing problems/opportunities.
The two sources of marketing problems are (1) unanticipated change and (2) planned change. Research on planned change tends to be proactive, while research on unanticipated, or unplanned, change tends to be reactive.

Learning Objective 4

Explain why the researcher must be actively involved in problem formulation.
Researchers play a key role in problem formulation because they bring a new perspective to the problem/opportunity situation. Managers often fall into routine ways of seeing the business and its environment;

researchers can help them get to the heart of the problem.

Learning Objective 5

Distinguish between two types of decision problems.

A decision problem is the basic problem or opportunity facing the manager. Discovery-oriented decision problems typically ask "what" or "why" and generate information that can be used by managers to make important decisions. Strategy-oriented decision problems are usually directed at "how" planned change should be implemented and focus on making decisions.

Learning Objective 6

Distinguish between a decision problem and a research problem.

A decision problem is the problem/opportunity as seen by managers. Research problems restate the decision problem in research terms, from the researcher's perspective.

Learning Objective 7

Describe the research request agreement.

The research request agreement summarizes the problem formulation process in written form and is submitted to managers for approval. It includes the following sections: origin, decision problem,

research problem(s), use, targets and their subgroups, and logistics.

Learning Objective 8

Outline the various elements of the research proposal.

Most research proposals contain the following elements: tentative project title, statement of the marketing problem, purpose and limits of the project, outline, data sources and research methodology, estimate of time and personnel requirements, and cost estimates.

Learning Objective 9

Describe types of research that should be avoided.

Several types of research should be avoided, including unethical research (e.g., sugging, advocacy research); research to support a decision that has already been made; research for which adequate resources are unavailable; and research in which the costs involved outweigh the benefits to be obtained.

Learning Objective 10

Describe the purpose of a request-for-proposal (RFP).

A request-for-proposal is issued by a company in order to solicit proposals from research providers. The RFP should be specific enough to allow easy comparisons across vendors.

KEY TERMS

decision problem (page 60)
discovery-oriented decision problem
    (page 61)
strategy-oriented decision problem
    (page 61)

research problem (page 64)
research request agreement (page 66)
research proposal (page 68)
request-for-proposal (RFP) (page 72)

REVIEW QUESTIONS

1.   What does it mean when we say that problems and opportunities are two sides of the same coin?

2.   What are the sources of marketing problems or opportunities? Are different sources typically associated with different research objectives? Explain.

3.   What is "normal thinking"? Why is it a problem when defining the marketing problem/opportunity?

4.   What is the basic nature of a decision problem?

5. What are the fundamental characteristics of the two types of decision problems?

6. What is a research problem? Why is it important to develop the full range of possible research problems?

7. What is involved in a research request agreement? What is included in the written statement?

8. How does the research proposal differ from the research request agreement?

9. What is "death wish" research? Why should it be avoided?

10. What factors should be considered when choosing a research supplier?

11. What are the benefits of using a request-for-proposal?

DISCUSSION QUESTIONS, PROBLEMS, AND PROJECTS

1. Identify one possible research problem for each of the following decision problems. Tell whether the decision problems are discovery oriented or strategy oriented.

   a. Why have sales of my brand decreased?

   b. Is my advertising working?

   c. What pricing strategy should I choose for a new product?

   d. Should I increase the level of expenditures on print advertising?

   e. How can I increase in-store promotion of existing products?

   f. Should I change the sales force compensation package?

2. Given the following research problems, identify a corresponding decision problem for each which the research problem might address.

   a. Design a test market to assess the impact on sales volume of a particular discount theme.

   b. Evaluate the stock level at the different warehouses.

   c. Evaluate the sales and market share of grocery stores in a particular location.

   d. Develop sales forecasts for a particular product line.

   e. Assess the level of awareness among students, faculty, and staff about the benefits of a new software package.

   f. Assess attitudes and opinions of customers toward existing theme restaurants.

3. Briefly discuss the difference between a decision problem and a research problem.

4. In each of the following situations, identify the fundamental source of the marketing problem or opportunity, a decision problem arising from the marketing problem or opportunity, and a possible research problem.

   a. Apex Chemical Supply is a manufacturer of swimming pool maintenance chemicals. Recently, a malfunction of the equipment that mixes anti-algae compound resulted in a batch of the product that not only inhibits algae growth but also causes the pool water to turn a beautiful shade of light blue (with no undesirable side effects).

   b. State University's director of recruitment for the M.B.A. program recently extended offers to 20 promising students. Only five offers were accepted. In the past, acceptance rates averaged 90%.

c. Montgomery Candy Company has enjoyed great success in its small regional market. Management attributes much of this success to Montgomery's unique distribution system, which ensures twice weekly delivery of fresh product to retail outlets. The directors of the company have instructed management to expand Montgomery's geographical market if it can be done without altering the twice weekly delivery policy.

5. You are the marketing manager of a mid-size manufacturing firm. Your company would like to gauge customer satisfaction. Prepare a simple RFP to be used to solicit proposals from marketing research companies.

6. Describe three situations in which marketing research should not be undertaken. Explain why this is true.

PART 2

RESEARCH DESIGN

CHAPTER 5   Types of Research Design and
             Exploratory Research

CHAPTER 6   Descriptive and Causal Research Designs

Measuring Scion's Buzzworthiness

It's cool, it's edgy, it's even polarizing (and it thinks that's a good thing). It's owned by Internet-savvy multi-taskers who are design conscious and highly elusive (and they think that's a good thing, too). It wants to be mentioned in the same breath as trendsetting brands like Apple, Nike, and Helio. Its owners are helping it get there via blogs, enthusiast clubs, and social networking sites.

It is Scion, a division of Toyota Motor Corporation. Its owners are dedicated to interactive media. The relationship between Scion and its owners has been closely followed by Nielsen BuzzMetrics, a subsidiary of The Nielsen Company, focused on measuring consumer-generated media (CGM) and word-of-mouth communication.

The Scion story actually starts with a failure. Toyota was looking to reach younger market segments, primarily Generation Y consumers, after research revealed that the average Toyota consumer was 54 years old.

After limited release in southern California some years later, Scion started generating buzz. It was attracting attention with its boxy design and generating traffic at its Web site want2bsquare.com. The Web site was established as a viral marketing presence, one meant to promote interactive content and sharing. Scion needed to measure the CGM it was attempting to facilitate, and BuzzMetrics had the tools to do it.

BuzzMetrics measured and gauged consumer reaction to the radical Scion xB, which received mixed reviews after its launch. Analyses reported what consumers were saying about the vehicle on blogs, message boards and other online—months before survey information would be available. In addition, BuzzMetrics addressed Scion's key concern by reassuring the company that the new xB was polarizing and was not perceived as a mainstream vehicle thanks in part to Scion's marketing campaign and vehicle styling.

Remember that the long-term goal was to attract younger consumers? Eighty percent of Scion buyers are new to Toyota with an average age of 39 years old, the youngest in the auto industry. Square is cool.

Part 2 of the text provides an overview of the different ways to design research projects. As this example demonstrates, there is more than one way to address research questions efficiently. Just within the Scion story, we see examples of the use of both exploratory and descriptive research designs. Each of these, along with causal designs, will be discussed in this section.

Source: Scion Case Study downloaded from http://www.nielsenbuzzmetrics.com/files/uploaded/NBZM_Scion_Case_Study.pdf, August 5, 2008.

Types of Research Design and Exploratory Research

Learning Objectives

1. Explain what a research design is.
2. List the three basic types of research design.
3. Describe the major emphasis of each type of research design.
4. Describe the basic uses of exploratory research.
5. Specify the key characteristics of exploratory research.
6. Discuss the various types of exploratory research and describe each.
7. Identify the key person in a focus group.
8. Discuss two major pitfalls to avoid with focus groups (or any other form of exploratory research).

Introduction

A **research design** is simply the framework or plan for a study used as a guide in collecting and analyzing data. It is the blueprint that is followed in completing a study. It resembles the architect's blueprint for a house. While it is possible to build a house without a blueprint, the results will probably be a little different than what the buyer had in mind: Rooms are too small or too big; something important was left out. And the house will usually end up costing more than necessary, as changes are made to fix problems as they arise.

It's possible to do marketing research without a detailed blueprint, but like a building project without a plan, the results are almost always less than desirable. If the results from such projects are usable at all, they often provide little more than interesting information that does little to address the real marketing problem.

research design
The framework or plan for a study that guides the collection and analysis of the data.

The research design ensures that the study (1) will be relevant to the problem and (2) will use economical procedures. There are multiple research design frameworks, just as there are many different kinds of house designs. Fortunately though, research designs can be broken into three basic types: exploratory, descriptive, or causal.[1]

Learning Objective

1. Explain what a research design is.

TYPES OF RESEARCH DESIGN

Learning Objective

2. List the three basic types of research design.

The goal of **exploratory research** is to discover ideas and insights. A soft drink manufacturer faced with an unexpected drop in sales might conduct an exploratory study to generate possible explanations. Sometimes exploratory research is necessary to adequately define the manager's decision problem.

Descriptive research is typically concerned with determining the frequency with which something occurs or the relationship between two variables. It is usually guided by one or more initial hypotheses. An investigation of the trends in the consumption of soft drinks with respect to such characteristics as age, sex, and geographic location would be a descriptive study.

A **causal research** design is concerned with determining cause-and-effect relationships. Causal studies typically take the form of experiments, because experiments are best suited to determine cause and effect. For instance, a soft drink manufacturer may want to determine which of several different sales promotions is most effective. One way to proceed would be to use different sales promotions (e.g., coupons) in different geographic areas and investigate which approach generated the highest sales. If the study was designed properly, the company might have evidence to suggest that one or the other promotional approaches caused the higher rate of sales.

So which is the best research design for a particular situation? Most, but not all, projects involve some degree of exploratory and descriptive research; only some call for causal research. The choice of research design hinges mostly on how much managers already know about the issue to be studied. When a decision problem has arisen from unplanned changes in the environment, there is usually a need for exploratory research to better understand what is happening and why it is happening, and exploratory research should be used to get insights into the situation. Sometimes, however, managers have a great deal of knowledge about the situation—they know what the key issues are and what questions need to be asked—and the focus quickly shifts to descriptive research that is geared more toward providing answers than generating initial insights. When a company needs precise answers about the effects of various proposed marketing actions on important outcomes, managers use causal research.

The three basic research designs can be viewed as stages in a continuous process. Figure 5.1 shows the interrelationships. Exploratory studies are often seen as the initial step. Consider, for example, the following problem: "Brand X's share of the soft drink market is slipping. Why?" This statement is too broad to serve as a guide for detailed descriptive or causal research. Exploratory research should be used to narrow and refine the problem. The goal would be to find possible explanations for the sales decrease. These tentative explanations, or hypotheses, would then serve as specific guides for descriptive or causal studies.

Suppose the tentative explanation that emerged was that "Brand X is an economy-priced soft drink. Individuals have more money today than when the brand was first introduced and are willing to pay more for higher-quality products. It stands to reason that our market share would decrease." These tentative explanations, or hypotheses, that people have more real income to spend and that a larger proportion of that money is going toward higher-priced soft drinks could be examined in a descriptive study.

If the descriptive study did support the hypotheses, the company might then wish to determine whether individuals were, in fact, willing to pay more for soft drinks.

exploratory research
Research design in which the major emphasis is on gaining ideas and insights; it is particularly helpful in breaking broad, vague problem statements into smaller, more precise subproblem statements.

descriptive research
Research design in which the major emphasis is on determining the frequency with which something occurs or the extent to which two variables covary.

Learning Objective

3. Describe the major emphasis of each type of research design.

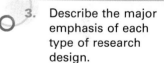

causal research
Research design in which the major emphasis is on determining cause-and-effect relationships.

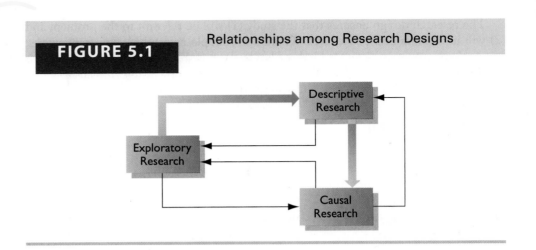

FIGURE 5.1   Relationships among Research Designs

MANAGER'S FOCUS

In several of the preceding Manager's Focus sidebars we have emphasized the importance of your learning how to evaluate for *yourself* the appropriateness of proposed research methods. Mastering the material in this chapter will be your first major step toward developing those capabilities. Specifically, it is essential that you be able to determine whether an exploratory, descriptive, or causal research design is most suitable given what you currently know about your marketing situation.

If you stop and analyze your own personal experience, much of what you have learned has resulted from asking yourself questions and then seeking answers to those questions. But the questions you ask differ depending on the nature of your circumstances and your understanding of them. For example, when something occurs that you do not expect, meaning you do not understand your situation very well, you likely ask yourself "What might be some reasons why this happened to me?" You need to identify some possible answers to this question before you can have any idea what some appropriate responses to the situation might be. As you begin to better formulate some *possible* explanations for the event, you might begin to ask "how large and important is this new situation I am facing?" Answering this question can help you begin to determine some ways you might respond to the situation, and whether it is in your best interest to respond at all. Later you may determine that there are several reasonable ways you might respond to

your situation and for each alternative you might ask the question "If I respond in this manner, what effect will I likely have on the situation?" The answers will help you determine which alternative action to take.

As you will see in this chapter, determining the most appropriate type of research design is really nothing more than identifying what type of question you should be asking yourself at this point in time *given what you currently know about your marketing situation*. Exploratory research designs are used when you don't understand your current situation very well. You "explore" to find answers to "What might be?" types of questions. In contrast, descriptive research designs are used to answer "How large?" types of questions. You are "describing" the degree to which groups have certain characteristics or the size of the association between two or more variables. Finally, causal research designs are utilized to answer questions such as, "If we do this, what impact will we likely have in the marketplace?"

How do you know which type of question you should be asking? The answer is really quite simple. If you have carefully completed the problem formulation stage using the research process, the type of question you should be asking yourself now will have been identified already. The key, then, is to be certain the type of research design employed actually fits the type of question you are trying to answer.

Further, the managers might want to determine what attributes (such as sweeter taste, fewer calories, type of artificial sweetener) were most important to consumers. This might be accomplished through a test market study, a causal design.

Although we've presented the different research designs as if they must proceed in order, that's not always the case. Sometimes managers will get results from descriptive or causal projects that lead to more questions which lead to more exploratory research. The smaller arrows in Figure 5.1 demonstrate the different ways in which the types of research design can be interrelated.

EXPLORATORY RESEARCH

The general objective in exploratory research is to gain insights and ideas. When conducted correctly, exploratory research should provide a better understanding of the situation; this kind of research is not designed to come up with final answers and decisions. At the end of the exploratory phase, researchers hope to have generated hypotheses about the key aspects of a situation. A **hypothesis** has been described as an educated guess; in more formal terms, it is a statement that specifies how two or more measurable variables are related.

In the early stages of research, we usually don't know enough about a problem or an opportunity to formulate a specific hypothesis. There are often several tentative explanations for a given marketing phenomenon. For example, sales are off because our price is too high, our dealers or sales representatives are not doing the job they should, or our advertising is weak. Exploratory research can be used to establish priorities in studying these competing explanations. Top priority would usually be given to whichever hypothesis appeared most promising in the exploratory study.

Exploratory research is also used to increase a researcher's familiarity with a problem, especially when the researcher is new to the company and/or problem. For example, a marketing research consultant who is working with a company for the first time will likely need to develop a working knowledge of the industry, company, and specific problem area. Exploratory research is good for this.

An exploratory study may also be used to clarify concepts. For instance, if management is considering a change in service policy intended to increase dealer satisfaction, an exploratory study could be used to (1) clarify what is meant by dealer satisfaction and (2) develop a method by which dealer satisfaction could be measured.

An exploratory study can be used for

■ Better formulating the manager's decision problem

■ Developing hypotheses

■ Increasing the researcher's familiarity with the problem

■ Clarifying concepts

In general, exploratory research is appropriate for any problem about which little is known. It becomes the foundation for a good study. Exploratory studies are typically small scale and quite flexible.

Small Scale Regardless of the particular methods employed, exploratory studies should almost always be relatively small in size. Researchers simply can't afford to devote the bulk of the research budget to exploratory research. What would be the point, anyway? Answers and decisions will flow from descriptive and/or causal research, not from the exploratory research. Having said this, however, we want to emphasize that enough resources must be devoted to exploratory research to ensure that the problem has been adequately defined. Sometimes that may mean spending a little more money on the exploratory phase than originally planned, but it's money

Learning Objective

4. Describe the basic uses of exploratory research.

hypothesis
A statement that specifies how two or more measurable variables are related.

Learning Objective

5. Specify the key characteristics of exploratory research.

Learning Objective

6. Discuss the various types of exploratory research and describe each.

literature search
A search of statistics, trade journal articles, other articles, magazines, newspapers, and books for data or insight into the problem at hand.

well spent if the problem/opportunity is brought more clearly into focus and the optimal research problem(s) can then be addressed.

Flexibility Because so much is often unknown at the beginning of a project, exploratory studies are very flexible with regard to the methods used for gaining insight and developing hypotheses. Basically, anything goes! Exploratory studies rarely use detailed questionnaires or involve probability sampling plans. Instead, researchers frequently use multiple methods, perhaps changing methods as they learn more about the problem. Investigators often follow their intuition in an exploratory study. While exploratory research may be conducted in a variety of ways, literature searches, depth interviews, focus groups, nominal groups, case analyses, and projective methods are among the most common approaches (see Figure 5.2).

Literature Search

One of the quickest and least costly ways to discover hypotheses is to conduct a **literature search**. Almost all marketing research projects should start here. There is an incredible amount of information available in libraries, through online sources, in commercial databases, and so on. The literature search may involve conceptual literature, trade literature, or published statistics from research firms or governmental agencies.

A few years ago, Miller Business Systems, Inc., was able to respond effectively to a competitive threat because of its ongoing effort to review trade literature. Using published industry sources, the company developed profiles of its competitors, which it then kept in its database. The company regularly scanned the database to monitor competitive actions. Based on this information, the company noticed that a competitor had hired nine furniture salespeople in a 10-day period. This was a tip-off to a probable push by the competitor in the office-furniture market. Miller was able to schedule its salespeople to make extra sales calls and hold on to their accounts.[2] As another example, researchers at Silver Dollar City, the theme park located in Branson, Missouri, regularly monitor all sorts of literature for insights into customers, markets, and competitors.

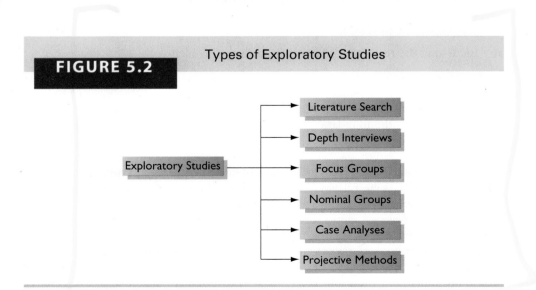

FIGURE 5.2   Types of Exploratory Studies

MANAGER'S FOCUS

Knowledge about marketing research will be most helpful to you as a manager if you acquire the ability to "connect the dots" between the different concepts presented in this book. At every opportunity ask yourself, "How does this relate to what I've studied so far?" For example, how might literature searches play a role in the development and maintenance of an MIS (marketing information system)? Remember, every effort should be made to obtain marketing intelligence from existing sources (see discussion of secondary data) before any new marketing research studies should be conducted (see discussion of primary data). Literature searches are efficient ways of gathering market intelligence that can be fed into an organization's MIS. Indeed, smaller companies with limited budgets should have personnel who regularly monitor the available literature for relevant market information that can be distributed to decision makers.

Sometimes conceptual literature is more valuable than trade literature. For example, a firm with concerns about customer satisfaction might begin its exploratory research by reviewing academic studies and industry reports on the topic, with an eye toward uncovering factors that have been shown to drive satisfaction. The issue of how to measure customer satisfaction could be researched at the same time.

Suppose a firm's problem was one that typically triggers much marketing research: "Why are sales revenues down?" Initial insights into this problem could easily be obtained by analyzing published data and trade literature. Such an analysis would quickly indicate whether the problem was an industry problem (everyone's sales are down) or a firm problem (other firms' sales have held steady or even increased). The results would then lead to very different kinds of descriptive and/or causal research.

A company's own internal data should be included in the literature examined in exploratory research, as Mosinee Paper Company once found to its pleasant surprise. The company was about to drop one of its products because of its dismal sales performance. First, however, the company took a closer look and found that only one salesperson was selling that specific grade of industrial paper. Upon further investigation, Mosinee discovered how the buyers were using the paper—an application that had been known only to the one salesman and his customers. This information enabled management to educate the rest of its sales force as to the potential market for the paper, and sales rose substantially. This example also highlights the need for knowledge management within organizations.

It is important to remember that in a literature search, as with all other kinds of exploratory research, the major emphasis is on the discovery of ideas and tentative explanations of the phenomenon and not on drawing conclusions. Finding answers and drawing conclusions is better left to descriptive and causal research. Thus, researchers must be alert to the hypotheses that can be derived from available material, both published material and the company's internal records.

Depth Interviews

Depth interviews (sometimes called "in-depth interviews") attempt to tap the knowledge and experience of those with information relevant to the problem or opportunity at hand. For example, a San Francisco builder focused on architects and designers when trying to get a handle on its competitors. The company asked these people to describe the traits of builders that tended to turn off buyers of expensive homes. Some of the answers included bad manners, workers who tracked dirt across carpets, and beat-up construction trucks parked in homeowners' driveways. Based on this information, the company bought a new truck, had its estimators wear jackets

depth interview
Interviews with people knowledgeable about the general subject being investigated.

and ties, and made sure its work crews were impeccably polite. In less than two years, the company's annual revenue more than quintupled.

Anyone who has any association with the issue at hand is a potential candidate for a depth interview. This could include current customers, members of the target market, executives and managers of the company, sales representatives, wholesalers, retailers, and so on. It can literally include anyone with insights into the situation. For example, a children's book publisher gained valuable information about a recent sales decline by talking with librarians and schoolteachers. These discussions indicated that more and more people were using library facilities, while book sales were decreasing. The increase in library usage was, in turn, traced to an increase in federal funds, which had enabled libraries to buy more books for their children's collections. Similarly, some years back, Ford Motor Co. designed a medium-duty truck intended for beverage distribution, among other things, after seeking feedback from fleet owners, mechanics, and drivers.[3]

As with other types of exploratory research, depth interviews are quite flexible. Participants are selected based on their likely ability to provide usable information. Certainly, there is no need to attempt a random sample. It is important to include people with differing points of view and opinions.

Sometimes the questions asked are the same across respondents, and sometimes they differ. It is not a good idea to use a formal questionnaire at this point, unless it is short and designed to start or guide the conversation. Instead, because this is exploratory research, the questions should be general, allowing the participants a great deal of leeway in how they answer. As a general rule, respondents should be given freedom in choosing issues to be discussed, although it is the role of the researcher to keep the depth interview in the topic area.

As the name suggests, the point of a depth interview is to encourage the respondent to offer as much information as possible. As a result, sometimes depth interviews can last for an hour or more. Because there is so much information collected, it is often a good idea to have two interviewers, one for asking questions and one for observing and taking notes, perhaps participating from time to time. It is always advisable to have an audio or video recording of the interview. Interviewers must be carefully trained; they perform an important balancing act between keeping the interview on track while allowing the respondent to take the conversation where he or she sees fit. This task isn't easy.

A series of depth interviews can be very expensive. Well-trained interviewers command higher salaries, data are collected from one respondent at a time, and audio/video recordings must be transcribed, coded, and analyzed. This technique, however, can yield important insights and more often than not is well worth the effort.

At first glance, depth interviews seem similar to the personal interview method of collecting descriptive research data. Exhibit 5.1 presents key differences between the two techniques.

Focus Groups

Focus group interviews are among the most often used techniques in marketing research. Some would argue that they are among the most *over*used and *mis*used techniques as well, a point we'll return to later. In a **focus group**, a small number of individuals are brought together to talk about some topic of interest to the focus group sponsor. The discussion is directed by a **moderator**. The moderator attempts to follow a rough outline of issues while simultaneously having the comments made by each person considered in group discussion. Participants are thus exposed to the ideas of others and can respond to those ideas with their own.

Group interaction is the key aspect that distinguishes focus group interviews from depth interviews, which are conducted with one respondent at a time. It is also the primary advantage of the focus group over most other exploratory techniques. Because of their interactive nature, ideas sometimes drop "out of the blue" during a focus group discussion. Further, ideas can be developed to their full importance because of the

Learning Objective

7. Identify the key person in a focus group.

focus group
An interview conducted among a small number of individuals simultaneously; the interview relies more on group discussion than on directed questions to generate data.

moderator
The individual that meets with focus group participants and guides the session.

Exhibit 5.1	**Depth Interviews versus Personal Interview Surveys**

In-depth interviewing is usually done at the beginning of a major research project, when you will be studying a population that you have never researched before. In-depth interviews—also called "semistructured interview[s]," or "informal interviews"—are very different from survey interviews. They are much more similar to journalistic interviews. Some of the differences between survey interviewing and in-depth interviewing are as follows:

- A survey usually has at least 100 interviews, but with informal research, 20 respondents [are] often enough.

- A survey has a fixed questionnaire. All the respondents are asked the same questions (except those skipped), in the same order. But with in-depth interviewing, there are no specific questions. Instead of beginning with "Which of the following statements . . ." an informal interviewer might say "Can you tell me about a time when you . . ."

- With in-depth interviewing, there is no specific order. The respondent may jump from one subject to another. The interviewer has a list of things to be discovered, but the wording and sequence of the "questions" depend on the "answers" the respondent gives.

- Instead of using a fully random sample, in-depth interviews are usually done with people who are deliberately chosen to be as different as possible from each other.

The reason for these differences between survey interviewing and in-depth interviewing is that their purposes are different. Unlike survey interviewing, in-depth interviewing does not claim to obtain results that can be generalized to a whole population.

Source: Excerpted from Dennis List, *Know Your Audience: A Practical Guide to Media Research* (Wellington, New Zealand: Original Books, 2005). Downloaded from the Audience Dialogue Web site, http://www.audiencedialogue.net, August 10, 2008.

snowballing effect: A comment by one individual can trigger a chain of responses from other participants. The presence of other people and the opportunity to listen to their comments often allows individuals to "warm up" to the topic and become willing to express their ideas and expose their feelings. As a result, responses are often more spontaneous and less conventional than they might be in a depth interview.

Characteristics of Focus Groups   Although focus groups vary in size, most consist of eight to 12 members. Smaller groups are too easily dominated by one or two members; with larger groups, frustration and boredom can set in, as individuals have to wait their turn to respond or get involved.

Respondents are usually selected so that the groups are relatively homogeneous. That is, the goal is to include people who are more or less like one another. This promotes better discussion as people realize that they have things in common with

MANAGER'S FOCUS

As a manager, you must think carefully before utilizing focus groups. Focus groups can be helpful in the right circumstances, but there are several alternative exploratory research techniques available, and you should select one or more that best fit the types of questions you are trying to address. In our opinion, focus groups are used far more often than they ought to be. Research firms too often recommend focus groups simply because they specialize in them, not because they are the most appropriate exploratory tool. Relatively few firms have the expertise necessary to competently perform the entire range of exploratory methods. Therefore, when you need exploratory information, you should interview prospective firms by asking them to thoroughly discuss the advantages and disadvantages of alternative exploratory methods as they apply to your current information needs. You should then select the firm that speaks most authoritatively about alternative approaches and presents a compelling case for why a particular technique best fits the questions you are addressing. Under no circumstances should you select a firm or a method simply because it is used frequently by other organizations.

other participants. It also helps prevent individuals from being intimidated by other participants, thus stifling their contribution to the discussion. For example, perceived differences in social status or other socioeconomic factors might discourage some from speaking at all while encouraging others to dominate the discussion. Indeed, keeping everyone involved while allowing none to take over the discussion is one of the key roles of the moderator. Research Window 5.1 offers a humorous true account of what happened in a group discussion when one individual tried to take over a group discussion.

Most firms conducting focus groups use screening interviews to determine the individuals who will compose a particular group. Clients will normally have specific criteria for the kinds of participants they seek. In fact, under normal circumstances, the more specific the criteria, the more useful the results will be. A critical task is to recruit participants who meet the requested criteria. Often, this isn't easy.

One type of individual who recruiters must try to avoid is the "professional" respondent who has participated before—perhaps regularly—in other focus groups. At best, the results will be tainted because professional respondents don't usually meet all of the relevant criteria to be included. At worst, the results can be worthless if the individual acts as an "expert" and dominates the discussion. Such respondents want to participate because the incentives, monetary or otherwise, are often generous.

research window 5.1

Shut Up, Jimmy!

In the summer of the year 199__, I arrived in the small town of N____ (as a Victorian novelist might begin). This was in western Australia, where I was conducting a series of focus groups. The participants had been organized by a market research company in Perth. All I needed to do was arrive at the right time and get them talking.

I found the venue: a back room in a shabby hotel. A century earlier, it would have been a splendid building, but now it was simply down-at-heel. The evening sun poured in through the west-facing windows, revealing the effect on the woodwork of 100 years of beer drinking. I set up the tape recorder, and the people began to arrive.

"Hello Joe," said the first participant to the second. "Haven't seen you for a long time. What are you doing these days?"

I hadn't counted on this. The town, with a population of 5,000 or so, was small enough that everybody seemed to know everybody else. Normally, focus groups are done in cities, and you can safely assume that nobody knows anybody else. Here, though, most of them knew each other.

In this case, when the group began talking, one man dominated the proceedings. This is not uncommon, and usually a few hints from the moderator (e.g., "Does anybody else have anything to say on this matter?") will dissuade the dominator. But this guy wouldn't stop. He had a bee in his bonnet about something.

To my amazement, he started trying to run the group like a public meeting. "I move that we are dissatisfied with the radio service in N____" he boomed. "All in favor say Aye."

I was about to step in and point out that this wasn't how focus groups work, but another participant—a middle-aged woman—got in before me.

"Would you just shut up, Jimmy?" she snapped. "We've all had enough of your carrying on like this. What will this man think of the people of N____ if you behave in this way?" (By "this man" she meant me.)

After a great uproar of general agreement, Jimmy became silent. He hardly said a word for the next hour or two.

I was amazed. Obviously something had happened in this group (or some of them) in the past, and I was at a disadvantage for not understanding it.

Source: Excerpted from Dennis List, "Small-Town Group Discussion," June 17, 2002, downloaded from http://www.audiencedialogue.net, August 10, 2008. Reprinted by permission.

Firms must recognize that the more specific the screening criteria, the greater the incentive for recruiters to use professional respondents. They are often easier to find than people who actually qualify to participate.

As you might expect, many different types of participants have been involved in focus groups. Exhibit 5.2 describes how several different organizations have used focus groups; a wide variety of participants are represented. The important thing, of course, is to recruit from the audience that can offer the exploratory insights that the company is seeking. Harley-Davidson conducted focus groups composed of current owners, those who wanted to own Harleys, and those who currently owned other brands to better understand how people viewed the company's motorcycles (see Research Window 5.2).

Given that the participants in any one group should be reasonably homogeneous, how can a firm be sure that the full range of opinions will be represented? The best way is to hold multiple groups. That way, the characteristics of the participants can vary across groups. Ideas discovered in one group session can be introduced in later group sessions for reaction. A typical project has four groups, but some may have up to 12 or more. The issue is whether the later groups are generating additional insights. When they show diminishing returns, the groups are stopped.

The typical focus group session lasts from one and a half to two hours. Most groups are held at facilities designed especially for them, although they can be held at other places. The typical setup includes a conference room with nice furniture and

---

> ### *Exhibit 5.2*   **Examples from the Wide World of Focus Groups**
>
> - Aeropostale has become one of the hottest performing clothing chains for teens. Unlike some clothing marketers, the company has no interest in setting clothing trends. Instead, it works diligently to follow clothing trends using a variety of exploratory research techniques, including focus groups with high school students.
>
> - Public officials in Great Britain have been struggling with a sticky problem—how to clean used gum from public sidewalks. In a recent 5-year period, gum sales have escalated over 30% in Great Britain. Much of the cast-off gum, unfortunately, seems to have ended up on the sidewalks of towns and cities. Estimates place the cost of removing the gum at $285 million per year. The Environment and Rural Affairs Department commissioned a series of focus groups to study chewers' attitudes. The results? Everyone interviewed admitted having tossed their gum aside at least occasionally, and the researchers were able to identify a number of different segments of "gum droppers," ranging from an "excuses" segment [who] felt guilty and tried to drop gum discreetly to a "bravado" group who enjoyed openly tossing their gum and then kicking it for good measure.
>
>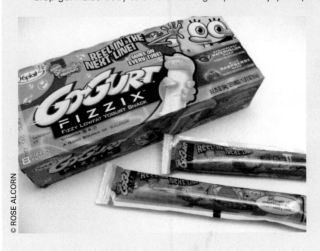
>
> - The explosive growth and success of Bratz dolls, from toymaker MGA Entertainment Inc., can be traced in part to the company's exploratory research with young girls. New ideas for products often come from girls who participate in focus groups. Bratz dolls almost single-handedly forced Mattel to redesign its icon Barbie dolls.
>
> - At Yoplait, yogurt moved from cups to tubes. Yoplait's Fizzix also moved from simple yogurt cultures to include carbonation. This was the step taken to make yogurt more palatable to tweens. According to focus group results, tweens seemed to love it, while it was anything but a hit with grown-ups. The focus group results so convinced Yoplait's president that he skipped regional pilot testing for Fizzix and went straight to a national rollout for the product.
>
> **Sources:** "Online Extra: Targeting the Universal American Kid," *BusinessWeek online*, June 7, 2004, downloaded from http://www.businessweek.com, August 10, 2008; Beth Carney, "Britain's Very Sticky Problem," *BusinessWeek online*, March 7, 2005, downloaded from http://www.businessweek.com, August 10, 2008; Christopher Palmeri, "Hair-Pulling in the Dollhouse," *BusinessWeek online*, May 2, 2005, downloaded from http://www.businessweek.com, August 10, 2008; and Matthew Boyle, "Carbonated Yogurt: Sizzle or Fizzle?" *Fortune online*, September 18, 2007, downloaded from http://money.cnn.com/, August 10, 2008.

research window 5.2

Experience of Harley-Davidson with Focus Groups

After making a remarkable comeback in the 1980s, motorcycle manufacturer Harley-Davidson had buyers on 2-year-long waiting lists all over the country. But that success placed the company in a familiar quandary: Should Harley expand and risk a market downturn, or should it stay the course, content with its good position in the industry?

"To invest or not to invest, that was the question," said Frank Cimermancic, Harley's director of business planning. "Dealers were begging us to build more motorcycles," he said. "But you have to understand our history. One of the things that caused past problems was a lack of quality, and that was the result of a too-rapid expansion. We did not want to relive that situation."

The company's dilemma was complicated by the fact that the market for heavyweight bikes was shrinking. "We were doing fine, but look at the market," Cimermancic said. "Maybe, we thought, we could reverse these trends and become an industry leader, something we hadn't been for a long time."

A new kind of customer seemed to hold the keys to market growth. White-collar motorcycle enthusiasts, or "Rubbies" (rich urban bikers), started to shore up Harley sales in the mid-'80s, adding to the company's success and image. But whether these were reliable, long-term customers was another question.

"Are those folks going to stay with us, or are they going to move on when the next fad comes along?" Cimermancic asked. "If we got the answer right, we could become a force in the industry. If we got it wrong, we would go right back to the early '80's. Nobody wanted to make the wrong decision and watch 20 percent of our employees walk away with their possessions in a cardboard box."

Harley also needed to know if it should market its products differently to different audiences. A core clientele of traditional "bikers" had kept Harley afloat during its leanest years, and they could not be alienated. "We had to understand the customer mindset," Cimermancic said. "Was there a universal appeal to owning a Harley?"

To find out, the company first invited focus groups made up of current owners, would-be owners, and owners of other brands to make cut-and-paste collages that expressed their feelings about Harley-Davidsons. Whether long-time Harley riders or fresh prospects, common themes emerged in the artwork: enjoyment, the great outdoors, freedom.

Harley-Davidson then mailed more than 16,000 surveys "with a typical battery of psychological, sociological, and demographic questions you typically see in studies," Cimermancic said, as well as subjective questions such as "Is Harley typified more by a brown bear or a lion?" The questionnaire got a 30% response rate, with no incentive for return.

From the responses, Harley identified seven core customer types: the Adventure-Loving Traditionalist, the Sensitive Pragmatist, the Stylish Status-Seeker, the Laid-Back Camper, the Classy Capitalist, the Cool-Headed Loner, and the Cocky Misfit. All of them appreciated Harley-Davidson products for the same reasons.

"Independence, freedom, and power were universal Harley appeals," Cimermancic said. "It didn't matter if you were the guy who swept the floor of the factory or if you were the CEO at that factory, the attraction to Harley-Davidson was very similar. We were surprised by a tremendous amount of loyalty across the board."

That loyalty meant the company could build and sell more motorcycles, without having to overextend itself. In 1990, Harley-Davidson built 62,800 bikes; the company plans to ship between 303,500 and 307,500 bikes in 2008.

Sources: Ian P. Murphy, "Aided by Research, Harley Goes Whole Hog," *Marketing News* 30, December 2, 1996, pp. 16–17. See also Rick Barrett, "Harley Drops Earnings Forecast," *The Milwaukee Journal Sentinel*, April 13, 2005, downloaded from Newspaper Source database, June 16, 2005; Ted Shelsby, "Harley Sales Go Hog Wild," *The Baltimore Sun*, November 25, 2001, p. 1c; and "Harley-Davidson Announces 2008 Second Quarter Results, July 17, 2008, downloaded from http://investor.harley-davidson.com, August 1, 2008.

fixtures that can comfortably hold the participants. Traditionally, at one end of the conference room will be a 1-way mirror, with space behind the mirror to house audiovisual equipment for recording the focus group interview as well as seating for researchers, clients, and/or advertising agency representatives. One advantage of these facilities is that they can incorporate the latest in technology because of the large number of groups held there. For example, videoconferencing technology can be used to link groups in different locations, allowing participants at the various locations to interact directly with each other.

Advancing technology has also created an explosion in the use of online, Internet-based focus groups. Such "groups," in which multiple respondents can "meet" electronically via chat rooms, instant messaging, Web cameras, and the like, offer tremendous speed and cost benefits, particularly when using an established online panel of respondents. There are other advantages of online focus groups, including the ability to form groups

This focus group is listening attentively to its facilitator and is an example of a more up close and personal session, as opposed to an online session.

composed of people from far-flung locations, or to deal with sensitive topics. According to Susan Roth, the director of qualitative research at Greenfield Online, "You can do international groups, or groups about subjects of sensitive nature, like HIV or impotence, where being anonymous can be better."[4] Online focus groups can be an effective tool for producing useful exploratory insights.

Should these approaches be categorized as focus groups, however? Our observations suggest that most should not be. As noted above, the key advantage and distinguishing feature of a focus group is the synergy obtained by having the participants meet together, experience each other's presence, and feed off one another's comments. While electronic interaction is possible, we suspect that the true value of focus group research cannot be duplicated very effectively online except, perhaps, when working with very specific target populations. This method of gathering exploratory data is certainly valid—again, with exploratory research, anything goes—but they are not focus groups in the classic sense.[5]

In general, focus groups are less expensive to conduct than are individual depth interviews, mostly because multiple respondents are handled simultaneously. That's not to say that they are inexpensive, however. By the time an experienced moderator has been hired to conduct the session and write the report, the facility rented, and incentives paid to participants, a focus group has become costly. And that's just one focus group; add a series of focus groups and the costs can really rise.

The Role of the Moderator The moderator in the focus group plays the single most important—and most difficult—role in the process. For one thing, the moderator typically translates the study objectives into a guidebook. The **moderator's guidebook** lists the general (and specific) issues to be addressed during the session, placing them in the general order in which the topics should arise. In general, the funnel approach is used, in which the moderator introduces broad general topics or tasks first and then the conversation begins to focus on the key issues under study.

To develop the guidebook and conduct a focus group effectively, the moderator needs to understand the background of the problem and the most important information the client hopes to obtain from the research process. The moderator also needs to understand the overall plan for the use of focus groups: how many will be held, how many participants will be in each, what kinds of people will be involved, and how the sessions might be structured to build on one another.

moderator's guidebook

An ordered list of the general (and specific) issues to be addressed during a focus group; the issues normally should move from general to specific.

MANAGER'S FOCUS

We have emphasized throughout this chapter that managers must be very careful not to misuse exploratory research findings. The findings from focus group interviews are among those most frequently misused by managers, even by managers who should know better. We once observed the president of an advertising and marketing research consulting firm announce that his company was launching a new service because "the focus group findings were all positive." Focus groups, when used properly, are uniquely capable of capitalizing on group dynamics to generate new ideas or insights that would not emerge if respondents were interviewed separately and could not help build on other people's ideas. It is important for you to always remember that these ideas and insights can be very useful in helping you create new marketing strategies. But exploratory techniques should not be used to make final decisions about implementing a particular marketing strategy. You need other kinds of research (descriptive or causal) to make decisions, especially decisions like this that are central to the company's future success.

The moderator must lead the discussion so that all objectives of the study are met and that interaction among the group members is stimulated. The focus group session cannot be allowed to dissolve into a series of individual depth interviews in which the participants each take turns responding to a predetermined set of questions. As a result, the moderator's role is extremely delicate. It requires someone who is intimately familiar with the purpose and objectives of the research and at the same time possesses good interpersonal communication skills. One important measure of a focus group's success is whether the participants talk to each other, rather than the moderator. Some of the key qualifications moderators must have are described in Exhibit 5.3.

The Dark Side of Focus Groups Despite their benefits, focus groups have two major weaknesses. Actually, these weaknesses have little to do with focus groups as a technique. Instead, they arise from how they are used. The first great weakness has to do with how the results of a focus group session are interpreted. When managers—or researchers, for that matter—bring preconceived ideas about what they want or expect to see, it's no surprise when they find evidence in one or more of the group discussions that supports their position. Because executives have the ability to observe the discussions through 1-way mirrors or to review recordings of the sessions, focus groups are more susceptible to executive and researcher biases than most other exploratory techniques. These biases may not be intentional, but they can still be harmful. And many managers find it too easy to use focus group data to intentionally support their positions. As one observer put it, "The primary function of focus groups is often to validate the sellers' own beliefs about their product."[6] Research Window 5.3, on page 92, offers an example of what can happen when a company loses its sense of caution and objectivity about focus group results.

A few years ago, the president of a sizable chain of restaurants based in the southwestern United States gave a presentation about his company's marketing efforts. He discussed how focus groups had been used to test an upcoming advertising campaign. In fact, he had observed at least one of the focus groups and could recall the words of one particular focus group participant, which coincidentally expressed his own feelings about the campaign very well. When the president of an organization can remember the words of a single participant in a single focus group, watch out. The exploratory research is about to be used in ways in which it was never intended, nor is well suited.

Here is our second big concern about how focus groups are being used: Many companies and the researchers advising them seem to believe that almost any need

Learning Objective

8. Discuss two major pitfalls to avoid with focus groups (or any other form of exploratory research).

Exhibit 5.3	**Seven Characteristics of Good Focus Group Moderators**

Superior Listening Ability It is essential that the moderator be able to listen to what the participants are saying. A moderator must not miss the participants' comments because of lack of attention or misunderstanding. The effective moderator knows how to paraphrase, to restate the comments of a participant when necessary, to ensure that the content of the comments is clear.

Excellent Short-Term Auditory Memory The moderator must be able to remember comments that participants make early in a group, then correlate them with comments made later by the same or other participants. A participant might say that she rarely watches her weight, for example, [and] then later indicate that she always drinks diet soft drinks. The moderator should remember the first comment and be able to relate it to the later one so that the reason for her diet soft drink consumption is clarified.

Well Organized The best moderators see things in logical sequence from general to specific and keep similar topics organized together. A good moderator guide should be constructed logically, as should the final report. An effective moderator can keep track of all the details associated with managing the focus group process, so that nothing "falls through the cracks" that impacts negatively on the overall quality of the groups.

A Quick Learner Moderators become intimately involved in a large number of different subject areas—and for only a very short time in each. An effective moderator is able to learn enough about a subject quickly in order to develop an effective moderator guide and conduct successful group sessions. Moderators normally have only a short period of time to study subject areas about which they will be conducting groups. Therefore, the most effective moderators can identify the key points in any topic area [and] then focus on them, so that they know enough to listen and/or probe for the nuances that make the difference between an extremely informative and an average group discussion.

High Energy Level Focus groups can be very boring, both for the participants and for the client observers. When the tenor of a group gets very laid back and lifeless, it dramatically lowers the quality of the information that the participants generate. The best moderators find a way to inject energy and enthusiasm into the group so that both the participants and the observers are energized throughout the session. This ability tends to be most important during late evening groups, when observers and participants are frequently tired because of the late hour, and can become listless if they are not motivated to keep their energy and interest levels high. The moderator must be able to keep his or her own energy level high so that the discussion can continue to be very productive to the end.

Personable The most effective moderators are people who can develop an instant rapport with participants, so that the people become actively involved in the discussion in order to please the moderator. Participants who don't establish rapport with the moderator are much less likely to "open up" during the discussion, and the output from the group is not as good.

Well-Above-Average Intelligence This is a vital characteristic of the effective moderator, because no one can plan for every contingency that may occur in a focus group session. The moderator must be able to think on his or her feet: process the information that the group is generating [and] then determine what line of questioning will most effectively generate further information needed to achieve the research objectives.

Source: Thomas L. Greenbaum, *The Handbook for Focus Group Research*, 2nd ed. (Thousand Oaks, Calif.: Sage Publications, 1998), pp. 77–78.

for information can be answered by conducting a series of focus groups. Focus groups are only one type of exploratory research, yet for whatever reason they have grown in popularity to the point where they are just about the only kind of research—exploratory or otherwise—that some companies will use. Managers (and researchers, too, unfortunately) tend to forget that the discussion—and consequently, the results—are greatly influenced by the moderator, the screening criteria, and the particular people who end up participating in the group. Focus group results are not representative of what would be true for the general population and are not projectable. Like other forms of exploratory research, focus groups are better for generating ideas and insights than for systematically examining them. They are not designed to provide final answers, yet they are often used for that very purpose.

Why is focus group research so popular? Well, when used appropriately, it can be very effective, and this accounts in part for its popularity. We believe, however, that focus groups often get a bigger share of the research budget than they probably deserve simply because managers can be involved in the process. They are more comfortable supporting an activity in which they can participate and observe, plus, conducting focus groups has simply become the "norm" over the years. If everyone else is doing them, focus groups become the safe option for researchers to recommend, regardless of whether or not they are actually the best option in a given situation. As one critic bluntly stated, "Focus groups are the crack cocaine of market research. You get hooked on them and you're afraid to make a move without them."[7]

research window 5.3

What Women Want

Focus groups failed a company targeting products to teenage girls. MIT professor, Justine Cassell, author of a thought-provoking piece entitled "What Women Want" reports her experience working with the company. Following a series of focus groups the company concluded that what teenage girls wanted was technologically enhanced nail polish. This was a happy coincidence as technologically enhanced nail polish was precisely what the company produced! However, in Cassell's own research with 3,062 children (60% of whom were girls) in 139 countries, in which the children were invited to describe what they would like to use technology for, not a single one of them said technologically enhanced nail polish!

Source: Excerpted from Philip Hodgson, "Focus Groups: Is Consumer Research Losing Its Focus?" *Userfocus*, June 1, 2004, downloaded from http://www.userfocus.co.uk, August 10, 2008.

© DIGITAL VISION/GETTY IMAGES

MANAGER'S FOCUS

Managers commonly attend focus group sessions and observe with varying degrees of attention from behind 1-way mirrors. Researchers sometimes joke about how managers sit distractedly in the back room eating gourmet food, while the focus group participants talk and eat cheap snacks. The managers may be served gourmet food because research firms have a vested interest in pleasing their clients. Unfortunately, this desire to please the client can carry over into how a focus group is conducted. One way this can occur is when managers send new questions in to the moderator during the focus group session. Sometimes these questions prompt a fruitful discussion; other times they merely redirect the conversation in the way the manager wants it to go. This can be detrimental to the objectivity and usefulness of the findings.

Many managers have a predisposition toward seeking research findings that confirm what they already believe to be true. The essence of sound exploratory research is to generate ideas that have never occurred to managers. When you are a manager, attending a focus group session could be a very thought-provoking experience for you. However, for it to stimulate your thinking the way it should, you need to make an effort to avoid doing anything during the session that will influence either the moderator or the participants toward your preconceived ideas. Similarly, you may learn a great deal by "listening in on" depth interviews as they take place, but again, for the best results to emerge, you must guard against biasing the process in any way. If you have any doubt about your ability to do this, or if you have any reason to believe your presence will influence the interviewer, it is in your own best interest (and your company's) to stay away and allow the professional interviewers to gather objective information on your behalf.

Nominal Groups

Nominal group interviews are similar in characteristics to focus group interviews. Each enlists eight to 12 people to participate, is directed by a moderator, and focuses on group interaction. The primary difference is that nominal groups require written responses by participants before open group discussion. It was noted earlier that smaller groups can be too easily dominated by one or two members or that larger groups can lead to frustration or boredom as individuals wait to respond or get involved. Nominal groups hope to ensure that these issues are avoided, regardless of group size, by asking people to think and write before speaking. Here's how a nominal group interview works.

First, the moderator proposes the question or topic for discussion. Once it is clear that all participants fully understand the issue, participants are invited to think about and then record their thoughts on paper. Second, the moderator asks respondents one by one to reveal their written responses. Often, the moderator will write the individual responses for all group members to see. Individuals are encouraged to record new ideas stimulated by the sharing from others. At the same time, verbal discussion between group members is discouraged until after all participants have had a chance to reveal their ideas. Next, the complete set of individual responses is reviewed by the group and the moderator. Discussions center around clarification of existing thoughts and elimination of duplication. Finally, group members are asked to prioritize the group's ideas. The ideas with the highest priority, as agreed upon by the group, are now the focus of the group discussion.

Nominal groups limit respondent interaction initially in an effort to maximize individual input. Like focus groups, it is a terrific technique for generating new ideas. In fact, nominal groups can produce more, and more varied, ideas than focus groups due to their concentration on individual participation. It also minimizes any potential concerns of "group think," domination by a few individuals, or the lack of involvement by respondents who are generally more quiet or shy.[8]

nominal group
A group interview technique which initially limits respondent interaction to a minimum while attempting to maximize input from individual group members.

Case Analyses

Case analysis involves the study of selected examples or cases of the phenomenon about which insights are needed. Researchers may examine existing records, observe the phenomenon as it occurs, conduct unstructured interviews, or use any one of a variety of other approaches to analyze what is happening in a given situation. The focus may be on entities (individual people, households, or other institutions) or groups of entities (sales representatives or distributors in various regions).

For example, when asked how Aeropostale selects the clothes it wants to carry in its stores, CEO Julian Geiger had this to say: "We don't look at what's on the selling floor of our competitors. We look at what's on the backs of our customers. Our design group goes all over. Sure, everybody goes to London and Paris and Barcelona. But we go to Great Adventure and concerts, spring break, train stations, and airports to see what the real kids are wearing. We feel we're targeting the real, universal American kid, who comes to the mall with $40 in their pocket."[9]

Case analyses can be performed in lots of different ways, but there are a couple of general things to keep in mind.[10] First, it is important to record all relevant data, not just data that support any initial hypotheses that researchers or managers have already formed. Second, the success of the case analysis approach depends upon the researcher's ability to interpret the diverse mass of information that is collected

case analysis
Intensive study of selected examples of the phenomenon of interest.

© ROB BRINSON/GETTY IMAGES

In case analysis, researchers can observe a phenomenon as it occurs, such as teens shopping.

ETHICAL DILEMMA 5.2

Prompted by an increasing incidence of homes for sale by owner, the president of a local real estate company asks you to undertake exploratory research to ascertain what kind of image realtors enjoy in the community. Unbeknownst to your current client, you undertook a similar research study for a competitor two years ago and, based on your findings, have formed specific hypotheses about why some homeowners are reluctant to sell their houses through realtors.

- Is it ethical to give information obtained while working for one client to another client who is a competitor? What should you definitely not tell your current client about the earlier project?
- Is it ethical to undertake a research project when you think that you already know what the findings will be? Can you generalize findings from two years ago to today?
- Should you help this company define its problem, and if so, how?

across cases. The researcher must be able to sort through the data and see the "big picture," or insights that apply across multiple cases, not just details that apply only to individual cases. Finally, as with all other forms of exploratory research, the goal is to gain insights, not to test explanations.

Consider a study aimed at improving the productivity of the sales force of a particular company. The researcher chose to carefully study several of the company's best salespeople and to compare them to several of the worst. Although their backgrounds and degree of experience were similar, observing the salespeople in the field suggested an important difference between the high and low performers. The best salespeople were checking the stock of retailers and pointing out items on which they were low; the low performers were not taking the time to do this. Placing the researcher in the field with the salespeople allowed an insight that might not have been uncovered otherwise.

Case analyses seem to be especially effective for generating insights when the cases chosen reflect recent changes in behavior. For example, the way a market adjusts to the entrance of a new competitor can reveal a great deal about the structure of the industry. Similarly, a company can probably learn more from a long-time customer that has defected to a competitor than it can from a long-time customer that stays with the company.

Cases that reflect extremes of behavior are also good candidates for study. The company noted above that compared the best and worst performing salespeople offers an example. To determine the factors responsible for the differences in unit sales across a company's sales territories, a researcher will probably learn more by comparing the best and worst territories than by looking at all territories.

benchmarking
Using organizations that excel at some function as sources of ideas for improvement.

Benchmarking A frequently used example of using case analysis to develop insights is benchmarking. **Benchmarking** involves identifying one or more organizations that excel at carrying out some function and using their practices as a source of ideas for improvement. For example, L.L.Bean is noted for its excellent order fulfillment. Even during the busy Christmas season, the company typically fills over 99% of its orders correctly. Therefore, other organizations have sought to improve their own order fulfillment by benchmarking L.L.Bean.

Organizations carry out benchmarking through activities such as reading about other organizations, visiting or calling them, and taking apart competing products to see how they are made. The process of benchmarking varies according to the information needs of the organization and the resources available.

Xerox is widely credited with the first benchmarking project in the United States. In 1979, Xerox studied Japanese competitors to learn how they could sell mid-size copiers for less than what it cost Xerox to make them. Today, many companies including AT&T, Eastman Kodak, and Motorola use benchmarking as a standard research tool.

ethnography
The detailed observation of consumers during their ordinary daily lives using direct observations, interviews, and video and audio recordings.

Ethnography An increasingly popular form of case analysis is ethnography. These procedures, which have been adapted from anthropology, involve the detached and prolonged observation of consumers' emotional responses, cognitions, and behaviors during their ordinary daily lives. Unlike anthropologists, however, who might live in the group being studied for months or years, ethnographers use a combination of direct observations, interviews, and video and audio recordings to make their observations more quickly. Research Window 5.4 provides more insights into the philosophy behind and methods used in ethnographic research.

research window 5.4

Underlying Philosophy and Methods Used in Ethnographic Research

Imagine being a fly on the wall at your consumers' homes: You would know exactly what products the consumer was using, when, and how. No more guessing about what a consumer wants.

That's why more and more companies are using ethnographic research as a tool to better understand how products fit into the context of consumers' lifestyles and, in turn, provide a basis for generating innovative new-product concepts. Ethnography allows one to observe consumer behavior where the person uses the product, whether it is in the home, on the go, at school, or in the office.

Ethnography is an anthropologic view of the marketplace. It deals with the scientific description of contemporary cultures. It uses anthropology to understand what the consumer needs but cannot adequately articulate. It records insights into the consumer experience with the product.

With ethnography, a consumer is viewed using products in his or her natural environment. For example, an ethnographer with a video camera becomes an observer at a consumer's home, perhaps "viewing" the inside of kitchen cabinets or the freezer compartment to get an accurate assessment of storage products' uses.

It should be obvious that this procedure shifts the focus to what consumers actually do, versus what they say they do. It draws hypotheses from the activities or behavior of the consumer rather than from their expressed attitudes. By closely observing and evaluating these patterns of behavior, we are able to draw conclusions for potential new-product ideas.

Perhaps the greatest benefit of such an ethnographic approach is the marketers' ability to view the consumer actually using the product, taking the concept of a "taste test" to a whole new realm. Rather than having a consumer test a product and provide feedback, consumers are using the product where and when they are most comfortable.

This exactness of ethnography is appealing. Consumers can't alter their response to a question about a product if they are being videotaped.

Among the most important approaches to ethnography are (1) in-home observation of consumers, (2) having consumers photograph usage occasions or environments, and (3) in-field observation of consumers.

In-home observation is most desired when the product's use is home related. An interviewer and videographer might enter the respondent's home and ask specific questions under the watchful eye of the camera.

The second method involves having a consumer videotape or photograph the product in the home. For storage containers, for instance, the consumer might take pictures or videotape her cabinets, freezer, refrigerator, pantry, or any other place storage containers are used, providing a comprehensive photographic record of the product in use.

In the third method, in-field observation, a videographer, interviewer, and anthropologist go out to the field—a supermarket, picnic area, or daycare facility—to view the intended product.

While skeptics feel the presence of a camera hinders respondents from behaving naturally, there are ways to structure the observation so that it seems as though the camera isn't even there.

There are many other methods to obtain a record of consumers' attitudes and behaviors. One involves having consumers take photographs of products throughout their homes. These allow consumers to express in a visual way the impact of products on specific parts of their lives. These photographs then are brought to an "ideation" session for generating new-product ideas.

In another method, consumers keep diaries of their responses to products, how they use certain products, when, and where. The diary is kept for a specified time and is used as a written recording of consumers' interaction with products.

Source: Adapted from Marvin Matises, "Send Ethnographers into New—SKU Jungle," *Brandweek* 41, September 25, 2000, pp. 32–33.

Like other methods of case analysis, ethnography is useful as an exploratory research tool because it can allow insights based on real behavior, rather than on what people say. For example, an academic researcher conducted a 16-month ethnography of households and the brands in their kitchen pantries. She used interviews and observation, as well as projective techniques such as sentence completion and a drawing task (see next section), to gain an understanding of the perception of brands in consumer households.

MANAGER'S FOCUS

"Best practices" studies have become popular methods by which businesses benchmark against highly successful companies. While they can provide valuable results, it is also possible for managers to misunderstand the underlying reasons for successful performance when they analyze only the highest performing organizations. As a manager, you are probably more likely to pinpoint the underlying drivers of relative success and failure in an industry if you compare and contrast organizations representing the whole spectrum of market performance.

One family that she studied (a couple in their forties and their 14-year-old son) clearly demonstrated the insights that can be generated through ethnography. The family's kitchen has an old-fashioned "general store" look and they prefer that their groceries simply blend into the background. In fact, they often remove products from their original packaging and place them in more discreet containers. They also place the more flashy brands that the son purchases out of general view. When asked about the importance they place on food brands, the couple made comments such as, "I really don't pay attention to brands," "We aren't brand loyal," and "I don't have any real preferences for brands." Based on these answers, a marketer conducting traditional research may have expected this family to be completely unaffected by brand names and packaging.

Observation of the family, however, made it evident that they bought many of the same brands over and over again. In particular, the family bought the Dominick's store brand for many of its food choices. The couple describes this brand as "not flashy," "discreet," and "subtle." While consciously attempting to avoid nearly all things related to branding, the couple was unknowingly becoming very loyal to a brand that they valued for its ability to simply blend in, evidence that consumers' expressed beliefs do not always indicate their purchasing behaviors.[11]

Some companies and researchers, seeking the benefits of ethnography without the tremendous time and monetary costs, practice a sort of "light" version of the technique, spending as little as a day or a few hours on site with research participants. The Ford Motor Company has been developing a gasoline–electric hybrid sport utility vehicle for some time. Researchers began by holding focus groups with the two segments of consumers, environmentally conscious consumers and technology fans, whom they thought would be most receptive to the vehicle. Next, they selected a handful of consumers who agreed to let Ford marketers spend a day of "ethnographic immersion" with them in their homes. Ford was surprised to learn that the fans of the new hybrid SUV tended to be very mainstream; they were not hardcore environmentalists.[12]

Despite the current popularity of ethnography and other forms of case analysis, we need to offer some words of caution about their (mis)use. As with other forms of exploratory research, the usefulness of the technique for generating insights depends on the quality and objectivity of the analysis. Interpreting the rich, qualitative data produced by these techniques is very difficult to do. Remaining objective about the results (that is, not allowing preconceived ideas and expectations to influence the interpretation) may be even harder to do. And here's another point that you've heard before: Exploratory methods should be used to generate insights and hypotheses. They are not useful for discerning final answers and making decisions, although some researchers attempt to use them for that purpose. Research Window 5.5 presents a cautionary note from an executive with the J. Walter Thompson advertising agency.

research window 5.5

The Case Against Ethnography

At its worst, ethnography could become the reality TV of marketing information—entertaining, easy, and quick, but superficial. I am always interested in original approaches to analyzing problems, but my concern about ethnography in a commercial context is that it will not lead to original explanation, but to microscopic reflections of the everyday.

It is neither as long term nor as rigorous as academic study, and risks becoming an excuse for unedited reportage masquerading as "important" information.

Ever since we sold our souls to the god of insights—an all-powerful, but unforgiving and often unknowable master—there seems to be a desire for more observations and examples of customer behavior, which can be reported back as insightful.

It is the actions of people that are the "insights." It is not the way we interpret them, how we might apply them to the problem, or what they signify, but literally the behavior itself.

Ethnography can be an additional input, but it is no replacement for thoughtful and intelligent analysis. At worst, ethnography is the enemy of good analysis. But, as in every other field, it depends more on the quality of the person in charge of the project than the technique itself.

Source: Excerpted from Marco Rimini, Executive Planning Director, J. Walter Thompson, as quoted in Louella Miles, "Living Their Lives," *Marketing*, December 11, 2003, p. 27, downloaded via ProQuest, June 29, 2004.

Projective Methods

Sometimes individuals have difficulty expressing their true feelings, beliefs, and behaviors. Consumers won't describe many of their motives and reasons for choice because a truthful description would be damaging to their egos. This is especially the case when there is pressure, real or imagined, to think, feel, or behave in certain ways. Other motives they cannot describe, either because they do not have the words to make their meaning clear or because their motives exist below the level of awareness. Yet marketers need to understand what motivates consumers and how they really feel about phenomena in order to create truly satisfactory exchanges with their customers (see Research Window 5.6). Asking direct questions, however, can sometimes produce answers that are either useless or misleading.

Researchers have tried to overcome subjects' reluctance to discuss their feelings and/or to provide truthful answers through the use of **projective methods.** Projective methods encourage respondents to reveal their own feelings, thoughts, and behaviors by shifting the focus away from the individual through the use of indirect tasks. The basic assumption with projective methods is that an individual's reaction to an ambiguous stimulus is an indicator of the person's basic perceptions of the phenomenon. For example, giving a high school student a picture of a young man seated in a classroom and then asking the student what the young man is doing or thinking encourages the student to project his or her needs, motives, and values. With projective methods, the respondent chooses his or her own interpretation, description, and evaluation of the ambiguous stimulus.

In general terms, then, a projective technique involves the use of a vague stimulus that an individual is asked to describe, expand upon, or build a structure around. Many different approaches have been used, ranging from asking people to describe what a brand would be like if it came to life to asking respondents to draw or select pictures of the kinds of people who would use certain products. Among the most common techniques are word association, sentence completion, storytelling, and role playing.

projective methods
Methods that encourage respondents to reveal their own feelings, thoughts, and behaviors by shifting the focus away from the individual through the use of indirect tasks.

research window 5.6

The Secret Life of Brands: The Hidden Motivations for the Things We Buy

There's more at play in purchases than meets the eye, and you can't position your brand if you don't understand its secret life. And to do that, you need to be able to answer this question: What do people buy when they buy your brand?

If people bought brands solely on the basis of quality, price convenience, service, and other rational attributes, the lives of marketers would be much simpler. But purely rational appeals are not sufficient in a competitive marketplace. In understanding the secret lives of brands, one not only needs to know the rational and tangible elements of human purchasing behavior and the emotional and intangible elements—but also the unconscious motivations as well.

Let's take insurance for example. Our work has shown that at the tangible level, consumers are buying mitigation of risk, replacement of objects, preservation of wealth, etc. At the intangible level, they are buying security, control, "I am taking care of my family" and, "It is what my father would do." But at the unconscious level, they are buying something bigger—a higher power to protect them from things they can't defend themselves against; they are buying a sort of magic.

How does understanding these unconscious programs help in a marketing context?

A major U.S. brokerage firm asked us to help it create a stronger relationship between the company and its clients. It wished to create stronger loyalty to its own brand and differentiate itself from competitors. It also hoped to reduce the client attribution that invariably occurs when an individual broker moves to another firm.

We demonstrated that many investment decisions were driven by feelings of fear about the future and related feelings of helplessness. There were already many rational techniques in place for addressing these fears—diversification, asset allocation, investment strategies, technology, electronic communication, etc. However, the relationship with the broker was the only way that the strong emotional needs of the clients could be addressed. Weakening the relationship with the broker in an attempt to strengthen the client's relationship and loyalty to the company brand would have only served to increase client attrition. So we designed a unique model of broker/client relationship that was subsequently successfully piloted.

If you believe that consumers are buying your product because of good, solid, rational reasons, you are missing the most important aspect of their motivation. In order to understand consumer motivations, you have to understand the hidden, unconscious meanings of your brand or product. When these motivations are uncovered, you can connect with your customers at a deep emotional level that goes way beyond how they feel when they use your brand. When you understand what people are actually buying, then you can sell.

Source: Excerpted and adapted from Thelma Beam and Hugh Oddie, "The Hidden Motivations for the Things We Buy," *Strategy Magazine*, April 19, 2004, downloaded from http://www.strategymag.com, August 1, 2008.

---

word association
A projective method in which respondents are asked to respond to a list of words with the first word that comes to mind.

Word Association With word association, subjects respond to a list of words with the first word that comes to mind. The test words are intermixed with neutral words to conceal the purpose of the study. Suppose that a research team is doing a study on people's feelings about ecology and pollution. Some of the key words that might be used for a word association task could include *traffic, lakes, smokestacks,* and *city,* mixed in with words such as *margarine, blue jeans,* and *government.*

Responses to each of the key terms are recorded word for word and later analyzed for their meaning. The responses are usually judged in three ways: by the frequency with which any word is given as a response, by the average amount of time that elapses before a response is given, and by the number of respondents who do not respond at all to a test word after a reasonable period of time.

To determine the amount of time that elapses before a response is given to a test word, a stopwatch may be used or the interviewer may count silently while waiting for a reply. Respondents who hesitate (which is usually defined as taking longer than three seconds to reply) are judged to be sufficiently emotionally involved in the word so as to provide not their immediate reaction but rather what they consider to be an acceptable response. If they do not respond at all, their emotional involvement is judged to be so high as to block a response. An individual's pattern of responses, along with the details of the response to each question, are then used to assess the person's attitudes or feelings on the subject.

Sentence Completion   Sentence completion requires that the respondent complete a number of sentences with the first thoughts that come to mind. The responses are recorded word for word and are later analyzed.

sentence completion
A projective method in which respondents are directed to complete a number of sentences with the first words that come to mind.

While the analysis of qualitative responses is subjective, sometimes the results are clear enough that there would be good agreement in their interpretation as follows:

People who are concerned about ecology *care about the future.*
A person who does not use our lakes for recreation is *being thoughtful about the ecosystem.*
When I think of living in a city, I *can't help but think of the smog over LA.*

Compare those responses to these of another person:

People who are concerned about ecology *are just tree-huggers who want to run up my taxes.*
A person who does not use our lakes for recreation is *a person who doesn't enjoy water sports.*
When I think of living in a city, I *think about cruising my car downtown on Saturday night!*

Presumably, these two respondents could easily be characterized as belonging to segments of consumers who are more and less ecologically concerned.

One advantage of sentence completion over word association is that respondents can be provided with a more directed stimulus. There should be just enough direction to evoke some association with the concept of interest. The researcher needs to be careful not to convey the purpose of the study or provoke the "socially acceptable" response. Obviously, skill is needed to develop a good sentence-completion or word-association test.

Storytelling   The storytelling approach often relies on pictorial material such as cartoons, photographs, or drawings. Basically, respondents are asked to tell stories about the pictures. The pictures can be of anything that might somehow lead to relevant insights about the problem/opportunity at hand. The way an individual responds to the pictures or drawings helps researchers interpret that individual's values, beliefs, attitudes, and personality.[13]

storytelling
A projective method of data collection relying on a picture stimulus such as a cartoon, photograph, or drawing, about which the subject is asked to tell a story.

With respect to the pollution example, the stimulus might be a picture of a city, and the respondent might be asked to describe what it would be like to live there. The analysis of the individual's response would then focus on the emphasis given to pollution in its various forms. If no mention were made of traffic congestion, dirty air, noise, and so on, the person would be classified as displaying little concern for pollution and its control.

Role Playing   The role playing technique is similar in many ways to storytelling. With role playing, however, the researcher will introduce a scenario or context and ask respondents to play the role of a person in the scenario. The researcher might ask how "people you know" or "the average person" or "people like you" or even how the respondents themselves would react in the situation. As with other projective methods, the goal is to get a glimpse into respondents' own feelings, beliefs, actions, and so on, by shifting the focus away from them and onto the task itself.

role playing
A projective method in which a researcher will introduce a scenario or context and ask respondents to play the role of a person in the scenario.

Suppose, for example, that the pollution researchers wanted exploratory feedback on city residents' likely reactions to a number of pollution control efforts being considered by local officials. Rather than ask residents direct questions about whether or not they are in favor of—or would abide by—new regulations about carpooling or time of day restrictions on lawn mowing, the researchers might instead use a scenario in which the regulations were being introduced in another city. They could then ask the research participants how a resident of that city is likely to feel and respond to the regulations. In the process of describing the anger, feelings of being hassled, frustration, willingness to obey the law, or positive feelings of being able to "do my part" likely to be felt by residents of the other city, the respondents will reveal a great deal about their own feelings.

The usual concerns about the difficulty of data analysis and interpretation apply to projective methods, just as they apply to other forms of exploratory research. And, as always, researchers must keep in mind that no form of exploratory research, including projective methods, is designed to get final answers or make decisions.

SUMMARY

Learning Objective 1

Explain what a research design is.
A research design is the framework or plan for a study and guides the collection and analysis of data.

Learning Objective 2

List the three basic types of research design.
One basic way of classifying designs is in terms of the fundamental objective of the research: exploratory, descriptive, or causal.

Learning Objective 3

Describe the major emphasis of each type of research design.
The major emphasis in exploratory research is on the discovery of ideas and insights. Descriptive research is typically concerned with determining the frequency with which something occurs or the relationship between variables. A causal research design is concerned with determining cause-and-effect relationships.

Learning Objective 4

Describe the basic uses of exploratory research.
Exploratory research is useful for helping formulate the manager's decision problem, developing hypotheses, gaining familiarity with a phenomenon, and/or clarifying concepts. In general, exploratory research is appropriate for any problem about which little is known. The output from exploratory research is ideas and insights, not answers.

Learning Objective 5

Specify the key characteristics of exploratory research.
Exploratory studies are typically small scale and are very flexible; anything goes.

Learning Objective 6

Discuss the various types of exploratory research and describe each.
Common types of exploratory research include literature searches, depth interviews, focus groups, nominal groups, case analyses, and projective methods. Literature searches involve reviewing conceptual and trade literature, or published statistics. Depth interviews attempt to tap the knowledge and experience of those familiar with the general subject being investigated. Focus groups involve a discussion among a small number of individuals, normally eight to 12, simultaneously. Nominal groups aim to maximize individual input in group discussion settings. With case analyses, researchers study selected cases of the phenomenon under investigation; ethnographic research is a popular example. Finally, projective methods encourage respondents to reveal their own feelings, thoughts, and behaviors by shifting the focus away from the individual through the use of indirect tasks.

Learning Objective 7

Identify the key person in a focus group.
The moderator is key to the successful functioning of a focus group. The moderator

must not only lead the discussion so that all objectives of the study are met but must also do so in such a way that interaction among group members is stimulated and promoted.

Learning Objective 8

Discuss two major pitfalls to avoid with focus groups (or any other form of exploratory research).

Researchers and managers must consciously work to remain as objective as possible when reviewing and interpreting exploratory data. It is very easy to see what you expect or want to see in qualitative data. The second pitfall to avoid is to use exploratory research to obtain answers and decisions rather than the ideas, insights, and hypotheses that these techniques were designed to deliver.

KEY TERMS

research design (page 78)
exploratory research (page 79)
descriptive research (page 79)
causal research (page 79)
hypothesis (page 81)
literature search (page 82)
depth interview (page 83)
focus group (page 84)
moderator (page 84)
moderator's guidebook (page 89)

nominal group (page 93)
case analysis (page 93)
benchmarking (page 94)
ethnography (page 94)
projective methods (page 97)
word association (page 98)
sentence completion (page 99)
storytelling (page 99)
role playing (page 99)

REVIEW QUESTIONS

1. What is a research design? Is a research design necessary to conduct a study?

2. What are the different types of research designs? What is the basic purpose of each?

3. What are the basic uses for exploratory research?

4. What are the key characteristics of exploratory research?

5. What is a literature search? What kinds of literature might be searched?

6. What are the characteristics of a depth interview? Who should be interviewed?

7. How does a focus group with eight to 12 people differ from a series of depth interviews with eight to 12 people? How does a focus group differ from a nominal group?

8. What characteristics should a good focus group moderator possess? Why is each important?

9. How might focus groups be misused?

10. What are two common approaches to the use of case analyses?

11. What is the basic point of projective methods? What are some popular approaches?

DISCUSSION QUESTIONS, PROBLEMS, AND PROJECTS

1. The Communicon Company was a large supplier of residential telephones and related services in the southeast United States. The R&D group at the company recently designed a prototype with a memory function that could store the number of calls and the contents of the calls for a period of 72 hours. A similar product, introduced by a competitor six months earlier, was marginally successful. However, both models suffered from a technical flaw. The audio quality on calls that lasted for over 20 minutes would

begin to deteriorate due to technical limitations. Despite the flaw, management was excited about the new product and decided to do a field study to gauge consumer reaction. A random sample of 1,000 respondents was to be chosen from three major metropolitan centers in the Southeast. The questionnaires were designed to find out respondents' attitudes and opinions toward this new instrument.

In this situation, is the research design appropriate? If yes, why? If no, why not?

2. For each of the situations described below, which type of research design is most appropriate? Why?

   a. Frank's Flies is a fishing lure manufacturer. Frank's management has decided to enter the lucrative market for trout flies, an area in which the company has little experience. The fly development department has decided that it needs more information concerning trout fishing in general before it can begin designing the new product line.

   b. The management team at Aardvark Audio strongly suspects that the company's current advertising campaign is not achieving its stated goal of raising consumer awareness of the company's name to a 75% recognition level in the target market. The team has decided to commission a research project to test the effectiveness of the various ads in the current campaign.

   c. Ace Fertilizer Company is trying to decide where advertisements for its vegetable garden fertilizers should be placed. Management is contemplating a research project to determine which publications home gardeners read on a regular basis.

3. A medium-sized manufacturer of high-speed copiers and duplicators was introducing a new desktop model. The vice president of communications had to decide between two advertising programs for this product. He preferred advertising program Gamma and was sure it would generate more sales than its counterpart, advertising program Beta. The next day, he was to meet with the senior vice president of marketing to plan an appropriate research design for a study that would aid in the final decision as to which advertising program to implement.

   What research design would you recommend? Justify your choice.

4. A local mail-order firm was concerned with improving its service. In particular, management wanted to assess if customers were dissatisfied with current service and the nature of this dissatisfaction.

   What research design would you recommend? Justify your choice.

5. The Write-It Company was a manufacturer of writing instruments such as fountain pens, ballpoint pens, soft-tip pens, and mechanical pencils. Typically, these products were sold through small and large chains, drugstores, and grocery stores. The company had recently diversified into the manufacture of disposable cigarette lighters. The distribution of this product was to be restricted to drugstores and grocery stores because management believed that its target market of low- and middle-income people would use these outlets. Your expertise is required in order to decide on an appropriate research design to determine if this would indeed be the case.

   What research design would you recommend? Justify your choice.

6. Feather-Tote Luggage is a producer of cloth-covered luggage, one of the primary advantages of which is its light weight. The company distributes its luggage through major department stores, mail-order houses, clothing retailers, and other retail outlets such as stationery stores, leather goods stores, and so on. The company advertises rather heavily, but it also supplements this promotional effort with a large field staff of sales representatives, numbering around 400. The number of sales representatives varies, and one of the historical problems confronting Feather-Tote Luggage has been the large number of resignations. It is not unusual for 10 to 20% of the sales force to turn over every year. Since the cost of training a new person is estimated at $5,000 to $10,000, not including the lost

sales that might result because of a personnel switch, Mr. Harvey, the sales manager, is concerned and has been conducting exit interviews with each departing sales representative. On the basis of these interviews, he has concluded that the major reason for this high turnover is general sales representatives' dissatisfaction with company policies, promotional opportunities, and pay. But top management has not been sympathetic to Harvey's pleas regarding the changes needed in these areas of corporate policy. Rather, it has tended to counter Harvey's pleas with arguments that too much of what he is suggesting is based on his gut reactions and little hard data. Before it would be willing to make changes, top management wants more systematic evidence that job satisfaction, in general, and these dimensions of job satisfaction, in particular, are the real reasons for the high turnover. Harvey has called on the marketing research department at Feather-Tote Luggage to assist him in solving his problem.

a. As a member of this department, identify the general hypothesis that would guide your research efforts.

b. How might each type of research design be effectively used in this case? What would you recommend to Harvey?

7. Cynthia Gaskill is the owner of a clothing store that caters to college students. Through informal conversations with her customers, she has begun to suspect that a video-rental store specifically targeting college students would do quite well in the local market. While her conversations with students have revealed an overall sense of dissatisfaction with existing rental outlets, she hasn't been able to isolate specific areas of concern. Thinking back to a marketing research course she took in school, Gaskill has decided that focus group research would be an appropriate method to gather information that might be useful in deciding whether to pursue further development of her idea to open a video rental store (e.g., a formal business plan, store policies).

a. What is the decision problem and resulting research problem apparent in this situation?

b. Whom should Gaskill select as participants for the focus group? Exactly what criteria would you establish for recruiting participants?

c. Where should the focus group session be conducted?

d. What would you need the moderator of the focus group to know before the session?

e. Develop the moderator's guidebook for the focus group.

8. The exploratory techniques of focus group research and depth interviews are similar in many ways, yet each offers distinct advantages, depending on the objectives of the research project. What are some of the similarities and differences in these techniques?

9. A large retail chain focusing on athletic shoes has noticed some recent slippage in same-store sales, in particular for stores located in suburban areas; sales in urban stores have increased slightly. Managers are concerned that the styles the stores offer may no longer be in fashion among some target groups. Because the chain manufactures it own line of shoes, styles must be chosen at least 10 to 12 months before they hit the stores to allow time for manufacturing. Managers have always assumed that athletic shoes are selected and purchased primarily for their functional attributes but are beginning to think that the more symbolic attributes may play a larger role than previously believed. Your research firm has been contracted to provide marketing research into these issues.

a. Which research design might be most appropriate under the circumstances? Why?

b. Assuming that you planned to conduct exploratory research, how might a literature search be employed?

c. Discuss two ways in which case analyses could be conducted to provide useful information.

10. Pick three of your friends and conduct a depth interview with each of them to determine their feelings toward purchasing athletic shoes.

   a. What factors were mentioned in the first interview?

   b. What factors were mentioned in the second interview?

   c. What factors were mentioned in the third interview?

   d. Based on the findings for Questions a, b, and c, what specific hypotheses would you suggest?

   e. Briefly discuss the strengths and weaknesses of depth interviews.

11. Design and administer a word-association test to determine a student's feelings toward eating out.

   a. List 10 stimuli and the subject's responses and the amount of time that elapsed before the subject reacted to each stimulus.

Stimulus	Response	Time
1.		
2.		
3.		
4.		
5.		
6.		
7.		
8.		
9.		
10.		

   b. On the basis of your minisurvey, what tentative conclusions can you infer regarding the person's feelings toward eating out?

   c. Briefly discuss the strengths and weaknesses of this technique.

12. Design and administer a sentence-completion test to determine a student's feelings toward coffee consumption.

   a. List at least eight sentences that are to be used in the sentence-completion exercise.

   1. _____

   2. _____

   3. _____

   4. _____

   5. _____

   6. _____

   7. _____

   8. _____

   b. On the basis of the respondent's reactions, how would you describe the respondent's attitudes toward drinking coffee?

   c. How would a researcher analyze the responses?

13. Design and administer a storytelling test to determine a student's reasons for not living in a residence hall, or dormitory.

    a. Develop a stimulus (verbal or pictorial) for the story-completion exercise. (*Hint:* It might be easier to use a verbal stimulus.)

    b. Based on this exercise, what are your findings as to the person's reasons for not living in a residence hall?

Descriptive and Causal Research Designs

Introduction

In the preceding chapter, we learned that research designs typically fall into one of three categories: exploratory, descriptive, or causal research. We examined exploratory research and noted that one of its primary uses is to generate ideas and insights for additional, more targeted research. In this chapter, we introduce some basic ideas about descriptive research. We then look at how causal research might be used to test the validity of the hypotheses that exploratory studies generate.

DESCRIPTIVE RESEARCH DESIGNS

Learning Objective

1. Cite three major purposes of descriptive research.

Descriptive research is very common in business and other aspects of life. In fact, most of the marketing research that students have heard about or participated in before taking a research course can be categorized as descriptive research. With a descriptive research design we are usually trying to describe some group of people or other entities. Much of the information in this book deals with how to collect descriptive data.

We use descriptive research for the following purposes:

1. **To describe the characteristics of certain groups.** For example, a research group gathered information from individuals who had eaten at a particular barbecue restaurant chain in a midwestern U.S. city to help managers develop a profile of the "average user" with respect to income, sex, age, and so on. The managers were surprised to learn that about half of their customers were women; they had started with the mistaken belief that a clear majority of their customers were men.

2. **To determine the proportion of people who behave in a certain way.** We might be interested, for example, in estimating the proportion of people within a specified radius of a proposed shopping complex who currently shop or intend to shop at the center. Most behavioral data (see Chapter 11) are collected via descriptive research. For example, when a shopper makes a purchase at most retailers, the purchase behavior is recorded as part of scanner data.

3. **To make specific predictions.** We might want to predict the level of sales for each of the next five years so that we could plan for the hiring and training of new sales representatives.

Learning Objective

2. List the six specifications of a descriptive study.

Descriptive research can be used to accomplish a wide variety of research objectives. However, descriptive data become useful for solving problems only when the process is guided by one or more specific research problems, much thought and effort, and quite often exploratory research to clarify the problem and develop hypotheses. A descriptive study design is very different from an exploratory study design. While exploratory studies are flexible in nature, descriptive studies can be considered rigid. They require a clear specification of the who, what, when, where, why, and how of the research.

Suppose a chain of electronics stores is planning to open a new store, and the company wants to determine how customers decide to visit a new store. Consider some of the questions that would need to be answered before data collection for this descriptive study could begin.

- **Who** should be considered a customer? Anyone who enters the store? What if someone doesn't buy anything but just participates in the grand-opening prize giveaway? Perhaps a customer should be defined as anyone who purchases anything from the store. Should customers be defined on the basis of the family unit, or should they be defined as individuals, even though the individuals come from the same family?

- **What** characteristics of customers should be measured? As we'll note in Chapter 12, when we ask questions or observe people or things, we are really just attempting to take measures of their attributes and characteristics. Are we interested in their age and sex, or in where they live and how they came to know about the store?

- **When** will we measure characteristics of the customers—while they are shopping or later? Should the study take place during the first weeks of operation of the store, or should it be delayed six months? For example, if we are interested in word-of-mouth influence, we'll need to wait until that influence has a chance to operate.

■ **Where** will we measure the customers? Should it be in the store, immediately outside the store, or should we attempt to contact them at home?

■ **Why** do we want to measure them in the first place? Are we going to use these measurements to plan promotional strategy? In that case, the emphasis might be on measuring how people become aware of the store. Or are we going to use these measurements as a basis for deciding where to place other stores? In that case, the emphasis might shift more to determining the trading area of the store.

■ **How** should we measure the customers? Do we use a questionnaire, or should we observe their purchasing behavior? If we use a questionnaire, what form will it take? Will it be highly structured? Will it be in the form of a scale? How will it be administered? By telephone? By mail? By e-mail? Maybe by personal interview?

Some of the answers to these questions will be fairly obvious from the hypotheses that guide the descriptive research. Others, however, will not be obvious. The researcher may not have answers until after much thought or even after a small pilot or exploratory study. In any case, the researcher should delay data collection until hypotheses are developed and clear judgments of the who, what, when, where, why, and how of descriptive research are made.

Learning Objective

3. Explain what a dummy table is.

dummy table
A table (or figure) with no entries used to show how the results of the analysis will be presented.

The Importance of Dummy Tables

Data collection must be delayed until it is clear how the data will be analyzed. To accomplish this, a series of dummy tables should be prepared before beginning the collection process. A **dummy table** is simply a table (or figure) used to show how the results of the analysis will be presented. It is a "dummy" table because there are no actual data in the table; data haven't been collected yet. Preparing a complete set of dummy tables forces you to think carefully about each piece of information to be

MANAGER'S FOCUS

Producing a set of empty tables is not an exciting proposition for anybody. As you read this section, you may be wondering if this task is really necessary—or maybe it's something that can be left to the researchers. The reality is that researchers and managers too often skip this step, either because it doesn't occur to them or they simply don't want to devote the necessary time. Skipping this step now, however, is simply inviting trouble later.

Rather than viewing this process as unnecessary or tedious, you should treat it as a valuable mid-project opportunity to meet with your research provider to make sure that the study's results will be useful to you. Working with your research supplier to create an exhaustive set of dummy tables will force you to carefully consider all of the information you'll need for your

management purposes. The benefits to you for investing this time and cognitive energy are immense, including (a) making certain you have communicated to the researcher all of your needs and expectations, (b) ensuring that the data collection instrument will capture all of the necessary variables and will measure them in the proper format, (c) providing a clear roadmap to the researchers for how the data will need to be analyzed, and (d) specifying the precise format in which the information should ultimately be reported to you. It is really a small price to pay to avoid a host of unpleasant surprises that can easily occur in the absence of proper planning. If your research provider does not raise the issue of creating dummy tables, you should bring it up yourself.

E x h i b i t 6 . 1	**Dummy Table: Athletic Shoe Store Preference by Age**

Age	Store Preference			Total
	Finish Line	**Foot Locker**	**The Athlete's Foot**	**Total**
Less than 18	xx%	xx%	xx%	100%
18–29	xx	xx	xx	100
30–39	xx	xx	xx	100
40 or over	xx	xx	xx	100

(Sample size = xx)

collected. It also takes the guesswork out of the analysis phase of the project. Some will be simple tables or figures that show the results of individual items; others may show relationships between important variables. Exhibit 6.1 shows a dummy table that might be used by an athletic shoe retailer preparing to investigate whether its customers are mostly from one age group and, if so, how that group differs from the customers who prefer competitors' stores.

Note that the table lists the age segments the company managers want to compare. It is crucial that the exact variables and categories being investigated are specified before researchers begin to collect the data. The statistical tests that will be used to uncover the relationship between age and store preference in this case should also be specified before data collection begins. Inexperienced researchers often question the need for such hard, detailed decisions before collecting the data. They assume that delaying these decisions until after the data are collected will somehow make the decisions easier. Just the opposite is true.

Once the data have been collected and analysis is begun, it's too late to say, "If only we had collected information on that variable," or "If only we had measured that variable using a different scale." Correcting such mistakes simply isn't possible without collecting more data, often at great expense. These issues must be handled before the data are collected. The researcher must know in advance the objective of each question, the reason the question is included in the study, the particular analysis in which the question will be used, and the way the results will appear using dummy tables. Dummy tables are particularly valuable in providing clues on how to phrase the individual questions and code the responses.

Two Types of Descriptive Studies

Figure 6.1 is an overview of various types of descriptive studies. The basic distinction is between cross-sectional designs, which are the most common, and longitudinal designs. Typically, a **cross-sectional study** involves researching a sample of elements from the population of interest. Characteristics of the elements, or sample members, are measured only once.

A **longitudinal study**, on the other hand, involves a panel, which is a fixed sample of elements. The elements may be stores, dealers, individuals, or other entities. The panel, or sample, remains relatively constant through time, although members may be added to replace dropouts or to keep it representative. The sample members in a panel are measured repeatedly, in contrast with the one-time measurement in a cross-sectional study. Both cross-sectional and longitudinal studies have weaknesses and advantages.

Longitudinal Analysis: Consumer Panels There are two types of panels: continuous panels (sometimes called true panels) and discontinuous panels (sometimes called

Learning Objective

4. Discuss the difference between cross-sectional and longitudinal designs.

cross-sectional study
Investigation involving a sample of elements selected from the population of interest that are measured at a single point in time.

longitudinal study
Investigation involving a fixed sample of elements that is measured repeatedly through time.

Learning Objective

5. Explain what is meant by a panel in marketing research and explain the difference between a continuous panel and a discontinuous panel.

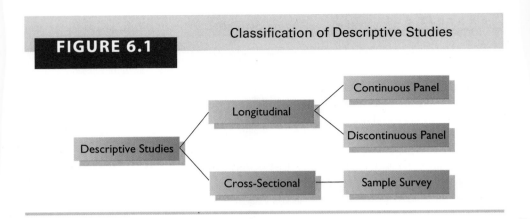

FIGURE 6.1   Classification of Descriptive Studies

```
Descriptive Studies ──┬── Longitudinal ──┬── Continuous Panel
                      │                  │
                      │                  └── Discontinuous Panel
                      │
                      └── Cross-Sectional ── Sample Survey
```

continuous panel
A fixed sample of respondents who are measured repeatedly over time with respect to the same variables.

discontinuous panel
A fixed sample of respondents who are measured repeatedly over time but on variables that change from measurement to measurement.

omnibus panels). **Continuous panels** rely on repeated measurements of the same variables. For example, Nielsen's Homescan product uses a panel consisting of more than 260,000 households across 27 countries to provide continuous tracking of consumer product purchases. The NPD Group maintains an online panel of over 3 million consumers who regularly report purchases across a wide variety of product and service categories. The operations of panels will be detailed in the section on standardized marketing information services in Chapter 8. The important point to note now is that each panel member is repeatedly measured with respect to the same characteristics.

With a **discontinuous panel**, the information collected from panel members varies. At one time, it may be attitudes with respect to a new product. At another time, the panel members might be asked to evaluate alternative advertising copy. In each case, a sample might be selected from the larger group, which is in turn a sample of the population. The subsample might be drawn randomly. More likely, however, participants with the desired characteristics will be chosen from the larger panel. For example, imagine that an automobile manufacturer had put together a panel of 5,000 car enthusiasts. The company might select members of the panel to help evaluate new car concepts. If they were developing a new type of fuel efficient vehicle, researchers might select only members of the panel who had previously indicated a preference for this type of automobile. With discontinuous panels, those chosen and the information sought vary from project to project. Several large marketing research companies operate discontinuous panels. For example, Synovate offers its Global Omnibus discontinuous panel, which has been in operation since 1986 and collects data via telephone survey.

The distinction between the traditional continuous panel and the discontinuous panel is important. True longitudinal analysis, also called *time series analysis,* can be performed only with repeated measurements of the same variables for the same entities over time. This is a real advantage compared with discontinuous panels and cross-sectional studies. Technically Speaking 6.1, on page 112, demonstrates one of the advantages of continuous panels.

COMING SOON
CVS/pharmacy
America's #1 Pharmacy

© TERRI L. MILLER/VISUAL COMMUNICATION, INC.

Descriptive studies can help retail companies determine how consumers become patrons of a new store or a new location of a familiar store.

MANAGER'S FOCUS

The benefits of longitudinal analysis (monitoring consumer processes over time) should be immediately obvious to you as a marketing manager. Utilizing the panel services of marketing research companies, however, is only one way of achieving these benefits. Companies as diverse as John Deere, Kellogg, and ESPN have established proprietary online panels with which they can continuously monitor specific variables over time (use as continuous panels) or measure a variety of variables on an *ad hoc* basis (use as discontinuous panels). Because they obtain panel data on a regular basis, maintaining their own panels enables them to reduce costs while increasing the speed with which they can access the panel. This approach, however, is more feasible for larger companies that have the necessary financial and technological resources. It also helps when your products and services have an inherent appeal to consumers or business customers so that they can enjoy serving on the panel.

If you think broadly, you may begin to recognize other ways various organizations obtain longitudinal data. For example, many supermarkets have programs for which they provide pricing incentives to customers who register their purchases using a store card. This enables them to track purchases for customers on an ongoing basis. Similarly, online merchants, both large and small, employ a variety of technologies that enable them to monitor online behavior and measure such variables as Web site access rates, conversion rates, and repeat purchases. It is also important that the information uncovered should feed into the organization's decision support system to maximize its usefulness to managers. Throughout your career, you'll always want to think creatively about how to leverage existing technology to acquire relevant data, including longitudinal data where possible.

The other advantages and disadvantages of both types of panels compared with cross-sectional studies are about the same. For example, panels are probably a researcher's best format for collecting detailed demographic information, such as respondents' incomes, ages, education levels, and occupations. Cross-sectional studies are limited in this respect, because respondents being contacted for the first and only time are rarely willing to give lengthy, time-consuming interviews. Panel members are usually compensated for their participation, so interviews can be longer and more involved, or there can be several interviews. The sponsoring firm can afford to spend more time and effort securing accurate classification information, because this information can be used in a number of studies.

Panel data are also believed to be more accurate than cross-sectional data, especially when it comes to measuring things like purchasing behavior and watching and listening to media outlets. With cross-sectional designs, respondents are asked to remember and report their past behaviors, a process that inevitably leads to error because people tend to forget. In a panel, on the other hand, behavior can often be recorded as it occurs, so less reliance is placed on memory. When diaries are used to record purchases, the problems should be virtually eliminated because the respondent is instructed to record the purchases immediately upon returning home. When other behaviors, such as television viewing, are of interest, actual viewing behaviors can be recorded electronically as they occur, thus minimizing the possibility that they will be forgotten or distorted. Research Window 6.1, on page 114, details how Arbitron uses diaries to determine radio station listening audiences. This information is then used by radio stations to make programming decisions and by advertisers to determine which programs to sponsor.

The main disadvantage of panels is that they are nonrepresentative and/or nonrandom. The agreement to participate involves a commitment on the part of the designated sample member, and many individuals do not want to make this commitment. They do not wish to be bothered with testing products, evaluating advertising copy, or filling out consumer diaries. Because these activities require a

technically speaking   6.1

Brand-Switching Analysis

Brand-switching analysis has been around for a long time and demonstrates the single most important advantage of true panel data: the way it lends itself to analysis. Suppose that we can obtain consumer purchase data from a panel of 1,000 families, and that we manufacture a laundry detergent called Sudsy. Sudsy has three main competitors: Sunshine, Sparkle, and Silky.

We have recently changed the package design for Sudsy, and are interested in determining what impact the new design has on sales. We'll consider the performance of our brand before the change (time period t_1) and after the package change (time period t_2).

We could perform several types of analyses on these data. We could look at the proportion of those in the panel who bought our brand in period t_1. We could also

calculate the proportion of those who bought our brand in period t_2. Suppose these calculations generated the data shown in Exhibit A, which indicates that the package change was successful. Sudsy's market share increased from 20% to 25%. Plus, Sudsy seemed to make its gain at the expense of Sunshine and Sparkle, whose market shares decreased. Notice that if we rely just on sales data, this is about all we can tell.

But that isn't the whole story. Because we can identify panel participants and we have repeated measures from those participants, we can count the number of families who bought Sudsy in both periods, those who bought the other brands in both periods, and those who switched brands between the two periods. Suppose the information in Exhibit B was a result of these tabulations. This table,

Exhibit A — Number of Families in Panel Purchasing Each Brand

Brand Purchased	During First Time Period (t_1)	During Second Time Period (t_2)
Sudsy	200	250
Sunshine	300	270
Sparkle	350	330
Silky	150	150
Total	1,000	1,000

Exhibit B — Brand-Switching Matrix

		During Second Time Period (t_2)				
		Bought Sudsy	Bought Sunshine	Bought Sparkle	Bought Silky	Total
During First Time Period (t_1)	Bought Sudsy	175	25	0	0	200
	Bought Sunshine	0	225	50	25	300
	Bought Sparkle	0	0	280	70	350
	Bought Silky	75	20	0	55	150
	Total	250	270	330	150	1,000

(Continued)

Exhibit C		**Brand Loyalty and Brand-Switching Probabilities among Families in Panel**				
		During Second Time Period (t_2)				
		Bought Sudsy	**Bought Sunshine**	**Bought Sparkle**	**Bought Silky**	**Total**
During First Time Period (t_1)	Bought Sudsy	.875	.125	.000	.000	1.000
	Bought Sunshine	.000	.750	.167	.083	1.000
	Bought Sparkle	.000	.000	.800	.200	1.000
	Bought Silky	.500	.133	.000	.367	1.000

which is known as a brand-switching matrix or turnover table, contains the same basic information as Exhibit A. That is, we can still see that 200, or 20%, of the families bought Sudsy in period t_1, while 250, or 25%, did so in period t_2. But Exhibit B also shows that Sudsy didn't make its market share gains at the expense of Sunshine and Sparkle, as we originally thought when we had only sales data but instead captured some of the families who previously bought Silky; 75 families switched from Silky to Sudsy in period t_2. And, as a matter of fact, Sudsy lost some of its previous users to Sunshine during the period; 25 families switched from Sudsy to Sunshine in period t_2.

Exhibit B also allows the calculation of brand loyalty. Consider Sudsy, for example: 175 of the 200, or 88%, of those who bought in period t_1 remained "loyal to it" (bought it again) in period t_2. Simply divide each cell entry by the row total to calculate these brand loyalties. Exhibit C, produced by such calculations, tells us that Sudsy exhibited the greatest buying loyalties and Silky the least. This is important to know because it indicates whether families like the brand when they try it.

Brand-switching analysis can be performed only when there are repeated measures over time for the same variables for the same subjects, which is the purpose of a continuous panel. It is not appropriate for discontinuous panel data, in which the variables being measured are constantly changing, nor is it appropriate for cross-sectional studies, even if successive cross-sectional samples are taken.

sizable time commitment, families in which both husband and wife work, for example, may be less well represented than those in which one partner works and the other is at home. Even when the companies who run these panels attempt to match the composition of the panel with the demographics of the target population, the results still cannot be projected to the population because the participants were not randomly drawn from the population (see Chapter 15).

Most consumer panels have cooperation rates of 50% or less—and that is among households that agreed to participate in the panel. A large percentage of consumers choose not to join a panel in the first place. As might be expected, cooperation rates tend to be higher when consumers find the topic interesting or when less work is required of them (for example, using a Nielsen television meter versus keeping a diary by hand of all grocery purchases).

The better ongoing panel operations select prospective participants very systematically. They attempt to generate and maintain panels that are representative of the total population of interest (though they will still be nonrandom). Quite often, to create a representative panel, they will use quota samples, in which the proportion of sample members possessing a certain characteristic is approximately the same as the proportion possessing that characteristic in the general population. As a very simplified

research window 6.1

The Arbitron Radio Listening Diary—From Beginning to End

Producing the most reliable radio listening estimates is not as simple a process as asking, "What did you listen to today?" There are many steps between the selection of a sampled household and the electronic publication of the Radio Market Report, now known as "Arbitron eBookSM"; nevertheless, the Radio Listening Diary remains the center of the whole process. It is best to think of the diary process in terms of nine separate, yet equally important, steps:

1. Contact

In most cases, the first contact with potential diarykeepers is made by mail. This mailing informs the household of their selection for the survey and alerts them to the phone call they will soon receive from Arbitron. The letter also provides the household the option of consenting online via a secure Web site, if they prefer. The next contact with each selected household is by telephone. Arbitron's Interviewing Center places more than 4 million calls every year to randomly selected households, soliciting their consent to participate in a survey. Prompted by a standardized script, Interviewing Center representatives speak with potential diarykeepers to determine survey eligibility, ask for agreement to participate in the survey, and collect selected demographic information about the household. Bilingual interviewers in English and Spanish are available when needed.

2. Mailing

After a household agrees to participate in the survey, a package of survey materials is mailed. The package contains the following key items:

- A 7-day radio listening diary for each eligible member of the household age 12 and over (up to a maximum of nine persons per household) that includes:

    Easy-to-follow diary instructions

    Checklist

    Mailing instructions

- A Q&A brochure about the Arbitron survey
- A thank-you letter for participation
- Cash premiums for each person

Hispanic households receive bilingual Spanish-English diaries and support materials.

3. Survey Week

Arbitron diarykeepers record their radio listening in the diary for one week and send the diary back to Arbitron's Columbia, Maryland, facility for processing. For a diary to be tabulated in a survey, the diarykeeper must return the diary soon after the survey week.

---

example of this, consider an organization that wishes to study sports car owners. If the organization knows that in the general population of interest, 52% are men and 48% are women, then it will want its quota sample to reflect that percentage.

All the research organization can do, however, is designate families or respondents to be included in the sample. Researchers cannot force anyone to participate, nor can they require continued participation from those who initially agreed to cooperate. Even when researchers offer premiums or payment, a significant percentage of panel members often do not cooperate—or drop out quickly once the panel has begun. Some individuals are lost to the panel because they move away or die. Depending on the type of cooperation needed, the refusal and mortality, or drop-out, rate might run over 50%. Then the question arises as to whether the panel is still representative of the population.

Learning Objective

6. Describe the emphasis in sample surveys.

Cross-Sectional Analysis: Sample Survey Despite the advantages of longitudinal analysis, in practice the cross-sectional design is probably the more important

4. Follow-Up Calls and Support for Diarykeepers

Arbitron provides a variety of support options to diary-keepers during the survey period to help ensure diaries are filled out correctly and returned promptly. During the survey week, Arbitron calls consenting households to answer any questions participants may have, to encourage them to fill out their diaries, and to remind them to return the diaries on time. In addition, diarykeepers have access to a toll-free phone support line as well as a Web site designed specifically for them: www.arbitronratings.com. The site contains answers to frequently asked questions, an overview of Arbitron Ratings, information on contacting Arbitron for help via both phone and e-mail, and some radio "fun facts."

5. Receipt

Upon arrival at Arbitron's Columbia processing facility, each diary's ID bar code is wanded and entered into the receipt control system.

6. Scanning

Images of the diary's cover, individual day pages, qualitative pages, and comments page are captured using the most current OCR (optical character recognition) technology. Respondent data from the diary day pages are then key-entered into Arbitron's master database for processing.

7. Processing

Arbitron's Diary Processing staff assigns credit to domestic and satellite radio stations based on the respondent data. Crediting decisions are made by reconciling the diarykeeper's response and Arbitron's Radio Station Information File. The result of this crediting process is the raw material of the Radio Market Report, also referred to as the "Arbitron eBook."

8. Data Release

The data are organized, sorted, and tabulated for release as "ArbitrendsSM" in continuously measured markets; Arbitrends is a service offered to subscribing clients that provides 3-month trended estimates on a monthly basis prior to release of the Arbitron eBook. Each quarter, the data are then released electronically as the Arbitron eBook and through various other services, such as Maximi$er®, Tapscan®, Arbitron Integrated Radio Systems (IRS)^{SM}, and third-party processors.

9. Client Review

Subscribers who wish to review the crediting process can schedule a visit to Arbitron's Client Services suite in Columbia, Maryland. There, using the Electronic Diary Storage and Retrieval (EDSR) system, subscribers can view diary day page images, diary comments pages, and diary processing results. Arbitron's Interviewing center places more than 4 million calls every year to randomly selected households.

Source: "The Arbitron Radio Listening Diary," downloaded from the Arbitron Web site, http://www.arbitron.com/downloads/diary.pdf, July 10, 2008, with the permission of Arbitron Inc.

---

descriptive design. The cross-sectional study has two key features that distinguish it from longitudinal studies. First, it provides a snapshot of the variables of interest at a single point in time, as opposed to a series of pictures that, when pieced together, provide a movie of the situation and the changes that occur. Second, in the cross-sectional study, the sample of elements is typically selected to be representative of some known universe, or population. Therefore, a great deal of emphasis is placed on selecting sample members, usually with a probability sampling plan. That is one reason the technique is often called a **sample survey**.

A cross-sectional sample survey offers two strong advantages over panel designs. For one thing, very specific populations can be targeted and the members of those populations recruited to participate in the survey. Targeted recruitment is possible with consumer panels, but only using the data that have been collected about the participating individuals or households. For example, if a retail store located in a mid-sized city in the northeastern United States decided to conduct a satisfaction study among its customers, unless the store has created its own panel, it is highly unlikely

sample survey
Cross-sectional study in which the sample is selected to be representative of the target population and in which the emphasis is on the generation of summary statistics such as averages and percentages.

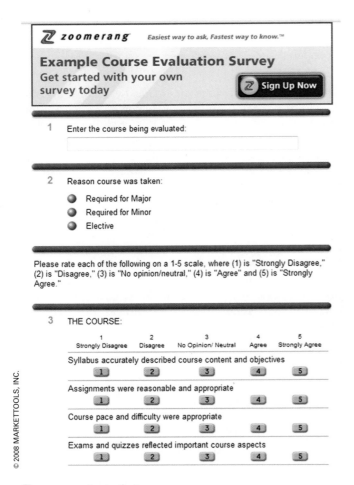

Zoomerang touts that users can set up a Web-based survey in minutes to research, review, analyze, and evaluate every kind of feedback a company could possibly want to help it succeed.

that an existing panel is going to be as efficient as simply sampling from its customer database and using a sample survey.

A second advantage of sample surveys is the ability to use a probability sampling plan that will allow the results of the sample to be projected to the overall population. As we'll discuss later, this is a very important issue, because managers are more concerned about answers that apply to everyone in the population rather than answers that apply only to the people who provided the information.

Although the sample survey is commonly used, it has several disadvantages. These include superficial analysis of the phenomenon, high cost, and the technical sophistication required to conduct survey research. We'll consider each disadvantage in turn.

One common criticism of survey data is that they typically do not penetrate very deeply below the surface, because breadth is often emphasized at the expense of depth. There is ordinarily an emphasis on the calculation of statistics that efficiently summarize the wide variety of data collected from the sometimes large cross-section of subjects. Yet the very process of generating summary statistics to describe the phenomenon suggests that the eventual "average" might not accurately describe any individual entity making up the aggregate.

Second, a survey is expensive in terms of time and money. It could be months before a single hypothesis can be tested because of necessary preliminaries so vital to survey research. The entire research process—from problem definition through measuring instrument development, design of the sample, collecting the data, and editing and coding the data—must be executed before an analyst can begin to examine the hypotheses that guide the study. As we discuss in later chapters, each of these tasks can be challenging. Each can require large investments of time, energy, and money.

Survey research also requires a good deal of technical skill. The research analyst must either have the technical skills required at each stage of the process or have access to technical consultants. Only rarely will a person be able both to develop an attitude scale and to design a complex probability sample.

CAUSAL RESEARCH DESIGNS

Sometimes managers want stronger evidence that a particular action is likely to produce a particular outcome. For example, if a price change is planned, a manager may want to test this hypothesis: "A 5% increase in the price of the product will have no significant effect on the amount of the product that customers will buy." If she is considering a change in product packaging, a brand manager may first want to test this hypothesis: "A redesign of the cereal package so that it is shorter and less likely to tip over will improve consumer attitudes toward the product."

When the research question can be stated this explicitly, a causal research design would be the method of choice. Descriptive research is fine for testing hypotheses about relationships between variables, but it is not as effective as causal designs for testing cause-and-effect relationships.

MANAGER'S FOCUS

One of the limitations of sample surveys is that they are often developed too quickly, without enough preliminary effort to fully understand the issues being studied. We hope that you are beginning to recognize how different types of research designs, and corresponding techniques, can be used in combination with one another. In Chapter 5, we discussed how exploratory research can be used to clarify the meaning of concepts. For example, depth interviews (an exploratory research technique) can be used effectively to explore the complexities of the issues you want to address in a survey (a descriptive research technique). By incorporating the insights drawn from depth interviews, the questionnaire used in a sample survey can be designed to cover the key concepts much more effectively and completely.

Poor surveys are usually produced by people who haven't been trained in the art and science of questionnaire design. Managers sometimes (often?) think that they can develop their own questionnaires because "anyone can ask questions." It just isn't that simple. Well-done performances of any kind (ballet, theater, sports . . . even hair styling) look easy to those observing the performance. The performer, however, understands the amount of training, effort, and experience required to make it look so easy. We urge managers to resist temptation and enlist the services of a professional marketing researcher (inside or outside the firm) to create survey instruments. Even better, find one that routinely employs exploratory research techniques, especially literature searches and depth interviews, as part of the process of developing questionnaires.

Concept of Causality

Everyone is familiar with the general notion of causality, the idea that one thing leads to the occurrence of another. The scientific notion of causality is quite complex, however, and a detailed discussion of it is beyond the scope of this book. An important point to recognize at this stage is that we can never really prove that one thing causes another. As discussed in Technically Speaking 6.2, establishing that variable X causes variable Y requires meeting a number of conditions, including the elimination of all other possible causes of Y. Because we can never know for certain that we have eliminated all other possible causes, no matter how carefully we have planned and conducted our research, we can never say with absolute certainty that X causes Y.

Does this mean that researchers shouldn't bother trying to establish causal relationships? Not at all! Although we can't prove with certainty that a change in one variable produces a change in another, we can conduct research that helps us narrow down the likely causal relationship between two variables by eliminating the other possible causes that we are aware of. With typical descriptive research designs, we do this by measuring the other variables and attempting to control their effects on the outcome variable via statistical techniques. With causal research designs, we work toward establishing possible causal relationships through the use of experiments.

Experiments as Causal Research

An **experiment** can provide more convincing evidence of causal relationships than an exploratory or descriptive design can because of the control it gives investigators. In an experiment, a researcher manipulates, or sets the levels of, one or more causal variables (independent variables) to examine the effect on one or more outcome variables (dependent variables) while attempting to account for the effects of all other possible causal variables, usually by holding them constant. Because investigators are able to control the levels of the independent variable(s), they can be more confident that the relationships discovered are so-called true relationships.

experiment
Scientific investigation in which an investigator manipulates and controls one or more independent variables and observes the degree to which the dependent variables change.

technically speaking   6.2

Evidence of Causality

Three conditions must be met before we can say that one thing "caused" another: (1) There must be consistent variation between the cause and the effect, (2) the time order of the cause and the effect must be correct, and (3) other explanations must be eliminated.

Consistent Variation

Suppose that an auto manufacturer wanted to test the relationship between customer satisfaction with its dealerships and the company's market share in different areas. If dealership satisfaction leads to higher market share (this is our hypothesis), we will find the following: In territories where our dealers receive high marks for customer satisfaction, we should have higher market shares than in territories with poor levels of customer satisfaction. If we find, however, that there is no relationship between dealership satisfaction and market share (for example, if dealerships with higher levels of customer satisfaction don't have higher market shares), we would conclude that either our hypothesis is faulty or that there are additional factors involved.

If market share increases as dealership satisfaction increases across the dealerships that we are studying, we have found evidence of consistent variation. The cause-and-effect variables change in a consistent way. The pattern of change is also consistent with our expectations about what ought to occur, or our theory.

A consistent pattern of variation or relationship between two variables is not enough to conclude that one caused the other, however. All we can conclude is that the association makes the hypothesis more likely; it does not prove it. We are always inferring, rather than proving, that a causal relationship exists. Similarly, the lack of an association between two variables is not enough to conclude that one could not have caused the other, because sometimes other variables can be related to the cause-and-effect variables in such a way that the true relationship between them is hidden.

Time Order

This one is easy: Causes cannot come after effects. Suppose that the auto manufacturer studied the relationship between dealership customer satisfaction and market share over time and found the following consistent pattern: Within 24 months after a substantial increase in market share, customer ratings of customer satisfaction increased. As before, there is consistent variation between the proposed cause-and-effect variables. However, our proposed causal variable (customer satisfaction with the dealership) has occurred after our proposed effect variable (market share), which disproves our hypothesis. Instead, we might develop a new hypothesis that improving market share may lead to greater resources to provide a better quality dealership. The situation is actually a little more complicated than this (for example, it is technically possible for causes and effects to occur simultaneously, or for two variables to each cause the other), but the main idea remains the same: Causes cannot come after effects.

Elimination of Other Explanations

The final condition for establishing causality is also the most difficult to meet and the primary reason that we cannot "prove" that one thing causes another. To fully establish causality, the researcher must eliminate all other possible causes for the outcome variable. This may mean physically holding other factors constant in a lab experiment, or it may mean adjusting the results to remove the effects of other possible causal factors. Here's the kicker: Even if we've held constant or accounted for all the other possible causes we can think of, we can *never* be certain that there's not another potential cause that we don't know about yet.

Consider again the automobile manufacturer trying to determine if dealership satisfaction influences market share. Establishing that there is a relationship between customer

(*Continued*)

> satisfaction and market share and that the changes in market share followed the changes in dealership quality would successfully achieve the first two conditions for determining causality. It would also be necessary to demonstrate that pricing strategies, new models of cars, competitive actions, the overall economic environment in different regions, and so on, didn't cause the changes in market share. Even if we hold some of these things constant (for example, no price incentives in the markets under study during the test period) and control others by measuring them and accounting for them statistically (for example, competitors' pricing strategies), we still can't prove that there isn't one or more additional variable that might have caused the changes in market share.

There are two basic types of experiments—laboratory experiments and field experiments. Each has its own advantages and disadvantages, and researchers need to be familiar with both.

Laboratory Experiments A laboratory experiment is one in which we create a situation with the desired conditions and then manipulate some variables while controlling others. By holding other variables constant while manipulating the independent variable(s), we can observe and measure the effect of the manipulation of the variables while the effect of other factors is minimized.

Researchers recently used a laboratory study to better understand "trip chaining," the practice of driving to more than one retail shop on the same shopping trip (as opposed to making separate trips to each retailer).[1] The researchers believed that consumers prefer to drive short distances between retailers (that is, the retailers are "clustered") rather than to drive longer distances between retailers ("nonclustered" retailers)—even when the total distance traveled from home, to the retailers, and back home again was the same. To test this proposition, the researchers developed detailed maps and driving directions for both clustered and nonclustered trip chains and presented them to undergraduate students who agreed to serve as experimental subjects. Street names were changed and some streets removed from the maps presented to subjects; in this way, prior knowledge of the geographic area could be controlled. Students saw both the clustered and the nonclustered manipulations of trip chains and then indicated which would be their preferred route. Confirming the researchers' hypothesis, 74% chose the clustered route.

In some ways, the task presented to subjects was similar to that confronting consumers in real life. For example, when we shop for various items, we must choose which routes to take. In other respects, however, the study wasn't as realistic: these were not the real consumers living in the real geographic area represented on the maps.

Because we are able to produce a somewhat "sterile" environment in which outside variables are held constant, lab experiments generally have relatively high degrees of internal validity. Internal validity refers to our ability to attribute the effect that was observed to the experimental variable and not to other factors. This is important; marketing managers need to know whether or not changes in the experimental variable (degree of clustering) actually produced the observed changes in the outcome variable (consumer preference) so that they can formulate marketing strategy.

Field Experiments A field experiment is a research study in a realistic or natural situation, although it, too, involves the manipulation of one or more variables under as carefully controlled conditions as the situation will permit. The field experiment differs from the laboratory experiment primarily in terms of environment.

The researchers studying consumer preferences for clustered (versus nonclustered) trip chains also conducted a field experiment. In this case, the experiment

Learning Objective

7. Clarify the difference between laboratory experiments and field experiments.

laboratory experiment
Research investigation in which investigators create a situation with exact conditions in order to control some variables, and manipulate others.

internal validity
The degree to which an outcome can be attributed to an experimental variable and not to other factors.

field experiment
Research study in a realistic situation in which one or more independent variables are manipulated by the experimenter under as carefully controlled conditions as the situation will permit.

was conducted with residents who actually lived in the area that had been mapped for subjects in the lab experiment. For the field study, however, researchers used a telephone survey and based the study on the subjects' home address and actual locations of retailers who were known to the subjects. Subjects were asked to imagine that they needed to make trips to the two kinds of retailers and were then presented with two alternative routes (one that was clustered and one that was nonclustered). As in the laboratory experiment, subjects for whom the overall travel distance was about the same regardless of which alternative was chosen expressed a preference for the clustered trip chain compared with the nonclustered trip chain.

Note the distinction between the two studies. In the field experiment, no attempt was made to set up special conditions. Manipulation of the experimental variable—the degree to which the trip chain was clustered or not—was imposed in a natural environment. The laboratory experiment, on the other hand, was contrived. Subjects were not real consumers considering real shopping trips that they might make to real retailers located in their real home environments. Research Window 6.2 demonstrates how Frito-Lay used field experiments to test elements of its promotional campaign.

Field studies usually have higher degrees of external validity than do lab studies. **External validity** refers to the extent to which the results of an experiment can be generalized, or extended, to other situations. Field studies have higher external validity because of the more realistic conditions of the experiment. In our example, real consumers were reporting their preferences about shopping behavior in their own geographic area. Note, however, that external validity and internal validity work against one another: having greater external validity means giving up a degree of internal validity and vice versa. For example, to gain greater internal validity, we must hold more elements in the situation constant across conditions, and this makes the experiment less realistic, thereby lowering external validity. Similarly, if we want more external validity, the more realistic environment that is required serves to decrease internal validity.

So, which type of validity is more important? The answer is that both types are important. Both internal and external validity are matters of degree rather than all-or-nothing propositions. A study with little internal validity is worthless; on the other hand, a study with little external validity won't help a marketing manager very much either. One possible strategy is to conduct both types of experiments. The laboratory experiment can be used to establish the basic cause-and-effect relationship between one or more independent variables and the dependent variable(s), and the field experiment can be used to confirm the effect in a more natural environment, thus providing some evidence of external validity.

Online retailers have been able to use experimentation quite successfully. Crayola LLC wanted to investigate ways of attracting potential customers to its Crayola.com Web site and getting them to purchase products from its online store. After experimentally varying a number of elements of the e-mail messages sent to prospective customers, the company was able to identify one message that was three times as effective as others at getting individuals to visit the Web site. The company credits its online experimentation with helping to make its online efforts profitable. In this situation, the research would be categorized as a field experiment because the company was working with actual shoppers (and buyers) in the actual online shopping environment.[2]

Learning Objective

8. Explain which of the two types of experiments has greater internal validity and which has greater external validity.

external validity
The degree to which the results of an experiment can be generalized, or extended, to other situations.

ETHICAL DILEMMA 6.1

The regional sales manager for a large chain of men's clothing stores asks you to establish whether increasing her salespeople's commission will result in better sales performance. Specifically, she wants to know whether increasing the commission on limited lines of clothing will result in better sales on those lines, but with the penalty of fewer sales on the remaining lines, and whether raising the commission on all lines will produce greater sales on all lines. Suppose that you think the best way to investigate the issue is through a field experiment in which some salespeople receive increased commission on a single line, others receive increased commission across the board, and still others make up a control group, whose members receive no increase in commission.

- Are there ethical problems inherent in such a design?
- Is the control group being deprived of any benefits?

research window 6.2

How Frito-Lay Used Experiments to Test Advertising Effectiveness

John Wanamaker made a fortune in retailing but is better known for a statement so widely quoted that it has become a marketing cliché: "I know that half of my advertising doesn't work. The problem is, I don't know which half." Marketers still repeat his lament—which is surprising, given modern research techniques.

One company that has *not* been content to complain is Frito-Lay. Several years ago, the snack-food giant carried out a series of experiments, based on earlier work by Leonard Lodish of the University of Pennsylvania's Wharton School of Business.

Professor Lodish and his colleagues tested common assumptions about advertising. They examined historical data from Behaviorscan, a database of purchases by thousands of households, collected using store scanners. The households in the Behaviorscan panel receive all of their television programming on cable, so marketers can add or remove advertisements and identify whether their ads are associated with a change in purchases. The researchers matched advertising for certain products with sales volume and market share for those products, testing common assumptions, such as the following:

- Marketers assume that spending more than competitors on advertising leads to increased sales. But this was not necessarily the case. Some ads were effective; spending more on those ads led to a significant sales increase. Other ads were ineffective; increased spending on those ads did not make much difference in sales.

- Advertisers believe that TV ads require a long time to produce a sales increase. Again, this assumption did not hold up. The effective ads typically boosted sales within six months.

Lodish's study also looked for factors associated with advertising effectiveness. The researchers compared households exposed to the same ad, but with different frequencies and amounts of exposure. They also compared households exposed to different ads for the same product, but with the same frequencies and amounts of exposure. In all cases, they studied advertising of low-priced packaged goods purchased often.

The study found that advertising was associated with greater sales volume and market share under certain conditions. For example, increasing the amount and frequency of advertising was particularly effective for smaller, less-established brands. The common practice of scheduling advertising to run for a few weeks and then take a break for a few weeks (called "flighting") was not effective. New ad messages were associated with greater sales; old copy was less effective. Standard methods of measuring advertising "success"—recall of the ad and statements that the ad was persuasive—were not associated with sales increases.

Looking at such historical data is interesting, but Frito-Lay needed information for decisions about the future. Frito-Lay set research objectives of developing guidelines for managing television advertising and setting priorities for advertising campaigns. The company focused on television advertising because it receives the bulk of Frito-Lay's advertising budget.

The research plan was to test a series of hypotheses that an ad would produce increased sales. Researchers assigned Behaviorscan households randomly to "ad" or "no ad" conditions. Frito-Lay tested ads that were already approved during the company's regular media-planning process. Each household assigned to the "ad" condition received the ads in the media plan. Households in the "no ad" condition received public service announcements in place of Frito-Lay's TV ads.

The experiment lasted four years, during which Frito-Lay tested each brand's advertising in at least two markets for 12 months. At the end of the four years, the company learned that 57% of its advertisements resulted in sales increases that were significantly larger in the "ad" households than in the "no ad" households. Frito-Lay's experience resembled Wanamaker's retailing career—half its advertising worked. The research data would help Frito-Lay decide which half was working.

Frito-Lay's advertising produced many results similar to Lodish's study of historical data. In 88% of the cases when ad content introduced something new, such as a new brand or new product features, the ad led to significant sales increases. In all but one case, the impact on sales was noticeable within the first three months. Not only were results rapid, but they also tended to last. A follow-up study found that the ads producing a gain in the short term also had a long-term effect, approximately doubling the short-term sales increase. The average short-term impact of an effective ad was a 15% increase in sales.

The research also looked at advertising weight—the amount and frequency of the advertising. The data

(Continued)

showed that 61% of Frito-Lay's advertising was not responsive to weight changes (changes in weight for that advertising did not explain changes in sales). Marketers could apply that result by testing specific ads to see whether lowering the advertising weight resulted in a sales decline in the test market. If not, the marketer could save money by lowering the frequency of those ads.

Frito-Lay learned some other important lessons as well. One is that its ads should deliver "news." Another lesson is to test ads and target spending on the most effective ads. A 15% boost in sales for a big consumer-products company like Frito-Lay amounts to millions of dollars. Spending hundreds of thousands of dollars to choose the right advertising is a logical management decision. With data from services such as Behaviorscan, Frito-Lay can say, "We know which half of our advertising works."

Source: This research is described in Leonard Lodish, "When Do Commercials Boost Sales?" *Financial Times*, August 7, 2002.

MARKET TESTING

market testing (test marketing)
A controlled experiment done in a limited but carefully selected sector of the marketplace.

Experiments in marketing were rare before 1960 but have become more common in the years since then. One of the most significant growth areas has been in **market testing**, or test marketing. Market testing involves the use of a controlled experiment done in a limited but carefully selected sector of the marketplace. Market testing is often used to predict the sales or profit outcomes of one or more proposed marketing actions. Very often, the action in question is the marketing of a new product or service. For example, in response to the rising popularity of specialty coffee drinks, McDonald's used test markets to determine that a market existed for McDonald's own higher-end coffee drink before beginning the commercialization process on a larger scale. Interestingly, Starbucks has confirmed that it is test marketing a lower-priced, smaller version of its coffees in some U.S. stores.[3]

Even if a company has performed previous tests of the product concept, the product package, the advertising copy, and so on, the test market is still the final gauge of consumer acceptance of the product. For example, a study on consumer packaged goods brands conducted by Information Resources reported that 80% of brands that are successful in live test markets go on to commercial success. Similarly, ACNielsen data indicate that roughly three out of four products that have been test-marketed succeed, while four out of five that have not been test-marketed fail.[4]

Test marketing is not restricted to testing the sales potential of new products; it has been used to examine the sales effectiveness of almost every element of the marketing mix. General Motors, for example, used its Cadillac car division to test market a proposed alteration in the distribution strategy for all its car lines. The Florida test involved keeping 1,200 new cars at a regional distribution center in Orlando for delivery to the state's 42 dealerships within 24 hours of an order. The approach was intended to whittle down the costly inventory that dealers have to maintain, improve manufacturing efficiency, and increase sales by allowing consumers to take quick possession of precisely the Cadillac model they wanted.[5]

Market tests have also been used to measure the sales effectiveness of new displays, the responsiveness of sales to shelf-space changes, the impact of changes in retail prices on market shares, the price elasticity of demand for products, the effect of different commercials on sales of products, and the differential effects of price and advertising on demand.

Key Issues in Market Testing

Learning Objective

9. List the three major considerations in test marketing.

The three key considerations of market testing are cost, time, and control.

Cost Always a major consideration in test marketing, the cost includes the normal research costs associated with designing the data-collection instruments and the sample, the wages paid to the field staff who collect the data, and several other indirect expenses as well. General Mills, for example, spent $2.8 million testing and refining its chain of Olive Garden restaurants.[6] Ideally, the test market should reflect the marketing strategy to be used on the national scale, so the test can also include marketing costs for advertising, personal selling, displays, and so on.

With new product introductions, there are also the costs associated with producing the merchandise. To produce the product on a small scale is typically inefficient. Yet to gear up immediately for large-scale production can be tremendously wasteful if the product proves a failure.

Time The time required for an adequate test market can also be substantial. In the 1960s, Procter & Gamble spent eight years testing Pampers disposable diapers before launching the product in the United States. In today's faster-paced global environment, this approach simply leaves a company much too vulnerable to attack from more agile competitors.

There is pressure to extend the period of test marketing because a test market's accuracy increases with time. Experiments conducted over short periods do not allow the cumulative impact of marketing actions. Consequently, a year is often recommended as a minimum before any kind of "go–no go" decision is made. Longer tests allow researchers to account for possible seasonal variations and to study repeat-purchasing behavior. For example, Altria tested a new cigarette called *Marlboro Ultra Smooth*—which was designed to be safer than regular cigarettes—for over three years in Atlanta, Tampa, and Salt Lake City before deciding to discontinue the product; consumers didn't seem to care for the product.[7] Such lengthy experiments are costly, however, and raise additional problems of control and competitive reaction.

Control The problems associated with control manifest themselves in several ways. First, there are the control problems in the experiment itself. What specific test markets will be used? How will product distribution be organized in those markets? Can the firm get wholesalers and retailers to cooperate? Can the test markets and control cities be matched sufficiently to rule out market characteristics as the primary reason for different sales results?

Chain retailers may have some advantage when it comes to control, because they can identify individual stores to serve as test sites and control the marketing mix elements inside the stores—including the products and services offered—in those specific geographic areas. For example, McDonald's is testing a variety of drinks such as Red Bull and Coca-Cola's Vitaminwater in 150 of its stores, including 20 in the New York City area. Rite Aid Pharmacies introduced two Spanish-language stores in northern Philadelphia with bilingual staff, product selections, and in-store messages designed to appeal to the Hispanic market. Finally, Coach regularly tests new handbag and accessory ideas in a limited number of stores in North America six months before full commercialization of the product.[8]

One of the chief concerns about market testing is the opportunity it provides competitors to see a company's new product before it is fully commercialized. With many market tests, there are few secrets. When a Frito-Lay assistant brand manager

Learning Objective

10. Distinguish between a standard test market and a controlled test market.

standard test market
A test market in which the company sells the product through its normal distribution channels.

would fly to a test-market city in Iowa to follow up with test sites selling the company's new Baked Lays product, the gate attendant at the small airport would routinely tell her which other snack foods companies had also had representatives in town to check the progress of the new product. In addition, competitors can, and do, sabotage marketing experiments by cutting the prices of their own products or by gobbling up quantities of the test marketer's product—thereby creating excitement and false confidence on the part of the test marketer.

Test marketing has been called the most dangerous game in all of marketing because of the great opportunity it affords for misfires, as shown by the examples in Exhibit 6.2. Some of these misfires represent mistakes made by the company testing the new product (including the failure to test the product, in some cases), and some demonstrate competitive reactions. Others simply reflect the true value of a market test: the ability to spot problems early, before they become even more costly and embarrassing. And in some cases, it's too late.

Marketing managers who are thinking about a market test must weigh the costs of such a test against its likely benefits. While it may serve as the final yardstick for consumer acceptance of the product, in some cases it may be less effective and more expensive than a carefully controlled laboratory or in-home test.

Types of Test Markets

There are three general categories of test markets: standard, controlled, and simulated. In a **standard test market**, such as those we've been describing, a company develops a product and then attempts to sell it through the normal distribution channels in a number of test-market cities. The potential success of the product can be gauged, and different elements of the marketing mix for the product can be experimentally varied with an eye toward developing the best marketing mix combination for the product. A key distinguishing feature of a standard test market is that the producer must sell the product to distributors, wholesalers, and/or retailers just as it would any other product.

What makes some cities better than others for standard test markets? Several factors are involved. The proposed test-market city needs to be demographically representative of the larger market in which the product will ultimately be sold. Most popular test-market cities are reasonably representative of the overall population, although some are more representative than others. Exhibit 6.3, on page 126, lists some of the best and worst U.S. test-market metropolitan areas based on the degree to which the population in the area "mirrors" the characteristics of the U.S. population. If the product is geared more toward a specific segment of the population, however, then markets should be chosen with high representation of that segment. For example, for products targeted toward Hispanic consumers, test markets with higher proportions of Hispanic residents are obviously desirable.

Popular standard test-market cities also possess other features prized by researchers. The test market should be large enough that it has media outlets (e.g., newspapers and radio and television stations) of its own, which allow tests of advertising and promotion. It must also be large enough to have a sufficient number of the right kind of retail outlets. When Taco Bell was looking for a test market for its Grilled Stuft Burrito, for example, it was important to find a market with a good mix of company and franchise-owned restaurants and Fresno, California, was selected.[9] It is also important that test markets be geographically isolated from other cities in order to avoid

Exhibit 6.2	**Misfires in Market Testing**

- When asked, consumers will often indicate a desire for healthier menu selections at fast-food restaurants. In response, some time ago, McDonald's developed and introduced the McLean Deluxe into all of its U.S. locations without doing its normal market testing. The product never caught on and was discontinued a few years later.

- A few years ago, Snell (Booz Allen's design and development division, which does product development and work under contract) developed a nonliquid temporary hair coloring that consumers used by inserting a block of solid hair dye into a special comb. "It went to market and it was a bust," a company manager recalled. On hot days when people perspired, any hair dye excessively applied ran down their necks and foreheads. "It just didn't occur to us to look at this under conditions where people perspire," he says.

- Frito-Lay test-marketed its Max potato, corn, and tortilla chips containing the Olestra fat substitutes in Grand Junction, Colorado; Eau Claire, Wisconsin; and Cedar Rapids, Iowa. A TV crew sampled the chips and succumbed to diarrhea, and then broadcast a report about it, creating lots of bad publicity for the chips.

- In focus groups, consumers raved about Oven Lovin', a new cookie dough developed by Pillsbury that was packaged in resealable tubs and loaded with Hershey's chocolate chips, Reese's Pieces, or Brach's candies. Based on these positive reactions, the company skipped market testing and immediately rolled out the product, supporting it with heavy television advertising and some 200 million coupons. Sales took off like a rocket, rising from zero to almost $6 million a month. After three months, however, sales began to crumble and were almost nonexistent two years later. Although consumers still maintained they liked the product and resealable package, "many shoppers found they ended up baking the entire package at once—or gobbling up leftover raw dough instead of saving it—eliminating the need for the . . . package." In sum, the package provided a benefit consumers didn't really need, particularly given the fact that it contained only 18 ounces of dough, compared with 20 ounces in a tube of Pillsbury Best dough that was priced comparably.

- McDonald's tested its McRib sandwich while noting that it was a "limited time only" menu option. Because promoting a time constraint on an offering will affect the immediate demand for the product, the results of the market test were not accurate at predicting longer term sales of the item.

- When Campbell Soup first test-marketed Prego spaghetti sauce, Campbell marketers say they noticed a flurry of new Ragu ads and cents-off deals that they feel were designed to induce shoppers to load up on Ragu and to skew Prego's test results. They also claim that Ragu copied Prego when it developed Ragu Homestyle spaghetti sauce, which was thick, red, flecked with oregano and basil, and which Ragu moved into national distribution before Prego.

- Procter & Gamble claims that competitors stole its patented process for Duncan Hines chocolate chip cookies when they saw how successful the product was in test market.

- A health and beauty aids firm developed a deodorant containing baking soda. A competitor spotted the product in test market, rolled out its own version of the deodorant nationally before the first firm completed its testing, and later successfully sued the product originator for copyright infringement when it launched its deodorant nationally.

- When Procter & Gamble introduced its Always brand sanitary napkin in a test market in Minnesota, Kimberly-Clark Corporation and Johnson & Johnson countered with free products, lots of coupons, and big dealer discounts, which caused Always not to do as well as expected.

- Campbell Soup spent 18 months developing a blended fruit juice called Juiceworks. By the time the product reached the market, three competing brands were already on store shelves. Campbell dropped its product.

- Spurred by its incredible success with Fruit 'N' Juice Bars, Dole worked hard to create a new fruity ice cream novelty product with the same type of appeal. Company officials expected that the product that resulted from this development activity, Fruit and Cream Bars, which it test-marketed in Orlando, Florida, would do slightly less well because it was more of an indulgence-type product. However, the test-market results were so positive that Dole became the number-one brand in the market within three months. The company consequently shortened the test market to six months. When it rolled out the product, however, the company unhappily found four unexpected entrants in the ice cream novelty category. Due to the intense competition, Fruit and Cream sales fell short of expectations.

- In a move to speed products to market, Procter & Gamble decided to reserve the use of test marketing mainly to new products that would require investing in new plants and equipment. As a result, the company failed to test Pampers Rash Guard, a premium diaper, only to see the product fail to meet sales goals.

- Sunlight dishwashing liquid was confused with Minute Maid lemon juice by at least 33 adults and 45 children, who became ill after drinking it.

(Continued)

- When a large packaged goods company set out to introduce a squirtable soft drink concentrate for children, it held focus groups to monitor user reaction. In the sessions children squirted the product neatly into cups. Yet once at home, few could resist the temptation to decorate their parents' floors and walls with colorful liquid. After a flood of parental complaints, the product was withdrawn from development.

Sources: Bret Thorn, "Lesson Learned: Menu Miscues," *Nation's Restaurant News,* May 20, 2002, downloaded via ProQuest, June 23, 2005; Ann Lynn and Michael Lynn, "Experiments and Quasi-Experiments: Methods for Evaluating Marketing Options," *Cornell Hotel and Restaurant Administration Quarterly,* April 2003, downloaded via ProQuest on June 16, 2005; Annetta Miller and Karen Springen, "Will Fake Fat Play in Peoria?" *Newsweek,* June 3, 1996, p. 50; Kathleen Deveny, "Failure of Its Oven Lovin' Cookie Dough Shows Pillsbury Pitfalls of New Products," *The Wall Street Journal,* June 17, 1993, pp. B1 and B8; Jack Neff, "Is Testing the Answer?" *Advertising Age,* July 9, 2001, p. 13; Annetta Miller and Dody Tsiantor, "A Test for Market Research," *Newsweek* 110, December 28, 1987, pp. 32–33; Leslie Brennan, "Test Marketing Put to the Test," *Sales and Marketing Management* 138, March 1987, pp. 65–68; Kevin Wiggins, "Simulated Test Marketing Winning Acceptance," *Marketing News* 19, March 1, 1985, pp. 15 and 19; Eleanor Johnson Tracy, "Testing Time for Test Marketing," *Fortune* 110, October 29, 1984, pp. 75–76; Damon Darden, "Faced with More Competition, P&G Sees New Products as Crucial to Earnings Growth," *The Wall Street Journal,* September 13, 1983, pp. 37 and 53; Annetta Miller and Dody Tsiantor, "A Test for Market Research," *Newsweek* 110, December 28, 1987, pp. 32–33; Lynn G. Reiling, "Consumer Misuse Mars Sampling for Sunlight Dishwashing Liquid," *Marketing News* 16, September 3, 1982, pp. 1 and 12; Betty Morris, "New Campbell Entry Sets Off a Big Spaghetti Sauce Battle," *The Wall Street Journal,* December 2, 1982, p. 31; and Roger Recklefs, "Success Comes Hard in the Tricky Business of Creating Products," *The Wall Street Journal,* August 23, 1978, pp. 1 and 27.

controlled test market

An entire test program conducted by an outside service in a market in which it can guarantee distribution.

"spillover" effects from nearby markets where testing is not taking place. Such spillover effects might include advertising and other promotion or a significant percentage of consumers in the test market traveling outside the test market to shop.

An alternative to the standard test market is the **controlled test market**, sometimes called the forced-distribution test market. In the controlled test market, the entire test program is conducted by an outside service. The service pays retailers for shelf space and can therefore guarantee distribution to those stores that represent a predetermined percentage of the marketer's total food store sales volume. A number of research firms operate controlled test markets, including GfK Group, a large research company based in Germany, and Information Resources, Inc.

Exhibit 6.3	**Best and Worst Test Markets**

1. Albany-Schenectady-Troy, N.Y.
2. Rochester, N.Y.
3. Greensboro–Winston-Salem–High Point, N.C.
4. Birmingham, Ala.
5. Syracuse, N.Y.
6. Charlotte–Gastonia–Rock Hill, N.C.-S.C.
7. Nashville, Tenn.
8. Eugene-Springfield, Oreg.
9. Wichita, Kans.
10. Richmond–Petersburg, Va.
    .
    .
    .
141. El Paso, Tex.
142. Columbia, Mo.
143. Tallahassee, Fla.
144. Brownsville–Harlingen–San Benito, Tex.
145. Provo-Orem, Utah
146. Ocala, Fla.
147. McAllen–Edinburg–Mission, Tex.
148. Honolulu, Hawaii
149. San Francisco, Calif.
150. New York, N.Y.

Source: "Best and Worst Test Markets," downloaded from http://www.acxiom.com, July 7, 2004. According to information on the Acxiom Corporation Web site, the "rankings are based on how closely the population of the metropolitan area 'mirrors' the characteristics of the U.S. consumer population as a whole."

Several research providers have taken the controlled test market a step further by recruiting a panel of households in the test-market area from which they secure a great deal of demographic information. Purchasing behavior for these households is typically recorded by handheld scanners used at home and/or via identification cards that automatically record purchases at participating retailers. In some cases, the research companies can monitor each panel household's television-viewing behavior—and some can even deliver different test commercials to different households, allowing them to test not only consumer acceptance of a product but also various other parts of the marketing program. Del Monte, for example, has used controlled test markets for media-weight, pricing, and promotion tests, in addition to new product evaluations. As another example, when eight varieties of Ferrero chocolates were introduced in Aldi stores in southern Germany, GfK Group tested the impact on sales of the products through Aldi—and through other retailers—with actual sales results and through feedback from its consumer panel in the area.[10]

Information Resources, Inc. (IRI) is a leading supplier of controlled test-market services. Its Behaviorscan service uses five demographically representative cities. Within each city several thousand panel households carry cards that are scanned when they purchase items from a variety of retail stores. When marketers are planning to launch a new product, Behaviorscan gives them control over many important marketing and environmental variables. IRI maintains its own warehouse and distribution system in each city, and IRI employees routinely visit the stores each week to see that the distribution, shelf location, and point-of-sale promotions are executed as planned. The company also controls direct-to-consumer promotions and the targeting of specific advertising to subsets of the panel households.[11]

Bank of America teamed with Yahoo! en Español to create a Spanish-language financial Web site—accessible anywhere—enabling marketing and advertising to be geared toward this specific demographic group.

MANAGER'S FOCUS

As a manager, you need to be fully cognizant of the risks inherent in standard market tests. The obvious goal of such testing is to get an advantage over your competitors. Implementing your marketing strategy in selected markets will make your company vulnerable to a variety of competitive responses. So, when deciding whether or not to use a standard market test, an important decision criterion is the degree to which your company has some type of reasonable protection. This can come from the legal system (e.g., trademarks, copyrights, patents) or barriers to market entry such as the need for large capital investments, long product development time frames, or dominant brand equity that would enable your company to overcome any threat imposed by a competitor that attempted to steal your idea and beat you to the market with it. In the absence of such protection, it may be in your company's best interest to utilize an alternative such as a simulated market test. Due to competitive risk factors, even companies as large and dominant as Procter & Gamble have limited their use of standard market tests and have increased their use of less risky approaches.

In most situations, if it's financially feasible, you should employ some type of market test before implementing a new or revised marketing strategy. Because managing a market test can be a complex undertaking, it is often wise to hire a firm that specializes in market tests to handle the process for you.

simulated test market (STM)
A study in which consumer ratings are obtained along with likely or actual purchase data often obtained in a simulated store environment; the data are fed into computer models to produce sales and market share predictions.

Another variation in market testing is the **simulated test market (STM)**. A simulated test market differs from standard and controlled test markets in that consumers do not purchase the product (or service) being tested from a retail store. In fact, in many cases, the product has not even been put into production. Instead, researchers will typically recruit consumers to participate in the simulated study. Consumers are shown the new product or product concept and asked to rate its features. They may be shown commercials for it and for competitors' products. Often, in a simulated store environment, they are then given the opportunity to buy the product, perhaps at a discounted rate. If the product is in tangible form, researchers may follow up with participating consumers after a predetermined use period to assess their reactions to the product and likely repeat-purchase intentions.

All the information is fed into a computer model, which has equations for the repeat purchase and market share likely to be achieved by the test model. The key to successful simulation is the equations built into the computer model. Nielsen's BASES simulation approach, an industry leader, reports that in 90% of cases, its STM models can come within 20% of actual results in the marketplace.[12]

MANAGER'S FOCUS

In Chapter 5, we cautioned you to avoid using focus group interviews until you are convinced that doing so is truly the most appropriate way of gathering exploratory data. You should understand that sample surveys can be overused in much the same way as focus groups. Much of the time, researchers are quick to recommend them, and managers readily approve them, without carefully considering whether there might be a more appropriate way to collect the needed information. As a manager, you should specifically discuss with researchers whether a given situation would be best addressed with descriptive research or causal research. Managers are too often willing to make decisions based on associations found in sample surveys (because they are relatively simple to obtain), and too seldom insist on research that will enable them to infer cause-and-effect relationships. The danger of this common approach can be seen in the following example.

A friend, whose identity will be kept anonymous, was the CEO of a company that grew produce items that were marketed through grocery stores. When developing new packaging for a product, the CEO hired the services of a marketing research consultant. The consultant completed a series of focus group interviews in which questions were asked about the features of

packages that consumers found to be most desirable. Based on this information, several prototype packages were designed. In personal interviews (sample surveys), consumers evaluated the alternative package designs, and the one most preferred by the target consumer groups was selected. After the new packaged items arrived in supermarkets, the company was dismayed to discover that consumers were not buying them. The CEO visited stores to observe consumers' buying processes. He repeatedly witnessed consumers picking up the new packages, looking them over, placing them back down, and ultimately buying a competitor's brand. When he asked consumers why they had chosen not to buy his brand, most of them told him that while the new packages were attractive in appearance, they did not permit the consumer to see the produce inside. The CEO was embarrassed to realize that he and his research consultant never bothered to test for actual market response before implementing the new package.

Managers must recognize that descriptive survey data generally are a poor substitute for market tests when trying to gauge how the target market will respond to changes in marketing strategy. Consumers' responses to questions on surveys do not always correspond well with their actual behavior in the marketplace.

Most simulated test-market data are collected via the Internet using consumer panels, although other data collection approaches are used where necessary. Members of an online panel may be recruited for participation in a particular study by letter and e-mail which provide access to an online survey. Over the years, most simulated test markets have been conducted for consumer nondurable products. In recent years, however, more and more studies have focused on financial services, healthcare, consumer durables, pharmaceuticals, and other industries.[13]

Comparing the Three Types of Test Markets Marketers who need to test-market a new product or to fine-tune an element of a marketing program must choose which type of test market to use. Each of the approaches has advantages and disadvantages.

A prime advantage of simulated test markets is the protection they provide from competitors. They are also good for assessing trial and repeat-purchasing behavior. They are faster and cheaper than full-scale tests and are particularly good for spotting weak products, which allows firms to avoid full-scale testing of these products. The primary disadvantage of simulated test markets is that they do not provide any information about the firm's ability to secure trade support for the product or about what competitive reaction is likely to be. Thus, they are more suited for evaluating product extensions than for examining the likely success of radically different new products.

Learning Objective

11. Discuss the advantages and disadvantages of simulated test marketing.

Controlled test markets are more expensive than simulated test markets, but less costly than standard test markets. One reason they cost less than standard test markets is that the research supplier provides distribution. The manufacturer does not need to use its own sales force to convince the trade that stocking the product is worthwhile. The manufacturer can rest assured that the new product will obtain the right level of store acceptance, will be positioned in the correct aisle in each store, will receive the right number of facings on the shelf, will have the correct everyday price, will not experience any out-of-stock problems, and will receive the planned level of promotional displays and price features.

This perfect implementation of the marketing plan also represents one of the weaknesses of the controlled test market. Acceptance or rejection of the new product by the trade in the "real world" is typically critical to the success of any new product. A controlled test market guarantees acceptance by the trade for the duration of the test, but acceptance will not be guaranteed during the actual marketing of the product. When a new product fits in nicely with a company's existing line, for which it already has distribution, the controlled test market is a fairly good indicator. When the product is new or represents a radical departure for the manufacturer, the question of trade support is much more problematic, and the controlled test is much less useful under these circumstances.

The traditional, or standard, test market provides a more natural environment than either the simulated or the controlled test market and, as a result, offers the greatest degrees of external validity and prediction accuracy. These advantages must be balanced against some important disadvantages, however. Standard test markets are the most expensive, take the most time, and are the most likely to tip off competitors compared with the other approaches. Even so, the standard test market may be a logical choice when (1) it is important for the firm to test its ability to actually sell to the trade and get distribution for the product; (2) the capital investment is significant and the firm needs a prolonged test market to accurately assess its capital needs or its technical ability to manufacture the product; and/or (3) the company is entering new territory and needs to build its experience base so that it can play for real but wants to learn how to do so on a limited scale.

The relative advantages and disadvantages of the three basic types of test markets are shown in Exhibit 6.4.

Relative Advantages and Disadvantages of Different Types of Test Markets

	Simulated	Controlled	Standard
Speed	1	2	3
Cost	1	2	3
Security	1	2	3
Validity			
*Internal	1	2	3
*External	3	2	1
Prediction accuracy	3	2	1

1 = most favorable 3 = least favorable

SUMMARY

Learning Objective 1

Cite three major purposes of descriptive research.

Descriptive research is used when the purpose is to (1) describe the characteristics of certain groups, (2) determine the proportion of people who behave in a certain way, and (3) make specific predictions.

Learning Objective 2

List the six specifications of a descriptive study.

Descriptive studies require a clear specification of the answers to who, what, when, where, why, and how in the research.

Learning Objective 3

Explain what a dummy table is.

A table (or figure) used to show how the results of the analysis will be presented. A series of dummy tables that are complete except for the actual data should be prepared *before* data are collected in order to guide data collection and analysis.

Learning Objective 4

Discuss the difference between cross-sectional and longitudinal designs.

A cross-sectional design involves researching a sample of elements from the population of interest. Various characteristics of the elements are measured once. Longitudinal studies involve panels of people or other entities whose responses are measured repeatedly over a span of time.

Learning Objective 5

Explain what is meant by a panel in marketing research and explain the difference between a continuous panel and a discontinuous panel.

A panel is a fixed sample of elements. In a continuous panel, a fixed sample of subjects is measured repeatedly with respect to the same type of information. In a discontinuous panel, a sample of elements is still selected and maintained, but the information collected from the members varies with the project.

Learning Objective 6

Describe the emphasis in sample surveys.

The sample survey involves the study of a number of cases at the same point in time. The survey attempts to be representative of some known population.

Learning Objective 7

Clarify the difference between laboratory experiments and field experiments.

Laboratory experiments differ from field experiments primarily in terms of environment. The researcher creates a setting for a laboratory experiment; a field experiment is conducted in a natural setting. Both types, however, involve control and manipulation of one or more presumed causal factors.

Learning Objective 8

Explain which of the two types of experiments has greater internal validity and which has greater external validity.
The laboratory experiment typically has greater internal validity because it allows greater control of the variables. Field experiments are generally considered more externally valid, meaning that their results are better able to be generalized to other situations.

Learning Objective 9

List the three major considerations in test marketing.
Three of the more important issues in test marketing are cost, time, and control.

Learning Objective 10

Distinguish between a standard test market and a controlled test market.
A standard test market is one in which companies sell the product through their normal distribution channels, and results are typically monitored by a standard distribution service. In a controlled test market, the entire program is conducted by an outside service. The service pays retailers for shelf space and therefore can guarantee distribution to those stores that represent a predetermined percentage of the marketer's total store sales volume.

Learning Objective 11

Discuss the advantages and disadvantages of simulated test marketing.
Simulated test-marketing studies provide the following advantages: (1) They protect a marketer from competitors, (2) they are faster and cheaper than full-scale tests, and (3) they are particularly good for spotting weak products. However, they do have disadvantages in that they cannot provide any information about the firm's ability to secure trade support for a product or indicate what competitive reaction is likely to be.

KEY TERMS

dummy table (page 108)
cross-sectional study (page 109)
longitudinal study (page 109)
continuous panel (page 110)
discontinuous panel (page 110)
sample survey (page 115)
experiment (page 117)
laboratory experiment (page 119)

internal validity (page 119)
field experiment (page 119)
external validity (page 120)
market testing (test marketing) (page 122)
standard test market (page 124)
controlled test market (page 126)
simulated test market (STM) (page 128)

REVIEW QUESTIONS

1. What are the basic uses of descriptive research?
2. What are the six specifications of a descriptive study?
3. What are the main types of descriptive studies, and what do their differences mean?
4. What are the basic types of panels, and how important are the differences between them?
5. What is a sample survey? What are its advantages and disadvantages?
6. What types of evidence are necessary to establish that one variable "causes" another?
7. What is an experiment?

8. What is the distinction between a laboratory and a field experiment?

9. What is the difference between internal and external validity?

10. What is a test market? For what kinds of investigations can test markets be used? What are the problems associated with test markets?

11. What is the primary difference between a standard test market and a controlled test market?

12. How does simulated test marketing (STM) work? What are its main advantages and disadvantages compared to full market tests?

13. How is a simulated test market typically conducted?

14. Under what conditions is a standard test market a better choice than either simulated or controlled test markets?

DISCUSSION QUESTIONS, PROBLEMS, AND PROJECTS

1. The management of a national book club was convinced that the company's market segment consisted of individuals in the 25- to 35-year-old age group, while its major competitor's market segment seemed more widely distributed with respect to age. It attributed this difference to the type of magazines in which the competitor advertised. Management decided to do a study to determine the socioeconomic characteristics of its own market segment. Management formed a panel of 800 heads of households who had previously shown a strong interest in reading. Mail questionnaires would be sent to all the panel members. One month after receiving all the questionnaires, the company would again send similar questionnaires to all the panel members. In this situation, is the research design appropriate? If yes, why? If no, why not?

2. The Nutri Company was a medium-sized manufacturer of highly nutritional food products. The products were marketed as low-fat foods with high nutritional content. The company was considering marketing these products as snack foods but was concerned about its present customers' reaction to the change in the products' images. The company decided to assess customers' reaction by conducting a study using one of the established types of consumer panels. What type of panel would you recommend in this situation? Why?

3. Super Savers is a chain of department stores located in large towns and metropolitan centers in the northeastern United States. In order to improve its understanding of the market, management has decided to develop a profile of the "average" customer. You are requested to design the study.

   a. What kind of research design will you select? Justify your choice.

   b. List at least 10 relevant variables.

   c. Specify at least four hypotheses. (*Note:* Remember that a hypothesis is an educated guess about how two or more variables are related. You should indicate how each of the variables would be measured.)

   d. Construct dummy tables for four of the variables that you specified in part (b) of this problem and two of the hypotheses developed for part (c).

4. Consider the following statement: "The increase in sales is due to the new sales personnel recruited over the last several years. Sales of the new salespeople are up substantially, while sales for longer-term salespeople have not increased."

   a. Identify the causal factor (X) and the effect factor (Y) in the above statement.

   b. Discuss the evidence that would be necessary to establish that factor (X) caused factor (Y) in the above statement.

5. The research department of the company in Problem 4 investigated the change in sales for each of the company's salespeople. Using criteria supplied by management, the department categorized all territory sales changes as "increased substantially," "increased marginally," or "no increase." Consider the following table, in which 260 sales personnel have been classified as old or new.

| Salesperson Assigned | Territory Sales Change | | | |
	Increased Substantially	Increased Marginally	No Increase	Total
New	75	30	5	110
Old	50	40	60	150

a. Does this table provide evidence of consistent variation? Justify your answer.

b. What conclusions can be drawn about the relationship between X and Y on the basis of the table?

6. The product development team at Busby's Briquets has been working on several modifications of Busby's highly successful line of charcoal briquet. The most promising development is a new briquet that provides a unique smoky flavor to grilled meat. Management, based on favorable feedback from a few employees who have tested the product in their homes, feels that the new briquet has the potential to become a major seller.

At a recent strategy session, the vice president of marketing suggested a test-marketing program before committing to introduction of the new briquet. He pointed out that a test market would be a good way to evaluate the effectiveness of two alternative advertising and promotional campaigns that have been proposed by Busby's ad agency. He feels that effectiveness should be evaluated in terms of the trial- and repeat-purchasing behavior engendered by each program. He also wants to gauge Busby's current distributors' acceptance of the new product.

The CEO of Busby's, however, is not very enthusiastic about the idea of test marketing. She pointed out several of her concerns, among them the fact that Busby's competitors could easily duplicate the new briquet, the fact that the company is nearing the limit of budgeted costs for developing the new briquet, and the fact that the seasonal nature of briquet sales makes it imperative to reach a "go–no go" decision on the new briquet by mid-December, only four months away.

The director of marketing research stated that she felt a test market could be devised that would satisfy both the vice president of marketing and the CEO. She was instructed to submit a preliminary proposal at the next strategy session.

a. What information should be obtained from the test market in order to satisfy the vice president of marketing?

b. Under what constraints must the test-marketing plan operate in order to satisfy the CEO?

c. Given your answers to (a) and (b), what method of test marketing should the director recommend? Why?

7. Schedule an interview with the marketing manager of a consumer products company. In the interview, discuss the use of test marketing by the firm. Attempt to find answers to the following questions: How important is test marketing in the firm's product-development process? Does the firm normally progress through different types of test marketing for a specific product (as suggested in this text), or is only one type commonly used? What does your contact see as the advantages and disadvantages of various methods of test marketing? Have successful test-marketing

episodes always led to successful product introductions for the firm? What does your contact perceive as the most promising avenue for future development of test-marketing procedures?

Write a report of your interview, highlighting information that you obtained that was not discussed in the text, or that seems at odds with the textbook discussion.

PART 3

DATA COLLECTION METHODS

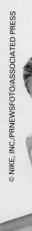

NikeWomen: Progressive Marketing Through Research

© NIKE, INC./PRNEWSFOTO/ASSOCIATED PRESS

Delphine Delsalle, France: "Here I Am."

Simona La Mantia, Italy: "Here I Am."

Nicola Sanders, United Kingdom: "Here I Am."

Maria Sharapova, Russia: "Here I Am."

Nicola Spirig, Switzerland: "Here I Am."

Outside of Maria Sharapova, you might not be familiar with the ladies listed above. The sports in which they compete—track and field events, triathlons, and judo—are not as high profile internationally as tennis. However, all five are featured in a new marketing campaign from NikeWomen. Their message: "Women gain social community and mental strength through sports."

The campaign is a direct result of an online survey conducted by TNS Global. TNS was commissioned by NikeWomen to survey 10,000 women between the ages of 16–30 from nine Pan-European countries (France, Germany, Italy, The Netherlands, Russia, Spain, Sweden, Turkey, and the United Kingdom). The results indicated that playing sports on a regular basis helps young women feel healthier, more confident, and more successful in life. Moreover, the results also indicated that European women are far less competitive about sports than men and enjoy the social aspects and community building opportunities associated with participation in sports.

With survey results in hand, NikeWomen then turned to long-time agency partner Wieden+Kennedy (W+K) to develop a campaign centered around the themes of developing greater self-confidence and self-empowerment. It was W+K that employed the phrase, "Just Do It" in 1988 but decided it needed something different based on this research. "Here I Am" met Nike's needs on multiple levels.

Nike does not presently have a slogan aimed at women in the United States. It is also not planning to use this European campaign in the United States. The ads starring Delsalle, La Mantia, Sanders, Sharapova, and Spirig can be seen worldwide online at popular sites like YouTube and nike.com/nikewomen/, but the other elements of the campaign are strictly available only in Europe.

From a marketing research perspective, it is interesting to see how research, more specifically an online survey, leads to the creative execution of a new campaign with a new slogan. Part 3 of the text focuses on data collection methods with primary emphasis given to the various ways a firm can gain information from consumers and other constituent groups.

Source: Aaron O. Patrick, "Softer Nike Pitch Woos Europe's Women," *The Wall Street Journal* (September 11, 2008) downloaded from www.wsj.net on September 15, 2008; Jeff Beer, "Nike Declares European Women Have Arrived," *Creativity* (September 11, 2008) downloaded from creativity-online.com on September 15, 2008.

Secondary Data

Introduction

Once a research problem is defined and clearly specified, the research effort turns to data collection. The natural temptation is to begin designing a survey immediately—however, survey data should only be collected if absolutely necessary. Instead, first attempts at data collection should focus on secondary data, information not gathered for the immediate study at hand but previously gathered for some other purpose. Information originated by the researcher for the purpose of the investigation at hand is called primary data.

If Frigidaire conducted a survey on the demographic characteristics of refrigerator purchasers to determine who buys the various sizes of refrigerators, this would be primary data. If, instead, the company used its existing files and compiled the same data from warranty cards its customers had returned, or if it used already published industry statistics on refrigerator buyers, the information would be considered secondary data.

secondary data
Information not gathered for the immediate study at hand but for some other purpose.

primary data
Information collected specifically for the investigation at hand.

In the course of doing exploratory research via literature reviews, researchers will sometimes stumble onto useful secondary data. It is important for researchers to understand that successful projects should start with a careful search for existing secondary data. But most people usually have no idea just how much secondary data are available. Exhibit 7.1 lists some of the information on people and households collected by the U.S. Bureau of the Census, readily available for use by researchers. It is important to know what is available in secondary sources, not just to avoid "reinventing the wheel," but also because secondary data possess some significant advantages over primary data. Some types of marketing research—in particular, market analysis—rely almost exclusively on secondary data. Research Window 7.1 explores how Arby's, the fast-food chain, blends available secondary data with on-site analysis to identify promising locations for new stores.

Learning Objective

1. Explain the difference between primary and secondary data.

ADVANTAGES OF SECONDARY DATA

The most significant advantages of secondary data are the time and money they can save. If the information being sought is available as secondary data, the researcher can simply go to the library or go online, locate the appropriate source(s), and gather the information desired. This should take little time and involve little cost. If the

Learning Objective

2. Cite two advantages offered by secondary data.

Exhibit 7.1

Information Available from the 22nd Census of Population and Housing

100 percent characteristics (short form): A limited number of questions were asked of every person and housing unit in the United States. Information is available on

Household relationship	Race
Sex	Tenure (whether the home is owned or rented)
Age	Vacancy characteristics
Hispanic or Latino origin	

Sample characteristics (long form): Additional questions were asked of a sample (generally 1 in 6) of persons and housing units. Data are provided on

Population	*Housing*
Marital status	Value of home or monthly rent paid
Place of birth, citizenship, and year of entry	Units in structure
School enrollment and educational attainment	Year structure built
Ancestry	Number of rooms and number of bedrooms
Migration (residence in 1995)	Year moved into residence
Language spoken at home and ability to speak English	Plumbing and kitchen facilities
Veteran status	Telephone service
Disability	Vehicles available
Grandparents as caregivers	Heating fuel
Labor force status	Farm residence
Place of work and journey to work	Utilities, mortgage, taxes, insurance, and fuel costs
Occupation, industry, and class of worker	
Work status in 1999	
Income in 1999	

Sources: "Introduction to Census 2000 Data Products," p. 1, downloaded from http://www.census.gov/dmd/www/products.html, September 13, 2008.

research window 7.1

How Arby's Uses Secondary Data and Site Visits to Select Retail Locations

Pulling off the freeway just north of Los Angeles, Barbara Vinson spotted some promising signs. A Home Depot. A Target. An upscale mall called The Oaks. As she scanned the mall parking lot, she said, "I get really excited if I see a lot of Beemers . . . or anything that is more than an $18,000 car." Ms. Vinson, the top scout for Arby's Inc., does a job critical to the growth of the fast-food business: finding new places to sell sandwiches. In the past, many restaurants simply followed the growing highway system, or plopped themselves next to a McDonald's to piggyback on the No. 1 burger chain's market research.

But now the United States has 277,208 fast-food outlets from coast to coast—one for every 1,000 people in the country, according to Technomic Inc., a food-consulting firm. That's up from one for every 1,400 people in 1990, and every 2,000 people in 1980. The claustrophobic conditions have cut the industry's sales-growth rate in half over the past decade and left chains struggling to find spots for new stores that won't cannibalize nearby locations. So chains employ scouts such as Ms. Vinson to sniff out promising real estate. They comb through maps pinpointing existing fast-food outlets, and then reconnoiter the sites in person, armed with mapping data, demographic analyses, and an eye for spotting details that don't show up in the numbers. One trick of the trade: Look for a spot next to a Walmart.

Arby's parent, holding company Triarc Cos., has said its franchisees are committed to building at least 530 units by 2011, and that the chain could grow to 4,000 to 5,000 units in the next six to 10 years. That's where Ms. Vinson comes in. Hired from drive-in burger chain Sonic Corp., where she worked her way up from secretary to market analyst, the 48-year-old grandmother melds technical mapping and demographic analysis with what she calls a "gut feeling" in picking hot real estate.

At Sonic, Ms. Vinson selected sites across the United States, including one of Sonic's hottest markets for new openings, Tampa, Florida.

Before she flies off from her home base in Moore, Oklahoma, where she grew up, Ms. Vinson maps out the location of every Arby's in a given market. The company doesn't allow stand-alone Arby's stores to be built within a mile of each other. She then plots out where all the competitors are in the market, and their sales figures, which Arby's buys from an independent firm that surveys the restaurants. In the past, she paid particularly close attention to Wendy's International Inc., which markets itself as the upper end of fast food and thus serves as a good benchmark for Arby's. If Wendy's could do well in a certain area, the logic goes, so could Arby's. This logic could also be one of the reasons Triarc acquired Wendy's in 2008.

After she maps out a market's fast-food picture, Ms. Vinson—like scouts for many fast-food companies and small stores—looks for big retailers in the area that will generate traffic. Twice a month, Wal-Mart Stores Inc. sends fast-food companies and other businesses a list of available land on existing and future Walmart sites, including its Supercenter and Sam's Club formats.

Many Walmart stores also own real estate nearby, which they sell to fast-food chains or other retailers. About half of the sites being studied as possible Arby's locations are near a Walmart or another big retailer such as Target Corp.'s Target or Home Depot Inc. "A fast-food place is like a fish that follows a shark," says Arby's CEO Michael Howe.

Arby's doesn't think it's risky to tie its fortunes so closely to those of another company. "They do their homework as much as we do and probably even further," says Bob Cross, Arby's vice president of business development. "If you are going to purchase that large a piece

same information were to be collected using a survey, the following steps would have to be taken: data collection form designed and pretested; field interviewing staff selected and trained; sampling plan devised; data gathered and then checked for accuracy and omissions; data coded and analyzed. As a conservative estimate, this process would take two to three months and could cost thousands of dollars, since it would include expenses and wages for a number of additional field and office personnel.

With secondary data, the expenses incurred in collecting the data have already been paid by the original compiler of the information. Even if there is a charge for using the data (unlike statistics compiled by government or trade associations, commercial data are not free), the cost is still substantially less than if the firm collected the information itself.

of property and invest that much money, you better make sure you're going to make it a success."

Demographic data also go into Ms. Vinson's mix. Ideal Arby's sites need only a surrounding population of 20,000—with at least 3,000 of those hanging around during the day, not commuting to another place—and an average household income of $35,000.

When her maps are complete, Ms. Vinson hits the road to fill in the blanks. In a typical month, she travels 12 to 15 days, immersing herself in the market. With a map in her lap, one hand on the steering wheel and the other on a tape recorder, she spends hours cruising roads.

Spotting a promising parcel of land on a recent afternoon, she stopped to snap pictures and plot the geographic coordinates on her hand-held global-positioning-system device. Checking that against her maps, she got some good news: There are no other Arby's in the area—and one nearby Wendy's generates 24% higher sales than the chain's average. Best yet, the Wendy's isn't visible from the site of the potential Arby's, so Arby's customers wouldn't get lured away. She marked the empty lot as planned restaurant No. 243.

In judging a site, Ms. Vinson also looks for large numbers of rooftops, suggesting a cluster of customers, and follows local traffic to see where everyone's heading. While Walmarts and Targets are obvious draws, grocery stores and post offices also excite her because people need to go there at least once a week. "I'm getting to the point where I can sniff out shopping," she says.

Ms. Vinson will often examine the same sites on her way out of town to see where people are on the weekends, as opposed to weekdays. By the time she finishes a report, she typically has driven several thousand miles crisscrossing the same streets. Along the way, she'll drop into a McDonald's or other competitor that's doing well, chatting up people behind the counter for local insights.

Once Ms. Vinson picks a site, Arby's franchisees, who own all of the restaurants in the chain, foot the average $1.6 million cost to buy or lease land and build the store. Arby's provides the franchises with a team of real-estate managers who help them close the deals.

© ROSE ALCORN

Sources: Excerpted from Shirley Leung, "Where's the Beef? A Glutted Market Leaves Food Chains Hungry for Sites," *The Wall Street Journal*, October 1, 2003, p. A1, accessed via ProQuest, September 13, 2008. Michael J. de la Merced, "Peltz Offer Is Accepted by Wendy's," *New York Times*, April 25, 2008, p. C1, accessed via ProQuest, September 13, 2008.

Given the substantial amount of time and money at stake, we offer this advice: Begin with secondary data, and only when the secondary data are exhausted or show diminishing returns, proceed to primary data. Sometimes the secondary data are sufficient, especially when all you need is a ballpark estimate, which is often the case. Although it is rare that secondary data completely solve the problem under study, they usually will (1) help the investigator to better state the problem under investigation, (2) suggest improved methods or further data that should be collected, and/or (3) provide comparative data that can help interpret primary data if such data are eventually collected.

DISADVANTAGES OF SECONDARY DATA

3. Specify two problems common to secondary data.

Two problems that commonly arise with secondary data are (1) they do not completely fit the problem, and (2) they are not totally accurate.

Problems of Fit

Because secondary data are collected for other purposes, it is rare when they perfectly fit the problem as defined. In some cases, the fit will be so poor that the data are completely inappropriate. Usually, the poor fit is due to (1) different units of measurement, (2) different class definitions, or (3) the age of the data.

The size of a retail store, for instance, can be expressed in terms of gross sales, profits, square feet, and number of employees. Consumer income can be expressed by individual, family, household, and spending unit. So it is with many variables, and a common source of frustration in using secondary data is that the source containing the basic information desired presents that information in units of measurement different from that needed.

Assuming the units are consistent, we find that the class boundaries presented are often different from those needed. If the problem demands income by individual in increments of $5,000 (0–$4,999, $5,000–$9,999, and so on), it does the researcher little good if the data source offers income by individual using boundaries $7,500 apart (0–$7,499, $7,500–$14,999, and so on).

Finally, secondary data are often out of date. The time from data collection to data dissemination is often long, sometimes as much as two to three years, as, for example, with much government census data. Although census data have great value while current, this value diminishes rapidly with time. Most marketing decisions require current, rather than historical, information.

Problems of Accuracy

4. List the three criteria researchers should use in judging the accuracy of secondary data.

The accuracy of much secondary data is also questionable. As we'll show you, there are lots of sources of error possible in the collection, analysis, and presentation of marketing information. When a researcher is collecting primary data, firsthand experience helps in judging the accuracy of the information being collected. But when using secondary data, the task of assessing accuracy is more difficult. It may help to consider the primacy of the source, the purpose of publication, and the general quality of the data collection methods and presentation.

primary source
The originating source of secondary data.

secondary source
A source of secondary data that did not originate the data but rather secured them from another source.

Primacy of Source   First, consider the source. Secondary data can be secured from either a primary source or a secondary source. A **primary source** is the source that originated the data. A **secondary source** is a source that in turn took the data from a primary source. The *Statistical Abstract of the United States*, for example, contains a great deal of useful information for many research projects. It is a secondary source of secondary data. All of its data are taken from other government and trade sources. If you stopped searching for secondary data with the *Statistical Abstract*, you would violate the most fundamental rule in using secondary data—always use the primary source of secondary data.

The owner of GrandKids Ltd. violated that rule when she planned the launch of her store in Pelham, New York. She thought her upscale suburb was an ideal location for a store catering to grandparents eager to spoil their grandchildren. After all, specialty stores of this type were the largest segment of the clothing market for infants and toddlers. She checked secondary data from the school district and a company that produces advertising circulars, and estimated that there were about 10,000 families in Pelham—enough, she reasoned, to support her store. But three years after the founding, she closed for lack of business. She had grossly overestimated her market. Census data recorded 12,000 residents and fewer than 3,500 families. Furthermore,

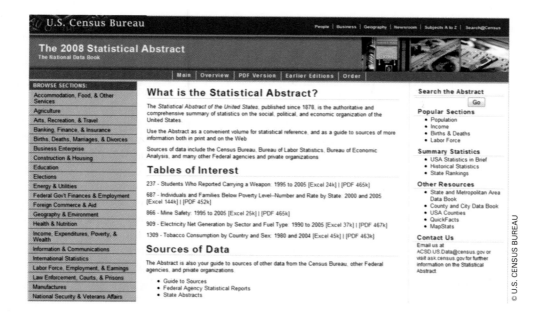

© U.S. CENSUS BUREAU

less than one-third of Pelham's residents were in her targeted age group of people 50 and older.[1]

There are two main reasons for using a primary source. First and foremost, the researcher will need to search for general evidence of quality (e.g., the methods of data collection and analysis). The primary source will typically be the only source that describes the process of collection and analysis and, as a result, is the only source by which this judgment can be made. Second, a primary source is usually more accurate and complete than a secondary source. Secondary sources often fail to include important information such as footnotes that the original researchers included with the research results. Errors in transcription can also occur in copying data from a primary source. Once made, transcription errors seem to hold on tenaciously, as the following example illustrates.

In 1901, Napoleon Lajoie produced the highest batting average ever attained in the American League when he batted .422 on 229 hits in 543 times at bat. In setting the type for the record book after that season, a printer correctly reported Lajoie's .422 average but incorrectly reported his hits, giving him 220 instead of 229. A short time later, someone pointed out that 220 hits in 543 at-bats yields a batting average

Learning Objective

5. State the most fundamental rule in using secondary data.

Manager's Focus

We have emphasized several times how important it is for you to learn how to evaluate the quality of marketing research information. You should make extensive use of secondary information that is relevant to your marketing efforts. However, you should *never* use secondary data without first scrutinizing its quality. At times, managers can be too trusting of external secondary data, assuming its quality must have been verified before it was published. The information presented in this chapter will help you understand why this is a dangerous assumption and give you appropriate criteria to employ when evaluating secondary data. In addition, the knowledge about research methods you acquire from this book will enable you to better judge the appropriateness of the methods originally used to generate the secondary data. When you have the expertise to make these assessments, you can have much greater confidence as you make decisions based on the vast array of market intelligence available.

of .405, and so Lajoie's reported average was changed. The error persisted for some 50 years, until an energetic fan checked all the old box scores and discovered the facts.[2]

Purpose of Publication   A second way to judge the accuracy of secondary data is the purpose of publication. Consider the following example: According to the results of a survey, almost one-third of respondents have talked to a doctor about a treatment they saw advertised. Of those who asked their doctor for a drug they saw advertised, half were given a prescription for it. Three-quarters of respondents said ads for prescription drugs showed both the risks and benefits of the medicine.[3] The results were released at a time when the Food and Drug Administration was preparing new guidelines for advertising prescription drugs directly to consumers (rather than promoting them only to physicians). Would your reaction to this information be different if you knew that the survey was sponsored by *Prevention* magazine, which publishes health-related articles and advertisements from prescription drug companies? Do you now have the same confidence in the objectivity of the results? Probably not; this suggests that the source is one criterion for evaluating the accuracy of secondary data.

Research that has been collected in such a way that the results will support a particular position is often referred to as advocacy research. With **advocacy research**, the goal is to support a position, not to uncover the truth about an issue. Researchers pursuing this type of research may word questions in such a way that they get the answers they want; select a nonrepresentative sample (e.g., only surveying people known to support the position the researcher wants); or any number of other unethical practices.

This doesn't mean that all data collected or sponsored by an interested party should automatically be rejected as advocacy research. Instead, we simply suggest that such data should be viewed critically by the research user. A source that publishes secondary data as its primary function deserves confidence. Companies whose primary business is to publish secondary data must maintain high quality. These firms have no reason to publish inaccurate information and would probably lose business if they did so. The success of any organization supplying data as its primary purpose depends on the long-run satisfaction by its users that the information supplied is accurate.

General Evidence of Quality   A third standard by which the accuracy of secondary data can be assessed is through the general evidence of quality. One way of determining this quality is to evaluate the ability of the supplying organization to collect the data. The Internal Revenue Service, for example, has greater leverage in securing income data than an independent marketing research firm. However, researchers also have to weigh whether this additional leverage may introduce bias. Would a respondent be more likely to hedge in estimating her income in completing her tax return or in responding to a consumer survey?

In judging the quality of secondary data, a user also needs to understand how the data were collected. A primary source should provide a detailed description of the data collection process, including definitions, data collection forms, method of sampling, and so forth. If it doesn't, be careful! Such omissions are usually indicative of sloppy methods (at best) or advocacy research (at worst).

When the details of data collection are provided, the user of secondary data should examine them thoroughly. Was the sampling plan sound? Was this type of data best collected through questionnaire or by observational methods? What about the quality of the field force? What kind of training was provided? What kinds of checks of the fieldwork were used? What was the extent of nonresponse due to refusals, not at homes, and by item? Are these statistics reported? Is the information presented in a well-organized manner? Are the tables properly labeled, and are the data within them internally consistent? Are the conclusions supported by the data? As these questions suggest, you need to be familiar with the research process and the potential sources of error in order to gauge the quality of secondary data. The remainder of this book provides much of the needed insight for evaluating secondary data.

advocacy research
Research conducted to support a position rather than to find the truth about an issue.

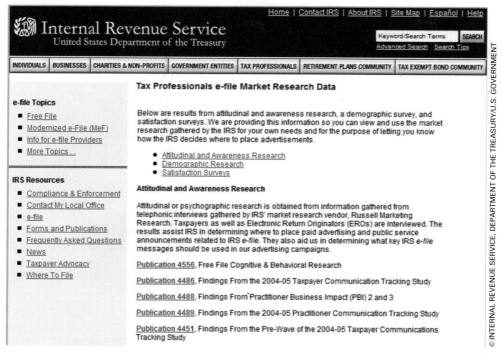

The IRS indicates that it obtains its demographic survey results from information included on taxpayer returns. This information assists the IRS in segmenting the population into various and/or specific market segments for the purpose of knowing and understanding its customers (taxpayers as well as tax professionals).

TYPES OF SECONDARY DATA: INTERNAL AND EXTERNAL

The most common way of classifying data is by source, whether internal or external. **Internal data** are those found within the organization for whom the research is being done; **external data** are those obtained from outside sources. The external sources can be further split into those that regularly publish statistics and make them available to the user at no charge (e.g., the U.S. government), and those commercial organizations that sell their services to various users (e.g., Nielsen). In the remainder of this chapter and its appendix, we will review some of the main types and sources of published statistics; in the next chapter, we will review some of the more important sources of commercial statistics. Figure 7.1 provides an overview of these sources.

Internal Secondary Data

Internal data that were collected for some purpose other than the study at hand are internal secondary data. For example, the sales and cost data compiled in the normal accounting cycle represent promising internal secondary data for many research problems—such as evaluation of past marketing strategy or assessment of the firm's competitive position in the industry. Much of the information in a company's marketing information system or decision support system might be considered internal secondary data if the information can be used to address new issues.

Generally, for manufacturers the one most productive source document is the sales invoice. It usually contains the following information:

- Customer name and location

- Product(s) or service(s) sold

- Volume and dollar amount of the transaction

Learning Objective

6. Explain the difference between internal and external data.

internal data
Data that originate within the organization for which the research is being done.

external data
Data that originate outside the organization for which the research is being done.

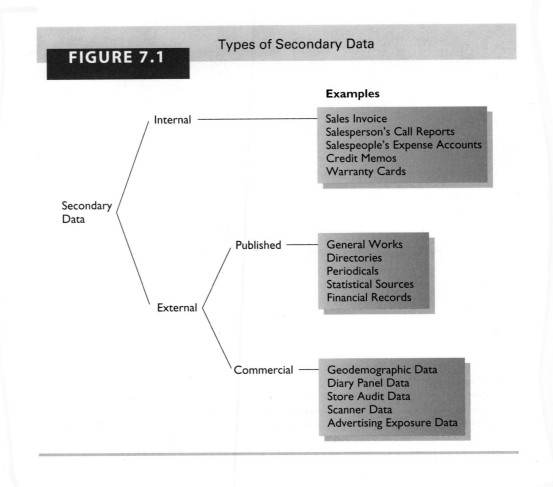

FIGURE 7.1 · Types of Secondary Data

Examples

Secondary Data

Internal
- Sales Invoice
- Salesperson's Call Reports
- Salespeople's Expense Accounts
- Credit Memos
- Warranty Cards

External

Published
- General Works
- Directories
- Periodicals
- Statistical Sources
- Financial Records

Commercial
- Geodemographic Data
- Diary Panel Data
- Store Audit Data
- Scanner Data
- Advertising Exposure Data

MANAGER'S FOCUS

Managers are sometimes too quick to file away marketing research reports once the current information need has been met. These managers fail to recognize how these reports can be a valuable source of internal secondary data when facing new business situations. Sometimes managers do this because they have taken "ownership" of the information and don't want to share it with other managers in the organization who might benefit from it when addressing various marketing issues. This tendency is particularly pronounced among managers who initiate marketing research studies to confirm what they believe to be true or to provide political cover for decisions they want to make or have already made. For example, in the middle of a project a client once told us, "I have already implemented my decision. If the results support what I did, I will broadcast them throughout the company. But, if they don't, I'll bury them so deeply nobody will ever see them."

When you are a manager and commission marketing research studies, please take the necessary steps to make certain your organization gets maximum benefit from its investment. Remember that being market oriented means sharing marketing intelligence throughout your organization. Instead of squirreling away marketing research reports, you should work with the information technology staff to feed the findings into your information systems to make them available for use by anyone in your organization.

▓ Salesperson (or agent) responsible for the sale

▓ End use of the product sold

▓ Location of customer facility where product is to be shipped and/or used

▓ Customer's industry, class of trade, and/or channel of distribution

▓ Terms of sale and applicable discount

▓ Freight paid and/or to be collected

▓ Shipment point for the order

▓ Transportation used in shipment

Other documents provide more specialized input. Some of the more important of these are listed in Exhibit 7.2. Most companies are likely to use only two or three of these sources of sales information in addition to the sales invoice. Those used depend on the company and the types of analyses used to plan and evaluate the marketing effort.

Even something as simple as a product registration card can be used for marketing intelligence. Years ago, when the Skil Corporation was launching a cordless power screwdriver, management was surprised to find that a substantial proportion of the new screwdrivers were being sold to elderly people, based on information obtained from registration cards. Although marketing managers had positioned the product for the "do-it-yourself" target market, the ease of use made the product attractive to older consumers. The company began advertising in publications targeting older Americans.[4]

At larger companies with active marketing research programs, another useful source of internal secondary data is prior marketing research studies on related topics. Even when the topics don't match up perfectly with the current need for information, there can still be a wealth of information in the reports. For example, previous reports and their results may offer new perspectives on the current situation. You might gain insights into better ways of asking certain questions or even find results that can serve as baseline measurements for the current research effort. The point is to look at any report that is in any way related to the current decision problem.

Internal secondary data are the least costly (and most readily available) of any type of marketing research. If maintained in an appropriate form, internal sales data can be used to analyze the company's past sales performance by product, geographic location, customer, channel of distribution, and so on; cost data help in determining how profitable these segments of the business are. Most studies should begin with a search for internal secondary data. For example, common questions that confront marketing managers are: How do we maximize sales (and profits) within our existing product lines? When consumers enter a store, what else might they also buy? What are they least likely to buy? Internal sales data are a great place to start when attempting to answer these types of questions.

Exhibit 7.3, on page 147, illustrates how secondary data—both available within the firm and through an external vendor—can be successfully used to answer these questions with greater depth. The first form of secondary data can be provided by a retailer based on proprietary internal sales data. The second form is centered on a database and software application developed by Spectra Marketing, a Nielsen subsidiary. One of the strengths of Spectra's data is to identify cross-merchandising opportunities based on clusters of products often purchased during consumers' visits. A retailer can import data on past sales and Spectra will identify clusters of products most often purchased together and compare the clusters to its database. Take simple products like a greeting card or motor oil and Spectra's analysis will prioritize which other products are most likely to be purchased as well. In this case, consumers purchasing a greeting card are 92% more likely to also purchase store-brand candy.

| Exhibit 7.2 | Some Useful Sources of Internal Secondary Data |

Document	Information Provided
Cash register receipts	Type (cash or credit) and dollar amount of transaction by department by salesperson
Salesperson's call reports	Customers and prospects called on (company and individual seen; planned or unplanned calls)
	Products discussed
	Orders obtained
	Customer's product needs and usage
	Other significant information about customers
	Distribution of salesperson's time among customer calls, travel, and office work
	Sales-related activities: meetings, conventions, and so on
Salesperson's expense accounts	Expenses by day by item (hotel, meals, travel, etc.)
Individual customer (and prospect) records	Name and location and customer number
	Number of calls by company salespersons (agents)
	Sales by company (in dollars and/or units, by product or service, by location of customer facility)
	Customer's industry, class of trade, and/or trade channel
	Estimated total annual usage of each product or service sold by the company
	Estimated annual purchases from the company of each such product or service
	Location (in terms of company sales territory)
Financial records	Sales revenue (by products, geographic markets, customers, class of trade, unit of sales organization, etc.)
	Direct sales expenses (similarly classified)
	Overhead sales costs (similarly classified)
	Profits (similarly classified)
Credit memos	Returns and allowances
Warranty cards	Indirect measures of dealer sales
	Customer service

Thus, it is in the retailer's best interest to position these products next to one another in the store if they aren't already. In the case of motor oil, the results differ slightly based on the product being a premium or private label brand. In the case of premium grade motor oil, consumers are 50% more likely to purchase a riding lawn mower and 22% less likely to purchase imported beer. In terms of private label motor oil, buyers are 78% more likely to also buy hunting apparel. The combination of internal and external sources of data provides new retailing opportunities.

Searching for Published External Secondary Data

Although most people underestimate what is available, there is likely to be relevant external secondary data on almost any problem a marketer might confront. The fundamental problem is not availability; it is identifying and accessing what is there. Even researchers who do have an inkling of how much valuable secondary data exists are typically unsure of how to go about searching for it. Figure 7.2 provides some guidelines that can be used to get started on a search of secondary data on a particular topic.[5]

Exhibit 7.3	Cross-Merchandising Opportunities Based on Past Purchase Behavior				

Most Likely to Purchase with

Greeting Cards		Premium Motor Oil		Private Label Motor Oil	
Store-Brand Candy	192*	Riding Lawn Mowers	150	Hunting Apparel	178
Sweet 'N Low	171	Hunting Apparel	149	Riding Lawn Mowers	165
Russell Stover Candies	164	Domestic Beer	125	Saw Blades	126

Least Likely to Purchase with

Greeting Cards		Premium Motor Oil		Private Label Motor Oil	
Canada Dry Diet Ginger Ale	121	Imported Beer	78	Imported Beer	90
Pepsi Caffeine Free Diet Cola	122	Light Domestic Beer	98	Light Domestic Beer	103
Parker Pens/Pencils	123	Batteries	99	Batteries	107

*100 equals the U.S. average demand for the product. Numbers greater than 100 indicate higher than average likelihood of purchase; numbers less than 100 indicate lower than average likelihood of purchase.

Sources: Spectra EnLighten Custom Store Facts Data Importer, downloaded from http://us.acnielsen.com/products/documents/SpectraEnlighten-CustomStoreFactsDataImporter.pdf, September 13, 2008 and Cross-Merchandising Opportunities: Greeting Cards/Motor Oil, December 1, 2001, downloaded from http://www.allbusiness.com/, September 13, 2008.

FIGURE 7.2   How to Get Started When Searching Published Sources of Secondary Data

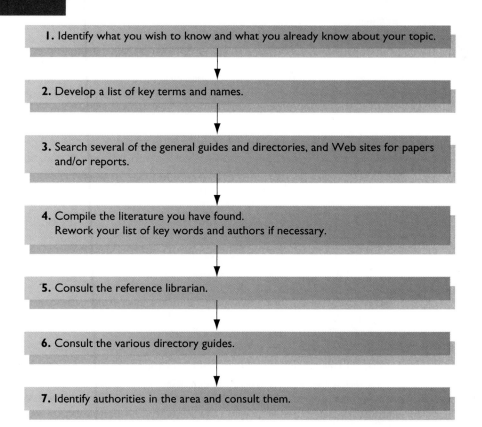

1. Identify what you wish to know and what you already know about your topic.

2. Develop a list of key terms and names.

3. Search several of the general guides and directories, and Web sites for papers and/or reports.

4. Compile the literature you have found. Rework your list of key words and authors if necessary.

5. Consult the reference librarian.

6. Consult the various directory guides.

7. Identify authorities in the area and consult them.

Step 1 The first step in the process is to identify what you want to know and what you already know about your topic. This may include relevant facts, names of researchers or organizations associated with the topic, key papers and other publications with which you are already familiar, and any other information you may have.

Step 2 A useful second step is to develop a list of key terms and authors. These terms and names will provide access to secondary sources. Unless you have a very specific topic of interest, it is better to keep this initial list long and quite general.

Step 3 In Step 3, you are ready to use the library or the Internet for the first time. It is useful to begin your search with several of the directories and guides listed in Appendix 7A or Web sites that deal with the subject. One way to identify information sources on the Internet is to start with an InfoTech Marketing Web site called The Sales & Marketing Source (http://www.smsource.com). It offers hundreds of links to sites that InfoTech has reviewed for relevancy to marketing issues, including published reports, newspapers and magazines, government data sources, and sources of data about specific companies. Some of the links are to free data.

Step 4 Now it is time to compile the literature you have found. Is it relevant to your needs? You may be overwhelmed by information at this point, or you may have found little that is relevant. If you need more information, rework your list of key words and authors and expand your search to include a few more years and a few additional sources. Once again, evaluate your findings. By the end of Step 4, you should have a clear idea of the nature of the information you are seeking and sufficient background to use more specialized sources.

Step 5 One very useful specialized source is a reference librarian. Reference librarians are specialists who have been trained to know the contents of many of the key information sources in a library and on the Web, as well as how to search those sources most effectively. A reference librarian can usually uncover information that is relevant to your current problem. The reference librarian will need your help, however, in the form of a carefully constructed list of key words or topics. You need to remember that the reference librarian cannot be of much help until you can provide specific details about what you want to know.

Step 6 If you have had little success or your topic is highly specialized, consult one of the general guides to information listed in Appendix 7A. These are really directories of directories, which means that this level of search will be very general. You will first need to identify potentially useful primary directories, which will then lead you to other sources.

Step 7 If you are unhappy with what you have found or are otherwise having trouble, and the reference librarian has not been able to identify sources, use an authority. Identify some individual or organization that might know something about the topic. The *Consultants and Consulting Organizations Directory*, *Encyclopedia of Associations*, or *Research Centers Directory* may help you identify sources. The Bureau of the Census puts out a list of department specialists whom users can contact for information on any of the bureau's studies. These people are often quite knowledgeable about related studies in their areas of expertise. Faculty at universities, government officials, and business executives can also be useful sources of information.

Some Key General Sources of External Secondary Data

In addition to the key role played by reference librarians, some important sources of external secondary data are associations, general guides to useful marketing information, and online computer searches.

Associations Most associations gather and often publish detailed information on such things as industry shipments and sales, growth patterns, environmental factors affecting the industry, operating characteristics, and so on. Trade associations can often secure information from members that other research organizations cannot, because of the working relationships that exist between the association and the firms that belong to it. Two useful sources for locating associations serving a particular industry are the *Directories in Print* and the *Encyclopedia of Associations*, described in Appendix 7A.

General Guides to Secondary Data The general guides to secondary data are also described in Appendix 7A. Exhibit 7.4, for example, lists what the *Encyclopedia of Business Information Sources* says about data sources on the electronic security systems industry. Aspiring researchers should also become familiar with the more important general sources of marketing information so that they know what statistics are available and where they can be found. Many of the most important of these are listed and briefly described in Appendix 7A.

Online Computer Searches Online computer searches have become increasingly popular for locating published information and data. Many public libraries, as well as college and university libraries, have invested in the equipment and personnel necessary to make database searching available to their patrons. There are now thousands of databases to choose from, with many of them applying to business. Companies use online databases to search for journal articles, reports, speeches, marketing data, economic trends, legislation, inventions, and many other types of information on a particular topic.

When accessing a database online, users typically pay whether they get the answer or not. The more information they get, the more they pay. The overall cost of using an online database may include (1) planning and executing the search, (2) telephone line charges, (3) connection charges, and (4) citation and printing charges. The big advantage of online searching is time savings. Some of the more well-known database vendors are Dialog, Dow Jones, and Lexis/Nexis.

Databases are typically defined by the type of information they contain. For example, bibliographic databases provide references to magazine or journal articles. They will list the name of the article, the author, the title of the journal, and the date of publication. They are likely to include some key words that describe the contents of the article. Most bibliographic databases also provide an abstract or summary of the article. Some of the useful databases for marketers are included in Appendix 7A.

In addition to using online databases, researchers can use the Internet for general searches of the Web to locate secondary data on a subject. To do so requires Web access through an access provider and one or more search engines. Search engines are needed because the Internet contains many billions of words in documents that are not arranged for retrieval. Creators of search engines compile and index an electronic catalog of Web content, then provide the software needed to search through the index for key words or concepts specified by the user. The most popular search engine is Google (http://www.google.com), which conducts over half of all searches done via search engine.[6]

ETHICAL DILEMMA 7.2

A marketing manager for a dog food manufacturer stumbled onto an important piece of competitive intelligence while visiting a local printer near her company's plant. While waiting to speak with the salesperson who handled her company's account, the manager noticed some glossy advertising proofs for one of its competitor's products. The ad highlighted some new low prices. When she mentioned the prices to the printer, she was told that they were part of a new advertising campaign. On her return to headquarters, the marketing manager called a meeting of her own company's management. As a result of that meeting, the company initiated a preemptive, price-cutting campaign of its own that effectively neutralized the competitor's strategy.

- Did the marketing manager act ethically in reporting the information back to her own company?
- Would your judgment be different if the proofs were in a folder and the marketing manager casually and somewhat inadvertently opened the folder while standing there? What if she did so on purpose after noticing that the folder pertained to the competitor?
- Should information like this be entered into the firm's decision support system?

Learning Objective

7. List some of the key sources researchers should consider in conducting a search process.

| Exhibit 7.4 | Sources of Data on the Electronic Security Systems Industry |

ELECTRONIC SECURITY SYSTEMS

See also: INDUSTRIAL SECURITY PROGRAMS

DIRECTORIES

Automotive Burglary Protection and Mechanical Equipment Directory. Underwriters Laboratories, Inc. ● Annual. $10.00. Lists manufacturers authorized to use UL label.

National Burglar and Fire Alarm Association Members Services Directory. National Burglar and Fire Alarm Association. ● Annual. Membership. Names and addresses of about 4,000 alarm security companies. Formerly *National Burglar and Fire Alarm Association-Directory of Members.*

Security Distributing and Marketing-Security Products and Services Locator. Cahners Business Information. ● Annual. $50.00. Formerly *SDM: Security Distributing and Marketing-Security Products and Services Directory.*

Security: Product Service Suppliers Guide. Cahners Business Information. ● Annual. $50.00. Includes computer and information protection products. Formerly *Security—World Product Directory.*

HANDBOOKS AND MANUALS

Burglar Alarm Sales and Installation. Entrepreneur Media, Inc. ● Looseleaf. $59.50. A practical guide to starting a burglar alarm service. Covers profit potential, start-up costs, market size evaluation, owner's time required, pricing, accounting, advertising, promotion, etc. (Start-Up Business Guide No. E1091.).

Effective Physical Security: Design, Equipment, and Operations. Lawrence J. Fennelly, editor. Butterworth-Heinemann. ● 1996. $36.95. Second edition. Contains chapters written by various U.S. security equipment specialists. Covers architectural considerations, locks, safes, alarms, intrusion detection systems, closed circuit television, identification systems, etc.

PERIODICALS AND NEWSLETTERS

9-1-1 Magazine: Public Safety Communications and Response. Official Publications, Inc. ● Bimonthly. $31.95 per year. Covers technical information and applications for public safety communications personnel.

Security Distributing and Marketing. Cahners Business Information. ● 13 times a year. $82.00 per year. Covers applications, merchandising, new technology and management.

Security Management. American Society for Industrial Security. ● Monthly. Free to members; nonmembers, $48.00 per year. Articles cover the protection of corporate assets, including personnel property and information security.

Security Systems Administration. Cygnus Business Media. ● Monthly. $10.00 per year.

Security: The Magazine for Buyers of Security Products, Systems and Service. Cahners Business Information. ● Monthly. $82.90 per year.

TRADE/PROFESSIONAL ASSOCIATIONS

ASIS International (American Society for Industrial Security). 1625 Prince St., Alexandria, VA 22314-2818. Phone: (703)519-6200 Fax (703)519-6299. URL: http://www.asisonline.org.

Automatic Fire Alarm Association. P.O. Box 951807, Lake Mary, FL 32795-1807. Phone: (407)322-6288 Fax: (407)322-7488. ● URL: http://www.afaa.org.

Central Station Alarm Association, 440 Maple Ave., Suite 201, Vienna, VA 22180-4723. Phone (703)242-4670 Fax: (703)242-4675 E-mail: communications@csaaul.org.

National Burglar & Fire Alarm Association. 8300 Colesville Rd., Ste. 750, Silver Spring, MD 20910. Phone: (301)907-3202 Fax: (301)907-7897 E-mail: staff@alarm.org ● URL: http://www.alarm.org.

Source: Linda D. Hall, ed., *Encyclopedia of Business Information Sources*, 20th Edition (Detroit: Thomson Gale, 2005), pp. 305–307.

MANAGER'S FOCUS

We hope that you now see how secondary data can be a cost-effective, useful resource for you and your organization. We want you to also recognize that the quality of the services provided by external marketing research firms can be considerably enhanced by "opening the vaults" of your secondary data resources. Having access to a company's reserves of external and internal secondary data (including past marketing research reports) will help your research providers better understand your marketing environment. This will enable them to guide you more precisely through the problem formulation stage and to help them design research studies that genuinely meet your needs.

SUMMARY

Learning Objective 1

Explain the difference between primary and secondary data.
Secondary data are statistics not gathered for the immediate study, but for some other purpose. Primary data are originated by the researcher for the purpose of the investigation at hand.

Learning Objective 2

Cite two advantages offered by secondary data.
The most significant advantages offered by secondary data are time savings and money savings for the researcher.

Learning Objective 3

Specify two problems common to secondary data.
Two problems that commonly arise when secondary data are used are (1) they do not completely fit the problem, and (2) they are not completely accurate.

Learning Objective 4

List the three criteria researchers should use in judging the accuracy of secondary data.
The three criteria researchers should use in judging the accuracy of secondary data are

(1) the source, (2) the purpose of publication, and (3) general evidence regarding the quality of the data.

Learning Objective 5

State the most fundamental rule in using secondary data.
The most fundamental rule in using secondary data is to always use the primary source of secondary data.

Learning Objective 6

Explain the difference between internal and external data.
Internal data are those found within the organization for which the research is being done; external data are those obtained from outside sources.

Learning Objective 7

List some of the key sources researchers should consider in conducting a search process.
The key sources researchers should keep in mind in conducting a search process are reference librarians, associations, online computer searches, and general guides to useful marketing information.

KEY TERMS

secondary data (page 136)
primary data (page 136)
primary source (page 140)
secondary source (page 140)

advocacy research (page 142)
internal data (page 143)
external data (page 143)

REVIEW QUESTIONS

1.   What is the difference between primary and secondary data?

2.   What are the advantages and disadvantages of secondary data?

3.   What criteria can be used to judge the accuracy of secondary data?

4.   What is the difference between a primary source and a secondary source of secondary data? Which is preferred? Why?

5.   What distinguishes internal secondary data from external secondary data?

6.   How would you go about searching for secondary data on a particular topic?

7. How would you perform an online computer search? What types of information would you be hoping to find?

DISCUSSION QUESTIONS, PROBLEMS, AND PROJECTS

1. List some major secondary sources of information for the following situations:

   a. The marketing research manager of a national soft-drink manufacturer has to prepare a comprehensive report on the soft-drink industry.

   b. Mr. Baker has several ideas for instant cake mixes and is considering entering this industry. He needs to find the necessary background information to assess its potential.

   c. Mr. Adams has heard that the profit margins in the fur business are high. The fur industry has always intrigued him, and he decides to do some research to determine if the claim is true.

   d. A recent graduate hears that condominiums are the homes of the future. She decides to collect some information on the condominium market.

   e. Owning a grocery store has been Mrs. Smith's dream, and she finally decides to make it a reality. The first step she wishes to take is to collect information on the grocery business in her hometown.

2. For many years, Home Decorating Products had been a leading producer of paint and painting-related equipment such as brushes, rollers, turpentine, and so on. The company is now considering adding wallpaper to its line. At least initially, it did not intend to actually manufacture the wallpaper but, rather, to subcontract the manufacturing. Home Decorating Products would assume the distribution and marketing functions.

   Before adding wallpaper to its product line, however, Home Decorating secured some secondary data assessing the size of the wallpaper market. One mail survey made by a trade association showed that, on the average, families in the United States wallpapered two rooms in their homes each year. Among these families, 60% did it themselves. Another survey, which had also been done by mail but by one of the major home magazines, found that 70% of the subscribers answering the questionnaire had wallpapered one complete wall or more during the previous 12 months. Among these families, 80% had done the wallpapering themselves. Home Decorating Products thus has two sets of secondary data on the same problem, but the data are not consistent.

   Discuss the data in terms of the criteria one would use to determine which set, if either, is correct. Assume that you are forced to make the determination on the basis of this information. Which would you choose?

3. Assume that your school is interested in developing a marketing plan to boost sagging attendance at major athletic events, particularly home football games. As an initial step in developing the new marketing plan, the athletic department has decided that it needs demographic and lifestyle profiles of people who currently attend games on a regular (season-ticket) basis. Fortunately, the ticket office maintains a listing of all season-ticket purchasers (including names and addresses) from year to year. What potential sources of internal secondary data might the athletic department first investigate before considering the collection of primary data?

4. Using the current U.S. *Statistical Abstract*, answer the following questions:

   a. Which metropolitan statistical area in the United States has the largest population?

   b. What is the population of this metropolitan area?

   c. What is the estimated median age of the U.S. population?

   d. Complete the following table:

Marital Status of U.S. Population	Number (million)	Percent of Total
Total		
Never Married		
Married		
Widowed		
Divorced		

e. Complete the following table on school enrollment:

	18–19 years old	20–21 years old	25–29 years old
Number of Students			

f. Complete the following table:

Income Category	Number of Households
Under $10,000	
$10,000 to $14,999	
$15,000 to $24,999	
$25,000 to $34,999	
$35,000 to $49,999	
$50,000 to $74,999	
$75,000 and over	

g. What was the consumer price index for all items? What was the base year? What does that indicate?

5. The *Statistical Abstract* is a secondary source of secondary data. Because it is always better to use the primary source, start with the *Statistical Abstract* and identify the primary source for the following data.

a. The estimated median age of the U.S. population.

b. The height of males and females ages 20–29.

c. The consumer price indexes by major groups.

d. The manufacturing corporations' profits, stockholders' equity, sales, and debt ratios.

6. John Smith is interested in becoming a wholesaler in household appliances. He has collected some general information but requires your help in finding answers to the following questions:

a. What is the North American Industry Classification System (NAICS) code for household appliance manufacturers?

b. How many retail establishments sell household appliances in the United States?

c. What are the total sales of all the retail establishments?

Instead of attempting to handle all household appliances, John is considering specializing in household refrigerators and freezers.

d. What are the total number of establishments manufacturing household refrigerators and freezers?

e. How many wholesale establishments are there in the United States dealing in this category?

John thinks that Dayton, Ohio, would be a profitable place to locate. He needs to know the following:

f. What is the total population of Dayton?

g. What is the total civilian labor force in Dayton?

h. How many persons are employed in Dayton?

i. In what county is Dayton, Ohio, located? What is the total number of furniture and home furnishing stores within this county?

(*Hint:* To complete this exercise, refer to the *Economic Census: Manufacturing Sector; Retail Trade Sector; Wholesale Trade Sector;* and *County and City Databook.*)

7. Carefully read the information in Research Window 7.1 about how Arby's chooses new locations for its restaurants.

a. List the different sources or types of secondary information used in identifying potential locations.

b. Think carefully about the area in which you live. Using secondary sources, screen at least one potential location for an Arby's restaurant in your area. Can you find one or more locations that fit the criteria established by Arby's? Why or why not?

8. Assume that you have recently begun work as a researcher with a very large management consulting organization. One of your first assignments is to prepare a thorough profile of a specific industry based on secondary data. For a significant industry of your choosing, develop such a profile. Your report should contain industry information related to major products, largest producers, primary inputs on the supply side, NAICS codes, unions, trade magazines, and other information you feel is useful (including financial information). The information should be addressed to other businesspeople—not academics—and should be presented in a readable manner using a format similar to the following:

I. Executive Summary (including a synopsis of your opinion on the state of the industry along with the reasons for your opinion)

II. Major Industry Competitors (including financial information)

III. Major Industry Products (including export information)

IV. Primary Industry Inputs (including import information)

V. Human Resource/Labor Unions

VI. Ownership Trends

VII. Technology

VIII. Governmental Regulation

Include two special exhibits with your profile—a timeline showing important events in the history of the industry, especially during the past 10 years and a flowchart of a typical firm in the industry showing inputs, primary products, channels of distribution, major customers, and so on.

You are encouraged to use as many sources as possible, including financial databases, business periodicals, and government reports. Prepare a complete bibliography of all sources used in preparing your report. In addition, carefully identify all sources throughout your report, including sources for graphs and charts.

Secondary Data Sources

There is so much published secondary data that it is impossible to mention all of it in a single appendix. Thus, we present only a representative cross-section of the available material. These secondary sources are organized into six sections, according to the type of information they contain. Several sources of electronic online search services are included. First, however, we present a brief discussion of governmental sources of secondary data.

Census Data and Other Government Publications: Overview

The Bureau of the Census of the United States Department of Commerce is the largest gatherer of statistical information in the world. The original census was the Census of Population, which was required by the Constitution to serve as a basis for apportioning representation in the House of Representatives. The first censuses were merely head counts. Not only has the Census of Population been expanded, but the whole census machinery has also been enlarged. At this point, there are nine different censuses, all of which are of interest to the marketing researcher. Exhibit 7.1, for example, listed some of the most useful data on population and housing that are available in the Census of Population. Exhibit 7A.1 lists some of the most useful data that are collected in the various economic censuses shown in the following sections.

Industry Information

Almanac of Business and Industrial Financial Ratios (Englewood Cliffs, N.J.: Prentice Hall)

Business & Industry (Detroit: Gale Group)

Census of Agriculture (U.S. Department of Agriculture: National Agricultural Statistics Service, http://www.agcensus.usda.gov/)

Census of Governments (U.S. Bureau of the Census: Government Printing Office, http://www.census.gov/govs/www/cog2007.html)

Commodity Yearbook (New York: Commodity Research Bureau)

Economic Census (U.S. Bureau of the Census: Government Printing Office, http://www.census.gov/econ/census07) Some of the more important sectors are: Construction, Manufacturing, Mining, Retail Trade, Transportation and Warehousing, and Wholesale Trade.

Guide to Industrial Statistics (Washington, D.C.: U.S. Bureau of the Census)

Industry Norms and Key Business Ratios (Murray Hill, N.J.: Dun & Bradstreet)

Information, Finance and Services USA: Industry Analyses, Statistics, and Leading Organizations (Detroit: Gale Group)

Manufacturing and Distribution USA: Industry Analyses, Statistics, and Leading Companies (Detroit: Gale Group)

Mergent's Industry Review (New York: Mergent FIS)

North American Industry Classification System (NAICS) (Washington, D.C., Executive Office of the President, Office of Management and Budget, http://www.census.gov/eos/www/naics/)

Predicast's Overview of Markets and Technology (PROMT) (Detroit: Thompson Gale)

RMA Annual Statement Studies (Philadelphia: The Risk Management Association)

Standard & Poor's Industry Surveys (New York: Standard & Poor's Corp.)

Standard Industrial Classification Manual (Springfield, Va.: Office of Management and Budget, National Technical Information Service) The SIC system was used for federal economic statistics classified by industry but is being replaced with the *North American Industrial Classification System (NAICS)*.

Company Information

Companies and Their Brands, 18th ed. (Detroit: Gale Group)

Corporate Affiliations (New Providence, N.J.: LexisNexis)

Dun & Bradstreet Regional Business Directory (Bethlehem, Pa.: Dun & Bradstreet, Inc.)

Fortune 500 Directory (New York: CNNMoney.com, http://money.cnn.com/magazines/fortune/fortune500/2008/index.html)

Hoover's Handbook of American Business (Austin, Tex.: Hoover's Business Press, Some information is available at no cost at http://www.hoovers.com/free/)

How to Find Information About Companies (Washington, D.C.: Washington Researchers, 1999)

International Directory of Company Histories (Chicago: St. James Press)

Mergent's Manuals (New York: Mergent)

Million Dollar Databases (New York: Dun & Bradstreet, http://www.dnbmdd.com/mddi)

	Manufacturing	Mining	Construction	Retail Trade	Wholesale Trade	Management of Companies	All Other Sectors
Number of establishments and firms							
Establishments with payroll	A, Z	S	S	A, Z	A	A	A, Z
Establishments without payroll (nonemployers)			S	S			S
Single-unit and multiunit establishments	N	N	N	N	N	N	N
Establishments by legal form of organization	N	N	N	N	N	N	N
Firms	N	N		N	N	N	N
Employment							
All employees	A	S	S	A	A	A	A
Production (construction) workers/hours	A	S	S				
Employment size of establishment	A, Z	N	S	N, Z	N	N	N, Z
Labor costs							
Payroll, entire year	A	S	S	S	A	A	A
Payroll, first quarter				A	A	A	A
Worker wages	A	S	S				
Supplemental costs	S	S	S	e	e	e	e
Cost of contract labor				e	e	e	e
Sales, receipts, or value of shipments/construction work done							
Establishments with payroll	A	S	S	A	A	A	A
By specific product, line, or type of construction	S	S	S	M	M		S
Sales/receipts size of establishments			S	N, Z	N		N, Z
Class of customer				N	N		N
Type of structure			N				
E-commerce sales	S	S	S	S	S		S
Expenses							
Total				e	N		N
Cost of materials, parts, etc.	A	S	S	e	e	e	
Cost of fuels	S	S	S	e	e	e	e
Energy consumed	S	S					
Cost of electricity	S	S	S	e	e	e	e
Cost of other utilities				e	e	e	e
Products bought for resale	S	S		e	e		
Taxes and license fees				e	e	e	e
Cost of office supplies				e	e		e
Depreciation charges	S	S		e	e	e	E
Commission expense					e		

(Continued)

	Manufacturing	Mining	Construction	Retail Trade	Wholesale Trade	Management of Companies	All Other Sectors
Purchased services:							
Advertising	N			e	e	e	e
Rental payments	S	S	S	e	e	e	e
Legal services	N			e	e	e	e
Accounting services	N			e	e	e	e
Data processing services	N			e	e	e	e
Refuse removal	N						
Communications services	N	S	S	e	e	e	e
Purchased repairs	N		S	e	e	e	e
Cost of contract work	S	S			e		
Assets, capital expenditures, inventories							
Capital expenditures, total	S	S	S				
Depreciable assets, gross value	S	S	S				
Value of inventories	S	S	S	e	A		

Sources: Downloaded from the U.S. Census Bureau Web site, http://www.census.gov/epcd/ec02/g02items.htm, September 13, 2008.
Legend: A – All areas except ZIP Codes; Z – ZIP Codes and States; M- MA's, states, and National; S – States and National; N – National only; e – National data only in Business Expenses

Standard & Poor's Corporation Records (New York: Standard & Poor's Corp.)

Standard & Poor's Register of Corporations, Directors and Executives (New York: Standard & Poor's Corp.)

Thomas Food and Beverage Market Place (Millerton, N.Y.: Grey House Publishing Co.)

Thomas Register of American Manufacturers and Thomas Register Catalog File (New York: Thomas Publishing Co.)

Value Line Investment Survey [New York: Value Line Publishing, http://www.valueline.com (for subscribers)].

Market and Consumer Information

Aging America—Trends and Projections (U.S. Senate Special Committee on Aging and the American Association of Retired Persons: Government Printing Office)

Census of Housing (U.S. Bureau of the Census: Government Printing Office, http://www.census.gov/hhes/www/housing.html)

Census of Population (U.S. Bureau of the Census: Government Printing Office, http://www.census.gov/main/www/cen2000.html)

County and City Databook (U.S. Bureau of the Census: Government Printing Office, http://www.census.gov/prod/www/ccdb.html)

County Business Patterns (U.S. Department of Commerce: Government Printing Office, http://www.census.gov/epcd/cbp/view/cbpview.html)

Data Sources for Business and Market Analysis, 4th ed., ed. John Ganly (Metuchen, N.J.: Scarecrow Press, 1994)

Editor and Publisher Market Guide (New York: Editor and Publisher Co.)

A Guide to Consumer Markets (New York: The Conference Board)

The Insider's Guide to Demographic Know-How (Chicago: Probus Publishing Co.)

International Marketing Handbook (Detroit: Gale Research)

Journal of Consumer Research (Chicago: The University of Chicago Press)

Rand McNally Commercial Atlas and Marketing Guide (Chicago: Rand McNally Company)

State and Metropolitan Area Data Book (U.S. Department of Commerce: Government Printing Office, http://www.census.gov/statab/www/smadb.html)

Survey of Buying Power and Media Markets (New York: Sales and Marketing Management)

General Economic and Statistical Information

Business Statistics (U.S. Department of Commerce: Government Printing Office)

Economic Indicators (Council of Economic Advisers: Government Printing Office, http://www.economicindicators.gov)

Economic Report of the President (U.S. Government: Government Printing Office, http://www.gpoaccess.gov/eop)

Federal Reserve Bulletin (Washington, D.C.: Federal Reserve System Board of Governors, http://www.federalreserve.gov/pubs/bulletin/default.htm)

Historical Statistics of the United States from Colonial Times to 1970 (U.S. Bureau of the Census: Government Printing Office)

Monthly Labor Review (U.S. Bureau of Labor Statistics: Government Printing Office, http://www.bls.gov/opub/mlr)

Standard & Poor's Statistical Service (New York: Standard & Poor's Corp.)

Statistical Abstract of the United States (U.S. Bureau of the Census: Government Printing Office, http://www.census.gov/compendia/statab/)

Statistics of Income (Internal Revenue Service: Government Printing Office, http://www.census.gov/hhes/www/income/income.html)

Survey of Current Business (U.S. Bureau of Economic Analysis: Government Printing Office, http://www.bea.gov/scb/date_guide.asp)

United Nations Statistical Yearbook (New York: United Nations)

World Almanac and Book of Facts (New York: Press Publishing Co.)

General Guides to Business Information

American Marketing Association Bibliography Series (Chicago: American Marketing Association)

Business A to Z Source Finder (Annapolis, Md.: Beacon Bay Press)

Business Information: How to Find It, How to Use It, 2d ed., ed. Michael R. Lavin (Phoenix, Ariz.: Oryx Press, 1992)

Business Information Sources, 3d ed., ed. Lorna M. Daniells (Berkeley: University of California Press, 1993)

Census Catalog and Guide (U.S. Bureau of the Census: Government Printing Office, http://www.census.gov/prod/www/abs/catalogs.html)

Encyclopedia of Business Information Sources, 16th ed. (Detroit: Gale Research, 2002)

The Federal Data Base Finder (Potomac, Md.: Information USA Inc.)

Finding Answers in U.S. Census Records (Orem, Utah: Ancestry Publishing)

Guide to American and International Directories, 15th ed. (Nyack, N.Y.: Todd Publications, 2002)

Guide to Foreign Trade Statistics (Washington, D.C.: U.S. Bureau of the Census, 1999, http://www.census.gov/foreign-trade/guide/sec2.html)

A Handbook for Business on the Use of Government Statistics (Charlottesville, Va.: Tayloe Murphy Institute)

Statistics Sources, 25th ed., ed. Jacqueline Wasserman O'Brien et al. (Detroit: Gale Group, 2001)

A User's Guide to BEA Information (U.S. Bureau of Economic Analysis: Government Printing Office)

Indexes

ABI/Inform (Ann Arbor, Mich.: UMI)

American Statistics Index (Washington, D.C.: Congressional Information Service)

Business Index (Foster City, Calif.: Information Access Company)

Business Periodicals Index (Bronx, N.Y.: The H. W. Wilson Company)

Communication Abstracts (Thousand Oaks, Calif.: Sage Publications)

Dissertation Abstracts International (Ann Arbor, Mich.: University Microfilms International)

Index to International Statistics (Washington, D.C.: Congressional Information Service)

Journal of Marketing, "Marketing Literature Review" (Chicago: American Marketing Association)

Social Sciences Citation Index (Philadelphia: Institute for Scientific Information)

Statistical Reference Index (Washington, D.C.: Congressional Information Service)

The Wall Street Journal Index (New York: Dow Jones)

Specialized Directories

The Advertising Red Books: Advertisers (New Providence, N.J.: LexisNexis Group)

The Advertising Red Books: Agencies (New Providence, N.J.: LexisNexis Group)

American Business Locations Directory (Detroit: Gale Group)

Business Organizations, Agencies, and Publications Directory, 16th ed. (Detroit: Gale Group, 2004)

Consultants and Consulting Organizations Directory, 24th ed. (Detroit: Gale Research, 2001)

Directories in Print, 21st ed. (Detroit: Gale Research, 2001)

Encyclopedia of Associations (Detroit: Gale Group)

FINDEX, The Directory of Market Research Reports, Studies and Surveys (Bethesda, Md.:

Cambridge Information Group, http://www.market research.com)

Gale Directory of Databases (Detroit: Gale Research)

The Green Book (New York: American Marketing Association, New York Chapter)

Hoover's Masterlist of Major U.S. Companies (Austin, Tex.: Hoover's Business Press)

Information Industry Directory (Detroit: Gale Research)

Standardized Marketing Information Services

Learning Objectives

1. List three common uses of the information supplied by standardized marketing information services.
2. Define *geodemography.*
3. Describe the operation of a diary panel.
4. Describe the operation of store audits.
5. Define *UPC.*
6. Define *single-source measurement.*
7. Discuss the purpose and operation of people meters.

Introduction

The many standardized marketing information services that are available are important sources of secondary data for the marketing researcher. These commercial services are more expensive than using published information, but they are usually much less expensive than collecting primary data. Suppliers of these data sell them to multiple companies, allowing the costs of collecting, editing, coding, and analyzing them to be shared. Because multiple companies must be able to use the data, however, the data to be collected—and how they are to be collected—must be standardized. As a result, such data may not always be a perfect fit for a company. This is the primary disadvantage of standardized marketing information. This chapter describes some of the main types and sources of standardized marketing information service data.

PROFILING CUSTOMERS

Learning Objective

1. List three common uses of the information supplied by standardized marketing information services.

Market segmentation is common among businesses seeking to improve their marketing efforts. Effective segmentation demands that firms group their customers into relatively homogeneous groups. That enables them to tailor marketing programs to the individual groups, thereby making the programs more effective. A common segmentation base for firms selling industrial goods takes into account the industry designation or designations of its customers, most typically by means of the North American Industry Classification System (NAICS) codes. The NAICS codes are a system developed by the U.S. Bureau of the Census for organizing the reporting of business information, such as employment, value added in manufacturing, capital expenditures, and total sales. These codes are used by federal statistical agencies as a replacement of the Standard Industrial Classification (SIC) system. In both systems, major industry sectors are given a two-digit code number, and the types of businesses making up the industry are given additional digits. Exhibit 8.1 demonstrates how a U.S. industry is coded using the NAICS system.

Learning Objective

2. Define *geodemography*.

One of the commercial services that is especially popular among industrial goods and service suppliers is the Dun & Bradstreet International Business Locator, an index that provides basic data on over 28 million public and private companies worldwide. These records allow sales management to construct sales prospect files, define sales territories and measure territory potentials, and isolate potential new customers with particular characteristics. They allow advertising management to select potential customers by size and location; to analyze and select the media to reach them; to build, maintain, and structure current mailing lists; to generate sales leads qualified by size, location, and quality; and to locate new markets for testing. Finally, they allow marketing research professionals to assess market potential by territory, to measure market penetration in terms of numbers of prospects and numbers of customers, and to make comparative analyses of overall performance by districts and sales territories and in individual industries.

Firms selling consumer goods don't normally target individual customers, because no single customer is likely to buy much of any product or service. Rather, firms need to target groups of customers. Their ability to do this has increased substantially since the 1970 census, which was the first electronic census. Since that time, the Census Bureau has made available computer tapes of the facts that have been gathered and, more recently, CD and online formats, which make the data easily usable. Having the data available in electronic form allows them to be analyzed by arbitrary geographic boundaries, and an entire industry has developed to take advantage of this capability. The **geodemographers**, as they are typically called, combine census data with their own survey data or data that they gather from administrative records such as motor vehicle registrations or credit transactions, to produce customized products for their clients.

geodemography
The availability of demographic, consumer-behavior, and lifestyle data by arbitrary geographic boundaries that are typically quite small.

Exhibit 8.1

NAICS Hierarchy and Codes

Level	Code	Title
Sector	31–33	Manufacturing
Subsector	334	Computer and Electronic Product Manufacturing
Industry Group	3346	Manufacturing and Reproducing of Magnetic and Optical Media
Industry	33461	Manufacturing and Reproduction of Magnetic and Optical Media
U.S. Industry	334612	Prerecorded Compact Disc (except Software), Tape, and Record Reproducing
Product Class	3346120	Reproduction of Recording Media

Mapping software, often called a geographic information system (GIS), combines various kinds of demographic data with geographic information on maps. The user can draw a map showing average income levels of a county and then zoom closer to look at particular towns in more detail. Most GIS programs on the market can show information as detailed as a single block; some programs can show individual buildings. Seeing the information on a map can be more useful than merely reading tables of numbers.

Chase Manhattan Bank used GIS analysis to determine that only two-thirds of one branch's customers lived in its trade area, with the other customers working in the area but living elsewhere. Further analysis indicated that many of the customers who lived out of the area worked at nearby medical centers and that, as a group, the remote customers might represent more than a half billion dollars in potential deposits. They also discovered that a competing bank was actually in a better location to attract this potential business. Based on the GIS analysis, Chase was able to identify options for relocating the existing branch.[1]

GISs once required mainframe computers and were quite expensive, but today's applications are usually off-the-shelf programs that can run on personal computers and can be very inexpensive. Many GIS packages are now available, including BusinessMAP (from ESRI), GeoMedia (Intergraph), Maptitude (Caliper Corporation), MapInfo (Pitney Bowes), and MapLinx (Linxoft Solutions).

Another thing that geodemographers do is regularly update the census data through statistical extrapolation. The data can consequently be used with much more confidence during the years between the censuses. Another value-added feature that has had a great deal to do with the success of the industry has been the analysis performed on the census data. Firms supplying geodemographic information have cluster-analyzed the census-produced data to produce "homogeneous groups" that describe the American population. Figure 8.1 shows the results of some of these data.

For example, Nielsen Claritas (the first firm to do this and still one of the leaders in the industry as a member of the Nielsen Company) uses hundreds of demographic variables in its PRIZM (Potential Ratings for Zip Markets) system when classifying residential neighborhoods. This system breaks down over 250,000 neighborhood areas in the United States into 66 types based on consumer behavior and lifestyle. Each of the types has a name that theoretically describes the type of people living there, such as Upward Bound, Boomtown Singles, Money and Brains, and Gray Power.

MEASURING PRODUCT SALES AND MARKET SHARE

Firms need to have an accurate assessment of how they are doing if they are to succeed in an increasingly competitive environment. One way to accomplish this is to review internal records and determine how much they have sold into the channel of distribution (that is, wholesalers, distributors, retailers, and the like). Knowing how much product has been shipped to wholesalers and retailers doesn't provide a timely understanding of how the product is doing with consumers, however. In addition, simply totaling sales invoices provides no information at all about how a company's product is doing relative to products from other companies. Historically, there are several ways of measuring sales to final consumers, including the use of diary panels of households and the measurement of sales at the store level.

FIGURE 8.1	Sample Median Household Income Demographic Data

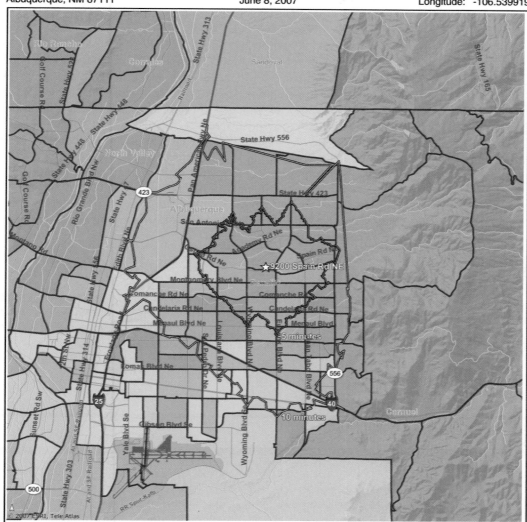

2007 Median Household Income by Census Tract

9200 Spain Rd NE
Albuquerque, NM 87111

Sample
June 8, 2007

Latitude: 35.138763
Longitude: -106.539919

2007 Median Household Income by Census Tract

- $0 - $32,000
- $32,001 - $38,000
- $38,001 - $44,500
- $44,501 - $55,200
- $55,201 - $500,001

About Your Map...

This map shows 2007 Median Household Income by Census Tract.

Source: http://www.esri.com/software/bao-us/pdfs/onlinethematic_map.pdf downloaded on December 20, 2008.

Learning Objective

3.   Describe the operation of a diary panel.

(Online) Diary Panels

Diary panels are an important source of information about products purchased by households. Whether recorded on paper or reported online, the key feature of a diary panel is that a representative group of individuals or households keeps track of purchases made or products consumed over a given period of time. In this way, purchasing and/or consumption behavior can be extrapolated to the larger population.

The NPD Group tracks a number of food-related trends in the United States. For example, the National Eating Trends (NET) service has operated a household diary panel since 1980. Participants keep a record of all food and drink consumed by all household members for a period of two weeks. Participation is spread across a one-year period, with about 50 households beginning the recording process each week. During the two-week period, respondents are asked to record the name and brand of all food and drink products consumed by all members of the household. At the end of each day, respondents report that day's food consumption back to the NPD Group's offices, where they are collected and analyzed. The panel is demographically balanced, reflecting U.S. Census Bureau statistics.[2]

The NPD Group also offers results from a large online consumer panel. The panel offers access to more than 3 million adults and teens who have agreed to respond to surveys and to provide information on purchasing behavior. Ongoing tracking services are provided for a variety of product categories, ranging from automotive to fashion to toys.[3]

Learning Objective

4.   Describe the operation of store audits.

Store Audits

Another way to assess product sales and market share is to work with retailers, rather than a panel of consumers, to get the data. In working with retailers, there are two basic approaches, store audits and scanners; each involves an actual physical count of products being sold. Scanners reflect the new way, store audits, the old. The vast

MANAGER'S FOCUS

Although the fees for standardized marketing information services are lower than the costs of conducting customized marketing research, they can still represent a significant financial investment for your organization. Therefore, it is important to carefully evaluate the likely usefulness of any standardized information before purchasing it. The steps for defining a marketing problem are as pertinent to assessing the relevance of standardized marketing information services as they are to designing a primary marketing research study. A key distinction here, however, is that the provider of standardized information services will not guide you through the problem formulation process. Learning to navigate the problem formulation steps yourself is one reason this book should be relevant to you as a manager.

Some standardized information services are available on a subscription basis. You may find yourself, therefore, in situations where your organization already purchases certain types of standardized marketing information on an ongoing basis. In such circumstances, it is a good idea to periodically *audit* the degree to which your organization actually uses the information it is receiving. This review may reveal how your organization is not taking advantage of its resources, which may prompt you to better utilize the standardized marketing information you already have. The audit might also lead you to conclude the information is unnecessary. Once again, if you have carefully defined the marketing problems you are facing, you will be in a good position to determine whether subscriptions to standardized marketing information services should be continued or terminated.

majority of consumer products in the United States are now tracked via scanner. However, audits are still used in some U.S. stores and in stores in many international markets.

Here's how a store audit works. The research firm sends field workers, called auditors, to a select group of retail stores at fixed intervals. On each visit, the auditors take a complete inventory of all products designated for the audit. The auditors also note the merchandise moving into the store by checking wholesale invoices, warehouse withdrawal records, and direct shipments from manufacturers. Sales to consumers are then determined by the following calculation:

> Beginning inventory
>
> + Net purchases (from wholesalers and manufacturers)
>
> − Ending inventory
>
> = Sales

The store audit was pioneered by ACNielsen and served as the backbone of the Nielsen Retail Index for many years. The method is still used to measure sales in situations where it may not be possible to rely on scanner data, for whatever reason. For example, most convenience stores do not scan products at the point of sale. ACNielsen offers its Convenience Track service, assessing product sales through convenience stores in 30 local markets. Products audited include soft drinks, gum, candy, tobacco products, and other products often sold through this channel. The company takes the auditing records and generates information for each brand of each of the products audited. This information is then available for purchase.[4]

Scanners

Learning Objective

5. Define *UPC*.

Since the late 1970s, ACNielsen has been replacing its Retail Index service with its SCANTRACK service. The SCANTRACK service emerged from the revolutionary development in the grocery industry brought about by the installation of scanning equipment to read Universal Product Codes (UPCs). Universal Product Codes are 12-digit numbers imprinted on products themselves or on tags attached to the products. In general, the first six digits identify the manufacturer, and the next five a particular product of the manufacturer, be it a different size, variety, or flavor. See Figure 8.2.

There is a unique 12-digit code for each product.[5] As the bar code is read by a fixed or handheld **scanner**, the scanner identifies the 12-digit number, looks up the price in the attached computer, and immediately prints the description and price of the item on the cash register receipt. At the same time, the computer can keep track of the movement of every item that is scanned.

Scanners are now so pervasive that the majority of retail sales information today is based on scanner data. Using either a sample of stores to represent a channel or a census of all stores to represent a retail organization, scanner data are available across multiple outlets, including grocery, mass merchant, drug, special warehouse clubs, and selected convenience stores (though, as we noted above, store audits are necessary with many convenience stores). Where scanning is available, weekly sales (units sold at what price) are collected from a retailer's system. ACNielsen takes these data and matches the UPC to a description to make the information more useful (for example, share of category, full fat versus low fat). In addition, other data sources can be combined with this information.

For example, causal data are collected to help explain the "causes" of changes in sales. Causal data include:

scanner
An electronic device that automatically reads the Universal Product Code imprinted on a product, looks up the price in an attached computer, and instantly prints the description and price of the item on the cash register receipt.

- Display information—stores are audited and items on display are recorded.

- Feature information—features are collected and coded to identify items being advertised.

- Price changes—the system identifies changes via comparisons to historical prices.

FIGURE 8.2

Behind the Bars: The Technology of a Bar Code

Since the introduction of the Universal Product Code (UPC) over 30 years ago, the symbology has allowed supermarkets to control their inventory more efficiently, automate the task of reordering stock, provide a faster and more accurate checkout for customers, and gather information for accurate and immediate market analysis. But when you get down to the bare bars, how exactly does the bar code work?

A UPC bar code symbol consists of patterns of black vertical bars with white spaces and numbers at the bottom of the symbol. Together these bars make up the symbology of the code. Beneath these bars is a series of numbers called a standard. The thickness of the bars and the distance between them define the numbers contained in the bar code.

A set of two black bars appear at the beginning, middle, and end of the symbology and are called guard patterns. These patterns provide start-and-stop signals to tell a scanner where it is reading within the code.

The three parts that make up the bar code number are:

- *UCC Company Prefix*—the number that identifies a company, assigned and licensed by the UCC (in the example, the UCC Company Prefix is *614141*).
- *Item Reference Number*—the number that identifies a company's individual products, assigned by the company (in the example, the Item Reference Number is *00179*).
- *Check Digit*—a digit calculated from the UCC Company Prefix and Item Reference Number, used to ensure uniqueness of the number (in the example, the check digit is the *8* to the far right).

UCC Company Prefix and Item Reference

Check Digit

Source: Adapted and excerpted from http://www.uc-council.org/pdf/2003_UCC_Press_Kit.pdf, October 6, 2008.

Learning Objective

6. Define *single-source measurement*.

single-source data
Data that allow researchers to link together purchase behavior, household characteristics, and advertising exposure at the household level.

By combining the retail sales and causal data, the effectiveness of various marketing actions can be assessed. This is accomplished by estimating what "base" sales would have been without the presence of the action. The data allow clients to evaluate the effectiveness of short-term promotions, evaluate pricing changes, follow new product introductions, and monitor unexpected events such as product recalls and shortages.

The effect of scanners on the collection of sales and market share data has been profound. Scanners can also be used to link purchase behavior with demographic information. Before scanners were available, the link was usually made using diaries that are still used effectively. A problem with diaries, however, is that they depend for their accuracy on the conscientiousness of those in the panel to record their purchases as they occur. Scanner data are not subject to such recording biases. Several firms, including Information Resources, Inc. (IRI) and ACNielsen, use scanners and consumer panels to link purchase behavior to particular households. Some systems take it a step further and measure or control media exposure in these households. Combining all of these data sources at the household level produces what has become known as **single-source data**.

British Sky Broadcasting (BSkyB), a major satellite television company in Great Britain, has teamed up with TNS Media Intelligence in an effort to track satellite customer exposure to interactive advertising and gauge its influence on customer purchasing behavior. To accomplish this, some of the BSkyB customers will be participants on TNS panels, enabling advertising exposure to be matched with household demographics and purchasing behavior. According to Robert Leach, head of interactive services at BSkyB: "We will be able to say that this person saw the ad for Knorr Soup, they interacted with it for 10 minutes, they went to the shop and bought this many packets when prior to [watching the ad] they only bought this many packets. You will start to get real single-source data back, which will be useful in measuring effectiveness but also in terms of targeting advertising."[6]

ACNielsen's system is designed to measure natural consumer behavior as well as test the effects of different promotions or advertising. Its Homescan Panel service maintains a panel of 125,000 participating households whose purchases are measured using a handheld scanner they use to scan the UPC codes on products brought into the house. The electronic unit then asks them a number of questions such as where the purchase was made, age and sex of the shopper, and price paid.[7]

Although single-source measurement offers the opportunity for new market insights, firms subscribing to these services need to prepare themselves for the incredible amounts of data they produce. Without proper planning, firms can literally drown in these data. That is why decision support systems for analyzing data (particularly expert systems) are becoming increasingly important in marketing research.

MEASURING ADVERTISING EXPOSURE AND EFFECTIVENESS

Learning Objective

7. Discuss the purpose and operation of people meters.

Another area in which there is a great deal of commercial information available for marketers relates to the assessment of exposure to, and effectiveness of, advertising. Most suppliers of industrial goods advertise most heavily in trade publications. To sell space more effectively, the various trade publications typically sponsor readership studies that they make available to potential advertisers. Suppliers of consumer goods and services also have access to media-sponsored readership studies. In addition, a number of services have evolved to measure consumer exposure to the various media.

Television and Radio

The Nielsen television ratings produced by Nielsen Media Research are probably the most familiar form of media research to most people. Almost everyone has heard of the Nielsen ratings and their impact on which television shows are canceled by the networks and which are allowed to continue. The ratings themselves are designed to provide estimates of the size and nature of the audience for individual television programs.

Data needed to compute the Nielsen ratings are gathered in a variety of ways. **People meters** attempt to measure not only the channel to which a set is tuned, but also who in the household is watching. Each member of the family has his or her own viewing number. Whoever turns on the set, sits down to watch, or changes the channel is supposed to enter his or her number into the people meter. All of this information is transmitted to a central computer for processing. In addition, Nielsen supplements people meter data with information collected using simple electronic meters that record what channels are being watched (but nothing about who is watching), consumer diaries, and telephone interviews.

people meter
A device used to measure when a television is on, to what channel it is tuned, and who in the household is watching it.

Through the data provided by these basic records, Nielsen develops estimates of the number and percentage of all television households viewing a given television show. Nielsen also breaks down these aggregate ratings by numerous socioeconomic and demographic characteristics, including territory, education of head of house, household income, occupation of head of house, household size, and so on. These

breakdowns assist the television networks in selling advertising on particular programs, while they assist the advertiser in choosing programs that reach households with the desired characteristics. Research Window 8.1 provides a more detailed overview of how Nielsen produces its television ratings.

Advertisers buying radio time are also interested in the size and demographic composition of the audiences they will be reaching. Radio-listening statistics are typically gathered using diaries that are placed in a panel of households. Arbitron, for example, generates telephone numbers randomly to ensure that it is reaching households with unlisted numbers and sends diaries to household members who agree to participate. Most radio markets are rated only once or twice a year, although some of the

research window 8.1

Behind the Nielsen TV Ratings

Clients use Nielsen Media Research's television audience research information to buy and sell television time as well as to make program decisions. That information is the currency in all the transactions between buyers and sellers, which adds up to more than $60 billion in national and local advertising spending in the United States each year.

In the United States, the National People Meter service provides audience estimates for all national program sources, including broadcast networks, cable networks, Spanish language networks, and national syndicators. Local ratings estimates are produced for television stations, regional cable networks, MSOs, cable interconnects, and Spanish language stations in each of the 210 television markets in the United States, including electronic metered service in 56 markets.

How the Data Are Collected

National Measurement The heart of the Nielsen Media Research national ratings service in the United States is an electronic measurement system called the Nielsen people meter. These meters are placed in a sample of 9,000 households in the United States, randomly selected and recruited by Nielsen Media Research. The people meter is placed on each TV set in the sample household. The meter measures two things—what program or channel is being tuned and who is watching.

Which TV source (broadcast, cable, etc.) is being watched in the sample homes is continually recorded by one part of the meter that has been calibrated to identify which station, network, or satellite is carried on each channel in the home. Channel changes are electronically monitored by the meter.

Who is watching is measured by another portion of the Nielsen people meter that uses an electronic "box" at each TV set in the home and accompanying remote control units. Each family member in the sample household is assigned a personal viewing button (identified by name or symbol) on the people meter. Whenever the television set is turned on, a red light flashes from time to time on the meter, reminding viewers to press their assigned button to indicate if they are watching television.

Local Measurement In 56 of the largest markets in the United States, a different metering system provides TV ratings information on a daily basis. This information is used by local television stations, local cable systems, advertisers, and their agencies to make programming decisions as well as to buy and sell commercial advertising. In each of these markets, approximately 400 to 500 households are recruited, and electronic meters are attached to each TV set in the sample home. Homes recruited for local samples are not equipped with people meters, so the information is limited to "set tuning" information from which Nielsen Media Research can determine which channel the TV set is tuned.

larger ones are rated four times a year. The April/May survey is conducted in every Arbitron market and consequently is known as the "sweeps" period. Radio ratings are typically broken down by age and sex and focus more on individual than household behavior, in contrast with television ratings.

Arbitron has also introduced a portable people meter, or PPM, which is in use in several countries. The PPM is a pager-sized device to be carried by consumers. The devices sense inaudible codes embedded into programming by radio and television broadcasters (including cable TV) so that an accurate record can be made of actual exposure to media. The PPMs are even equipped with a motion sensor to verify that the device has been moved (and presumably carried by the respondent), a basic requirement for proper use. Each night, the participants recharge the unit in a base station that also automatically sends the data collected during the day back to a central computer for processing.[8]

Diary measurement is used to collect viewing information from sample homes in every one of the *210 television markets in the United States* in November, February, May and July of each year. These measurement periods are known in the industry as *"the sweeps."* This local viewing information provides a basis for advertising decisions and program scheduling.

How the Data Are Processed

Household tuning data from both the national and local metered samples for each day are stored in the in-home metering system until they are automatically retrieved by Nielsen Media Research's computers each night. Data include when the set is turned on; which channel is tuned; when the channel is changed; when the set is off; and, for the people meter households, who is viewing, and when that person's viewing starts and stops.

Nielsen Media Research's Operations Center in Dunedin, Florida, processes this information each night for release to the television industry the next day. To comprehend the dimension of the task, consider that Nielsen Media Research collects information from approximately 25,000 households starting about 3 a.m. each day, processes approximately 10 million viewing minutes each day, and has more than 4,000 gigabytes of data available for customer access the next day.

© MATJAZ BONCINA/ISTOCKPHOTO

Source: Excerpted from "About Nielsen Media Research" and "Inside TV Ratings," downloaded from http://www .nielsenmedia.com, October 6, 2008.

Print Media

There are several services that measure exposure to, and readership of, print media. For example, the Starch Ad Readership program measures the effectiveness of magazine advertisements. Many thousands of advertisements in hundreds of individual issues are assessed each year. For each magazine issue, respondents are asked to indicate whether they have read each ad. Four degrees of reading are recorded:

1. **Noted**—a person who remembered seeing any part of the advertisement in that particular issue.

2. **Associated**—a person who not only noted the advertisement but also saw the advertiser's name.

3. **Read Some**—a person who read any of the advertising copy.

4. **Read Most**—a person who read more than half of the advertising copy.

During the course of the interview, respondents also offer comments on the advertisements themselves as well as the brands featured in them.

Starch Readership Reports provide insights into readership for the ads; they also attempt to gauge reader interest and reactions to the editorial content and advertising in the magazine. An important feature of the reports is the ability to compare readership scores for a particular ad against (a) the other ads in the issue, and (b) ads of similar size, color, and product category. These features of Starch scores help make them effective in assessing changes in theme, copy, layout, use of color, and so on.[9]

Internet

Advertisers also need information about consumers' online activities. It is relatively easy to count the number of times that a site or banner ad has been accessed, along with revenues from online transactions. As with other forms of media, however, it is a little more complicated to determine the demographics of those accessing a Web site—and this is important for decisions about which Web sites to choose for advertising purposes. Nielsen/NetRatings offers its audience measurement service NetView, a syndicated service that assesses Internet usage at work and at home.

Regular reports detail a site's audience size and composition, time spent at the site, and so on. Exhibit 8.2 lists the top 10 Internet brands based on the number of different Internet users who visited the brand's site(s) during a recent one-month period. For example, the top brand, Google, was visited by over 120 million people during the time period. Users spent over three hours at second place Yahoo! sites on average over the course of the month.

WebTrends is recognizing the growing use of video online and has produced a new tracking system to assess visitor patterns for Web sites using video regardless of media format. WebTrends Analytics generates real-time insights into online video use and tracks daily viewing trends, including exit points from the video to other Web destinations.

One final area of Internet-oriented measurement is in the media consumption over cellular phones. Nielsen Wireless recognizes the growing trends in mobile entertainment and advertising. Mobile phones are not only used for making calls, but are also increasingly being used to surf the Web and watch video clips. As such, Nielsen Wireless will track how people use mobile Internet (both the Web and e-mail), view videos, and make purchases like ring tones.

Exhibit 8.2

Top Ten Web Sites by Brand, June 2008

Brand	Unique Audience (000)	Time per Person (hh:mm:ss)
1. Google	120,496	1:17:09
2. Yahoo!	113,187	3:06:57
3. MSN/Windows Live	99,747	2:05:25
4. Microsoft	93,786	0:40:11
5. AOL Media Network	91,167	3:35:11
6. YouTube	71,398	0:55:59
7. Fox Interactive Media	70,039	2:04:36
8. Wikipedia	52,747	0:21:01
9. eBay	52,509	1:51:34
10. Apple	49,911	1:08:33

Source: "Nielsen Online Reports Topline U.S. Data for June 2008," press release (July 14, 2008), downloaded from the Nielsen Online Web site, http://www.nielsen-online.com, August 5, 2008.

Multimedia Services

Experian Consumer Research (formerly Simmons Market Research) uses a national probability sample of about 25,000 adult respondents (plus children in the randomly selected households) and serves as a comprehensive data source allowing the cross-referencing of product usage and media exposure through its National Consumer Survey. Using stratified sampling, Experian recruits at the household level for participation. Those agreeing to participate are sent a household survey booklet that collects information about household usage of an extensive list of products and services. In addition, each member of the household is sent a personal survey booklet that collects extensive media usage measures as well as personal information on demographics and

MANAGER'S FOCUS

Because the providers of standardized marketing information services present themselves as experts in specific fields and can legitimately claim that other organizations are already purchasing their services, it would be easy for you as a manager to conclude that the information they provide is of high quality. This is not necessarily the case, especially since the criteria for determining quality and appropriateness differ across marketing situations.

Remember, the providers of standardized marketing information services do not collect data specifically for your organization. Representatives of these information suppliers have—at best—a limited understanding of your unique marketing problems and corresponding marketing intelligence needs. As a result, the burden is on you to evaluate the quality of standardized marketing information before purchasing it.

Standardized marketing information services are nothing more than commercial sources of secondary data. Researchers should feel free to ask a variety of important questions to help evaluate the quality of standardized marketing information (secondary data). These questions will help you assess the extent to which the information (a) fits your specific needs and (b) is accurate.

Evaluating the accuracy of secondary data includes an assessment of what is called "the general evidence of quality." This involves a careful review of the ability of the secondary marketing information service to collect the data and the appropriateness of the methods it uses. Don't be afraid to ask questions; legitimate providers of sound marketing information have nothing to hide. Beware of "super-secret" methods and sources that can't be shared. There's really no need for much mystery in the process of data collection, just sound methods and hard work.

lifestyle, product/service usage, shopping behavior, and so on. By taking into account both media habits and product usage, the Experian data allow companies to better segment, target, and communicate to the most promising groups.[10]

Mediamark Research Inc. also makes available information on exposure to various media and household consumption of various products and services. Its annual survey of over 26,000 adult respondents covers magazines, national and local newspapers, radio, television, and about 550 product and service categories.[11] Information is gathered from respondents by two methods. First, a personal interview is used to collect demographics and psychographics and data pertaining to media exposure. Magazine readership is measured by a recent-reading method that asks respondents to sort a deck of magazine logo cards according to whether they (1) are sure they have read, (2) are not sure they have read, and (3) are sure they have not read a given magazine within the previous six months.

Newspaper readership is measured using a yesterday-reading technique in which respondents are asked which of the daily newspapers on the list of papers that circulate in the area were read or looked at within the previous seven days. For Sunday and weekend papers, a four-week time span is used. Radio listening is determined through a yesterday-recall technique in which respondents are shown a list of five day parts and are asked how much time was spent listening to a radio during each time period on the previous day. They are then asked what stations were listened to. Television-audience data are collected in a similar manner.

When the interview is completed, interviewers then leave a questionnaire booklet with respondents. The interviewer personally picks up the booklet, which covers personal and household usage of approximately 550 product and service categories and 6,000 brands, after a short time. The respondents for the Mediamark reports are selected using probability sampling methods.

SUMMARY

Learning Objective 1

List three common uses of the information supplied by standardized marketing information services.
The information supplied by standardized marketing information services is commonly used to (1) profile customers, (2) measure product sales and market share, and (3) measure advertising exposure and effectiveness.

Learning Objective 2

Define geodemography.
Geodemography refers to the availability of demographic, consumer-behavior, and lifestyle data by arbitrary geographic boundaries that are typically small.

Learning Objective 3

Describe the operation of a diary panel.
The key feature of a diary panel, whether recorded on paper or reported online, is that a representative group of individuals or households keeps track of purchases made or products consumed over a given period of time.

Learning Objective 4

Describe the operation of store audits.
Store audits involve sending field workers, called auditors, to a select group of retail stores at fixed intervals. On each visit, the auditors take a complete inventory of all products designated for the audit. The auditors also note the merchandise moving into the store by checking wholesale invoices, warehouse withdrawal records, and direct shipments from manufacturers and from this information determine sales to consumers.

Learning Objective 5

Define UPC.
The Universal Product Code (UPC) is a 12-digit number imprinted on products or price tags that identifies the product manufacturer and the particular product. The UPC is read by a scanner at the time of purchase.

Learning Objective 6

Define single-source measurement.
Single-source measurement refers to organizations that have the capability to monitor product-purchase data and

advertising-exposure data by household and to relate that information to the demographic characteristics of the households.

Learning Objective 7

Discuss the purpose and operation of people meters.

People meters attempt to measure which household members are watching which television channels at what times. Each member of the family has his or her own viewing number. Whoever turns on the set, sits down to watch, or changes the channel is supposed to enter his or her number into the people meter, which is an electronic device that stores and transmits this information to a central computer for processing.

KEY TERMS

geodemography (page 161)
scanner (page 165)

single-source data (page 166)
people meter (page 167)

REVIEW QUESTIONS

1. What is the basic operation of a store audit?

2. Describe how a type of business can be more successfully targeted using the Dun's Business Locator.

3. What does it mean to "profile" customers or prospects?

4. If you were a product manager for Brand X detergent and you needed up-to-date market share information by small geographical sectors, would you prefer diary panel data or store audit data? Why?

5. What are the key distinctions between diary panel data and scanner data?

6. What is the advantage of using single-source data?

7. How are Starch scores determined?

8. What is the basis for the Nielsen television ratings?

9. How do multimedia services operate?

DISCUSSION QUESTIONS, PROBLEMS, AND PROJECTS

1. Several scenarios are presented below. In each case, there is a need for standardized marketing information. Recommend a service or services that could provide the required information. Explain your choice.

   a. As part of its advertising-sales strategy, radio KZZD wants to stress the fact that its programming appeals to young adults between the ages of 19 and 25. The advertising salespeople need "numbers" to back up this claim.

   b. Pulitzer Peanut Company has developed a unique sales promotion and television ad campaign for its 36-ounce container of Spanish peanuts. It needs to know the following in order to evaluate the campaign:

      1. Are people more likely to use a coupon when they've also seen the television ad?
      2. What is the median size of the households using a coupon?
      3. What is the proportion of new purchasers to past purchasers among the users of a coupon?

c. EMM Advertising Agency assured one of its clients that despite the $200,000 cost of placing a half-page ad in one issue of a national magazine, the actual cost per reader of the ad would be less than two cents. EMM is preparing a report to the client and needs data to back its assurance.

d. Eco-Soft, Inc., is introducing a software package that will make long-range forecasts of contaminant buildup levels in plants that manufacture polyester fibers. It needs a current listing of potential customers, organized by plant sales volume, in order to prioritize its sales calls for the new package.

e. The advertising agency for a leading brand of disposable razors for men needs to choose which network television shows might be best for its ads.

2. Interview representatives of your local media outlets (e.g., radio stations, television stations, and newspapers) and determine the extent to which they utilize sources of standardized marketing information. You may wish to use the following questions as a guideline for your interviews.

a. Which sources do they use?

b. What specific types of information do they obtain from the source?

c. How do they use the information?

d. How important is the information in how they do business?

e. How do they rate the accuracy of the information?

f. Do they supplement the standardized information with locally collected primary data?

Collecting Primary Data

Introduction

Advantages of using secondary data include it being fast, inexpensive, and fairly easy to obtain. However, such data also have certain shortcomings and will rarely provide a complete solution to a research problem. The units of measurement or classes used to report the data may be wrong; the data may be nearly obsolete by the time of their publication; the data may be incomplete; and so on. When these conditions occur, the researcher usually turns to primary data.

This chapter serves as an introduction to the subject of primary data. In this chapter, we will discuss the various types of primary data researchers collect from and about subjects.

The information of interest that marketing researchers collect falls into one of the following categories: (1) demographic/socioeconomic characteristics, (2) psychological/lifestyle characteristics, (3) attitudes/opinions, (4) awareness/knowledge, (5) intentions, (6) motivation, and (7) behavior. It is important to understand each type and the issues involved in collecting it. We also examine the two main methods that are used to collect these types of information: communication and observation. In the following chapters, we explore each of these methods in more detail.

Learning Objective

1.   List the kinds of demographic and socioeconomic characteristics that interest marketers.

TYPES OF PRIMARY DATA

Demographic/ Socioeconomic Characteristics

One type of primary data of great interest to marketers is the respondent's demographic and socioeconomic characteristics, such as age, education, occupation, marital status, gender, income, and social class. These variables are often used to cross-classify the collected data to help interpret the consumers' responses. Suppose we are interested in people's attitudes toward the natural environment. We might find that attitudes toward green marketing are related to the respondents' level of education or are different for men and women. Similarly, marketers frequently ask whether the consumption of particular products (for example, SUVs, disposable diapers, vacation golf packages) is related to a person's age, education, income, and so on.

Demographic variables are often used as a basis for market segmentation. For example, gender has been used to segment categories as diverse as cigarettes (Marlboro versus Virginia Slims), razors (Gillette Fusion versus Venus), and athletic shoes (Foot Locker versus Lady Foot Locker). Lots of other demographic and socioeconomic variables have been used as well.

Some demographic variables, such as a respondent's age, gender, and level of formal education, can be readily verified. Some, such as social class, cannot be verified except very crudely, because they are relative and not absolute measures of a person's standing in society. A person's income can also be a fairly difficult piece of information to verify. Although the amount a person

The varying storefront colors and layouts illustrate the appeal to the demographic variable of gender.

© ROSE ALCORN

earns in a given year is an absolute instead of relative quantity. Money, in our society, is such a sensitive topic that exact numbers may be hard to determine.

Personality/Lifestyle Characteristics

personality
Normal patterns of behavior exhibited by an individual; the attributes, traits, and mannerisms that distinguish one individual from another.

Another type of primary data of interest to marketers is the respondent's psychological and lifestyle characteristics in the form of personality traits, activities, interests, and values. **Personality** refers to the normal patterns of behavior exhibited by an individual—the attributes, traits, and mannerisms that distinguish one individual from another. We often characterize people by the personality traits—aggressiveness, dominance, friendliness, sociability—they display. Marketers are interested in personality because it seems as if it would affect the way consumers and others in the marketing process behave. Many marketers maintain, for example, that personality can affect a consumer's choice of stores or products, or an individual's response to an advertisement or point-of-purchase display. Similarly, they believe that successful salespeople are more likely to be extroverted and understanding of other people's feelings than are unsuccessful salespeople. Although the empirical evidence regarding the ability of personality to predict consumption behavior or salesperson success is weak, personality remains a very popular variable with marketing researchers.

MANAGER'S FOCUS

Effective marketing decision making requires an ability to accurately predict how consumers or organizational buyers will behave in response to alternative marketing actions. How will organizational buyers respond if we increase our prices? If we change the positioning emphasis of our advertisements, how will our target consumers react? How will existing and prospective organizational customers respond if we add a new model to our product line? If we increase the quality of our product, and market it through more exclusive retail outlets, how will target consumers react? Making these types of predictions involves modeling *consumer or organizational buyer behavior*.

A hypothesis specifies how two or more measurable variables are related. When you read this, you may have wondered "what exactly are *'measurable variables'*?" We begin to answer that question in this chapter by describing some of the general types of variables commonly measured in marketing research studies. As a manager, you need to (a) determine which variables are most relevant to your marketing situation and (b) formulate hypotheses about how the variables are related to one another. Don't forget that exploratory research can help you gain useful insights in these areas. They can help you identify which characteristics, attitudes, knowledge issues, motivations, and so on, appear to correspond with one another and ultimately with buyers' behavior. These hypothesized relationships represent a working model of buyer behavior pertaining to your marketing circumstances.

The relationships between variables are much easier for you to recognize if you have a strong understanding of *buyer behavior theory*. This is why you may have taken (or may take in the future) a *buyer behavior* (or consumer behavior) course. Studying buyer behavior theory is really just a form of exploratory research. Specifically, it is an extensive literature search in which you examine how different buyer-related variables have been found to correspond with one another in previous research contexts. Through this secondary research process, you will learn about many generalizable models of buyer behavior that represent possible relationships between variables in the specific marketing situations you will face as a manager.

With an understanding of buyer behavior theory, you will become a much more effective user of marketing research services. As a manager, you will draw upon your prior managerial experiences, your understanding of buyer behavior theory, and the findings of exploratory research performed on your behalf in order to formulate sound hypotheses (a buyer behavior model) pertaining to your organization's marketing problems. Once you have decided on your hypothesized model, you will need to employ your marketing research expertise to select and work with a research supplier to complete descriptive and/or causal research to test your hypotheses. The goal, however, is not to merely confirm or disconfirm your hypotheses—it is to achieve marketing success by developing a thorough understanding of the issues that drive your target customers' behaviors.

Lifestyle analysis (sometimes called psychographic analysis) rests on the premise that a company can plan more effective strategies to reach its target market if it knows more about its customers in terms of how they live, what interests them, and what they like. For example, Frito-Lay conducted research that identified two broad categories of snackers, which it called "compromisers" and "indulgers." The compromisers are typically female and are more likely to exercise, read health and fitness magazines, be concerned about nutrition, and read product labels. Frito-Lay appeals to this group with its Baked Lay's potato chip, a reduced-fat snack. Frito-Lay's traditional potato chips are targeted to the other psychographic category, the indulgers, who are mostly male, in their late teens and early twenties, snack heavily, feel unconcerned about what they eat, and hesitate to sacrifice taste for a reduction in fat.[1]

The NPD Group taps its ongoing panel of consumers regularly to assess their lifestyles as well as their category-specific (e.g., apparel, food, sporting goods) purchase behaviors. Exhibit 9.1 contains the list of characteristics that are usually assessed when measuring lifestyle. The analysis attempts to identify groups of consumers who are likely to behave similarly toward a product and who have similar lifestyle profiles. Research Window 9.1 recognizes the reality that people with similar demographic/socioeconomic characteristics often have dissimilar consumption patterns. Finally, Exhibit 9.2 (on page 181) shows six international segments that have been identified from applying values and lifestyle surveys to teenagers.

Attitudes/Opinions

Some authors distinguish between attitudes and opinions, while others use the terms interchangeably. Usually, **attitude** refers to an individual's overall evaluation of something; **opinions** are attitudes expressed verbally. We treat attitudes and opinions interchangeably as representing a person's global evaluation of a specific object or idea.

Attitude is one of the more important notions in the marketing literature, since it is generally thought that attitudes are related to behavior.[2] In general, if a person has a positive attitude toward a product or brand, the person is more likely to buy that product or to choose that brand. Because attitudes influence behavior in this way, marketers want to shape attitudes or target people with favorable attitudes. Thus, marketers often want to learn people's attitudes toward product categories, brands, Web sites, retailers, and a whole host of other things. They also want to know what factors influence people's attitudes. For example, findings from recent studies suggest

> **Learning Objective**
>
> 2. Discuss the rationale for lifestyle analysis.

attitude
An individual's overall evaluation of something.

opinion
Verbal expression of an attitude.

E x h i b i t   9 . 1   **Lifestyle Dimensions**

Activities	Interests	Opinions
Work	Family	Themselves
Hobbies	Home	Social issues
Social events	Job	Politics
Vacation	Community	Business
Entertainment	Recreation	Economics
Club membership	Fashion	Education
Community	Food	Products
Shopping	Media	Future
Sports	Achievements	Culture

Sources: Adapted from Joseph T. Plummer, "The Concept and Application of Life Style Segmentation," *Journal of Marketing* 38, January 1974, p. 34. Published by the American Marketing Association. See also Ronald D. Michman, *Lifestyle Market Segmentation* (New York: Praeger Publishers, 1991).

research window 9.1

New-Vehicle Buyers and Psychographics

J. D. Power and Associates and Mediamark Research Inc. (MRI) are working together to inform auto marketers about psychographics of new-vehicle buyers. These data were previously unavailable according to the two companies.

"We are very excited about the J. D. Power and Associates-MRI products, which are truly a breakthrough for the industry," said Gene Cameron, vice president of media solutions at J. D. Power. "Prior to this study, marketers had to infer psychographics from the total audience of a magazine and not specifically to new-vehicle buyers. As auto marketers offer more models to serve customers' lifestyles and attitudes, we can now provide them with guidance on where and how to advertise to reach those specific customers."

Kathi Love, president and CEO of MRI, had this to say about the relationship, "MRI is considered the 'go to' company for marketers who need a high resolution view of consumers—who they are, what they buy, how they think and how to reach them. In recent years we've added hundreds of psychographic questions to our *Survey of the American Consumer*, because people with similar demographics often have dissimilar approaches to consumer products and product categories."

While MRI psychographics are widely used and respected, linking them with consumption patterns of new-vehicle buyers as measured by J. D. Powers provides greater focus and insights for marketers.

Source: "J. D. Power and Associates Announces Collaboration with Mediamark Research Inc. to Offer Psychographic Data on New-Vehicle Buyers," April 23, 2007, downloaded from http://www.jdpower.com/corporate/news/releases/pressrelease.aspx?ID=2007060, October 8, 2008.

that teenagers' attitudes toward brand-name goods have declined, perhaps to a historic low. Energy/BBDO stated in its GenWorld Report that two-thirds of the 3,322 young people surveyed worldwide are apathetic about brands, and only 37% like to wear the logos of their favorite brands.

In the United Kingdom, Carlson Marketing Group found that only three in 10 people are committed to certain brands. Another global youth study found that young people ranked brand names as fifth out of eight possible factors in teenage purchasing decisions.[3] Research Window 9.2, on page 182, demonstrates how consumers' attitudes can sometimes be wildly different toward the same company. Attitude is such a pervasive notion in behavioral science, and particularly in marketing, that Chapter 14 is devoted to various types of instruments used to measure it.

Learning Objective

3. Cite the three main approaches used to measure the effectiveness of magazine ads.

awareness/knowledge
Insight into, or understanding of facts about, some object or phenomenon.

Awareness/Knowledge

Awareness/knowledge as used in marketing research refers to what respondents do and do not know or believe about some product, brand, company, advertisement, or so on. For instance, marketers are always interested in judging the effectiveness of ads in TV, radio, magazine, billboard, and Web banners. One measure of effectiveness is the product awareness generated by the ad, using one of the three approaches described in Exhibit 9.3, on page 183. All three tests of memory (unaided recall, aided recall, and recognition) are aimed at assessing the respondent's awareness of, and knowledge about, the ad. They are assumed by advertisers to reflect differences in the extent to which consumers have cognitively processed (in detail or just superficially) the ad, the brand name, the featured attributes, and so on. Consumers have retained more knowledge from the ad when they can state the brand in an unaided recall test compared to a recall test where they have been given hints, and that both of these show superior knowledge and retention over simple recognition.

Exhibit 9.2			Segments Identified Using Values Surveys among Teens Worldwide		
Segment	**%**	**Key Countries**	**Enjoy**	**Worry About**	**Own/Wear/Do**
Thrills and chills (sensations)	18	Germany, United Kingdom, Lithuania, Greece, Netherlands, South Africa, United States	going out to eat, going to a bar, drinking, smoking cigarettes, going to a party, going on a date, dancing; have most online access	finding love, unplanned pregnancy, own attractiveness	fast food, acne medication, perfume, would dye hair, would like tattoo or nose ring, do *not* have a job or attend church
Upholders (family, tradition)	16	Vietnam, Indonesia, Taiwan, China, Italy, Peru, Venezuela, Puerto Rico, India, Philippines, Singapore	reading books, spending time with family and visiting relatives; have least online access	not living up to others' expectations; believe the world will improve in their lifetime	do *not* have jobs to earn money, eat fast food, wear deodorant, wear tattoos or nose rings, carry guns; girls do *not* wear makeup
Quiet achievers (success, anonymity)	15	Thailand, China, Hong Kong, Ukraine, Korea, Lithuania, Russia, Peru	studying, listening to music, visiting museums; do *not* enjoy going to parties or drinking wine/ beer	not living up to others' expectations; believe the world will improve in their lifetime; do *not* worry about finishing education, pregnancy, AIDS, or drugs	do *not* have jobs, or backpacks, blue jeans, or athletic shoes; girls do *not* wear makeup
Resigned (low expectations)	14	Denmark, Sweden, Korea, Japan, United Kingdom, Norway, Germany, Belgium, France, Netherlands, Spain, Argentina, Canada, Turkey, Taiwan	do *not* enjoy doing something artistic/ creative, attending opera, play, or ballet, or visiting relatives	do *not* worry about going to college, the economy, rain forest, global warming, living up to others' expectations	have or would dye hair; do *not* care about access to new technology
Boot-strappers (achievement, individualism)	14	Nigeria, Mexico, United States, India, Chile, Puerto Rico, South Africa, Venezuela, Colombia	spending time with family and visiting relatives	do *not* worry about not having friends or being lonely; believe education is good preparation for future and that they will have a good life	attend religious services; do *not* receive allowances
World savers (environment)	12	Hungary, Brazil, Philippines, Venezuela, Spain, Colombia, Belgium, Argentina, Russia, Singapore, France, Poland, Ukraine, Italy, South Africa, Mexico, United Kingdom	attending opera, plays, and ballet, doing something artistic/creative (such as taking photos), going camping/hiking, going to a bar, dancing	racism, poverty for others, environment, AIDS, war, terrorism, being able to have children, finding love	would *not* carry gun

For more information, see Elissa Moses, *The $100 Billion Allowance: Accessing the Global Teen Market* (New York: Wiley, 2000), pp. 80–103.

One of the common indices used to measure the short-term success and impact of an ad is "day-after recall" (or DAR), which is a phone survey made the day following the airing of a new ad (such as the day after the Super Bowl). The DAR scores are compared to the ad agency's databank of such indices to project sales by using other recent ads that had achieved similar DAR scores as benchmarks.

Increasingly, psychologists and advertising researchers are exploring the idea that consumers do not have to explicitly remember an ad for that ad to have an impact on their behavior. For example, after airing an ad for Reebok, the researcher might

MANAGER'S FOCUS

"Attitudes/Opinions" represent a very broad class of variables. Although you might not have recognized it, several of the concepts you have studied in marketing such as assessments of value, satisfaction, brand image, and quality are like "attitudes" because they are special types of *evaluations* made by consumers. *Value perceptions* are evaluations of a marketing offering in terms of the benefits it provides relative to the costs of acquiring and using it. *Satisfaction*, in contrast, is an evaluation of a marketing offering involving a comparison of benefits actually received with the benefits expected before purchase and use. *Brand image* is an evaluation of the degree to which various characteristics and cultural symbols are associated with a brand as well as the favorability/desirability of those associations. Finally, *quality perceptions* are evaluations of the features and performance of a product or service.

In addition to predicting buyer behavior, marketing managers frequently use measures of attitudinal variables to monitor and control marketing performance. Franchisers in the services sector, for instance, commonly measure the satisfaction of their franchisees' customers. Some require franchisees to maintain satisfaction at or above a specific level in order to retain their franchise. Given the prevalence of attitudinal measurement in marketing, it is essential that you understand what this broad class of variables encompasses, and how to appropriately measure each specific type of attitude. As you will learn in later chapters, there are many common pitfalls to avoid when measuring attitudes and other variables.

research window 9.2

Wal-Mart is the best! No, wait, it's the worst!

Pick A or B:

A. Wal-Mart has the most believable advertising of any company in America, scores first in retail customer service, and ranks as the second-most trustworthy corporation in the nation.

B. Wal-Mart has the least believable advertising of any company in America, scores worst in customer service, and ranks as the second-least trustworthy company in America—right behind Enron.

The correct answer is C: all of the above, according to the American Demographics Perception Study, an online survey of 1,133 adults fielded for *Ad Age* by Aegis Group's Synovate.

What gives? Consumers are deeply divided over the behemoth from Bentonville, sending Wal-Mart to the top of the charts as both the best and the worst. When consumers were asked to name the "most trustworthy company in America," Wal-Mart tied for second (with General Electric Co.), behind Ford Motor Co. But more people picked Wal-Mart in a separate question as the "least trustworthy" company, putting it second on the rogue's list.

It's not unusual for giant companies to have lots of fans and foes. Ford and General Motors Corp., for example, both ranked in the top five for most and least trustworthy companies. But Wal-Mart is the most extreme example. It's a lightning rod, sparking widely divergent views within the same age, income, education, and regional demographic groups.

Wal-Mart leads the way in truth in advertising—and fiction. It far and away scored tops among adults in questions both on what company had the "most believable" advertising and what company's ad pitch was "most at odds with its image, reputation or product."

Source: Excerpted from Bradley Johnson, "Wal-Mart Is the Best! No, Wait, It's the Worst!" *Advertising Age*, June 13, 2005, p. 14, accessed via ProQuest, August 12, 2008. Reprinted by permission.

Exhibit 9.3   **Approaches Used to Measure Awareness**

Unaided recall: Without being given any clues, consumers are asked to recall what advertising they have seen recently. An ad or a brand that can be remembered with no clues at all is presumed to have made a deep impression. As a result, unaided recall represents the highest level of awareness.

Example: What ads for products and brands do you remember seeing?

Aided recall: Consumers are prompted, typically with a category cue. That is, they are asked to remember all ads/brands that they have seen for products and services in a particular product category. Aided recall represents a relatively high level of awareness, but the presence of the cue makes the task easier than unaided recall.

Example: Do you remember recently seeing ads for personal computers?

Recognition: Actual advertisements, brand names, or logos are shown or described to consumers, who are asked whether they remember seeing each one. Because the task is simply to recognize whether or not they have seen an ad, the recognition task is much easier for respondents but represents a lower level of awareness.

Example: Do you remember seeing this ad for Dell?

choose to use "implicit" or indirect tests of memory. Rather than asking, "Do you remember any recent ads for athletic shoes or Reeboks?" the researcher might instead ask consumers to list brand names of sneakers, their choice of sporting shoes, shoes affiliated with athlete spokespersons, and so on, to assess the number of times the Reebok brand name appears. Researchers have even asked such questions as, "Name all the brands of any kind of product that start with R" to see how often Reebok would appear, along with names such as Reese's, Rolex, and Ramada. The assumption in these tests is that if Reebok appears disproportionately more than it should (based on market shares), the ad was successful in bringing the Reebok brand name to mind.

Would an ad such as this one for Reebok be memorable in an implicit or explicit test of memory? What would be most memorable in this ad?

In addition to ad testing, memory measures are used to assess awareness and knowledge of brands, products, companies, and the like. Marketers are often interested in understanding what different audiences know or believe about their brands and companies. This is the basis of countless brand image or company image studies. In addition, this information, sometimes in combination with attitudes (that is, evaluations of the brand or company based on the knowledge or beliefs held in memory), are key inputs into positioning studies based on perceptual mapping. In general, awareness questions help the marketer assess consumers' knowledge of any element of the consumer experience—advertisements, products, retail stores, etc.

Intentions

A person's **intentions** refer to the individual's anticipated or planned future behavior. Marketers are interested in people's intentions primarily with regard to purchase behavior. One of the better known studies regarding purchase intentions is that conducted by the Survey Research Center at the University of Michigan. The center regularly conducts surveys to determine the general financial condition of consumers and their outlook with respect to the state of the economy in the near future. The center phones a sample of 500 households monthly, asking 50 core questions about

intentions
Anticipated or planned future behavior.

consumer confidence and buying intentions for durable goods such as appliances, automobiles, and homes during the next few months. The responses are then analyzed and used as one indicator of future economic activity. In marketing, intentions are often gathered by asking respondents to indicate which of the following best describes their plans with respect to a new product or service:

☐ definitely would buy

☐ probably would buy

☐ undecided

☐ probably would not buy

☐ definitely would not buy

Intentions receive less attention in marketing than do other types of primary data, because there is often a big difference between what people say they are going to do and what they actually do. Estimating demand for products and services is very difficult—for example, in one study, consumers were told of a new pricing option for a service to which they already subscribed. They were asked to indicate how likely they were to buy the service when it became available. Less than half of the people who indicated that they *definitely would buy* the service actually did so within the first three months of its availability. And some of the respondents who indicated that they would not buy it actually did so.[4] Practicing marketing researchers have learned that they must discount people's stated intentions in most situations, based on the researchers' past experience in similar situations.

While the prediction of behaviors by intentions is not perfect, sometimes behavioral data are too expensive, difficult, or even impossible to obtain. For example, if Apple were to create a new version of its popular iPod that was solar-powered and could receive satellite radio broadcasts, by definition no purchase data would exist because the product would not have been available yet for purchase. If the marketer had access to data on purchase levels of iPods, solar-powered radios, and satellite radio subscriptions among the target market, it might be possible to develop a rough sales forecast for the new product (this would require lots of assumptions, of course). Still, in many circumstances, consumer judgments of their purchase intentions are as close to actual behaviors as marketers can get.

It is difficult to garner true and realistic purchase intentions when offering new, and untried, features for a product, such as the iPod.

The iPod example also demonstrates one of the chief difficulties with obtaining accurate projections of future demand for new products and services. Until the product or service can be examined and tried out by consumers, it is very difficult for them to know how they might behave with respect to the offering in the future. Artist renderings, written product concepts, and computer simulations simply can't replace product trial and use. Standard test markets are more accurate than simulated test markets. This is one reason why.

Purchase intentions are most often used when studying the purchase of "big-ticket" (that is, expensive) items, such as an automobile for a family, or plant and equipment for a business. The general assumption is that the larger the dollar expenditure, the more preplanning necessary and the greater the correlation between anticipated and actual behavior.

Motivation

A **motive** is a need, a want, a drive, an urge, a wish, a desire, an impulse, or any inner state that directs or channels behavior toward goals. Marketers often appeal to these motives in their communications efforts. For example, the motive that underlies an ad for life insurance may be the desire to make certain that the family has adequate financial resources should something happen to a parent.

Learning Objective

4.   Give two reasons why researchers are interested in people's motives.

A marketing researcher's interest in motives typically involves determining *why* people behave as they do. There are several reasons for this interest. In the first place, researchers believe that a person's motives tend to be more stable than an individual's behavior and therefore offer a better basis for predicting future behavior than does past behavior.

The second reason researchers are interested in motives is that by understanding what drives a person's behavior, it is easier to understand the behavior itself. A desire for status may motivate one car buyer to purchase a Mercedes-Benz; a concern for safety may send another to the local Volvo showroom. If researchers understand the forces underlying consumer behavior, they are in a better position to design and offer products and services that can satisfy the motives driving that behavior.

motive

A need, a want, a drive, a wish, a desire, an impulse, or any inner state that energizes, activates, or moves and that directs or channels behavior toward goals.

Behavior

Behavior concerns what subjects have done or are doing. In marketing, this usually means purchase and use behavior. Said differently, this could represent the distinction between a customer (purchaser) and consumer (user). Behavior is a physical activity or action that takes place under specific circumstances, at a particular time, and involves one or more actors or participants. A marketing researcher investigating behavior would be interested in a description of the activity and its various components. Exhibit 9.4 is a checklist of the key elements involved in customer and consumer behavior. Researchers can use a checklist like this one to design data collection instruments.

behavior

What subjects have done or are doing.

As a researcher fills in each category, he or she must make a decision about what information to include or omit. Consider the "where" category, for example. The "where of purchase" may be specified with respect to type of store, the location of the store by broad geographic area or specific address, size of the store, or even the name of the store. So it is with each of the many categories. The study of behavior, then, involves the development of a description of the purchase or use activity, either past or current, with respect to some or all of the characteristics contained in Exhibit 9.4.

Behavior data may also be obtained by asking consumers to remember and report their behaviors. As we note elsewhere, however, this approach is subject to more forms of bias because it depends on respondents' ability to accurately remember and report their prior behaviors. Even so, asking about specific behaviors performed during a specific time frame can yield solid information.

Behavioral data are becoming increasingly available through various technologies (for example, scanners and the Web) and increasingly important to marketers, such as in building relationships with customers. Scanner data are probably the most common type of behavioral data.

Exhibit 9.4	**Behavior Checklist**	
	Purchase Behavior	**Use Behavior**
What and how much		
How		
Where		
When		
Who		

MANAGER'S FOCUS

The types of primary data discussed in this chapter are useful only if they deepen marketers' understanding and ability to predict consumer (or organizational) behavior. After all, the bottom line for organizations is how target markets respond to their marketing efforts. Later in this chapter, you will learn about the relative merits of collecting primary data by either communication or observation. Traditionally, managers have probably relied too heavily on communications—asking consumers about their thoughts, feelings, past behaviors, and intended future behaviors—and have underutilized observational methods that would enable them to *directly measure*

consumers' *actual* behavior. This has been due to managers' relative unawareness of observational research techniques and their assumption that monitoring behavior in most situations is difficult or impossible.

With the advent of new technology, managers have at their disposal many innovative and effective ways of tracking consumer behavior. As a result, companies are increasingly placing a higher priority on tracking the behavior of target markets. Observational research could help you become more creative in identifying ways your organization might generate highly valuable behavioral data.

A different technology that yields similar behavioral data is the Web and all it entails, including the production of personal profile data, click-stream trails, and records of response to Web advertising. The process of tracking behavioral information via the Web is often referred to as *Web analytics*. A revolution is occurring regarding data access. The marketer talented at analyzing these data sets will derive great insights.

Learning Objective

5. Describe the two basic means of obtaining primary data.

communication
A method of data collection involving questioning of respondents to secure the desired information, using a data collection instrument called a questionnaire.

observation
A method of data collection in which the situation of interest is watched and the relevant facts, actions, or behaviors are recorded.

Learning Objective

6. State the specific advantages of each method of data collection.

OBTAINING PRIMARY DATA

Once you've decided to collect primary data, there are still several choices to make about the method to use (see Figure 9.1). The primary decision is whether to use communication or observation. **Communication** involves questioning respondents to secure the desired information, using a data collection instrument called a questionnaire. The questions may be verbal or in writing, and the responses may also be given in either form. **Observation** does not involve questioning. Instead, the situation of interest is scrutinized and the relevant facts, actions, or behaviors are recorded. The observer may be a person or a mechanical device. For instance, supermarket scanners may be used to determine how many boxes of a particular brand of cereal are sold in a given region in a typical week. Alternatively, a researcher interested in the brands of canned vegetables a family buys might arrange a pantry audit in which the family's shelves are checked to see which brands they have on hand. Some studies use both communication and observation to collect primary data, as the example in Research Window 9.3, on page 188, demonstrates.

Choosing a primary method of data collection also requires additional decisions. For example, should the questionnaires be administered by mail, over the telephone, or in person? Should the purpose of the study be disguised or remain undisguised? Should the answers be open-ended, or should the respondent be asked to choose from a limited set of alternatives? Although Figure 9.1 implies that these decisions are independent, they are actually intimately related. For instance, a decision with respect to method of administration has serious implications regarding the degree of structure that must be imposed on the questionnaire.

Both the communication and observation methods have advantages and disadvantages, which are reviewed in the remainder of this chapter. In the next chapter, we discuss the decisions that must be made when using the communication method, and in the following chapter, the decisions involved in the observation method. In general, the communication method of data collection has the general advantages of versatility, speed, and cost; observational data are typically more objective and accurate.

Versatility

Versatility is the ability of a technique to collect information on the many types of primary data of interest to marketers. A respondent's demographic/socioeconomic characteristics and lifestyle, the individual's attitudes and opinions, awareness and knowledge, intentions, the motivation underlying the individual's actions, and the person's behavior may all be obtained by communication. All we need to do is ask, although the replies will not necessarily be truthful.

Not so with observation. Observation techniques can provide us only with information about behavior and certain demographic/socioeconomic characteristics. Even here, our observations are limited to present behavior, for example. We cannot observe a person's past behavior. Nor can we observe the person's intentions as to future behavior. If we are interested in past behavior or intentions, we must ask.

ETHICAL DILEMMA 9.1

A national department store chain with a relatively sophisticated image is planning to open a store in an area inhabited by professionals. The marketing research director of the company wants a detailed profile of the residents' characteristics and lifestyles in order to tailor the new store to the tastes of this lucrative new market. He suggests that you, a member of his staff, contribute to the research effort by spending a month observing the residents going about their daily affairs of eating in restaurants, attending church, shopping in other stores, socializing with one another, and so on. You are then to prepare a report on what expenditures support their lifestyles.

- Are there ethical problems involved in observing people in public places? Do the ethical problems become more serious if you socialize with your subjects?
- Who has ethical responsibility for your behavior: the marketing research director? You? Both?

FIGURE 9.1

Basic Choices among Means for Collecting Primary Data

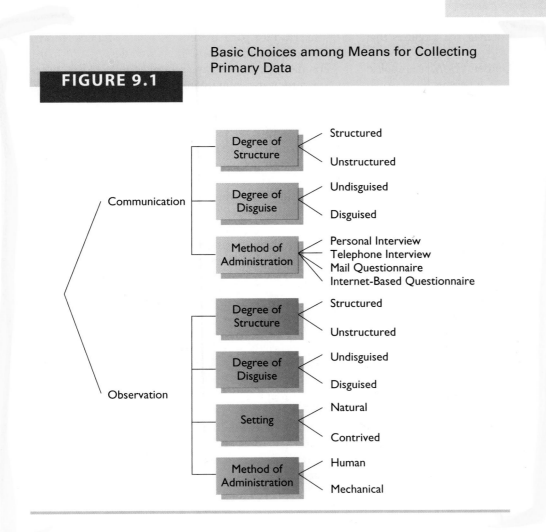

research window 9.3

The Naked Truth about Shower Heads

A few years ago, Moen Inc. arranged for a marketing research firm to watch individuals take showers. Strange as that may sound, the observations were part of a well-planned research project.

Moen sells plumbing fixtures, and its brand of faucets is the market leader in that category. Until a few years ago, Moen sold all its faucets and sinks through plumbing supply houses. To build sales, the company decided to begin selling shower heads to consumers through hardware and home-center stores. Existing data showed that although the average price of a shower head was below $20, more than half of total sales dollars came from higher-priced models. Moen decided to enter the market at the high end by developing a superior product. For this, it would need to know what consumers value in a shower.

Moen's marketing research director, Jack Suvak, hired QualiData Research to help Moen answer some very basic questions: What do consumers do in the shower? What benefits do they associate with taking a shower? How do they go about buying a new shower head? How can a shower head deliver the qualities that consumers value most?

As Suvak and QualiData founder Hy Mariampolski discussed these issues, it became apparent they would need to combine several forms of research. They could get some basic data by asking consumers to provide information about their behavior and attitudes. Consumers could record their time in the shower and their opinions about showering and shower heads. But Mariampolski's background as a sociologist told him that people often have difficulty putting into words their thoughts about everyday activities like showering. They may be so used to the pleasures and irritations of their morning or evening shower that they don't consciously notice those experiences anymore. As Suvak later explained to a newspaper reporter, "The obvious things don't bubble to the surface all the time." To find the issues that don't "bubble to the surface," the researchers would need to watch what consumers actually do.

The decision to use observation gave rise to another set of challenges. To learn about consumers' purchasing behavior, the researchers could observe consumers as they shopped in a store's plumbing aisle. But how could they observe consumers in the shower without offending them? The solution would require a combination of technology to carry out the observations and careful recruiting to find people who were not too self-conscious yet appropriately motivated. Moen also wanted subjects to be a diverse slice of American consumers.

QualiData recruited subjects to keep diaries of their shower habits and then visit a testing facility for in-depth interviews and actual showers. At a Lowe's home center, researchers used hidden cameras to observe customers in the shower head aisle and then surveyed shoppers as they left.

Perhaps the biggest challenge was finding subjects for the in-shower observations. Brainstorming, Mariampolski and his research team identified a logical source: social nudists, whose philosophy is that nudity is natural, not embarrassing. Internet bulletin boards for such groups were one of the recruiting sources, and members of nudist groups were a sizable portion of the approximately 20 subjects. Volunteers were screened to ensure their motives were appropriate and not wholly focused on the $250 fee paid for participating. Also, researchers selected a variety of ages, body types, and ethnicities.

For the test, showers were hooked up to a computer to measure water temperature and flow. A heat- and moisture-resistant video camera was mounted next to the shower head. From these measurements, researchers identified significant patterns of behavior. For example, they determined that adjusting a shower head can be tricky, because people often have their eyes closed and are holding accessories like soap or a washcloth. The surveys told Moen that consumers want to adjust the shower head to meet the needs of different household members or to achieve different benefits (such as stress relief or an early-morning wakeup). Thus, an easily adjustable shower head would meet a need.

The research into shopping behavior also provided insights. Moen learned that most shoppers spent about five minutes looking at shower heads and then walked away without speaking to a store employee. That meant the shower head's packaging would have to catch shoppers' eyes quickly and sell them on the product. Shoppers also tested the weight of different shower heads, suggesting they use weight as an indicator of sturdy construction and high quality.

(Continued)

Moen's engineers used this information to develop a new shower head that looks and feels substantial. They placed a control dial below the water stream so consumers can easily use one hand to adjust the shower's force, frequency, and coverage. To catch consumers' eyes on store shelves, package designers created holographic images on wedge-shaped boxes. When it was introduced, it quickly began to fly off store shelves.

Sources: Dina ElBoghdady, "Naked Truth Meets Market Research: Perfecting a New Shower Head? Try Watching People Shower," *The Washington Post*, February 24, 2002, downloaded from the Dow Jones Interactive Publications Library; Moen, "Extensive Research by Moen Provides What Consumers Want in a Great Shower Experience," news release, July 17, 2001, downloaded from the Moen Web site, http://www.moen.com; and Fortune Brands, "Home Products," downloaded from Fortune Brands' Web site, http://www.fortunebrands.com, February 11, 2003.

Some demographic/socioeconomic characteristics can readily be observed. Gender is the most obvious example. Others can be observed, but with less accuracy. A person's age and income, for example, might be inferred by closely examining the individual's mode of dress and purchasing behavior. Clearly, though, both of these observations may be in error, with income likely to be the furthest off. Still others, such as social class, cannot be observed with any degree of confidence about the accuracy of the recorded data.

The other basic types of primary data cannot be measured by observation at all. We can't observe an attitude or opinion, a person's awareness or knowledge, or motivation. We could attempt to make inferences about these variables on the basis of the individual's observed behavior, but behaviors and the underlying psychological factors and processes are different things. For instance, if we watch a person purchase a can of a new flavor of Campbell's soup, we might infer that the person has a favorable attitude toward Campbell's, but we don't know that to be true. It may be that the person has no attitude at all toward Campbell's and is simply trying it for the first time. It might also be that the person doesn't like Campbell's soup at all but is buying it for someone else. Generalizing from observed behavior to states of mind is risky, and researchers need to recognize this. Questioning clearly allows us to gather more types of primary data.

Speed and Cost

The speed and cost advantages of the communication method are closely intertwined. Assuming the data lend themselves to either, communication is often a faster means of data collection than observation, because it provides a greater degree of control over data-gathering activities. With the communication method, researchers are not forced to wait for events to occur, as they would be with the observation method. In some cases, it is impossible to predict when an event will occur precisely enough to observe it. For other behaviors, the time interval between events can be substantial. For instance, an observer seeking to determine the brand purchased most frequently

ETHICAL DILEMMA 9.2

A marketing research firm was hired by a candy manufacturer to gather data on the alternatives consumers consider when deciding to buy a candy bar. Tom Samuelson, the person in charge of the research, believed that the best way to collect accurate information was through an observation study done in major supermarkets, drugstores, and discount stores in a number of large cities. Unfortunately, at that time, the personnel of the firm were stretched to the limit because of a number of other assignments. The company simply did not have sufficient personnel available to do the study using personal observation and still meet the client's deadline. Samuelson consequently decided that he would propose to the client a mail study utilizing the research firm's panel of households. Not only would this place fewer demands on the research firm's personnel, but the cost to the client would be about 25% less than with personal observation.

- Does Samuelson have an obligation to the client to disclose why he is recommending the mail panel?
- Is it ethical for a research firm to use alternative methods of gathering data because of internal constraints? What if the alternatives reduce the charges to the client?
- Who should make the decision as to the best way to approach the project—the client or the research supplier?

Barcode scanners, such as shown in this photo, enable instantaneous recording of purchased items.

in one of several appliance categories might have to wait a long time to make any observations at all. Much of the time the observer would be idle ... but still getting paid, raising the overall cost of the project. Events that last a long time can also cause difficulty. An observational approach to studying the relative influence of a husband and a wife in the purchase of an automobile would be prohibitive in terms of both time and money.

There are instances when observation is faster and costs less than communication. A primary example involves the purchase of consumer nondurables. The use of scanners, for example, allows many more purchases to be recorded and at less cost than if purchasers were questioned about what they bought.

Objectivity and Accuracy

Although the observation method has some serious limitations in terms of scope, time, and cost, it has great advantages with regard to objectivity and accuracy. Data that can be gathered by either method will typically be more accurately secured by observation. This is because the observation method is independent of the respondent's unwillingness or inability to provide the information desired. For example, respondents are often reluctant to cooperate whenever their replies might place them in an unfavorable light. Sometimes respondents conveniently forget embarrassing events; in other cases, the events are not of sufficient importance for them to remember what happened. Because observation allows the recording of behavior as it occurs, it is not dependent on the respondent's memory or mood in reporting what occurred.

Observation usually produces more objective data than does communication. Sometimes people are not even aware they are being observed, so they are not tempted to tell the interviewer what they think the interviewer wants to hear or to give socially acceptable responses that are not truthful. With observation, the objectivity of the results depends upon the selection, training, and control of the observers and is not influenced by the subject's perceptions.

MANAGER'S FOCUS

By now, you should be able to see how understanding the issues involved in later research stages can help you work more effectively with researchers in the earlier stages. For example, understanding the different types of consumer variables discussed in this chapter will enhance your ability to specify the marketing problem your organization is confronting. You will be more proficient at recognizing how consumers' characteristics, thoughts, feelings, and motivations might be influencing their behavioral responses to your marketing efforts, and those of your competitors. This, in turn, should help you be more creative in identifying alternative actions that can be tested through research to determine which one is likely to produce the most desirable consumer responses.

SUMMARY

Learning Objective 1

List the kinds of demographic and socioeconomic characteristics that interest marketers.

Marketers are interested in such socioeconomic and demographic characteristics as age, education, occupation, marital status, sex, income, and social class.

Learning Objective 2

Discuss the rationale for lifestyle analysis.

Lifestyle analysis rests on the premise that a company can plan more effective strategies to reach its target market if it knows more about its customers in terms of how they live, what interests them, and what they like.

Learning Objective 3

Cite the three main approaches used to measure the effectiveness of magazine ads.

The three main approaches used to measure awareness of magazine ads are (1) unaided recall, in which the consumer is given no clues at all; (2) aided recall, in which the consumer is given some prompting; and (3) recognition, in which the consumer is actually shown an advertisement and asked whether or not he or she remembers seeing it.

Learning Objective 4

Give two reasons why researchers are interested in people's motives.

First, researchers believe that motives tend to be more stable than behavior and therefore offer a better basis for predicting future behavior. Second, researchers believe that by understanding what drives a person's behavior, it is easier to understand the behavior itself.

Learning Objective 5

Describe the two basic means of obtaining primary data.

The two basic means of obtaining primary data are communication and observation. Communication involves questioning respondents to secure the desired information, using a data collection instrument called a questionnaire. Observation involves scrutinizing the situation of interest and recording the relevant facts, actions, or behaviors.

Learning Objective 6

State the specific advantages of each method of data collection.

In general, the communication method of data collection has the advantages of versatility, speed, and cost, whereas observation data are typically more objective and accurate.

KEY TERMS

personality (page 178)
attitude (page 179)
opinion (page 179)
awareness/knowledge (page 180)
intentions (page 183)

motive (page 185)
behavior (page 185)
communication (page 186)
observation (page 186)

REVIEW QUESTIONS

1. What types of primary data interest marketing researchers most? What are the differences between the types of data?

2. What is an attitude? Why do marketers care about attitudes?

3. In what areas of marketing research are measures of awareness and/or knowledge most common?

4. What is the basic problem in measuring consumers' intentions about future behaviors?

5. What are the general advantages and disadvantages associated with obtaining information by questioning? By observation? Which method provides more control over the sample?

DISCUSSION QUESTIONS, PROBLEMS, AND PROJECTS

1. The Metal Product Division of Miracle Ltd. devised a special metal container to store plastic garbage bags. Plastic bags pose household problems, as they give off unpleasant odors, look disorderly, and provide a breeding place for insects. The container overcomes these problems, as it has a bag-support apparatus that holds the bag open for filling and seals the bag when the lid is closed. In addition, there is enough storage area for at least four full bags. The product is priced at $53.81 and is sold through hardware stores. The company has done little advertising and relies on in-store promotion and displays. The divisional manager is wondering about the effectiveness of these displays. She has called on you to do the necessary research.

    Should the communication or the observation method be used in this situation? Justify your choice.

2. Friendship is a national manufacturer and distributor of greeting cards. The company has recently begun distributing a low-priced line of cards using a lower-grade paper. Quality differences between the higher- and lower-priced cards do not seem to be noticeable to consumers. The company follows a policy of printing its name and the price on the back of each card. The initial acceptance of the new line of cards has convinced the vice president of production, Sheila Howell, that the company should use this lower-grade paper for all its cards and increase its profit margin from 12% to 15%. The sales manager is strongly opposed to this move and has commented, "Sheila, consumers are concerned about the quality of greeting cards; a price difference of 5 cents on a card does not matter." The vice president has called upon you to undertake the study.

    Should the communication or the observation method be used in this situation? Justify your choice.

3. Stop-Buy, Inc., recently opened a new convenience store in Galveston, Texas. The store is open every day from 7:00 a.m. to 11:00 p.m. Management is interested in determining the trading area from which this store draws its customers, so that it can better plan the location of other units in the Galveston area.

    How would you determine this information by the questionnaire method? By the observation method? Which method would be preferred? Be sure to specify in your answer how you would define "trading area."

4. Following are several objectives for marketing research projects. For each objective, specify the type(s) of primary data that would be of use and a possible method of data collection.

    a. Assess "people flow" patterns inside a shopping mall.

    b. Gauge the effectiveness of a new advertisement.

    c. Gauge a salesperson's potential for success.

    d. Segment a market.

e. Identify the shopper types that patronize a particular store.

f. Discover how people feel about a new package design.

5. Lifestyle analysis collects data concerning three dimensions of a respondent's lifestyle (see Exhibit 9.1). Compare and contrast these dimensions. Are the three dimensions exhaustive, or can you suggest others that should be included?

Collecting Information by Communication

Learning Objectives

1. Explain the concept of *structure* as it relates to questionnaires.
2. Cite the drawbacks of using high degrees of structure.
3. Explain what is meant by *disguise* in a questionnaire context.
4. Discuss two situations in which disguise might be desirable.
5. Differentiate among the main methods of administering questionnaires.
6. Discuss three important aspects used to compare the four different methods of administering questionnaires.
7. Explain why sampling control is difficult with telephone interviews and how this problem can be overcome.
8. List and discuss two types of Internet-based questionnaires.

Introduction

In this chapter, we look closely at communication techniques, one of the two most common methods to gather primary data. We'll discuss the three key decisions that researchers must make regarding communication: the degree of structure to use, whether or not to disguise the questionnaire, and which method to use. The chapter will close with a comparison of primary communication techniques across three levels of research control.

STRUCTURED VERSUS UNSTRUCTURED COMMUNICATION

Learning Objective

1. Explain the concept of *structure* as it relates to questionnaires.

If researchers choose to use the communication method of gathering data, they must decide how much structure, or standardization, to use on the questionnaire. In a highly structured questionnaire, the questions to be asked and the response categories provided to respondents are completely predetermined. Most of the surveys that you have completed probably have featured a high degree of structure: Everyone received the same questions, and everyone responded by choosing from among the same set of possible answers. These are known as fixed-alternative questions, or closed-ended questions, and they are very commonly used to collect primary data.

Consider the following question regarding attitudes toward a company.

structure
The degree of standardization used with the data collection instrument.

> **Considering all aspects, what is your overall evaluation of Microsoft Corporation?**
> ☐ Extremely unfavorable
> ☐ Unfavorable
> ☐ Neither favorable nor unfavorable
> ☐ Favorable
> ☐ Extremely favorable

fixed-alternative questions
Questions in which the responses are limited to stated alternatives.

Notice that the question itself is standardized and so are the response categories. Everyone asked to answer the question will get the identical question and respond with one of the five possible answers. These questions are like multiple-choice questions on an exam.

Now consider another way of asking a similar question, one involving much less structure.

> **Overall, how do you feel about Microsoft Corporation? Please write your answer in the space provided.**
> _____
> _____
> _____

This is an example of an open-ended question, a type of question for which respondents are free to reply using their own words and are not limited to a fixed set of possible answers. Most open-ended questions used for collecting primary data for descriptive research have a standardized question that everyone receives, but everyone gets to answer in any way that they choose. These questions are similar to essay questions on an exam. Questionnaires used for depth interviews, an exploratory research technique, usually have even less structure because the questions and the way they are posed to respondents can change based on answers to previous questions.

open-ended question
A question for which respondents are free to reply in their own words rather than being limited to choosing from among a set of alternatives.

Advantages and Disadvantages of High Structure

Learning Objective

2. Cite the drawbacks of using high degrees of structure.

Highly structured questionnaires have several advantages over questionnaires with lower degrees of structure. For one thing, they are simple to administer. Regardless of method of administration, once the questionnaire items have been developed and the questionnaire finalized, it's a relatively straightforward matter to conduct the interviews, send out the questionnaires, distribute them via the Internet, and so on. There is little need for extensive interviewer training, other than to be able to answer questions that arise; there are no probing or follow-up questions. Respondents respond, and that's about it.

The use of high structure also greatly simplifies data coding and analysis. Open-ended questions are much more difficult to code, which typically means converting answers into code numbers, than are questions with a limited number of possible responses.

High degrees of structure are also usually associated with greater reliability, or consistency, of the answers obtained. That is, if respondents were asked the same fixed-alternative question again, they would tend to provide the same answer again (assuming that nothing has happened to cause the answer to change). Highly structured questions also help improve reliability across different respondents because standardized questions and responses provide respondents with an identical frame of reference. In contrast, consider the question, "How often do you watch television?" If no alternatives were supplied, one respondent might say "every day," another might say "regularly," and still another might respond with the number of hours per day. Responses from such an open-ended question would be far more difficult to interpret than those from a fixed-alternative question limiting replies to the categories of "every day," "at least three times a week," "at least once a week," or "less than once a week."

Providing alternative responses also often helps to make the question clear. "What is your marital status?" is less clear than "Are you married, single, widowed, or divorced?" The latter question provides the dimensions in which to frame the reply.

There are certain disadvantages associated with high degrees of structure, however. Although fixed-alternative questions tend to provide the most reliable responses, they may also encourage misleading answers. For example, fixed alternatives may force an answer to a question on which the respondent has no

MANAGER'S FOCUS

The degree of structure can differ significantly across the various items included on a questionnaire. As a manager, you play an important role in helping researchers determine how much structure to employ in each area. Your level of knowledge about a marketing situation is the primary driver of the type of general research design used (i.e., exploratory, descriptive, or causal). Your input to decisions about structure is quite similar—you must work with the researcher by articulating what you already know about each issue that will be addressed in the questionnaire, and how much of this was learned from statements made by individuals in the target population.

Relatively structured questions are utilized in situations where previous research and experience have given you considerable insight into what a particular topic encompasses from the perspective of the consumer or business buyer. This represents descriptive research in the purest sense because your current purpose is to ask "how large" types of questions. Conversely, relatively unstructured (open-ended) questions are used when you believe you need greater insight into the nature or parameters of a topic. Due to your limited knowledge, you want respondents to reply in their own words so you can learn more about the meaning of the topic from their perspective. In a very real sense, whenever you ask open-ended questions, you are performing exploratory research—even when most of the other questions are highly structured, and the overall purpose of the study is descriptive in nature.

An example of this type of mixed structure is when respondents are first asked to rate something (such as a brand) using a standardized or structured scale. They are then asked *why* they rated the item that way. The first question is descriptive in nature, and the second is more exploratory in nature. Despite this difference in the focus of the questions, the responses to such open-ended questions are ultimately classified (coded) and tallied and thus presented in a descriptive format. The key point, though, is that it is your responsibility as a manager to highlight for researchers the relevant topic areas where more insight is needed through relatively unstructured questions.

opinion. Suppose that an individual had never heard of Microsoft but encountered the first question shown above. Does this necessarily mean that he won't check one of the boxes? Some people would simply skip the question; others will provide an answer so they don't appear to be unknowledgeable. We could include a "don't know" or "no opinion" response option, but if we do, some people are likely to choose this option as a way to hurry through the questionnaire without having to think about it.

Fixed-alternative responses may also produce inaccuracies when the response categories themselves introduce bias. This is particularly true when a reasonable response is omitted because of an oversight or insufficient exploratory research regarding the response categories that are appropriate. The provision of an "other" category does not eliminate this bias either, since subjects are often reluctant to respond in the "other" category.

The fixed-alternative question is most useful when possible replies are well known, limited in number, and clear-cut. They work well for securing factual information (age, education, home ownership, amount of rent, and so on) and for obtaining expressions of opinion about issues on which people hold clear opinions. They are not very appropriate for securing primary data on motivations but could certainly be used to collect data on attitudes, intentions, awareness, demographic/socioeconomic characteristics, and behavior.

Advantages and Disadvantages of Low Structure

Questionnaires with low degrees of structure also have advantages and disadvantages, and as you might guess, they tend to be opposite those of questionnaires with high structure. By not limiting the respondent to a fixed set of replies, open-ended questions can provide a more accurate picture of the respondent's true position on, or knowledge of, some issue. The information obtained from consumers "in their own words" through open-ended questions in interviews and on surveys can also be extremely rewarding and insightful. It can also be clear whether or not a respondent has really thought much about a topic, providing the researcher a clue as to how much credence to give the respondent's expressed opinions.

On the downside, interpreting open-ended responses so that they can be analyzed can be difficult and time consuming. One or more skilled researchers are typically required to interpret the responses—and this raises costs significantly. Plus, writing out a thoughtful answer places more burden on the respondent in the first place. The lack of structured response categories also makes it easier for researchers to put their own bias into the interpretation of open-ended responses. More than one researcher has seen what he or she expected to see in open-ended responses, just as managers and researchers often find what they are looking for in focus group interviews.

Some of the problems with coding open-ended questions are changing in response to new technology. Researchers are increasingly feeding respondents' answers into computers programmed to recognize a large vocabulary of words in their search for regularities in the replies. Consumers' responses are usually first broken into "thought units." For example, if a consumer is asked, "Tell me about the last time you had poor service at a restaurant," and answers, "Well, the service was slow and the waiter was rude," the sentence would be divided into "service was slow" and "waiter was rude," because they express different qualities and would need to be coded differently. Computer analysis can quickly rank each word that respondents use by the frequency of usage and can then print out sentences containing the keywords. Detailed analysis of these sentences allows researchers to recognize recurring themes. This process is traditionally referred to as content analysis. More recently, the term *text mining* has also been used to associate the concept with data mining.

DISGUISED VERSUS UNDISGUISED COMMUNICATION

Learning Objective

3.   Explain what is meant by *disguise* in a questionnaire context.

disguise

The amount of knowledge about the purpose or sponsor of a study communicated to the respondent. An undisguised questionnaire, for example, is one in which the purpose of the research is obvious.

Learning Objective

4.   Discuss two situations in which disguise might be desirable.

The second consideration in the use of communication to gather primary data concerns disguise. A disguised questionnaire attempts to hide the purpose of the study. An undisguised questionnaire makes the purpose of the research obvious, either in the introduction given, the instructions provided, or the questions asked. For example, if Ford Motor Co. wanted to determine its customers' satisfaction with its cars and trucks, it could simply send out a survey with a cover letter printed on Ford letterhead stationery and the Ford logo appearing on the questionnaire itself. Doing so, however, means that respondents' answers are very likely biased toward Ford, because the survey's purpose and sponsor are clear. If Ford wants more objective data, it might go without the letterhead, or go through an outside marketing research agency, or ask its drivers about Ford, GM, and Honda cars. In this scenario, the target of the research is less clear, and it is expected that the customer would answer more truthfully.

There are two general situations in which the use of disguise is often necessary. The Ford example illustrates the first: when knowledge of the sponsor or topic of the survey is likely to cause respondents to change their answers. Here's another example of this: Imagine asking people to "name the first three brands of cars that come to mind" or to "indicate their top two choices among the following brands of cars" when they can clearly see that the survey is sponsored by Ford. The researcher has "primed" a particular response, and the results will be of little value. Many times, respondents will not even know that they are changing their responses, although sometimes they do. There are several different sorts of these response biases; chief among them are an ingrained tendency to offer positive answers (sometimes referred to as "yeah-saying" bias), particularly when responding directly to the focal person or organization, and the general desire to tell others what we think they want to hear. If the sponsor and purpose are hidden from respondents, concerns about these sorts of biases are greatly reduced.

Disguise is also used to help create a more natural environment in which to collect data from individuals. While this can apply to questionnaires, it more often applies to experimental research. As an example, suppose that Ford researchers were interested in comparing two possible television advertisements for their ability to create awareness of a new Ford pickup truck. The researchers decided to run a lab study in which two groups of consumers were each shown one of the television ads. Further, the ads were imbedded into a 30-minute television show along with lots of other ads, and the consumers were told to watch the show as if they were watching television at home. Later, the participants were asked to recall as many of the brands advertised during the show as possible.

What will happen if the sponsor and purpose of the study are fully disclosed? The subjects will be watching for anything in the show or advertisements related to Ford products and, as a result, recall for the test ads will be much higher than it would otherwise have been. In short, the results would be useless. An alternative strategy would be to tell participants that the project was sponsored by the producers of the television show who wanted their feedback about the program. In this way, no extra attention is directed at the Ford commercials—in fact, attention is directed to where it normally would be for people viewing at home: on the program itself. The researchers have at least partially re-created a more natural environment that will produce results that come closer to the true situation.

The Ethics of Disguise

It seems a little strange to suggest that deception can be used to get at the truth in a situation, doesn't it? The use of disguise makes some people and researchers uncomfortable. Any way you look at it, the use of disguise amounts to a conscious effort to deceive the respondent, or at least to withhold information. Under the deontological perspective on marketing ethics, using disguise necessarily means a violation of a respondent's right to know why he is being asked to provide answers, how those answers will be used, and/or who will use the information. Researchers almost

MANAGER'S FOCUS

Sometimes managers or researchers choose not to disguise the purpose of their research because they hope to influence respondents' answers in a way that will help them or their companies look better. Here's an example: Mitchell's,* an independent restaurant, conducted a customer satisfaction survey using the following introduction:

> **You can expect More from us**
>
> **100% SATISFACTION is Mitchell's Guarantee**
>
> Because at Mitchell's your guaranteed satisfaction is our number one goal.
>
> Mitchell's has been an area tradition for residents and visitors alike. A tradition built on the finest ingredients, friendly atmosphere, and great service.
>
> PLEASE HELP us as we strive to make your next visit to Mitchell's even better.

It seems to us that the restaurant wanted to make respondents completely aware of the purpose of the questionnaire. The restaurant's managers apparently wanted to motivate patrons to complete the questionnaire by suggesting it was in their best interest to do so. This is not necessarily a bad thing—a good introduction is essential for securing cooperation in a study.

Subtle issues, however, can adversely affect information accuracy. For example, by repeatedly stating their commitment to satisfying customers, the restaurant managers may have introduced a positive bias in how respondents answered the satisfaction questions. Similarly, by claiming a strong tradition of having "the finest ingredients, friendly atmosphere, and great service," the managers may have prompted respondents to evaluate these aspects of the restaurant differently.

This example is nothing compared to the experience one of the authors had while buying a new car. During the process of completing the required paperwork, the purchaser was informed that he would soon receive a satisfaction survey in the mail and to please inform the salesperson if there was any reason that he couldn't give the highest satisfaction rating on key aspects. They even spelled out what the highest satisfaction rating would be on the scales to be included on the forthcoming survey. On the one hand, we could conclude that this was simply an effort to make certain that our needs were being met, and that the survey would provide confirmation that our needs were, in fact, met. On the other hand, let's call it what it really was: a blatant attempt to influence the dealership's satisfaction score at a time when corporate managers and consumers were placing increasingly greater emphasis on satisfaction measures generated internally and by outside sources (for example, J. D. Power and Associates).

It is important to recognize that there are many degrees of disguise. When measuring customers' satisfaction with specific products, services, or companies, it is almost impossible to disguise the purpose of the study. Nevertheless, it is generally good policy to reveal only what is necessary about the purpose of the study to secure cooperation from prospective respondents. You must never reveal your goals as a manager or other underlying purposes for the study if they have any potential to alter how people respond to questions. Similarly, you must resist the temptation to promote your products or services when gathering research data, because doing so is highly likely to influence how current or prospective customers respond to your questions. You may color respondents' views of the issues and/or make respondents skeptical about the integrity of the study. In addition, if you think about it, a questionnaire is an extremely poor promotional platform—it reaches a very limited number of people—so why sacrifice information integrity? Research is research, and promotion is promotion . . . and the two functions must *never* be combined in a single effort.

---

*Not the real name, although the restaurant is no longer in business.

universally agree, however, that the benefits of true, usable information outweigh the costs of the deception to respondents (note the use of the teleological perspective), provided that respondents are given appropriate information following the task. This process is known as **debriefing**.

How much information should be shared in the debriefing process? Rarely do researchers offer full disclosure. Most of the time, in fact, there is probably no great need to identify the specific sponsor of a project or the specific purpose of the research. Respondents usually don't care, and sponsors normally prefer to remain anonymous. This recommendation applies to situations in which information has been withheld. When disguise has involved an active deception, it is necessary to tell respondents that they have been misled, explain why the deception was needed, and provide a general overview of the purpose of the project. For the most part, the use of disguise and the amount of debriefing necessary involve judgment calls on the part of the researcher.

debriefing
The process of providing appropriate information to respondents after data have been collected using disguise.

METHODS OF ADMINISTERING QUESTIONNAIRES

The third decision that researchers must make when collecting primary data via communication is which method(s) to use. The main methods include personal interviews, telephone interviews, mail questionnaires, and Internet-based questionnaires. Although there are others, most approaches can be categorized into one of these four types. In this section, we'll discuss each of these methods and compare them on important attributes.

For each general method, we consider three key aspects. *Sampling control* refers to the ability of a particular method to identify and obtain responses from a sample of respondents from the target population. Obtaining lists of population members and likely response rates are key issues in sampling control. *Information control* is concerned primarily with the number and types of questions that can be used and the degree to which researchers and/or respondents might introduce error into the answers or their interpretation. Finally, *administrative control* refers to resource issues such as the time and monetary costs of the different approaches.

Learning Objective

5. Differentiate among the main methods of administering questionnaires.

Personal Interviews

A **personal interview** involves a direct face-to-face conversation between an interviewer and the respondent. Generally, the interviewer asks the questions and records the respondent's answers, either while the interview is in progress or immediately afterward. Sometimes, the interviewer may give all or part of the questionnaire to the respondent and be available to answer questions. In still other cases, the researcher may choose to secure the cooperation of the respondent, leave the questionnaire, and return to pick it up later (or have the respondent return the questionnaire via mail). Questionnaires that are administered in residential areas sometimes use this approach. Even though the questionnaire is completed without the researcher's presence, we still consider this a form of personal interview because of the initial face-to-face contact. The "drop-off" approach shares many similarities with mail questionnaires, however.

personal interview
Direct, face-to-face conversation between a representative of the research organization, the interviewer, and a respondent, or interviewee.

Personal interviews can take place just about anywhere. They can be conducted in a respondent's home or office or at the researcher's office in a central location. The location is dictated by the needs of the research and the convenience of the respondents. For example, if the interview is to be accompanied by an audit of food brands in a household's pantry or observation of how an individual uses a product at home, then the interview needs to take place at the consumer's residence. On the other hand, most of the time there is little need to actually visit the consumer's home, and researchers may choose to use a central location, such as a shopping mall. Research Window 10.1 provides one participant's humorous experiences with a personal interview conducted at a shopping center.

Learning Objective

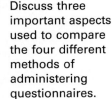

6. Discuss three important aspects used to compare the four different methods of administering questionnaires.

research window 10.1

Me, Doctor Mullet, and a Market-Research Mess

As a professional marketer, how could I resist experiencing what it's like to be on the consumer's side of a survey-taker's clipboard?
I did something unethical recently. Unethical in the same way that an undercover officer lies about his occupation in the line of duty. Meaning, it's really okay to lie when it's your job. Right? Anyway, it's all Subaru's fault. So when I'm at the gates of Hell, I'll have an alibi.

First, I have to tell you that I drive a Subaru. I know 40% of Americans need a monster truck to get to the grocery store, but I just need a car that can go anywhere without breaking. My Subaru Outback tells me I'm adventurous, rugged, and environmentally friendly, and in four years it's never had a mechanical failure. I have an expedition rack on the roof to personalize my brand bio by displaying snowboard, mountain bike, and the jumbo box of diapers that doesn't fit in the trunk with the groceries. I love my car.

So when the local Subaru dealer sent me a mailer with a $100 offer to answer a market-research survey, I was stoked. It was like someone offering money to eat chocolate cake. I'm happy to talk about my car and I'm happy to take a check, but I'm really happy to be on the consumer end of a market-research survey, taking note of whatever new techniques are being used by the big guns in retail marketing. I'm just weird that way. The concept of being a lab monkey for Subaru's market research was exhilarating, so I set up an appointment with an interviewer at the local mall.

Hide and Freak

I don't know how many times you've been intercepted at the mall to answer a "short survey," but you can spot the surveyors from a mile away—they're the only human beings on the planet who still carry clipboards. It's their distinguishing mark, like FBI agents with those-flesh-colored ear phones. What I didn't realize is that those surveyors actually live in the mall. They have their own storefront with a small reception area that hides all the cages in the back where they conduct lab tests on mall rats in exchange for movie tickets and candy.

I check into the lab, where a nice receptionist asked me to fill out a demographic survey and a release form. She pulled the form from a manila folder titled "Subaru Test," and then quickly covers up the title when she

realizes I can see over the counter. Apparently I'm supposed to be unaware that I'm taking part in a Subaru study, even though I was invited by Subaru. So she discretely hides the folder in a large tray clearly titled "Subaru." I'm also supposed to be double blind.

When I finished the form, she called to the back for my interviewer. I'm not sure exactly what I was expecting in a market researcher, but I suppose I have something professional in mind. A guy stepped into the doorway right off the set of an Eighties new wave video, complete with hair gel, dangle earring, and some kind of tunic shirt. He pulls it all together, though, with a white lab coat. He's, like, Dr. Mullet, and he walks me through a hallway, past convenience-store refrigerators filled with an odd assortment of generic products, and seats me in one of a handful of curtained cubicles containing a computer, monitor, and two chairs.

Watch and Learn

My task is to watch a series of commercials. They look like real commercials at first, but I don't recognize the products.

Is this bait and switch? Did they pull me in under the guise of talking about Subaru, when they really want to measure my response to this new product? Fine Pet Food? Good Quality Life Insurance? Wait a minute, these aren't real commercials. They're generic commercial pap, though I'm kind of frightened now that I can tell the difference.

But finally, sandwiched in the middle of a bunch of obviously fake commercials for nonexistent brands, I get the new Subaru message. A heart-pounding, adrenaline pumping commercial with Lance Armstrong riding like a warrior on a mountain bike over rocks and through streams. Is that what I look like? I do drive a Subaru, and I do ride a mountain bike. Boy am I cool! And I feel good about my choice to buy a Subaru.

Pat Answers

When the commercials are over, I wait a few minutes while Dr. Mullet chats in the hall with the receptionist about a popcorn taste test. He finally pulls back the curtain and sits down to his computer to ask me some

(Continued)

questions. First question: "Which brands do you recall from the commercials?"

Well, golly gee, let me think. I was invited to this gig by Subaru, and when I arrived I found out it was called the Subaru Test. I know I saw some vague commercials about fuzzy cats and old people. "Uh, Subaru?"

The doctor looks pleased. But somehow I'm sensing he's not happy for Subaru, simply relieved that the survey will go down easy. Second question: "How did the Subaru commercial make you feel?"

Questionable Questioning

Hmmm. With my palate cleansed by a course of happy household settings, calming music, and no discernible message, that hard-rocking music video with stunt cars and extreme sports stood out a bit. I look at Dr. Mullet and suddenly find myself feeling as clinically detached as he is. It's as if I, too, am a detached observer of my animalistic consumer responses.

"I felt. Excited. Energized," I respond. Dr. Mullet, typing at the computer, appreciates the concise responses. And at that moment, I realize why marketers like me are not supposed to play this game. As Dr. Mullet asks me a string of questions testing my recall and preference, I'm analyzing the questions, as well as my responses. I know what I want Subaru to read from my survey, and I know how the questions are designed to measure response, so I start calibrating my answers to achieve a consistent profile. Is this wrong? I like Subaru, and I like these commercials. And they obviously segmented their audience well if they're showing me images of rugged athletes. But man, I start to realize, this really is a poorly implemented survey.

As the string of questions drags on, Dr. Mullet gets impatient. Now, he's reading the questions as if in a hurry, and where before he had painstakingly typed every word I said, he now seems to be abbreviating. It seems to me that he's only half-reading the questions, and I kinda suspect he's typing in his own answers. Really, Scout's honor—although, in the interest of full disclosure, I only earned one badge in the Webelos. I'm outraged. Subaru is paying good money for this.

"Care for Pudding?"

I'm contemplating whether I should call Dr. Mullet's bluff on this farce of a market-research survey when he abruptly clasps his hands and says we're done. "Thank you for your time," he says, and I smile weakly. Perhaps sensing my disappointment, he smiles brightly in return and asks if I have time to try a new popcorn flavor. I don't, but I eye all the packages in the refrigerator on the way out with interest. Pudding. Fruit roll-ups—all signs of a mall-rat demographic. Is that my family?

The receptionist breaks away from a conversation with a young woman in a mall-store uniform to cut me a check and ask if I'm interested in future surveys. Many of them pay well she assures me. Sure, why not, but somehow the excitement is gone. Is this really how the big guys are tuning their products and messages? As I'm heading out the door she calls out to Dr. Mullet, "Hey Brian, run Julie on the popcorn test, and then do the frozen dinner with her, okay?" Julie must be the control group.

Source: Christopher Kenton, "Me, Dr. Mullet, and a Market-Research Mess," originally published in *BusinessWeekonline*, June 25, 2004, downloaded from Chris Kenton's Web site, http://www.chriskenton.com/marketonomy/articles/bw040625_Suburu.html, October 28, 2008. Reprinted by permission.

mall intercept
A method of data collection in which interviewers in a shopping mall stop or interrupt a sample of those passing by to ask them if they would be willing to participate in a research study.

Mall intercepts are popular for conducting personal interviews among consumers. The technique involves exactly what the name suggests: Interviewers intercept, or stop, people in a shopping mall and ask them to participate in a research study. If you've spent much time in a regional shopping mall, you've probably seen interviewers in action. You may even have participated in an interview. Those who agree to participate are typically taken to the firm's office in the mall, where the interview is then conducted. Research participants often receive incentives such as coupons or small gifts for their cooperation and time.

Mall intercepts are popular because they place the researcher in a location where people naturally gather together—consumers in their natural habitat. Simply put, this approach is convenient for finding consumers to answer our questions. There's a cost to this convenience, however. For most purposes, it will be impossible to draw a random sample of consumers, because not all consumers shop at malls. Only those who happened to visit the particular mall during the particular time frame had a chance of being included in the study. In addition, the people conducting the research typically choose which consumers to approach. These factors limit our ability to project results to the overall population. Still, for exploratory research and situations in which a nonrandom sample will work, mall intercepts can be quite useful.

Sampling Control   In some cases, a random sample can be used with the personal interview method. For some populations (for example, doctors, architects, or businesses), a list of population members (often called *population elements*) from which a sample can be drawn may readily be available from trade associations or in trade directories. When researchers want to draw a random sample of consumers or households, they often use area sampling, in which geographic areas (blocks, neighborhoods) and/or housing units (apartment buildings) are randomly selected and people within those areas are approached for personal interviews. The important point is that it is possible to draw a type of random sample when implementing data collection via personal interview. Still, developing a list of population members for personal interviews tends to be a little more difficult than for most other methods.

It is one thing to figure out whom to contact in a study; it is something else entirely to get that person to agree to participate. In this respect, the personal interview offers more sample control than other approaches. To start, the interviewer can verify the identity of the respondent; there is little opportunity for anyone else to reply. Response rates are also higher for personal interviews than most other methods of gathering communication data. The personal appeal makes it harder for respondents to say "no" compared with, say, simply tossing a mail questionnaire in the trash can. Sometimes a problem occurs with potential respondents not being at home, but this can often be handled by coming back at more appropriate times.

Information Control   The personal interview can be conducted using questionnaires with any degree of structure, from purely open-ended questions to purely fixed-alternative questions or any combination in between. One of the great strengths of personal interviews is the ability to explain or rephrase questions and to have respondents explain their answers. In addition, the personal nature of the interaction allows the interviewer to show the respondent pictures, examples of advertisements, lists of words, scales, and so on, as stimuli. The ability to gain a rapport and develop trust with a respondent is also a strong point for personal interviews.

A lot of information can be gathered in a personal interview, more so than with any other approach under normal circumstances. Because of the personal interaction aspect, researchers can usually get respondents to spend more time in a face-to-face interview. Personal interviews also allow the sequence of questions to be changed by the researcher fairly easily in response to the answers provided by respondents. For example, if the answer to a question about home ownership is "no," the researcher can skip questions about length of ownership, satisfaction with the current lender, recent remodels, and so on, and proceed to another point in the survey form, all without the respondent's knowledge.

Personal interviews are subject to several kinds of error that can bias the results obtained away from the truth in a situation. For

Learning Objective

7.   Explain why sampling control is difficult with telephone interviews and how this problem can be overcome.

ETHICAL DILEMMA 10.1

Pharmaceutical Supply Company derived its major source of revenue from physician-prescribed drugs. For quite some time, Pharmaceutical Supply had maintained a dominant position in the market. A new competitor had entered the market, however, and was quickly gaining market share.

In response to competitive pressure, Pharmaceutical Supply's management decided that it needed to conduct an extensive study concerning physician decision making with regard to selection of drugs. Janice Rowland, the marketing research director, decided that the best way to gather this information would be through the use of personal and telephone interviews.

Rowland directed the interviewers to represent themselves as employees of a fictitious marketing research agency, as she believed that a biased response would result if the physicians were aware that Pharmaceutical Supply was conducting the study. In addition, the interviewers were instructed to tell the physicians that the research was being conducted for the research agency's own purpose and not for a particular client.

- Was Rowland's decision to withhold the sponsor's true name and purpose a good one?
- Did the physicians have a right to know who was conducting the research?
- It has been argued that use of such deception prevents a respondent from making a rational choice about whether or not to participate in a study. Comment on this.
- What kind of results might have been obtained if the physicians had known the true sponsor of the study?
- What are the consequences for the research profession of using this form of deception?

example, we noted earlier that the interpretation of open-ended responses can be influenced by the biases of the researcher. In the classic form of a personal interview, the researcher is asking questions and then recording the respondent's answers; from hearing the answer, to writing it down, to interpreting it later, opportunities for researcher bias abound. And if the researcher changes the wording of questions or even the inflection in his or her voice . . . more possible error. Add to this the bias from the respondent's side of the equation—in particular the (un)conscious desires to appear knowledgeable, socially acceptable, and helpful to the researcher—and it should be clear that personal interviews must be undertaken with great care, including substantial interviewer training.

Administrative Control In most cases, personal interviews cost more to conduct than any other communication method. It's easy to see why: Interviews take place one at a time; interviews tend to last longer; researchers must often travel from one interview to the next (unless all interviews are conducted in a central location, which leads to greater office overhead expense); interviewers must be well trained, which is expensive, and when they are trained, they command higher salaries; and coding and analysis can be much more involved, particularly if open-ended questions have been used.

As you might also guess, using personal interviews generally takes a great deal of time. For each interviewer, there is unproductive time between each interview while the interviewer travels to the next respondent. If we want to speed up the process, the size of the field force must be increased. However, as the number of interviewers increases, so do problems of interviewer-related bias and costs of training. One potentially promising approach to overcoming these costs is computer-assisted interviewing tools. Not only do the time and speed issues of interviewing become less relevant, but data quality concerns such as variability in voice inflection become nonissues.[1]

Telephone Interviews

A **telephone interview** is similar in some ways to a personal interview, except that the conversation between researcher and respondent takes place over the telephone. It is still a social process involving direct interaction between individuals (with the exception of in-bound telephone surveys; see page 208). In part because of the social aspect, response rates are usually quite reasonable, whereas costs are much lower than personal interviews. As a result, telephone interviews have been a very popular means of securing communication data for many years. Still, there's a downside to not being able to know exactly what's on the other end of the telephone line, as researchers in Australia once discovered (see Research Window 10.2).

Sampling Control Many companies generate and sell lists of consumer or business telephone numbers from which to draw a random sample. These lists can often be selected based on particular geographic or demographic variables, or even on variables representing consumer interests, occupations, lifestyles, hobbies, and so on. One or more telephone books might also serve as a list of potential sampling elements. Phone book sampling frames are usually inadequate, however, because they do not include those without phones or those who have unlisted numbers including most mobile telephone users.

The overall penetration rate of telephones in the United States is quite high—over 90%—however, there is a dramatic shift in the types of service maintained. Landline or wireline phones are giving way to wireless subscribers (see Figure 10.1). Characteristically, wireless telephone numbers are not available in telephone directories. This increases the challenge of sampling control.

Studies that rely on phone books also underrepresent households that move from one geographic area to another. Anywhere from 12 to 15% of the residential numbers in a typical telephone directory are disconnected when called. Phone books also

research window 10.2

Tales from the Field: Persistence Pays Off

In 1993, we were doing a phone survey throughout country areas of western Australia. One night, an interviewer dialed a number in the Geraldton area. It rang and rang. As several attempts had already been made to do an interview at this number, she thought maybe it was a farm. Bearing in mind that some farmers install enormous phone bells outside their houses, and run from great distances whenever they hear the bells, she let it ring on and on.

At last a guy answered.

"I'd like to speak to the oldest man living in your household," said the interviewer. "That's me," he said.

The interview continued for ten or fifteen minutes, covering his radio listening, his opinions about programs, and so on. Finally they reached the demographic questions at the end of the questionnaire. The interviewer collected his age group, occupation, and so on. Last of all she asked: "How many people live at that address with you?"

"None!" he said, laughing. "They wouldn't fit in. This is a phone box."

"But . . . but . . . but" said the interviewer, puzzled.

"Look, I was walking down the street and I passed this phone box. The phone kept ringing, so I answered it."

do not include numbers that were assigned after the current directory was published, or numbers for people who have requested an unlisted telephone number. The unlisted segment has been growing steadily and now represents a sizable portion of U.S. telephone households.

The fact that some households don't have telephones in any form, the shift from resident to wireless service, and the fact that many telephone numbers are unlisted poses a problem known as noncoverage error when using telephone directories. These individuals or households have no opportunity to participate in the telephone

FIGURE 10.1 Monthly Personal Consumption Expenditures for Telephone Service per Household

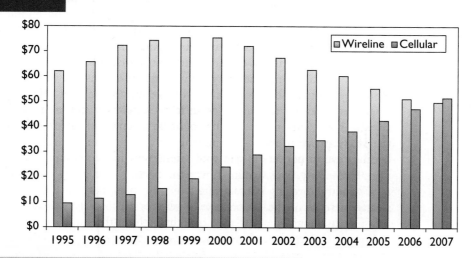

Source: United States Federal Communication Commission.

random-digit dialing (RDD)
A technique used in studies using telephone interviews, in which the numbers to be called are randomly generated.

interviews. This becomes a serious problem when they are different in some way (demographically, attitudinally, etc.) from people who are on the list.

Fortunately, there are a couple of ways of overcoming the error caused by unlisted numbers (though these techniques cannot overcome the lack of telephones in some households). The first approach, random-digit dialing (RDD), uses a computer to randomly generate numbers to be called. These systems usually automatically dial the calls as well. As a result, when a working number is reached, it makes no difference whether or not that number was listed in the telephone directory. Tests comparing RDD to the white pages of telephone listings found slightly better response rates for white-page calls, but no significant differences in demographic or other self-reported profile data between the RDD and white-page samples.[2]

As you might imagine, RDD systems are fairly inefficient because there are many millions of possible number combinations, but only a limited number of valid telephone numbers. Even when the possible combinations are limited by using only known area-code-prefix combinations, leaving only the final four digits to be randomly generated, RDD will produce several times more nonworking numbers than working numbers. An alternative scheme to random digit dialing is plus-one sampling, in which a random sample of phone numbers is selected from the telephone directory and a single, randomly determined digit is added to each selected number.

plus-one sampling
A technique used in studies employing telephone interviews, in which a single, randomly determined digit is added to numbers selected from the telephone directory.

Finding a working number from a list vendor, from the telephone book, or by RDD or plus-one sampling is only the first step, however, in securing feedback from a sample with the telephone interview method. The respondent must also be near the phone when it rings, answer the call, agree to participate, and then actually do so. Response rates that have traditionally been fairly good have begun to suffer in recent years, most likely from increasing use of caller ID and answering machines and personal voicemail to screen calls. Despite call screening, research firms can still generally get through to talk to a live consumer, however. Doing so simply requires persistence; more contacts to a given number must be attempted.[3] Fortunately, calling back is much simpler and more economical than following up personal interviews. The relatively low expense of a telephone contact allows a number of follow-up calls to secure a needed response, whereas the high cost of field contact restricts the number of follow-ups that can be made in studies using personal interviews.

Panel A in Exhibit 10.1 illustrates the percentage of respondents who were contacted on the first, second, third, and so on, attempted contact for a study conducted by one of the authors. This was a follow-up study conducted at the end of a school year among students about to graduate from college. The overall response rate was very high (94%), but only because we didn't stop making callbacks after the first or second try. Panel B in Exhibit 10.1 presents similar information for a telephone survey of faculty coordinators for fire science training programs across the United States. These results are consistent with other studies that have indicated that four to five calls are often needed to reach three-fourths of the elements in a sample.

Figure 10.2, on page 208, presents an analysis of answering machine rates, contact rates, refusal rates, and overall response rates for a telephone survey conducted by the Gallup Organization. The survey involved Internet usage, was conducted each quarter in the United States over a six-year period (September 1997 through September 2003), used exactly the same design in each quarter, and used up to five callbacks to any given working number. Although the reported rates are specific to this project, the study provides an ideal opportunity for examining changes in rates over time because everything about the study itself remained constant. As the chart indicates, overall response rates declined over the period. The cause of this decline appears to be a steadily lowering contact rate which, in turn, may have been caused in part by a steady increase in the proportion of phones picked up by answering machines. The refusal rate remained about the same throughout the study.

One additional consideration that may be affecting response rates to telephone surveys is the National Do-Not-Call (DNC) Registry, which prohibits telemarketers from calling registered U.S. households. The DNC Registry has been a rousing

Exhibit 10.1	Percentage of Respondents Reached with Each Call in a Telephone Survey

Panel A: Telephone Survey, University Seniors

Call	Number of Respondents	Percent*	Cumulative Percent*
1	35	20%	20%
2	31	18	38
3	34	20	58
4	14	8	66
5	40	23	89
6	17	10	99
7	1	1	100

*Percentages are based on total number of completed interviews. When refusals (4) and not-at-homes (2) are included, the overall response rate was 94%.

Panel B: Telephone Survey, Faculty Coordinators for Fire Science Training Programs

Call	Number of Respondents	Percent	Cumulative Percent
1	33	19%	19%
2	38	22	41
3	22	13	54
4	18	10	64
5	15	9	73
6	11	6	79
7	7	4	83
8	9	5	88
9	5	3	91
10	1	1	92
11	2	1	93
12	2	1	94
13	1	1	95
14	2	1	96
15	0	0	96
16	1	1	97
17	2	1	98
18	2	1	99
19	0	0	99
20	0	0	99
21	1	1	99
22	0	0	99
23	1	1	100

Panel B example courtesy Dr. Christine A. Johnson, Director, Oklahoma State University Bureau for Social Research.

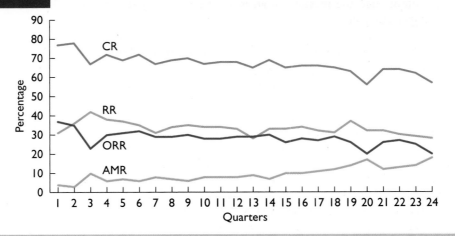

FIGURE 10.2

Recent Trends in Answering Machine Rate, Contact Rate, Refusal Rate, and Overall Response Rate for a Telephone Survey

Source: Robert D. Tortora, "Response Trends in a National Random Digit Dial Survey," *Metodoloski zvezki*, No. 1, 2004, downloaded from http://mrvar.fdv.uni-lj.si/pub/mz/default1.htm, October 28, 2008.

success by any measure. Current estimates suggest that over 75% of households have registered. Although marketing research and public opinion telephone interviews are *not* restricted by the DNC, some researchers have expressed concerns about its possible negative impacts on this communication method. In particular, if DNC household members become hardened in their belief that they should not be receiving any calls, it may prompt a quicker refusal than might otherwise have occurred. Countering this, however, is the fact that the presence of the DNC Registry has greatly reduced the number of unwanted calls in DNC households, effectively lowering competition for household members' attention—and possibly improving response rates in these households as a result.[4]

So far, we've assumed that a list of population members can be obtained, or at least that the purpose of the telephone interview is general enough that a sample from a telephone book or a number generated randomly will do. What happens, however, when the group you need to question is small and can't be identified on a list somewhere? Using telephone books, RDD, or plus-one sampling would be far too inefficient as a means of hunting for needles in the haystack. In this situation, many researchers have turned to **in-bound telephone surveys**. With in-bound surveys, respondents place the call to the researcher rather than the other way around (thus the call is "in-bound"). Actually, in virtually all cases, the respondents place a call that is answered by a computer and the respondent then uses the buttons on the telephone to answer questions prepared by the researchers and communicated through the computer. The computer can also record answers to open-ended questions. The in-bound call can be placed at any time by the respondent, day or night, whenever it is most convenient. At the conclusion of the interview, respondents typically receive a code number that allows them to obtain a discount or free gift of some sort from the survey sponsor.

In our experience, restaurants seem to be the most frequent users of in-bound telephone surveys. And this approach makes a lot of sense for restaurants or any businesses that cater to a unique clientele or that want to measure service quality or satisfaction while the experience is fresh in the consumer's mind. Imagine that a restaurant needed to determine the satisfaction level of customers who only visited the restaurant to pick up "to-go" meals to be eaten elsewhere. No one would offer a list of such customers, and starting with a general sample of residents in the area

in-bound telephone surveys
A method of data collection in which respondents place a telephone call at their convenience to a research firm and answer questions, typically by pressing buttons on the telephone.

would be terribly inefficient—it's hard enough to get consumers on the telephone in the first place without having to screen out the 95% or so who haven't ordered take-out food from the particular restaurant during the designated time period. In this situation, handing the consumer a coupon at the time of purchase with instructions to dial the telephone number and the promise of an incentive for doing so may be a cost-effective means of gathering the required data.

Information Control   As with personal interviews, it is possible to use both fixed-alternative and open-ended questions with telephone interviews. Most of the time, however, researchers tend to focus more on fixed-alternative questions that can easily be explained by the interviewer and easily answered by the respondent. The ability to sequence questions based on the answers to earlier questions is quite strong with telephone interviews, especially with the use of **computer-assisted interviewing (CAI)** software.

Computers were first used in the early 1970s to assist with telephone interviews. Interviewers would read the questions displayed on the computer screen and then key in the answers to a file that was sent to a mainframe computer. The early systems saved so much time and money that they created a revolution in data collection. Partly because of the advantages gained with computer administration of questionnaires, telephone interviews have become the most popular technique for gathering information by communication. One of the most important advantages of CAI is the information control it allows. The computer displays each question exactly as it should be asked and will go on to the next question only after an acceptable answer has been entered to the previous question. Question sequencing is handled seamlessly: Depending on the answer to the current question, the appropriate next question is automatically shown on the screen for the interviewer to ask the respondent. This saves considerable time and confusion in administering the questionnaire and permits a more natural flow of the interview. As we'll see in a later section, computer administration is the heart and soul of Internet-based surveys.

Telephone interviews allow probing and follow-up on respondent answers where necessary. Questions and instructions can be repeated and answers verified. Because of the human contact, a degree of trust can be developed, particularly on longer surveys. Because of the general focus on closed-ended questions that are easy to interpret and code, less bias due to interaction between interviewer and respondent probably enters the results. The presence of human interaction creates a social encounter, however, and data collected via telephone interview should not be assumed to be completely free of this sort of bias.

One of the biggest disadvantages of the telephone interview method is the limited amount of information that can be gathered from any given individual. Unless the topic is of great interest to respondents (or they are bored enough to talk to *anybody*, which actually happens), most are not going to be excited about staying on the telephone for an extended period of time. How long should a telephone interview be? It depends on the likely interest level of the topic, but we recommend trying to keep the interview to 5 to 10 minutes. Longer interviews are certainly possible, but you need to consider the possible adverse effects on response rates, not only to this particular survey, but also to future surveys these respondents might be asked to complete. The quality of the answers obtained from respondents whose patience has been exhausted is also an issue.

If the questionnaire to be used in the telephone interview is developed correctly, a considerable amount of information can be collected in 5 to 10 minutes, although all else equal, more information can usually be obtained using one of the other communication methods. For one thing, it is wise to use common rating scales and response categories with which people are familiar. Remember that respondents are *listening* to the survey and cannot see it. For example, many respondents probably have used 1–10 rating scales, formally and informally, for most of their lives. Similarly, they have little trouble understanding response categories anchored with words such as

computer-assisted interviewing (CAI) Using computers to manage the sequence of questions and to record the answers electronically through the use of a keyboard.

"not important–important," "unfavorable–favorable," "strongly disagree–strongly agree," and the like. Using familiar scales shortens the amount of time needed for instructions on how to respond. Unless absolutely necessary, we also recommend *not* trying to explain the meaning of every scale position ("... use a 1–5 scale, where 1 = very unlikely, 2 = unlikely, 3 = neutral ...") with telephone interviews. If respondents understand the meaning of the lowest position and the highest position, they should be just fine—and the interviewer can save some time. A final trick is to group all questionnaire items that use the same response categories together so that the interviewer isn't constantly taking time to instruct respondents on how to use the scales.

It is very difficult to use visual materials with telephone interviews. It might be possible to send pictures, graphics, logos, and the like, in advance, or to encourage respondents to go to a particular Web site during the telephone interview, but unless they are very motivated to respond, these options are not very realistic. If respondents need to respond to visual stimuli, other methods will almost always be preferred.

Administrative Control   Although it is usually more costly to collect data using telephone interviews compared with mail or Internet-based questionnaires, higher response rates for this method have traditionally kept the cost-per-contact quite reasonable. As rates decrease for telephone services, the largest portion of overall cost continues to be interviewer labor. Interviewers must be recruited and trained, and as with personal interviews, each interviewer can visit with only one respondent at a time. Unlike personal interviews, however, it is not uncommon for companies providing telephone interviewing services to employ small armies of interviewers on any given project. The training is not as intense as with personal interviews, and quality control can be assured by having supervisors periodically listen in on interviews in progress. As a result, data from telephone interviews can be collected in a matter of days, rather than weeks or months.

Mail Questionnaires

Who hasn't received a **mail questionnaire**? The classic form involves surveys sent to designated respondents with an accompanying cover letter and reply envelope. Respondents complete the questionnaire at their leisure and mail their replies back to the research organization. Variations to the classic form also exist. For example, a questionnaire might be dropped off at a residence (without direct contact between researcher and respondent), along with instructions to complete it and return it by mail to the researchers. Faxed surveys operate just like mail questionnaires, except that they are faxed to and from the recipients, typically businesses. Questionnaires for a "mail" administration may simply be attached to products or printed in magazines and newspapers or even stuffed in shopping bags. The key feature of all these approaches is a questionnaire that is completed by the respondent when and where he or she chooses, without personal communication with the researcher, and returned to the researcher typically through the mail.

Sampling Control   One key to effective mail questionnaires is obtaining one or more accurate mailing lists of people in the population of interest. This is no problem for companies doing customer surveys based on updated customer records in its database. In addition, some firms have established panels, which can be used to answer mail questionnaires and which are representative of the population in many important respects. In other cases, companies can purchase mailing lists, often for very specific populations. Business-to-business marketing research is usually easier in this regard— the mailing list and lists of phone and fax numbers are more stable than those for consumers, and businesses are fewer in number.

When a mailing list is purchased from a list company, it is normally purchased for a one-time use. Since the names and addresses on a mailing list can be delivered in a variety of formats, including as an electronic database file that can be stored on the client company's computer system, how does the list provider know that its list has been used only once? It's easy: Providers normally include one or more "dummy" addresses that are delivered back to the list company or its employees. If a company tries to use the list more than once, the owner of the list will soon know about it.

Purchased lists are usually reasonably accurate. Accuracy takes two forms when it comes to mailing lists. First is the accuracy of the actual addresses. List providers usually guarantee that at least 95% of the addresses are current, and the researcher can verify this based on the number of pieces that are returned because they cannot be delivered. The second type of accuracy, which is more difficult to determine, concerns whether or not the list contains the specific types of elements (for example, households in which the head of the household is African American, with household incomes above $50,000) that it is supposed to contain. Including questions on the survey to verify the selection criteria (ethnic background, household income) is about the only way to verify that the list was accurately selected.

As we noted, sometimes the list is generated internally. Spurred on by technical advances, a number of firms are developing greater capabilities to target questionnaires or other mailings to specific households. For example, American Express, with its image-processing technology, is now able to select all its cardholders who made purchases from golf pro-shops, who traveled more than once to Europe, who attended symphony concerts, or who made some other specific purchase using their American Express card. Databases are continually updated, so they also serve as an excellent resource for surveying current customers.

The quality of the mailing list determines the sampling control in a mail study. If there is an accurate, applicable, and readily available list of population elements, the mail questionnaire allows a wide and representative sample, since it costs no more to send a questionnaire across the country than it does to send one across town. Even ignoring costs, it is sometimes one of the only means of contacting the relevant population, such as busy executives who will not participate in an arranged personal or telephone interview but may respond to a mail questionnaire or Internet-based survey. The key is addressing the questionnaire to a specific respondent rather than to a title or position.

Mail questionnaires provide little control in securing a response from the intended respondent. The researcher can carefully identify desired respondents and offer them incentives, but he or she cannot control whether or not the respondents actually complete and return the questionnaires. With no direct contact between researcher and respondent, there is less social pressure to agree to the researcher's request to complete the questionnaire. Although there are circumstances in which a high proportion of people will return the surveys, this is not normally the case. Response rates for mail questionnaires are usually lower than for personal interviews or telephone interviews. Often, only those most interested in the survey topic will respond. And some people *can't* respond, because they are illiterate, or at least cannot read the language in which the questionnaire is written. Whatever the reason, higher levels of nonresponse with this method create greater opportunities for error to enter the process.

There's one final problem with mail questionnaires when it comes to sampling control. There is no way to determine if the intended respondent really completed a returned questionnaire, or if someone else may have completed it. This is probably more of a problem with questionnaires sent to businesses than with consumer projects. Many surveys intended for upper-level managers get completed and returned by their assistants—and there's no really good way for researchers to tell the difference. Even if code numbers are placed on the questionnaires (a practice we usually discourage), the researcher would only be able to determine which survey was returned—not who actually completed it.

Information Control Mail questionnaires offer a couple of nice advantages when it comes to information control. For one thing, with written questions, there is no opportunity for interviewer bias from the wording of questions or the way that the questions are asked. It is also possible to include graphics, pictures, or other artwork if respondents need to see a stimulus in order to respond effectively. It may also be possible to collect a bit more information with mail surveys than with telephone interviews, but there are clearly limits on the amount of time respondents are willing to spend on written questionnaires. As with all other methods, it depends on how interested they are in the topic, but it is usually advisable to keep mail surveys under four pages long. Better yet, keep the survey to two pages (that is, one page, printed on both sides) if at all possible.

One of the biggest advantages of mail questionnaires is the anonymity offered the respondent. People are likely to be more candid in their responses when they believe that the responses cannot be traced directly back to them. If your topic revolves around a sensitive issue (for example, sexual behavior, participation in illegal or socially undesirable activities), the normal recommendation is to use mail questionnaires.

Despite these advantages, there are some shortcomings of mail questionnaires with respect to information control. Most importantly, mail questionnaires do not allow clarification of questions or response categories, nor can researchers ask follow-up questions or clarify answers. If open-ended questions are included, individuals must write out their answers, which is more difficult than answering a question orally. All else equal, more work for respondents translates into fewer questionnaires returned.

Here's another disadvantage: If they choose, respondents can review the entire questionnaire before answering the questions. This is a real problem if the researcher wants to assess awareness for certain brands and also ask specific questions about those brands in the same survey. If respondents see questions about Target in a survey, don't be surprised if "Target" is one of the most often mentioned answers to the item "list the first three department stores that come to mind." In addition, instructions for question sequencing ("If the answer to the previous question is "no" go to question 7") can quickly become complicated and should be avoided if possible with mail questionnaires.

Administrative Control   Given low response rates and the problems with information control noted above, why would anyone continue to use mail questionnaires? Probably the biggest reason, other than the anonymity we discussed earlier, is the fact that mail questionnaires can typically be implemented at lower cost than personal interviews or telephone interviews. (Internet-based surveys cost even less, but often have even lower response rates and cannot guarantee anonymity.) Compared with hiring and training interviewers, it just doesn't cost a lot to print surveys, buy a mailing list, and pay postage (outbound and inbound). If the response rate is too low with mail, however, it is possible for cost-per-contact to actually be lower for telephone interviews.

Quality control is a plus for mail surveys, compared with telephone interviews, and especially, personal interviews. Supervisory responsibilities are limited to the management of the mailing process, both outgoing and incoming. This also serves to lower costs.

The only administrative disadvantage of mail questionnaires is that they take longer to implement than do most telephone surveys—but they're faster than personal interviews. It takes longer because the surveys must go through the postal system going and coming, and respondents are free to answer at their own convenience. As a result, you should budget at least two extra weeks in the timeline of a project using this approach. If you include follow-up mailings, which is often the case with mail surveys as a means of increasing the response rate, the time required increases substantially. By the way, here is another difference between mail surveys (or Internet-based projects) when it comes to administration time: It takes as long to get replies from a small sample as it does from a large sample. This is not the case with personal and telephone interviews, where there is a direct relationship between the number of interviews and the time required to complete them.

Internet-Based Questionnaires

Internet-based questionnaires share many of the qualities of mail questionnaires but utilize the Internet for distribution (most of the time) and completion/receipt (virtually all of the time) of participants' responses. There are two general forms of these surveys. The first relies completely on e-mail; the survey is included in the text of the e-mail message or in an attachment to the e-mail and the respondent completes the survey and sends it back by replying to the e-mail. It is possible that the respondent would be asked to return the survey in some other fashion (in person, by mail, or via telephone), but not very likely.

The second form of Internet-based questionnaire utilizes a survey placed on a Web site. With this approach, respondents can be recruited in a variety of ways (but usually via e-mail) and directed to the Web site to complete the questionnaire. This method of gathering communication data is increasing in popularity as more and more households gain Internet access. Dozens of companies offer online survey services; many of these companies offer assistance with survey design and analysis along with basic data collection. Note that this approach is much like an in-bound telephone interview: Respondents must decide to contact the researcher to gain access to the survey.

Sampling Control   As with all techniques, the ability to obtain an accurate list of population members' contact information is the first key aspect of sampling control. With all e-mail surveys and most Web surveys, this means obtaining lists of e-mail addresses. Before going any further, you must recognize that not all people have e-mail addresses or have easy access to the Internet, facts that some proponents of Internet-based questionnaires seem to forget. For many of us, especially younger people and those who have learned to use e-mail as a key communications tool, these technologies have been integrated into our everyday lives. This isn't the case, however, for everyone; unless your population contains a high proportion of people likely to utilize the Internet on a regular basis, one of the other approaches should

Learning Objective

8. List and discuss two types of Internet-based questionnaires.

Internet-based questionnaire
A questionnaire that relies on the Internet for recruitment and/or completion; two forms include e-mail surveys and questionnaires completed on the Web.

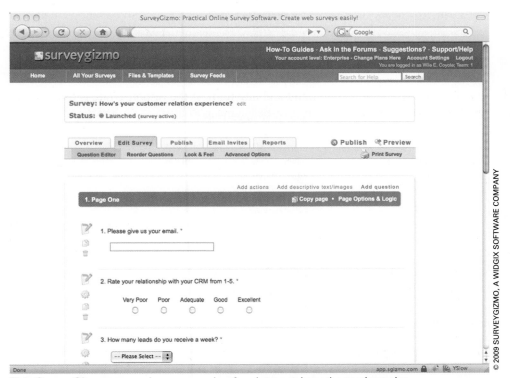

This SurveyGizmo survey is an example of an Internet-based questionnaire.

© 2009 SURVEYGIZMO, A WIDGIX SOFTWARE COMPANY

probably be used. Think about it this way: A very large percentage of people and/or households have telephones and mailing addresses. Although Internet-based communication is growing in popularity in the United States and around the world, in the general population the penetration level of these approaches simply doesn't compare with the established methods.

Lists of e-mail addresses are available from numerous sources. Much like mailing lists, these lists can often be selected based on respondent demographics, interests, and so on. As an example, the online survey company Zoomerang boasts its ZoomPanel of over 2.5 million participants who have agreed to complete surveys. Exhibit 10.2 includes the variables available for fine-tuning sample selection. You should note, however, that many e-mail samples are developed by encouraging individuals to join a panel in exchange for gifts and/or other incentives. These samples, even if they are carefully built to reflect the overall population under study, do not meet the requirements necessary for projecting results to the population. It isn't the incentives that cause the problem; it's the fact that not everyone in the designated population had the chance to be included—some because they don't have e-mail or Web access and some because they simply didn't sign up to be part of a sample. On the other hand, if all or most members of a particular population do have e-mail and Internet access and all or most are

---

Exhibit 10.2   **Sample Selection Variables Available through Zoomerang**

Demographic Variables

Gender
Age
Children in Household
Annual Household Income
Occupation
Education
Ethnicity
Marital Status
Home Ownership
Pet Ownership
Children's Dates of Birth
Language

Geographic Variables

Country
State
Zip Code
Metropolitan Statistical Area

Technographic Variables

Internet Access Speed
Internet Access Location
Internet Usage

Occupation/Business Variables

Occupational Title
Functional Area
Industry
Number of Employees
Annual Revenue
Business Owner

Shopping/Consumption/Ownership Variables

Home Electronics Purchase Intent
Home Electronics Ownership

Consumer Goods Purchase Frequency for over 75
   Specific Products
Online Purchases/Purchase Intent
Channel Shopping Frequency at Convenience,
   Discount, Club, Drug, Supermarket, Electronics,
   Book, Automotive, and Apparel Stores
Channel Shopping Purchases at Convenience,
   Discount, Club, and Drug Stores
Restaurant Dining Frequency at over 20 Specific
   Restaurants
Pet Ownership
Home Ownership

Health/Wellness Variables

Dietary Restrictions
Organic Product Purchase Frequency
Health Conditions/Ailments

Automotive Variables

Purchase Intent
Number of Vehicles
Make, Model, Year of Vehicles
Automotive Store Shopping Frequency

Personal Finance Variables

Investments
Online Investing
Credit Services
Online Purchasing
Online Insurance Purchasing

Interest Variables

Books
Music
Computers
Health/Exercise/Sports

Source: Downloaded from the Zoomerang Web site, http://www.zoomerang.com/resources/Panel_Profile_Book.pdf, October 27, 2008.

included on a list of the population members, then a sample can probably be drawn using some random technique and the results can be projectable. By the way, this problem isn't specific to Internet-based questionnaires alone. It applies to any situation in which a relatively complete list of population members is not available or cannot be developed. Compared with mail questionnaires and telephone interviews, however, the problem is more severe with Internet-based surveys.

Even if e-mail addresses are available for a particular population, we still face the daunting task of getting them to respond to the questionnaire. Our experience suggests that Internet-based questionnaires often have the lowest response rates of any method of collecting communication data. Sure, it's possible to end up with a large sample size by sending millions of e-mail requests to participate, but if only 2 to 3% (or less) of these people respond, there is an increased possibility (probability?) that the people who respond are different in important ways from the people who don't respond. And as a result, we can have little confidence in the results that we produce.

With e-mail surveys, it isn't likely that someone other than the intended respondent will reply, given that the questionnaires reside in personal e-mail accounts. This is an advantage compared with mail surveys, which are normally truly anonymous. Of

MANAGER'S FOCUS

New technologies often seem to be promoted with exaggerated claims about the benefits they produce. This has certainly been the case with some Internet-based research methods. For example, some research firms specializing in Web-based surveys have promised prospective customers extraordinarily high "response rates." As with any other numerical figure, though, the meaning of "response rate" depends on how it is calculated.

Response rates should be calculated by using as the base the number of people from a population who were predesignated to be respondents. In other words, the base is the number of people the firm attempts to contact to be in the study, after adjusting for invalid e-mail addresses, mailing addresses, and telephone numbers. Dividing the number of people who actually respond to the questionnaire by this base produces the response rate.

Some Web-based survey companies focus more on the completion rate than the actual response rate. The completion rate represents the proportion of people who complete the survey after opening the survey Web page. Naturally, the completion rate always is going to be much higher than the overall response rate, unless virtually everyone contacted about a study actually goes to the survey Web site—and our experience with Web-based questionnaires suggests that that is almost never going to happen. Although a high completion rate is a desirable outcome, it is *not* the same thing as a high response rate. As a manager, you'll need to compare

claims by different online research suppliers about "response rates" to make certain they are all talking about the same thing.

One other caution is related to some of the material discussed in this chapter. When you assess the response rates produced by Web-based survey companies, you need to determine whether the survey was administered to a sample *generated specifically for the study*, or if it was administered to members of an *existing* panel. Web-based surveys are often administered to panels that are said to be "representative" of populations based on demographic characteristics, even though they may not be representative in terms of many other important characteristics. Because panel members have agreed beforehand to participate in surveys, the response rates tend to be higher, enabling an organization to generate a larger sample at a relatively low cost.

As discussed in this chapter, panels can provide useful information for some purposes. However, when you need to project or generalize the findings to the overall market (population), panels are not particularly good data sources and probability samples should be utilized instead. When knowing what would be true for the overall population (within a margin of sampling error), as opposed to what is true for the particular people who participate in the project, is important, it is probably better to obtain data from a small-sized probability sample than to collect data from a larger sample generated from an existing panel.

course, if anonymity is needed due to sensitive questions and the like, the ability to personally identify a respondent becomes a disadvantage in terms of information control.

Most of the time, Internet-based questionnaires should be used with caution. Assuming that you can reach the right kinds of people and get them to respond, however, they can be used as an exploratory research tool. And under the right circumstances (that is, a population in which all or most members are Internet savvy and have access, an accurate list that contains all or most population members, and motivated respondents), they may be the most effective means of collecting descriptive data as well.

For one recent project, we used a Web-based questionnaire to collect data from sales consultants with three large direct selling companies. Each of the companies routinely used e-mail as a means of communicating with the sales consultants, so the e-mail address lists were current and the consultants mostly were comfortable with the technology. We drew random samples of sales consultants meeting our criteria and had the companies send e-mails from someone within the company encouraging (but not requiring) each sales consultant to participate. The e-mail, which contained a link to the Web-based questionnaire, assured potential respondents that their answers would be held in confidence. The overall response rate across the companies was 12%, which is probably a little lower than we would have expected with mail questionnaires. As we'll discuss below, however, Internet-based questionnaires can be much less expensive than any other approach, which explains in part their appeal.

Information Control Internet-based questionnaires, especially those conducted via the Web, can effectively use pictures and other graphics with the questionnaire. Consistent with mail surveys, the amount of information collected can be more substantial than with telephone interviews, there is essentially no interviewer bias in the way questions are asked, and any type of question can be used. This approach also shares a disadvantage with mail surveys: There is no ability to probe, to explain questions, or to ask for respondents to explain their answers.

With Web surveys, question sequencing can be programmed into the survey, ensuring that the appropriate next question appears on the screen for the respondent. This feature offers greater flexibility with Web surveys than with e-mail or mail surveys. As noted, e-mail questionnaires offer little anonymity. Many people are also concerned about privacy when it comes to Web activity as well, believing that their answers could be traced back to them if someone wanted to do so. Still, the comfort level of respondents is likely higher with Web-based questionnaires than with those conducted via e-mail.

Administrative Control One of the greatest advantages of Internet-based surveys is that they provide the marketing researcher the quickest turnaround. Many e-mail surveys are completed and returned the same day they are sent. There are other administrative advantages as well. Most companies already employ Internet servers, so the necessary hardware is likely already in place and paid for should a company decide to implement Internet-based questionnaires on its own, and the services of online survey providers are relatively inexpensive should researchers choose that option. Even better, because responses are normally automatically recorded in data files (and only valid responses are accepted), respondents effectively code their own responses when they reply to the questions on the survey. This eliminates one step (that is, data coding) where error can enter into the data set, not to mention a great deal of potential cost.

Comparing Methods of Administering Questionnaires

Each of these methods of communication possesses advantages and disadvantages. These are summarized in Exhibit 10.3. When discussing the pros and cons, the pure cases logically serve as a frame of reference. When a modified form of administration is used, the general advantages and disadvantages may no longer hold. The advantages

MANAGER'S FOCUS

Sampling Control, Information Control, and *Administrative Control* may appear to be primarily concerns for researchers. After all, it is generally the researcher's responsibility to propose a method by which to administer the data collection instrument. Nevertheless, it isn't wise to assume that researchers always propose a method of administration after carefully weighing these issues.

Always remember that one of your central responsibilities as a manager is to evaluate research proposals for ways to gather the information *you* need to make marketing decisions. As a result, it is critical that *you* carefully consider the control factors described above when evaluating a research provider's proposal.

You should ask yourself whether it appears the proposed method of questionnaire administration is well justified through a discussion of these control issues, or if it was likely selected as a matter of cost or convenience to the researcher. It is not uncommon for research providers to have a "preferred" method of administration, the one they use in most research studies, and the preference may or may not correspond with your organization's specific needs. If it is not clear to you why a particular method has been proposed, you should probe for the research supplier's motivation by asking a series of questions concerning the various control considerations.

E x h i b i t   1 0 . 3   **Primary Communication Methods of Data Collection: Relative Advantages (+) and Disadvantages (−)**

	Personal Interviews	Telephone Interviews	Mail Questionnaires	Internet-Based Questionnaires
SAMPLING CONTROL				
Ability to secure list of population members		+	+	−
Ability to secure correct respondent	+	+	−	+ (E)*
Response rate	+	+	−	− −
INFORMATION CONTROL				
Ability to probe for detailed answers	+ +	+	−	−
Ability to handle complex information	+	− −	−	+ (W)
Ability to clarify questions	+ +	+	−	−
Amount of information obtained	+	−		
Flexibility of question sequencing	+	+	−	+ (W)
Protection from interviewer bias	− −	−	+	+
Ability to obtain personal information	−	−	+	− (E)
Ability to show visual displays	+	−	+	+
Ability to offer anonymity	−	−	+	− (E)
ADMINISTRATIVE CONTROL				
Time requirements	− −	+	−	+ +
Cost requirements	− −	+	+	+ +
Quality control/supervisory requirements	− −	−	+	+
Computer support		+	−	+ +

*(E) = e-mail questionnaire, (W) = Web questionnaire

and disadvantages may also not apply when dealing with different countries with different cultures. We have provided a general overview.

The specific situation surrounding a project often dictates the actual approach chosen. For example, no matter how much the research team may want to use personal interviews, the budget may not support that option, and researchers must do the best they can with the budget allocated, even if the final approach is suboptimal. Similarly, researchers will need to endure the disadvantages of mail questionnaires if this is the only reasonable method of reaching the designated population.

Combining Administration Methods While none of the methods we have described for collecting communication data is superior in all situations, the research problem itself will often suggest one approach over the others. It is also possible that a combination of approaches may be more productive. For example, a business manager could receive a letter, an e-mail, or a phone call asking for his or her help in a study, and after this notification the survey could be sent to his or her place of business. Web surveys can be initiated either by sending an e-mail to the sample of potential respondents that asks them to visit a certain Web address to complete the survey form, or by a cooperative relationship with another Internet vendor by placing a banner at its site. The respondent then just clicks through the survey. Self-administered questionnaires can be hand-delivered to respondents along with product samples, and telephone interviews can be used for follow-up.

SUMMARY

Learning Objective 1

Explain the concept of *structure* as it relates to questionnaires.

The degree of structure in a questionnaire is the degree of standardization imposed on it. In a highly structured questionnaire, the questions to be asked and the responses permitted by the subjects are completely predetermined. In a questionnaire with less structure, the response categories are not provided; sometimes even the questions can vary.

Learning Objective 2

Cite the drawbacks of using high degrees of structure.

Fixed-alternative questions may force a subject to respond to a question on which he or she does not really have an opinion. They may also prove inaccurate if none of the response categories allows the accurate expression of the respondent's opinion. The response categories themselves may introduce bias if one of the probable responses is omitted because of an oversight or insufficient prior research.

Learning Objective 3

Explain what is meant by *disguise* in a questionnaire context.

The amount of disguise in a questionnaire is the amount of knowledge hidden from the respondent as to the purpose and/or sponsor of the study. An undisguised questionnaire makes the purpose of the research obvious by the questions posed; a disguised questionnaire attempts to hide the purpose of the study.

Learning Objective 4

Discuss two situations in which disguise might be desirable.

Disguise is useful when knowledge of the purpose of the study or its sponsor would cause respondents to change their answers. Disguise is also used to help re-create a more natural environment for those participating in research, especially experimental research.

Learning Objective 5

Differentiate among the main methods of administering questionnaires.

Personal interviews imply a direct face-to-face conversation between the interviewer and the respondent, as opposed to *telephone interviews*. In both types, the interviewer asks the questions and records the respondents' answers, either while the interview is in progress or immediately afterward. *Mail questionnaires* are sent to designated respondents with an accompanying cover letter. The respondents complete the questionnaire at their leisure and mail their replies back to the research organization. *Internet-based questionnaires* involve either e-mails sent to respondents, who in turn reply to the e-mail with their answers, or surveys that are completed by respondents via the Web.

Learning Objective 6

Discuss three important aspects used to compare the four different methods of administering questionnaires.

Sampling control concerns the ability to identify, reach, and receive answers from population members. Information control involves the amount, type, and quality of information that can be retrieved from respondents. Administrative control is concerned with the degree of quality control possible and time and cost requirements.

Learning Objective 7

Explain why sampling control is difficult with telephone interviews and how this problem can be overcome.

Many individuals and households either do not have a telephone, have an unlisted telephone number, or have moved since the most recent telephone directory was published. As a result, studies using telephone interviews based on samples drawn from telephone directories will not include many people who are members of the particular population being studied. Random-digit dialing overcomes this problem by randomly generating telephone numbers to be dialed. Plus-one sampling addresses the problem by taking valid telephone numbers and adding a randomly determined single digit to the number. In-bound telephone surveys have respondents place a call to a computer at a research provider's office and answer questions typically by using the buttons on the telephone's keypad. This approach overcomes the problem of developing a list of population members when population members are hard to identify and/or other methods would be inefficient.

Learning Objective 8

List and discuss two types of Internet-based questionnaires.

The two types of Internet-based questionnaires include e-mail surveys and Web surveys. With e-mail surveys, the data collection instrument is sent in the body of the e-mail or as an attachment. Web surveys require respondents to go to a Web page, typically by clicking a link, where they complete the survey.

KEY TERMS

structure (page 195)
fixed-alternative questions (page 195)
open-ended question (page 195)
disguise (page 198)
debriefing (page 200)
personal interview (page 200)
mall intercepts (page 202)
telephone interview (page 204)

random-digit dialing (RDD) (page 206)
plus-one sampling (page 206)
in-bound telephone surveys (page 208)
computer-assisted interviewing
    (CAI) (page 209)
mail questionnaire (page 210)
Internet-based questionnaires (page 213)

REVIEW QUESTIONS

1. What are the advantages of higher degrees of structure? What do researchers gain through the use of lower structure?

2. What is a disguised questionnaire? What are the ethical considerations in using disguise?

3. Why are telephone interviews a popular choice for collecting communication data?

4. Why do you think Internet-based questionnaires are growing in popularity?

5. How do personal interviews, telephone interviews, mail questionnaires, and Internet-based questionnaires differ with respect to the following:

   a. sampling control

   b. formation control

   c. administrative control

6. How might a researcher combine different methods of communication in the same project? Give an example.

DISCUSSION QUESTIONS, PROBLEMS, AND PROJECTS

1. Suppose you were asked to design an appropriate communication method to find out students' feelings and opinions about the various food services available on campus.

   a. What degree of structure would be appropriate? Justify your choice.

   b. What degree of disguise would be appropriate? Justify your choice.

   c. What method of administration would be appropriate? Justify your choice.

2. Ann Avery is the general manager of Taylor's, a steakhouse located in a southwestern U.S. city that has been open for about a year. The restaurant has been a success so far, but Avery doesn't yet have a grasp of exactly who her customers are. The lunch customers seem to be quite different from those who visit Taylor's for the evening meal. She needs your help in designing a project designed to develop a better understanding of her customers.

   a. What degree of structure would be appropriate? Justify your choice.

   b. What degree of disguise would be appropriate? Justify your choice.

   c. What method of administration would be appropriate? Justify your choice.

   d. Suppose that the key issue is to determine the overall awareness level for Taylor's among residents of the city. Would this change your answers to any of the above questions?

3. Which method of gathering data would you use in each of the following situations? Justify your choice.

   a. Administration of a questionnaire to determine the number of people who listened to the "100 Top Country Tunes in 2008," a program that aired on December 31, 2008.

   b. Administration of a questionnaire to determine the number of households having a mentally ill individual in the household and the history of mental illness in the family.

   c. Administration of a questionnaire by a national manufacturer of microwave ovens in order to test people's attitudes toward a new model.

   d. Administration of a questionnaire by a local dry cleaner who wants to determine customers' satisfaction with a recent discount promotion.

   e. Administration of a questionnaire by the management of a small local hotel that wants to assess customers' opinions of its service.

4. You have been asked to conduct a survey of graduating seniors at your school about their plans following graduation. Very little money is available to support the research, and your client has asked you to use an Internet-based questionnaire. Prepare and discuss a list of key advantages and disadvantages of this communications method in this situation. Based on your analysis, how would you design the study, if at all? If you did not want to

use Internet-based questionnaires, what other option would you recommend given the budget restrictions?

5. Arrange an interview with a member of the marketing faculty at your school (other than your instructor in this course) who is actively engaged in academic marketing research. Discuss the objectives of the faculty member's research and what type of method(s) she or he uses to collect primary data. Report on the advantages and disadvantages of the data collection method(s) used in relation to the research objective. Try to determine if trade-offs have been necessary (e.g., cost against speed; structure against disguise) in order to collect the data, and if so, the reasons for those trade-offs. Be sure to address the broad issues of structure, disguise, sampling control, information control, and administrative control in your report.

Collecting Information by Observation

Introduction

One means for researchers to gather data is via communication: asking questions and receiving answers. When it comes to the measurement of behavior, however, more reliable data can often be obtained through observation. The reason is obvious—with interviews and surveys, there are lots of ways for error to enter into the analysis, things like people forgetting, trying to look better in the eyes of the interviewer, misunderstanding the question or the answer, and so on. Although observational research is not completely free from error, it is often the best method for generating valid data about what people *do*. We focus on this topic in this chapter.

OBSERVATION RESEARCH

Observation is a fact of everyday life. We are constantly observing other people and events as a means of gaining information about the world around us. When researchers use this approach, however, the observations are systematically planned and carefully recorded. For example, when researchers watched consumers buy dog food, they found that adults focused on buying dog food, but that senior citizens and children bought a bigger proportion of dog treats. Unfortunately for these seniors and small children, the treats were usually stocked on the top shelf. The researchers' cameras "witnessed one elderly woman using a box of aluminum foil to knock down her brand of dog biscuits." When the retailer moved the treats to where children and older people could reach them more easily, sales soared.[1] The insights gathered by watching that lady maneuver to get her favorite brand might have taken much longer to obtain—if they could be uncovered at all—using communication.

Observation is often more useful than surveys in sorting fact from fiction with respect to behaviors, particularly "desirable" behaviors. For example, most people wouldn't want to acknowledge that they spend more on cat food than on baby food, but consumers can be observed doing so. In another study, parents were asked whether the color of a new toy would matter; all the parents said no. At the end of the study, as a small reward for their participation, researchers offered the parents a toy to take home to their child, and all the parents clamored for the purple and blue toys.

Examples of Observation Research Observation research involves watching a situation of interest and recording relevant facts and behaviors. Sometimes researchers use *direct observation*, which means watching the actual activity. For example, Hewlett-Packard's medical products division sent its researchers to watch surgeons operate. They noticed that monitors portraying electronic video of scalpel movement were often blocked by other staff members walking between the physician and the monitor, so HP created a surgical helmet that casts images in front of a surgeon's eyes.[2] In other cases, researchers use *indirect observation*, in which the outcomes of the behavior are observed, rather than the behavior itself. For example, Timothy Jones, an archeologist and garbologist at the University of Arizona, has dug through Tucson trashcans in search of empty toothpaste tubes and used dental floss to see which dental hygiene practices seem to work, and which don't, based on correlating what he finds in the garbage with local dental records.[3]

Observation research does not have to be sophisticated to be effective. It can be as basic as the retailer who used a different color of promotional flyer for each zip code to which he mailed. When customers came into the store with the flyers, he could identify which trading areas the store was serving. Similarly, nonprofit groups using various mailing lists to solicit donations can easily determine which lists are more effective by coding the response forms or envelopes. And consider these straightforward indirect measures of behavior:

- A car dealer in Chicago checked the position of the radio dial of each car brought in for service. The dealer then used this information to decide on which stations to advertise.

- The number of different fingerprints on a page has been used to assess the readership of various ads in a magazine, and the age and condition of cars in a parking lot have been used to gauge the affluence of those patronizing a particular store.

- Scuff marks on museum floor tile have long been used as a means of measuring the popularity of a display.

MANAGER'S FOCUS

The marketing research process is often considered the "ears" of an organization because it involves "listening to the voices" of target customers. This is certainly a reasonable depiction, but marketing research can also be considered the "eyes" of the organization. Without a doubt, regularly hearing the voice of the market is an important part of being market oriented. Some data simply cannot be obtained in any other way. In our view, however, researchers are often too quick to use communication methods (that is, interviews and questionnaires of various types) when observational methods would be more appropriate and helpful. Managers need to reprogram their thinking so their first impulse is not to conduct surveys when information is needed to predict market responses.

As we have emphasized before, consumers can easily tell you what they will do in the future ... it's just that what they say they will do and what they actually do are often different. As a result, you are treading on thin ice when you make important decisions based only on what consumers tell you about their likely future purchasing behavior. Consumers' prior behavior is almost always a better predictor of their future behavior.

Your effectiveness as a marketing decision maker will be enhanced if you regularly commission research to observe target customers' buying and consumption behavior. For this reason the methods discussed in this chapter are very important to your future success even though they have not traditionally been utilized as frequently as communication techniques. As you will see, innovative organizations are increasingly finding clever ways to use technology to monitor marketplace behavior for opportunities and threats. You may not always have the resources necessary to perform the more sophisticated forms of observation you will read about here, but you should do whatever observation you can to understand how consumers actually behave relative to your offerings and those of your competitors.

Learning Objective

2. List the important considerations in the use of observational methods of data collection.

Sometimes observational research is more sophisticated. Consumers have been watched through one-way mirrors trying to assemble a computer or using the computer to surf the Internet. Many shopping malls determine their trading areas by hiring people to walk the parking lot of the mall and record every license number they find. These data can then be fed into computers that match the license plates to zip code areas or census tracts and prepare color-coded maps showing customer density from the various areas. And sometimes the degree of sophistication reaches levels that would make James Bond proud. A large sports/convention arena located in the eastern United States once built sensors into its outside walls that could determine which radio stations were tuned in on cars driven in its parking lot. This information would be useful for deciding which stations to use for advertising upcoming events at the arena.

Researchers have inventoried or photographed the contents of consumers' refrigerators, their

Researchers can check what radio stations are preset in a vehicle to gauge which stations to advertise on.

© JOHN LAMM/TRANSSTOCK/JUPITERIMAGES

medicine cabinets, their closets, and their garages. Photos of a medicine cabinet will indicate not only what products it contains, and what brands and sizes, but also their arrangement—items stored front and center are probably used most frequently. Researchers for *Gourmet* magazine have moved right into their readers' homes to "look into their cabinets," "pore over their Visa bills," or "snip labels out of their clothes." *Gourmet* especially wanted to understand its younger readers—readers who are affluent, knowledgeable about food trends, and know hot restaurants and fine wines. A sample of readers were given disposable cameras and asked to take photos of cherished household belongings. Knowing what customers treasure can yield insight into cross-selling opportunities, or even subtle messages in ads to appeal to this target group's values.[4]

Increasingly, marketing managers, consultants, and researchers have lobbied for observational research over communication research when it comes to assessing consumer behavior. We agree with the sentiment presented in Research Window 11.1. It is often better to measure consumers' actual behavior and then work backward to determine what led to that behavior than it is to measure their attitudes and intentions and then hope that their future behavior matches their intentions. Doing it this way will almost certainly be more expensive, because the behaviors must be recorded and then connected back to their potential causes, which may mean developing a method of connecting each individual's attitudes, awareness, motivations, and the like, with his or her actual behaviors, but the information will almost always be far more useful. Tesco, the British grocery chain, is among the best companies in the world in understanding its customers and tracking their behavior. Research Window 11.2, on page 228, describes how Tesco has taken the dominant position in U.K. grocery retailing based largely on its Clubcard program.

Like communication methods, observation methods may be structured or unstructured, disguised or undisguised. Further, as Figure 11.1 shows, the observations may be made in a contrived or a natural setting and may be secured by a human or a mechanical observer.

Structured versus Unstructured Observation

The distinction between structured and unstructured observation is similar to that between structured and unstructured communication methods. **Structured observation** applies when the problem has been defined precisely enough so that the

structured observation
The problem has been defined precisely enough so that the behaviors that will be observed can be specified beforehand, as can the categories that will be used to record and analyze the situation.

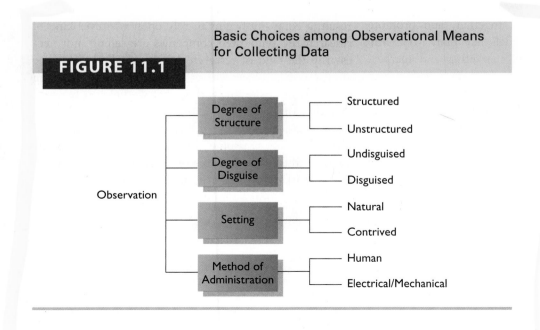

FIGURE 11.1

Basic Choices among Observational Means for Collecting Data

Observation
- Degree of Structure
  - Structured
  - Unstructured
- Degree of Disguise
  - Undisguised
  - Disguised
- Setting
  - Natural
  - Contrived
- Method of Administration
  - Human
  - Electrical/Mechanical

research window 11.1

What's Wrong with Marketing Research? An Interview with Don Schultz

Don E. Schultz is professor emeritus-in-service, Integrated Marketing Communications, Northwestern University, and president of Agora Inc., an integrated marketing company with clients located around the globe. He has received numerous teaching awards, worked with countless corporate clients, and was named by Sales and Marketing Management *magazine as one of the most influential people in America.*

Through his interactions with managers at the highest levels in companies, agencies, and the media, he's had the chance to observe the role of marketing research within many companies. Here's what he has to say about the current practice of marketing research in organizations.

Q: You have said traditional marketing is in rapid decline, and that marketing research might be the prime cause of this decline. Why is that?

The American Marketing Association (AMA) developed a new definition of "marketing" in 2004. (It was revised in 2007.) The 2004 definition was the first the AMA ever had that included anything about customers or consumers. That's important because the difficulty the industry and the academic community have always had is that they have been primarily focused on the four P's [product, price, promotion, place] ... in the four P's there's an assumption that the customer is considered, but I think what has happened is that too many people take it literally. So managers say "let's make a product, put a price on it, and get a distribution system together, and promote it like crazy." In business models like that, where the focus is on the supply chain, marketing and marketing research are not terribly important. The firm assumes it is going to make these or those products. Marketing's job is to get rid of what has been made. I think that has caused more problems for marketing than anything else. Marketing has been marginalized to the point that it is just another function in an organization, not a way of doing business. If you isolate marketing—put it in one of the functional silos—it allows everyone else in the organization to say "well, I don't have to worry about customers, because that's marketing's job." As a result, I think it's given the operations people, the finance people, the human relations people, and everyone else an excuse to say that customers are not their responsibility, so let's go ahead and do what we want to do, how we want to do it, and so on. Let marketing worry about customers, not us.

Q: So what's happened to marketing research within these companies?

If marketing is being marginalized within the organization, marketing research—which has usually been seen as a marketing support activity, rather than as a support for the organization itself—has been pushed further down into the firm. It has no relevance to anyone except marketing. No impact on the firm—that's what has happened in many organizations. In my view, two things have driven down the current value of marketing research within organizations. The first is the dismantling of strong research departments in companies and advertising agencies. Increasingly, companies have substituted the thinking of the marketing research function with the purchase of syndicated research data ... the research people have become the *purchasers* of research data rather than the *doers* of marketing research. As a result, a company begins to rely upon whatever kind of research the syndicated companies are selling, not necessarily the kind of research that it actually needs. The company buys research as a bundle, never thinking about "is this relevant, is this what we need to know, is this the kind of information we need?" In truth, in many cases, the syndicated research services simply furnish data. They assume the organization will do the analysis. But, with the demise of the research function in the marketing firms and their agencies, little analysis generally occurs or if it is done, it is done by junior people or relatively untrained brand managers. So ... that's one thing.

The other thing is that traditional marketing research has been based on an approach that was developed decades ago, before we had access to large amounts of customer purchase behavior data. Back then, researchers focused on collecting attitudinal data, using a psychological model that suggests that if we can change attitudes, then we can change behaviors. Thus, the research industry developed tools that allowed them to "sample and project" from various populations—they would draw samples and then look for common traits or tendencies in that population. Always looking for the "normal curve" from which they could base projections or probabilities. In the past 10 to 15 years, things have changed to the point that companies no longer lack behavioral data ... they just don't know how to manage the data they have. Our marketing research tool set is not as relevant as it used to be. We don't have a whole lot of people out there who understand or know how to manage huge census data sets. We have a lot of research techniques, capabilities, and management processes that are 50, 60, 70 years old and no one has really questioned them. We just keep using them whether they are relevant or not because that's what the research firms do or provide.

Q: Behavioral data—particularly in the form of scanner data—have been around for a long time. Why haven't companies used these data more effectively?

I've been doing scanner panel analysis since the 1970s. With scanner data, you can observe consumer behaviors, but you don't really understand why those behaviors happened. We can make some assumptions, as we do with marketing mix analysis, but we really don't know the internal drivers. Therefore, I can observe consumers' behaviors, but then I must go back and ask the respondents "Why did you do that?" or try to uncover why they

did what they did, based on the observations we have made. We've got the tools backwards; most of the time we're asking about attitudes and trying to predict behavior, when we ought to be observing behavior and then going back and trying to explain that behavior. If I can observe your behavior, most of the time you can tell me why you did that specific something and I can understand your reasoning. But, if I ask you to predict what you're going to do going forward, real problems occur. Most people are not really sure what they're going to do tomorrow, what products they're going to buy, and so on. So, they guess or they provide the answer they think the researcher wants to hear.

As an example, if I go into a grocery store with the intent to buy a certain brand of cereal, I may walk out with something totally different. I can tell you why I bought what I bought after I walk out the door, but I can't always tell you, and be very accurate, about what I'm going to buy when I go in. Most of our research techniques are an attempt to predict, when we should be trying to explain. If we can explain, then I think that we can make some relatively reasonable projections going forward. I'm *not* saying that we should only use behavioral data. I'm saying that we ought to start with the behavioral data and then go back upstream to understand why those behaviors occurred.

We're stuck with this old psychologically based model ... when we didn't have any data, and we couldn't get any data, the easiest thing was to get a representative sample, ask them some relatively inane questions, and try to project the future behaviors of the relevant set. In essence, today we've got all the behavioral data any researcher will need about any product or service. When we didn't have these data, we made do ... but we don't need to make do anymore. Unfortunately, we keep on using the same tools, primarily because we're comfortable with them. And, because that's what the research vendors are offering.

research window 11.2

Scoring Points: How Tesco Is Winning Customer Loyalty

Go into any Tesco store in the United Kingdom and you'll see the vast majority of shoppers pulling a plastic card out of their purses or wallets when it's time to make their purchases. This is Tesco's Clubcard, a shopping card that rewards customers points based on the amount of their purchases. Every three months, over 14 million Clubcard owners receive quarterly statements with vouchers that can be redeemed like cash in Tesco stores. The vouchers can also be redeemed online at Tesco.com. In addition to the vouchers, each member receives carefully targeted coupons for products that she or he purchases regularly as well as coupons for products not currently purchased but favored by other shoppers who are similar to the Clubcard holder in important ways. This highlights the real value of the Clubcard: Tesco knows more about its customers and their shopping habits and preferences than probably any other company in the world.

Background

Tesco was founded in Great Britain in 1956. Operating with what customers perceived as a "pile it high, sell it cheap" mentality, the company eventually became the second-largest supermarket chain in the United Kingdom. By the early 1990s, however, the company had seemingly stalled in its pursuit of market leader Sainsbury's. There was a sense that change was necessary to take the company to the next level. It was at this point that the idea of implementing a loyalty program—but one unlike any other—began to take shape.

Implementing Clubcard

Three factors were critical in the decision to develop Clubcard. Competitive pressure from above (Sainsbury's, the market leader) and below (other supermarket chains, including the discount providers) heightened the need to keep current customers, making Tesco's board of directors more receptive to the idea of Clubcard. At the time, some of Tesco's competitors, including Sainsbury's, were investigating and testing loyalty programs. Finally, technological advances made it possible to process the huge volumes of transaction data that would be required.

Initial tests on the concept began in three stores in 1993. Implementing the system required updates in card reader technologies in the test stores and the development of secure data collection and information management systems. Further, staff had to be trained and customer service monitored—and an appealing Clubcard program would have to be designed and effectively communicated to Tesco customers.

Those working on the development of Clubcard recognized an important point early on: Customers had to view the card as a reward for their current business, not as an incentive to get more business from them. Although the company would use the relationship with customers formed through Clubcard as a means of distributing incentives for future product purchases, from the beginning the focal point of the program has been the rewards provided to customers in the form of vouchers. The "Clubcard Customer Charter" serves to reinforce the relationship that Tesco wants to establish with each of its customers.

© GHISLAIN AND MARIE DAVID DELOSSY/THE IMAGE BANK/GETTY IMAGES

How It Works

Customers obtain Clubcard in any Tesco store by completing a brief application. When purchasing goods in a Tesco store, the card is scanned, effectively tying the card owner to his or her purchases. Online purchases at Tesco.com are also tracked. With each purchase, the customer earns points. Every three months, Clubcard holders receive a mailing that includes vouchers based on the points earned and representing 1% of the amount spent at the store during the preceding three months. The vouchers can be spent like cash in any Tesco store.

For the company, the biggest benefit from the cards is the customer data they generate. Before Clubcard, managers could track the sales of every item purchased in a Tesco store (which store, which item, what price, when was it purchased), but they lacked a vital piece of information: Exactly *who* purchased the item? With Clubcard, they could begin to answer that question. When customers signed up for the card at the test stores, they were asked to provide the following information: names, addresses, size and ages of family. They received a plastic card, vouchers for a free cup of tea or coffee, and a letter from the store manager. A data revolution was underway at Tesco.

Less than a year after launching the test in three stores, 60% of sales in those stores were from Clubcard holders—and the percentage of sales captured on Clubcard continued to rise. Based on initial analyses of the data generated through the test stores, the company sent its first direct mail pieces in September 1994. The initial segmentation was very basic (high spenders vs. low spenders received different offers), but the results were staggering: in some cases, 70% of the coupons were redeemed.

Based on the initial test results, Tesco made the decision to implement Clubcard in all its locations. In an atmosphere of secrecy—because competitors were rumored to be working on their own shopping card systems—Tesco feverishly prepared for the February 1995 national launch.

The Results

Two weeks after the national launch, 7 million Clubcards were delivered to stores for distribution to Tesco customers. Within days, 70% of all Tesco sales were being matched with particular customers. Overall, sales growth settled in well above 2%, after spiking nearly 4% in response to the initial introduction of the

program. The company was able to shift budget away from mass advertising, which was unnecessary and inefficient when it could go directly to customers with targeted appeals. For example, Christmas 1995 was considered a success for Tesco, even though it ran no television ads at all—something it had never tried before.

By the time of the first quarterly mailing (just three months after the national rollout), 5 million Clubcard owners had used their cards to earn points. Vouchers worth £14 million were sent to Clubcard owners. (Today, the quarterly vouchers exceed £50 million.) The quarterly mailings also include coupons that are targeted to the individual Clubcard holder. Initially, the ability to target was limited, and only 12 different message/offer combinations could be utilized for different segments. Still, the coupons had redemption rates of between 20 and 40%, compared with less than 5% for normal sales promotion efforts. Eighteen months later, there were 1,800 different combinations based on lifestyle, demographic, and purchase behavior segmentation variables. By the end of 2002, Tesco had effectively achieved one-to-one marketing: Each Clubcard owner received a mailing with coupons that were customized to his or her specific characteristics and purchase history. This was tremendously important; the goal of the entire program was to create a stronger relationship between the customer and Tesco that benefits both parties. Sending coupons for discounts on beef products would do little to further the relationship with a vegetarian.

Through careful targeting and a resulting increase in revenues, the Clubcard program has paid for itself since the very first quarterly mailing in 1995; in fact, it has always turned a profit. It took Sainsbury's a year and a half to respond to the Clubcard program. In that time, customers spent 28% more at Tesco—and decreased spending at Sainsbury's by 16%. By the end of 1996, there were 8.5 million customers actively using their Clubcards, and Tesco had overtaken Sainsbury's as the United Kingdom's number one retailer, a position it maintains today.

The real benefit of the program from Tesco's perspective is the ability to develop competitive advantage based on the data the company collects from millions of transactions each day. The company established its Customer Insight Unit, a group of researchers whose job is to crunch the Clubcard data looking for patterns that lead to new insights. Members of the original Customer Insight Unit were drawn from the company's market research group. These researchers had previously used geodemographic databases for selecting sites for new Tesco stores. There's

(Continued)

a key difference between geodemographic databases and the Clubcard database, however. Geodemography is based on secondary data and essentially says "you are where you live." The Clubcard database is based on actual customer behavior and says "you are what you buy." Profiles based on arbitrary geographic boundaries cannot be nearly as accurate as profiles based on months and years of real purchase behavior.

Tesco uses its wealth of customer information to customize its communications with its customers via the quarterly statements and *Clubcard Magazine* (different versions are sent to different segments of customers). The data are also used for price sensitivity analyses, adjusting product selections in particular stores based on the specific shopping habits of the customers who shop those stores and adjusting in-store promotions. Probably most importantly, the customer data are used to develop a much richer profile of Tesco customers, to the point that the company believes that it can understand the motivations behind customer purchases.

Based on insights generated from the Clubcard research program and its other initiatives, Tesco continues to expand its dominance of the U.K. market, even as it expands globally. The company's 31% share of Britain's grocery trade was nearly twice the size of its nearest competitor, Asda (which is owned by Wal-Mart). Tesco is the largest private employer in the United Kingdom and is the world's largest Internet supermarket, with over 400,000 regular shoppers and 1 million home deliveries—and its online business has had operating profits since the late 1990s. Through Tesco Personal Finance, the company is also one of Europe's fastest-growing financial services companies, with 3.4 million customers. Maybe most importantly, customers now see Tesco as a progressive company that delivers on its promises. And the company's behavioral research has played a fundamental role in its success.

Sources: "Tesco Profit Tops $3.8 Billion," *CNN.com*, April 12, 2005, downloaded from http://www.cnn.com, November 17, 2008; David Derbyshire, "Tesco Takes £1 in Every Three We Spend at Supermarkets," *Telegraph*, April 12, 2005, downloaded from http://telegraph.co.uk, November 17, 2008; Clive Humby, Terry Hunt, and Tim Phillips, *Scoring Points* (London: Kogan Page, 2003); Becky Barrow, "£2.5bn Profit for Tesco as Supermarket Vows to Get Bigger," *Mail Online*, April 18, 2007, downloaded from http://www.dailymail.co.uk, November 17, 2008; John Penman, "Tesco to Take on High-Street Banks," *Times Online*, November 16, 2008, downloaded from http://business.timesonline.co.uk, November 17, 2008. Reprinted by permission.

unstructured observation

The problem has not been specifically defined, so a great deal of flexibility is allowed the observers in terms of what they note and record.

behaviors that will be observed can be specified beforehand, as can the categories that will be used to record and analyze the situation. **Unstructured observation** is used for studies in which the problem has not been so specifically defined, so that a great deal of flexibility is allowed the observers in terms of what they note and record. Unstructured observation is much more likely to be used in exploratory research than in descriptive or causal research.

Imagine a study designed to investigate how consumers make decisions about purchasing soup. On the one hand, the observers could be told to stand at one end of a supermarket aisle and record whatever behavior they think is appropriate with respect to each sample customer's deliberation and search. This might produce the following record:

> Purchaser first paused in front of the Campbell's brand. He glanced at the price on the shelf, picked up a can of Campbell's, glanced at its picture and list of ingredients, and set it back down. He then checked the label and price for Progresso. He set that back down and after a slight pause, picked up a different flavor can of Campbell's than he originally looked at, placed it in his cart, and moved down the aisle.

Alternatively, observers might be told to record a number of things, including the first soup can examined, the total number of cans picked up by any customer, the brand of soup selected, and the time in seconds that the customer spent in front of the soup shelves—and to record these observations by checking the appropriate boxes on the observation form. This last situation represents a good deal more structure than the first:

Record #: ___*83*___
❑ male   ☑ female
First soup can picked up for examination: ☑ Campbell's
                                                       ❑ Progresso
                                                       ❑ Lipton
                                                       ❑ Knorr
                                                       ❑ other: _____

Total # cans picked up for examination, any brand: ___*3*___
Brand selected: ☑ Campbell's
(leave blank if none selected)   ❑ Progresso
                                                       ❑ Lipton
                                                       ❑ Knorr
                                                       ❑ other: _____
Time (in front of soup shelves):   ___*12*___ seconds

To use the more structured approach, researchers must decide precisely which behaviors are to be observed and which specific categories and units will be used to record the observations. In order to make such decisions, researchers must have specific hypotheses in mind. Thus, the structured approach is again more appropriate for descriptive and causal studies than for exploratory research. The unstructured approach would be useful in generating insights about the various aspects of the search and deliberation behavior in the preceding example. But it is less useful for

MANAGER'S FOCUS

Whenever you use unstructured (open-ended) questions, you are, in essence, performing exploratory research. The same is true when you employ unstructured observation. Imagine for a moment how actively observing consumers, without any preconceived ideas of what behaviors are important or relevant, might help you generate new and innovative marketing ideas.

The unexpected behaviors observed might reveal new uses for your product that could be promoted to prospective new customers. Or, they might divulge features that could be redesigned to enhance your product's functionality or convenience. The observed behaviors may even demonstrate how two seemingly unrelated products could effectively be bundled together to augment their overall usefulness to consumers.

The ultimate goal, though, is to uncover breakthrough opportunities for new products or services that would satisfy important unmet needs for consumers. For example, by freely watching the actions of consumers, and applying creativity, you might identify a remedy for a "problem" consumers do not currently realize exists because they never dreamed of doing something in a new or different way. In such situations, exploratory communication techniques such as focus groups, depth interviews, or unstructured questions in a survey would be incapable of generating these insights because it would never occur to consumers to state them verbally.

testing hypotheses about it. Since so many different kinds of behaviors could be recorded, it would be difficult for researchers to code and quantify the data in a consistent manner.

The advantages and disadvantages of structure in observation are very similar to those in communication. Structuring the observation reduces the potential for bias and increases the reliability of observations. However, the reduction in bias may be accompanied by a loss of validity, since the number of seconds spent in deliberation or the number of cans of soup picked up and examined may not represent the complete story of deliberation and search. What about the effort spent in simply looking at what is available but not picking them up, or the discussion between husband and wife as to which brand to buy? A well-trained, highly qualified observer might be able to interpret these kinds of behaviors and relate them in a meaningful way to search and deliberation.

Disguised versus Undisguised Observation

In **undisguised observation**, people know they are being observed; in **disguised observation**, they do not. In the soup purchase study described earlier, observers could stand next to the soup shelves in the grocery store in plain sight of customers, pencil and clipboard in hand, announcing their purpose to each customer. They would then get to watch consumers take much greater care than normal to read the labels for nutrition content, determine the best value, and all the other things that "smart" shoppers do, because the shoppers know they are being observed. On the other hand, the researchers might find a position where shoppers are less likely to notice them, or they could even observe the behavior using hidden cameras. The consumers' shopping behavior would be natural, but as with disguised communication methods, each consumer's right to be informed has been violated and debriefing would likely take place at the conclusion of the consumer's visit to the store. It is also possible that individuals could be told when they enter the store that their actions would be observed for research purposes and to please shop as they normally would. Most consumers will forget within minutes that they are being observed, that is, unless they see people walking around with white lab coats and clipboards!

Sometimes disguise is accomplished by having observers become part of the shopping scene. This is typically the case when it is the service worker or organization that is being observed, rather than the consumer. For example, some firms use paid observers disguised as shoppers, to evaluate important aspects of the shopping process. Krispy Kreme is one company that has hired mystery shoppers to visit their stores. The mystery shoppers use tiny cameras to record such things as the evenness of the jelly in doughnuts and the cleanliness of bathrooms. AT&T Wireless used mystery shoppers to visit its 2,700 locations. At a cost of about $50 per visit, the mystery shoppers visited each store monthly.[5] The Federal Trade Commission also employs mystery shoppers to ensure that children and teenagers cannot buy M-rated video games and R-rated DVDs.[6] Mystery shopping has even moved into the online shopping arena as well—see Research Window 11.3.

No matter whether consumers or workers are being observed, researchers use disguise to control the tendency for people to behave differently when they know their actions are being watched. You need to consider a couple of issues about disguised observation, however. We've already noted the first: There are ethical concerns involved in observing people without their prior

undisguised observation
The subjects are aware that they are being observed.

disguised observation
The subjects are not aware that they are being observed.

Learning Objective

3. Cite the main reason researchers may choose to disguise the presence of an observer in a study.

© COMSTOCK/JUPITERIMAGES

Mystery shoppers might be used to gauge the aesthetics and appeal of baked goods displays.

research window 11.3

Using Mystery Shoppers to Evaluate Online Retailers

Future Now, Inc.'s 2007 Online Retail Study for Customer Focused Excellence sent out independent mystery shoppers as well as its own Web site conversion specialists to over 300 top retailers' Web sites. Their mission was to analyze how customer focused the retailers' Web sites were once a customer identified the product they wanted to purchase.

Methodology: 2007 Online Retail Study for Customer-Focused Excellence

The study consisted of mystery shoppers visiting a retailer's Web site and answering a series of Yes or No questions about the availability of 69 different customer experience factors. The factors were weighted based on 10 years of optimizing retail Web site experiences and totaled to arrive at an eventual score for each site. The maximum possible score is 100.

The factor-based questions include:

- the quality and detail of images (could the shopper zoom in or did the retailer provide images from multiple angles);

- did the product copy description answer the shopper's questions;

- whether the retailer offers customer reviews;

- how well did retailers do at meeting shopper's gift buying needs (e.g., did the retailer offer gift wrapping, messaging, or gift certificates);

- ease and simplicity of checkout (how many pages did it take to check out and did the retailer provide a progress indicator);

- retailer's ability to address the shopper's concerns (e.g., return policies, guarantees, third-party seals, and security assurances);

- ease and clarity of retailer return policies;

- providing of shipping and tax totals early in the checkout process;

- offering multiple payment options (e.g., pay by check, PayPal, etc.);

- offering estimated delivery times and showing in-stock availability for items;

- offering pick-up where physical stores exist.

The Results: 2007 Online Retail Study for Customer-Focused Excellence

Congratulations to the top 10 retailers for their efforts at providing visitors a customer-centric experience. The overall leaders:

1. SmartBargains.com 67
2. BestBuy.com 66
3. CompactAppliance.com 66
4. BlueNile.com 65
5. EasternMountainSport 64
6. BackCountry.com 63
7. TigerDirect.com 63
8. CDUniverse.com 63
9. Ebags.com 63
10. Staples.com 63

The Leaders by Category:

Apparel/Fashion

1. Ebags.com
2. Landsend.com
3. Lids.com, Bluefly.com, LLBean.com

Electronics

1. BestBuy.com
2. TigerDirect.com
3. Crutchfield.com

Food

1. SurLaTable.com
2. Cooking.com
3. Berries.com

Jewelry

1. BlueNile.com
2. Ice.com
3. Diamond.com

(Continued)

Children/Toys

1. OneStepAhead.com
2. KBToys.com
3. BabyAge.com

Housewares/Kitchen

1. CompactAppliance.com
2. BedBathandBeyond.com
3. SurLaTable.com

Office

1. Staples.com
2. OfficeDepot.com
3. OfficeMax.com

Mass Merchants

1. SmartBargains.com
2. Walmart.com
3. Target.com

Source: Downloaded and excerpted from the Future Now Web site, http://www.grokdotcom.com, November 16, 2008. Reprinted by permission.

knowledge. Employees of an organization have reason to expect that their behaviors on the job will be observed; consumers do not. Thus, there are fewer ethical concerns with mystery shopping than with observing and recording consumer behavior. The second important issue with disguised observation is a practical one: How will you obtain other relevant background information, such as demographic and attitudinal information, if you don't identify yourself as a researcher? This highlights the primary difficulty with observational research in general: Many kinds of data simply cannot be observed. The use of disguise makes it even more difficult to tie data that might be obtained via communication to observational data.

Natural versus Contrived Setting for Observation

natural setting
Subjects are observed in the environment where the behavior normally takes place.

contrived setting
Subjects are observed in an environment that has been specially designed for recording their behavior.

Observations may be obtained in either natural or contrived settings. Sometimes the natural setting is altered to some degree for experimental purposes. In the soup study mentioned earlier, researchers might choose to keep the setting completely natural and study only the activities that normally go into the purchase of soup in the normal setting. Alternatively, they might want to examine the effectiveness of point-of-purchase display materials and could include such materials in the stores where observations were taken. One measure of effectiveness might be the amount of search and deliberation the materials stimulate for the particular brand being promoted.

If a contrived setting is desired, the researcher could bring a group of people into a very controlled environment such as a multiproduct display in a laboratory and ask them to pretend that they were shopping. This controlled environment might contain, for example, a soup display that would allow researchers to study the degree of search and deliberation that participants go through as they decide what to buy.

An increasingly popular method for assessing customer reactions in a contrived environment is computer simulations and virtual reality. These approaches allow marketers to display potential new products or product displays without going to the expense of physically building them. The advantage of virtual reality is that the objects appear in three dimensions, as if they are actually there. VirTra Systems, a company that specializes in three-dimensional (3-D) virtual reality, can customize the virtual experience to include vibration, smells, wind, and sounds in addition to sight. These tools could be used very effectively by marketing researchers to offer greater

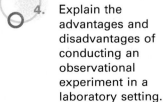

Learning Objective

4. Explain the advantages and disadvantages of conducting an observational experiment in a laboratory setting.

reality (and, thus, external validity) to studies conducted in contrived settings. Computer technology has also been used in consumer shopping experiments.[7]

The primary advantage of the laboratory environment is that researchers can control outside influences that might affect the observed behaviors; this allows higher levels of internal validity for the study. For example, a shopper in a natural setting might pause to chat with a friend while deciding what soup to buy. If researchers were measuring the time spent in deliberation, this interruption could distort the accuracy of the measurement. Another advantage of the contrived setting is that the researcher does not need to wait for events to occur but can instruct the participants to engage in the needed kind of behavior. This means that a great many observations can be made in a short period of time. Sometimes an entire study can be completed in a couple of days or a week, which can substantially reduce costs.

As you might guess, the great benefit of natural observation is that the recorded behaviors occur naturally, without prompting from researchers. In contrived observation, the prompting from researchers might be direct ("Pretend you are in a grocery store and show us how you would shop for soup") or through the creation of an artificial environment. Either way, the contrived setting may cause differences in behavior and thus raise real questions about the generalizability of the findings. This is much less of a problem with natural observation, and, as a result, external validity is greater with this approach. Research Window 11.4 discusses the use of natural observation to better understand the youth market.

human observation
Individuals are trained to systematically observe a phenomenon and to record on the observational form the specific events that take place.

electrical or mechanical observation
An electrical or mechanical device observes a phenomenon and records the events that take place.

Human versus Mechanical Observation

Much scientific observation is in the field, with researchers taking notes on the observations they make. With **human observation**, one or more individuals are trained to systematically watch consumers or other phenomena of interest and to record events that take place. Researchers commonly use written field notes to record their impressions at the time they are observed in the field and later develop theoretical and summary thoughts back at the office. While much field research is still of this pencil-and-paper variety, **electrical or mechanical observation** has grown substantially in importance in marketing research. With electrical/mechanical observation, the behaviors of interest are recorded electronically or mechanically for analysis by researchers. (To simplify things, we'll just use the traditional term "mechanical observation" to refer to any type of technology used to record data.) Although some technologies (such as tape recorders and video cameras) have been used for a long time, the development of new and less-expensive technologies is expanding the role and importance of mechanical observation. For example, ethnographic researchers increasingly rely on technology to assist them, particularly as various tools—such as audio and video recorders—get smaller in size, which means they are lighter in weight and less intrusive.

One of the most important methods of mechanical observation is the simple bar-code scanner. Bar codes are scanned 5 billion times a day; each item scanned is a potential data point for marketing researchers to analyze.[8] Tesco's hugely successful Clubcard program (see Research Window 11.2) relies on scanner data for its success. Research Window 11.5, on page 238, discusses the important role of scanners in marketing research.

Another well-known use of mechanical observation is ACNielsen's use of people meters for tracking which family members are watching which television shows and when they are watching them. People meters are far more reliable at measuring

ETHICAL DILEMMA 11.1

A leading manufacturer of breakfast cereals was interested in learning more about the kinds of processes that consumers go through when deciding to buy a particular brand of cereal. To gather this information, an observational study was conducted in the major food chains of several large cities. The observers were instructed to assume a position well out of the shoppers' way, because it was thought that the individuals would change their behavior if they were aware of being observed.

- Was it ethical to observe another person's behavior systematically without that person's knowledge? What if the behavior had been more private in nature? What if the behavior had been recorded on videotape?
- Does use of this method of data collection invade an individual's privacy?
- Even if there is no harm done to the individual, is there harm done to society?
- Does the use of such a method add to the concern over big brotherism?
- Can you suggest alternative methods for gathering the same information?

research window 11.4

Watch and Learn: Hang out with Youth Market in Their Element

Why tweens prefer one soft drink over another or why teenagers just can't seem to resist a certain brand of jeans are the kinds of mysteries more businesses want to get to the bottom of.

To find out why the youth market behaves a certain way as consumers, more research firms are using observational research techniques to better observe youths' reactions to certain products and styles.

"We have found that a lot of marketers today want to do [observational research] for the sake of being closer to the consumer . . . to make the experience as productively efficient as possible while the observers remain as unobtrusive as possible," says Peter Zollo, president of Northbrook, Illinois-based Teen Research Unlimited, a marketing research firm that specializes in the teen market. "We call these types of studies 'in-context research,' as we strive to place the client and the respondent in the context of the particular venue or situation, whether it's . . . in the gym, on the field, at a concert, or at the beach or the park. By [doing this], we're best able to understand the brand's context—how it fits into [young] consumers' lives and with their lifestyles."

Qualitative researchers in charge of such research should keep in mind a few things before and during a study. Experts in the field offer five tips they say will help gather more useful data and provide clients with a better return on their investment.

Recruit "Hip" Respondents

One of the first imperatives in setting up a so-called tag-along session—in which qualitative researchers go to a shopping mall, for example, with youth respondents—is to choose the most appropriate participants: kids who are hip.

Companies benefit from recruiting teen leaders—those who loyally follow trends—and bring them on as independent recruiters. In turn, the teen recruiters would be charged with the task of drafting the "hippest individuals" as respondents, notes Trenton Haack, director and practice leader of qualitative research for Cincinnati-based Burke Inc.

"It's important to get the right respondents in order to find out what the latest and greatest thing is," he says.

Ask Clever Questions

Once the researchers are out and about observing the tween or teen respondents in a real-world setting, researchers should then make it a point to step in and interact with the respondents by asking specific questions about why they're buying certain products, experts say.

Nino DeNicola, president of Dialogue Resource Inc., based in Fairfield, Connecticut, tells of a recent study when certain questions were asked of teen respondents on behalf of one of his clients, a blue jeans manufacturer. In this particular study, for example, Dialogue Resource asked about the jeans' design aspects and what the respondents thought about the way the jeans were packaged on the racks and shelves.

"Basically, you are trying to understand what the actual selection criteria [are]. How important is the brand? If it is, what do they look for in the way of specific product attributes? What's important about the jeans, and why?" DeNicola says.

Zollo adds that his firm often debriefs youth respondents immediately after an excursion.

"For example, after a shop-along exercise we'll convene at a nearly food court to talk about what we observed, asking questions about observed behavior and choices," he says. "As important as it is to be able to replicate real-world experiences in observational research, having the opportunity to probe for clarification on what was observed makes subsequent analysis easier and more accurate."

Make Them Feel Comfortable . . . They're the Experts!

Experts say not to forget to make youth participants feel as comfortable as possible during an observational research study. After all, they are the experts.

"Make sure the observations are in an environment that they are comfortable with," says Miguel Lyons-Cavazos, a partner at Redwood Shores, California-based Cheskin Research.

For example, Lyons-Cavazos says, teen respondents may feel more comfortable if they are participating in the study with their friends, even if their friends are not also official respondents in the study. He adds that researchers need to convey to the respondents that they are the "experts" about whatever it is—whether it has to do with music consumption or the latest skateboard design.

The More Respondents, the Better

Another sure-fire way to gather valuable data is by studying a large group of respondents over a long period of time, DeNicola notes.

The best way, he says, is to recruit 30 or 40 kids and observe eight a day, giving researchers more to work with and a wider range of opinions, as opposed to having just one group on one day.

Get out There

Finally, experts say that qualitative researchers need to "get out there" and "be themselves."

Researchers need to experience what the youth respondents are experiencing, whether it's buying clothes or other products in a shopping mall or at a music store listening to today's hottest music artists, Lyons-Cavazos says.

"Don't just be the researcher that gathers the info. Get out there and experience what [youth respondents] are," he adds. "Doing observational research is so much richer when you're a part of it, too."

Source: Deborah L. Vence, "Watch and Learn," *Marketing News*, September 1, 2004, downloaded via EBSCOhost, November 16, 2008. Reprinted by permission.

---

viewing behavior than would be surveying viewers or even having them keep detailed diaries. On the Internet, software like TrueActive Monitor records every activity on a computer. It is possible to track how visitors to a Web site navigate its pages, which pages they look at, which pages they exit from, which banner ads they click, and so on. This information is of enormous value for understanding consumer behavior.

Mechanical observation has also been used to try to gauge the strength of respondents' feelings and/or uncertainty when they are responding to questionnaires administered by computer or over the telephone. **Response latency** is the amount of

Learning Objective

5. Define response latency and explain what it measures.

response latency
The amount of time a respondent deliberates before answering a question.

MANAGER'S FOCUS

The usefulness of marketing research information is magnified substantially when managers and researchers employ techniques in creative ways. One form of creativity is to use multiple methods simultaneously. An example of this is when highly skilled focus group moderators ask participants to engage in activities during the early stages of the interview process. For example, moderators may ask the participants to collaborate on a task such as sorting various food items into different piles based on their perceptions of the degree to which the items represent "ethnic" or "international" cuisine. Certainly, this type of activity is intended to serve as an icebreaker, but it also represents a form of observation in a contrived setting. The participants talk with one another during the process, but they are not responding to questions

from the moderator, so their behaviors and their conversations are being "observed." Sometimes their behaviors toward other participants, or the task itself, are more revealing than anything they verbalize.

The research methods you are learning do not necessarily have to be used in isolation or in the same way every time. It is perfectly fine to modify them to meet your needs as long as you are working with a competent researcher who can help you assess the validity of the new approach. Good ideas for blending methods do not emerge exclusively from researchers. As a manager, you should freely share with your research suppliers any ideas you have for creating innovative ways to capture information that addresses your marketing problems.

research window 11.5

Scanning the Globe

As often happens with seemingly minor technological changes, bar codes have had a huge and unexpected impact. Cash registers had been mere repositories of money; post-UPC, they became data conduits par excellence. Each time a product is sold, a record of the item is now preserved. And as any student of Wal-Mart can tell you, that altered the balance of power between retailers and manufacturers. Once, manufacturers controlled data about product sales via warehouse inventories. They understood what was selling much better than the retailers. But now the stores had data, too—and both sides would learn to mine that information.

Case in point: In the early 1980s, a Pepsi brand manager named Scott Klein was called into the office of then-CEO John Sculley. As Klein recalls it, Sculley held up a can of soda and asked, "Have you ever noticed these bar codes that we put on all of our packages? If we can get our hands on some of this data, we might be able to learn something from it." Klein, now CEO of Information Resources Inc., which uses bar-code data for market research, says that was the beginning of a sea change. Pepsi soon began buying store sales data, and the daily figures showed, unsurprisingly, that volume surged around the time of sales promotions. But Pepsi staffers noticed something unusual: The increases occurred right *before* the sales began. They eventually realized that it wasn't the lower price that was driving higher volume as much as the big displays of Pepsi products, which stores tended to erect days before sales events began.

Market research was transformed. Where analysts used to wander up and down store aisles jotting observations in notebooks, there was now cold, hard data. Marketing maxims began to give way to numbers. Who needs gut instinct when you can get customized sales data? By creating databases of individual customers' ongoing purchasing information (by linking customers' loyalty card numbers, and any household information they submit, to their purchases), the bar-code data connected actual purchasing with specific shoppers.

Some businesses realized how little they knew their own customers. Consider the beef industry, which for various technical reasons was a bar-code laggard. According to Herb Meischen, a vice president for meat-packing giant Cargill, it's only in the past three or four years that his company realized who was actually buying its product. Companies had always considered steak a luxury item bought by affluent purchasers. But it turns out that the biggest steak eaters aren't wealthy at all, Meischen says: "They're rural. They're blue collar. They've got a median household income somewhere in the $40,000 range." Meischen says the information "blew the socks off our people here, and it blew the socks off retailers." That knowledge and subsequent bar-code data have allowed Cargill to improve the way it tailors product mix and adjusts pricing and product size at different supermarkets. He says that in the stores in which Cargill has been able to implement such strategies, beef sales are up an additional 10 to 12%.

Sources: Excerpted from Nicholas Varchaver, "Scanning the Globe," *Fortune*, May 31, 2004, downloaded from http://money .cnn.com, November 16, 2008. Reprinted by permission.

---

galvanometer
A device used to measure the emotion induced by exposure to a particular stimulus by recording changes in the electrical resistance of the skin associated with the minute degree of sweating that accompanies emotional arousal; in marketing research, the stimulus is often specific advertising copy.

time it takes a respondent to answer a question. Response time seems to be directly related to the respondent's uncertainty in the answer, and it assists in assessing the individual's strength of preference when choosing among alternatives. Measures of response latency can be programmed into the computerized survey, and respondents need never know that their answers were being timed.

Using Mechanical Observation in Advertising Tests   Other methods of mechanical observation have focused on testing advertising copy. The **galvanometer** is used to measure emotional arousal in response to seeing or hearing an ad. When a person experiences emotions, there are slight changes in the electrical resistance of the skin;

these changes cannot be controlled by the individual. The galvanometer records these changes in electrical resistance. For example, a person could be fitted with small electrodes to monitor electrical resistance and then shown different advertising copy. The strength of the current induced would then be used to infer the subject's interest or attitude toward the copy.

Voice-pitch analysis relies on the same basic premise as the galvanometer: Participants experience a number of involuntary physiological reactions, such as changes in blood pressure, rate of perspiration, or heart rate, when emotionally aroused by external or internal stimuli. Voice-pitch analysis examines changes in the relative vibration frequency of the human voice that accompany emotional arousal. Special audio-adapted computer equipment can measure abnormal frequencies in the voice caused by changes in the nervous system, changes that may not be discernible to the human ear. The more the voice pitch differs from the respondent's normal pitch, the greater the emotional intensity of the consumer's reaction is said to be.

The **eye camera** is used to study eye movements while a respondent reads advertising copy. Two aspects are particularly important. The first concerns where the eye is focused: Where did the individual look first? How long did the person linger on any particular place? Did the consumer read the whole ad or just part of it? Following eye paths has also been used to analyze package designs, billboards, and displays in the aisles of supermarkets. The second important aspect concerns pupil dilation, which is assumed to indicate a person's interest in the stimulus being viewed. Pupilmetrics have been used to evaluate color schemes in packaging and optimal advertisement placement in magazines.

To address a decline in click-through rates for Internet banner ads, researchers recently used eye-tracking devices to investigate Internet users' attention to online advertising. They then surveyed the users to take awareness measures on the banner ads they had encountered during the study. The results indicated that banner ads created much lower levels of awareness compared with rates normally found for television commercials and directory advertising.[9]

Learning Objective

6. Define voice-pitch analysis and explain what it measures.

voice-pitch analysis
Analysis that examines changes in the relative frequency of the human voice that accompany emotional arousal.

Learning Objective

7. Explain how researchers use eye cameras.

eye camera
A device used by researchers to study a subject's eye movements while he or she is reading advertising copy.

ETHICAL DILEMMA 11.2

You are running a laboratory experiment for the promotion manager of a soft drink company. The promotion manager has read a journal article indicating that viewers' responses to upbeat commercials are more favorable if the commercials follow very arousing film clips, and he is interested in testing this proposition with respect to his firm's commercials. To establish whether film clips that induce high levels of arousal result in more extreme evaluations of ensuing commercials than film clips that induce low levels of arousal, you are pretesting film clips for their arousing capacity. To do this, you are recording subjects' blood pressure levels as they watch various film clips. The equipment is not very intrusive, consisting of a finger cuff attached to a recording device. You are satisfied that the procedure does not threaten the subject's physical safety in any way. In addition, you have made the subjects familiar with the equipment, with the result that they are relaxed and comfortable and absorbed in the film clips. On getting up to leave at the end of the session, one subject turns to you and asks, "Is my blood pressure normal, then?"

- Is it ethical to give respondents information about their physiological responses that they can interpret as an informed comment on the state of their health?
- What might be the result if you do not tell the subject the function of the equipment?

SUMMARY

Learning Objective 1

Explain the primary advantage of collecting data via observation.

The primary advantage of observation over communication as a means of collecting data is that observation data are typically much more accurate when it comes to measuring individuals' behavior.

Learning Objective 2

List the important considerations in the use of observational methods of data collection.

Observational data may be gathered using structured or unstructured methods that are either disguised or undisguised. The observations may be made in a contrived or a natural setting and may be secured by a human or an electrical/mechanical observer.

Learning Objective 3

Cite the main reason researchers may choose to disguise the presence of an observer in a study.

Most often, an observer's presence is disguised in order to control the tendency of people to behave differently when they know their actions are being watched.

Learning Objective 4

Explain the advantages and disadvantages of conducting an observational experiment in a laboratory setting.

The advantage of a laboratory environment is that researchers are better able to control outside influences that might affect the observed behavior. The disadvantage of the laboratory setting is that the contrived setting itself may cause differences in behavior and thus threaten the external validity of the findings. A contrived setting, however, usually speeds the data collection process, results in lower cost research, and allows the use of more objective measurements.

Learning Objective 5

Define response latency and explain what it measures.

Response latency is the amount of time a respondent deliberates before answering a question. Because response time seems to be directly related to the respondent's uncertainty in the answer, it assists in assessing the individual's strength of preference when choosing among alternatives.

Learning Objective 6

Define voice-pitch analysis and explain what it measures.

Voice-pitch analysis examines changes in the relative vibration frequency of the human voice that accompany emotional arousal. The amount an individual is affected by a stimulus question can be measured by comparing the person's abnormal frequency to his or her normal frequency. The greater the difference, the greater the emotional intensity of the subject's reaction is said to be.

Learning Objective 7

Explain how researchers use eye cameras.

Eye cameras are used by researchers to study a subject's eye movements while he or she is reading advertising copy. The visual record produced can allow researchers to determine the part of the ad the subject noticed first, how long his or her eyes lingered on a particular item, and whether the subject read all the copy or only part of it.

KEY TERMS

structured observation (page 225)
unstructured observation (page 230)
undisguised observation (page 232)
disguised observation (page 232)
natural setting (page 234)
contrived setting (page 234)
human observation (page 235)

electrical or mechanical observation
    (page 235)
response latency (page 237)
galvanometer (page 238)
voice-pitch analysis (page 239)
eye camera (page 239)

REVIEW QUESTIONS

1. How can observational methods be classified? What are the key distinctions among the various types?

2. When should a higher degree of structure be used with observational research? When might a lower degree of structure be used?

3. What are mystery shoppers? What is their purpose?

4. What are the primary advantages and disadvantages of working in a natural setting as contrasted with a contrived setting?

5. What is the role of bar-code scanners in observational research?

6. What principle underlies the use of a galvanometer?

7. What is an eye camera?

8. What is voice-pitch analysis? What does it measure?

9. What does response latency assess? How is it measured?

DISCUSSION QUESTIONS, PROBLEMS, AND PROJECTS

Problems 1 and 2 could be assigned to pairs of students, with one student answering Problem 1 and the other answering Problem 2. The students could then compare their results and discuss the advantages and disadvantages of structure in observational research.

1. Be a mystery shopper and assess the service provided to customers at the check-out counter at two grocery stores in your area. Complete the following structured observation table for each:

Store _____   Date _____
Location _____   Time _____

Too few checkout counters	Yes	No
Long wait in line	Yes	No
Cashier: Quick and efficient	Yes	No
Cashier: Prices well recorded	Yes	No
Cashier: Friendly and pleasant	Yes	No
Purchases packed quickly	Yes	No
Purchases packed poorly	Yes	No
Bags carried to car	Yes	No
Bags provided were flimsy	Yes	No
Bags provided were attractive	Yes	No
Other facts _____		

2. Be a mystery shopper and assess the service provided to customers at the checkout counter at two grocery stores in your area. Record anything that you believe is relevant to the service provided customers.

3. Discuss the ethical ramifications of disguised observation versus undisguised observation.

4. Discuss the strengths and weaknesses of a natural setting versus a contrived setting.

5. Describe how each of the following instruments works and in what area of marketing they are most useful.

    a. galvanometer

    b. eye camera

6. If you were the product manager of a leading brand of toothpaste, how would each of the following help you do your job?

    a. observational studies in a retail store

    b. observational studies in the consumer's home

7. The Better Business Bureau (BBB) has received several complaints over the past six months that certain local automobile dealers are engaging in subtle forms of racial discrimination. The alleged discrimination concerns such things as overly restrictive credit terms, lack of salesperson assistance, and refusals to perform routine maintenance services in a timely manner. The BBB has surveyed the firms in question and found no evidence of discriminatory practices, yet complaints continue to be received. The BBB decided to call in professional researchers and has contracted with your marketing research firm to collect data for use in their investigation of these allegations.

    a. Briefly outline the manner in which you would collect information for the BBB using observation techniques. Be sure to address the issues of structure, disguise, setting, and mechanical versus human observers in your answer. Do you think an observational study will yield information as good as, better than, or worse than, the survey?

    b. Is it ethical and/or proper for a marketing research firm to conduct this type of research project? Why or why not?

8. Discuss the advantages and disadvantages of using electrical/mechanical methods of data collection versus using human observers. What criteria should the researcher consider when deciding which method to use for a particular project?

PART 4

DATA COLLECTION FORMS

Agree or Disagree Web 2.0 Style

It's Saturday night. You're sitting on the couch, perfect hair, pressed blue top, a decision looms. Do you move in or stay away? Get closer or keep your distance? It's a tough decision. You think about it, but rational thought doesn't help. It's an emotional decision, and one that needs to be made. Now.

It is Saturday night but the couch isn't real. It's virtual. You with your perfect hair and shirt aren't real either. It's an avatar you selected for the occasion. The occasion? The tough decision? You're answering a survey question about a brand or advertisement. Moving in to cuddle with it means you like it. Staying away means you don't. Getting closer brings a smile to your face. Keeping your distance provides a visual indication of remorse. This is the breakthrough technology of Conquest Research in London. The survey tool is called Metaphorix (www.metaphorixuk.com).

The concept of Metaphorix is Web 2.0 meets the tried-and-true seven-point agree/disagree scale. Surveys designed online have the opportunity for better graphical user interfaces and pictorial representation of data to the respondent. Behind the scenes, the data are still represented quantitatively just like on paper-and-pencil surveys.

Instead of allowing consumers words and numbers to express their reactions to brands and advertisements, Conquest believes emotional reactions are better. Body language, gestures, and facial expressions of avatars allow for a nonverbal medium that captures people's reactions more faithfully than the spoken word.

According to David Penn, managing director of Conquest Research, "If research were to be invented today, we wouldn't be doing it the way that we do. We still have a pen and paper mindset that reflects the technologies that were available 50 years ago." He continues, "But, for consumers there's nothing uplifting about being asked to answer 50 questions."

The virtual characters of Metaphorix are designed to be uplifting. They allow for the expression of happiness by having the avatar jump in the air and express emotional closeness by cuddling. The hope is that using these characterizations of emotions: (1) makes taking part in surveys fun thus enhancing the opportunity to overcome failing response rates across the industry and (2) allows people to express their feelings in ways words cannot.

"The problem . . . is that people can't put into words what they feel," says Penn. "By taking words out of the equation, you make it easier for people to express extremes of emotion spontaneously." It also adds a fun-based approach that is uncommon in the marketing research arena.

Part 4 provides an overview of the different data collection forms. Many different ways of designing surveys and questionnaires exist. From the happy and sad faces used with young, pre-reading children to sophisticated virtual reality contexts, the key is to get data that can be analyzed to produce decision-making information.

Sources: "Virtual Worlds are the Reality," *MarketingWeek* (July 3, 2008), downloaded from www.marketingweek.co.uk on December 3, 2008; www.metaphorixuk.com.

© O'LUK/ISTOCKPHOTO

Asking Good Questions: Measurement Basics

Learning Objectives

1. Define the term *measurement* as it is used in marketing research.
2. List the four types of scales that can be used to measure an attribute.
3. Explain the primary difference between a ratio scale and an interval scale.
4. Name the two types of error that may affect measurement scores and define each.
5. Explain the concept of validity as it relates to measuring instruments.
6. List three general types of validity that can be used to assess the quality of a measure.
7. Outline the sequence of steps to follow in developing valid measures of marketing constructs.

Introduction

Although we don't often think about it, most of us spend the day measuring things. We stagger out of bed when the clock tells us to get up. We climb onto the bathroom scale, hoping our diets and workouts have made a difference. We measure coffee into the coffee maker, or stir a teaspoonful of instant coffee into a cup of water. We keep an eye on the clock so we won't miss the bus or leave too little time to negotiate traffic on our way to work or class. We check a Web site for the score of the previous night's baseball game—and maybe *The Wall Street Journal* for the closing price on a favorite investment.

Most of the things we measure are fairly concrete: pounds on a scale, teaspoons of coffee, the amount of gas in a tank. But how can we measure a person's attitude toward bubble gum? The likelihood that a teenager will go see a particular new movie? A family's social class? Marketers are interested in measuring many attributes that most people rarely think of in terms of numbers.

All of the questions on a survey or marks on an observation form are attempts at measuring important attributes or behaviors of some group or situation that is of interest to marketing managers. In this chapter, we will discuss how marketing researchers go about assigning numbers to various objects and phenomena.

SCALES OF MEASUREMENT

Learning Objective

1.   Define the term *measurement* as it is used in marketing research.

Measurement consists of "rules for assigning numbers to objects in such a way as to represent quantities of attributes."[1] Note two things about this definition. First, it indicates that we measure the attributes of objects and not the objects themselves. We don't measure a person, for example—but we can measure his or her income, social class, education, height, weight, or attitudes, all of which are attributes of the individual. Second, the definition is broad in that it does not specify how the numbers are to be assigned. Researchers must be careful when designing a measure because the type of measure used will dictate the kinds of analyses and conclusions that will be possible with the data collected using the measure. We have to take care to not read more meaning into the numbers than they actually contain.

measurement
Rules for assigning numbers to objects to represent quantities of attributes.

For example, when we see the numbers 1, 2, 3, and 4, we usually assume that the number 1 stands for one object, 2 for two objects, and so on. Usually, we will say that 2 is larger than 1, and 3 is larger than 2; that the interval between 1 and 2 is the same size as the interval between 3 and 4; and that 3 is three times greater than 1, while 4 is four times greater than 1. Unfortunately, these assumptions are often not true when it comes to measuring attributes of objects. It is important that we first determine the properties of the attribute and then assign numbers so that they accurately reflect the properties of that attribute. The numbering system is simply a tool that

MANAGER'S FOCUS

In many ways, designing and conducting a marketing research study is similar to building a house. Just as you wouldn't begin constructing your future home without a good blueprint, proper planning is necessary before creating and using a measurement instrument such as a questionnaire. The development of a good blueprint for a house requires an understanding of the science of architectural engineering, an ability to discern the necessary relationships between the planned structure and the surrounding environment, and an eye for what will be functional and aesthetically pleasing for those who actually experience the home. Likewise, designing a good questionnaire requires an understanding of the science of measurement theory, an ability to discern the necessary relationships between the measurement instrument and the subjects being measured, and an eye for what will be useful and appropriate when interviewing future respondents.

Most of us do not have the expertise necessary to draw up a set of blueprints for a home or the skills required to follow blueprints in order to build a house. Because houses require a substantial investment, we would want the job done right and would hire a professional architect and general contractor. Unfortunately, managers too often do not exercise similar prudence

when it comes to designing and creating questionnaires, despite the significant investment necessary to conduct the survey and the even larger investment required to implement marketing actions based on the research information. Some managers assume "anyone can ask questions" and create their own questionnaires, or have their subordinates do so. The result is generally a questionnaire with very weak measurement properties.

This chapter focuses on some of the fundamental principles of measurement theory (or more formally, the scientific field of psychometrics). However, after reading this chapter, you still won't have the expertise necessary to design a good measurement instrument yourself (there are much more extensive works on these topics that you would need to master first). Instead, you should have enough of an appreciation of the properties of good measurement and the complexity of the measurement process to recognize why it's worth the investment to have a professional researcher do this work for you. Equally important, you will have enough of an understanding to ask prospective researchers meaningful questions to help you determine whether they truly understand the measurement process or if they are more inclined to simply ask questions clients say they want to ask. You should never hire researchers of the latter persuasion.

MANAGER'S FOCUS

The different levels of measurement may seem like esoteric abstractions for which only researchers would have any genuine concern. But this is not the case. Having an understanding of the different levels of measurement is extremely important and practical to you as a manager. Without this understanding you are quite likely to attribute inappropriate meanings to numbers generated in research studies, or to readily accept misinterpretations made by others who do research for you. Equipped with an understanding of measurement levels, you will be able to properly interpret the meaning of research findings and assess the appropriateness of techniques researchers propose using to analyze the data generated by the measurement instrument.

In addition, by understanding that there are different levels of measurement, you will be more discerning about the amount of information certain questions and scales can provide. Managers in particular have a propensity to be satisfied with "yes/no" questions, or similar ones that also produce nominal data—the lowest level of measurement. Generally, these same questions can easily be recast to produce ordinal, interval, or ratio levels of measurement. Given that higher levels of measurement provide greater information and more analysis options, variables should be measured at the highest levels permitted by the underlying concept and the willingness of respondents to disclose the desired information.

Learning Objective

2. List the four types of scales that can be used to measure an attribute.

must be used correctly in order to avoid misleading ourselves and those who are counting on the information we are delivering.

There are four types of scales used to measure attributes of objects: nominal, ordinal, interval, and ratio.[2] Exhibit 12.1 summarizes some of the more important features of these scales. These are often referred to as four "levels" of measurement

Exhibit 12.1	Scales of Measurement			
Scale	**Basic Comparison**[a]	**Measures of Typical Examples**	**Average**[b]	
Nominal	Identity	Male/Female User/nonuser Occupations Uniform numbers	Mode	
Ordinal	Order	Brand preference Social class Hardness of minerals Graded quality of lumber	Median	
Interval	Comparison of intervals	Temperature scale Grade point average Attitude toward brands	Mean	
Ratio	Comparison of absolute magnitudes	Units sold Number of purchases Income Age	Geometric mean Harmonic mean	

[a] All the comparisons applicable to a given scale are permissible with all scales below it in the table. For example, the ratio scale allows the comparison of intervals and the investigation of order and identity, in addition to the comparison of absolute magnitudes.

[b] The measures of average applicable to a given scale are also appropriate for all scales below it in the table; for example, the mode is also a meaningful measure of the average when measurement is on an ordinal, interval, or ratio scale.

because measures at higher levels of measurement (e.g., ratio scales) have more properties and can be used for more kinds of analyses than can measures at lower levels of measurement (e.g., nominal scales). For this reason, the highest level of measurement possible should normally be used when developing a measure for some attribute. However, it is important to remember that it is the properties of the attribute itself that determine which levels of measurement are possible.

Nominal Scale

One of the most basic uses of numbers is to *identify* particular objects. A person's social security number is a **nominal scale**, as are the numbers on football jerseys, lockers, and so on. These numbers simply identify the individual or object that has been assigned the number. In these examples, the numbers are used to uniquely identify individuals; nominal scales also allow us to categorize people or things into groups based on their attributes. For example, if we assign the number 1 to represent female respondents to a survey and the number 2 to represent male respondents, we have used a nominal scale that allows us to identify the gender of a particular respondent and to determine the relative proportions of females vs. males in our sample. Figure 12.1 uses the issue of a respondent's preferences for six different soft drinks to illustrate how questions about this issue might be framed to secure reactions on a nominal scale as well as other levels of measurement.

With nominal scales, the numbers don't mean anything other than simple identification. A basketball player wearing uniform number 15 isn't necessarily taller or a better shooter than a player wearing the number 14; we must use other measures with different scale properties to make those kinds of assessments. Similarly, the fact that females have been identified as 1 and males as 2 in our measurement system doesn't imply anything at all about females versus males on any attribute other than identification. Females are not necessarily "inferior" to males, or "less" than males or half as many as males—as the numbers 1 and 2 might indicate. We can just as easily reverse our coding procedure so that each female is a 2 and each male a 1.

The reason we can reverse our codes is that the only property conveyed by the numbers is identity. With a nominal scale, the only permissible operation is counting. As a result, the *mode* (the most frequently occurring category) is the only legitimate measure of central tendency or average. It does not make sense in a sample consisting of 60 men and 40 women to say that the average sex is 1.4, if males were coded 1 and females 2, even though the computer will calculate the mean *if you tell it to do so*. This is an incredibly important point: The numbers have been assigned by the researcher, and the researcher must be aware of what kinds of analyses are possible with different scales of measurement. In this example, all we can say is that there were more males in the sample than females, or that 60% of the sample was male. If we want to say more than that, we'll need to take additional measures.

Ordinal Scale

A useful property of all scales above the nominal level of measurement is that of *order*. Thus, with an **ordinal scale**, we could say that the number 2 is greater than the number 1, that 3 is greater than both 2 and 1, and that 4 is greater than all three of these numbers. The numbers 1, 2, 3, and 4 are ordered, and the larger the number, the greater the property. Note that the ordinal scale implies identity, since the same number would be used for all objects that are the

nominal scale
Measurement in which numbers are assigned to objects or classes of objects solely for the purpose of identification.

ordinal scale
Measurement in which numbers are assigned to data on the basis of some order (for example, more than, greater than) of the objects.

ETHICAL DILEMMA 12.1

José Cardenas, a research analyst for Quality Surveys, was working on a study attempting to assess the image of the various automobile dealers in a metropolitan area. The survey instrument asked about such things as the quality and promptness of the dealer's repair service; the courtesy, knowledge, and helpfulness of its salespeople; how competitive the dealer was with respect to its automobile assortment and prices; and so on. Altogether there were 35 items that addressed the various attributes by which customers might evaluate automobile dealers. Respondents were asked to evaluate the dealer with whom they were most familiar on each attribute using one of four categories: poor (1), fair (2), good (3), or excellent (4). Thus, the range of scores could run from 35 to 140. In presenting the results to the client, a Ford dealership, Cardenas stated that, on average, people in town had twice as favorable an attitude toward the Ford dealer as toward its nearest Chevrolet dealer. This was based on the average scores of 120 for the Ford dealership and 60 for the Chevrolet dealership.

- Could Cardenas rightly make such a claim? If not, what could he say?
- What were Cardenas's responsibilities to the client with respect to understanding measurement-scale issues?
- Did Cardenas's superiors have any responsibility in this regard?

	Assessing a Respondent's Preference for Soft Drinks with Nominal, Ordinal, Interval, and Ratio Scales
FIGURE 12.1	

NOMINAL SCALE

Which of the soft drinks on the following list do you like? Check all that apply.

_____ Coke
_____ DrPepper
_____ Mountain Dew
_____ Pepsi
_____ 7 Up
_____ Sprite

Mode

ORDINAL SCALE

Please rank the soft drinks on the following list according to your degree of liking for each, assigning your most preferred drink rank = 1 and your least preferred drink rank = 6.

_____ Coke
_____ DrPepper
_____ Mountain Dew
_____ Pepsi
_____ 7 Up
_____ Sprite

Mode
Median

INTERVAL SCALE

Please indicate your degree of liking each of the soft drinks on the following list by checking the appropriate position on the scale.

Mode
Median
Arithmetic Mean

	DISLIKE A LOT	DISLIKE	LIKE	LIKE A LOT
Coke	_____	_____	_____	_____
DrPepper	_____	_____	_____	_____
Mountain Dew	_____	_____	_____	_____
Pepsi	_____	_____	_____	_____
7 Up	_____	_____	_____	_____
Sprite	_____	_____	_____	_____

RATIO SCALE

Please divide 100 points among each of the following soft drinks according to your degree of liking for each.

Mode
Median
Arithmetic Mean
Geometric mean

_____ Coke
_____ DrPepper
_____ Mountain Dew
_____ Pepsi
_____ 7 Up
_____ Sprite
100

same. An example would be the assignment of the number 1 to identify first-year students, 2 to identify sophomores, 3, juniors, and 4, seniors. We could just as well use the numbers 10 for first-year students, 20 for sophomores, 25 for juniors, and 30 for seniors. This assignment would still indicate the class level of each person and the *relative standing* of two persons when compared in terms of who is further along in the academic program. Note that this is all that is conveyed by an ordinal scale. For example, the difference in ranks says nothing about the difference in academic achievement between two ranks.

Suppose that there were three new restaurants located in a mid-sized college town and that the general manager of one of the restaurants wanted to know where her restaurant ranks with college students relative to the others. A team of student researchers worked with the manager to develop a telephone survey that asked a sample of students to rank-order their preferences among the new restaurants, with 1 assigned to the first choice, 2 to the second choice, and 3 to the third choice. The manager was encouraged when she reviewed the results: 52% of respondents ranked her restaurant as their first choice, 40% ranked it as their second choice, and 8% ranked it as their third choice. Thus, the modal ranking for the restaurant was "first choice" because that is the largest category of respondents. Because there is an order for the responses (that is, first choice is better than second choice, and so on), however, we can also calculate an additional measure of central tendency: the *median*. If there were 100 students in our sample, imagine lining them up according to their ranking of the restaurant. First might come the 8 who ranked it as third choice, then would come the 40 who ranked it as second choice, followed by the 52 who ranked it as first choice. The median ranking for the restaurant would be the ranking provided by the person in the center of our line-up (with an even number of respondents, we would consider the scores of the two people in the center). In our example, the median ranking would thus be "first choice."

Both ordinal and interval scales can help assess preference for a restaurant.

Whether or not we can use the ordinal scale to assign numbers to objects depends on the attribute in question. The attribute itself must possess the ordinal property to allow ordinal scaling that is meaningful. In addition, we can transform an ordinal scale in any way we wish as long as we maintain the basic ordering of the objects, because the order of the objects is all that we know with an ordinal scale. It is impossible to say how much someone preferred one object to another; all we can say is that one is preferred over the other. In our restaurant example, one respondent might really like all three restaurants, ranking them in the following order: first-restaurant A, second-restaurant B, third-restaurant C. Another respondent might really dislike all three restaurants, yet still rank them in the same order. Still another student may like A and B and dislike C, and once again rank them in the same order. In each case, rank order is the same, while the underlying feelings about the restaurants are quite different. Representing those feelings requires a higher level of measurement.

Interval Scale

Some scales possess the following useful property: The *intervals* between the numbers tell us how far apart the objects are with respect to the attribute. This means that the differences can be compared. The difference between 1 and 2 is equal to the difference between 2 and 3.

Rating scales for measuring consumer attitudes are commonly used in marketing research and are great examples of **interval scales**. Consider the restaurant example again. Suppose that respondents were asked to rate their attitudes toward the three restaurants using 1–7 scales, where 1 = "extremely unfavorable" and 7 = "extremely favorable." Such an approach allows us to see the relative strength of a respondent's feelings toward each of the restaurants. A respondent who really likes all three restaurants might assign each of them high scores, such as 6 or 7. Similarly, someone who

interval scale
Measurement in which the assigned numbers legitimately allow the comparison of the size of the differences among and between members.

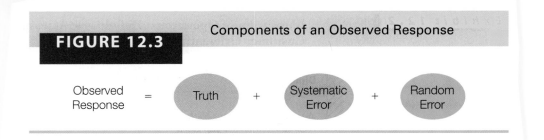

FIGURE 12.3   Components of an Observed Response

Observed Response = Truth + Systematic Error + Random Error

We'll call these response errors. These errors fall into two general categories, systematic error and random error. Figure 12.3 provides an illustration of these ideas. Our goal, of course, is to minimize error. As systematic and random errors decrease, the validity of the measure increases.

research window 12.1

Impact of Culture on Response Styles

One of the most important and dramatic ways culture impacts multicountry research is in the different ways people in various countries respond to survey questions and use questionnaire scales. In a carefully controlled experiment, GfK Custom Research Inc. (CRI) explored the use of different kinds of scales in new product research. The result: *We found extraordinary differences from country to country in the way respondents use common survey scales.* For example: Survey respondents in the Philippines and Italy are four times more likely than

respondents in Hong Kong or Japan to use the "top box" of a buying intent scale.

And these differences are clearly the result of culture, not economic levels. Japan and the United States, two of the most affluent countries in the world, are dramatically different on these measures. These differences must be understood and taken into account in analyzing multicountry studies. In the CRI experiment across 18 countries, here are a few of the differences we found on use of the buying intent scale:

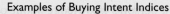

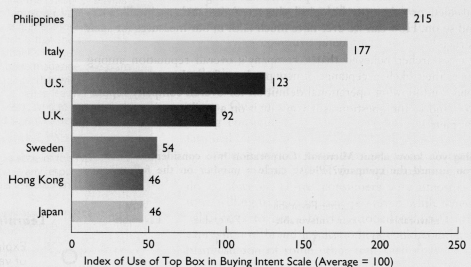

Examples of Buying Intent Indices

Country	Index
Philippines	215
Italy	177
U.S.	123
U.K.	92
Sweden	54
Hong Kong	46
Japan	46

Index of Use of Top Box in Buying Intent Scale (Average = 100)

Systematic error, which is also called constant error, is error that affects the measurement in a constant way. Imagine that the reputation question had been worded this way: "Taking everything you know about Microsoft Corporation into consideration, including its aggressive defense of its monopolistic market position, how favorable are you toward the company?" This is a leading question that would probably have caused you to choose a lower scale position when responding to the item. If you were to answer the same question at a later time, you would probably still choose the lower scale position. For that matter, if lots of people were asked to answer the same leading question, most of their responses would be lower than if they responded to the nonleading version of the question. As a result, using the leading question has systematically lowered scale scores.

Sometimes personality traits or other stable characteristics of individuals add systematic error to the measurement process. For example, Research Window 12.1 illustrates the impact culture has on people's response styles. Similarly, some people are more willing to express negative feelings than are other people; some people seem to

systematic error
Error in measurement that is also known as constant error since it affects the measurement in a constant way.

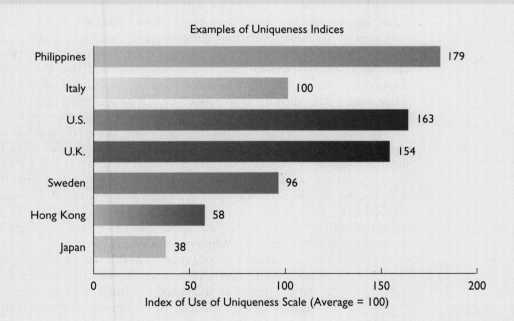

Examples of Uniqueness Indices

But the effect of cultural differences on scale use is even more complex: Differences even exist within the same country from one scale to another.

That is illustrated by comparing the example above, showing use of the uniqueness scale, with the previous example on buying intent. Italians are less bullish in their use of the uniqueness scale, while respondents in the United Kingdom are more aggressive in using the uniqueness scale than in stating buying intent.

This means there is no single, simple way to adjust for country-to-country differences. It requires experience across countries and a thorough understanding of how each scale is used differently country by country.

Sources: Jeffrey Pope, *How Cultural Differences Affect Multi-Country Research* (Minneapolis, Minn.: GfK Custom Research Inc., 1991). See also Irvine Clarke III, "Global Marketing Research: Is Extreme Response Style Influencing Your Results?" *Journal of International Consumer Marketing* 12, 4, 2000, pp. 91–111.

be systematically negative in all their responses. On the other side of the coin, some people follow the old advice, "If you can't say something nice, don't say anything at all." They have been asked to cooperate, so they respond, but not always truthfully. Their responses are likely to introduce systematic error on the positive side.

In general, people's responses to survey questions can be affected by a host of individual characteristics that systematically push responses away from the true score. As an example, research has demonstrated that consumers sometimes have a hard time accurately reporting how frequently they perform behaviors. Those who perform behaviors frequently tend to underreport the level of behavior and those who perform those behaviors less frequently tend to overreport the level of behavior. In a clever study, researchers demonstrated that consumers who make a lot of long-distance telephone calls report making fewer calls than they actually do; the reverse is true for consumers who make few long-distance calls. The same effect applied to estimates of how long the calls lasted.[5]

Differences in how surveys are administered can also introduce systematic error into a project. Much measurement in marketing involves the use of questionnaires administered by phone or in person. Because interviewers can vary in the way they ask questions, the responses also may vary as a function of the interviewer. Differences in method of administration can also make a difference in how people respond to survey items. Researchers at Silver Dollar City, a theme park located near Branson, Missouri, regularly assess visitors' satisfaction with the park a few days after they visit. While examining responses to telephone surveys versus e-mail surveys, they discovered that responses to the same satisfaction question were consistently higher when obtained via telephone compared with e-mail. Because there were no differences in answers for virtually all other questions, the researchers concluded that the telephone survey respondents were likely inflating satisfaction scores because of the social context: They were talking directly to someone else. There was apparently less social stigma associated with less flattering answers when delivered by electronic means.

random error

Error in measurement due to temporary aspects of the person or measurement situation and which affects the measurement in irregular ways.

The other general type of error, **random error**, is not constant but is due to temporary aspects of the person or measurement situation; this can affect the measurement in irregular ways. Random error is present when we repeat a measurement on an individual and don't get the same scores as the first time we did the measurement, even though the characteristic being measured hasn't changed. For example, if you responded to the original Microsoft reputation question with a "3" today, a "4" tomorrow, and a "1" next week—and nothing has happened to change how you feel about Microsoft—the error is random and not systematic.

A person's mood, state of health, fatigue, and so forth, may all affect his or her responses, yet these factors are temporary and can vary. Thus, if an individual has had a hard day and is temporarily seeing the negative side of everything and everybody, his survey responses (if he chooses to respond at all) will be more negative than they might be if he responded the next day. It works the other way, too. Maybe the individual is completing the survey after just receiving a promotion with a significant raise; everything and everybody looks a little better than it did before.

The situation surrounding the measurement also can affect the score in random ways. Maybe the room temperature is uncomfortably hot or cold when the survey was completed. Maybe the presence of someone else in the room causes the respondent to alter her responses, whether or not she even realizes it. For example, researchers studying the decision-making process of married couples have encountered a frequent situational influence on responses to survey items: When the husband is asked for the respective roles of husband and wife in purchasing a new automobile, for instance, one set of responses is secured; when the wife is asked, the responses are different; when the two are asked together, still a third set is

© EYEWIRE/GETTY IMAGES

One of the researcher's main tasks is to generate questions that mean the same thing to all respondents.

obtained. Which is correct? It is hard to say, since the fact remains that the situation surrounding a measurement can affect the scores that are obtained.

Finally, sometimes people respond differently to a questionnaire or an item on a scale because of differences in interpretation of an ambiguous or complex question rather than any fundamental differences in the characteristic we are attempting to measure. Even simple words can be open to misinterpretation. In measuring complex concepts such as attitudes, the possibilities for misunderstanding increase greatly. One of the researcher's main tasks is to generate items or questions that mean the same thing to all respondents. If we don't do this, we add random error as people interpret the question in all sorts of different ways.

THE ASSESSMENT OF VALIDITY AND RELIABILITY

Learning Objective

6. List three general types of validity that can be used to assess the quality of a measure.

The distinction between systematic error and random error is important because of the way the **validity**, or correctness, of a measure is assessed. Any scale or other measure that accurately assesses what it was intended to assess is said to have validity. While both systematic and random error lower a measure's validity, in some ways systematic error is less troublesome than random error. For example, even though cultural influences may cause respondents in a particular country to unconsciously raise or lower their responses on rating scales, we can still compare responses across individuals within that culture because the error is constant, more or less, across the individuals. For cross-cultural comparisons, it is possible to adjust scores to account for the systematic error associated with cultural differences so that the results are useful. Random error, on the other hand, is just that—random—and it cannot effectively be held constant or accounted for statistically. The best we can hope is that random errors cancel themselves out across respondents.

Building valid measures is a very difficult task. It is especially difficult when we try to measure hypothetical constructs. We must take the necessary steps to make certain that our measures are valid. Researchers often think about four key concepts related to the validity of their measures: reliability, predictive validity, content validity, and construct validity.

validity
The extent to which differences in scores on a measuring instrument reflect true differences among individuals, groups, or situations in the characteristic that it seeks to measure, or true differences in the same individual, group, or situation from one occasion to another, rather than systematic or random errors.

Reliability

Reliability refers to the ability of a measure to obtain consistent scores for the same object, trait, or construct across time, across different evaluators, or across the items forming the measure. *Consistency* is the hallmark of reliability; as a result, improving reliability requires decreasing random error.

Evaluating the reliability of any measuring instrument consists of determining how much of the variation in scores is due to inconsistencies in measurement. If a measure is reliable, it is not heavily influenced by transitory factors that cause random errors. However, a measure could be reliable, but not necessarily valid because of systematic error. A reliable measure is just consistent—it may not be measuring the right thing, but it returns consistent scores.

Suppose that a sportsman is comparing three different rifles—an old rifle and two new ones. He fires each of the rifles a number of times and each time he lines up the sights on the gun perfectly with the center of the target. Figure 12.4 illustrates the results for the three different rifles. The old rifle is unreliable; despite the fact that the sights are set on the center of the target, the shots go off in random directions. The first new rifle is relatively reliable—it hits about the same spot on the target each time—but its sights are set incorrectly in the center diagram. The error is systematic and not random, but the rifle still misses the mark. The right-hand diagram shows a new rifle with its sights set correctly. Only in the right-hand diagram could a user of any of the rifles be expected to hit the center of the target with regularity. This represents a measure that is both reliable *and* valid.

reliability
Ability of a measure to obtain similar scores for the same object, trait, or construct across time, across different evaluators, or across the items forming the measure.

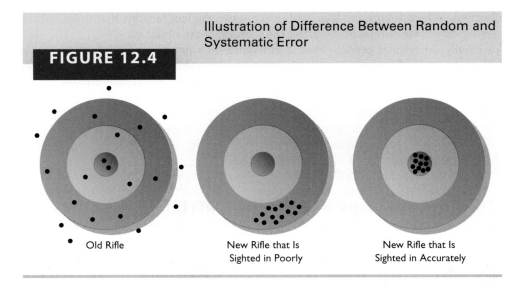

FIGURE 12.4

Illustration of Difference Between Random and Systematic Error

Old Rifle

New Rifle that Is
Sighted in Poorly

New Rifle that Is
Sighted in Accurately

How can we assess reliability? Suppose that we measured job satisfaction among a group of salespeople at the first of the month and then measured it again two weeks later. If our measure of job satisfaction is reliable, we would expect the scores to be highly correlated. If they aren't, the measure is unstable and its reliability must be questioned. This sort of reliability is known as *test–retest reliability*. Similarly, if we asked a group of salespeople to evaluate the quality of a new competing product that has just entered the market, we would anticipate that the product quality measures would be highly correlated across the group of salespeople. If so, the measure has demonstrated reliability through its consistency across the different evaluators. This latter form of reliability might be called *interjudge reliability* and is relevant to any situation in which multiple judges evaluate a single object. Common examples include talent and beauty contests and Olympic competitions such as diving and figure skating. Figure 12.5 depicts a situation in which the judgments of two different observers do not agree.

When we use multiple items to measure a hypothetical construct such as satisfaction, image, or many other constructs, we often assess reliability based on the *internal consistency* of the measures. That is, if all of the items are assessing some aspect of the hypothetical construct, then they ought to be highly correlated with one another.

FIGURE 12.5

A Situation in Which the Judgments of
Two Observers Do Not Agree

Hagar the Horrible

One popular means of assessing the internal consistency reliability of a measure is coefficient alpha, which provides a summary measure of the intercorrelations that exist among the set of items in a measure of a construct.

Although a measure that is reliable may or may not be valid, if it is not reliable, it is surely not valid. Thus, reliability is necessary, but not sufficient, for establishing the validity of a measure. Reliability is more easily determined than validity, however, so there has been a greater emphasis on it historically for gauging the quality of measures.

Predictive Validity

How well the measure actually predicts some characteristic or specific behavior of the individual, an organization, the marketplace, and so on, is its **predictive validity**. The Graduate Management Admissions Test (GMAT) provides a good example. This test has proven to be useful in predicting how well a student with a particular score on the exam will do in an accredited M.B.A. program. The test score is used to predict the criterion of performance. Similarly, if a measure of salesperson job satisfaction does a good job of forecasting which salespeople will actually quit over some time frame, then the job satisfaction measure is said to have predictive validity. Both of these examples illustrate predictive validity in the true sense of the word—that is, the use of the score to predict some future event—but predictive validity also applies when a measure is used to "predict" something that is happening at the same time. For example, most medical tests are meant to predict whether or not a person has specific medical problems at the present time, rather than at some point in the future.

If the number of birds sitting on a fence in your backyard is highly correlated with the average price of a company's shares on the New York Stock Exchange, then the number of birds is said to have predictive validity with respect to that company's stock price. It is completely irrelevant whether or not that relationship makes sense or can be explained. While easy to assess, predictive validity is rarely the most important kind of validity. We usually want more evidence that our measures are assessing what they are supposed to assess.

> **predictive validity**
> The usefulness of the measuring instrument as a predictor of some other characteristic or behavior of the individual; it is sometimes called *criterion-related validity*.

Content Validity

If your measure of some construct adequately covers the most important aspects of that construct, it has **content validity**, which is sometimes called *face validity*. Consider, for example, the construct "spelling ability," and suppose that the following list of words was used to assess an individual's general spelling ability: *catcher, shortstop, foul, strike, walk, pitcher, umpire, outfielder*. Now, you might object to this spelling test on the grounds that all the words relate to the sport of baseball and nothing else. A person who is basically a very poor speller could do well on this test simply because he or she is a baseball fan. A person with a good basic ability for spelling but little interest in baseball might, in fact, do very poorly. This test appears to lack content validity, since it does not properly sample the range of all possible words that could be used to assess general spelling ability.

Theoretically, to capture a person's general spelling ability (in English) most accurately, we would have to build a test that includes all the words in the English language. Since we can't really do this, we construct tests consisting of much smaller samples of words. The goal is simply to come up with a set of items that adequately represents the full range of words that could be included on the spelling test. Whether we have assessed the true characteristic depends on how well we have sampled the range of the characteristic. This is true not only for spelling ability, but it also holds for psychological characteristics.

How can we ensure that our measure will possess content validity? We can never guarantee it, because it is partly a matter of judgment. What we can do, however, is to be systematic in how we develop the items to be used as a measure of some construct. A systematic process usually starts with a review of any relevant literature to see how

> **content validity**
> The adequacy with which the important aspects of the characteristic are captured by the measure; it is sometimes called *face validity*.

other people have measured the concept in the past. Then a large number of possible items can be developed, with the goal of covering the entire range of the characteristic being measured. For example, a measure of a sales representative's job satisfaction might include items about each of the components of the job (duties, fellow workers, top management, sales supervisor, customers, pay, and promotion opportunities). The initial set of items must be large, so that after refinement the measure still contains enough items to adequately sample the entire range of the variable. The set of items can then be "purified" to a smaller set of items through discussion with experts in the area and/or through data collection and analysis. Again, the goal is to end up with a set of items that appears to adequately represent the construct being assessed.

Construct Validity

construct validity
Assessment of how well the instrument captures the construct, concept, or trait it is supposed to be measuring.

Construct validity is the most difficult type of validity to establish.[6] With predictive validity, the only concern was whether or not the measure was useful for predicting some phenomenon, and content validity involved an assessment of the degree to which the measure appeared to be measuring the full range of the construct. A measure is said to have **construct validity** if it actually measures the construct, concept, or trait it is supposed to be measuring. That is, each item in the instrument must reflect the construct and must also show a correlation with other items in the instrument.

Thus, a scale designed to measure attitude would have construct validity if it measured the attitude in question and not some other underlying characteristic of the individual that affects his or her score. Unfortunately, the process of establishing construct validity is not a simple one. It involves lots of considerations. Measures with construct validity are reliable and possess predictive validity and content validity, but that's only a starting point. Most researchers agree that establishing construct validity also involves demonstrating that a measure (a) is highly positively correlated with other measures of the same construct (convergent validity); (b) is *not* correlated highly with measures of other, preferably related, constructs (discriminant validity); and (c) is related to other constructs in theoretically predictable ways (nomological validity).

For example, consider our earlier example relating job satisfaction to job turnover among sales representatives. Suppose we had developed a new measure of job satisfaction and the task is to determine its degree of construct validity. Assuming that the

MANAGER'S FOCUS

Measuring virtually anything in any field of study involves some degree of measurement error. In marketing, we are often interested in quantifying intangible psychological variables such as attitudes, motives, satisfaction, or perceptions of a brand's image or position because we believe doing so will ultimately help us understand and predict behavior in the marketplace. However, there will almost always be a higher degree of measurement error when we endeavor to measure what we cannot directly experience with our senses. Stated differently, we are always less certain we have truly measured what we set out to measure when the variable

of interest is intangible. Construct validity is harder to establish with these sorts of concepts.

For these reasons, objectivity and accuracy are much greater for observational studies (in which behavior or physiological responses to marketing stimuli are measured) than for communication studies (in which people are asked to respond to questions pertaining to unobservable psychological variables). As a manager, then, it should be clear that the integrity of the market intelligence you have available to you will be greater if you commission observational studies, rather than surveys, whenever the variables of interest can be directly observed.

measure has content validity (that is, it appears to measure the full range of the job satisfaction construct as we have defined it), the next step would be to collect data from salespeople in order to determine the statistical relationships between the new measure and other measures.

If our new measure is really assessing job satisfaction, it is reasonable to expect the measure to be highly correlated with other existing measures of job satisfaction, particularly ones that have been validated in previous research. After all, two measures of the same thing ought to be highly related to one another. This would provide evidence of convergent validity. Demonstrating that the new measure of job satisfaction has correlations that aren't too high with measures of other job-related constructs like role conflict or organizational commitment would provide evidence of discriminant validity. Finally, we expect our measure of salesperson job satisfaction to predict a salesperson's intentions to quit, based on our theory about how these constructs are related to one another. Supporting that relationship offers evidence of nomological validity.

DEVELOPING MEASURES

Learning Objective

7. Outline the sequence of steps to follow in developing valid measures of marketing constructs.

It is easy to get confused about the process of developing measures of marketing constructs. How should a measure be developed, and how should you deal with the basic issues of reliability and validity? Figure 12.6 diagrams a sequence of steps that can be followed to develop valid measures of marketing constructs.

Step 1 in the process involves defining the construct that is to be measured. Researchers need to be careful in specifying what is included in the domain of the construct and what is excluded. Imagine that we were interested in measuring your degree of satisfaction with a new car you had just purchased. What attributes of the car and the purchase process should be measured to assess your satisfaction? Certainly, we would want to include lots of product features such as cost, durability, quality, operating performance, and style. But what about your reaction to the salesperson who worked with you or with the dealership itself? What about your reaction to news of some negative environmental effect of operating the vehicle? Should these things be included? Researchers need to be very careful in specifying what is to be included in the domain of the construct being measured and what is to be excluded.

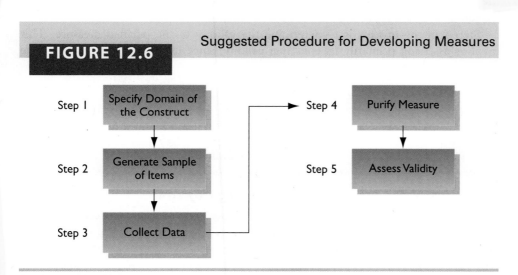

FIGURE 12.6   Suggested Procedure for Developing Measures

Step 1 — Specify Domain of the Construct
Step 2 — Generate Sample of Items
Step 3 — Collect Data
Step 4 — Purify Measure
Step 5 — Assess Validity

Source: Adapted from the procedure suggested by Gilbert A. Churchill, Jr., "A Paradigm for Developing Better Measures of Marketing Constructs," *Journal of Marketing Research* 16, February 1979, p. 66. American Marketing Association.

MANAGER'S FOCUS

Measurement is a process that extends well beyond merely writing and asking questions. Contrary to what you may previously have believed, the development of a sound measurement instrument requires a significant investment of both time and resources. For example, the development of an appropriate operational definition for a hypothetical construct might involve a considerable amount of time (1) reviewing published literature to determine how others have defined the construct, (2) conducting depth interviews with members of the target population to identify what issues are most relevant to them, or (3) performing other forms of exploratory research. The same types of exploratory research are necessary for generating a valid set of items (questions) for measuring the different components of a hypothetical construct. As a manager, you should encourage and financially support these acts of discovery, knowing they will likely improve measurement accuracy and thereby provide more trustworthy market intelligence with which to make future decisions.

Step 2 in the process is to generate items that capture the domain as specified. Techniques that are typically productive in exploratory research, including literature searches, experience surveys, focus groups, and so on, are generally productive here. The literature should indicate how the variable has previously been defined and how many dimensions or components it has. The search for ways to measure customer satisfaction would include product brochures, articles in trade magazines and newspapers, or results of product tests such as those published by *Consumer Reports*. The experience surveys and/or focus groups might include discussions with people in the product group responsible for the product, sales representatives, dealers, persons in marketing research, consumers, and outsiders who have a special expertise in heating equipment.

Step 3 involves collecting data about the concept from a relevant sample of the target population—for example, all those who have purchased an automobile from a specific dealership within the last six months.

Step 4 uses the data collected in Step 3 to purify the original set of items. Among other things, purification involves eliminating items that either seemed to create confusion among respondents or were not highly correlated with the other items in the measure.

Step 5 in the process is to determine the validity of the purified measure. This involves assessing primarily its construct validity, since its content validity will have largely been addressed in Steps 1 through 4.

SUMMARY

Learning Objective 1

Define the term *measurement* as it is used in marketing research.

Measurement consists of rules for assigning numbers to objects in such a way as to represent quantities of attributes.

Learning Objective 2

List the four types of scales that can be used to measure an attribute.

The four types of scales on which an attribute can be measured are nominal, ordinal, interval, and ratio scales.

Learning Objective 3

Explain the primary difference between a ratio scale and an interval scale.
In an interval scale, the zero point is established arbitrarily. The ratio scale possesses a natural, or absolute, zero—one for which there is universal agreement as to its location.

Learning Objective 4

Name the two types of error that may affect measurement scores and define each.
Two types of error may affect scores. The first type is systematic error, which affects the measurement in a constant way. The second type is random error, which is due to transient aspects of the person or measurement situation and which affects the measurement in irregular ways.

Learning Objective 5

Explain the concept of validity as it relates to measuring instruments.

Any scale or other measurement instrument that actually measures what it was intended to measure is said to have validity. As systematic and/or random error increases, the validity of a measure decreases.

Learning Objective 6

List three general types of validity that can be used to assess the quality of a measure.
The three types of validity are predictive validity, content validity, and construct validity.

Learning Objective 7

Outline the sequence of steps to follow in developing valid measures of marketing constructs.
The following sequence of steps is helpful in developing better measures of marketing constructs: (1) specify the domain of the construct, (2) generate a sample of items, (3) collect data, (4) purify the measure, and (5) assess validity.

KEY TERMS

measurement (page 245)
nominal scale (page 247)
ordinal scale (page 247)
interval scale (page 249)
ratio scale (page 250)
hypothetical construct (page 251)
conceptual definition (page 252)
operational definition (page 252)

systematic error (page 255)
random error (page 256)
validity (page 257)
reliability (page 257)
predictive validity (page 259)
content validity (page 259)
construct validity (page 260)

REVIEW QUESTIONS

1. What is measurement?

2. What are the scales of measurement? What comparisons among scores can be made with each?

3. What are some factors that may produce systematic errors? What factors may produce random errors?

4. What is reliability? What information does it contribute to determining if a measure is accurate?

5. How can we establish the reliability of measures?

6. What is validity?

7. What are the various types of validity?

DISCUSSION QUESTIONS, PROBLEMS, AND PROJECTS

1. Identify the type of scale (nominal, ordinal, interval, ratio) being used in each of the following questions. Justify your answer.

   a. *During which season of the year were you born?*
      ☐ winter ☐ spring ☐ summer ☐ fall

   b. *What is your total household income?* _____

   c. *Which are your three most preferred brands of cigarettes? Rank them from 1 to 3 according to your preference, with 1 as most preferred.*
      ☐ Marlboro   ☐ Salem
      ☐ Newport   ☐ Camel
      ☐ Benson and Hedges   ☐ Merit

   d. *How much time do you spend traveling to school every day?*
      ☐ under 5 minutes   ☐ 16–20 minutes
      ☐ 5–10 minutes   ☐ 30 minutes and over
      ☐ 11–15 minutes

   e. *How satisfied are you with* Newsweek *magazine?*
      ☐ very satisfied   ☐ dissatisfied
      ☐ satisfied   ☐ very dissatisfied
      ☐ neither satisfied nor dissatisfied

   f. *On average, how many cigarettes do you smoke in a day?*
      ☐ over 1 pack   ☐ less than 12 pack
      ☐ 12 to 1 pack

   g. *Which of the following courses have you taken?*
      ☐ marketing research   ☐ sales management
      ☐ advertising management   ☐ consumer behavior

   h. *What is the level of education for the head of household?*
      ☐ some high school   ☐ some college
      ☐ high school graduate   ☐ college graduate and/or graduate work

2. The analysis for each of the preceding questions follows. Is the analysis appropriate for the scale used?

   a. About 50% of the sample were born in the fall, while 25% of the sample were born in the spring, and the remaining 25% were born in the winter. It can be concluded that the fall is twice as popular as the spring and the winter seasons.

   b. The average income is $25,000. There are twice as many individuals with an income of less than $9,999 than individuals with an income of $40,000 and over.

   c. Marlboro is the most preferred brand. The mean preference is 3.52.

   d. The median time spent on traveling to school is 8.5 minutes. There are three times as many respondents traveling less than 5 minutes as respondents traveling 16 to 20 minutes.

   e. The average satisfaction score is 4.5, which seems to indicate a high level of satisfaction with *Newsweek* magazine.

   f. Ten percent of the respondents smoke less than one-half pack of cigarettes a day, while three times as many respondents smoke more than one pack a day.

   g. Sales management is the most frequently taken course, since the median is 3.2.

   h. The responses indicate that 40% of the sample have some high school education, 25% of the sample are high school graduates, 20% have some college education, and 10% are college graduates. The mean education level is 2.6.

3. You have developed a questionnaire designed to measure attitudes toward a series of television ads for a new snack food product. The respondents, as a group, will view the ads on a television set and then complete the questionnaire. Due to logistical circumstances beyond your control, you must split your sample of respondents into three groups and collect data on three separate days. What steps might you take in an effort to minimize possible variance in scores caused by the three separate administrations?

4. Many areas of marketing research rely heavily on measures of psychological constructs. What characteristics inherent in these constructs make them so difficult to measure? What tools can the marketing researcher use when evaluating the "correctness" of his or her measure? In other words, what can we do that allows us to state with some degree of confidence that we are indeed measuring the construct of interest?

5. Discuss the notion that a particular measure could be reliable and still not be valid. In your discussion, distinguish between reliability and validity.

6. Feather-Tote Luggage is a producer of cloth-covered luggage, one of the primary advantages of which is its light weight. The company distributes its luggage through major department stores, mail-order houses, clothing retailers, and other retail outlets such as stationery stores, leather good stores, and so on. The company advertises rather heavily, but it also supplements this promotional effort with a large field staff of sales representatives, numbering around 400. The number of sales representatives varies, and one of the historical problems confronting Feather-Tote Luggage has been the large number of sales representatives' resignations. It is not unusual for 10 to 20% of the sales force to turn over every year. Since the cost of training a new sales representative is estimated at $15,000 to $20,000, not including the lost sales that might result because of a personnel switch, Mr. Harvey, the sales manager, is concerned. He has been concerned for some time and thus has been conducting exit interviews with each departing sales representative. On the basis of these interviews, he has formulated the opinion that the major reason for this high turnover is general sales representatives' dissatisfaction with company policies, promotional opportunities, and pay. But top management has not been sympathetic to Harvey's pleas regarding the changes needed in these areas of corporate policy. Rather, it has tended to counter Harvey's pleas with arguments that too much of what he is suggesting is based on his gut reactions and little hard data. Before it would be willing to change things, top management desires more systematic evidence that job satisfaction, in general, and these dimensions of job satisfaction, in particular, are the real reasons for the high turnover.

   Describe the procedures you would use in developing a measure by which the job satisfaction of Feather-Tote Luggage sales representatives could be assessed. Indicate the type of scale you would use and why, and detail the specific steps you would undertake to assure the validity and reliability of this measure.

Measuring Attitudes and Other Variables

Learning Objectives

1. List the various ways by which attitudes can be measured.
2. List three general categories of ratings scales.
3. Explain the difference between a graphic-ratings scale and an itemized-ratings scale.
4. Name the most widely used attitude scaling techniques in marketing research and explain why researchers prefer them.
5. Explain how the constant-sum scaling method works.
6. List some other key decisions to be made when designing scales.
7. Explain how norms are useful for interpreting rating scale results.

Introduction

Marketers have a keen interest in consumers' attitudes towards products. Whether they are genuinely new products, simply "new and improved" versions of existing products, or existing products, corporate managers must often consider how groups ranging from consumers to government regulators to retailers to suppliers to employees feel about the company and its products and services. Poor perceptions and evaluations across any of these groups usually lead to poor performance. Because attitudes, perceptions, and other hypothetical constructs can be important determinants of the company's success, the marketer needs a way to measure such things. In this chapter, we review some specific methods used to measure attitudes and other important constructs.

Although the attitude concept is one of the most widely used in psychology, it is used inconsistently. Both researchers and practitioners have trouble agreeing on interpretations of its various aspects. However,

© ROSE ALCORN

most theorists agree that (1) an attitude is an individual's overall evaluation of an idea or object that can range from very negative to very positive; (2) an attitude that is strongly held is difficult to change; and (3) there is usually a consistency between attitudes and behavior.

MEASURING ATTITUDES

Learning Objective

1.   List the various ways by which attitudes can be measured.

Measuring things that can't be directly seen is tough. Researchers have developed quite a number of different approaches to attempt to measure attitudes over the years, including the idea of simply observing people's behavior and inferring their attitudes toward some object based on their behaviors with respect to the object. Although there is tremendous value in observational research, a behavior is not the same thing as an attitude. If we desire to measure attitudes, then a different sort of measure is necessary. In the next section, we'll go into detail about the use of self-report measures, the most common approach. First, however, we will briefly overview a couple of other approaches to attitude determination. These approaches might be used in situations where respondents would find it difficult to provide an unbiased direct response.

Performance of Objective Tasks

On the theory that people's **performance of objective tasks** will reflect their attitudes, we might ask a person to memorize a number of facts about an issue and then assess his or her attitude toward that issue from the facts that were successfully memorized. Imagine that researchers for a motorcycle manufacturer wanted to understand potential customers' attitudes toward proposed helmet use legislation. One way to proceed is to ask respondents to memorize such facts as (1) the number of lives saved by helmet usage, (2) the average cost of helmets, and (3) the number of states that have adopted a mandatory helmet law. The material should reflect both sides of the issue. The researcher then would determine what facts the person remembered. The assumption is that subjects would be more likely to remember those arguments that are most consistent with their own position.

performance of objective tasks
A method of assessing attitudes that rests on the presumption that a subject's performance of a specific assigned task (for example, memorizing a number of facts) will depend on the person's attitude.

Physiological Reaction

Another approach to attitude measurement involves **physiological reaction**. Here, through electrical or mechanical means, such as the galvanic skin response technique, the researcher monitors the subject's response to the controlled introduction of some stimuli. One problem that arises in using these measures to assess attitude is that, with the exception of voice-pitch analysis, the individual's physiological response indicates only the intensity of the individual's feelings and not whether they are negative or positive.

physiological reaction
A method of assessing attitudes in which the researcher monitors the subject's response, by electrical or mechanical means, to the controlled introduction of some stimuli.

SELF-REPORT ATTITUDE SCALES

Learning Objective

2.   List three general categories of ratings scales.

By far, the most common approach to measuring attitudes (and other hypothetical constructs) is to obtain respondents' **self-reports**, in which people are asked directly for their beliefs or feelings about something. On BizRate.com, consumers can self-report ratings of their purchase experience with companies such as Tower Hobbies, a nine-time platinum winner in BizRate's Toys and Games category. This online business rating service recognizes Circle of Excellence winners via graphic smiley/frowning face ratings so that both online businesses and prospective customers can easily gauge customer attitudes toward stores across many product categories.

self-report
A method of assessing attitudes in which individuals are asked directly for their beliefs about or feelings toward an object or class of objects.

Because attitude is such an important concept, it isn't surprising that researchers have developed a number of different self-report methods to measure it. There are three general categories of self-report ratings scales: graphic-ratings scales,

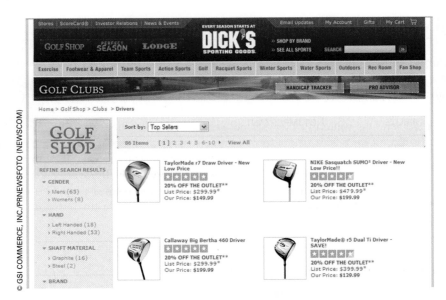

Dick's Sporting Goods Web site incorporates Web Shopping 2.0 Social Navigation technology from GSI Commerce Inc. and uses stars as its graphic-ratings scale.

itemized-ratings scales, and comparative-ratings scales. In this section, we review these approaches and provide some specific examples of how each might be used for measuring attitudes or other important marketing constructs.

Graphic-Ratings Scales

When using **graphic-ratings scales**, individuals indicate their rating by placing a check at the appropriate point on a line that runs from one extreme of the attribute to the other. Many variations are possible. The line may be vertical or horizontal; it may be unmarked or marked; if marked, the divisions may be few or many as in the case of a *thermometer scale*, so called because it looks like a thermometer. Figure 13.1 is an example of a horizontal, end-anchored only, graphic-ratings scale. Each individual would be instructed to indicate the importance of the attribute by checking the appropriate position on the scale. The importance value would then be inferred by measuring the length of the line from the left origin to the marked position.

One of the great advantages of graphic-ratings scales is the ease with which they can be constructed. They are also relatively easy for respondents to use, although the instructions must be clear. They also offer respondents the greatest degree of freedom in providing answers; in theory, there are an infinite number of possible response positions along the continuous scale. Just how useful such fine differences in responses are is questionable, however, and the actual physical measurement of responses takes researcher time and attention. For these reasons, itemized-ratings scales have proven to be much more popular with researchers.

graphic-ratings scale
A scale in which individuals indicate their ratings of an attribute typically by placing a check at the appropriate point on a line that runs from one extreme of the attribute to the other.

FIGURE 13.1	Graphic-Ratings Scale

Please evaluate each attribute, in terms of how important the attribute is to you personally, by placing an "X" at the position on the horizontal line that most reflects your feelings.

ATTRIBUTE	NOT IMPORTANT	VERY IMPORTANT
Courteous service		
Convenient location		
Convenient hours		
Low-interest-rate loans		

Itemized-Ratings Scale

The itemized-ratings scale is similar to the graphic-ratings scale except that the rater selects from a limited number of categories instead of placing a mark on a continuous scale. In general, five to nine categories work best; they permit fine distinctions and yet seem to be readily understood by respondents. As an example, Research Window 13.1 depicts the importance of various attributes of religious services for a sample of U.K. residents, as measured using itemized-ratings scales.

There are many different variations of itemized-ratings scales. Two very commonly used scales are summated-ratings scales and semantic-differential scales.

itemized-ratings scale
A scale on which individuals must indicate their ratings of an attribute or object by selecting the response category that best describes their position on the attribute or object.

MANAGER'S FOCUS

We recognize the tendency of managers, and others who are relatively unfamiliar with the measurement process, to ask questions at the nominal (lowest) level of measurement. For example, they may ask consumers "Are you satisfied with our service?" or "Did you like or dislike your experience in our store?" Think about these questions and try to identify (a) the managerially useful information they fail to generate and (b) how you could change them to provide more useful information.

As you are aware, some consumers may have mildly positive or negative evaluations of your marketing efforts; others may have very strong positive or negative assessments. Yes/No or Like/Dislike questions may provide a crude indication of whether an attitude is favorable or unfavorable, but they fail to capture the relative strength of attitudes across respondents. The self-report attitude scales discussed in this section provide ways of converting nominal (e.g., Yes/No or Like/Dislike) scales into interval scales. Rather than ask "Are you satisfied with our service?" you could ask "Using the five-point scale provided, please indicate how satisfied you are with our service." In other words, the self-report scales can help you follow our recommendation to always employ the highest level of measurement permitted by the subject matter as long as respondents are willing and able to provide the desired information.

research window 13.1

Importance of Selected Service Quality Dimensions as Applied to Religious Services

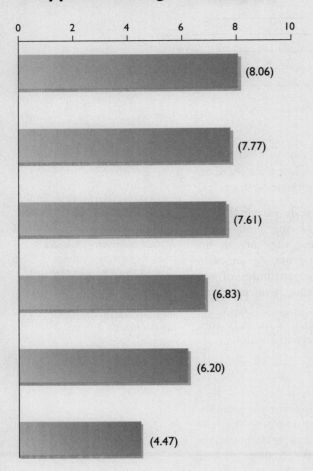

Responsiveness
Willingness to help customers and to provide prompt service, including giving an impression of interest in the customer and showing a willingness to serve, and to be concerned, sympathetic, and patient towards the customer

Credibility
Trustworthiness, believability, and honesty of the service provider

Courtesy
Politeness, respect, warmth, propriety, consideration, and friendliness of contact personnel

Communication
Customers are kept informed in language they can understand and are listened to, and service providers communicate with customers properly

Tangibility
Appearance of physical facilities, equipment, personnel, and communication materials including cleanliness and neat appearance, and the physical and psychological comfort of the service environment and facilities

Recovery
The way service providers deal with complaints, accept responsibility, and correct mistakes when the service delivery fails or breaks down

Note: Higher scores reflect higher levels of importance to respondents.

Source: Adapted from Jessica Santos and Brian P. Mathews, "Quality in Religious Services," *International Journal of Nonprofit and Voluntary Sector Marketing* 6, 3, 2001, pp. 278–288.

---

summated-ratings scale
A self-report technique for attitude measurement in which respondents indicate their degree of agreement or disagreement with each of a number of statements.

Summated-Ratings (Likert) Scale The summated-ratings scale, also called a *Likert scale*, is one of the most widely used attitude-scaling techniques in marketing research. It is particularly useful because it allows respondents to express the intensity of their feelings.[1]

With the summated-ratings scale, researchers write a number of statements that relate to the issue or object in question. Figure 13.2 is an example of a scale that might be used by a bank interested in comparing its image with that of its competitors. Subjects are asked to indicate their degree of agreement or disagreement with each statement in the series. The response categories represent various degrees of agreement and are assigned scale values. Let's assume the values 1, 2, 3, 4, and 5 are

FIGURE 13.2	Example of Likert Summated-Ratings Scale

	STRONGLY DISAGREE	DISAGREE	NEITHER AGREE NOR DISAGREE	AGREE	STRONGLY AGREE
1. The bank offers courteous service.	___	___	___	___	___
2. The bank has a convenient location.	___	___	___	___	___
3. The bank has convenient hours.	___	___	___	___	___
4. The bank offers low-interest-rate loans.	___	___	___	___	___

assigned to the respective response categories shown in Figure 13.2. A total score can then be calculated for each subject by adding (thus the name "summated-ratings") or averaging the scores across items.

Suppose that one customer of the bank checked "agree" on items 1 and 4 and "strongly agree" on items 2 and 3. This customer's total attitude score toward the bank would thus be 18 if we add the scores, or 4.5 if we calculate the mean score.

Researchers often use variations of the scale we've shown in Figure 13.2. For example, the version shown includes verbal descriptors, or *anchors*, for each scale position (i.e., "strongly disagree," "disagree," and so on). Some researchers will anchor only the endpoints of the scale, letting respondents infer the meaning of the internal scale positions. On the one hand, this introduces error to the degree that respondents interpret the nonanchored positions differently. On the other hand, such an approach may come closer to producing equal scale intervals if people are likely to interpret the verbal anchors differently.

Another variation of the summated-ratings scale asks respondents to circle a number representing the level of agreement rather than check the appropriate category. Further, some researchers offer more response categories than the traditional five categories shown in Figure 13.2. Regardless of how the particular scale is designed, the key features of the summated-ratings scale remain the same: a set of statements with which respondents indicate level of agreement.

Semantic-Differential Scale One of the most popular techniques for measuring attitudes in marketing research is the **semantic-differential scale**. It is particularly useful in corporate, brand, and product-image studies. The scale grew out of research concerning the underlying structure of words but has since been adapted to make it suitable for measuring attitudes.[2]

Semantic-differential scales consist of pairs of bipolar words or phrases that can be used to describe the attitude object. Let's look again at measuring attitude toward a bank. Using the semantic-differential approach, the researcher would first generate a list of bipolar adjectives or phrases. Figure 13.3 parallels Figure 13.2 in terms of the attributes used to describe the bank, but it is arranged in semantic-differential format. All we have done in Figure 13.3 is to try to express the things that could be used to describe a bank and thus serve as a basis for attitude formation, in terms of positive and negative statements. Respondents are instructed to read each set of bipolar phrases and to check the space that best represents their opinions for each set of phrases. A respondent who believed that the hours were terribly inconvenient might check the space closest to the phrase "Hours are inconvenient"; someone who was about neutral on this issue would select the middle position on the scale.

Learning Objective

4. Name the most widely used attitude scaling techniques in marketing research and explain why researchers prefer them.

semantic-differential scale
A self-report technique for attitude measurement in which the subjects are asked to check which cell between a set of bipolar adjectives or phrases best describes their feelings toward the object.

FIGURE 13.3 Example of Semantic-Differential Scaling Form

Service is discourteous.   :———:———:———:———:———:———: Service is courteous.

Location is inconvenient.   :———:———:———:———:———:———: Location is convenient.

Hours are inconvenient.   :———:———:———:———:———:———: Hours are convenient.

Loan interest rates are high. :———:———:———:———:———:———: Loan interest rates are low.

snake diagram

A diagram that connects the average responses to a series of semantic-differential statements, thereby depicting the profile of the object or objects being evaluated.

Semantic-differential scales are popular in marketing for several reasons. They are quite flexible and easy to administer from the researcher's perspective. They are easy for study respondents to understand and complete, with about any method of administration except by telephone. They are also quite good when it comes to presenting the results of a study. For example, suppose that respondents were asked to evaluate two or more banks using the same scale. When several banks are rated, the different bank profiles can be compared. Figure 13.4 (which is sometimes referred to as a snake diagram because of its shape) illustrates that Bank A is perceived as having more courteous service and a more convenient location and as offering lower interest rates on loans, but as having less convenient hours than Bank B. The plotted values represent the average score of all subjects on each descriptor. The profile that emerges gives a clear indication of how respondents perceive the differences between the two banks.

If you don't want to develop a profile, you can also total the scores on a semantic-differential scale in order to compare attitudes toward different objects. This score is computed by totaling or averaging the scores for the individual scales. As was true for summated-ratings scales, variations in scale design are common. Numbers are sometimes substituted for blanks, and different numbers of scale positions can be used.

Other Itemized-Ratings Scales There are lots of other possible variations of itemized-ratings scales. For example, Figure 13.5 depicts three different forms of itemized-ratings scales that have been used to measure customer satisfaction. The categories

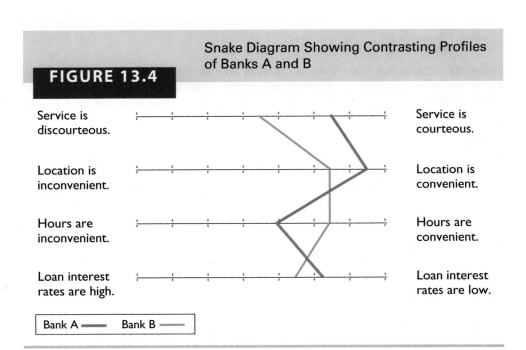

FIGURE 13.4 Snake Diagram Showing Contrasting Profiles of Banks A and B

Service is discourteous. — Service is courteous.

Location is inconvenient. — Location is convenient.

Hours are inconvenient. — Hours are convenient.

Loan interest rates are high. — Loan interest rates are low.

Bank A ——   Bank B ——

Three Forms of Itemized-Ratings Scales Used to Measure Satisfaction

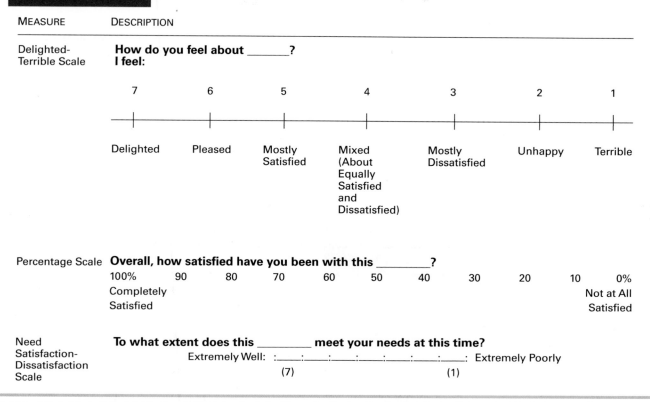

Source: Adapted from Robert A. Westbrook, "A Rating Scale for Measuring Product/Service Satisfaction," *Journal of Marketing* 44, Fall 1980, p. 69. Published by the American Marketing Association (Chicago, IL).

are ordered in terms of their scale positions; in some cases, the categories have verbal descriptions attached, and in other cases they do not. The distinguishing feature of an itemized scale is that the possible response categories are limited in number. Thus, a set of faces varying systematically in terms of whether they are frowning or smiling used to capture a person's satisfaction or preference (appropriately called a *faces scale*) would be considered an itemized scale. A summated-ratings statement is an example of an itemized-ratings scale, as is a semantic-differential scale. Figure 13.6 is an itemized-ratings scale used to measure importance values; this four-point scale has the descriptor labels attached to the end scale positions only.

A modification of the semantic-differential scale that has received some attention is the **Stapel scale**. It differs from the semantic-differential scale in that (1) adjectives or descriptive phrases are tested separately instead of simultaneously as bipolar pairs, (2) points on the scale are identified by number, and (3) there are 10 scale positions rather than 7. Figure 13.7 presents the same four attributes previously used to measure attitudes toward banks in a Stapel scale format. Respondents would be told to rate how accurately each of a number of statements describes the object of interest, Bank A.

Researchers who regularly use the Stapel scale point out that this method not only frees the researcher from the sometimes difficult task of developing bipolar adjectives for each of the items on the test but also permits finer discriminations in measuring attitudes. Stapel scales (or their variations) are also easier to administer over the telephone than are semantic-differential scales.

Stapel scale
A self-report technique for attitude measurement in which respondents are asked to indicate how accurately each of a number of statements describes the object of interest.

FIGURE 13.6	Itemized-Ratings Scale Used to Measure Importance Values

Please evaluate each attribute, in terms of how important the attribute is to you personally, by placing an "X" in the appropriate box.

ATTRIBUTE	NOT IMPORTANT			VERY IMPORTANT
Courteous service	☐	☐	☐	☐
Convenient location	☐	☐	☐	☐
Convenient hours	☐	☐	☐	☐
Low-interest-rate loans	☐	☐	☐	☐

FIGURE 13.7	Example of Stapel Scale

	−5	−4	−3	−2	−1	+1	+2	+3	+4	+5
Service is courteous.	☐	☐	☐	☐	☐	☐	☐	☐	☐	☐
Location is convenient.	☐	☐	☐	☐	☐	☐	☐	☐	☐	☐
Hours are convenient.	☐	☐	☐	☐	☐	☐	☐	☐	☐	☐
Loan interest rates are high.	☐	☐	☐	☐	☐	☐	☐	☐	☐	☐

comparative-ratings scale
A scale requiring subjects to make their ratings as a series of relative judgments or comparisons rather than as independent assessments.

Learning Objective

5. Explain how the constant-sum scaling method works.

constant-sum method
A comparative-ratings scale in which an individual divides some given sum among two or more attributes on a basis such as importance or favorability.

halo effect
A problem that arises in data collection when there is carryover from one judgment to another.

Comparative-Ratings Scale

In graphic and itemized scales, respondents are asked to consider attributes of an entity independently. For example, respondents may be asked to indicate how important convenient location is to them in choosing a bank, but not if convenient location is more or less important than convenient hours. In comparative-ratings scales, however, respondents are asked to judge each attribute with direct reference to the other attributes being evaluated.

The constant-sum scaling method is an example of a comparative-ratings scale. In the constant-sum method, the individual is instructed to divide some given sum among two or more attributes on some basis such as importance or favorability. Thus, in Figure 13.8, if the subject assigned 50 points to courteous service and 50 points to convenient location, the attributes would be judged to be equally important; if the individual assigned 80 to courteous service and 20 to convenient location, courteous service would be considered to be four times as important. Note the difference in emphasis with this method. All judgments are now made in comparison to some other alternative.

Although comparative scales require a different sort of judgment from the individual than either graphic or itemized scales, they do tend to eliminate the halo effect that is common in scaling. A halo effect occurs when there is carryover from one judgment to another. For example, suppose we are conducting a satisfaction study among recent shoppers of a department store and we are concerned about two key issues: satisfaction with service provided at the checkout counter and satisfaction with store location. If questions about these issues are asked back to back on the survey, a respondent with strong positive feelings about the service provided is likely to provide more positive assessments of store location than she or he might normally provide. In this case, the positive response to location may be due more to halo effects from the preceding question than to true feelings about the location. Comparative-ratings scales help control this problem by requiring respondents to consider two or more attributes in combination.

Another problem that researchers may encounter when using graphic or itemized scales to measure importance values is that respondents may be inclined to indicate that all, or nearly all, of the attributes are important. The comparative scaling methods usually allow more insight into the relative ranking, if not the absolute importance, of the attributes to each individual.

OTHER CONSIDERATIONS IN DESIGNING SCALES

There are a number of issues that must also be considered when designing scales for measuring concepts like attitudes. In this section, we'll deal with some of them.

Reverse Scaling

One of the problems that researchers often encounter, particularly when using multiple-item scales for measuring hypothetical constructs, is that respondents sometimes fall victim to response set bias. **Response set bias** refers to error that enters into our measures when respondents begin to answer all the questions in a similar way, often due to boredom or lack of attention (possibly caused by poor questionnaire design). Such respondents are "set" in their responses. For example, we have had whole sections of surveys returned in which respondents circled exactly the same response for every item (for example, circling the 6 on a 1–7 itemized-ratings scale for 20 questions in a row).

Response set bias clearly creates error in our attempts to accurately measure things. One technique designed to deal with this issue is **reverse scaling**, in which some of the items in a multi-item scale for measuring a construct are written in the negative form so that the most positive responses to the item are actually at the opposite end of the scale from where they would normally be. This technique is designed to encourage respondents to pay greater attention to the items and to help identify cases where response set bias has likely become a problem. For example, look back at Figure 13.2 and the example of the Likert, or summated-ratings, scale. Suppose that the second item were worded as follows: "The bank has an inconvenient location." From the bank's perspective, what would

ETHICAL DILEMMA 13.1

An independent researcher was hired by a national chain of department stores to develop a scale by which the chain could measure the image of each of its stores. The researcher thought that the best way to do this was through a semantic-differential scale. Since she was interested in establishing her credentials as an expert on store-image research, however, she decided to also develop items for a Likert scale and to administer both of the scales to designated participants. She realized that this might induce greater respondent fatigue and perhaps lower-quality responses, but she was willing to take the chance because she knew that the client would not sanction or pay for administering the second survey to an independent sample of respondents.

- Was it ethical for the researcher to accept the risk of lowering the quality of the data addressing the client's issue so that she could further her own goals and career?
- What if the data collected by the two instruments provided stronger evidence that store image had indeed been measured even more adequately than if data had been collected through the sole use of the semantic-differential scale?
- Would it make any difference if there had been a reasonable chance that the Likert format would produce a better instrument for measuring retail image than a semantic-differential format?

Learning Objective

6. List some other key decisions to be made when designing scales.

response set bias
A problem that arises when respondents answer questionnaire items in a similar way without thinking about the items.

reverse scaling
A technique in which some of the items on a multi-item scale are written so that the most positive responses are at the opposite end of the scale from where they would normally appear.

FIGURE 13.8

Constant-Sum Comparative-Ratings Scale

Please divide 100 points between the following two attributes in terms of the relative importance of each attribute to you.

Courteous service _____

Convenient location _____

be the most positive response to this item? The most positive response would be "strongly disagree." Here's the important part: A respondent who checked "strongly agree" on all four items may well have been responding more to response set than to the actual items. The usual recommendation is to reverse scale half of the items in a multiple-item measure. Then, if a respondent provides the same response to all the items, we can be fairly certain that response set bias is present, and researchers must decide whether to eliminate the questionnaire completely or to discard responses only in that section.

Before we rush off and reformat half of the items on our scales, however, we want you to consider the other side of the story. While it is true that response set bias is a problem, there is some evidence that the cure (reverse scaling) may be worse than the disease. In short, the practice of negatively wording some of the items often seems to introduce a sort of negativity bias that may distort responses even more than response set bias does. In some cases, respondents seem to react more to the negative wording than to the actual content of the question.[3] As a result, reverse scaling should be used only sparingly. Instead, researchers should rely on the physical inspection of questionnaires to identify obvious response set bias. Another option is to include a number of items that are designed to generate negative responses but that are unrelated to any of the other scales in the questionnaire. Unfortunately, space on a questionnaire is usually limited, and adding items solely for the detection of response set bias may not always be justified.

Number of Items in a Scale

Another consideration involves exactly how many items are needed to measure the construct. Should attitude toward a company be assessed using a single item, 3 items, 10 items, or 35 items? The answer depends on the purpose of the measure. If an overall summary judgment of how consumers feel about the company is needed, then a single-item global measure of attitude on a "very unfavorable–very favorable" scale may be enough. The goal of a global measure is to provide a succinct assessment of some object or idea. Consider the following global measure of corporate reputation.

global measure
A measure designed to provide an overall assessment of an object or phenomenon, typically using one or two items.

What is your overall evaluation of Microsoft Corporation? (Circle a number)				
Very Unfavorable		Neither Favorable nor Unfavorable		Very Favorable
1	2	3	4	5

Sometimes, however, we need to develop a more comprehensive measure of a construct that will provide more information about how respondents view various aspects of the phenomenon being studied. These types of measures, often called composite measures, are more diagnostic in the sense that they provide more information for identifying strong or weak areas, particularly when aspects can be compared with one another or with measures for other entities. Research Window 13.2 presents a measure of company reputation used by the Reputation Institute who conducts an annual corporate reputation survey published in Forbes magazine. Rather than a global measure, this approach assesses reputation across four aspects of a firm.

composite measure
A measure designed to provide a comprehensive assessment of an object or phenomenon, with items to assess all relevant aspects or dimensions.

As another example, suppose that marketing managers for a major discount chain are concerned about customer satisfaction. A global measure of satisfaction would provide an overall indication of how things are going, but a composite measure, consisting of measures of satisfaction with the location, product selection, prices, employees, and so on, would allow the managers to more easily diagnose any problem areas. The managers would benefit even more if they had similar satisfaction ratings for competing discount stores (see "Interpreting Rating Scales: Raw Scores versus Norms" on page 279).

research window 13.2

The Most Respected Companies in the United States

The Reputation Institute in New York conducts an annual survey to determine the companies with the best corporate reputations. "When people trust, admire and have a good feeling about a company, they are willing to support and recommend the company to others," explains Anthony Johndrow, Managing Director.

In order to assess corporate reputation, four indicators—trust, esteem, admiration, and good feeling—were scored from 0–100 by a representative sample of 100 local respondents who were familiar with the companies. Overall measures of reputation were averaged and placed in one of five categories: Excellent/Top Tier (average of 80–100), Strong/Robust (70–79), Average/Moderate (60–69), Weak/Vulnerable (40–59), and Poor/Lowest Tier (0–40).

The most recent rankings of the top 15 companies are as follows:

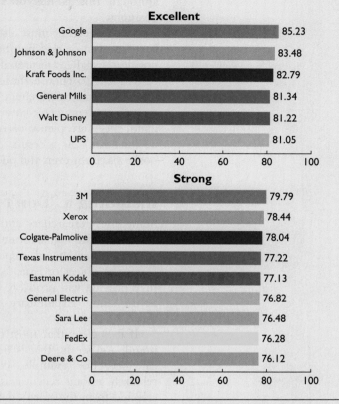

Excellent

Company	Score
Google	85.23
Johnson & Johnson	83.48
Kraft Foods Inc.	82.79
General Mills	81.34
Walt Disney	81.22
UPS	81.05

Strong

Company	Score
3M	79.79
Xerox	78.44
Colgate-Palmolive	78.04
Texas Instruments	77.22
Eastman Kodak	77.13
General Electric	76.82
Sara Lee	76.48
FedEx	76.28
Deere & Co	76.12

Source: "The Most Respected Companies in the United States—Reputation Institute Releases Results of Its Global Pulse U.S. 2008 Study," June 4, 2008, downloaded from www.reputationinstitute.com on February 14, 2009.

How many items should be used with a composite measure? As many as it takes to fully capture the phenomenon being measured. For a measure to have content validity it must adequately represent the domain of the concept. That may mean 3 or 4 items, or it may require 50 or more. An extensive study of the marketing literature over a 20-year period confirmed that the reliability of a measure increases with an increasing number of items, suggesting that more items are better than fewer items.[4] This advice must be balanced, however, with concerns about questionnaire length. Researchers must use their judgment to ensure that the construct is adequately represented and reliable, yet is not so long as to create unnecessary burdens for respondents.

Number of Scale Positions

Researchers must also decide how many scale positions to include when designing measures. For most purposes, a minimum of five response categories should be included. Research has demonstrated that extreme response style effects become problematic with fewer than five positions and that measure reliability seems to increase as the number of scale positions increases.[5]

What is the upper limit on number of scale positions? Theoretically, there is no limit. For example, with a graphic-ratings scale, there are an infinite number of positions along the line between, say, "not important" and "very important" (see Figure 13.1), although a finite scale will be imposed when measuring the distance from the start of the line to the point at which the respondent indicated his or her response. With itemized-ratings scales, there seems to be a general consensus that

10 or 11 scale positions are more than sufficient for capturing the variation on an item among a group of respondents. In fact, scales with five to nine positions work quite well and are used routinely in marketing research. As a practical matter, going beyond five to nine scale positions becomes quite difficult for researchers who have chosen to anchor, or attach descriptive labels to, each scale position, although this is less of a problem for those who anchor only the end scale positions.

The researcher must also make an important decision with respect to whether to have an even or odd number of scale positions. An odd number allows for a center position, usually interpreted as "neutral" by respondents. Sometimes it is easier for a respondent to choose the center position than to actually think carefully about an item, so some researchers use an even number of scale positions to ensure that the respondent won't just opt for the middle position and go on. On the other hand, there are plenty of issues on which a perfectly well-thought-out answer may be "neutral." As a result, some researchers routinely use an odd number of scale positions. Both even and odd numbers are used regularly in practice.

Including a "Don't Know" Response Category

Sometimes researchers choose to include a "don't know" or "no opinion" option along with the regular scale positions for an item. This may be a good idea if a fairly sizable percentage of respondents are likely not to have encountered or thought about the object or issue being addressed in the study. Otherwise, any answers that they provide will probably have little meaning and as a result will simply add error to the study. Exploratory research and pilot studies can be used to shed light on the issue.

If it is clear that most of the respondents have come in contact with the store, brand, and so on, that is being studied, we advise against including a "don't know" category. For example, consider a retailer who regularly conducts satisfaction research among recent customers of the store whose names have been randomly selected from the store's database. It is quite reasonable to expect the respondents to be able to answer questions about satisfaction with the store, products purchased, and so on, because we know that they are recent customers of the store. If the store conducted the research by randomly selecting names from the local telephone directory, a "don't know" option might be appropriate.

A word of caution: If you include the "don't know" option, you can be assured that some respondents will choose it—including some who are simply looking for the easiest way to complete the survey. In fact, research has indicated that no opinion options are more frequently chosen (1) by individuals with lower levels of education, (2) by those answering anonymously, (3) for questions that appear later in a survey, and (4) by respondents who indicated that they had devoted less effort to the task of completing a survey.[6] As a result, including a "don't know" option may often do more harm than good.

This is an important issue because the results for a question can vary a lot depending upon whether or not a "don't know" or "no opinion" option is included. For example, in a national telephone survey of 1,422 adults, results differed according to whether respondents were given a "don't know" option. The poll, jointly sponsored by the Kaiser Family Foundation, National Public Radio, and Harvard's Kennedy School of Government, asked a variety of questions to gauge public opinion about education issues.[7] Two questions asked about attitudes toward issues that had received considerable media attention: school vouchers and charter schools. Half of the respondents were given two choices: whether they favor or oppose these programs. The other half of the respondents were given three choices: whether they favor or oppose the programs or haven't heard enough about the issue to have an opinion. As Figure 13.9 shows, people who heard this third choice were much more likely to say they didn't know enough to have an opinion.

	Differences in Response with Use of a "Don't Know" Option
FIGURE 13.9	

Questions about Vouchers

"Do you favor or oppose . . . 'vouchers' . . . ?"

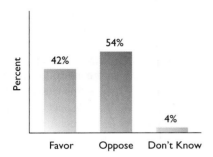

"Do you favor or oppose 'vouchers' . . . , or haven't you heard enough about that to have an opinion?"

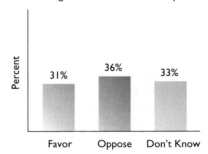

Questions about Charter Schools

After defining "charter schools": "Do you favor or oppose such a program?"

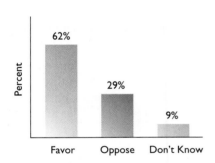

After defining "charter schools": "Do you favor or oppose such a program, or haven't you heard enough about that to have an opinion?"

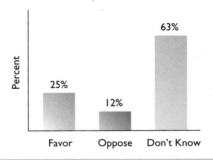

Note: The results are from a random telephone survey of 1,422 adults (18 and over) nationwide, developed jointly by National Public Radio, the Henry J. Kaiser Family Foundation, and Harvard University's Kennedy School of Government and administered by ICR/International Communications Research in June and July 1999.

Source: "NPR/Kaiser/Kennedy School Education Survey," downloaded from National Public Radio Web site, http://www.npr.org, September 9, 1999.

Determining Which Type of Scale to Use

Many beginning researchers are baffled by the choices that confront them when it comes to designing the questionnaire. Should they use summated-ratings scales, semantic-differential scales, other forms of itemized-ratings scales, or constant-sum scales to measure the concepts they need to assess? Many times, several approaches might work equally well, and researchers should let common sense guide their choices. All the scales have proven useful at one time or another. All rightly belong in the researcher's measurement tool kit.

The nature of the problem and the planned mode of administration will affect the final choice. So will the characteristics of the respondents, their commitment to the task, and their experience and ability to respond. In some cultures, graphic-ratings scales may be unknown, and respondents with low levels of education may not even be able to conceptualize a continuous scale from extreme dissatisfaction to extreme satisfaction, say, that is divided into equal increments of satisfaction. In other cultures, the use of these scales may be a very new experience for most research participants, and interviewers may need to spend considerable time explaining the scale. In still other situations, it might be necessary to develop new scales.

INTERPRETING RATING SCALES: RAW SCORES VERSUS NORMS

One of the biggest difficulties with rating scales is trying to interpret what the scores obtained using the scales actually mean. Some time ago, we were asked to develop a scale for measuring patients' perceptions of the quality of service they received from endodontists, dentists who provide specialized dental services such as root canals and oral surgery. We developed a composite scale consisting of 23 items covering two primary dimensions: (a) the procedure and service provided by the endodontist and (b) the service provided by the endodontist's staff. Each of the items described an aspect of the service and asked patients how performance on each aspect compared with their expectations using a seven-point scale anchored by "much less than I expected" and "much more than I expected" (the center position was anchored by "about what I expected"). Scores were averaged across the items in each dimension

MANAGER'S FOCUS

Marketing research studies are born out of a need to understand your marketing situation better. Measurement scales help answer the important "how much?" questions you face as a manager. How satisfied are your customers? How strong are consumer reactions to your products, marketing communications messages, prices, and so on? How attractive are various product features or benefits? How strongly is your brand positioned on a set of attributes? All of these types of questions, and many others, can be answered in descriptive studies employing self-report attitude scales.

If all marketing variables were measured on ratio scales, managers could look at the numbers and draw relatively clear and unambiguous conclusions about where they stand with consumers. This is because ratio scales represent direct levels of the variables measured. Unfortunately, about the only marketing variables for which ratio measurement is possible are observable behaviors (e.g., the number of purchases made in a particular time frame) and some demographic variables. As we have emphasized throughout Chapter 13, however, most marketing variables are not directly observable, which means they cannot be measured on scales representing absolute levels. The self-report scales presented in this chapter typically represent the interval level of measurement, and the numbers produced are less precise than ratio scales in terms of the meaning they convey.

For this reason, managers need to be more careful when they interpret the implications of interval scales.

Norms can help in the interpretation of ratio scales and are particularly important when identifying the managerial implications of interval scales. By definition, interval scales represent "relative" values or differences. If something is "relative," then its meaning can be determined only through some type of comparison. One solution is to invest the money necessary to produce norms within a specific study. The primary way of doing this is to obtain ratings of your competitors that serve as norms for the ratings of your brand or company. However, in some situations, it is difficult to produce these sorts of norms. For example, a restaurant or hotel may measure satisfaction levels among customers who just experienced their services. In order to identify the actual implications of such ratings, managers should invest in "tracking studies" that assess the construct of interest from respondents at regular time intervals. With tracking studies, the managerial implications of the ratings can be determined by examining changes or differences in ratings across time periods. The bottom line is that you should not take unnecessary risks by attempting to directly interpret the meaning of scale values that are inescapably "relative" in nature—you need to establish and use appropriate norms.

to get a composite rating for each dimension, and the composite scores for the two dimensions were averaged to get an overall service quality score. A total of 95 endodontists and 7,479 of their patients participated in the project.

One endodontist earned an overall service quality score of 5.13. How would you interpret his performance? Is this good, average, or poor performance? The score is well above the middle position on the 1 to 7 scale, so most people would probably conclude that his performance was above average based only on the raw score. To do so without a point of comparison, however, would be a mistake. What if 5.40 were the lowest score achieved by any of the other 94 endodontists? If that were the case, his performance was nothing short of awful. What if the highest score achieved by other endodontists was a 4.88? In this case, a score of 5.13 would represent an outstanding achievement. Here's the point: *It is very difficult to interpret a rating scale score using only the score itself and the scale on which it was obtained to provide meaning.*

When we compare the one endodontist's score against those of the others in the study, it turns out that 75% of the endodontists posted higher scores than he did. Armed with this knowledge, we can say with more confidence that this level of performance was relatively poor, even though the raw score suggested otherwise. In psychological scaling, researchers need to develop **normative standards**, or norms, for use in interpreting raw scores. In this case, norms also come in handy for diagnosing the likely causes of the poor performance. While the overall score was 5.13, the average score for the first dimension (covering aspects of the procedure and the endodontist) was 5.26 and that for the second dimension (covering the staff) was 5.00, suggesting that the endodontist should focus his attention on improving the quality of service provided by the staff. Right? Unfortunately for the endodontist, the comparison of raw scores against norms again points to another conclusion. The staff score was actually much stronger, ranking at the 42nd percentile (meaning that this staff outperformed 41% of the others in the study). The endodontist's score, even though it was higher, placed him only at the 17th percentile when compared to scores for other endodontists on this dimension.[8]

There are two general kinds of norms that can be used, population-based and time-based norms. Population-based norms, such as the example we've been using, give meaning to scores by comparing them to scores obtained by similar entities. For example, a department store chain might choose to compare the satisfaction score for a particular store with those of all other stores in the chain. Similarly, a researcher investigating consumer perceptions of a particular producer, service provider, product, or brand should also measure consumer perceptions of competing producers, service providers, and so on, in order to gain a better understanding of what the raw scores mean.

Time-based norms track scores for an entity over time. For example, suppose that the endodontist in our example decided to implement changes in the way service was delivered. To monitor the effectiveness of the changes, he decided to collect service quality information from patients on an annual basis. The ratings from earlier time periods serve as norms for ratings in future time periods. Although time-based norms are less informative than population-based norms (because there is no way to tell how scores at any given time compare against similar entities), they are still very useful for tracking progress and identifying problem areas. And they are certainly better than relying on raw scores alone for meaning.

normative standard
A comparative standard used to provide meaning to raw scale scores.

ETHICAL DILEMMA 13.2

The Samuelson Research Firm was contacted by Larkin Electronics, a manufacturer of small electronic radio parts, to conduct a survey of Larkin's employees. The purpose of the research was to determine the state of worker morale and the importance of certain employee grievances so that Larkin's management could gauge the strength of its position in collective bargaining with the employee union. Samuelson Research agreed to conduct the study.

- What are the consequences for employees who participate in such a survey?
- Would cooperating in this research be detrimental to the employees' immediate self-interest?
- Do researchers have the right to ask questions concerning this issue?
- Does this research undercut the position of labor's representatives since they have no corresponding way of gauging the intensity of management's opinions?
- If you had been director of the research, what kind of questions might you have asked of Larkin's management?
- Would you have agreed to conduct such a survey?
- In general, should a researcher be concerned with the uses of the research that he or she conducts or its effects on the research participants?

Sometimes it is possible to utilize both kinds of norms. This is the approach taken with the American Customer Satisfaction Index (ACSI) in measuring customer satisfaction with products and services. To compute the ACSI, researchers conduct telephone interviews of people who have recently bought or used a company's product or service, asking them about three determinants of satisfaction: their expectations, perception of quality, and perception of value. Using a sophisticated model, ACSI researchers use their responses to rate organizations and industries on a 1 to 100 scale of satisfaction, as well as to produce a national customer satisfaction score. An organization can track its own performance since the baseline measure was made in 1994, or it can compare its performance to industrywide numbers, or its industry to overall customer satisfaction. For example, customer satisfaction with the U.S. Postal Service had risen from a low of 61 in 1994 to 74 in 2008. In contrast, customer satisfaction with AT&T Corporation had fallen from a high of 85 to a low of 70 in 2007 while rising slightly to 75 in 2008.[9]

SUMMARY

Learning Objective 1

List the various ways by which attitudes can be measured.
Attitudes can be measured by self-reports, performance of objective tasks, and physiological reactions.

Learning Objective 2

List three general categories of ratings scales.
Three general categories of rating scales are the graphic, the itemized, and the comparative scales. Summated-ratings, semantic-differential, and Stapel scales are all examples of itemized-ratings scales.

Learning Objective 3

Explain the difference between a graphic-ratings scale and an itemized-ratings scale.
The itemized-ratings scale is similar to the graphic-ratings scale except that the rater must select from a limited number of categories instead of placing a mark on a continuous scale. In general, five to nine categories work well.

Learning Objective 4

Name the most widely used attitude scaling techniques in marketing research and explain why researchers prefer them.
The Likert scale, or summated-ratings scale, and the semantic-differential scale are the most widely used attitude scaling techniques in marketing research. Both are particularly useful because they allow respondents to express the intensity of their feelings.

Learning Objective 5

Explain how the constant-sum scaling method works.
In the constant-sum method of comparative rating, the individual is instructed to divide some given sum among two or more attributes on the basis of their importance to him or her. Respondents are generally asked to compare two attributes in this method, although it is possible to compare more.

Learning Objective 6

List some other key decisions to be made when designing scales.
Other key considerations include whether or not to use reverse scaling, whether to use a global or a composite scale, how many scale positions to use (and whether to use an even number or an odd number of scale positions), whether or not to include a "don't know" response category, and which type of scale to use.

Learning Objective 7

Explain how norms are useful for interpreting rating scale results.
A rating scale score, interpreted in isolation, can provide misleading information. Whenever possible, a rating scale score should be compared against scores obtained for similar entities (i.e., population-based norms) or for the same entity in prior time periods (i.e., time-based norms) to gain a better understanding of what the score really means.

KEY TERMS

performance of objective tasks (page 267)
physiological reaction (page 267)
self-report (page 267)
graphic-ratings scale (page 268)
itemized-ratings scale (page 269)
summated-ratings scale (page 270)
semantic-differential scale (page 271)
snake diagram (page 272)
Stapel scale (page 273)

comparative-ratings scale (page 274)
constant-sum method (page 274)
halo effect (page 274)
response set bias (page 275)
reverse scaling (page 275)
global measure (page 276)
composite measure (page 276)
normative standard (page 281)

REVIEW QUESTIONS

1. What are the major ways that have been used to measure attitudes?

2. How do you construct a Likert summated-ratings scale? How are subjects scaled with a Likert scale?

3. What is a semantic-differential scale? How is a person's overall attitude assessed with a semantic-differential scale?

4. How does a Stapel scale differ from a semantic-differential scale?

5. What is a graphic-ratings scale? An itemized scale? A constant-sum scale?

6. What is reverse scaling? Why is it used? What is a potential problem with its use?

7. What is the difference between a global measure and a composite measure? When might each be used effectively?

8. What is the key issue involved in the decision to use an even or an odd number of scale positions?

9. How can norms be developed? Why are they important?

DISCUSSION QUESTIONS, PROBLEMS, AND PROJECTS

1. a. List at least eight attributes that students might use in evaluating bookstores.

    b. Using these attributes, develop eight summated-ratings items and eight semantic-differential items by which attitudes toward (i) the university bookstore and (ii) some other bookstore can be evaluated.

    c. Administer each of the scales to 10 students.

    d. What are the average sample scores for the two bookstores using the scale of summated ratings? What can be said about students' attitudes toward the two bookstores?

    e. Develop a snake diagram using the semantic-differential scale scores for both bookstores.

    f. Based on the semantic-differential scales, what can be said about students' attitudes toward the two bookstores?

2. a. Assume that a manufacturer of a line of cheese products wanted to evaluate customer attitudes toward the brand. A panel of 500 regular consumers of the brand responded

to a questionnaire that was sent to them. It included several attitude scales (in their traditional formats), which produced the following results:

i.   The average score for the sample on a 25-item summated-ratings scale was 105.

ii. The average score for the sample on a 20-item semantic-differential scale was 106.

iii. The average score for the sample on a 15-item Stapel scale was 52.

The vice president has asked you to indicate whether his customers have a favorable or unfavorable attitude toward the brand. What will you tell him? Please be specific.

b. Following your initial report, the vice president has provided you with more information. The following memo has been given to you: "The company has been using the same attitude measures over the past eight years. The results of the previous studies are as follows:

Year	Summated-Ratings	Semantic-Differential	Stapel
1	86	95	43
2	93	95	48
3	97	98	51
4	104	101	55
5	110	122	62
6	106	112	57
7	104	106	53
8	105	106	52

We realize there may not be any connection between attitude and behavior, but it must be pointed out that sales peaked in Year 5 and since then have been gradually declining." With this information, do your conclusions change? Can anything more be said about customer attitudes?

3. Generate five attributes that assess students' attitudes toward "take-home exams." Use (i) graphic-ratings scales, (ii) itemized-ratings scales, and (iii) comparative-ratings scales to determine the importance of each of these attributes in students' evaluation of take-home exams. Administer each of these scales to separate samples of five students.

a. What are your findings with the graphic-ratings scale? Which attributes are important?

b. What are your findings with the itemized-ratings scale? Which attributes are important?

c. What are your findings with the comparative-ratings scale? Which attributes are important?

4. You are a staff researcher for a manufacturer of a well-known laundry detergent. As more and more competing products enter the market, managers at the company have decided that it would be a good idea to seek feedback regularly from consumers on their level of satisfaction with the brand.

a. What are your recommendations about how satisfaction might be measured? Would you recommend using a global or composite measure? Why?

b. Assuming that you wanted to use a composite measure, what are some key attributes of the brand for which satisfaction might be assessed? List at least five attributes.

c. For each of the attributes you have listed in part (b), develop three different satisfaction scales: a graphic-ratings scale and two types of itemized-ratings scales.

5. Create two versions of a composite scale for measuring corporate reputation for some company *not* located where you live. (Feel free to use the Reputation Institute scale discussed in Research Window 13.2, or develop your own set of items.) The first version of the composite scale should include a "no opinion" or "don't know" option; the second version should have no such option.

 a. Have 10 people complete each version of the measure (20 people total).

 b. Using a calculator or simple spreadsheet program, calculate the mean score for each item on both versions of the measure (you'll exclude respondents who responded "don't know" or "no opinion" on the first version of the measure). Also, calculate the percentage of people who responded "don't know" or "no opinion" for each item on the first version of the questionnaire.

 c. Based on the results of part (b), which version of the measure would you recommend using if you were surveying the general public about corporate reputations?

Designing the Questionnaire or Observation Form

Learning Objectives

1. Explain the role of research hypotheses in developing a questionnaire.
2. Define *telescoping error* and *recall loss* and explain how they affect a respondent's ability to answer questions accurately.
3. Cite some of the techniques researchers use to secure respondents' cooperation in answering sensitive questions.
4. Explain what a multichotomous question is.
5. List some of the primary rules researchers should keep in mind in trying to develop bias-free questions.
6. Explain what the funnel approach to question sequencing is.
7. Explain what a branching question is and discuss when it is used.
8. Explain the difference between basic information and classification information and tell which should be asked first in a questionnaire.
9. Explain the role of pretesting in the questionnaire development process.

Introduction

Marketing researchers have the responsibility of understanding and applying the basics of the measurement process and some of the popular approaches for measuring attitudes, perceptions, and preferences when designing a questionnaire or observation form. In this chapter, we present the procedures researchers can follow in developing data collection forms that maximize the quality of data available to organizational decision makers.

QUESTIONNAIRE DESIGN

Most beginning researchers have no idea how difficult it is to develop an effective questionnaire. They say to themselves, "How hard can it be to write a few questions?" and usually fail to leave themselves enough time to adequately prepare and test the questionnaires they plan to use. They are often more concerned with obtaining a sample and actually collecting the data than they are with developing forms that are user-friendly and ask the right questions in the right way. That's a shame, because it doesn't matter how perfectly data collection goes if the questions themselves are suboptimal and introduce error into the data set. As you read this chapter, we hope that you have an appreciation for the importance of these issues and won't make the same mistakes.

1. Explain the role of research hypotheses in developing a questionnaire.

Figure 14.1 offers a method for developing an effective questionnaire.[1] Considering that many people think that 10 minutes is more than enough time to develop a questionnaire, a process with 10 steps may be surprising or seem a little extreme. As we describe these steps, however, we think you'll begin to understand why each is important.

Although we present the steps as a sequence (see Figure 14.1), it's rare that it actually works that way. Instead, the steps are sometimes taken out of order, or decisions at later steps cause you to go back and change something done at an earlier step. The point isn't so much the order to the steps; it's that each step must be considered in light of the other steps. If you find yourself circling back to rethink and rework certain aspects—good; that's the way it should be. And far too many researchers neglect Step 10 (pretesting), because they either don't care or are in a hurry and then regret it later. You'll learn a lot from pretesting that can literally save a project that's headed for failure.

Step 1: Specify What Information Will Be Sought

The first step in questionnaire design, deciding what information will be sought, is easy, provided that researchers have been careful at earlier stages in the research process. Careless earlier work will make this decision difficult.

FIGURE 14.1   Procedure for Developing a Questionnaire

Step 1 — Specify What Information Will Be Sought	Step 6 — Determine Question Sequence
Step 2 — Determine Method of Administration	Step 7 — Determine Physical Characteristics of Questionnaire
Step 3 — Determine Content of Individual Questions	Step 8 — Develop Recruiting Message or Script
Step 4 — Determine Form of Response to Each Question	Step 9 — Reexamine Steps 1–8 and Revise If Necessary
Step 5 — Determine Wording of Each Question	Step 10 — Pretest Questionnaire and Revise If Necessary

ETHICAL DILEMMA 14.1

A financial institution has developed a new type of savings bond. The marketing director of this institution has requested that a local research supply company design a questionnaire that will help quantify target consumers' interest in this new bond. However, the marketing director is concerned about the possibility of competitors hearing about the new product concept because of the survey. He requests that the questionnaire be written in such a way as to mask the true purpose of the study.

To mask the actual purpose of the study, the questionnaire primarily asks respondents for details of their holiday plans and budgets. Because respondents are asked questions about their finances only after multiple vacation-related questions, it is hoped that the respondents will assume the information is for a travel company. Moreover, the marketing director of the financial institution asks that interviewers tell respondents that the information is being gathered for a travel-related company.

- Discuss the implications of deceiving respondents on a questionnaire in this way.
- If the interviewers had not been told to explicitly tell respondents that the information was for a travel-related corporation, would the deception be acceptable?
- Are there ways of gaining this type of information without resorting to deception while still protecting the institution's new product idea?
- Discuss the validity issues associated with respondents knowing the purpose of the survey as they are completing it.

Both descriptive and causal research designs require that researchers have enough knowledge about the problem to frame some specific hypotheses to guide the research. The hypotheses also guide the questionnaire. They determine what information will be sought, and from whom, because they specify what relationships will be investigated. If researchers have already established a complete set of dummy tables to structure the data analysis, their job of determining what information is to be collected is essentially complete. A dummy table is a table designed to catalog the data that will be collected. The table is identical to the one that will be used in the actual research, but in this early stage it has no numbers. Researchers must collect information on the variables specified in the dummy tables from the right people and in the right units.

Sometimes you will discover other hypotheses that might be investigated during preparation of the questionnaire. If the new hypothesis is truly important to understanding the phenomenon, by all means include the appropriate questions on the survey. Be careful, though: If it simply represents something that might be "nice to know," but isn't central to the purpose of the study, forget about it. Including interesting but not vital items lengthens the questionnaire, causes problems in administration and analysis, and often causes response rates to go down.

Our comments so far are directed at descriptive projects. With exploratory research, anything goes. Questionnaires in exploratory studies are often loosely structured, with only a rough idea of the kind of information that might be sought.

Step 2: Determine Method of Administration

After specifying the basic information that will be sought, the researcher must determine how it will be gathered. This decision centers on the degree of structure and disguise to be used and whether it will be administered by personal interviews, telephone interviews, mail questionnaires, or Internet-based questionnaires. At this point, your job is to consider the specific circumstances of your project in light of the advantages and disadvantages of the different methods and determine the overall best method of administration.

The type of data to be collected (see Step 1) will naturally have an important effect on the method of data collection. For example, a few years ago, a research firm had a client that wanted to know what proportion of Internet users had various multimedia plug-ins for downloading and playing multimedia files. From experience, the researchers knew that many Internet users don't know which plug-ins they have, especially with respect to which version of the software it might be. It would have been a waste of time to call or write to computer users and pose such questions. Instead, the researchers set up an ingenious Web-based survey that simply asked respondents whether or not they could see a downloaded image. If they clicked "yes," the researchers knew, by the format used to create the image, precisely what plug-in they were using. This methodology let respondents provide data without knowing the technical details.[2]

Exhibit 14.1 (see pages 290–292) offers an example of a questionnaire. The goal is to measure the use of a number of brands of ground coffee and respondents' attitudes toward these brands. The questions are all very structured and undisguised. Any of the common methods of data collection might be used to gather this information, but which should you choose? It's probably a little too long and complex for telephone, and the degree of structure is quite high, which means that personal interviews would

MANAGER'S FOCUS

Although the first step in designing a data collection form is to "specify what information will be sought," you should have worked with your research provider much earlier in the project to complete the bulk of this step. As we keep pointing out to you, having a strong understanding of the later stages of the research process will help you collaborate more effectively with researchers in the earlier stages. We have urged you to invest time in helping your researchers specify the decision and research problems, formulate research hypotheses, and create dummy tables. If you follow our advice in these early stages, when it is time to design the data collection form, all that should be necessary is to visit with your researchers to make certain that none of your information needs have changed or been overlooked, and that they pursue any additional relevant issues that were discovered through the exploratory research they completed (e.g., literature searches, depth interviews, focus groups). In other words, being thorough at the beginning of the study will facilitate and guide all subsequent stages. Once you have done this, however, you should refrain from micromanaging the design of the data collection form and allow the research professionals to do their jobs without too much interference. Ask questions, provide ideas—but please don't be like some managers who believe that they can do a better job developing the data collection forms than can the professionals who have the experience and training to do it effectively.

deliver very little extra value for a whole lot of extra cost. As a result, the questionnaire should most likely be administered by mail or the Internet. An Internet-based questionnaire will require a sample with easy access to computers and the Internet. Lots of ground coffee is purchased by elderly people, and even though many of them are becoming regular Internet users, this group would probably be vastly underrepresented if we chose this approach. As a result, mail questionnaires may be the method of choice. In fact, this questionnaire was used with a mail panel. Of course, a mail questionnaire may not be the optimal choice for another situation. This example provides a simple illustration of the process that researchers must go through in selecting a method of administration.

Step 3: Determine Content of Individual Questions

The content of individual questions is mostly driven by decisions that researchers make during Steps 1 and 2. Knowing what information is needed, the degree of structure and disguise to be used, and the method of administration eliminates a lot of options when it comes to individual question content, and that's a good thing. But the researcher can and should ask some additional questions.[3]

Is the Question Necessary? Suppose an issue is important. Then the researcher needs to ask whether the point has been adequately covered by other questions. If not, a new question will be necessary. The question should then be framed to secure an answer with the required detail, but not an answer with more detail than needed. Very often in marketing, for example, we employ the concept of *stage in the life cycle* to explore family consumption behavior. Stage in the life cycle is a variable made up of several elements, including marital status, presence of children, and the ages of children. Rather than asking for the ages of all children in the household, however, it is often possible to ask for the age of the youngest child living at home. This single question will usually be enough to establish that aspect of stage in the life cycle and eliminates additional questions. As before, the study's hypotheses and dummy tables are useful for determining whether or not a question is necessary.

Are Several Questions Needed Instead of One? Sometimes you'll need to ask several questions instead of just one. As we noted, stage in the life cycle can't be assessed

| Exhibit 14.1 | Questionnaire for Caffeinated Ground Coffee Study |

1. What type of coffeemaker do you usually use to prepare your ground coffee at home? (CHECK *ONE* BOX)

- 1 ☐ Automatic drip
- 2 ☐ Electric percolator
- 3 ☐ Stove top percolator
- 4 ☐ Stove top dripolator
- ☐ Other (Specify): _____

2. a. Check all the brands of regular ground coffee that you have **ever used** at home. (CHECK *ALL* THAT APPLY)

b. Check the **one** brand you **use most often**. (CHECK *ONE* BOX)

c. Check all the brands you currently **have on hand**. (CHECK *ALL* THAT APPLY)

d. Check the **one** brand you will probably **buy next**. (CHECK *ONE* BOX)

e. For each brand please indicate how much you like the brand overall on a scale of **1** to **10** with "**1**" meaning **dislike it extremely** and "**10**" meaning **like it extremely**. Rate each brand, whether you have used the brand or not.

	"A" Ever Used	"B" Use Most Often	"C" Have On Hand	"D" Will Buy Next	Brand Rating "1" Dislike It Extremely ←----------------→ "10" Like It Extremely
Folgers	1 ☐	1 ☐	1 ☐	1 ☐	01 ☐ 02 ☐ 03 ☐ 04 ☐ 05 ☐ 06 ☐ 07 ☐ 08 ☐ 09 ☐ 10 ☐
Hills Brothers	2 ☐	2 ☐	2 ☐	2 ☐	01 ☐ 02 ☐ 03 ☐ 04 ☐ 05 ☐ 06 ☐ 07 ☐ 08 ☐ 09 ☐ 10 ☐
Maxwell House Regular	3 ☐	3 ☐	3 ☐	3 ☐	01 ☐ 02 ☐ 03 ☐ 04 ☐ 05 ☐ 06 ☐ 07 ☐ 08 ☐ 09 ☐ 10 ☐
Maxwell House Master Blend	4 ☐	4 ☐	4 ☐	4 ☐	01 ☐ 02 ☐ 03 ☐ 04 ☐ 05 ☐ 06 ☐ 07 ☐ 08 ☐ 09 ☐ 10 ☐
Yuban	5 ☐	5 ☐	5 ☐	5 ☐	01 ☐ 02 ☐ 03 ☐ 04 ☐ 05 ☐ 06 ☐ 07 ☐ 08 ☐ 09 ☐ 10 ☐
Other (Specify): _____	6 ☐	6 ☐	6 ☐	6 ☐	01 ☐ 02 ☐ 03 ☐ 04 ☐ 05 ☐ 06 ☐ 07 ☐ 08 ☐ 09 ☐ 10 ☐

3. What do you usually add to the coffee you drink? (CHECK *ALL* THAT APPLY)

- 1 ☐ Nothing (I drink it black)
- 2 ☐ A dairy creamer, like milk, cream, or Half and Half
- 3 ☐ A non-dairy creamer, powdered or liquid
- 4 ☐ Sugar
- 5 ☐ Artificial sweetener
- ☐ Something else (Specify): _____

4. Are you the principle coffee **purchaser** for your household?

- 1 ☐ Yes
- 2 ☐ No

with a single question; it requires multiple demographic questions to be able to segment the respondents.

There are other situations in which more than one question is needed to zero in on the information researchers are seeking. Consider the question, "Why do you use Crest?" One respondent may reply, "To reduce cavities," while another may reply, "Because our dentist recommended it." Two different frames of reference are being used to answer this question. The first respondent is replying in terms of why he is using it now; the second is replying in terms of how she started using it. It would be better to break this one question down into separate questions that reflect the possible frames of reference that could be used. For example,

How did you first happen to use Crest? _____
What is your primary reason for using it? _____

Many times, these sorts of subtle issues won't be discovered until the questionnaire is pretested with actual members of the population being studied. That's one reason that pretesting is so important—to make sure that a question won't be interpreted in different ways by different people. If it can, then either the wording of the question must be made more specific, or multiple questions will be needed.

Exhibit 14.1

Questionnaire for Caffeinated Ground Coffee Study (*continued*)

5. Please indicate how important it is to you that a ground coffee have each of the following characteristics.
   (CHECK *ONE* BOX FOR *EACH* CHARACTERISTIC)

	Not At All Important 01	02	03	04	05	06	07	08	09	Extremely Important 10
Rich taste	☐	☐	☐	☐	☐	☐	☐	☐	☐	☐
Always fresh	☐	☐	☐	☐	☐	☐	☐	☐	☐	☐
Gets the day off to a good start	☐	☐	☐	☐	☐	☐	☐	☐	☐	☐
Fill-bodied taste	☐	☐	☐	☐	☐	☐	☐	☐	☐	☐
Rich aroma in the cup	☐	☐	☐	☐	☐	☐	☐	☐	☐	☐

	Not At All Important 01	02	03	04	05	06	07	08	09	Extremely Important 10
Good value for the money	☐	☐	☐	☐	☐	☐	☐	☐	☐	☐
The best coffee to drink in the morning	☐	☐	☐	☐	☐	☐	☐	☐	☐	☐
Rich aroma in the can/bag	☐	☐	☐	☐	☐	☐	☐	☐	☐	☐
Smooth taste	☐	☐	☐	☐	☐	☐	☐	☐	☐	☐
Highest quality coffee	☐	☐	☐	☐	☐	☐	☐	☐	☐	☐

	Not At All Important 01	02	03	04	05	06	07	08	09	Extremely Important 10
Premium brand	☐	☐	☐	☐	☐	☐	☐	☐	☐	☐
Not bitter	☐	☐	☐	☐	☐	☐	☐	☐	☐	☐
The coffee that brightens my day the most	☐	☐	☐	☐	☐	☐	☐	☐	☐	☐
Costs more than the other brands	☐	☐	☐	☐	☐	☐	☐	☐	☐	☐
Strong taste	☐	☐	☐	☐	☐	☐	☐	☐	☐	☐

	Not At All Important 01	02	03	04	05	06	07	08	09	Extremely Important 10
Has no aftertaste	☐	☐	☐	☐	☐	☐	☐	☐	☐	☐
Economy brand	☐	☐	☐	☐	☐	☐	☐	☐	☐	☐
Rich aroma while brewing	☐	☐	☐	☐	☐	☐	☐	☐	☐	☐
The best ground coffee available	☐	☐	☐	☐	☐	☐	☐	☐	☐	☐
Enjoy drinking with a meal	☐	☐	☐	☐	☐	☐	☐	☐	☐	☐
Costs less than other brands	☐	☐	☐	☐	☐	☐	☐	☐	☐	☐

(Continued)

Do Respondents Have the Necessary Information? It makes little sense to ask questions for which the intended respondents probably won't have answers, but researchers have been known to do this. Respondents will give answers; whether the answers mean anything, however, is another matter. In a classic example, researchers once asked this question:[4]

Which of the following statements most closely coincides with your opinion of the Metallic Metals Act?

☐ It would be a good move on the part of the United States.
☐ It would be a good thing, but it should be left to the individual states.
☐ It is all right for foreign countries, but it should not be required here.
☐ It is of no value at all.
☐ No opinion.

The proportion of respondents checking each alternative was, respectively, 21%, 59%, 16%, 4%, and 0.3%. The only problem was that there is no Metallic Metals Act. The point of this example is that *most questions will get answers ... but do the answers mean anything?* Plenty of studies since have shown that people are more than willing to answer questions, even when they have no idea what they are talking about. For the

Exhibit 14.1 | **Questionnaire for Caffeinated Ground Coffee Study (*continued*)**

6. On a scale of **0** to **10** with "**0**" meaning **does not describe at all** and "**10**" meaning **describes completely**, please indicate how well the following statements describe **each** of the coffee brands listed below. Rate each brand, whether you have used the brand or not. Please write in the number which indicates your answer on the lines provided.

	Folgers	Hills Brothers	Maxwell House Regular	Maxwell House Master Blend	Yuban
Rich taste	___	___	___	___	___
Always fresh	___	___	___	___	___
Gets the day off to a good start	___	___	___	___	___
Fill–bodied taste	___	___	___	___	___
Rich aroma in the cup	___	___	___	___	___

	Folgers	Hills Brothers	Maxwell House Regular	Maxwell House Master Blend	Yuban
Good value for the money	___	___	___	___	___
The best coffee to drink in the morning	___	___	___	___	___
Rich aroma in the can/bag	___	___	___	___	___
Smooth taste	___	___	___	___	___
Highest quality coffee	___	___	___	___	___

	Folgers	Hills Brothers	Maxwell House Regular	Maxwell House Master Blend	Yuban
Premium brand	___	___	___	___	___
Not bitter	___	___	___	___	___
The coffee that brightens my day the most	___	___	___	___	___
Costs more than the other brands	___	___	___	___	___
Strong taste	___	___	___	___	___

	Folgers	Hills Brothers	Maxwell House Regular	Maxwell House Master Blend	Yuban
Has no aftertaste	___	___	___	___	___
Economy brand	___	___	___	___	___
Rich aroma while brewing	___	___	___	___	___
The best ground coffee available	___	___	___	___	___
Enjoy drinking with a meal	___	___	___	___	___
Costs less than other brands	___	___	___	___	___

7. Please indicate your **sex** and **age**.

1 ☐ Male
2 ☐ Female   Age: _____

Source: Contributed by NFO Research, Inc.

---

answers to be meaningful, the questions need to mean something to the respondent. This means that (a) the respondent needs to know something about the issue addressed by the question and (b) the respondent must remember the information.

Try answering this question: "How much does your family spend on groceries in a typical week?" Unless you do the grocery shopping or your family operates with a fairly strict budget, you probably don't know. In a situation like this, it might be helpful to ask a **filter question** (sometimes called a *screening* or *qualifying question*) before this question to determine if the individual is likely to have the information. A filter question might be, "Who does the grocery shopping in your family?" or "Do you do the grocery shopping for your family?" Filter questions are regularly used at the start of interviews or questionnaires to determine whether or not the respondent is actually a member of the population being studied, particularly when names have been drawn from general lists (for example, telephone directories). So, if the population includes residents of a certain city who have eaten in a restaurant named Mickey's within the previous six months, and names are selected randomly from a

filter question
A question used to determine if a respondent is likely to possess the knowledge being sought; also used to determine if an individual qualifies as a member of the defined population.

telephone directory for that city, a key filter question might be "Have you eaten at Mickey's restaurant, located at Sixth Street and Manvel Avenue, within the past six months?" If the answer is "no," the interview is terminated because the individual doesn't meet the qualifications to be included in the population.

Not only should the individual have the information sought, but she or he must be able to remember it. Our ability to remember various events is influenced by the event itself and its importance, the length of time since the event, and the presence or absence of stimuli that assist in recalling it. Important events are more easily remembered than unimportant events. While many older adults might be able to remember exactly where they were and what they were doing when they learned that President Kennedy had been shot, many of them will be unable to recall the particular television shows they watched last Wednesday evening. Returning to our toothpaste example, many people won't be able to recall the first brand they ever used, when they switched to their current brand, or why they switched. While the switching and use information might be very important to a brand manager for toothpastes, it is unimportant to most individuals. This is something we must keep in mind continually as we design questionnaires. We need to put ourselves in the shoes of the respondent, not those of the product manager, when deciding whether the information is important enough for the individual to remember.

In general, there are two forces, telescoping error and recall loss, that affect a respondent's ability to provide accurate answers to questions about their behavior over a specified time period. **Telescoping error** is the tendency to remember an event as having occurred more recently than it did:

> Suppose that a national sample of households are asked to report the amount of coffee they purchased in the past seven days and that this total is then compared with shipments of all coffee manufacturers or observed sales in retail outlets. These comparisons usually show that the amount reported is more than 50 percent higher than the amount manufactured and sold.[5]

Problems with telescoping error get worse as the time periods respondents are asked to consider get shorter, believe it or not. If a respondent misreports an event by one day over a three-day reporting period (that is, a purchase made last Tuesday was recalled as occurring during the Wednesday through Friday time frame asked about), the resulting overreporting will be greater than misreporting an event by one day over a three-week reporting period.

Recall loss, the tendency to forget an event entirely, is the second force that affects respondents' ability to report accurately on prior events and behaviors. As we all know, as time passes, we simply tend to forget things. As a result, problems with recall loss are reduced as the time periods respondents are asked to consider get shorter. Because recall loss and telescoping error work in opposite directions, in theory there will be an optimal time frame to use with a particular question. For many events and behaviors, the best time frame seems to be between two weeks and one month.[6]

Will Respondents Give the Information?   Even if respondents have the information, there is always a question of whether or not they will share it. People in different areas of the world vary in their openness in providing the information that marketing researchers seek. Eastern Europeans are wonderful in this regard.

> [U]nlike blasé Western consumers, people in Eastern Europe are more than willing to answer questions. After years of directives from the top, people are flattered to be asked their opinions, even if they're just being asked about the taste of a toothpaste or the feel of a shaving cream. Gallup's Mr. Manchin [a regional vice president] recounts how an old lady in Hungary thanked the interviewer at the end of an hour-long session. "It was such a wonderful experience to have a chance to talk to you for so long," she said. "How much do I pay you?"[7]

Researchers in many other parts of the world are not as fortunate and sometimes encounter situations in which respondents have the necessary information, but they

---

Learning Objective

2. Define *telescoping error* and *recall loss* and explain how they affect a respondent's ability to answer questions accurately.

telescoping error
A type of error resulting from the fact that most people remember an event as having occurred more recently than it did.

recall loss
A type of error caused by a respondent's forgetting that an event happened at all.

will not give it. Korean businesspeople are reluctant to share any sort of business information with outsiders, considering it to be disloyal to their employers. And Japanese businesspeople hesitate to complete surveys during work hours because it would take time away from their jobs.[8]

Learning Objective

3. Cite some of the techniques researchers use to secure respondents' cooperation in answering sensitive questions.

Unwillingness to respond to a question (or the whole questionnaire, for that matter) may be a function of the amount of work involved in producing an answer, the respondent's inability to express an answer, or the sensitivity of the issue. Although a purchasing agent might be able to determine to the penny how much the company spent on a particular brand of janitorial supplies last year, why would he or she be willing to take the time to look it up to reply to an unsolicited questionnaire? Would you? Questionnaire developers must always be very sensitive to how much effort it will take respondents to give the information sought. When the effort is excessive, the respondent is likely to give an approximate answer, ignore the question, or refuse to complete the survey at all. You'll be better off leaving out questions that require excessive effort, since they tend to irritate respondents and lessen their cooperation.

When an issue is embarrassing or otherwise threatening to respondents, they are naturally less likely to cooperate. Rule 1 about asking sensitive questions: Avoid them unless they are absolutely essential to your project. If you must ask one or more sensitive questions, do so with care. You must respect the privacy of your respondents by maintaining the security of the information you collect and by fulfilling any promises of anonymity or confidentiality you have given. Exhibit 14.2 offers several techniques that can be used to more effectively handle sensitive issues. Technically Speaking 14.1 (see page 296) provides more detail about one of these techniques, the randomized-response model.

randomized-response model

An interviewing technique in which potentially embarrassing and relatively innocuous questions are paired, and the question the respondent answers is randomly determined but is unknown to the interviewer.

Step 4: Determine Form of Response to Each Question

Once the content of the individual questions is determined, researchers must decide whether to use closed-ended questions or questions that allow for open-ended responses. Let's look at each in a little more detail.

Open-Ended Questions Respondents are free to reply to open-ended questions in their own words rather than being limited to choosing from a set of alternatives. Here are some examples:

1. How old are you? _____ years
2. How would you feel about laws requiring motorcycle riders to wear helmets?

   _____

   _____

   _____

3. Can you name three sponsors of the Monday-night football games?

   _____

   _____

   _____

4. Do you intend to purchase an automobile this year? _____

5. Why did you purchase a Sony brand HDTV television?

   _____

   _____

   _____

6. In the past month, how many times have you purchased gasoline from Ted's Texaco?

   _____ times

As these questions demonstrate, just about any kind of information can be gathered using open-ended questions. The questions shown seek information ranging

Exhibit 14.2	**Handling Sensitive Questions**

Here are some tips and techniques for obtaining sensitive information from respondents. We've already given you the most important tip: *Don't include sensitive questions unless you absolutely have to.* Here are some other ideas.

Tip: **Guarantee respondents that their answers will be completely anonymous**—but only if you will actually carry through on your promise. Anonymity is *possible* with any method of data collection, but with anything other than mail questionnaires, the respondent must rely on you to remove his or her name from the data record. If you cannot promise anonymity, at least promise that respondents' answers will be held in confidence and that information specific to them will not be given to anyone else. Then keep your word.

Tip: **Put any sensitive questions near the end of the questionnaire.** This will allow the researcher and the respondent a little time to develop trust and rapport, especially with personal interviews and telephone interviews. There's another practical advantage, too: If the respondent decides to stop answering questions at that point, at least they've already completed most of the interview!

Tip: **Use a counterbiasing statement that indicates that the behavior or attitude in question is not unusual.** For example, a question about household financial difficulties might be preceded by the following statement: "Recent studies show that one of every four households has trouble meeting its monthly financial obligations." Doing it this way makes it easier for a respondent to admit the potentially embarrassing information.

Tip: **Phrase the question in terms of other people and how they might feel or act;** for example, "Do you think most people cheat on their income taxes? Why?" Respondents are more likely to reveal their attitudes and behaviors in sensitive areas when asked about other people than if you ask them directly about their own attitudes and behaviors.

Tip: **Ask for general answers, rather than specific answers, when seeking sensitive information.** One frequently used approach is to measure the response by having respondents check one of several categories instead of providing the precise answer. If you need to know a respondent's age, for example, rather than ask for his actual age in years, let him check one of the following boxes:

> Less than 20
> 20–29
> 30–39
> 40–49
> 50–59
> 60–69
> 70 or older

Although you won't be able to calculate the precise average age for the sample respondents, it usually isn't necessary to do so anyway.

Tip: **Use the randomized-response model.** With this technique, the respondent is typically given two questions, either of which can be answered yes or no. One question deals with a simple, nonsensitive issue, while the other specifically addresses the sensitive issue being studied. Using some random approach, such as flipping a coin (a fair coin provides 50% probability), respondents are instructed to answer one or the other question . . . but the researcher never knows which question they actually answered. That's what makes the approach work: Respondents feel free to answer truthfully because they know that the interviewer will never know if "yes" is in reference to the sensitive or nonsensitive question. The rest is easy. Because we know the probability of a "yes" answer on the innocent question before asking it and the probability of answering the sensitive question (50% based on the coin flip), we can back our way into the proportion of the sample that answered "yes" to the sensitive question. **See Technically Speaking 14.1 for details of how the randomized-response model works.** Here's the only catch: Because we can never know specifically which respondents have admitted to the sensitive issue, there is no way for us to look at the relationship between their behavior and other variables such as demographic characteristics.

from demographic characteristics to attitudes and intentions, to motivations and behavior. Open-ended questions are quite versatile.

Open-ended questions are often used to begin a questionnaire. The general feeling is that it is best to move from the general to the specific in constructing questionnaires. So an opening question such as, "When you think of televisions, which brands come to mind?" gives some insight into the respondent's frame of reference and provides an easy way for the respondent to begin to focus on the topic at hand. The open-ended question is also often used to probe for additional information. The probes "Why do you feel that way?" and "Please explain" are often used to seek elaboration of a respondent's reply.

technically speaking 14.1

Operation of the Randomized-Response Model

Two questions are presented to a respondent:

A. Have you ever shoplifted?
   ☐ Yes   ☐ No

B. Is your birthday in January?
   ☐ Yes   ☐ No

We can use census data to determine the probability of a person's birthday being in January. Suppose that probability is 0.05.

Next, we hand a coin to the respondent and give the following instructions: "Please flip this coin, but do not let me (the interviewer) see the coin. If it comes up 'heads,' answer Question A. If it comes up 'tails,' answer Question B. When you answer yes or no, I'll never know which question you have answered."

Suppose that we completed this process with 100 respondents and that 20 of them responded "yes." How do we know what proportion have shoplifted? Here's how the math works.

Let

Y = The total proportion of "yes" responses = 0.20

p_s = Probability that the sensitive question was asked = 0.5 (the coin flip is 50/50)

$1 - p_s$ = Probability that the other question was asked = 0.5

P_B = The proportion of "yes" responses to the other question = 0.05

P_A = The proportion of "yes" responses to the sensitive question

$Y = (p_s \times P_A) + [(1 - p_s) \times P_B]$

$.20 = (.50 \times P_A) + (.50 \times .05)$

$P_A = 0.35,$ or 35%

As a result, we can estimate that 35% of the respondents have shoplifted.

4. Explain what a multichotomous question is.

multichotomous question

A fixed-alternative question in which respondents are asked to choose the alternative that most closely corresponds to their position on the subject.

You may have noticed that some of the open-ended questions we presented seemed very straightforward, while others were more subjective in nature. There are two general classes of open-ended questions. One type seeks factual information from a respondent. For example, consider questions 1, 3, 4, and 6. These questions seek direct answers from the respondent. There is a correct answer to each question, and the researcher assumes that the respondent can provide those answers (questions 1, 4, and 6) or is testing to see if the respondent is capable of providing the answers (question 3).

The other type of open-ended question is more exploratory in nature (see questions 2 and 5). Questions designed to uncover motivations and rich descriptions of feelings and attitudes (sometimes referred to as "touchy-feely" questions) are terrific for exploratory research and can also be used with descriptive research, although they are very difficult to code.

Closed-Ended Questions With closed-ended questions, respondents choose their answers from a predetermined number of responses. Many times, they respond using rating scales. In this section, we'll present several key issues with using closed-ended questions.

In a **multichotomous question**, respondents are asked to choose the one (or more) alternatives from several choices that most closely reflect their answer or position on the subject. If there are only two response categories, these questions are referred to as *dichotomous questions*. Exhibit 14.3 reframes some of the open-ended questions from the preceding list as multichotomous questions. Respondents would be instructed to check the box or boxes that apply.

The examples in Exhibit 14.3 illustrate some of the difficulties encountered in using closed-ended questions. None of the alternatives in the motorcycle helmet law

Exhibit 14.3	Examples of Multichotomous Questions

Age	HDTV Television Purchase
How old are you?	**Why did you purchase a Sony brand HDTV television (check all that apply)?**
☐ Less than 20 ☐ 20–29 ☐ 30–39 ☐ 40–49 ☐ 50–59 ☐ 60 or over	☐ Price was lower than other alternatives ☐ Feel it represents the highest quality ☐ Availability of local service ☐ Availability of a service contract ☐ Picture is better ☐ Warranty is better ☐ Other
Motorcycle Helmet Use Legislation	**Gasoline Purchase Frequency**
How would you feel about laws requiring motorcycle riders to wear helmets?	**In the past month, how many times have you purchased gasoline from Ted's Texaco?**
☐ Definitely needed ☐ Probably needed ☐ Probably not needed ☐ Definitely not needed ☐ No opinion	☐ 0 ☐ 1–2 ☐ 3 or more

question, for example, may correctly capture the respondent's true feeling on the issue. The individual's opinion may be more complex. He may feel that helmets should be required when riding on highways and streets but not on private land or dirt tracks. The multiple-choice question does not permit individuals to elaborate on their true position but requires them to condense their complex attitude into a single statement. If necessary, you could include additional questions that allow more elaboration, but you would need to be careful not to include so many questions and choices that the questionnaire becomes too long to be used effectively.

The helmet law question also illustrates a general problem in question design: Should respondents be provided with a "don't know" or "no opinion" option? The general rule is that if a sizable portion of respondents truly don't know an answer or hold an opinion on an issue, they ought to be allowed to say so. How do we define "sizable portion"? If exploratory research or questionnaire pretesting reveals that more than about 20 to 25% of respondents either don't know or hold an opinion, it's probably a good idea to include appropriate response categories to capture this. Another option is to use a filter question and avoid asking the question of these respondents altogether.

The HDTV television purchase question in Exhibit 14.3 illustrates another problem with fixed-alternative questions. The list of reasons provided for purchasing a Sony brand HDTV television may not include all the reasons that could have been used by the respondent. Maybe a respondent purchased a Sony out of loyalty to a friend who owns the local electronics store or for some other reason not included on the list of possible reasons. *Response categories must be exhaustive*; that is, all reasonable possible responses must be included. The "other" response category attempts to solve this problem, but if many people are forced to check this response, the results for that question aren't worth much. As a result, the researcher must be as certain as she can be that she has included all reasonable responses. How do you know that you've included all necessary responses? Through exploratory research and questionnaire pretesting. Always keep in mind, however, that people have limited capacity for processing long lists of things. Don't exhaust your respondents in your quest to be exhaustive.

Here's another thing to consider when determining the form of response for each question. If a respondent is supposed to select only one response category, then there must be only one response category that contains his answer. In addition to being exhaustive, *response categories must also be mutually exclusive.* Consider the age question in Exhibit 14.3. What would happen if the response categories were "less than 20," "20–30," "30–40," "40–50," and so on, and the respondent was 30 years old? Which category should he check, "20–30" or "30–40"? Unless a respondent is instructed to check all alternatives that apply, or is to rank the alternatives in order of importance, researchers must be very careful that a respondent's answer will fall into only one category. Notice that the television purchase question includes the instruction to "check all that apply" because there might be several legitimate reasons for purchasing the Sony. On the other hand, if the instructions had said "check the most important reason," the categories would have been mutually exclusive because each represents a different reason.

Response categories are also susceptible to response order bias. Response order bias occurs when responses are likely to be affected by the order in which the alternatives are presented. Research Window 14.1 shows how responses to a question changed when the order in which the response categories were listed was changed on two versions of a mail questionnaire. (It's worth noting that mail questionnaires are among the least likely to show order bias, because respondents can see all possible responses. The differences shown in Research Window 14.1, which are statistically significant, would have been much greater had the study been done by telephone.) The recommended procedure for dealing with order bias is known as the **split-ballot technique**. In this approach, multiple versions of the questionnaire are produced and distributed. Each version varies the order of the response categories, so that each response category will appear in each position (for example, first, in the middle positions, last) about equally across the sample. The idea is that any order biases will be averaged out across all respondents.

Step 5: Determine Wording of Each Question

Step 5 in the questionnaire development process involves the phrasing of each question. This is a critical task, because a poorly worded question can cause respondents to refuse to answer it. This is known as *item nonresponse*, and it can create many problems in data analysis. Even worse, poorly worded questions introduce error when people do respond, because people may misunderstand the question or interpret it in different ways. Sometimes the wording of the question leads people into a particular answer that doesn't reflect their true position on an issue.

Writing good questions is difficult. Here are some general rules of thumb that you can follow to avoid some of the more obvious problems. There is no substitute, however, for careful thought—and a good deal of pretesting to ensure that your respondents understand and can accurately respond to your questions.

Use Simple Words Most researchers are more highly educated than the typical questionnaire respondent, and sometimes they use words that they are familiar with but that are not understood by many respondents. A significant proportion of the U.S. population, for example, does not understand the word *Caucasian*, although most researchers do, and determining the best method of assessing ethnic background is an important issue in many projects. Your task is to use words that are precise enough to get the answers you need, but that will be understood by virtually everyone in the designated population. Technical language on a survey is fine, and maybe even desired for its precision, with a technically oriented research topic and population. When seeking answers from the general public, however, it would be wise to remember that the average person in the United States has a high school, not a college,

response order bias
An error that occurs when the response to a question is influenced by the order in which the alternatives are presented.

split-ballot technique
A technique used to combat response bias in which one phrasing is used for a question in one-half of the questionnaires while an alternative phrasing is used in the other one-half of the questionnaires.

research window 14.1

How the Order in Which the Alternatives Are Listed Affects the Distribution of Replies

[Compared to a year ago] the amount of time spent watching television by my household is . . .

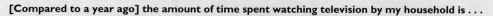

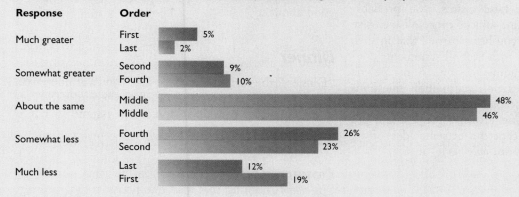

Response	Order	
Much greater	First	5%
	Last	2%
Somewhat greater	Second	9%
	Fourth	10%
About the same	Middle	48%
	Middle	46%
Somewhat less	Fourth	26%
	Second	23%
Much less	Last	12%
	First	19%

[Compared to a year ago] my household eats out at restaurants . . .

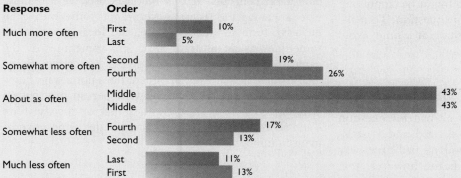

Response	Order	
Much more often	First	10%
	Last	5%
Somewhat more often	Second	19%
	Fourth	26%
About as often	Middle	43%
	Middle	43%
Somewhat less often	Fourth	17%
	Second	13%
Much less often	Last	11%
	First	13%

Most home repair or improvement projects completed in my home during the past years have been completed by . . .
[Base: Those completing a project.]

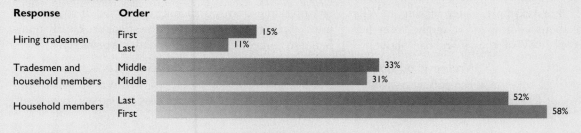

Response	Order	
Hiring tradesmen	First	15%
	Last	11%
Tradesmen and household members	Middle	33%
	Middle	31%
Household members	Last	52%
	First	58%

Source: "An Examination of Order Bias," *Research on Research* No. 1 (Chicago: Market Facts, Inc., undated). Reprinted with permission.

education and that many people have difficulty coping with such routine tasks as making change, reading job notices, or completing a driver's license application. Even common words can cause difficulty on questionnaires as Research Window 14.2 indicates. The best advice is to keep the words as simple as possible.

research window 14.2

Problem Words—Proceed with Caution!

All

"All" is one of those dead-giveaway words. From your own experience with true–false exams, you probably know that it is safe to count almost every all-inclusive statement as false. That is, you have learned that in such tests it is safe to follow the idea that all statements containing "all" are false, including this one. Some people have the same negative reaction to opinion questions that hinge on all-inclusive or all-exclusive words. They may be generally in agreement with a proposition, but nevertheless hesitate to accept the extreme idea of *all, always, each, every, never, nobody, only, none,* or *sure.*

And

The word "and" can signal that you might be combining two questions and asking them as one question. To make certain you're asking only one question at a time, avoid using the word "and" in your question.

Bad

In itself, the word "bad" is not at all bad for question wording. It conveys the meaning desired and is satisfactory as an alternative in a "good or bad" two-way question. Experience seems to indicate, however, that people are generally less willing to criticize than they are to praise. Since it is difficult to get them to state their negative views, sometimes the critical side needs to be softened. For example, after asking, "What things are good about your job?" it might seem perfectly natural to ask, "What things are bad about it?"

But if we want to lean over backward to get as many criticisms as we can, we may be wise not to apply the "bad" stigma, but to ask, "What things are not so good about it?"

Dinner

"Dinner," the main meal of the day, comes at noon with some families and in some areas. Elsewhere it is the evening meal. The question should not assume that it is either one or the other.

Government

"Government" is one of those words heavily loaded with emotional concepts. It is sometimes used as a definite word meaning the federal government, sometimes as an inclusive term for federal, state, and local government, sometimes as an abstract idea, and sometimes as the party in power as distinct from the opposition party. The trouble is that the respondent does not always know which "government" is meant. One person may have a different idea from another. It is best to specify if we want all respondents to answer with the same government in mind.

If

The word "if" is often associated with confusing directions or with skip patterns [branching questions]. If you need to use a skip pattern, be sure your questions are clearly numbered so that you can direct respondents properly.

Avoid Ambiguous Words and Questions Not only should the words and questions be simple, but they should also be unambiguous. Consider this multichotomous question:

> **How often do you rent movies from Blockbuster for viewing at home?**
> ☐ Never
> ☐ Occasionally
> ☐ Sometimes
> ☐ Often
> ☐ Regularly
> ☐ Always

Like

"Like" is on the problem list only because it is sometimes used to introduce an example. The problem with bringing an example into a question is that the respondent's attention may be directed toward the particular example and away from the general issue which it is meant only to illustrate. The use of examples may sometimes be necessary, but the possible hazard should always be kept in mind. The choice of an example can affect the answers to the question—in fact, it may materially change the question, as in these two examples:

Do you think that leafy vegetables like spinach should be in the daily diet?
Do you think that leafy vegetables like lettuce should be in the daily diet?

Not

Avoid using "not" in your questions if you're having respondents answer "yes" or "no" to a question. Using the word "not" can lead to double negatives and confusion.

Or

Similar to the word "and," the word "or" is often associated with a double question or with a false dilemma. (*Do you prefer the Republican or the Democratic candidate for governor?*) Be careful whenever you use the word "or" in a question.

Where

The frames of reference in answers to a "where" question may vary greatly. Consider the possible answers from this simple question:

Where did you read that?

Three of the many possible answers are:

In the New York Times.
At home in front of the fire.
In an advertisement.

Despite the seemingly wide variety of these three answers, some respondents could probably have stated them all: "In an ad in the *New York Times* while I was at home sitting in front of the fire."

You

"You" is extremely popular with question worders, since it is implicated in every question they ask. In most cases, "you" gives no trouble, since it is clear that it refers to the second person singular. However, and here is the problem, the word sometimes may have a collective meaning. Consider the question:

How many television sets did you repair last month?

The question seems to be straightforward, until it is asked of a repairman in a large shop, who counters with, "Who do you mean, me or the whole shop?"

Sometimes "you" needs the emphasis of "you yourself," and sometimes it just isn't the word to use, as in the above situation, where the entire shop is meant.

Sources: Excerpted from Norman Bradburn, Seymour Sudman, and Brian Wansink, *Asking Questions* (San Francisco, Calif.: Jossey-Bass, 2004), pp. 324–325, and Stanley L. Payne, *The Art of Asking Questions* (Princeton, N.J.: Princeton University Press, 1979), pp. 158–176.

For all practical purposes, the replies to this question would be worthless. The words *occasionally*, *sometimes*, *regularly*, and *often* are ambiguous. For example, to one respondent, the word "often" might mean "almost everyday." To another it might mean, "Yes, I use it when I have the specific need. This happens about once a week." The words *occasionally*, *sometimes*, and *regularly* could also be interpreted differently by different respondents. Even the words *never* and *always*, which are more concrete than the others on the list, can cause problems. To one person, "never" means "absolutely, positively, I have never, ever rented a movie from Blockbuster;" to another, it may mean "well, I *used* to rent movies from Blockbuster, but that was a long time ago, and I never do anymore." Thus, although this question would get answers, it would generate little real understanding of the frequency of the behavior in question.

MANAGER'S FOCUS

The process of designing a questionnaire should be guided by the science of measurement theory and the art of asking effective questions. Once again, these are areas in which your research provider should have extensive training and experience. Determining the wording of questions is a step where the input of managers can be very helpful, but it can also be detrimental. You can provide valuable assistance if you are able to give insight to the researcher about the terms used by people within your target population. Through your interactions with customers or prospects, previous research findings (particularly exploratory interviews), and other sources, you may have learned how the population communicates about key issues. However, management staffs have a tendency to develop their own vernacular about market-related issues. To the extent that these expressions diverge from how the target population communicates, they can be detrimental if they are used in the wording of questions.

For example, one of us had the embarrassing experience of working on a research project in which the client managers regularly used an acronym when referring to a competitor's brand. It was the first time our research firm had worked in this industry, and we assumed the acronym was how consumers also referred to the brand. At several points in the questionnaire, we used the acronym instead of the full brand name, and our clients approved this wording when reviewing our proposed questionnaire. Moreover, when we pretested the questionnaire, none of the respondents indicated they were unfamiliar with the acronym. We implemented the questionnaire only to notice after a full day of data collection that while none of the respondents objected to the acronym, most of them provided ratings that were more consistent with an unfamiliar brand than for one with a relatively strong market share. When we expressed concern to our clients, they acknowledged that they had made up the acronym and consumers would never have heard of it. We then had to revise the questionnaire and restart the data collection process. Without question, the mistake was ours, but our clients could have enabled us to avoid this embarrassing outcome by helping us understand the distinction between the way they communicated and the manner in which their target consumers communicated.

A much better strategy to use when asking about the frequency of some behavior is to ask how many times the behavior has been performed during a specific time period.

> **Over the past two weeks, how many movies have you rented from Blockbuster for viewing at home?**
> None
> ☐ 1
> ☐ 2
> ☐ 3
> ☐ 4
> ☐ 5
> ☐ more than 5

An even better approach might be to just let respondents provide the actual number:

> **Over the past two weeks, how many movies have you rented from Blockbuster for viewing at home? Write a number on the following line:**
> _____

leading question
A question framed so as to give the respondent a clue as to how he or she should answer.

Avoid Leading Questions Sometimes questions are written in such a way that they basically tell respondents what answer ought to be provided. A **leading question** might have been an accident by a careless researcher; more likely, it is an intentional attempt to manipulate the study's results by a researcher and/or manager. Remember that manipulating results produces advocacy research and is blatantly unethical. Under no circumstances should leading questions be used intentionally. Consider this question:

> **Do you feel that limiting taxes by law is an effective way to stop the government from picking your pocket every payday?**
> ☐ Yes
> ☐ No
> ☐ Undecided

This was one of three questions in an unsolicited questionnaire that one of the authors received as part of a study sponsored by the National Tax Limitation Committee. The committee intended to make the results of the poll available to Congress and to state legislators. Given the implied purpose, it is probably not surprising to see the leading words "picking your pocket" being used in this question, or the leading word "gouge" being used in another question. What is especially unfortunate is that it is unlikely that the questions themselves accompanied the report to Congress. Instead, it is more likely that the report suggested that some high percentage (for example, 90% of those surveyed) favored laws limiting taxes. Conclusion: Congress should pay attention to the wishes of the people and pass such laws.

Leading questions like this have become commonplace. The words that you use in a question can have a great deal of influence on the results, and sometimes it is very tempting to slant questions to get the answers we'd like to see. How else can we explain the conflicting survey results we see about any controversial issue such as abortion, capital punishment, war, and so on? The organizations that sponsor such studies usually want to support one side or the other. When the results of two projects focused on the same controversial topic conflict with one another, you can be almost certain that one or both were advocacy projects rather than attempts to get at the truth in the situation.

Here's a tip: When you see the results of surveys and public opinion polls presented in the news media, pay no attention whatsoever to any results that aren't accompanied by (a) the actual questions asked, (b) a description of how the study was conducted, and (c) what group was surveyed. Reputable media outlets will provide this information as a matter of routine.

Avoid Unstated Alternatives An alternative that is not expressed in the options is an **unstated alternative**. The results of one classic study from years ago demonstrate what can happen when unstated alternatives are made clear to respondents. Researchers wanted to know the attitudes of full-time homemakers toward the idea of having a job outside the home. They asked two random samples of homemakers the following two questions:[9]

unstated alternative
An alternative answer that is not expressed in a question's options.

Residential cleaning services, and other companies, can survey customers through rating scales in their "Tell us how we're doing?" online feature.

> **Would you like to have a job, if this were possible?** _____

> **Would you prefer to have a job, or do you prefer to do just your housework?** _____

While the two questions appear very similar, they produced dramatically different responses. In the first version, only 19% of the homemakers said "no." In the second version, 68% said they would prefer not to have a job—over three and one-half times as many as in the first version. The difference in the two questions is that the second version makes explicit an important alternative: Doing housework is a job in itself. As a general rule, you should avoid unstated alternatives; in this example, the second version of the question is better than the first. In many ways, this is consistent with our earlier advice that response categories must be exhaustive. Thorough exploratory research and questionnaire pretesting will help identify unstated alternatives.

Avoid Assumed Consequences A question should be framed so that all respondents will consider all relevant information as they respond. Unfortunately, it is easy to ask questions that don't spell out what might happen as a consequence of certain actions. These questions leave **assumed consequences**. The question "Are you in favor of placing price controls on crude oil?" will generate different responses from individuals, depending on whether they think price controls will result in rationing, long lines at the pump, or lower prices. A better way of asking this question is to clearly state the possible consequence(s). For example, the question could be changed to ask, "Are you in favor of placing price controls on crude oil if it would produce gas rationing?" Another possibility is to place a statement that explicitly notes what the consequences might be before asking the question:

assumed consequences
A problem that occurs when a question is not framed so as to clearly state the consequences, and thus it generates different responses from individuals who assume different consequences.

> **Many experts believe that placing price controls on crude oil will result in lower gasoline prices, but may also mean lower gasoline production, gasoline rationing, and longer lines at the pump. Are you in favor of placing price controls on crude oil?**
>
> ☐ Yes
> ☐ No
> ☐ Undecided

Figure 14.2 shows what can happen when the consequences are explicitly stated in a question. Version B makes the assumed consequence in Version A clear to respondents; the only way the helmet law could be effective would be if there were some penalty for not obeying the law. Yet, when there was no explicit statement about what would happen if a person did not comply with the proposed law, 73% were in favor of it.

Avoid Generalizations and Estimates Questions should always be asked in specific, rather than general, terms. Consider the question "How many salespeople did you see last year?" which might be asked of a purchasing agent. To answer the question, the agent would probably estimate how many salespeople call in a typical week and would multiply this estimate by 52. Don't place this sort of burden on your respondents. Instead, ask about a shorter time frame that won't force a respondent to provide an estimate. For this question, a more accurate estimate would be obtained if the purchasing agent were asked "How many representatives called last week?" and the researcher multiplied the answer by 52.

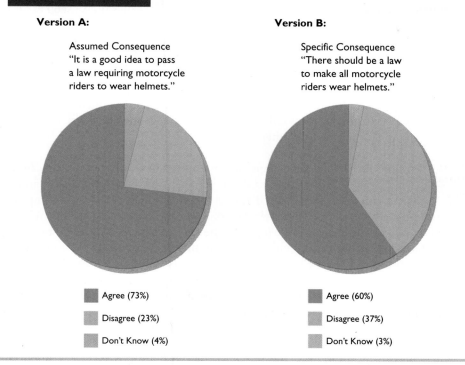

FIGURE 14.2 Illustration of What Can Happen When an Assumed Consequence Is Made Explicit

Version A:

Assumed Consequence
"It is a good idea to pass
a law requiring motorcycle
riders to wear helmets."

■ Agree (73%)

■ Disagree (23%)

■ Don't Know (4%)

Version B:

Specific Consequence
"There should be a law
to make all motorcycle
riders wear helmets."

■ Agree (60%)

■ Disagree (37%)

■ Don't Know (3%)

Source: Based on Albert J. Ungar, "Projectable Surveys: Separating Useful Data from Illusions," *Business Marketing* 71, December 1986, p. 90, Crain Communications, Inc.

Avoid Double-Barreled Questions Try to answer the following question:

> **Think back to the last meal you purchased at a fast-food restaurant. How satisfied were you with the price and the quality of service that you received?**
> ☐ Very Dissatisfied
> ☐ Dissatisfied
> ☐ Neutral
> ☐ Satisfied
> ☐ Very Satisfied

Was it difficult to answer the question? Maybe not, if both the price and service quality were consistently satisfactory or unsatisfactory. But what if the service was great but the price was too high? Now how should you answer the question? With **double-barreled questions**, two questions are rolled into one, leading to confusion for respondents.

Most of the time double-barreled questions are fairly easy to spot. Just look over your questionnaire closely, circling the words *and* and *or*. Finding one of these words doesn't necessarily mean you've written a double-barreled question, but it often does. Usually, a double-barreled question (or a *triple-barreled question*, for that matter) can easily be fixed by splitting the question into two or more separate questions.

double-barreled question
A question that calls for two responses and creates confusion for the respondent.

Step 6: Determine Question Sequence

Once the form of response and specific wording for each question have been decided, the researcher is ready to begin putting them together into a questionnaire. You must recognize immediately that the order in which the questions are presented can be crucial to the success of the research effort. Again, there are no hard-and-fast principles, but only rules of thumb to guide the researcher.

Learning Objective

6. Explain what the funnel approach to question sequencing is.

funnel approach
An approach to question sequencing that gets its name from its shape, starting with broad questions and progressively narrowing down the scope.

question order bias
The tendency for earlier questions on a questionnaire to influence respondents' answers to later questions.

Use Simple and Interesting Opening Questions   The first questions asked are critically important. If respondents cannot answer them easily—or if they find them uninteresting or threatening in any way—they may refuse to complete the remainder of the questionnaire. Thus, it is essential that the first few questions be simple, interesting, and in no way threatening to respondents. Questions that ask respondents for their opinion on some issue are often good openers, as most people like to feel their opinion is important. Sometimes it is helpful to use such an opener even when responses to it will not be analyzed, since opinion questions are often effective in relaxing respondents and securing their cooperation.

Use the Funnel Approach   One approach to question sequencing is the **funnel approach**, which gets its name from its shape, starting with broad questions and progressively narrowing down the scope. If respondents are to be asked, "What improvements can be made to improve your satisfaction with AAA Plumbing Company?" and also, "How do you evaluate the timeliness of the service provided?" the first question needs to be asked before the second. Otherwise, timeliness of service will be emphasized disproportionately in the responses simply because it is fresh in the respondents' minds. This is an example of **question order bias**, the tendency for earlier questions to affect respondents' answers to later questions. In general, the funnel approach helps prevent problems with question order bias. (Note that question order bias is not the same thing as response order bias, a topic we addressed earlier in this chapter.)

When measuring awareness, the sequence of the questions is a very important concern. Recall questions ("Which three financial institutions located in Taylorville come to mind first?") must always be asked before recognition questions ("Tell me whether or not each of the following financial institutions is located in Taylorville") if the results of the recall question are to be meaningful. Furthermore, with mail questionnaires, the recognition questions must be placed far enough away from the recall questions that respondents are not likely to see the recognition question at the time they answer the recall question.

There should also be some logical order to the questions. This means that sudden changes in topics and jumping around from topic to topic should be avoided. Transitional devices are sometimes necessary to smooth the flow when a change in subject matter occurs. Sometimes researchers will insert filter questions as a way to change the direction of the questioning. Most often, however, researchers will insert a brief explanation as a way of bridging a change in subject matter.

Learning Objective

7. Explain what a branching question is and discuss when it is used.

branching question
A technique used to direct respondents to different places in a questionnaire, based on their response to the question at hand.

Design Branching Questions with Care   A direction as to where to go next in the questionnaire based on the answer to a preceding question is called a **branching question**. For example, the initial question might be, "Have you bought a car within the last six months?" If the respondent answers "yes," she is then instructed to go to another place in the questionnaire, where questions are asked about specific details of the purchase. Someone replying "no" to the same question would be directed to skip the questions relating to the details of the purchase. The advantage to branching questions is that they reduce the number of alternatives that are needed in individual questions, while ensuring that those respondents capable of supplying the needed information still have an opportunity to do so. Those for whom a question is irrelevant are simply directed around it.

Through the use of computer technology, branching questions and directions are much easier to develop for telephone interviews, personal interviews, and Web-based questionnaires than they are for mail or e-mail surveys. With mail or e-mail questionnaires, the number of branching questions needs to be kept to an absolute minimum so that respondents do not become confused when responding, or refuse to cooperate because the task becomes too difficult.

Ask for Classification Information Last The typical questionnaire contains two types of information: basic information and classification information. *Basic information* refers to the subject of the study, for example, intentions or attitudes of respondents. *Classification information* refers to the other data we collect to classify respondents, typically for demographic breakdowns. For instance, we might be interested in determining if a respondent's attitudes toward a new product or service are in any way affected by the person's income. Income here would be a classification variable. Demographic/socioeconomic characteristics of respondents are often used as classification variables for understanding the results.

Except under rare circumstances, *basic information should be obtained first*, followed by classification information. There is a logical reason for this. The basic information is most critical. Without it, there is no study. The researcher shouldn't risk alienating the respondent by asking a number of personal questions before getting to the heart of the study, since it is not unusual for personal questions to alienate respondents most. Respondents who readily offer their opinions about television programming may balk when asked about their income. An early question aimed at determining their income may affect the whole tone of the interview or other communication. It is best to avoid this possibility by placing the classification information at the end.

Auto dealerships often ask customers to complete mail or online surveys on their products and services, using the funnel approach.

Place Difficult or Sensitive Questions Late in the Questionnaire The basic information itself can also present some sequence problems. Some of the questions may be sensitive. Early questions should not be sensitive, for the reasons we mentioned earlier. If respondents feel threatened, they may refuse to participate in the study. Thus, sensitive questions should be placed near the end of the questionnaire. Once respondents have become involved in the study, they are less likely to react negatively or refuse to answer when delicate questions are posed.

Step 7: Determine Physical Characteristics of Questionnaire

The physical characteristics of the questionnaire can affect the accuracy of the replies that are obtained. The Florida ballots in the 2000 U.S. presidential election and the controversy surrounding who actually won the electoral vote, George Bush or Al Gore, provide a vivid example. The physical characteristics of a questionnaire can affect how respondents react to it and the ease with which the replies can be processed. In determining the physical format of the questionnaire, a researcher wants to do those things that help get the respondent to accept the questionnaire, and facilitate handling and control by the researcher.

The physical appearance of the questionnaire can influence respondents' cooperation. This is particularly true with mail questionnaires, but it applies as well to any method in which respondents will be able to see the survey form. If the questionnaire looks sloppy, respondents are likely to feel the study is unimportant or unprofessional and refuse to cooperate no matter how important the researcher says it is. If the study is important (and why would you be conducting it if it isn't?), make the questionnaire reflect that importance.

Learning Objective

8. Explain the difference between basic information and classification information and tell which should be asked first in a questionnaire.

Here are some specific suggestions that can improve the initial "look" and likely acceptance of a questionnaire. All of these apply to mail questionnaires; many apply to other methods as well.

- Use good-quality paper and a good photocopier. If you will be distributing enough questionnaires to make it cost effective, have the surveys printed rather than photocopied.

- The questionnaire must not appear to be cluttered. Don't be afraid to leave margins and other empty space on the form, because this will make the questionnaire seem less intimidating to respondents.

- Keep the questionnaire to a single page, printed on front and back, if it is possible to do so. Almost every study has shown that shorter surveys achieve higher response rates than longer surveys, and the number of pages in the survey immediately communicates something about length. Even if you have to use a smaller font to keep the survey to a single page, we recommend that you do so. Use common sense, however. If your respondents are elderly and therefore more likely to have poor eyesight, don't try to use a very small font just to keep the survey on a single page. Plenty of three- to five-page surveys have been used effectively when necessary. When more than a single page is needed, make the questionnaire into a booklet rather than staple or paper-clip the pages together. It just looks better to the respondent.

- If you must use branching questions, make certain that the instructions are clear. It might even be possible to include arrows pointing from each answer on a branching question to the next question the respondent should read. Some researchers have effectively used color-coding to connect answers on a branching question to the next section to be completed.

- Use the graphics available in word processing software to improve the appearance of the survey form. Put boxes, lines, circles, shadows, shading, and so on, to good use.

- If your questionnaire will contain more than about 8 to 10 questions, try numbering the questions within sections. That is, if you had a 30-question survey, instead of numbering the questions 1 through 30, put the questions into sections and restart numbers within each section. So, the first four questions might be numbered 1-1, 1-2, 1-3, 1-4, and the next three questions numbered 2-1, 2-2, 2-3, and so on.

- Include the name of the sponsoring organization and the name of the project on the first page. Both of these lend credibility to the study. However, since awareness of the sponsoring firm may bias respondents' answers, many firms use fictitious names for the sponsoring organization.

There's one other thing to consider. Don't bother with long, drawn-out sets of instructions, unless you are doing something new and different and they are absolutely necessary. Most people have completed enough surveys to know how to respond to them, so a sentence or two ought to be enough. We learned this the hard way. One time we included a set of instructions that took up roughly a quarter of the first page of a survey. About 25% of our respondents didn't answer the first question, which closely followed the instructions and was a little wordy itself. We suspect that in their haste to skip over our burdensome instructions, most of these people never even saw the first question. Learn from our experience; keep instructions simple and short.

Step 8: Develop Recruiting Message or Script

The introduction to the research can also affect acceptance of the questionnaire. With personal interviews and telephone interviews, the opening script used to recruit potential respondents is probably your only chance to secure their participation, so put some thought into what you'll say. In fact, your "script" needs to be carefully developed and pretested to ensure that it is effective in getting people to agree to participate. Then you must make certain that the people making the contacts actually follow the script. Note that it is important that the recruiters practice the script until it sounds as natural as possible; nobody likes to hear someone reading or reciting a "canned" presentation to them.

With the nonpersonal methods of administration, the questionnaire will usually be introduced in written format, although Web surveys could use prerecorded audio. Because there is no direct social aspect to written requests to participate, the task of introducing the survey and securing respondent cooperation is even more difficult and must be approached with care.

Good cover letters and scripts are rarely written in a hurry. Like the questionnaire itself, they usually require a series of painstaking rewrites to get the wording just so. The most important things to communicate are (a) who you are, (b) why you are contacting them, (c) your request for their help in providing information, (d) how long it will take, (e) that their responses will be anonymous and/or confidential (if this is true), and (e) any incentives they will receive for participating. Research Window 14.3 lists important content considerations in the construction of cover letters for mail surveys; a similar approach might be used with other written formats such as Internet-based questionnaires. With personal and telephone interviews, the script is necessarily shorter. Regardless of method of administration, the recruiting message needs to convince respondents about the importance of the research and the importance of their participation.

research window 14.3

Contents of and Sample Cover Letter for a Mail Questionnaire

Panel A: Contents

1. Personal communication

2. Asking a favor

3. Importance of the research project and its purpose

4. Importance of the recipient

5. Importance of the replies in general

6. Importance of the replies when the reader is not qualified to answer most questions

7. How the recipient may benefit from this research

8. Completing the questionnaire will take only a short time

9. The questionnaire can be answered easily

10. A stamped reply envelope is enclosed

11. How recipient was selected

12. Answers are anonymous or confidential

13. Offer to send report on results of survey

14. Note of urgency

15. Appreciation of sender

16. Importance of sender

17. Importance of the sender's organization

18. Description and purpose of incentive

(Continued)

Panel B: Sample

The numbers refer to the corresponding items in Panel A.

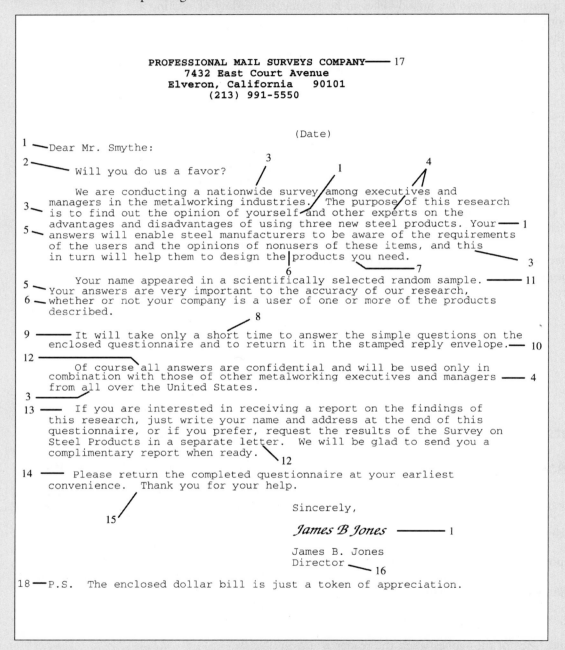

Source: Paul L. Erdos, *Professional Mail Surveys* (Melbourne, Fla.: Robert E. Krieger Publishing Co., Inc., 1983), pp. 102–103. Reprinted with permission.

Step 9: Reexamine Steps 1–8 and Revise If Necessary

A researcher should never expect the first draft of the questionnaire to be the one that is ultimately used. Questionnaire development is an iterative process, even for professional researchers. Each question should be reviewed to ensure that the question is easy to answer and not confusing, ambiguous, or potentially offensive to the respondent. Questions must not be leading or likely to bias respondents' answers. How can you tell? An extremely critical attitude and good common sense should help. You need to examine each word in each question. When a potential problem is discovered, the question should be revised. After examining each question, and each word in each question, for its potential meanings and implications, test the questionnaire by having different members of the research team answer the questions using the method of administration to be used in the actual study. Call them on the telephone, send them an e-mail, walk up and ask for their participation, or let them find the questionnaire with their mail. This sort of role playing should reveal some of the most serious shortcomings and should lead to further revision of the questionnaire.

Step 10: Pretest Questionnaire and Revise If Necessary

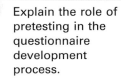

Learning Objective

9. Explain the role of pretesting in the questionnaire development process.

The real test of a questionnaire is how it performs under actual conditions of data collection. For this assessment, the questionnaire **pretest** is vital. The questionnaire pretest serves the same role in questionnaire design that test marketing serves in new product development. While the product concept, different advertising appeals, alternative packages, and so on, may all have been tested previously in the product development process, test marketing is the first place where they all come together. Similarly, the pretest provides the real test of the questionnaire and the mode of administration.

There are a number of interesting examples in the literature of questions with unintended implications that could have been avoided with an adequate pretest of the

pretest
Use of a questionnaire (or observation form) on a trial basis in a small pilot study to determine how well the questionnaire (or observation form) works.

MANAGER'S FOCUS

Pretesting does not guarantee there will be no problems with a questionnaire. Proper pretesting, however, will help researchers discover most problems. We all tend to believe we communicate far more clearly and effectively than is usually the case. The pretesting process quickly reveals how instructions, questions, and response formats we thought were perfectly clear can be easily misunderstood or misinterpreted by respondents. If these problems are not corrected, there will be a significant amount of unnecessary measurement error in our research findings.

Managers often do not appreciate the importance of pretesting, and unfortunately, some researchers don't

either. By this point in the research process, deadlines are becoming more pressing and it is tempting to conserve time by beginning the actual data collection process. But neglecting the pretest would be a major mistake that would probably lower the quality of the information obtained. It is quite rare that a pretest does not reveal one or more problems with how a questionnaire was originally designed. For this reason, pretesting is absolutely critical and under no conditions should you ever allow researchers to proceed without pretesting and revising a questionnaire. In fact, if your research provider does not suggest a pretest, or objects to the pretesting process, you probably need to find a different provider.

questionnaire. In one lifestyle study, for example, the following question was asked: "How would you like to be living two years from now?" While the question was intended to get at hoped-for lifestyles, a large group of the respondents simply replied "yes."[10]

Data collection should never begin until you have pretested—and probably revised again—the questionnaire. It is best if there are two pretests. The first should be done by personal interview, no matter how you actually plan to administer the actual survey. An interviewer can watch to see if people actually remember data requested of them, or if some questions seem confusing or produce resistance or hesitancy among respondents for one reason or another. The pretest interviews should be conducted among respondents similar to those who will be used in the actual study, by the firm's most experienced interviewers.

The personal interview pretest should reveal some questions in which the wording could be improved or the sequence changed. If the changes are major, the revised questionnaire should again be pretested in personal interviews. If the changes are minor, the questionnaire can be pretested a second time using mail, telephone, fax, e-mail, Internet, or personal interviews, whichever is going to be used for the full-scale study. This time, however, less-experienced interviewers should also be used in order to determine if typical interviewers will have any special problems with the questionnaire. The purpose of the second pretest is to uncover problems unique to the mode of administration.

Finally, the responses that result from the pretest should be coded and analyzed. We have previously discussed the need for the preparation of dummy tables prior to the development of the questionnaire. The analysis of pretest responses can check on the researcher's conceptualization of the problem and the data and method of analysis necessary to answer it. If there is no place in one of the dummy tables to put the responses to a question, the question is either not needed or the researcher has omitted some contemplated analysis. If some part of a dummy table remains empty, a necessary question may have been omitted. Trial analyses reveal better than any other alternative whether all the data collected will be put to use and that all needed data will be collected.

If you fail to pretest your data collection forms, you are asking for trouble. The pretest is the most inexpensive insurance the researcher can buy to ensure the success of the questionnaire and the research project. A careful pretest along with proper attention to the dos and don'ts presented in this chapter and summarized in Exhibit 14.4 should make the questionnaire development process successful.

OBSERVATION FORMS

There are generally fewer problems in constructing observation forms than in constructing questionnaires, because we don't have to worry about how questions and the way they are asked will affect the responses. Through proper training, observers can be taught how to handle the data collection instrument consistently. Alternatively, the researcher may simply use a mechanical device to measure the behavior of interest and secure complete consistency in measurement. This is not to imply that observation forms are always easy to develop. The researcher must make explicit decisions about what is to be observed and the categories and units that will be used to record this behavior. Figure 14.3 (see pages 315–317), which is the observation form used by a bank with mystery shoppers to evaluate the service provided by its customer contact employees, shows how detailed some of these decisions can be.

ETHICAL DILEMMA 14.2

A candy manufacturer tells you that he wants to raise the price of his gourmet chocolates and he needs you to establish the greatest price increase that shoppers will stand. He suggests that you interview patrons of gourmet candy shops without informing them of the sponsor or purpose of the research, describe the candy to them in general terms, and suggest prices that they might find acceptable, starting with the highest price.

- Is it ethical to ask people questions when their answer may be detrimental to their self-interest?
- Is it ethical not to reveal the purpose or sponsor of the research? If you did reveal the purpose of the research, would survey respondents give the same answers as otherwise?

| **E x h i b i t 1 4 . 4** | **Questionnaire Preparation Checklist** |

Step 1: Specify What Information Will Be Sought

☐ Make sure that you have a clear understanding of the issue and what it is that you want to know. Frame your research questions, but don't write the actual questions just yet.

☐ Make a list of your research questions. Review them periodically as you are working on the questionnaire.

☐ Use the dummy tables that were set up to guide the data analysis to suggest questions for the questionnaire.

☐ Conduct a search for existing questions on the issue and revise to meet your current purposes.

Step 2: Determine Method of Administration

☐ Use the type of data to be collected as a basis for deciding on the type of questionnaire.

☐ Use the degree of structure and disguise to guide selection of method of administration.

☐ Compare your situation against the advantages and disadvantages of the different approaches (see Exhibit 10.3).

Step 3: Determine Content of Individual Questions

☐ For each research question ask yourself, "Why do I want to know this?" Answer it in terms of how it will help your research. "It would be interesting to know" is not an acceptable answer.

☐ Make sure each question is specific and addresses only one important issue.

☐ Ask yourself whether the question applies to all respondents; if it doesn't, either the population must be redefined, or you need a filter question or branching question.

☐ Split questions that can be answered from different frames of reference into multiple questions, one corresponding to each frame of reference. If you don't need each frame of reference, carefully rephrase the question to provide only the perspective you need.

☐ Ask yourself whether respondents will be informed about, and can remember, the issue that the question is dealing with.

☐ Make sure the time period of the question is appropriate for the topic.

☐ Avoid questions that require excessive effort or that deal with sensitive (embarrassing or threatening) issues.

☐ If sensitive questions must be asked,
  (a) guarantee respondent anonymity or confidentiality.
  (b) make use of a counterbiasing statement.
  (c) phrase the question in terms of others and how they might feel or act.
  (d) put sensitive questions near the end.
  (e) use categories or ranges rather than specific numbers.
  (f) use the randomized-response model.

Step 4: Determine Form of Response to Each Question

☐ Determine which type of question—open-ended or closed-ended—provides data that fit the information needs of the project.

☐ Use structured questions whenever possible.

☐ Use open-ended questions that require short answers to begin a questionnaire.

☐ Try to convert open-ended questions to fixed-response questions to reduce respondent work load and coding effort for descriptive and causal studies.

☐ If open-ended questions are necessary, make the questions fairly specific to give respondents a frame of reference when answering.

☐ Provide for "don't know" and "no opinion" responses, if these are likely to apply to a significant proportion of the population.

☐ When using multichotomous questions, be sure the choices are exhaustive and mutually exclusive.

☐ Be sure that all reasonable alternative answers are included.

☐ If multiple responses are possible, use "check all that apply" in the instructions.

☐ Watch out for response order bias when using closed-ended questions. Consider the use of a split-ballot procedure to reduce order bias.

☐ Use the highest level of measurement possible for each question, unless there is a solid reason to do otherwise (see Chapter 13).

Step 5: Determine Wording of Each Question

☐ Use simple words.

☐ Avoid ambiguous words and questions.

(*Continued*)

| **Exhibit 14.4** | **Questionnaire Preparation Checklist** (*continued*) |

☐ Avoid leading questions.
☐ Avoid unstated alternatives.
☐ Avoid assumed consequences.
☐ Avoid generalizations and estimates.
☐ Avoid double-barreled questions.
☐ Make sure each question is as specific as possible.

Step 6: Determine Question Sequence
☐ Use simple, interesting questions for openers.
☐ Use the funnel approach, first asking broad questions and then narrowing them down.
☐ Design branching questions with care; prepare a flow chart whenever branching questions are being considered.
☐ Ask for classification information last so that if respondent refuses, the other data are still usable.
☐ Ask difficult or sensitive questions late in the questionnaire, when rapport is better.
☐ Watch out for question order bias; use a split-ballot procedure if necessary.

Step 7: Determine Physical Characteristics of Questionnaire
☐ Make sure the questionnaire looks professional and is relatively easy to answer.
☐ Use quality paper and printing.
☐ Attempt to make the questionnaire as short as possible while avoiding a crowded appearance; aim for a single page, printed on the back if necessary.
☐ Use a booklet format for ease of analysis and to prevent lost pages, if multiple pages are necessary.
☐ List the name of the organization conducting the survey on the first page.
☐ Number the questions to ease data processing; if there are more than about 8 to 10 questions, number within sections.
☐ Use concise, clear instructions, especially with branching questions.
☐ Use appropriate graphics to improve the appearance of the questionnaire.

Step 8: Develop Recruiting Message or Script
☐ Keep the message as brief as possible, especially with personal and telephone interview scripts, but include the following information at a minimum:
　(a) who you are.
　(b) why you are contacting them.
　(c) your request for their help in providing information.
　(d) approximately how long it will take to participate.
　(e) that their responses will be anonymous or confidential (if this is true).
　(f) any incentives they will be given.
☐ Practice the script until it sounds natural, rather than "canned" or memorized.

Step 9: Reexamine Steps 1–8 and Revise If Necessary
☐ Examine each word of every question to ensure that the question is not confusing, ambiguous, offensive, or leading.
☐ Have members of the research team complete the surveys using the method of administration selected.

Step 10: Pretest Questionnaire and Revise If Necessary
☐ Pretest the questionnaire first by personal interviews among respondents similar to those to be used in the actual study.
☐ Obtain comments from the interviewers and respondents to discover any problems with the questionnaire, and revise it if necessary. When the revisions are substantial, repeat Step 9 and pretest again with "real" respondents.
☐ Pretest the questionnaire by mail or telephone to uncover problems unique to the mode of administration.
☐ Code and analyze the pretest responses in dummy tables to determine if questions are providing adequate information.
☐ Eliminate questions that do not provide adequate information, and revise questions that cause problems.

FIGURE 14.3

Form Used by Observer Acting as Shopper to Evaluate Service Provided by Bank Employees

Bank _____

Date _____   Time _____   Shopper's Name _____

Nature of Transaction: ☐ Personal   ☐ Telephone

    Details _____

    _____

    _____

- -

A. FOR PERSONAL TRANSACTIONS

Bank Employee's Name _____

1. How was name obtained?
    ☐ Employee had name tag

    ☐ Nameplate on counter or desk

    ☐ Employee gave name

    ☐ Shopper had to ask for name

    ☐ Name provided by other employee

    ☐ Other _____

    _____

B. FOR TELEPHONE TRANSACTIONS

Bank Employee's Name _____

1. How was name obtained?
    ☐ Employee gave name upon answering the telephone

    ☐ Name provided by other employee

    ☐ Shopper had to ask for name

    ☐ Employee gave name during conversation

    ☐ Other _____

    _____

C. CUSTOMER RELATIONS SKILLS	YES	NO	DOES NOT APPLY
1. Did the employee notice and greet you immediately?	☐	☐	☐
2. Did the employee speak pleasantly and smile?	☐	☐	☐
3. Did the employee answer the telephone promptly?	☐	☐	☐
4. Did the employee find out your name?	☐	☐	☐
5. Did the employee use your name during the transaction?	☐	☐	☐
6. Did the employee ask you to be seated?	☐	☐	☐
7. Was the employee helpful?	☐	☐	☐

(Continued)

Form Used by Observer Acting as Shopper to Evaluate Service Provided by Bank Employees (*Continued*)

FIGURE 14.3

	YES	NO	DOES NOT APPLY
8. Was the employee's desk or work area neat and uncluttered?	☐	☐	☐
9. Did the employee show a genuine interest in you as a customer?	☐	☐	☐
10. Did the employee thank you for coming in?	☐	☐	☐
11. Did the employee enthusiastically support the bank and its services?	☐	☐	☐
12. Did the employee handle any interruptions (phone calls, etc.) effectively?	☐	☐	☐

Comment on any positive or negative details of the transaction that you found particularly noticeable.

_____

_____

_____

_____

_____

D. SALES SKILLS	YES	NO	DOES NOT APPLY
1. Did the employee determine if you had any accounts with this bank?	☐	☐	☐
2. Did the employee use "open-ended" questions in obtaining information about you?	☐	☐	☐
3. Did the employee listen to what you had to say?	☐	☐	☐
4. Did the employee sell you on the bank service by showing you what the service could do for you?	☐	☐	☐
5. Did the employee ask you to open the service which you inquired about?	☐	☐	☐
6. Did the employee ask you to bank with this particular bank?	☐	☐	☐
7. Did the employee ask you to contact him/her when visiting the bank?	☐	☐	☐
8. Did the employee ask you if you had any questions or if you understood the service at the end of the transaction?	☐	☐	☐
9. Did the employee give you brochures about other services?	☐	☐	☐
10. Did the employee give you his/her calling card?	☐	☐	☐
11. Did the employee indicate that you might be contacted by telephone, engraved card, or letter as a means of follow-up?	☐	☐	☐

FIGURE 14.3	Form Used by Observer Acting as Shopper to Evaluate Service Provided by Bank Employees (*Continued*)	

12. Did the employee ask you to open or use other services? Check the following if they were mentioned.   ☐   ☐   ☐

☐ savings account

☐ checking account

☐ automatic savings

☐ Mastercharge

☐ Master Checking

☐ safe-deposit box

☐ loan services

☐ trust services

☐ automatic payroll deposit

☐ bank-by-mail

☐ automatic loan payment

☐ bank hours

☐ other _____

Comment on the overall effectiveness of the employee's sales skills.

_____

_____

_____

_____

_____

Source: Courtesy of Neil M. Ford.

Almost any event can be described in a number of ways. When we watch someone making a soft-drink purchase, we might report that (1) the person purchased one 12-pack of soft drinks; (2) the *woman* purchased one 12-pack of soft drinks; (3) the woman purchased one 12-pack of *Coca-Cola* soft drinks; (4) the woman purchased one 12-pack of Coca-Cola soft drinks *after comparing the prices of Pepsi products*; (5) the woman, *after asking for and finding that the store was out of Dr. Pepper*, purchased one 12-pack of Coca-Cola soft drinks after comparing the prices of Pepsi products; and so on.

A great many additional variations are possible, such as adding the type, name, or location of the store where this behavior occurred. In order for this observation to be productive for scientific inquiry, we must predetermine which aspects of this behavior are relevant. In this particular example, the decision as to what to observe requires that the researcher specify the following:

■ Who should be observed? Anyone entering the store? Anyone making a purchase? Anyone making a soft-drink purchase?

■ What aspects of the purchase should be reported? Which brand they purchased? Which brand they asked for first? Whether the purchase was of 12-pack, 6-pack, 2-liter bottle, cans, or bottles? What about the purchaser? Is the person's gender to be recorded? Is the individual's age to be estimated? Does it make any difference if the person was alone or in a group?

■ When should the observation be made? On what day of the week? At what time of the day? Should day and time be reported? Should the observation be recorded only after a purchase occurs, or should an approach by a customer to a salesclerk also be recorded even if it does not result in a sale?

■ Where should the observation be made? In what kind of store? How should the store be selected? How should it be noted on the observation form—by type, by location, by name? Should vending-machine purchases also be noted?

You may notice that these are the same kinds of who, what, when, and where decisions that need to be made in selecting the research design. The why and how are also considered. The research problem should dictate the why of the observation; the how involves choosing the observation device or form that will be used. A paper-and-pencil form should be very simple to use. It should parallel the logical sequence of the purchase act (for example, a male walks down the beverage aisle, looks at the different brands of soft drinks, and so on, if these behaviors are relevant) and should permit the recording of observations by a simple check mark if possible. Again, careful attention to detail, careful development of the preliminary form, and an adequate pretest will be important in ensuring the quality of the observations made.

SUMMARY

Learning Objective 1

Explain the role of research hypotheses in developing a questionnaire.
Hypotheses guide questionnaire development by determining what information will be sought and from whom (since the hypotheses specify what relationships will be investigated). As a result, hypotheses also affect the type of question and the form of response used to collect it.

Learning Objective 2

Define *telescoping error* and *recall loss* and explain how they affect a respondent's ability to answer questions accurately.
Telescoping error refers to people's tendency to remember an event as having occurred more recently than it did. *Recall loss* means they forget it happened at all. The degree to which the two types of error affect the accuracy of the reported information depends on the length of the period in question. For long periods, the telescoping effect is smaller, while

the recall loss is larger. For short periods, the reverse is true.

Learning Objective 3

Cite some of the techniques researchers use to secure respondents' cooperation in answering sensitive questions.
When asking sensitive questions, researchers may find it helpful to (a) guarantee respondent anonymity or confidentiality; (b) make use of a counterbiasing statement; (c) phrase the question in terms of others and how they might feel or act; (d) put sensitive questions near the end; (e) use categories or ranges rather than specific numbers; or (f) use the randomized-response model.

Learning Objective 4

Explain what a multichotomous question is.
In a multichotomous question, respondents are asked to choose from a list of alternatives the one that most closely reflects their position on the subject.

Learning Objective 5

List some of the primary rules researchers should keep in mind in trying to develop bias-free questions.

Among the rules of thumb that researchers should keep in mind in developing bias-free questions are (1) use simple words, (2) avoid ambiguous words and questions, (3) avoid leading questions, (4) avoid unstated alternatives, (5) avoid assumed consequences, (6) avoid generalizations and estimates, and (7) avoid double-barreled questions.

Learning Objective 6

Explain what the funnel approach to question sequencing is.

The funnel approach to question sequencing gets its name from its shape, starting with broad questions and progressively narrowing down the scope. This is important for question sequencing, because asking for specific information early in a questionnaire will often influence respondents' answers to later questions, a source of error known as question order bias.

Learning Objective 7

Explain what a branching question is and discuss when it is used.

A branching question is one that contains a direction as to where to go next on the questionnaire based on the answer given. Branching questions are used to reduce the number of alternatives that are needed in individual questions, while ensuring that those respondents capable of supplying the needed information still have an opportunity to do so.

Learning Objective 8

Explain the difference between basic information and classification information and tell which should be asked first in a questionnaire.

Basic information refers to the subject of the study; classification information refers to the other data we collect to classify respondents so as to extract more information about the phenomenon of interest. The proper questionnaire sequence is to present questions securing basic information first and those seeking classification information last.

Learning Objective 9

Explain the role of pretesting in the questionnaire development process.

Questionnaire pretesting is the final step in the questionnaire development process. It is the last chance that the researcher has to ensure that the data collection form is working properly prior to data collection; pretesting must not be overlooked.

KEY TERMS

filter question (page 292)
telescoping error (page 293)
recall loss (page 293)
randomized-response model (page 294)
multichotomous question (page 296)
response order bias (page 298)
split-ballot technique (page 298)
leading question (page 302)

unstated alternative (page 303)
assumed consequences (page 304)
double-barreled question (page 305)
funnel approach (page 306)
question order bias (page 306)
branching question (page 306)
pretest (page 311)

REVIEW QUESTIONS

1. What role do hypotheses play in determining the information that will be sought?

2. Suppose you wanted to determine the proportion of men in a geographic area who dye their hair. How could the information be obtained by open-ended question and by closed-ended question? Which would be preferable?

3. How does the method of administration of a questionnaire affect the type of question to be used?

4. What criteria can a researcher use to determine whether a specific question should be included in a questionnaire?

5. What is telescoping error? What does it suggest about the period to be used when asking respondents to recall past experiences?

6. What are some recommended ways for asking for sensitive information?

7. What is an open-ended question? A multichotomous question? What are some of the key things researchers must be careful to avoid in framing multichotomous and dichotomous questions?

8. What is a split ballot, and why is it used?

9. What is an ambiguous question? A leading question? A question with unstated alternatives? A question with assumed consequences? A double-barreled question?

10. What is the proper sequence when asking for basic information and classification information? Why?

11. What is the funnel approach to question sequencing?

12. What is a branching question? Why are such questions used?

13. How can the physical features of a questionnaire affect its acceptance by respondents? Its handling and control by the researcher?

14. What is a cover letter? What key things should be included on a cover letter?

15. What decisions must the researcher make when developing an observational form for data collection?

DISCUSSION QUESTIONS, PROBLEMS, AND PROJECTS

1. Evaluate the following questions.

   a. **Which of the following magazines do you read regularly?**
      ☐ *Time*
      ☐ *Newsweek*
      ☐ *Business Week*

   b. **Are you a frequent purchaser of Birds Eye Frozen vegetables?**
      ☐ Yes   ☐ No

   c. **Do you agree that the government should impose import restrictions?**
      ☐ Strongly agree
      ☐ Agree
      ☐ Neither agree nor disagree
      ☐ Disagree
      ☐ Strongly disagree

   d. **How often do you buy detergent?**
      ☐ Once a week
      ☐ Once in two weeks
      ☐ Once in three weeks
      ☐ Once a month

e. **Rank the following in order of preference:**
   ☐ Kellogg's Corn Flakes
   ☐ Quaker's Life
   ☐ Post Bran Flakes
   ☐ Kellogg's Bran Flakes
   ☐ Instant Quaker Oatmeal
   ☐ Post Rice Krinkles

f. **Where do you usually purchase your school supplies?**

g. **When you are watching television, do you also watch most of the advertisements?**

h. **Which of the following brands of tea are most similar?**
   ☐ Lipton
   ☐ Twinings
   ☐ Bigelow
   ☐ Salada

i. **Do you think that the present policy of cutting taxes and reducing government spending should be continued?**
   ☐ Yes   ☐ No

j. **In a seven-day week, how often do you eat breakfast?**
   ☐ Every day of the week
   ☐ 5–6 times a week
   ☐ 2–4 times a week
   ☐ Once a week
   ☐ Never

2. Make the necessary corrections to the above questions.

3. Evaluate the following multichotomous questions. Rephrase them as dichotomous or open-ended questions if you think it would be more appropriate.

a. **Which one of the following reasons is most important in your choice of stereo equipment?**
   ☐ Price
   ☐ In-store service
   ☐ Brand name
   ☐ Level of distortion
   ☐ Guarantee/warranty

b. **Please indicate your education level.**
   ☐ Less than high school
   ☐ Some high school
   ☐ High school graduate
   ☐ Technical or vocational school
   ☐ Some college
   ☐ College graduate
   ☐ Some graduate or professional school

c. **Which of the following reflects your views toward the issues raised by ecologists?**
   ☐ Have received attention
   ☐ Have not received attention
   ☐ Should receive more attention
   ☐ Should receive less attention

d. **With which of the following statements do you most strongly agree?**
   - ☐ Delta Air Lines has better service than Northwest Airlines.
   - ☐ Northwest Airlines has better service than United Airlines.
   - ☐ United Airlines has better service than Delta Air Lines.
   - ☐ United Airlines has better service than Northwest Airlines.
   - ☐ Northwest Airlines has better service than Delta Air Lines.
   - ☐ Delta Air Lines has better service than United Airlines.

4. Evaluate the following open-ended questions. Rephrase them as multichotomous or dichotomous questions if you think it would be more appropriate.

   a. **Do you go to the movies often?**

   b. **Approximately how much do you spend per week on groceries?**

   c. **What brands of cheese did you purchase during the last week?**

5. Assume you are doing exploratory research to find out people's opinions about television advertising.

   a. Specify the necessary information to be sought.

   You have decided to design a structured, undisguised questionnaire and to use the personal interview method.

   b. List the individual questions on a separate sheet of paper.

   c. Specify the form of the response for each question. Provide justification for selecting a particular form of response.

   d. Determine the sequence of the questions. Reexamine and revise the questions.

   e. Attach the final version of the questionnaire.

   f. Pretest the questionnaire on a convenience sample of five students, and report the results of your pretest.

6. The objective of this study is to determine whether brand names are important for mothers purchasing children's clothing.

   a. Specify the necessary information that is to be sought.

   You have decided to use a structured, undisguised questionnaire and to use the telephone interview method.

   b. List the individual questions on a separate sheet of paper.

   c. Specify the form of the response for each question. Provide justification for selecting a particular form of response.

   d. Determine the sequence of the questions. Reexamine and revise the questions.

   e. Attach the final version of the questionnaire.

   f. Using the phone book as a sampling frame, pretest the questionnaire on a sample of five respondents, and report the results of your pretest.

7. A small brokerage firm was concerned with its declining number of customers and decided to do a quick survey. The major objective was to find out the reasons for patronizing a particular brokerage firm and to find out the importance of customer service. The following questionnaire was to be administered by telephone.

   Good Afternoon, Sir/Madam:

   We are doing a survey on attitudes toward brokerage firms. Could you please answer the following questions? Thank you.

1. Have you invested any money in the stock market?

☐ Yes   ☐ No

If respondent replies "yes" continue; otherwise terminate interview.

2. Do you manage your own investments, or do you go to a brokerage firm?

☐ Manage own investments   ☐ Go to brokerage firm

If respondent replies "go to a brokerage firm," continue; otherwise terminate interview.

3. How satisfied are you with your brokerage firm?

Very Satisfied	Satisfied	Neither Satisfied nor Dissatisfied	Dissatisfied	Very Dissatisfied
☐	☐	☐	☐	☐

4. How important is personal service to you?

Very Important	Important	Not Particularly Important	Not at All Important
☐	☐	☐	☐

5. Which of the following reasons is the most important in patronizing a particular firm?

☐ The commission charged by the firm
☐ The personal service
☐ The return on investment
☐ The investment counseling

6. Approximately how long have you been investing through the brokerage firm you are currently using?

☐ about 3 months   ☐ about 9 months
☐ about 6 months   ☐ about 1 year or more

7. How much capital do you have invested?

☐ $500–$750   ☐ $1,000–$1,500
☐ $750–$1,000   ☐ $1,500 or more

Good-bye, and thank you for your cooperation.

Evaluate the above questionnaire.

8. Assume that a medium-sized manufacturer of candy employs you to conduct an observation study in determining children's influence on adults in the purchase of candy.

a. List the variables that are relevant in determining this influence.

b. List the "observations" that might reflect each of these variables.

c. Develop an observation form that will enable you to collect the needed information.

d. Observe three such purchases in a store/supermarket or the location that you specified above.

e. Report your findings.

9. This observation task can be conducted near the vending machines in the cafeteria, library, or business school: The objective is to observe the deliberation time taken at the various machines and determine the factors that influence the deliberation time.

    a. List the variables that would be relevant in achieving the above objective.

    b. List the "observations" that would reflect each of these variables.

    c. Develop an observation form that will enable you to collect the needed information.

    d. Do five such observations and report your findings.

10. Your employer, a commercial marketing research firm, has contracted to perform a study whose objective is the investigation of usage patterns and brand preferences for premixed infant formula among migrant farm workers in the southeastern United States. You have been assigned to develop a suitable questionnaire and method of administration to collect the desired information. What potential problems might arise in design and administration due to the unique nature of the population in question? List these problems and provide solutions. What method of administration will you recommend?

11. Discuss various reasons a researcher might have for using an observation form as opposed to a questionnaire.

PART 5

SAMPLING AND DATA COLLECTION

CHAPTER 15   **Developing the Sampling Plan**

CHAPTER 16   **Determining Sample Size**

CHAPTER 17   **Collecting the Data: Nonsampling Errors and Response Rate Calculation**

© JIM R. BOUNDS/ASSOCIATED PRESS

NASCAR: Driving toward the Hispanic Market

Officials with the National Association for Stock Car Auto Racing (NASCAR) wanted to better understand how to make their sport more popular with America's Hispanic population. In recent years, NASCAR's "Drive for Diversity" campaign has helped produce several promising Latino drivers, including Michael Gallegos, Jesus Hernandez, Ruben Pardo, Rogelio Lopez, and Jose Luis Ramirez. Although the Hispanic fan base is growing, officials needed more information, including the following:

- How popular is the sport with Hispanics compared to the U.S. population as a whole?
- What sports compete with NASCAR for Hispanic attention?
- Are Hispanic NASCAR fans different demographically from nonfans or other NASCAR fans?
- What factors hold back NASCAR's appeal to Hispanics?

But how could the NASCAR managers obtain accurate, projectable results from a population that traditionally has been difficult to survey online effectively because of language, cultural, and technological barriers?

Enter Knowledge Networks, Inc., and its KNOWLEDGEPANEL® online research panel. Using KNOWLEDGEPANEL®, the company conducts syndicated research on a variety of topics, including information useful for answering the questions posed by NASCAR managers. The company's approach is unique because it (1) recruits respondents to the panel using random-digit dialing so that results can be projected to the entire population and (2) provides either laptops or MSNTV devices to households with no Internet access. Because 55% of Spanish-speaking Hispanics needed a laptop to participate, a sizable portion of the Hispanic market would have been excluded from more traditional online surveys.

Using KNOWLEDGEPANEL® members, the company first screened Hispanic respondents for their interest in NASCAR and then administered separate online surveys to NASCAR fans and nonfans. The initial results indicated that while the percentage of Hispanics who are NASCAR fans (38%) is close to the overall percentage of Americans who are fans (42%), only 3 percent of Hispanics are avid ("very interested") fans compared with 11 percent of the U.S. population as a whole. In fact, NASCAR was the 39th ranked sport among Hispanics (it was 5th for the U.S. population as a whole). NASCAR obviously has some work to do if it wants to achieve greater support in the Hispanic community.

Sources: "The Hispanic NASCAR Fan" (2008) provided by Patricia Graham of Knowledge Networks, Inc.; Daniel Soussa, "NASCAR Commissions Research on Hispanic Fanbase," *HispanicBusiness.com*, Oct. 22, 2008, downloaded from http://www.hispanicbusiness.com, Nov. 8, 2008; and Richard Lapchick, "NASCAR Making Strides in Drive for Hispanic Diversity," *ESPN.com*, Oct. 15, 2008, downloaded from http://sports.espn.go.com, Nov. 15, 2008.

Developing the Sampling Plan

Learning Objectives

1. Explain the difference between a census and a sample.
2. List the six steps researchers use to draw a sample of a population.
3. Explain the difference between a parameter and a statistic.
4. Explain the difference between a probability sample and a nonprobability sample.
5. Explain what a judgment sample is and describe its best use and its hazards.
6. Define *quota sample*.
7. Specify the two procedures that distinguish a stratified sample.
8. Cite two reasons researchers might choose to use a stratified sample rather than a simple random sample.
9. Explain the difference between a proportionate stratified sample and a disproportionate stratified sample.
10. List the steps followed in drawing a cluster sample.

Introduction

Once you've specified the problem, developed an appropriate research design, and carefully crafted your data collection instrument, the next step in a marketing research project is to develop the sampling plan. The sampling plan refers to the process of selecting the people or objects (that is, companies, products, etc.) to be surveyed, interviewed, or observed. One way to do this is to collect information from or about each member of the population—this is known as a **census**.

Another way would be to collect information from a portion of the population by taking a **sample** of elements from the larger group and, on the basis of the information collected from the subset, to make projections about what would be true for the population. As we'll see, the ability to make inferences about the overall population based on information collected from only some of the population members depends on how we select the sample.

census
A type of sampling plan in which data are collected from or about each member of a population.

sample
Selection of a subset of elements from a larger group of objects.

Figure 15.1 lays out a six-step process for drawing a sample and collecting data. In this chapter, we focus on the first three steps of the process. In Chapter 16, we'll consider sample size issues.

There are several reasons why working with a sample is often better than trying to conduct a census. First, complete counts on populations of even moderate size are often costly and time consuming. Often, the information will be obsolete by the time the census is completed and the information processed. In some cases, a census is impossible. If, for example, researchers wanted to test the life of a company's electric light bulbs by leaving all its inventory of bulbs on until they burned out, they would have reliable data, but no product to sell.

Finally—and this one may surprise you—a sample might give more accurate results than a census. Conducting a census rather than a sample will often require larger field staffs, which, in turn, introduces greater potential for some kinds of error. As an example, just how excited is a U.S. census worker likely to be about visiting a household on the tenth floor of an old apartment building with no working elevators in a crime-ridden part of town? It's no surprise that the U.S. census tends to under-count people in difficult areas. Because of things like this, the U.S. Bureau of the Census uses sample surveys to check the accuracy of various censuses.

> **Learning Objective**
>
> **1.** Explain the difference between a census and a sample.

DEFINING THE TARGET POPULATION

The first step in the process outlined in Figure 15.1 is to define the target population. By **population**, we mean all the individuals or objects that meet certain requirements for membership in the overall group. We often refer to those who qualify as *population elements*. For example, a study aimed at establishing a demographic profile of frozen pizza eaters requires specifying who is to be considered a frozen pizza eater. Anyone who has ever eaten a frozen pizza? Those who eat at least one frozen pizza a month? Those who eat a certain minimum number of frozen pizzas per month?

You must be very clear and precise in defining the population. For example, does the population consist of individuals, households, business firms, other institutions, credit card transactions, light bulbs on an assembly line, or something else? In making these decisions, it sometimes helps to specify what units are *not* to be included. Geographic boundaries and a time period for the study must always be specified, although additional restrictions are often placed on the elements. When the elements are individuals, for example, the relevant target population may be defined as all those over 18 years of age, or females only, or those with a high school education only, or those who have visited a certain restaurant within the last 30 days. When establishing

> **Learning Objective**
>
> **2.** List the six steps researchers use to draw a sample of a population.
>
> **population**
> All cases that meet designated specifications for membership in the group.

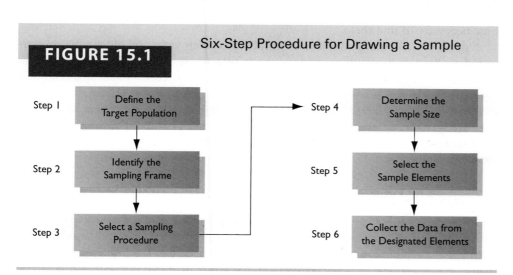

FIGURE 15.1   Six-Step Procedure for Drawing a Sample

Step 1 — Define the Target Population
Step 2 — Identify the Sampling Frame
Step 3 — Select a Sampling Procedure
Step 4 — Determine the Sample Size
Step 5 — Select the Sample Elements
Step 6 — Collect the Data from the Designated Elements

Researchers must carefully define a population in order to get accurate results. Should anyone who has ever eaten a frozen pizza be included when determining the demographics of frozen pizza eaters?

incidence

The percent of a general population or group that qualifies for inclusion in the population.

criteria for population membership, remember to think broadly, as the following classic example illustrates:

> Take the case of the manufacturer of dog food ... who went out and did an intensive market study. He tested the demand for dog food; he tested the package size, the design, the whole advertising program. Then he launched the product with a big campaign, got the proper distribution channels, put it on the market, and had tremendous sales. But two months later, the bottom dropped out—no follow-up sales. So he called in an expert, who took the dog food out to the local pound, put it in front of the dogs—and they would not touch it. For all the big marketing study, no one had tried the product on the dogs.[1]

Somewhere along the way it would have been helpful to have included a study in which dogs comprised the population. That didn't happen, however, probably because it is people who buy dog food and not the dogs themselves. Nevertheless, the careless specification of population elements can lead to bad consequences.

The problem of specifying the geographic boundaries for the target population is sometimes more difficult in international marketing research studies because of the additional complexity an international perspective introduces. For example, urban versus rural areas may be significantly different from each other in various countries. Also, the composition of the population can vary depending on the location within the country. In Chile, for example, the north has a highly centralized Indian population, whereas the south has high concentrations of persons of European descent.

In general, the simpler the definition of the target population, the higher the incidence and the easier and less costly it is to find the sample. **Incidence** refers to the proportion of a general grouping of people or objects that meets the criteria to be a member of the defined population. For example, if we start with the general public in the United States (that is, everybody living in the United States) and we define our study population to be all females living in the United States, the incidence rate is about 51%. Incidence has a direct bearing on the time and cost it takes to complete studies. When incidence is high (i.e., most elements in the general population qualify for the study because only one or very few easily satisfied criteria are used to screen potential respondents), the cost and time to collect data are minimized. Alternatively, as the number of criteria for population membership increases, so do the cost and time necessary to find them.

Exhibit 15.1 shows the number of people ages seven years and older who are estimated to have participated in various sporting activities during 2007. The data in Exhibit 15.1 suggest that it would be more difficult and costly to focus a study on people who play ice hockey, only 2.1 million people, than people who walk for exercise, 89.8 million people. Here's the important thing: You must be precise in specifying exactly what elements are of interest and what elements are to be excluded. A clear statement of research purpose is very important for determining the appropriate elements of interest.

Learning Objective

3.   Explain the difference between a parameter and a statistic.

Parameters versus Statistics

Before we go on, let's revisit why we are drawing a sample in the first place. Our goal with a sample is to determine what is likely to be true for a population based on data obtained from only a subset of that population. We typically work with a sample, rather than a census, because a sample is easier and less costly to obtain than is a census.

© TOM YANO/INDEX STOCK IMAGERY

Exhibit 15.1

Number of U.S. Participants in Various Sports (individuals seven years and older who participated more than once)

Sport	Number (in millions)
Exercise Walking	89.8
Exercising with Equipment	52.8
Swimming	52.3
Camping (vacation/overnight)	47.5
Bowling	43.5
Bicycle Riding	37.4
Fishing	35.3
Workout at Club	33.8
Weight Lifting	33.2
Boating, Motor/Power	31.9
Running/Jogging	30.4
Aerobic Exercising	30.3
Billiards/Pool	29.5
Hiking	28.6
Basketball	24.1
Golf	22.7
Target Shooting	20.9
Hunting with Firearms	19.5
Baseball	14.0
Soccer	13.8
Backpack/Wilderness Camp	13.0
Tennis	12.3
Dart Throwing	12.1
Volleyball	12.0
In-Line Roller Skating	10.7
Yoga	10.7
Scooter Riding	10.6
Skateboarding	10.1
Softball	10.0
Football (tackle)	9.2
Paintball Games	7.4
Mountain Biking (off road)	7.4
Target Shooting—Airgun	6.6
Archery (target)	6.6
Kayaking	5.9
Hunting w/Bow & Arrow	5.7
Skiing (alpine)	5.5
Water Skiing	5.3
Snowboarding	5.1
Mtn/Rock Climbing	4.6
Muzzleloading	3.6
Scuba Diving (open water)	2.4
Wrestling	2.1
Hockey (ice)	2.1
Skiing (cross-country)	1.7
Lacrosse	1.2

Source: ''2007 Participation—Ranked by Total Participation,'' National Sporting Goods Association, downloaded from http://www.nsga.org, August 4, 2008.

MANAGER'S FOCUS

Generating a representative sample is essential to producing useful market research intelligence. The first step in this process—defining the population—is more your responsibility than the researcher's. The definition of the target population should emerge directly from your market information needs. It involves answering the question "From whom do we need information?" Often, the answer to this question involves more than one group.

Target populations can be your current target markets, possible new target markets, former or disgruntled customers, loyal or important customers, key customer groups for competitors, certain types of marketing channel members, boundary-spanning employees within your own organization, or any other group that can provide information you need. Defining the population(s), therefore, is not an abstract statistical process but is instead a practical matter that is based directly on the marketing situations you are facing and the information you need to address those situations. Once you have guided the research provider to a proper definition of the target population(s) (which really should be done before the questionnaire is designed because researchers need to know with whom they will be communicating), your role in the sampling process is largely completed. You should step back and allow the researcher to create an appropriate plan for generating a sample from the target population(s).

---

parameter
A characteristic or measure of a population.

Any population has certain characteristics; these characteristics are called parameters, and we assume that if we could take measurements of these characteristics from all population elements without any kind of error getting into our data that we would know what is true about the population on these parameters. For example, suppose the population for a study consists of all adults living in Phoenix, Arizona. We could describe this population on a number of parameters, including average age, proportion with a college degree, range of incomes, attitude toward a new service offering, awareness of a new retail store that has just opened, and so on. Note that within the population, there is a real quantity or value for each of these parameters, even though we'll never know for sure what these true values are (because as a practical matter, we can never measure something without error).

statistic
A characteristic or measure of a sample.

When we work with a sample drawn from a population, we are attempting to describe the population parameters based on the measures we take from the sample members. That is, we calculate the average age, range of income, or awareness level for the sample as a means of gaining insights into what likely would be true for the population. In short, we work with statistics, which are characteristics or measures of a sample, to draw inferences about the larger population's parameters. When we work with a sample instead of a census, it is likely that our results will be at least a little different than they would have been had we gathered information from or about every member of the population. This difference is known as sampling error.

sampling error
The difference between results obtained from a sample and results that would have been obtained had information been gathered from or about every member of the population.

How big a problem is sampling error? It certainly is something that a researcher must take into account. Fortunately, sampling error can be estimated with relative ease, provided that you've drawn the right kind of sample. Plus, if a researcher wants to decrease sampling error, it is possible to do so—just increase the sample size. Because it is expensive to increase sample size, however, researchers must learn to balance the need for decreased sampling error (which results in greater precision and/or confidence in a statistic—see Chapter 16) against the costs of increasing the sample size.

IDENTIFYING THE SAMPLING FRAME

Once the population has been carefully defined, the next step is to find an adequate **sampling frame**, a listing of population elements from which the actual sample will be drawn. Suppose that the target population for a particular study is all the households in the metropolitan Dallas area. At first glance, the Dallas phone book would seem an easily accessible sampling frame. However, on closer examination, it becomes clear that the telephone directory provides an inaccurate listing of Dallas households, omitting those with unlisted numbers (and those without regular phones—many people now rely solely on cell phones) and double-counting those with multiple listings. People who have recently moved into the area and are not yet listed are also omitted.

sampling frame
The list of population elements from which a sample will be drawn; the list could consist of geographic areas, institutions, individuals, or other units.

Unfortunately, perfect sampling frames usually don't exist except in unusual circumstances. That makes developing an acceptable sampling frame one of a researcher's most important and creative tasks. In Chapter 10, we discussed random-digit dialing as one means of overcoming the lack of a solid sampling frame for telephone interview studies. Sometimes researchers sample geographic areas and then subsample within these areas when, say, the target population is individuals but a current, accurate list of appropriate individuals is not available—we'll have more to say on this later in this chapter.

Much of the time, researchers work with sampling frames that have been developed by companies that specialize in compiling databases and then selling the names, addresses, phone numbers, and/or e-mail addresses. For example, infoUSA, a database company located in Omaha, Nebraska, employs over 600 data compilers who gather information from a broad range of sources. Its list of millions of businesses is updated regularly based on telephone directory listings, annual reports, government data, the business press, and other sources. The company calls each business in its database to verify the accuracy of the information. As a result, researchers could easily develop a sampling frame for a fairly specific population of businesses, because lists can be screened by any information in the database, including industry, geographic location, size of company, credit rating, and so on. Research Window 15.1 provides information about several of the approaches used by Survey Sampling International to develop samples.

MANAGER'S FOCUS

A quick note about terminology might be helpful here. Nonresearchers commonly confuse the term "population parameter" with the criteria used to define the target population. For example, the target population might be defined as all women between the ages of 21 and 30 in Los Angeles, California. The criteria for defining this population are gender, age, and geographic location, but these are *not* population parameters. The population parameters are other characteristics about the population that we want to estimate. For example, we may want to estimate things like (a) income level, (b) educational attainment level, (c) attitudes toward brands in a specific product category, or (d) frequency of purchasing our brand in the last three months. These are the population parameters among Los Angeles women between the ages of 21 and 30 that we would like to estimate by generating statistics from our sample.

We have actually discussed population parameters at previous points without ever using the term. The information needs you identify when formulating the marketing problem as well as the variables you specify when creating dummy tables are in reality the population parameters you want to estimate in your study. As a result, in the earlier research stages you will have provided the researcher with the necessary input to understand what the relevant population parameters are.

research window 15.1

Survey Sampling International (SSI)

SSI specializes in the sample selection process across several methods of administration and across numerous countries.

Mail Samples

Using information collected from telephone white pages and other sources, SSI has developed the largest available national database of U.S. households. Samples can be drawn for specific geographic areas using the systematic sampling approach. The company notes that its deliverable rate is about 80% on mail surveys after accounting for wrong addresses.

Telephone Samples

SSI was one of the early innovators in telephone research products, including random-digit dialing (RDD). The company offers RDD in 21 countries for consumer and business samples as well as RDD for wireless/mobile telephones in nine countries in North America and Western Europe. Samples can be developed based on age, income, and ethnic background.

Online Samples

SSI manages proprietary online communities of research respondents in 22 countries including the United States (www.surveyspot.com) and China (www.opinionworld.cn). Very specific samples can be developed based on respondent purchases, age, or interests.

Source: Developed from information downloaded from http://www.surveysampling.com, August 6, 2008.

Learning Objective

4. Explain the difference between a probability sample and a nonprobability sample.

SELECTING A SAMPLING PROCEDURE

The third step in the procedure for drawing a sample involves selecting a particular sampling procedure—unless researchers have decided to attempt a census. For small populations of individuals, stores, or other objects, a census probably makes sense. Even if some individuals can't be reached or don't respond, if the number in the population is less than 400–500, it is usually reasonable to attempt to gather information from or about each population element. This is not a hard and fast rule, however. In some cases, it might be desirable to conduct a census when numbers are much higher, or to draw a sample when the population size is smaller. As is true for most aspects of the marketing research process, the needs of the particular research situation must be taken into account.

Most of the time, researchers find it necessary to draw a sample from the population. As we mentioned before, if managers and researchers are interested in what would likely be true for the whole population, as opposed to just the population elements that made it into the sample, it is important to draw the right kind of sample. Sampling techniques can be divided into two broad categories: probability and nonprobability samples. In a probability sample, each member of the target population has a *known, nonzero* chance of being included in the sample. The chances of each member of the target population being included in the sample may not be equal, but everyone has some chance of being included. Plus, there is a random component, not under the control of the researcher, in how population elements are selected for the sample.

With nonprobability samples, on the other hand, there is no way of estimating the probability that any target population element will be included in the sample. Thus, there is no way of ensuring that the sample is representative of the population. All nonprobability samples rely on personal judgment somewhere in the sample-selection process rather than on a random process to select sample members. While these judgments may sometimes result in good estimates of a population characteristic, there is no way of determining objectively if the sample is adequate. It is only when the target population elements have been selected with known probabilities that it is possible to evaluate the precision of a sample result. Knowing the precision of a result based on a sample is what allows us to draw inferences about the population from which the sample was drawn. For this reason, probability sampling is usually considered to be better than nonprobability sampling.

Samples can also be categorized by whether they are fixed or sequential samples, each of which can apply to both probability and nonprobability samples. In fixed samples, the sample size is decided before the study begins, and all the necessary information is collected before the results are analyzed. In a sequential sample, the number of elements to be sampled is not decided in advance but is determined by a series of decisions as the data are collected. For example, if the evidence is not conclusive with an initial small sample, more observations will be made. If the results are still inconclusive, the size of the sample will be expanded further. At each stage, a decision is made as to whether more information should be collected or whether the evidence is now sufficient to permit a conclusion. The sequential sample allows trends in the data to be evaluated as the data are being collected. It also allows researchers to reduce costs when it is clear that additional data would add little information.

Figure 15.2 shows the basic types of samples broken into two categories, nonprobability and probability samples. These basic sample types can be combined into more complex sampling plans when necessary. If you understand the basic types, though, you should be able to understand the more complex designs. In the following sections, we describe the different types of sampling plans.

probability sample
A sample in which each target population element has a known, nonzero chance of being included in the sample.

nonprobability sample
A sample that relies on personal judgment in the element selection process.

fixed sample
A sample for which size is determined in advance and needed information is collected from the designated elements.

sequential sample
A sample formed on the basis of a series of successive decisions.

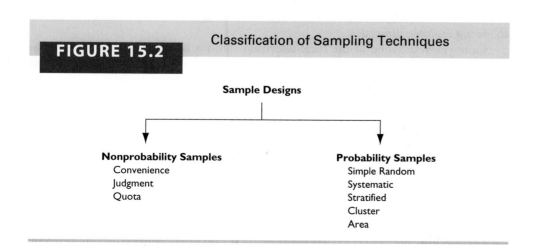

FIGURE 15.2   Classification of Sampling Techniques

Sample Designs

Nonprobability Samples
Convenience
Judgment
Quota

Probability Samples
Simple Random
Systematic
Stratified
Cluster
Area

NONPROBABILITY SAMPLES

Nonprobability samples involve personal judgment somewhere in the selection process. Sometimes the researcher chooses who should be included in the sample; sometimes field workers choose who they should approach; and sometimes the choices involve when and where to collect data. With all nonprobability samples, however, objectivity about which population elements get into the sample is missing and not all population elements have an opportunity to be included. As a result, it is impossible to assess the degree of sampling error. Without knowing how much sampling error results from a particular sampling procedure, we can't gauge the accuracy of the estimates with any precision. As a result, we know the results for the particular elements that made it into our sample, but we can't say anything at all about what would have been true for the overall population. Managers may still choose to act on the basis of results from nonprobability samples, but they are taking risks when they do so.

Convenience Samples

convenience sample
A nonprobability sample in which population elements are included in the sample because they were readily available.

With **convenience samples**, the name says it all: Inclusion in the sample is a matter of convenience. People or objects are selected for the sample because they happen to be in the right place at the right time to be included. Convenience samples are easy—just go out and find a location where lots of people who are likely to be members of the population are located and do interviews or pass out surveys. Lots of organizations put surveys on Web sites so that people who visit the sites can respond electronically—but what about people who don't visit the Web site? Sometimes radio and television programs invite their audiences to call a certain telephone number or to go to a particular Web site to respond to the "question of the day" or to vote for some option. All of these examples, and many more, amount to convenience samples. They are typically quick and easy ways of collecting data. If there is no need to ensure that the sample adequately represents the population, a convenience sample is probably the way to go. For instance, convenience samples are commonly used with exploratory research, where the goal is to generate insights or to develop hypotheses.

Problems arise, however, when people begin to draw important conclusions based on data from convenience samples. The main problem is that we have no way of knowing if those included in a convenience sample are representative of the larger target population. As a simple example, passing out surveys to passersby at the corner of Manvel Avenue and Tenth Street in a certain city during business hours on a Tuesday means that anyone who happened *not* to be at that corner during that time period had no chance of participating. It's very likely that important points of view may have been missed. Or maybe those points of view *were* represented—the problem is that we can never know for sure. As a result, we can't assume that the results of the study would apply to the whole population. And using bigger numbers of respondents doesn't necessarily make the sample any more representative, as the following example illustrates.

Some years ago, one of the local television stations in Madison, Wisconsin, featured a daily public opinion poll on topics of interest to the local community. The polls were labeled the "Pulse of Madison" and were conducted in the following way. During the 6 o'clock news every evening, the station would ask a question about some controversial issue to which people could reply with a yes or no. Persons in favor would call one number; persons opposed would call another. The number of viewers calling each number was recorded electronically. Percentages of those in favor and opposed would then be reported on the 10 o'clock news. With some 500 to 1,000 people calling in their opinions each night, the local television commentator seemed to interpret these results as reflecting the true state of opinion in the community.

On one 6 o'clock broadcast, the following question was posed: "Do you think the drinking age in Madison should be lowered to 18?" The existing legal limit was 21. Almost 4,000 people called in that night with 78% in favor of lowering the drinking

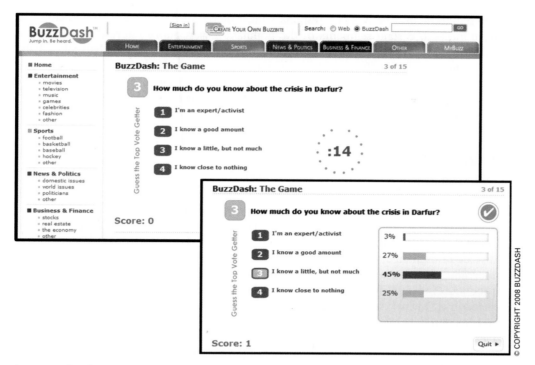

An example of a convenience sample could be asking a reader or viewer to go to a particular Web site to respond to the "question of the day" or to vote for some option.

MANAGER'S FOCUS

Each of the sampling methods discussed in this chapter can be useful in the right circumstances. What you need to understand, then, are the situations in which each is appropriate. You have just learned that for each type of nonprobability sample there is no way to know or estimate the likelihood of selecting or not selecting specific population members for inclusion in the sample. As a result, you have no way of assessing sampling error. This does not mean nonprobability samples are unrepresentative. It is possible for them to be highly representative, but the likelihood of this occurring is lower and there is simply no way to assess this likelihood.

Consequently, nonprobability samples are most useful when it is not necessary to assume responses came from a representative sample. This is only the case when we are conducting exploratory research where our primary aim is to gain tentative insights about what might be happening or important in a market situation. Nonprobability samples should be avoided when the purpose is to describe or profile a population or to identify cause-and-effect relationships between variables. In order to be confident in our descriptions of a population or in our inferences about what marketing variables cause specific outcomes, we need information about the

probability of population members being included in the sample. This means probability samples are more useful when conducting descriptive or causal studies.

Much too commonly, nonprobability samples, particularly convenience samples, are used in descriptive and causal studies in an effort to save time and money. If a sampling frame is available from which a probability sample can be drawn, it is unwise to trade off information about sample representativeness in favor of time or monetary savings. It is dangerous to make inferences about a population based on data from a nonprobability sample. If you choose to do so, you should understand that the little bit of money saved by employing a nonprobability sample may be offset by the costs of taking inappropriate marketing actions based on imprecise statistical estimates. In the long run, it is in your organization's best interest to invest in a quality probability sample to facilitate effective decision making. If you face a situation where it is very difficult or impossible to generate a probability sample, you should at least invest the time and money necessary to compare your nonprobability sample's characteristics against external information sources (such as census data) to determine how representative it is on key demographic or other characteristics.

age requirement. Surely 4,000 responses must be representative! Wrong. As you may have guessed, certain segments of the population were more interested in the issue than others. It was no surprise to later learn that university students had taken half-hour phone shifts on an arranged basis. Each person would call the yes number, hang up, call again, hang up, and so on, until it was the next person's turn. Thus, neither the size of the sample nor the proportion favoring the age change was surprising. The sample was simply not representative.

Judgment Samples

With judgment samples, the sample elements are handpicked by the researcher because it is expected that they can serve the research purpose. Procter & Gamble (P&G) used this method once when it advertised for "interns" ages 13 to 17 from the area around its Cincinnati headquarters. The company's food and beverage division hired this group of teenagers to serve as a kind of consumer panel. Working 10 hours a week in exchange for $1,000 and a trip to a concert, they reviewed television commercials, visited the mall with P&G managers to study retail displays, tested new products, and discussed their purchasing behavior. By selecting the panel members through a "hiring" process rather than randomly, the company could focus on traits it considered helpful—for example, the teenagers' ability to articulate their views clearly—at the risk that their views might not be representative of their age group.[2]

The snowball sample is a judgment sample that is sometimes used to sample special populations—populations with a low incidence rate within the general public, for example. This type of judgment sample relies on the researcher's ability to locate an initial set of respondents with the desired characteristics. These individuals are then used as informants to identify others with the desired characteristics.

Imagine, for example, that a company wanted to determine the desirability of a certain product that would enable deaf people to communicate over telephone lines. Researchers might begin by identifying some key people in the deaf community and asking them for names of other deaf people who might be used in the study. Those asked to participate would also be asked for names of others who might cooperate. In this way, the sample "snowballs" by getting larger as participants identify still other possible respondents.

As long as the researcher is at the early stages of research when ideas or insights are being sought—and when the researcher realizes its limitations—the judgment sample is perfectly appropriate. In some cases, it may be about the only way to develop a sample of people who meet specific criteria that don't occur frequently and/or cannot easily be observed. A judgment sample becomes dangerous, however, when it is used in descriptive or causal studies and its weaknesses are ignored.

Quota Samples

Researchers sometimes use another kind of nonprobability sample, the quota sample, in order to build a sample that mirrors the population on one or more important aspects. For example, imagine that you have been asked to draw a sample of 1,000 undergraduate students for short personal interviews on a college campus. If you used a quota sample, you'd make sure that your sample contained the right proportions of freshmen, sophomores, juniors, and seniors. You might also want to ensure that you had the right proportions of men and women in the sample, or maybe you'd want to have the right proportions of students from the various colleges or majors across campus. Again, the goal would be to build a sample that looked like the larger population of students.

Suppose that class and sex were the two most important variables and that 30% of the undergraduates on campus were freshmen, 25% were sophomores, 25% were juniors, and 20% were seniors. Furthermore, across all the classes, half of the students were men. Your quota sample would require that 300 respondents were first-year

---

students (150 men, 150 women), 250 were sophomores (125 men, 125 women), 250 were juniors (again, 125 men, 125 women), and 200 were seniors (100 men, 100 women). If you had hired interviewers, you would complete the project by giving each interviewer a quota—thus, the name *quota sample*—specifying the types of undergraduates he or she is to contact. For example, one interviewer might be instructed to find and collect data from 50 students according to the following quota:

- 20 freshmen—5 male and 15 female

- 15 sophomores—10 male and 5 female

- 10 juniors—5 male and 5 female

- 5 seniors—2 male and 3 female

A quota sample of students on a college campus should be sure to include equal proportions of freshmen, sophomores, juniors, and seniors.

Across all interviewers, the total number of student respondents would add up to 1,000, and if your interviewers successfully reached their quotas, the proportions in the sample will match those in the population. Note, however, that the specific sample elements (i.e., students) to be used would be left to the discretion of the individual interviewers. That's what makes a quota sample a nonprobabilistic sampling plan. And even though the resulting sample *looks* like the overall population on two key aspects, it may not accurately reflect other aspects of the population.

The key problem with quota samples and other types of nonprobabilistic sampling plans is that biases usually influence the selection of population elements to be included in the sample. It's no surprise that people would rather interview their friends and neighbors, conduct in-home surveys in nicer parts of town, or collect data in a convenient location with lots of potential respondents (e.g., a shopping mall, airline terminal, or business district). These sorts of biases may or may not actually change the results of the study, but we don't know and can't correct for them when analyzing the data. When the sample elements are selected objectively, on the other hand, using a probabilistic sample, researchers have certain tools they can rely on to make the question of whether a particular sample is representative less difficult. With probability samples, we rely on the sampling procedure and not on the composition of the specific sample to solve the problem of representation.

PROBABILITY SAMPLES

In a probability sample, we can calculate the likelihood that any given population element will be included, because the final sample elements are selected objectively by a specific process and not according to the whims of the researcher or field-worker. Since the elements are selected objectively, we can make inferences to the larger population based on the results from the sample. With a probability sample, we can assess the likely amount of sampling error, the difference between the sample results and what would have been true had we taken measures from all population members. In this section, we'll introduce several different types of probability samples, starting with the most well known, the simple random sample.

ETHICAL DILEMMA 15.1

You are designing an experiment to compare the effectiveness of different types of commercials and need to recruit a large group of subjects of varying ages to watch television for an hour every night for a week. You approach your local church minister and tell him that you will make a donation to the church restoration fund for every member of the congregation who agrees to participate.

- When might incentives be coercive?
- Is it ethical to coerce people to participate in research?
- Will the quality of the data suffer from the coercive recruitment of participants?

Simple Random Samples

simple random sample
A probability sampling plan in which each unit included in the population has a known and equal chance of being selected for the sample.

Most people have had experience with **simple random samples** either in beginning statistics courses or in reading about results from such samples in newspapers or magazines. In a simple random sample, each unit included in the sample has a known and equal chance of being selected for study, and every combination of population elements is a sample possibility. For example, if we wanted a simple random sample of all students enrolled in a particular college, we might have a computer pick a sample randomly from a list of students in that college.

Simple random samples and other types of probability samples depend on the sampling distribution of the particular statistic being considered for the ability to draw inferences about the larger population (see Appendix 15A at the end of this chapter for more details). Even though any particular sample of population elements may include some unusual or extreme cases, the principles underlying the sampling distribution of the statistic allow us to establish the range within which the population parameter is likely to fall if all cases in the population were considered. This range is known as the *confidence interval*; we discuss the calculation of confidence intervals in Chapter 19.

It is important that you recognize the difference between "random" in a scientific sense and "random" in an everyday sense. For many people, a "random sample" would simply mean walking down the street and passing out surveys to people they don't know, or going through the telephone book, haphazardly calling numbers "at random." To a researcher, however, a "random sample" is one in which the particular population elements are selected by some objective process outside the control of the researcher. Believe it or not, researchers have been known to roll dice, flip coins, or draw numbers out of a hat in order to create the randomness necessary with probabilistic samples. For simple random samples, in which each sampling element is selected randomly, random number tables generated by computers were often used in the past by researchers to select the sample. Now it is more likely that the computer will use an internal random-number generator to select the simple random sample.

The ability to draw a simple random sample depends to a great extent on the availability of a good sampling frame. For some populations, this is no problem—for example, imagine that you needed to conduct a study among *Fortune* magazine's list of the 500 largest corporations in the United States. The list is readily available, and a simple random sample of these firms could easily be selected. For many other target populations of interest (for example, all families living in a particular city), a list of population elements simply doesn't exist, and researchers often resort to other sampling schemes.

If the population is moderate to large in size, you'll want the computer to randomly select the sample from the sampling frame, so having a digital version of the sampling frame is important. Fortunately, this is commonly the case. If a computer file containing the sampling frame is not available, researchers again will likely want to utilize another form of probabilistic sampling plan.

Systematic Samples

Suppose that you were asked to conduct telephone interviews with 250 college students at a particular school and that the university published a directory that contained the names and telephone numbers of all 5,000 of its students. If you had access to a computer file containing the information, it would be a relatively easy matter to draw a simple random sample from the list. If you don't have such a computer file, however, drawing a simple random sample isn't so simple. It is difficult to randomly select each sample member.

systematic sample
A probability sampling plan in which every *k*th element in the population is selected for the sample pool after a random start.

A **systematic sample** offers an easy, but very effective, solution. With a systematic sample, researchers randomly select the first population element to be included in the sample and then select every *k*th element following it in the sampling frame. In our example, let's assume for a moment that we'll be able to interview all 250 college students who are selected for the sample. We'll end up interviewing one out of every 20 students on campus (5,000/250 = 20). So, you would randomly select one of the first 20 names in the student directory, then count down 20 names on the list and select that name, count down 20 more names and select that name, and so on, until you have gone through the entire directory. (It may not sound like it, but this is *much* easier than trying to randomly select each member of the sample by hand.)

So what makes this a probabilistic sampling plan? It's because the first element is randomly selected, and every other element selected for the sample is a function of the first element, which makes them all randomly selected, in effect. And if there is any sort of natural order within the sampling frame, using a systematic sample may well produce a sample that is more representative of the larger population than would a simple random sample. Imagine, for example, that our student directory groups the students by class; All first-year students are presented in the first section, in alphabetical order, followed by sophomores, juniors, and seniors. A systematic sample will necessarily produce a sample with the right proportions of student names drawn from each class; that won't necessarily happen with a simple random sample.

Calculating the **sampling interval** (that is, k, the number of names to count when selecting the sample members) is easy—sort of. In general, we simply divide the number of population elements in the sampling frame by the number of elements that we need to draw to obtain the sample size we want. In the example above, $k = 5,000/250$, so our sampling interval was 20. Here's where it gets a little tricky, though. Remember how we assumed that we could conduct telephone interviews with all 250 students selected for the sample? For lots of reasons, it almost never works out that way.

sampling interval
The number of population elements to count (k) when selecting the sample members in a systematic sample.

As we discuss in the following chapter, it's a relatively straightforward matter for researchers to decide how large or small a sample they need in a given research situation. Someone has decided that in the current situation a sample size of 250 students is sufficient. If we select only 250 students for our sample, however, it is almost a certainty that we'll end up with fewer than 250 respondents—maybe a whole lot fewer. Why? Some people won't be home to answer their telephones, even if we try multiple times to reach them. Others will have changed telephone numbers since the directory was published. And some people will refuse to answer our questions because they are too busy or just don't care to help. As a result, in almost all cases we need to start with a larger number of population elements in our initial sample pool in order to end up with the desired sample size. We refer to the total number of elements to be selected for inclusion in the initial sample pool as **total sampling elements (TSE)**.

total sampling elements (TSE)
The number of population elements that must be drawn from the population and included in the initial sample pool in order to end up with the desired sample size.

The notion of TSE is general and applies to any type of sample, not just systematic samples. Anytime it is necessary to select a larger initial sample in order to reach the necessary sample size, the calculation of TSE becomes important. Calculating TSE typically requires making predictions about the proportion of sample elements that (a) have incorrect contact information (telephone number, e-mail address, or mailing address); (b) are ineligible because they don't meet criteria for inclusion in the sample; (c) refuse to participate; and (d) cannot be contacted, even after multiple tries.

The formula for TSE looks like this:

$$\text{total sampling elements}(TSE) = \frac{\text{sample size}}{(1 - BCI)(1 - I)(1 - R)(1 - NC)}$$

where BCI = estimated proportion of bad contact information (wrong telephone numbers, mailing or e-mail addresses), I = estimated proportion of ineligible elements in the sampling frame (that is, people or entities that don't meet the criteria to be population members but were included in the sampling frame), R = estimated proportion of refusals, and NC = estimated proportion of elements that cannot be contacted after repeated attempts. The challenge, as you might imagine, is to estimate in advance the proportions needed for the formula in a given situation.

Returning to the current problem, we need a sample of 250 respondents from the 5,000 students in the directory. Even if the directory is updated annually, we should assume that some of the telephone numbers won't be working, because some people may have left school and others will have changed telephone numbers. Let's assume that percentage is 15%; thus, $BCI = 0.15$. Because some of the people who have left school, and therefore are no longer eligible to be included in the population, might still have working telephone numbers, we also need to include an ineligibility proportion. That proportion is likely to be low, however, so we'll set it at 2% ($I = 0.02$). Refusal rates aren't typically all that high, but we want to be conservative to ensure that we end up with at least 250 respondents, so we'll set the refusal rate at 20% ($R = 0.20$). Finally, and this is often the biggest issue of all—we'll assume that we won't be able to reach 30% of the people selected for the sample, even after trying three to four times at different times of the day and evening; thus, $NC = 0.30$. Putting it all together, we need to draw a total of 536 students from the population in order to obtain a sample size of 250:

$$\text{total sampling elements (TSE)} = \frac{250}{(1 - 0.15)(1 - 0.02)(1 - 0.20)(1 - 0.30)} = 536$$

Once we know how many elements we need to draw from the population, it's a simple matter to determine the sampling interval:

$$\text{sampling interval} = \frac{\text{number of elements in the sampling frame}}{\text{total sampling elements}} = \frac{5,000}{536} = 9.3$$

To draw the sample, you would randomly select one of the first 9 names in the directory, perhaps using a random-number generator on a computer or calculator or even something as straightforward as pulling a number out of a hat. Once that name is selected, every ninth name following the starting name will be drawn. Since drawing every ninth name will result in a list of 556 students instead of the 536 that you want, you might choose to count down 9 names to get the second sample element, another 9 names to get the third sample element—and then count down 10 names to get the fourth. It doesn't matter, provided that you follow the same pattern throughout the whole sampling frame (that is, down 9, down 9, down 10, down 9, down 9, down 10, and so on); each name after the first is still a function of the position of the randomly selected first sample element.

Stratified Samples

stratified sample
A probability sample in which (1) the population is divided into mutually exclusive and exhaustive subsets, and (2) a simple random sample of elements is chosen independently from each group or subset.

Our goal in drawing a probabilistic sample from a population is to describe the population's characteristics, or parameters, based on statistics calculated from the sample. Stratified samples sometimes allow researchers to do this more efficiently and/or more effectively. A **stratified sample** is a probability sample in which (1) the population is divided into mutually exclusive and exhaustive subgroups (that is, each population element fits into one—and only one—subgroup) and (2) samples are chosen from each of the subgroups.

Suppose that there are two major universities in your particular geographic region. The schools compete in many different areas: for budget dollars from the state, for students, for recognition, for victories across a host of different sporting events. Imagine that you have been hired to measure the image of one of the schools among residents in the region who are 18 years or older and have lived in the region for at least one year. You have developed a telephone survey with appropriate measures and now must draw a sample. One possibility for accomplishing this is to draw a simple random sample from the population of residents, collect the necessary data, and calculate sample statistics. In our randomly chosen set of respondents, we'll have some who went to the school in question, some who went to the rival school, and some who didn't go to college at all or went somewhere else. As a result, we'll probably have some who hold very positive perceptions of the school, some who are likely to hold more negative perceptions of the school, and others who fall in between the extremes, respectively. In short, the variation in the measured image of the school is likely to be quite large.

As we'll see in the following chapter, as the variance of a population parameter gets larger, the required sample size for reaching a desired margin of sampling error also gets larger, all else equal. In our case, to get the same level of precision, we'll have to include more residents in our sample than we would if the variation in the image of the university was smaller. A stratified sample, however, provides a way for us to achieve the same precision in our results with fewer respondents, which can reduce costs significantly.

Learning Objective

8. Cite two reasons researchers might choose to use a stratified sample rather than a simple random sample.

Here's how it works. We would first divide the population (as defined above) into three groups: (1) those who attended the target university, (2) those who attended the rival university, and (3) those who attended neither university. It is reasonable to expect that the vast majority of those who attended the target university will hold positive perceptions of the university and that the variation in their responses will be quite low (that is, everybody feels about the same way about the school). Similarly, it is reasonable to expect that the vast majority of those who attended the rival university will hold more negative perceptions of the target university and that variation in their scores will also be reasonably low (again, there would be little difference in the scores within the group). Scores within the third group might be all over the place, which would make the variation within that group potentially much larger. This is the important part: Because the variances of image scores within the first two groups are much lower than for the overall population, the necessary sample size within those groups goes down considerably, making the total sample size decrease, and reducing costs.

If you are having trouble grasping why this works, think about it like this: If you had a room full of people who absolutely loved the target university across every dimension and each would provide the highest image score possible if asked, how many people in the room would you need to talk with to understand how everyone in the room felt about the school? *Only one.* That's right, you'd only need feedback from one person in that group. Stratified samples work on the principle of building subgroups of population elements that are as similar as possible within the groups on the attribute being assessed so that efficiencies can be gained.

There's one other key reason that stratified samples might be used, and this has more to do with effectiveness than efficiency. Sometimes it is necessary to work with stratified samples as a means of ensuring that particular categories of respondents are included in the final sample. Suppose, for example, that a manufacturer of diamond rings wants to conduct a study of sales of the product by social class. Unless special precautions are taken, it is likely that the upper class—which represents only about 3% of the total population—will not be represented at all, or will be represented by too few cases. Yet this may be an extremely important segment to the ring manufacturer. It is often true in marketing that a small subset of the population of interest will account for a large proportion of the behavior of interest—for example, consumption of the product. It then becomes critical that this subgroup be adequately represented in the sample. Stratified sampling is one way of ensuring adequate representation from each subgroup of interest. This is a common approach and is especially useful when an important subgroup makes up only a small portion of the population.

Learning Objective

9. Explain the difference between a proportionate stratified sample and a disproportionate stratified sample.

Proportionate and Disproportionate Stratified Samples With a *proportionate stratified sample*, the number of observations in the total sample is allocated among the subgroups in proportion to the *relative* number of elements in each subgroup in the population. If a subgroup contained one-fifth of all the population elements, then one-fifth of the overall sample should come from that subgroup, and so on. With a *disproportionate stratified sample*, however, greater efficiencies with stratified samples can be achieved. As noted, smaller samples are needed from subgroups with less variation on the parameter being estimated, and costs are lowered because the overall sample size is reduced. On the other hand, if the budget allows for, say, 1,000 telephone interviews, and the researcher wants to use all possible respondents, subgroups with greater variation can be sampled more than proportionately to their relative size, which increases the precision of results for that subgroup and for the overall sample. Thus, the efficiencies associated with stratified samples can be taken in the form of reduced costs or increased precision in the results. Either way, the outcomes can be better with a stratified sample than with a simple random sample. It is important to note, however, that these efficiencies are possible only when meaningful subgroups can be identified and when variability is substantially reduced within one or more subgroups.

Cluster Samples

Learning Objective

10. List the steps followed in drawing a cluster sample.

cluster sample
A probability sampling plan in which (1) the parent population is divided into mutually exclusive and exhaustive subsets and (2) a random sample of one or more subsets (clusters) is selected.

Cluster samples are another probability sampling technique often used by researchers. Cluster sampling is similar to stratified sampling in that the population is divided into mutually exclusive and exhaustive subgroups, but the similarities stop there. With cluster sampling, one or more subgroups are randomly selected, and either all the elements included in those subgroups are selected for the sample (*one-stage cluster sampling*) or a sample of elements is selected probabilistically from the randomly selected subgroups (*two-stage cluster sampling*). Clusters can be set up based on a variety of approaches as illustrated in Exhibit 15.2.

With stratified sampling, a sample of elements is selected from each subgroup. Not so with cluster sampling. This has important implications for the composition of the subgroups, or clusters. Since only some clusters will be randomly selected, it is important that the full range of the key variables being studied be represented in each cluster. Each cluster should reflect the diversity of the whole population. The goal with cluster sampling is thus to have clusters that are as heterogeneous as possible on the key issues. That way, no matter which cluster(s) are randomly selected, the full range is represented. (Recall that we wanted the subgroups to be as homogeneous within each subgroup as possible with stratified sampling.)

Exhibit 15.2	**Possible Clusters to Use to Sample Various Types of Population Elements**
Population Elements	**Possible Clusters**
College students	Colleges
Elementary school students	Schools
Manufacturing firms	Counties
	Localities
Airline travelers	Airports
	Planes
Hospital patients	Hospitals
Government workers	Government buildings

Systematic sampling, which we discussed earlier, is technically a form of cluster sampling. Once the sampling interval (*k*) is calculated, the population is effectively broken into *k* clusters, and one of these clusters is selected when the initial element is randomly selected. For example, if the sampling interval $k = 2$, we've split the population into two clusters (that is, cluster 1 = first, third, fifth, seventh, etc., name in the list; cluster 2 = second, fourth, sixth, eighth, etc., name in the list), and we'll end up with one or the other cluster based on whether the first or second name is randomly selected, perhaps by a coin flip.

Area Samples In every probability sampling plan discussed so far, we need a list of population elements in order to draw the sample. What can a researcher do when such a list isn't available? What about when a sampling frame is available, but personal interviews are to be conducted and the costs of traveling from one interview to the next would be prohibitive? In both of these situations, an area sample might be the best choice.

Suppose, for example, that you needed to do a series of 1,000 personal interviews with the residents of a town or city near you. Directories of all those living in the city at that particular moment in time simply do not exist: People move, others die, new households are constantly being formed. Even though accurate lists of families most likely won't be available, you will probably have access to a tool essential for area sampling, a map of the city. An **area sample** is a form of cluster sample in which geographic areas (city blocks, neighborhoods, housing additions, etc.) serve as primary sampling units. In our situation, we would begin by identifying on the map the geographic areas in which families reside, breaking them into a number of clusters. It is best if the clusters contain approximately the same number of families, but it doesn't always work out that way. Once the clusters (again, geographic areas) have been identified, one or more areas are randomly selected.

With a *one-stage area sample*, researchers would attempt to contact each family living in the selected areas, perhaps by knocking on doors or by collecting addresses and attempting to match names to the addresses for initial contact by telephone or mail. With *two-stage area sampling*, researchers draw a probabilistic sample from each of the randomly selected areas.

How well do area samples meet the criterion of having heterogeneity on the important parameters within each area cluster? Often, not too well. People tend to live near other people who are similar to themselves, which means that any particular area in a city probably won't represent the whole city very well. This problem can be addressed somewhat by drawing multiple clusters/areas, but it doesn't make the problem go away. Still, the cost efficiencies of working with only a few clusters rather than a simple random sample of the whole population may outweigh representativeness issues. As with many other issues in marketing research, the key is to use common sense about the best approach in a specific situation.

area sample
A form of cluster sampling in which areas (for example, census tracts, blocks) serve as the primary sampling units. The population is divided into mutually exclusive and exhaustive areas using maps, and a random sample of areas is selected.

COMBINING SAMPLE TYPES

As you can probably tell by now, sample design is a very detailed subject. Our discussion has concentrated on only the basic types of samples. You should be aware that the basic types can be, and are, combined in large-scale field studies to produce some very complex designs. For example, it is possible to have several levels of stratification—such as by geographic area and density of population—precede several stages of cluster sampling. Research Window 15.2 discusses how Nielsen uses multiple sampling approaches in its people meter research to produce ratings for television programs.

You won't be a sampling expert based on the limited information we've provided in this chapter, but you should have a basic understanding of some key issues and the basic types of sampling plans.

research window 15.2

How Nielsen Develops a Sample of Households

Nielsen TV families are a cross-section of households from all over the United States. We carefully draw our samples in a way that offers every American household with a television an equal chance of being selected.

Sample design, selection, and maintenance for both the national and local market samples are the responsibility of highly skilled statisticians—Nielsen's guardians of sample quality. They stay abreast of new sampling methods developed by survey organizations, the U.S. Census Bureau, and other government agencies.

Our samples include homes from all 50 states, from cities to towns, from suburbs to rural areas. We have homeowners and apartment dwellers—some with children and some without—across a broad range of demographic categories. We include people of all ages, income groups, geographic areas, ethnicities, and educational levels—all in proportion to their presence in the population at large. Once homes are selected and their occupants agree to participate, we take great care to protect their identity and privacy, and no data about individuals or specific households are ever disclosed.

Can families volunteer to have their home chosen by Nielsen? While we'd like to accept volunteers in our panels, we are unable to do so. To include volunteers would violate basic laws of random sampling practice and skew our results. A truly representative sample of the population can only be generated using statistical methods of selection.

Selecting Households

Selecting a representative sample of homes is vital to collecting data that mirror the population's viewing habits. We select households through one of two different methods: geographic selection (area probability sampling) in the national sample and larger markets, and randomly generated telephone numbers (Total Telephone Frame) in smaller markets.

For area probability sampling, Nielsen's statistical research department begins with broad, U.S. Census-defined geographic areas. We dispatch field representatives to identify each and every housing unit in these areas, regardless of size or accessibility. Ultimately, we narrow the selection down to individual, randomly selected housing units. Using this method, all households have an equal probability of selection into the sample. This allows for complete coverage of the country, since no homes are excluded by design.

For Total Telephone Frame sampling, Nielsen's statistical research department uses random digit-dialing to generate a call list that includes both published and unpublished telephone numbers in a Designated Market Area (DMA). Rather than using recordings, our call center staffs in Florida and Kentucky personally make multiple attempts to reach households, ensuring that they have a chance to be included in the sample.

Source: "Sampling the Population," downloaded from http://www.nielsenmedia.com, July 15, 2008.

SUMMARY

Learning Objective 1

Explain the difference between a census and a sample.

Taking information from or about every member of a target population is called a census. A sample is a portion of the population taken from the larger group.

Learning Objective 2

List the six steps researchers use to draw a sample of a population.

The six steps researchers use in drawing a sample are (1) define the target population, (2) identify the sampling frame, (3) select a sampling procedure,

(4) determine the sample size,
(5) select the sample elements, and
(6) collect the data from the designated elements.

Learning Objective 3

Explain the difference between a parameter and a statistic.

A parameter is a characteristic of the population; if it were possible to take measures from all population members without error, we could arrive at the true value of a parameter. A statistic is a characteristic or measure of a sample; statistics are used to estimate population parameters.

Learning Objective 4

Explain the difference between a probability sample and a nonprobability sample.

In a probability sample, each member of the target population has a known, nonzero chance of being included in the sample. The chances of each member of the target population being included in the sample may not be equal, but everyone has a known probability of inclusion.

With nonprobability samples, on the other hand, there is no way of estimating the probability that any population element will be included in the sample. Thus, there is no way of ensuring that the sample is representative of the target population. All nonprobability samples rely on personal judgment at some point in the sample-selection process.

Learning Objective 5

Explain what a judgment sample is and describe its best use and its hazards.

In a judgment sample, sample elements are handpicked because they are expected to serve the research purpose. Sometimes the sample elements are selected because it is believed that they are representative of the population of interest.

As long as the researcher is at the early stages of research, when ideas or insights are being sought—or when the researcher realizes its limitations—the judgment sample can be used productively. It becomes dangerous, however, when it is used in descriptive or causal studies and its weaknesses are overlooked.

Learning Objective 6

Define *quota sample*.

The quota sampling technique attempts to ensure that the sample is representative of the population by selecting sample elements in such a way that the proportion of the sample elements possessing a certain characteristic is approximately the same as the proportion of the elements with the characteristic in the target population. This is accomplished by assigning each field-worker a quota that specifies the characteristics of the people the interviewer is to contact.

Learning Objective 7

Specify the two procedures that distinguish a stratified sample.

A stratified sample is a probability sample that is distinguished by the following two-step procedure: (1) The parent population is divided into mutually exclusive and exhaustive subsets, and (2) a simple random sample of elements is chosen independently from each group or subset.

Learning Objective 8

Cite two reasons researchers might choose to use a stratified sample rather than a simple random sample.

Stratified samples can produce sample statistics that are more precise, meaning they have smaller error due to sampling than simple random samples. Stratification also allows the investigation of the characteristics of interest for particular subgroups.

Learning Objective 9

Explain the difference between a proportionate stratified sample and a disproportionate stratified sample.

With a proportionate stratified sample, the number of observations in the total sample is allocated among the subgroups, or strata, in proportion to the relative number of elements in each stratum in the population. Disproportionate stratified sampling involves balancing the two criteria of strata size and variability. With a fixed sample size, strata exhibiting more variability are sampled more than proportionately to their relative size. Conversely, those subgroups that are very homogeneous are sampled less than proportionately.

Learning Objective 10

List the steps followed in drawing a cluster sample.

Cluster sampling involves the following steps: (1) The parent population is divided into mutually exclusive and exhaustive subsets, and (2) a random sample of the subsets is selected.

KEY TERMS

census (page 326)
sample (page 326)
population (page 327)
incidence (page 328)
parameter (page 330)
statistic (page 330)
sampling error (page 330)
sampling frame (page 331)
probability sample (page 333)
nonprobability sample (page 333)
fixed sample (page 333)
sequential sample (page 333)

convenience sample (page 334)
judgment sample (page 336)
snowball sample (page 336)
quota sample (page 336)
simple random sample (page 338)
systematic sample (page 338)
sampling interval (page 339)
total sampling elements
    (TSE) (page 339)
stratified sample (page 340)
cluster sample (page 342)
area sample (page 343)

REVIEW QUESTIONS

1.   What is a census? What is a sample?

2.   Is a sample ever preferred to a census? Why?

3.   What distinguishes a probability sample from a nonprobability sample?

4.   What is a convenience sample?

5.   What is a judgment sample?

6.   Explain the operation of a quota sample. Why is a quota sample a nonprobability sample? What kinds of comparisons should you make with the data from quota samples to check their representativeness, and what kinds of conclusions can you legitimately draw?

7.   What are the distinguishing features of a simple random sample?

8.   How should a simple random sample be selected? Describe the procedure.

9.   What is a systematic sample? How are the random start and sampling interval determined with a systematic sample?

10.   What is a stratified sample? How is a stratified sample selected?

11.   Is a stratified sample a probability or nonprobability sample? Why?

12.   Which sampling method typically produces more precise estimates of a population mean—simple random sampling or stratified sampling? Why?

13.   What is a proportionate stratified sample? What is a disproportionate stratified sample? What must be known about the population to select each?

14.   What is a cluster sample? How is a cluster sample selected?

15. What are the similarities and differences between a cluster sample and a stratified sample?

16. What is an area sample? Why are area samples used?

DISCUSSION QUESTIONS, PROBLEMS, AND PROJECTS

1. For each of the following situations, identify the appropriate target population and sampling frame.

   a. A local chapter of the American Lung Association wants to test the effectiveness of a brochure entitled "12 Reasons for Not Smoking" in the city of St. Paul, Minnesota.

   b. A medium-sized manufacturer of cat food wants to conduct an in-home usage test of a new type of cat food in Sacramento, California.

   c. A large wholesaler dealing in household appliances in the city of New York wants to evaluate dealer reaction to a new discount policy.

   d. A local department store wants to assess the satisfaction with a new credit policy offered to charge account customers.

   e. A national manufacturer wants to assess whether adequate inventories are being held by wholesalers in order to prevent shortages by retailers.

   f. A manufacturer of cake mixes selling primarily in the Midwest wants to test-market a new brand of cake mix.

2. The management of a popular tourist resort on the West Coast had noticed a decline in the number of tourists and length of stay over the past three years. An overview of industry trends indicated that the overall tourist trade was expanding and growing rapidly. Management decided to conduct a study to determine people's attitudes toward the particular activities that were available at the resort. It wanted to cause the minimum amount of inconvenience to its customers and hence adopted the following plan: A request was deposited in each hotel room of the two major hotels in the resort, indicating the nature of the study and encouraging customers to participate. The customers were requested to report to a separate desk located in the lobby of the hotels. Personal interviews, lasting 20 minutes, were conducted at this desk.

   a. What type of sampling method was used?

   b. Critically evaluate the method used.

3. A national manufacturer of baby food was planning to enter the Canadian market. The initial thrust was to be in the provinces of Ontario and Quebec. Prior to the final decisions of launching the product, management decided to test-market the products in two cities. After reviewing the various cities in terms of such external criteria as demographics, shopping characteristics, and so on, the research department settled on the cities of Hamilton, Ontario, and Sherbrooke, Quebec.

   a. What type of sampling method was used?

   b. Critically evaluate the method used.

4. The Juno Company, a manufacturer of clothing for large-size consumers, was in the process of evaluating its product and advertising strategy. Initial efforts consisted of a number of focus-group interviews. The focus groups consisted of 10 to 12 large men and women of different demographic characteristics who were selected by the company's research department using on-the-street observations of physical characteristics.

   a. What type of sampling method was used?

   b. Critically evaluate the method used.

5. The Hi-Style Company is a chain of beauty salons in San Diego, California. During the past five years, the company has seen a sharp increase in the number of shops it operates and in the company's gross sales and net profit margin. The owner plans to offer a free service of hair analysis and consultation, a service for which competing salons charge a substantial price. In order to offset the increase in operating expenses, the owner plans to raise the rates on other services by 5%. Prior to introducing this new service and increasing rates, the owner wants to do a survey using her customers as a sample and employing the method of quota sampling. Your assistance is required in planning the study.

    a. On what variables will you suggest the quotas be based? Why? List the variables with their respective levels.

    b. The owner has kept close track of the demographic characteristics of her customers over a five-year period and decides that these would be most relevant in identifying the sample elements to be used.

Variable	Level	Percent of Customers
Age	0–15 years	5%
	16–30 years	30
	31–45 years	30
	46–60 years	15
	61–75 years	15
	76 years and over	5
Sex	Male	24
	Female	76
Income	$0–$9,999	10
	$10,000–$19,999	20
	$20,000–$29,999	30
	$30,000–$39,999	20
	$40,000 and over	20

    Based on these three quota variables, indicate the characteristics of a sample of 200 subjects.

    c. Discuss the possible sources of bias with the sampling method.

6. The Minnesota National Bank, headquartered in Minneapolis, Minnesota, has some 400,000 users of its credit card scattered throughout the state of Minnesota. The application forms for the credit card asked for the usual information on name, address, phone, income, education, and so on, that is typical of such applications. The bank is now very much interested in determining if there is any relationship between the uses to which the card is put and the socioeconomic characteristics of the using party; for example, is there a difference in the characteristics of those people who use the credit card for major purchases only, such as appliances, and those who use it for minor as well as major purchases?

    a. Identify the population and sampling frame that would be used by Minnesota National Bank.

    b. Indicate how you would draw a simple random sample from the above sampling frame.

    c. Indicate how you would draw a stratified sample from the above sampling frame.

    d. Indicate how you would draw a cluster sample from the above sampling frame.

    e. Which method would be preferred? Why?

7. Exclusive Supermarkets is considering entering the Boston market. Before doing so, however, management wishes to estimate the average square feet of selling space among

potential competitors, in order to plan the size of the proposed new store. A stratified sample of supermarkets in Boston produced the following results:

Size	Total Number in City	Number of This Size in Sample	Mean Size of Stores in Sample (sq. ft.)	Standard Deviation of Stores in Sample (sq. ft.)
Small supermarkets	1,000	20	4,000	2,000
Medium supermarkets	600	12	10,000	1,000
Large supermarkets	400	8	60,000	3,000

Was a proportionate or disproportionate stratified sample design used in determining the number of sample observations for each stratum? Explain.

8. Store-More is a large department store located in Lansing, Michigan. The manager is worried about the constant overstocking of a number of items in the various departments. Approximately 3,000 items ranging from small multipurpose wrenches to lawn mowers are overstocked every month. The manager is uncertain whether the surpluses are primarily due to poor purchasing policies or poor store layout and shelving practices. The manager realizes the difficulty of scrutinizing the purchase orders, invoices, and inventory cards for all the items that are overstocked. She decides on choosing a sample of items but does not know how to proceed.

a. Identify the population elements and sampling frame.

b. What sampling method would you recommend? Why? Be specific.

c. How would you draw the sample based on this sampling method?

9. The university housing office at a nearby university has decided to conduct a study to determine what influence living in dormitories versus off-campus housing has on the academic performance of the students. You are required to assist the housing office.

a. What sampling method will you recommend? Why? Be specific.

b. How would you draw the sample based on this sampling method?

10. Maxwell Federated operates a chain of department stores in a major metropolitan area. The management of Maxwell Federated has been concerned of late with tight money conditions and the associated deterioration of the company's accounts receivable. It appears on the surface that more and more customers are becoming delinquent each month. Management wishes to assess the current state of delinquencies, to determine if they are concentrated in particular stores, and to determine if they are concentrated among any particular types of purchases or purchasers.

a. What sampling method would you recommend? Why? Be specific.

b. How would you draw the sample based on this sampling method?

11. A retailer of household appliances is planning to introduce a new brand of dishwashers to the local market and wishes to estimate demand for the product. He has decided to use two-stage area sampling and has secured an up-to-date map of your area, but he does not know how to proceed and requires your assistance. Outline a step-by-step approach you will recommend for conducting the study.

12. In February, a Midwestern city instituted a mandatory recycling plan for certain types of household waste. A marketing research firm was hired to evaluate the progress of the plan in July. Among several measures of effectiveness to be used, the researchers wished to compare the weight of recyclables collected per household per week with a pre-implementation estimate of 10 pounds per week. In order to do this, the following sampling procedure was used. First, the city was divided into 840 blocks. The blocks were then arrayed from largest to smallest based on the estimated number of households they

contained and, based on the selection of a random number, every twelfth block was selected. Researchers then accompanied collectors on their weekly rounds and weighed each bag of recyclables collected on the specified blocks. (Assume each household puts out one bag per week.)

a. What are the population elements and the sampling frame?

b. What are the primary sampling units?

c. Describe the sampling plan used by the researchers?

d. What is the approximate probability that a household will be included in the sample?

In this appendix, we'll share a few of the statistical principles that make it possible to make projections to the population based on results obtained from a sample. We'll spare you many of the details, but these concepts are so important that they merit more attention than we gave them in the chapter.

Consider the hypothetical population of 20 individuals shown in Exhibit 15A.1. Now, most of the populations that marketers work with are much larger than this, but a small population allows us to calculate the true population parameter (mean monthly gross income in this example) and compare it to the estimates we would obtain from various samples drawn from the population.

For the population included in Exhibit 15A.1, the population mean (μ) is calculated as follows:

$$\text{population mean } (\mu) = \frac{\text{sum of population elements}}{\text{number of population elements}}$$

$$= \frac{\$5,600 + \$6,000 + \cdots + \$13,200}{20} = \$9,400$$

Next, let's see how well we can estimate this value based on samples drawn from the population.

Exhibit 15A.1	Population

Population Element	Monthly Income (Dollars)
1 A	$ 5,600
2 B	6,000
3 C	6,400
4 D	6,800
5 E	7,200
6 F	7,600
7 G	8,000
8 H	8,400
9 I	8,800
10 J	9,200
11 K	9,600
12 L	10,000
13 M	10,400
14 N	10,800
15 O	11,200
16 P	11,600
17 Q	12,000
18 R	12,400
19 S	12,800
20 T	13,200

Derived Population

The *derived population* consists of all the possible samples that can be drawn from the population under a given sampling plan. As discussed in the chapter, a statistic is a characteristic or measure of a sample; we use sample statistics to estimate population parameters. The value of a statistic used to estimate a particular parameter depends on the particular sample selected from the parent population under the sampling plan specified. Different samples yield different statistics and different estimates of the same population parameter.

Consider the derived population of all possible samples that could be drawn from our population using a sample size of $n = 2$ and a simple random sample. Suppose that the information for each population element—in this case, the person's name and gross monthly income—is written on a disk, placed in a jar, and shaken thoroughly. The researcher then reaches into the jar, pulls out one disk, records the information on it, and puts it aside. She does the same with a second disk. Then she places both disks back in the jar and repeats the process. Exhibit 15A.2 shows the many possible results—190 combinations—of following this procedure. In addition, the exhibit includes the mean income for each sample combination. So, for sample number 1, which includes population elements A and B, the sample mean ($\bar{x}$) is calculated as follows:

$$\text{sample mean} (\bar{x}) = \frac{\text{sum of sample elements}}{\text{number of elements in sample}}$$

$$= \frac{\$5,600 + \$6,000}{2} = \$5,800$$

Figure 15A.1 displays the sample mean monthly income for samples 25, 62, 108, 147, and 189. It also indicates the amount of error that would occur if each of the samples was used to estimate the population parameter.

There are a couple of things to keep in mind about the derived population. Although we demonstrated the concept by drawing all possible samples under our sampling plan (see Exhibit 15A.2), it is not necessary to do so in practice. Instead, we draw a single sample and rely on the *concept* of the derived population and the related sampling distribution to make inferences about the population based on the sample. Picking a sample of size = 2 from the population is equivalent to picking 1 of the 190 possible combinations out of the derived population. This fact is basic in making statistical inferences.

A second thing to note is that the derived population is defined as the population of all possible distinguishable samples that can be drawn under a *given sampling plan*. Change any part of the sampling plan, and the derived population will also change. For

Derived Population of All Possible Samples of Size $n = 2$ with Simple Random Selection

Sample	Elements	Mean	Sample	Elements	Mean	Sample	Elements	Mean	Sample	Elements	Mean
1	AB	5,800	49	CO	8,800	97	FR	10,000	145	JT	11,200
2	AC	6,000	50	CP	9,000	98	FS	10,200	146	KL	9,800
3	AD	6,200	51	CQ	9,200	99	FT	10,400	147	KM	10,000
4	AE	6,400	52	CR	9,400	100	GH	8,200	148	KN	10,200
5	AF	6,600	53	CS	9,600	101	GI	8,400	149	KO	10,400
6	AG	6,800	54	CT	9,800	102	GJ	8,600	150	KP	10,600
7	AH	7,000	55	DE	7,000	103	GK	8,800	151	KQ	10,800
8	AI	7,200	56	DF	7,200	104	GL	9,000	152	KR	11,000
9	AJ	7,400	57	DG	7,400	105	GM	9,200	153	KS	11,200
10	AK	7,600	58	DH	7,600	106	GN	9,400	154	KT	11,400
11	AL	7,800	59	DI	7,800	107	GO	9,600	155	LM	10,200
12	AM	8,000	60	DJ	8,000	108	GP	9,800	156	LN	10,400
13	AN	8,200	61	DK	8,200	109	GQ	10,000	157	LO	10,600
14	AO	8,400	62	DL	8,400	110	GR	10,200	158	LP	10,800
15	AP	8,600	63	DM	8,600	111	GS	10,400	159	LQ	11,000
16	AQ	8,800	64	DN	8,800	112	GT	10,600	160	LR	11,200
17	AR	9,000	65	DO	9,000	113	HI	8,600	161	LS	11,400
18	AS	9,200	66	DP	9,200	114	HJ	8,800	162	LT	11,600
19	AT	9,400	67	DQ	9,400	115	HK	9,000	163	MN	10,600
20	BC	6,200	68	DR	9,600	116	HL	9,200	164	MO	10,800
21	BD	6,400	69	DS	9,800	117	HM	9,400	165	MP	11,000
22	BE	6,600	70	DT	10,000	118	HN	9,600	166	MQ	11,200
23	BF	6,800	71	EF	7,400	119	HO	9,800	167	MR	11,400
24	BG	7,000	72	EG	7,600	120	HP	10,000	168	MS	11,600
25	BH	7,200	73	EH	7,800	121	HQ	10,200	169	MT	11,800
26	BI	7,400	74	EI	8,000	122	HR	10,400	170	NO	11,000
27	BJ	7,600	75	EJ	8,200	123	HS	10,600	171	NP	11,200
28	BK	7,800	76	EK	8,400	124	HT	10,800	172	NQ	11,400
29	BL	8,000	77	EL	8,600	125	IJ	9,000	173	NR	11,600
30	BM	8,200	78	EM	8,800	126	IK	9,200	174	NS	11,800
31	BN	8,400	79	EN	9,000	127	IL	9,400	175	NT	12,000
32	BO	8,600	80	EO	9,200	128	IM	9,600	176	OP	11,400
33	BP	8,800	81	EP	9,400	129	IN	9,800	177	OQ	11,600
34	BQ	9,000	82	EQ	9,600	130	IO	10,000	178	OR	11,800
35	BR	9,200	83	ER	9,800	131	IP	10,200	179	OS	12,000
36	BS	9,400	84	ES	10,000	132	IQ	10,400	180	OT	12,200
37	BT	9,600	85	ET	10,200	133	IR	10,600	181	PQ	11,800
38	CD	6,600	86	FG	7,800	134	IS	10,800	182	PR	12,000
39	CE	6,800	87	FH	8,000	135	IT	11,000	183	PS	12,200
40	CF	7,000	88	FI	8,200	136	JK	9,400	184	PT	12,400
41	CG	7,200	89	FJ	8,400	137	JL	9,600	185	QR	12,200
42	CH	7,400	90	FK	8,600	138	JM	9,800	186	QS	12,400
43	CI	7,600	91	FL	8,800	139	JN	10,000	187	QT	12,600
44	CJ	7,800	92	FM	9,000	140	JO	10,200	188	RS	12,600
45	CK	8,000	93	FN	9,200	141	JP	10,400	189	RT	12,800
46	CL	8,200	94	FO	9,400	142	JQ	10,600	190	ST	13,000
47	CM	8,400	95	FP	9,600	143	JR	10,800			
48	CN	8,600	96	FQ	9,800	144	JS	11,000			

Several Possible Samples and Their Respective Errors When Estimating the Population Mean

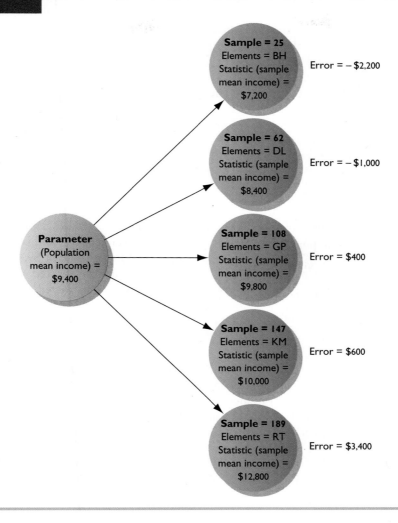

example, with samples of size 3 instead of 2, *ABC* is a sample possibility, and there are a number of additional possibilities as well—1,140 versus the 190 with samples of size 2. Change the method of selecting elements by using something other than simple random sampling, and the derived population will also change.

Sample Mean versus Population Mean

If we want to evaluate the income of those in a simple random sample, can we assume that the sample mean will equal the parent population mean? No, it's not especially likely that any particular sample will produce a sample mean that equals the population mean, but if we have drawn a probabilistic sample, certain statistical principles allow us to assume a relationship between the sample mean and population

mean. But how much error is there likely to be in using the sample to estimate something about the population?

Suppose we added up all the sample means in Exhibit 15A.2 and divided by the number of samples; that is, suppose we were to average the averages. By doing this, we would get the following:

$$\frac{\$5,800 + \$6,000 + \cdots + \$13,000}{190} = \$9,400$$

This is the mean of the parent population that we calculated earlier. Thus, *the mean of all possible sample means is equal to the population mean.* Note, however, that any particular estimate may be very far from the true population value—for example, the sample means for sample 1 or sample 190 provide very poor estimates of the population mean. In some cases, the true population value may even be impossible to achieve with any possible sample; this is not true in our example, however, since a number of sample possibilities—for example, sample 19—yield a sample mean that equals the population average.

Next, it is useful to look at the spread of these sample estimates, and particularly the relationship between this spread of estimates and the dispersion of incomes in the population. A very useful measure of spread is the population variance. To compute the population variance, we calculate the deviation of each value from the mean, square these deviations, sum them, and divide by the number of values making up the sum. Letting σ^2 denote the population variance, the calculation yields

population variance (σ^2)

$$= \frac{\text{sum of squared differences of each population element from the population mean}}{\text{number of population elements}}$$

$$= \frac{(5{,}600 - 9{,}400)^2 + (6{,}000 - 9{,}400)^2 + \cdots + (13{,}200 - 9{,}400)^2}{20}$$

$$= 5{,}320{,}000$$

The variance of *mean incomes* could be calculated similarly. That is, we could calculate the variance of mean incomes by taking the deviation of each mean around its overall mean, squaring and summing these deviations, and then dividing by the number of cases. Alternatively, we could determine the variance of mean incomes indirectly by using the variance of

incomes in the population, since there is a direct relationship between the two quantities. It turns out that when the sample is only a small part of the population, the variance of sample mean incomes is equal to the population variance divided by the sample size. In symbols, this means that

$$\sigma_{\bar{x}}^2 = \frac{\sigma^2}{n}$$

where $\sigma_{\bar{x}}^2$ is the variance of sample mean incomes, while σ^2 is the variance of incomes in the population, and n is the sample size. So, *the variance of sample means is related to the population variance.*

Finally, consider the distribution of the estimates from the derived population in contrast to the distribution of the mean monthly incomes in the population. Figure 15A.2 indicates that the population distribution, depicted by Panel A, is flat—each of the 20 values occurs once—and is symmetrical around the population mean value of $9,400. The distribution of estimates from the derived population, displayed in Panel B, was constructed by grouping the sample means from Exhibit 15A.2 into categories ($6,000 or less; $6,100 to $6,600; and so on) and then counting the number contained in each category. Panel B presents a simple bar chart, known as a histogram, showing the number of sample means that fell into each category. This is the *sampling distribution* of the statistic. Notice that *the sampling distribution is mound shaped,* even though the population distribution is flat.

The notion of sampling distribution is the single most important notion in statistics; it is the cornerstone of statistical inference procedures. If you know the sampling distribution for the statistic in question,

---

FIGURE 15A.2   Population Distribution versus Sampling Distribution

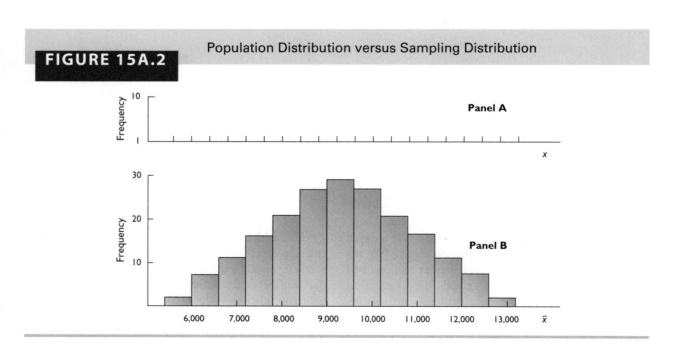

you can make inferences about the corresponding population parameter. If, on the other hand, you only know that a particular sample estimate will vary with repeated sampling but you have no information about *how* it will vary, then it is impossible to estimate sampling error. Because the sampling distribution of an estimate describes how that estimate will vary with repeated sampling, it provides a basis for determining the reliability of the sample estimate. This is why probability sampling plans are so important to statistical inference. When we know the probability that any population element will be included in the sample, we can derive the sampling distribution of various statistics. Researchers then rely on the sampling distributions to make inferences from single samples to population values.

Central-Limit Theorem

The mound-shaped sampling distribution provides initial evidence that the *central-limit theorem* is in operation. The central-limit theorem holds that if simple random samples of a given size n are drawn from a parent population with mean equal to μ, and variance equal to σ^2, then when the sample size n is large, the *distribution of sample means* will be approximately normally distributed with its mean equal to the population mean and its variance equal to the parent population variance divided by the sample size; that is,

$$\sigma_{\bar{x}}^2 = \frac{\sigma^2}{n}$$

The approximation will become more and more accurate as n becomes larger. Note what this means: Regardless of the shape of the parent population, the distribution of *sample means will be normal* if the sample is large enough. How large is large enough? If the distribution of the variable in the parent population is normal, then the distribution of means of samples of size $n = 1$ will be normal. If the distribution of the variable is symmetrical but not normal, then samples of very small size will produce a distribution in which the means are normally distributed. If the distribution of the variable is highly skewed in the population, then samples of a larger size will be needed.

Here's the bottom line: We can assume that the sampling distribution of sample means is normal as long as we work with a sample of sufficient size. We don't have to assume that the variable is normally distributed in the population in order to make inferences using the normal curve. Instead, we rely on the central-limit theorem and adjust the sample size according to the population distribution so that the normal curve can be assumed to hold. Fortunately, the normal distribution of the statistic occurs with samples of relatively small size—the normal standard is a sample size of 30, and sometimes even fewer are required. (You will usually need more cases than this to achieve reasonable levels of precision and confidence, but the sampling distribution becomes approximately normally distributed with around 30 cases.)

Determining Sample Size

Learning Objectives

1. Cite three factors researchers must take into account when determining sample size.
2. Specify the relationship between precision and confidence.
3. Explain in what way the size of the population influences the size of the sample.
4. Specify the circumstances under which the finite population correction factor should be used.
5. List four methods of determining sample size for a project.

Introduction

So far, our discussion of sampling has concentrated on different types of samples. Another important consideration is sample size. Unless you are using a sequential sample, you will need to determine the necessary sample size before beginning data collection.

You might be tempted to assume that the sample should be as large as the client can afford, but the question of sample size is complex. It depends on, among other things, the type of sample, the statistic in question, the homogeneity of the population, and the time, money, and personnel available for the study. We can't discuss all of these issues adequately in one chapter, but we'll provide an overview of the basics of determining sample size. We focus on simple random samples and two of the more popular sample statistics, means and proportions. If you want more information about how sample size is determined for stratified or cluster samples, there are other sources that can give you the detail you'll need.[1]

One other note before we move forward. There are computer programs that exist to calculate the necessary sample size in a given research situation; researchers routinely use them and avoid the formulas and hand calculations that we're about to give you. We think it is important, however, that you understand the simple factors that influence the size of sample needed. The best way for you to see these factors is to work through the formulas a time or two.

BASIC CONSIDERATIONS IN DETERMINING SAMPLE SIZE

Learning Objective

1. Cite three factors researchers must take into account when determining sample size.

Three basic factors affect the size of sample needed when working with a probabilistic sample. The first of these, the amount of diversity or variation of the parameter in question within the population, is beyond the control of the researcher. Do you remember from the previous chapter that one reason for using a stratified sampling plan is the efficiency obtained by grouping together population elements that are likely to be homogeneous, or similar, on the parameter to be estimated? The same principle holds for the overall population: When there is very little variation across elements on some characteristic, it doesn't require a very large sample to estimate the value of that characteristic. As variation increases, larger samples are required, all else equal.

A second consideration is how precise the estimate must be—this is under the control of the client/researcher and depends on the importance of the issue. For example, suppose that a researcher has been asked to develop a profile of the "average" diner in a particular restaurant. One thing the client will probably want to know is the mean income of the restaurant's diners. Should the sample estimate be within $100, high or low, of the true population value? Or can we get by with a less precise estimate—say, within $500 or $1,000 of the true value? The closer we need the estimate to be to the true value in the population, the larger the sample that will be required, all else equal. **Precision** is the acceptable amount of error in the estimate. If millions of dollars and hundreds of employees' jobs ride on the results of the study, the acceptable range of error is likely to be small. It is critical to obtain one or more managers' input as to the importance of a particular issue in determining the necessary precision of an estimate.

precision
The degree of error in an estimate of a population parameter.

The other factor that affects sample size is the degree of confidence that managers and/or the researcher require in the estimate. By **confidence**, we mean the degree of certainty that the true value of the parameter that we are estimating falls within the precision range that we have established. For example, suppose that you have decided that in describing the average diner in the restaurant, an acceptable precision range for mean income is +/−$500 and that the mean income in the sample is $45,300. Does this mean that mean income for the population *necessarily* falls between $44,800 and $45,800 in the population? No, it doesn't. Because we are working with the sampling distribution of sample means, however, we can have a certain level of confidence that the population parameter does fall within the precision range that we have established. How much confidence? With a given precision range, the amount of confidence is directly related to the size of the sample; the bigger the sample, the more certain we can be that the true value in the population falls within the precision range which is calculated based on the sample estimate.

confidence
The degree to which one can feel confident that an estimate approximates the true value.

Learning Objective

2. Specify the relationship between precision and confidence.

At any given sample size, there is a trade-off between degree of confidence and degree of precision. The most precise measure of mean income for our restaurant diners would be a *point estimate* of the mean, which is an estimate that involves a single value with no associated bounds of error. In our study, the sample mean income was $45,300. This point estimate is our best guess about the overall population mean, but it is almost certain to be off by at least a little bit, and thus we can have virtually no confidence in it despite its preciseness. On the other hand, we might have complete confidence in an estimate that the population mean income is between zero and $10 million—but that estimate is too imprecise to be of any practical value. The

The degree of homogeneity in the population on the characteristic to be estimated directly influences sample size.

desire for precision and confidence must be balanced. It might be entirely reasonable, for example, to end up being 95% confident that the population parameter lies between $44,800 and $45,800.

Here's another example that illustrates the relationship between confidence and precision: Suppose we wanted to estimate the proportion of restaurant diners who are female and that 37% of the people within our probabilistically drawn sample were women. We would probably be hesitant to conclude (that is, we would have virtually no confidence) that *exactly* 37% of all diners at this particular restaurant were female. On the other hand, we might feel quite confident in the less precise estimate that the true proportion of women lies somewhere between 33 and 41%. Again, precision and confidence are inversely related.

In sum, in order to determine the necessary sample size with a simple random sample, we only need three basic pieces of information: (1) how homogeneous or similar the population is on the characteristic to be estimated, (2) how much precision is needed in the estimate, and (3) how confident you need to be that the true value falls within the precision range you've established. Homogeneity is a function of the population itself and cannot be controlled by the researcher. The degrees of precision and confidence are established by the client and researcher and depend upon the needs of the research situation.

DETERMINING SAMPLE SIZE WHEN ESTIMATING MEANS

Imagine that the Division of Tourism in a certain state wants to know the average amount that people spend each year on food and lodging while on fishing trips within the state. Our job as researchers is to use a simple random sample to estimate the mean annual expenditure of those people, using a list of all those who applied for fishing licenses within the year. The director of tourism wants the estimate to be within +/−$25 of the population mean. She also wants to be 95% confident that the precision interval the researcher constructs will contain the true population mean.

The formula for calculating the necessary sample size for estimating the population mean is straightforward:

$$n = \frac{z^2}{H^2} \left(\text{est } \sigma^2 \right)$$

where n = required sample size, z = z-score corresponding to the desired degree of confidence, H = half-precision (or how far off the estimate can be in either direction, which would represent half of the full precision range), and σ^2 = the variance in expenditures in the population.

As you might recall from a basic statistics course, the z-score corresponding to 95% confidence is equal to 1.96. Here are the most common z-scores used by marketing researchers:

90% confidence: $z = 1.65$

95% confidence: $z = 1.96$

99% confidence: $z = 2.58$

Look at the sample size formula and notice what will happen to the required sample size (n) if we increase the desired degree of confidence. If we want greater confidence (represented by z in the formula) that our precision interval will capture the true value in the population, the required sample size increases.

The director of tourism wants our estimate to be within $25 (in either direction); as a result, the full precision range is $50, and half-precision ($H$) equals $25. Once again, look at the formula to see what would happen if we wanted to increase the precision of the answer. Because increased precision means decreasing the precision interval (that is, H gets smaller in the formula), as precision increases, so will the necessary sample size.

The only remaining piece of information we need in order to calculate sample size when working with mean values is an estimate of the variance of the characteristic in the population. But how can a researcher get such an estimate before he conducts the study? Sometimes we can look at prior research studies conducted on this or related topics, so secondary data would be a very good place to start when they are available. Another option is to conduct a pilot study; since it's almost always a good idea to conduct a pilot study prior to the major data collection effort (to check measures, data collection forms, and so on), this is an attractive option. Sometimes the variance can be estimated from the conditions surrounding the approach to the problem. Research Window 16.1, for example, discusses the estimation of the variance when rating scales are used to measure the important variables.

Yet another possibility for estimating population variance is to take into account the fact that for a normally distributed variable, the range of the variable is approximately equal to plus or minus three standard deviations. As a result, if you can estimate the likely range of the variable in the population, you can estimate the standard deviation by dividing by 6. In the current situation, there would be some licensed fishermen who would spend zero dollars on food and lodging while on fishing trips, since they would only be making one-day trips. Some might also be expected to go on one or more overnight trips a year. Suppose that 10 days a year were considered typical of the upper limit, and food and lodging expenses were calculated at $75 per day; the total dollar upper limit would be $750. The range would also be $750 ($750 − $0 = $750), and the estimated standard deviation would then be $125 ($750/6 = $125).

With desired precision of +/−$25 and a 95% confidence interval, the calculation of sample size looks like this:

$$n = \frac{z^2}{H^2}\left(\text{est } \sigma^2\right) = \frac{(1.96)^2}{(25)^2}(125)^2 = 96$$

We would then determine the number of total sampling elements (TSE; see Chapter 15) to be drawn randomly from the list of people who had applied for fishing licenses in the past year. Our goal is to ultimately achieve a sample size of at least 96 to reach the level of precision (and/or confidence) that we desire.

ETHICAL DILEMMA 16.1

Researchers in the laboratory of a regional food manufacturer recently developed a new dessert topping. This topping was more versatile than those currently on the market because it came in a greater variety of flavors than existing dessert toppings. Although the manufacturer believed that the product had great promise, management also thought it would be necessary to convince the trade (that is, wholesalers and retailers) of its sales potential in order to get them to handle it. The manufacturer consequently decided to test-market the product in a couple of areas where it had especially strong distribution. It selected several stores with which it had a long working relationship to carry the product. During the planned two-month test period, product sales did not begin to compare with sales of other dessert toppings. Feeling that such evidence would make it very difficult to gain distribution, the manufacturer decided to do two things: (1) run the test for a longer period and (2) increase the number of accounts handling the test product. Four months later, the results were much more convincing, and management felt more comfortable in approaching the trade with the test-market results.

- Is it ethical to conduct a test market in an area where a firm's distribution or reputation is especially strong?
- Is it ethical not to report this fact to potential customers, thereby causing them to misinterpret the market response to the item?
- Is it ethical to increase the size of the sample until one secures a result one wants? What if the argument for increasing sample size was that the product was so novel that two months simply was not enough time for consumers to become sufficiently familiar with it?
- Would it have been more ethical to plan initially for a larger and longer test than to adjust the length and scope of the test on the basis of early results? Why or why not?

DETERMINING SAMPLE SIZE WHEN ESTIMATING PROPORTIONS

Marketers are also often interested in estimating other parameters, such as the population proportion, π. In our example, the researcher might be interested in determining the proportion of licensed fishermen who are from out of state, or from rural areas, or who took at least one overnight trip.

research window 16.1

Guidelines for Estimating Variance for Data Obtained Using Rating Scales

Rating scales are doubly bounded: On a five-point scale, for instance, responses cannot be less than 1 or greater than 5. This constraint leads to a relationship between the mean and the variance. For example, if a sample mean is 4.6 on a five-point scale, there must be a large proportion of responses of 5, and it follows that the variance must be relatively small. On the other hand, if the mean is near 3.0, the variance can be potentially much greater. The nature of the relationship between the mean and the variance depends on the number of scale points and on the "shape" of the distribution of responses (e.g., approximately normal or symmetrically clustered around some central scale value, or skewed, or uniformly spread among the scale values). By considering the types of distribution shapes typically encountered in practice, it is possible to estimate variances for use in calculating sample size requirements for a given number of scale points.

The table lists ranges of variances likely to be encountered for various numbers of scale points. The low end of the range is the approximate variance when data values tend to be concentrated around some middle point of the scale, as in a normal distribution. The high end of the range is the variance that would be obtained if responses

were uniformly spread across the scale points. Although it is possible to encounter distributions with larger variances than those listed (such as distributions with modes at both ends of the scale), such data are rare.

In most cases, data obtained using rating scales tend to be more uniformly spread out than in a normal distribution. Hence, to arrive at conservative sample size estimates (i.e., sample sizes that are *at least* large enough to accomplish the stated objectives), it is advisable to use a variance estimate at or near the high end of the range listed.

Number of Scale Points	Typical Range of Variances
4	0.7–1.3
5	1.2–2.0
6	2.0–3.0
7	2.5–4.0
10	3.0–7.0

Source: *Research on Research*, No. 37 (Chicago: Market Facts, Inc., undated).

As we discussed earlier, we need three pieces of information for estimating sample size: the desired levels of precision and confidence and an estimate of how variable a characteristic is within the population. As with the calculation of sample size for estimating means, the specific requirements of the research problem determine how the first two items will be specified. With percentages, however, precision means that the estimate will be within plus or minus so many percentage points of the true value. For example, a recent Harris Poll of 1,010 U.S. adults, conducted by telephone, found that 66% of all adults are "cyberchondriacs:" people who have looked online for health information. At the 95% confidence level, the degree of sampling error (that is, precision) on this estimate was +/−3 percentage points. Thus, while our best guess is that 66% of U.S. adults are cyberchondriacs, we are 95% confident that the true percentage could be anywhere between 63 and 69%.[2]

The other piece of information needed to estimate sample size with proportions concerns the variability of the characteristic being estimated. When we were estimating population means, we were necessarily working with population parameters with interval or ratio level measurement properties for which calculating mean scores was appropriate (look back at Chapter 12 for a quick refresher if necessary). For these types of characteristics, the variance is the appropriate measure of variability—recall that we used an estimate of population variance to calculate sample size for estimating a population mean.

MANAGER'S FOCUS

Let's assume that your company initiated an annual national tracking study two years ago. The proportion of your customers who were "Dissatisfied" or "Very Dissatisfied" (the bottom two points on a five-point scale) with your services was 0.23 the first year and 0.28 the second year. You have since implemented some service changes with the goal of reducing this proportion to 0.15 this year.

The sample size was set at 400 for each of the first two tracking surveys simply because that was as large as your research budget would allow. This year, there is more money available and you would like to determine the appropriate sample size for the tracking study using a statistical approach. You talked with the manager of the field research firm that administered the survey last year. She said it was somewhat difficult to reach the designated respondents in the sample, and on average each telephone interviewer was able to obtain only 2.13 completed questionnaires per hour. Assuming the same response rate this year, she indicated it would cost $32.00 per completed questionnaire.

You decide to use the formula presented in this section to help you determine the appropriate sample size. After reflecting a while, you decide you definitely want the degree of confidence to be 95%. You also conclude it would be fine to have a precision level of +/−0.04. Using 0.15 (the level to which you are trying to reduce

dissatisfaction) as the estimate of the population proportion, you calculate you should have a sample size of 306. This means the data collection expenses would be $9,792 (roughly $3,000 less than last year).

These calculations were much lower than you were expecting, so you decide it would be nice to increase the level of precision to +/−0.02. The other specs are kept the same, and you calculate the sample size should be 1,225. This would cause the data collection costs to jump to $39,200. Staggered by this increase in sample size and data collection expenses, you slightly decrease the precision level to +/−0.03. Keeping the other specs unchanged, you calculate a new sample size of 544 with associated data collection expenses of $17,408.

You may be surprised to see how such small changes in your specifications can produce such large changes in the sample size and corresponding data collection costs. Which sample size should you ask your researchers to generate? There is a tendency among managers to believe that larger sample sizes are always preferable. But, you should ask yourself if a small increase in precision is worth paying substantially more for data collection. If the increased precision is unlikely to change how you will respond to the market information, then it is poor financial management to pay for a substantially larger sample.

With proportions, however, we are working with population parameters with nominal- or ordinal-level measurement properties. With these characteristics, each population element either falls into a certain category or it doesn't. In our example, imagine that 26% of people with fishing licenses are from out of state (that is, 26% possess the characteristic of residing in another state, and 74% do not possess that characteristic). How can we estimate population variability for parameters with only two levels (possess the characteristic, do not possess the characteristic)? *The proportion itself serves this purpose.* Think about it this way: What would a completely homogeneous population look like on a particular nominal or ordinal characteristic? Everyone (100%) would possess the particular characteristic. Or no one (0%) would possess the characteristic. Either way, everyone is exactly alike on the characteristic in question. As the population becomes more heterogeneous, the percentage who possess (or do not possess) the characteristic moves away from the extremes toward 50%, the level representing the most heterogeneity on the characteristic within the population.

This presents an interesting dilemma for a researcher. To estimate the variability of the characteristic being estimated, it is necessary to estimate the very quantity the study is being designed to discover in the first place! As strange as this may sound, it's true—the researcher will need to make a judgment about the approximate value of the parameter in order to determine sample size. To arrive at an initial estimate, you can look for past studies, consult other sources of secondary data, or conduct a pilot

In order to determine the sample size for a study of the proportion of fishermen who make overnight trips, a researcher would first have to estimate the number of fishermen who do so. To make that estimate, the researcher might need to begin by conducting a pilot study or by using previously published data.

study. If none of these options is a possibility, just try to make the most informed guess that you can make. If all else fails, the most conservative position is to assume the greatest heterogeneity possible: 50%. (Look at the next formula to see why estimating the population proportion at 50% will produce the largest sample size, all else equal.)

Sample size for estimating proportions is given by the formula

$$n = \frac{z^2}{H^2} \pi(1 - \pi)$$

where n = required sample size, z = z-score corresponding to the desired degree of confidence, H = half-precision (or how far off the estimate can be in either direction), and π = the population proportion.

Suppose the Division of Tourism is interested in knowing the proportion of all out-of-state fishermen who took at least one overnight fishing trip in the past year. Suppose also that they wanted this estimate within $+/-2$ percentage points, and they wanted to be 95% confident ($z = 1.96$) in the result. A similar study had been conducted two years ago and found that 18% of the respondents were from out of state and had taken at least one overnight fishing trip. Since that time, however, the Division of Tourism had advertised the state's outdoor activities quite heavily in neighboring states and they knew that the overall percentage of fishing licenses to out-of-state fishermen had increased a little in the most recent year. As a result, their best guess as to the current proportion of out-of-state fishermen who had taken at least one overnight fishing trip was about 25%.

Substituting these values in the formula yields

$$n = \frac{z^2}{H^2} \pi(1 - \pi) = \frac{(1.96)^2}{(0.02)^2} 0.25(1 - 0.25) = 1,800$$

As before, we would then determine the number of total sampling elements to be randomly drawn from the list of people who had applied for fishing licenses in the past year. The goal is to draw enough so that we would end up with the 1,800 that we need.

You probably noticed that in the first example we ended up with a sample size of 96 and in the second we needed 1,800. Why such a large difference? Remember that sample size is calculated for a particular parameter based on the needs of the research situation. It is possible that there would be different sample sizes for each parameter that might be estimated in a study. In the current situation, there must have been differences in confidence level, precision, or variability of the characteristic being estimated in the population. It appears that much of the difference is due to the need for considerably more precision when estimating the proportion of the population that traveled from out of state for at least one overnight fishing trip. To see this, take a quick look at the precision interval as a proportion of the normal range of the characteristic in the population. In the earlier case, we wanted to be within $25 of the mean amount spent on food and lodging and we calculated that a reasonable range of the amount spent in the population would be from $0 to $750. The overall precision interval ($50) works out to be 0.067 of the range of the variable ($50/$750 = 0.067). In estimating the percentage of people from out of state who made at least one overnight trip, the desired precision interval was $+/-2\%$, for an overall precision interval of 4%, which is 0.04 of the range of the variable (0% to 100%). All else equal, the

Exhibit 16.1	Sample Size Needed to Estimate Each of Three Parameters		

| | **Variable** | | |
	Mean Expenditures on Food and Lodging	**Mean Miles Traveled**	**Percent Staying Overnight**
Confidence level	95%	95%	95%
Desired precision	+/−$25	+/−50	+/−2%
Estimated population variation	$\sigma = \$125$	$\sigma = 500$	$\pi = 25\%$
Required sample size	96	384	1,800

increased precision desired for the proportion contributed greatly to the need for a larger sample size. Since the desired confidence level was the same in both cases, the remainder of the difference in required sample size is due to greater estimated variability of the characteristic in the population with the second characteristic (proportion staying overnight at least once).

MULTIPLE ESTIMATES IN A SINGLE PROJECT

You may be asking yourself by now, "How do I calculate sample size if I'm asking more than one question on a survey?" Researchers rarely conduct a study to estimate only one parameter. It is much more typical for a study to involve multiple estimates. Because this is the more likely situation, let's revisit our previous example of fishermen and assume that the researcher has also been asked to estimate the average number of miles traveled on fishing trips in a year. There are now a total of three parameters to be estimated. Suppose each is to be estimated with 95% confidence, and the desired precision and estimated variation in the population are as given in Exhibit 16.1. Exhibit 16.1 also contains the sample sizes needed to estimate each variable.

The three characteristics and their associated requirements produce conflicting sample sizes. Depending on the variable being estimated, *n* should equal 96, 384, or 1,800. The researcher must somehow reconcile these values to come up with a sample size suitable for the study as a whole. The most conservative approach would be to choose *n* = 1,800, the largest value. This would ensure that each variable would be estimated with the required precision, assuming that the estimates of population variation were accurate.

However, suppose that of the three parameters to be estimated, the estimate of the percentage staying overnight is the least critical. If so, for the other estimates, it would be wasteful of resources to use a sample size that large. A better approach would be to focus on those variables that are most critical and to select a sample sufficient in size to estimate them with the required precision and confidence. The variables for which a larger sample size is needed would then be estimated with either a lower degree of confidence or less precision than planned.

POPULATION SIZE AND SAMPLE SIZE

You may not have noticed it before, but here is an interesting observation: *The size of the population does not enter into the calculation of the size of the sample.* Except for one slight modification that we will discuss shortly, the size of the population has *no direct effect* on the size of the sample.

Learning Objective

3. Explain in what way the size of the population influences the size of the sample.

ETHICAL DILEMMA 16.2

A young marketing researcher was about to prepare a research proposal in response to a request-for-proposal (RFP) issued by a moderate-sized healthcare company. The company wants to gauge target market awareness of the services that it offers. This will be the researcher's third attempt at winning a contract from the company in the past 18 months. To prepare the first two proposals (which were for other types of projects), the researcher was careful to assess the situation, to get management feedback on the importance of the project, and to develop cost-conscious proposals with sample sizes that were sufficient for the purposes as described by managers. In each case, however, the projects were awarded to companies that proposed much larger sample sizes. Feedback from managers indicated that they simply didn't believe that his results would be "valid" unless he had many more respondents than proposed. It was clear to the researcher that the managers didn't really understand what they needed. For the current proposal, the researcher has decided to double the proposed sample size—that is, he plans to use twice as many respondents as he believes are necessary to deliver the levels of precision and confidence needed.

- Is it ethical to include additional respondents because managers (mistakenly) believe a study's results to be less valid with a smaller sample?
- Suppose that the researcher carefully explained to the managers why a smaller sample would adequately deliver the necessary levels of confidence and precision *and* save the company a great deal of money. If the managers still insisted on the larger sample, would the decision to propose the larger sample be ethical?

Learning Objective

4. Specify the circumstances under which the finite population correction factor should be used.

Learning Objective

5. List four methods of determining sample size for a project.

Although this statement may not seem intuitive at first, consider it carefully and you'll see why it is true. As we've noted before, if all population elements have exactly the same value of the characteristic (for example, if each of our fishermen spent exactly $74 per year on food and lodging), then a sample of 1 is all that is needed to determine the mean. This is true whether there are 1,000, 10,000, or 100,000 elements in the population. What directly affects the size of the sample is the variability of the characteristic in the population.

Suppose that our example state offered some of the best fishing in the country and drew fishermen from across the nation as well as locally. If the parameter we sought to measure was mean number of miles traveled annually on fishing trips, there would be great variation in the characteristic. The more variable the characteristic, the larger the sample needed to estimate it with some specified level of precision. This idea not only makes intuitive sense, but we can also see it directly expressed in the formulas for determining sample size to estimate a population mean. Thus, population size affects sample size only indirectly through variability. In most cases, the larger the population, the greater the *potential* for variation of the characteristic.

The population size also does not affect sample size when estimating a proportion. With a proportion, the determining factor is the estimated proportion of the population possessing the characteristic; the closer the proportion is to 0.5, the larger the sample that will be needed, regardless of the size of the population.

The procedures we have discussed so far apply to situations where the target population is large relative to the size of the sample to be drawn. This is the case in most consumer goods studies. However, we mentioned that there was one modification to the general rule that population size has no direct effect on sample size. In cases where the sample represents a large portion of the population, the formulas must be altered or they will overestimate the required sample. Since the larger the sample, the more expensive the study, the *finite population correction factor* should be used when applicable.

When the estimated sample represents more than 5 to 10% of the population, the calculated size should be reduced by the finite population correction factor. If, for example, the population contained 100 elements and the calculation of sample size indicated that a sample of 20 was needed, fewer than 20 observations would, in fact, be taken if the finite population correction factor were used.

The required sample would be given as $n' = n[N/(N + n - 1)]$, where n was the originally determined size, n' was the revised size, and N is population size. Thus, with $N = 100$ and $n = 20$, only 17 sample elements would, in fact, be used.

OTHER APPROACHES TO DETERMINING SAMPLE SIZE

So far, we've taken a statistical approach to calculating sample size. Researchers and companies often use other approaches instead of—or in addition to—the statistical approach we've presented. In this section, we discuss a few of these approaches, including the research budget, anticipated cross classifications, and historical precedent.

Sample Size Determination Using the Research Budget

As you may have concluded by now, marketing research can be an expensive process. While there are some aspects of the process that can be relatively inexpensive, obtaining high-quality information can require significant monetary resources. For the most part, data collection is a variable cost; the bigger the sample size, the greater the cost. The same thing is true for exploratory research. More depth interviews, focus groups, and so on, serve to increase the cost of the project.

The other aspects of the research process are, more or less, fixed in terms of cost. For example, it takes about the same amount of money to design a data collection form for a project with 100 respondents as it does for a project with 10,000 respondents. As a result, for projects with limited budgets, it is usually either the amount and quality of exploratory research or the sample size for the primary data collection (or both) that are reduced to make the project fit the budget. This is unfortunate, but it is often a fact of life for researchers. As a practical matter, then, when the budget is limited, sample size is a function of the amount of money "left over" after taking other research costs into consideration. The available budget is divided by the expected cost per contact of the method of administration utilized to arrive at the sample size. The cost per contact information will be based on historical information from other similar projects conducted by the research department or by the marketing research provider.

MANAGER'S FOCUS

Ideally, your research budget would be established based on whatever tasks needed to be accomplished (including generating a sample of appropriate type and size) to acquire information of the desired quality. However, business realities do not always permit us to pursue what is "ideal." How, then, should the sampling process be approached when the budget is limited?

All too often, managers (aided by compliant researchers) resort to nonprobability samples as an affordable means of obtaining what they believe to be necessarily large sample sizes. For example, surveys may be conducted (a) at malls using convenience samples (intercept interviewing) or (b) on the Web using online panels. The problem with this approach, as we have highlighted in earlier chapters, is that while the sample size might look "respectable," there is a good chance (and there is no way of estimating what that chance is) that the nonprobability sample will not be representative of the target population. Having a large sample size does not

improve the accuracy of your findings in the least if you are using an approach that generates an unrepresentative sample. In other words, if your statistics do not correspond with the population parameters, it doesn't matter whether they came from the responses of 100 or 1,000 people, they are still inaccurate.

A limited research budget is not a reason for abandoning sound research methods. Rather than generating a large nonprobability sample, it would be far better to utilize the probability sampling approach that best fits the purpose of your study and sacrifice sample size. The smaller sample size may somewhat reduce the precision of your statistical estimates, but your researcher will be in a position to estimate for you the range of precision attained. We believe it is better to know the sampling error limitations of a smaller data set than to ignore the much more dangerous errors associated with a larger nonprobability sample.

Each stage of the research process is interrelated and research teams should consider the entire process before undertaking any data collection.

Sample Size Determination Using Anticipated Analyses

One of the more important practical bases for determining the size of sample that will be needed is the analysis to be conducted on the data. Suppose that in our task of estimating the proportion of all fishermen who took at least one overnight fishing trip in the past year, we also wanted to determine whether this pattern of behavior was somehow related to an individual's age and income. Assume that the age categories of interest were as follows: younger than 20, 20–29, 30–39, 40–49, and 50 and older. The income categories were as follows: less than $15,000, $15,000–$29,999, $30,000–$44,999, $45,000–$59,999, and $60,000 and over. There are thus five age categories and five income categories for which the proportion of fishermen taking an overnight trip would be estimated.

While we could estimate proportions for each of these variables separately, we should also recognize that the two variables are interrelated in that increases in incomes are typically related to increases in age. To allow for this interdependence, we need to consider the impact of the two variables simultaneously. The way to do this is through a cross-tab analysis in which age and income jointly define the cells or categories in the table. (We'll go into more detail about this type of analysis in Chapter 20.)

Exhibit 16.2 is a cross-tab table that could be used for the example at hand. Note that this dummy table is complete in all respects except for the numbers that actually go in each of the cells. These would, of course, be determined by the data actually collected on the number and proportion of all those sampled who actually made at least one overnight trip. In the table, there are 25 cells that need estimation. It is unlikely, however, that the decision maker for whom our study is designed is going to be comfortable with an estimate based on only a few cases of the phenomenon. Yet even with a sample of, say, 500 fishermen, there is only a potential of 20 cases per cell (i.e., 500 cases divided by 25 cells) if the sample is evenly divided with respect to the age and income levels considered. And it is very unlikely that the sample would split this way, which would put the researcher in the position of

E x h i b i t 1 6 . 2	**Number and Proportion of Fishermen Staying Overnight as a Function of Age and Income**				
			Age		
Income	Younger than 20	20–29	30–39	40–49	50 and Older
Less than $15,000					
$15,000–$29,999					
$30,000–$44,999					
$45,000–$59,999					
$60,000 and over					

estimating the proportion in a cell engaging in this behavior on the basis of fewer than 20 cases.

If we were to determine sample size based on this particular anticipated analysis, we would start by determining the minimum number of respondents needed in each cell. The bare minimum number of cases falling into a cell is normally taken to be 5, but if this cross tab is central to the purpose of the study, the general rule of thumb is that 100 or more cases are needed in each cell. For issues of secondary importance, 20 to 50 cases are recommended.[3] In our example, if this analysis is the main reason the study was conducted, we would need a sample size of at least 2,500 (25 cells × 100 cases per cell = 2,500 cases). And this assumes that the 2,500 cases will spread themselves out evenly across the 25 cells, which basically never happens, so it would be necessary to raise the required sample size based on the expected distribution of the cases across the cells.

Maybe another type of analysis will be used. If so, the same arguments for determining sample size apply. That is, you need enough cases to satisfy the requirements of the technique, and different techniques have different sample size requirements. We don't need to get into those kinds of details in this book, but we do want to remind you once again that the stages in the research process are very much related, and a decision with respect to one stage can affect all the other stages. In this case, a decision with respect to method of analysis can have an important impact on the size of the sample that should be selected. As always, you must think through the entire research process, including how the data will be analyzed, before beginning the data collection process.

Determining Sample Size Using Historical Evidence

One final method by which some researchers and companies determine the size of the sample is to use the size that others have used for similar studies in the past. Although this may be different from the ideal size in a given problem, the fact that the contemplated sample size is in line with that used for similar studies is psychologically comforting, particularly to inexperienced researchers. One of us once had a client who had just taken a marketing research position with an organization. She would periodically ask for guidance with respect to marketing research projects that her company was conducting. When asked about the sample size that she had selected on a particular project, the client responded with a particular number of mail surveys that were going to be sent. When asked how she had arrived at that number, she said "because we always send out that many." Many companies operate in a similar fashion.

Sometimes, using history as a guide may not be a bad strategy. At some point in time, someone may have determined that a certain number of mail surveys sent will deliver enough confidence and precision for the types of assessment needed by the client company. Until things change—more confidence or precision is needed, response rates decrease significantly, or a parameter with much wider variation in the population is estimated—the necessary sample size probably won't change much.

ETHICAL DILEMMA 16.3

A recent discussion between the account manager for an independent research agency and the marketing people for the client left the account manager feeling perplexed. After numerous discussions, the account manager believed that she had a good handle on the client's problem and major concerns. On the basis of this understanding, she had developed a set of dummy tables by which the client's concerns could be investigated. During the most recent meeting, she had presented these to the client. The client had completely accepted the account manager's recommendation about how the data would be viewed and closed the meeting by asking how large a sample the account manager would recommend and how much the study would cost. The account manager's anxiety was caused by the fact that she believed from the earlier discussions and some preliminary investigation that two of the seven hypotheses were especially promising. The sample size that was needed to investigate these two hypotheses was almost 60% smaller than that needed to address some of the other hypotheses because of the fewer cells in the cross-classification table. The account manager was in a dilemma about whether she should take the safe route and recommend the larger sample size to the client and thereby assure that all the planned cross-classifications could be completed or whether she should go with her instinct and recommend the smaller sample size and save the client some money.

- What would you recommend that the account manager do?
- Is it ethical for the account manager to recommend the larger sample size when she is fairly certain that the smaller one will provide the answers the client needs? Is it ethical to do the reverse and recommend the smaller sample when there is some risk that the smaller sample will not adequately answer the problem that the firm was hired to solve?
- What are the account manager's responsibilities to the client in a case like this?

| Exhibit 16.3 | | Typical Sample Sizes for Studies of Human and Institutional Populations | | |

Number of Subgroup Analyses	People or Households		Institutions	
	National	Regional or Special	National	Regional or Special
None or few	1,000–1,500	200–500	200–500	50–200
Average	1,500–2,500	500–1,000	500–1,000	200–500
Many	2,500+	1,000+	1,000+	500+

Exhibit 16.3, which summarizes the evidence, provides a crude yardstick for using other studies as a guide for the sample size needed in a current study. Note that national studies typically involve larger samples than regional or special studies. Note further that the number of subgroup analyses has a direct impact on sample size.

SUMMARY

Learning Objective 1

Cite three factors researchers must take into account when determining sample size.
When estimating a sample size, researchers must consider (1) how precise the estimate must be, (2) the degree of confidence that the population parameter falls within the precision interval, and (3) how much variation there is on the parameter of interest in the population.

Learning Objective 2

Specify the relationship between precision and confidence.
There is a trade-off between degree of confidence and degree of precision. All else equal, if a researcher wants greater confidence, it is necessary to give up precision. If greater precision is necessary, then confidence must be reduced. It is only when sample size is allowed to vary that it is possible to achieve given levels of both precision and confidence. The determination of sample size involves balancing the two considerations against each other.

Learning Objective 3

Explain in what way the size of the population influences the size of the sample.

In most instances, the size of the population has no direct effect on the size of the sample but affects it only indirectly through the variability of the characteristic in the population.

Learning Objective 4

Specify the circumstances under which the finite population correction factor should be used.
In general, when the sample size will represent more than 5–10% of the population, the calculated sample size should be reduced by the finite population correction factor.

Learning Objective 5

List four methods of determining sample size for a project.
Researchers might determine the required sample size (1) using a statistical approach in which the desired levels of confidence and precision, as well as the estimated variability of the characteristic in the population, are taken into account; (2) using the available research budget as a guide; (3) using anticipated analyses and the number of cases necessary to perform those analyses; and (4) using historical evidence of sample sizes in similar studies.

KEY TERMS

precision (page 357)   confidence (page 357)

REVIEW QUESTIONS

1. In determining sample size, what factors must an analyst consider?

2. What is the difference between degree of confidence and degree of precision?

3. How do you determine the sample size necessary to estimate a population mean with some desired degree of precision and confidence?

4. What effect would relaxing the precision with which a population mean is estimated have on sample size? Decreasing the degree of confidence from 95 to 90%?

5. Suppose that you wanted to estimate a population proportion within +/−3 percentage points at the 95% level of confidence. How would you proceed, and what quantities would you need to estimate?

6. Where can you go for the estimates of population variance needed for calculating sample size for a mean?

7. If you had absolutely no idea about a population proportion but wanted to use the most conservative position possible, what would your estimate be? Why?

8. What is the correct procedure for choosing sample size when making multiple estimates?

9. How is sample size determined based on anticipated cross-tab analyses?

DISCUSSION QUESTIONS, PROBLEMS, AND PROJECTS

1. A survey was being designed by the marketing research department of a medium-sized manufacturer of household appliances. The general aim was to assess customer satisfaction with the company's dishwashers. As part of this general objective, management wanted to measure the average maintenance expenditure per year per household, the average number of malfunctions or breakdowns per year, and the number of times a dishwasher is cleaned within a year. Management wished to be 95% confident in the results. Furthermore, the magnitude of the error was not to exceed +/−$4 for maintenance expenditures, +/−1 for malfunctions, and +/−4 for cleanings. The research department noted that while some households would spend nothing on maintenance expenditures per year, others might spend as much as $120. Also, while some dishwashers would experience no breakdowns within a year, the maximum expected would be no more than three. Finally, while some dishwashers might not be cleaned at all during the year, others might be cleaned as frequently as once a month.

   a. How large a sample would you recommend if each of the three variables were considered separately? Show all your calculations.

   b. What size sample would you recommend *overall* given that management felt that the expenditure on repairs was most important and the number of cleanings least important to know accurately?

2. The management of a major dairy wanted to determine the average ounces of milk consumed per resident in the state of Montana. Past trends indicated that the variation in milk consumption(s) was four ounces. A 95% confidence level is required, and the error is not to exceed +/−12 ounces.

    a. What sample size would you recommend? Show your calculations.

    b. Management wanted to double the level of precision and increase the level of confidence to 99%. What sample size would you recommend? Show your calculations. Comment on your results.

3. The manager of a local recreational center wanted to determine the average amount each customer spent on traveling to and from the center. On the basis of the findings, the manager was planning on raising the entrance fee. The manager noted that customers living near the center would spend almost nothing on traveling. On the other hand, customers living at the other side of town had to travel about 15 miles and spent about 30 cents (U.S.) per mile on average. The manager wanted to be 95% confident of the findings and did not want the error to exceed +/−10 cents. What sample size should the manager use to determine the average travel expenditure? Show your calculations.

4. A large manufacturer of chemicals recently came under severe criticism from various environmentalists for its disposal of industrial effluent and waste. In response, management launched a campaign to counter the bad publicity it was receiving. A study of the effectiveness of the campaign indicated that about 20% of the residents of the city were aware of the campaign and the company's position. In conducting the study, a sample of 400 was used and a 95% confidence level was specified. Three months later, it was believed that 30% of the residents were aware of the campaign. However, management decided to do another survey and specified a 99% confidence level and a margin error of +/−2 percentage points. What sample size would you recommend for this study? Show all your calculations.

5. Score-It, Inc. is a large manufacturer of video games for game systems. The marketing research department is designing a survey to determine attitudes toward the products. Additionally, the percentage of households owning game systems and the average usage rate per week are to be determined. The department wants to be 95% confident of the results and does not want the error to exceed +/−3 percentage points for video game ownership and +/−1 hour for average usage rate. Previous reports indicate that about 70% of the households own game systems, and the average usage rate is 20 hours with a standard deviation of 10 hours.

    a. What sample size would you recommend, assuming only the percentage of households owning video games is to be determined? Show all your calculations.

    b. What sample size would you recommend, assuming only the average usage rate per week is to be determined? Show all your calculations.

    c. What sample size would you recommend, assuming both the above variables are to be determined? Why?

6. The local gas and electric company in a city in the northeast United States recently started a campaign to encourage people to reduce unnecessary use of gas and electricity. To assess the effectiveness of the campaign, management wanted to do a survey to determine the proportion of people that had adopted the recommended energy-saving measures. What sample size would you recommend if the error was not to exceed +/−0.025 percentage point and the confidence level was to be 90%? Show your calculations.

7. Assume you are a marketing researcher analyst for TV Institute, and you have just been given the assignment of estimating the percentage of all American households that watched the ABC movie last Sunday night. You have been told that your estimate should have a precision of +/−1% and that there should be 95% confidence in the results. Your first task is to choose a sample of the appropriate size. Make any assumptions that are necessary.

a. Compute the sample size that will satisfy the required specifications.

b. What is the required sample size if the precision is specified as +/−2 percentage points?

c. What would be the sample size if the confidence level were decreased to 90%, keeping the precision at +/−1 percentage point?

d. If you had only enough time to take a sample of size 100, what precision could you expect from your estimate? (Assume a 95% confidence interval.)

e. Assume that instead of taking a sample from the entire country, you would like to restrict yourself to one state with 1 million households. Would the sample size computed in (a) be too large? Too small? Explain.

8. The manager of a local bakery wants to determine the average expenditure per household on bakery products. Past research indicates that the standard deviation is $10.

a. Calculate the sample size for the various levels of precision and confidence. Show your calculations:

	Desired Precision (+/−)	Desired Confidence	Estimated Sample Size
1	0.50	0.95	
2	1.00	0.99	
3	0.50	0.90	
4	0.25	0.90	
5	0.50	0.99	
6	0.25	0.95	
7	1.00	0.90	
8	1.00	0.95	
9	0.25	0.99	

b. Which alternative gives the largest estimate for sample size? Explain.

9. A manufacturer of liquid soaps wishes to estimate the proportion of individuals using liquid soaps as opposed to bar soaps. Prior estimates of the proportions are listed below.

a. For the various levels of precision and confidence indicated, calculate the needed sample size.

	Desired Precision in Percentage Points (+/−)	Desired Confidence	(%) Estimated Proportion	Estimated Sample Size
1	6	0.99	20	
2	2	0.90	10	
3	6	0.99	10	
4	4	0.95	30	
5	2	0.90	20	
6	2	0.99	30	
7	6	0.90	30	
8	4	0.95	10	
9	4	0.95	20	

b. Which alternative gives the largest estimate of the sample size? Explain.

10. Your World, Inc., is a large travel agency located in Cincinnati, Ohio. Management is concerned about its declining leisure travel-tour business. It believes that the profile of those engaging in leisure travel has changed in the past few years. To determine if that is indeed the case, management decides to conduct a survey to determine the profile of the current leisure travel-tour customer. Three variables are identified that require particular attention. Prior to conducting the survey, the three dummy tables shown below were developed. How large a sample would you recommend be taken? Justify your answer.

	Age			
Income	**18–24**	**25–34**	**35–54**	**55+**
0–$9,999				
$10,000–$19,999				
$20,000–$29,999				
$30,000–$39,999				
$40,000 and over				

	Education			
Age	**Some High School**	**High School Graduate**	**Some College**	**College Graduate**
18–24				
25–34				
35–54				
55+				

	Education			
Income	**Some High School**	**High School Graduate**	**Some College**	**College Graduate**
0–$9,999				
$10,000–$19,999				
$20,000–$29,999				
$30,000–$39,999				
$40,000 and over				

11. You are the assistant director of political research for the ABC television network, and two candidates, Joseph Thomas and Ann Martin, are running for president of the United States of America. You need to furnish a prediction of the percentage of the vote going to Martin, assuming the election was held today, for tomorrow's evening newscast. You want to be 95% confident in your prediction and desire a total precision of 6%.

a. Assume that you have no reliable information concerning the percentage of the population that prefers Martin. What sample size will you use for the project?

b. Assume that a similar poll, taken 30 days ago, revealed that 40% of the respondents would vote for Martin. Taking this information into account, what sample size will you use for the project?

c. Which of the two sample sizes you have just calculated would you prefer to use for your study? Why?

d. Most polls of this type are conducted by telephone. When a potential respondent answers the phone, what is the *first* question you should ask? Why?

Collecting the Data: Nonsampling Errors and Response Rate Calculation

Learning Objectives

1. Describe four basic types of nonsampling errors.
2. Discuss noncoverage error and how it can be reduced.
3. Explain what nonresponse error is.
4. Identify the two main sources of nonresponse error.
5. Define response error and discuss some of its causes.
6. Discuss how interviewers can contribute to response error.
7. Cite the standard definition for response rate.
8. Discuss several ways in which response rates might be improved.

Introduction

To most people, the words "marketing research" mean the data collection process. At this stage, data are collected either in the field or by phone, mail, e-mail, and so on. In this chapter, we focus on the various things that can go wrong in conducting a study, with special emphasis on sources of error we haven't discussed in earlier chapters. Understanding the possible sources of error in data collection is important for understanding how much faith to put into the results of a study. In this chapter, we also show you how to calculate a study's response rate, an important consideration for assessing the overall quality of the data collection effort. Finally, we offer several suggestions for improving response rates.

IMPACT AND IMPORTANCE OF NONSAMPLING ERRORS

Two basic types of errors arise in research studies: *sampling errors* and *nonsampling errors*. We defined sampling error earlier as the difference between results obtained for a sample and the results we would have obtained had we gathered information from the whole population. As we saw, the degree of sampling error can be estimated (assuming probability sampling procedures are used) and can be reduced by increasing sample size.

Nonsampling errors reflect the many other kinds of error that can arise in research, and they apply to data collected from a sample or from a census. Nonsampling errors can be *random* or *nonrandom*. Nonrandom nonsampling errors are more troublesome. Random errors produce estimates that vary from the true value; sometimes these estimates are above and sometimes below the true value, but on a random basis. As a result, random errors tend to cancel each other out. Nonrandom nonsampling errors, on the other hand, tend to produce mistakes in only one direction. They bias the sample statistic away from the true value of the population parameter. Nonrandom errors can occur because of errors in conception, wording of questions, interpretation of replies, statistics, arithmetic, analysis, coding, or reporting.

Unfortunately, nonsampling errors are quite common because of the many ways they can creep into a project. Worse, nonsampling errors are not as manageable as sampling errors, which decrease with increases in sample size. Nonsampling errors do not necessarily decrease with increases in sample size. They may, in fact, increase. Furthermore, it is difficult to even estimate the size and effects of nonsampling errors.

As an example of the impact of sampling versus nonsampling error, consider how a sample of consumers might respond to the following question on a survey: "On average, how many times per week do you brush your teeth?" Suppose that we collected data from a random sample of consumers and found that the mean response was 21 brushings per week. Further, we could be 95% confident that had we talked with all consumers in the population the answer would fall between 19 and 23. In our analysis, we have fully accounted for possible sampling error. Accounting for sampling error, however, does not help with the fact that many people will have overstated their brushing behavior in order to be seen as socially acceptable. The appropriate allowance for sampling error provides accurate insights into how the population would have responded to the question given the data collection method but provides very little insight into the validity of the manner in which the data were collected or the question itself.

As you can begin to see from this example, nonsampling errors are frequently the most important errors that arise in research. Nonsampling error has consistently been shown to be the major contributor to total survey error, while sampling error has minimal impact.[1] Nonsampling errors can be reduced, but doing so depends on improving the method of data collection—primarily through effective exploratory research and careful pretesting of data collection forms—rather than increasing sample size.

nonsampling error
Error that arises in research that is not due to sampling; nonsampling error can occur because of errors in conception, logic, interpretation of questions and replies, statistics, arithmetic, analyzing, coding, or reporting.

TYPES OF NONSAMPLING ERRORS

There are four main categories of nonsampling error: noncoverage error, nonresponse error, response error, and office error. The first two types are sometimes referred to as nonobservation errors, because either part of the population of interest was not included, or because some respondents selected (randomly or otherwise) for inclusion in the sample did not participate. Response errors and office errors are sometimes called observation errors. In these cases, data were obtained from the appropriate sample elements, but the data were either inaccurate or mistakes were made during the coding, analysis, or reporting stages of the research.

Learning Objective

1. Describe four basic types of nonsampling errors.

noncoverage error
Nonsampling error that arises because of a failure to include some units, or entire sections, of the defined target population in the sampling frame.

Noncoverage Errors

Noncoverage error arises because of a failure to include some part of the defined population in the sampling frame. That is, one or more consumers, households, and so on, that meet the criteria for membership in the population are not included in the list of population members and thus have no chance of being included in the sample. Noncoverage error, then, is essentially a sampling frame problem.

Researchers realize that the telephone directory, for instance, does not provide a complete sampling frame for most general surveys. Many households no longer have regular telephones, instead choosing to use cell phones for which directories are not available. And not all people with regular telephones have their numbers listed in the directory. On top of that, important demographic differences have always existed between those who have phones and those who do not. Noncoverage error tends to be much less of a problem in surveys of businesses or other institutions for which directory listings are almost always available.

Noncoverage is also a problem in mail and e-mail surveys. The mailing and e-mail lists dictate the sampling frame. If the lists inadequately represent segments of the population, the survey will also suffer from noncoverage error. Almost all mailing lists or lists of e-mail addresses do not exactly capture the population the researcher wishes to study, even though mailing lists are available for very specific population groups.

When data are to be collected by personal interview in the home, some form of area sample is typically used to pinpoint respondents. In this case, the sampling frame is one of areas, blocks, and dwelling units, rather than a list of respondents. However, this does not eliminate potential noncoverage error. Maps of the city may not be totally current, so the newest areas may not have a proper chance of being included in the sample. The instructions to the interviewer may not be sufficiently detailed. The evidence indicates that lower-income households are avoided when the selection of households is made by the field staff rather than the home office. This means that a portion of the intended population is underrepresented in the study, while the accessible segment is overrepresented.

There are also sampling frame problems when personal interviews in shopping malls are used to collect data. For one thing, there is no list of population elements. Rather, only those who shop in a particular mall have a chance of being included in the study. This is why quota samples are often used in mall intercept studies. Unfortunately, using quota samples doesn't eliminate noncoverage bias. For example, interviewers typically underselect in both the high- and low-income classes.

Noncoverage error is not a problem in every survey. For some studies, clear, convenient, and complete sampling frames exist. For example, a department store wishing to conduct a study among its charge-account customers should have little trouble with frame bias. The sampling frame is simply those with charge accounts. Similarly, a firm should experience little noncoverage bias in conducting a study among its employees. The population of interest here would be the firm's employees, and it could be expected that the list of employees would be current and accurate since it is needed to generate the payroll.

The rise and popularity of cell phones increases the problem of noncoverage error when working with a telephone directory as a sampling frame.

Given that noncoverage bias is likely, what can the researcher do to lessen its effect? The most obvious step is to improve the quality of the sampling frame. This may mean taking the time to bring available city maps up to date, or taking a sample to check the quality and representativeness of a mailing list with respect to a target population. The unlisted-number problem common to telephone surveys can be handled by random-digit or plus-one dialing, although this will not provide adequate sample representation of those without phones.

We should mention one other relatively common problem with sampling frames. *Overcoverage error* can arise because of duplication in the list of sampling units. Units with multiple entries in the sampling frame—for example, families with several phone listings—have a higher probability of being included in the sample than do sampling units with one listing. For most surveys, however, noncoverage is much more common and troublesome than overcoverage.

Nonresponse Errors

Nonresponse error can occur when you fail to obtain information from elements of the population that were selected for the sample. Suppose that five years from now a university were to conduct a mail survey among this year's senior class to update records and to determine how "successful" the school's graduates were. Included on the survey was an item assessing current salary. Who is most likely to complete and return the survey? Probably those who are pleased with their salaries. Who is least likely? Probably those who are not happy with their salaries. As a result, there is a very real possibility that those who respond to the survey are different from those who do not respond to the survey on a key dimension, current salary, and the results with respect to salary will be systematically biased upward. This upward bias reflects nonresponse error.

Nonresponse error is a potential problem in any project for which data are not collected from all respondents selected for the sample. It is a *potential* problem, because it only occurs when those who respond are systematically different from those who do not respond in some important way. The degree of nonresponse error, however, is difficult to assess because we obviously do not have answers from those who do not respond. Exhibit 17.1 presents several possible methods of determining if nonresponse error is likely to be a problem in a particular study.

The two main sources of nonresponse bias are refusals, which apply to projects using all forms of data collection, and not-at-homes, which apply mainly to telephone surveys and some types of personal interviews.

Refusals In almost every study, some respondents will refuse to participate. The rate of refusals depends on many factors, including the nature of the respondent, the nature of the organization sponsoring the research, the circumstances surrounding the contact, the topic of the study, and the skill of the interviewer in the case of telephone and personal interviews. Even the culture of the country can affect the refusal rate. For example, in some cultures like Saudi Arabia, it is difficult to interview women. Research Window 17.1 (on page 379) reports data from The Council for Marketing and Opinion Research on the percentage of people who report that they have refused to participate in a survey in the prior year. The trend has been rising over a period of years.

As we discussed in Chapter 10, the method used to collect the data also makes a difference. All else equal, personal interviews seem to be most effective, and mail and Internet-based questionnaires least effective, in generating a response. Telephone interviews are usually less successful than personal interviews in getting target respondents to cooperate, but they typically have higher response rates than do other types of surveys. The most obvious reason for the superiority of personal interviews and telephone surveys over mail surveys is the social nature of the contact: A respondent doesn't run the risk of hurting someone's feelings by throwing a mail survey in the nearest trash can.

Learning Objective

3. Explain what nonresponse error is.

nonresponse error
Nonsampling error that represents a failure to obtain information from some elements of the population that were selected and designated for the sample.

Learning Objective

4. Identify the two main sources of nonresponse error.

refusals
Nonsampling error that arises because some designated respondents refuse to participate in the study.

| **Exhibit 17.1** | **Three Methods for Diagnosing Nonresponse** |

Method 1 Contact a sample of nonrespondents. If a researcher can identify persons who have not responded to a survey (perhaps after several attempts), it is sometimes possible to select a sample of the nonrespondents and contact them again, typically using a different method of contact. This time, however, the goal is not to get the respondent to complete the entire survey, but instead to simply answer one or two questions that focus on the key issue in the project. The answers from this "nonrespondent" sample on these items are then compared with those from the initial sample. If the responses from the two samples are not different on the key items (see Chapter 21 for methods of testing for statistically significant differences), then nonresponse error is probably not an issue in the project. This is the preferred method of diagnosing nonresponse bias, but it is also the most difficult under normal circumstances.

Method 2 Compare respondent demographics against known demographics of population. Sometimes researchers conduct sample surveys among populations for which data about the population are available from other sources. For example, suppose that you were conducting a telephone survey among the residents of a particular state in the United States and that when you completed the data collection process you computed the various demographic characteristics of your sample (e.g., gender, age, education). These sample statistics could then be compared to statistics from other sources such as U.S. census data to determine if certain demographic groups are over- or underrepresented in the sample, which would indicate the possibility of nonresponse error. Note, however, that this result might also be an indication of noncoverage error if the sampling frame is less than adequate. Further, even if the sample demographic statistics match perfectly with the known population parameters, we haven't eliminated the possibility of nonresponse error, because the key issues being addressed may be completely unrelated to the demographic variables we are considering. In that case, those who respond may be systematically different from those who don't respond, yet still have the same demographic characteristics on average. Despite its shortcomings, however, this approach is much better than simply assuming that those who don't respond are no different than those who do respond.

Method 3 Conduct an analysis of late responders versus early responders. With data collection methods that allow subjects to respond at their convenience (e.g., mail, e-mail, Internet, fax), it is possible to compare the responses of those who respond early with those who respond late. The idea is that those who respond late will be more like those who don't respond at all than are those who respond early. If the analysis indicates that scores on key issues are different for, say, the first 20% of respondents versus the last 20% of respondents, then the responses of those who didn't respond at all are likely to differ from those who did respond, indicating the possibility of nonresponse bias. If late responders are no different from early responders, it is less likely that nonresponse bias is a problem.

In general, there is a tendency for females, nonwhites, those who are less well educated, those who have lower incomes, and those who are older to be more likely to refuse to participate in a study.[2] In addition, the type of organization sponsoring the research can also make a difference in the number of refusals. As a general rule, most people are probably more inclined to "help" a not-for-profit entity than a for-profit enterprise by taking the time to respond to a survey, especially when the cause is one they support.

Sometimes the circumstances surrounding the contact can cause a refusal. A respondent may be busy, tired, or sick when contacted. And the subject of the research also affects the refusal rate. Those interested in the subject are most likely to respond. Commonly cited reasons for refusing to participate in a survey include lack of time, contacting respondents at an inappropriate time, and lack of interest in the subject matter.

Finally, interviewers themselves can have a significant impact on the number of refusals they obtain. Their approach, manner, and even their own demographic characteristics can affect a respondent's willingness to participate.

Not-at-Homes With refusals, we can be fairly certain that at least we contacted a potential respondent (or his or her household) and provided an opportunity to respond. We may not like the response (i.e., a refusal), but at least we received one. Not-at-homes present a different sort of problem. Sometimes we simply cannot reach designated sampling units at home during the data collection time frame. The percentage of not-at-homes has been increasing for a long time. The probability of finding someone home traditionally has been greater for low-income families, rural families, and families with younger children. Seasonal variations, particularly during the holidays, occur, as do weekday-to-weekend variations. And it's much easier to find a "responsible adult" at home than a specific respondent. Thus, the choice of the basic sampling unit is important in the not-at-home problem.

not-at-homes
Nonsampling error that arises when replies are not secured from some designated sampling units because the respondents are not at home when the interviewer calls.

research window 17.1

Past Year Refusals (Random-Digital Dialing Samples)

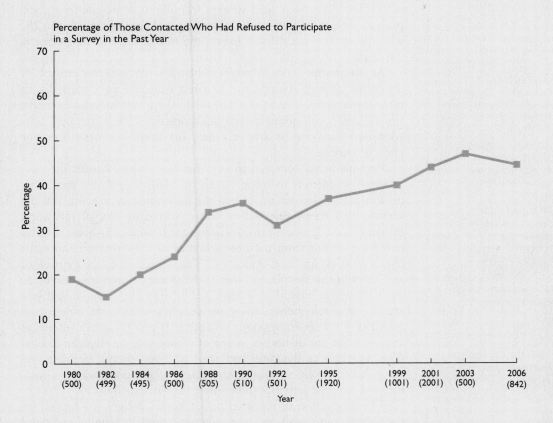

Percentage of Those Contacted Who Had Refused to Participate in a Survey in the Past Year

Source: "The Research Profession Image Study," Patrick Glaser, Director of Respondent Cooperation, The Council for Marketing and Opinion Research, May 2007.

Technological advancements have made the not-at-home problem even worse, especially with telephone surveys. As answering machines have become more prevalent in households, more and more people are using them to screen their calls. A substantial portion of households—not to mention individuals with cell phones—use caller ID, a technique for identifying the source of an incoming telephone call, to screen calls. Many people ignore calls coming from sources they do not recognize.

Several things can be done to reduce the incidence of not-at-homes. For example, in some studies, the interviewer might make an appointment in advance with the respondent. Although this approach is particularly valuable in surveys of busy executives, it may not be justifiable in an ordinary consumer survey. A commonly used technique in the latter instance is the *callback*, in which an interviewer attempts to reach a sample element again on different days and times. (The name comes from the telephone survey context, but the approach can apply to other methods of data collection as well.) The nonresponse problem due to not-at-homes is so important to the accuracy of most surveys that experts have been suggesting for many years that small samples with multiple callbacks are better than large samples without callbacks, unless the percentage of initial response can be increased considerably above normal levels.[3]

This is an important general point, so we'll repeat it: It is usually better to work hard at generating responses from a smaller sampling pool (that is, lower TSE) and perhaps end up with a smaller sample than to start with a (much) larger sampling pool

A well-known car agency needed to make a decision about whether to import a relatively unknown line of foreign cars to complement its domestic line. To aid in its decision making, the agency contracted a research firm to conduct a study to determine potential consumer interest and demand for this foreign car line. The results indicated that substantial awareness and interest existed, and consequently the decision was made to take on the new line.

To publicize the new line, a special preview was arranged for interested community members such as local newspaper and radio people, executives in related automotive industries, filling station and repair shop owners, and leaders of men's and women's clubs. The agency's owners also wanted to invite the survey participants who had expressed an interest in the car and consequently asked the research firm to provide them with the respondents' names. The research firm refused to comply with this request, arguing that to do so would be a violation of the respondents' promised anonymity.

- Should the research firm have complied with the agency's request?
- Did the car agency have the right to receive the participants' names since it had paid for the research?
- Would it have made a difference if the study had not been one to determine sales potential?
- What would be some of the consequences of making the respondents' names known to the car agency?
- If the question had been anticipated before the survey was begun, could the interview structure have avoided the dilemma in which the research company and the agency now find themselves?

and obtain a larger sample without concern for obtaining feedback from nonrespondents. Stated differently, with a fixed budget it is better to get a higher response rate from a smaller group of respondents than a lower response rate from a larger group of respondents, even if the result is a considerably smaller sample size. Beware of any data collection tool that offers thousands of respondents but must send surveys to millions of people to accomplish it. Unless the 98% who do not respond are the same as the 2% who do respond on the key issues, the risk of nonresponse error is too high.

An alternative to the straight callback is the *modified callback*. If the initial contact attempt and first few callbacks were made by an interviewer and a contact was not established, the interviewer might simply mail a self-administered questionnaire with a stamped, self-addressed envelope or drop a survey off at the contact's home or place of business.

Perhaps it has occurred to you that one way to handle the not-at-home problem is to substitute the house or apartment next door or, in a telephone survey, to call the next name on the list. On the surface, this seems reasonable, but it is actually one of the worst things you could do. All it does is substitute more "at-homes" (who may be different from the not-at-homes in a number of important characteristics) for "not-at-homes." This increases the proportion of at-homes in the sample and makes the potential nonresponse error problem worse instead of solving it. For example, imagine that you are doing a telephone survey on people's enjoyment of outdoor activities for a sporting goods company. If you routinely substitute at-homes for not-at-homes (many of whom may be engaged in outdoor activities at the time you tried to reach them), nonresponse error is very likely to cause an estimate of the population's enjoyment of outdoor activities to be lower than it actually is.

The proportion of reported not-at-homes is likely to depend on the interviewer's skill and the judgment used in scheduling initial contacts and callbacks. This suggests that one way of reducing not-at-home nonresponse bias is by better interviewer training, particularly with respect to scheduling callbacks more efficiently.

Response Errors

Response error occurs when an individual provides a response to an item, but the response is inaccurate for some reason. There are many factors that can cause response error, ranging from poorly written items that respondents misinterpret, to characteristics of the respondent that subconsciously influence his or her responses, to researcher misinterpretation of an individual's responses. Blame for response errors, therefore, can lay with the researcher, the respondent, or both.

The possible causes of response error are so broad that it is often difficult for researchers to grasp their likely effect on survey results. The following series of questions are useful for considering the different ways response errors can affect individuals' responses.[4] These questions might also be used to anticipate possible problems when developing questionnaire items in the first place.

Does the respondent understand the question? As previously mentioned, survey items must be written using simple, direct language, especially when a general audience is being surveyed. If respondents don't understand a question, one of two things is likely to happen: They will either skip the question, leading to potential nonresponse error, or they will answer the question based on their interpretation, which may not match your intended interpretation of the item. Neither of these outcomes is good. Pretesting the questionnaire with members of the relevant population can usually eliminate this source of error.

Several years ago, we conducted a satisfaction study among patients of a number of healthcare providers. The questionnaire included items assessing patient expectations and perceptions of service-provider performance across a range of relevant dimensions. Respondents were instructed to provide answers to each item on the rating scales we provided. One respondent appeared to have read the directions and (we presume) accurately responded to the first of the items on the rating scale, then proceeded to provide open-ended responses to most of the other items. For example, in response to an item that read "How physically comfortable I was during the procedure," this respondent penciled in "very comfortable" instead of responding on the scale we provided. The respondent, a 92-year-old woman, was doing her best to answer our questions. It was clear that she understood the questions, for the most part, but she didn't understand how we wanted her to respond. Was this her fault? Not really; it was our job to make sure that the instructions were clear.

Does the respondent know the answer to the question? Just because a respondent understands a question correctly doesn't mean that she or he actually knows the answer to the question. The problem is that many respondents will answer the question anyway. This is especially common with closed-ended questions for which respondents simply choose a response category. Dealing with this issue is a bit trickier. Providing a "don't know" response category is one option, but this strategy will often create difficulties in data analysis (i.e., lots of missing cases). People will sometimes select the "don't know" option as a way of not having to think about a particular item, even when they do know the answer to the question. A preferred strategy is to perform sufficient exploratory research and questionnaire pretesting to understand what population members are likely—and not likely—to know.

Is the respondent willing to provide the true answer to the question? Respondents who understand a question and know the answer don't always provide a truthful answer. There are lots of reasons for this. Respondents may consciously lie because they want to make themselves look better or to avoid appearing "dumb" when they don't really know the answer to a question. Sometimes respondents are angry or in a bad mood and they knowingly provide inaccurate answers. Some respondents just don't care about their responses, even though they could understand the questions and provide accurate responses if they wanted to. Others simply don't want to say something negative about a product, store, or service provider.

To study people who buy and fly airplanes, the Advanced General Aviation Transport Experiment (AGATE) conducted online surveys. The developers of the AGATE questionnaire noted that when surveys ask how much people are willing to pay for some item, respondents typically give an answer near the bottom of the true acceptable range, whereas asking a yes/no question like "Are you willing to pay $200?" generates more accurate responses, but only about that particular price. So the AGATE researchers set up a questionnaire format that used random numbers to select prices to present to

AGATE used online surveys to study aviation enthusiasts.

© HONDA/PRNEWSFOTO (AP TOPIC GALLERY)

respondents. Thus, no respondent would have the burden of evaluating all the price points. Rather, each person answered a few dozen randomly selected questions, and the results were pooled to create graphs showing the percentages of respondents who said each choice was acceptable.[5]

We once conducted a study where one of the goals was to examine the relationship between patients' self-reported mood prior to receiving a root canal and their perceptions of the service quality provided by their endodontists. One of our measures of mood was a global six-point semantic differential scale ranging from "bad" to "good." One elderly respondent was less than thrilled with our questionnaire, writing on the form that he was "crotchety enough without seeing questionnaires like this!" His attitude toward the questionnaire also seemed to influence his response to the global mood item: he checked the category nearest "good" and added, "I always experience absolute euphoria at the prospect of going to the endodontist. I sing the 'Ode to Joy' at the top of my lungs all the way."

What can be done about these sorts of response errors? Once again, the key is thorough exploratory research and questionnaire pretesting. Questions that are likely to cause respondents to be even slightly defensive—especially sensitive questions—must be carefully designed and tested. When the data collection forms are designed, careful attention must be given to the questions (and the order in which they are asked) so as to hold the respondent's attention.

Is the wording of the question or the situation in which it is asked likely to bias the response? As noted, the wording of a question and its response categories has a strong influence on individuals' responses. Leading questions must be avoided, and researchers must be careful not to accidentally use "loaded" words if they are to uncover the truth about an issue. Interviewers must also be trained not to let the tone of their voice or inflections in their speech vary from one interview to the next. With personal interviews, interviewer nonverbal communication also becomes a potential influence on individuals' responses.

While errors in asking questions can arise with any of the basic question types, the problem is particularly acute with open-ended questions where probing follows the initial response. No two interviewers are likely to use the same probes, creating clear situational differences between respondents. The content, as well as the timing, of the probes may differ. This raises the possibility that the differences in answers may be due to the probes that are used rather than any "true" differences in the position of the respondents.

Surprisingly, closed-ended questions also possess great potential for interviewer bias, because the interviewer may place undue emphasis on one of the alternatives in stating the question. Slight changes in emphasis or tone can change the meaning of the entire question. Most surveys, therefore, are conducted using a rigid set of procedures that interviewers must follow. The instructions should be clear, should be written, and should clearly state the purpose of the study. They should describe the materials to be used, such as questionnaires, maps, time forms, and so on. They should describe how each question should be asked, the kinds of answers that are acceptable, and the kinds and timing of probes that are to be used, if any. Practice training sessions will often be necessary.

There are two other sources of response error that the interviewer might cause. One of the interviewer's main tasks is to keep the respondent interested and motivated. At the same time, the interviewer must try to record what the respondent is saying by carefully writing down the person's answers to open-ended questions or checking the appropriate box with closed-ended questions. These responsibilities are sometimes incompatible, resulting in data recording errors. Interviewers may not correctly "hear" what the respondent is actually saying, hearing instead what they want to hear and recording what they want to record.

Recording errors can be forgiven; interviewer cheating is another matter. Cheating can range from the fabrication of a whole interview to making up one or

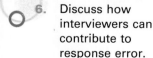

Learning Objective

6. Discuss how interviewers can contribute to response error.

two answers to make the response complete. Because of interviewer cheating, most commercial research firms validate 10 to 20% of the completed interviews through follow-up telephone calls or by sending postcards to a sample of respondents to verify that they have, in fact, been contacted.

Office Errors

Problems with nonsampling errors do not end with data collection. Office error can arise in the editing, coding, and analyzing of the data. For the most part, these errors can be reduced, if not eliminated, by exercising proper controls in data processing. We address some of these issues in the following chapter.

office error
Nonsampling error due to data editing, coding, or analysis errors.

Total Error Is the Key

It is important to understand that total error, rather than any single type of error, is the key in a research investigation. We believe that far too many researchers focus too intently on decreasing sampling error when they should be focusing more closely on potential sources of nonsampling error. Managers, students (especially those with a course in statistics behind them), and some researchers often argue for the "largest possible sample," reasoning that a large sample is much more likely to produce a "valid" result than a small sample is. Increasing the sample size does, in fact, decrease sampling error, but it also can increase nonsampling errors. Nonsampling error is a much more troublesome error than sampling error. Sampling error can be estimated. Many forms of nonsampling error cannot, and new sources of nonsampling error are

Manager's Focus

Sampling error is certainly a concern, but you should be aware that it is only one of many sources of error, and every type of error keeps you from accurately understanding your market. During election cycles, for example, we regularly hear claims that poll results have a margin of error of plus or minus a small number of percentage points. Yet many political polls prove to be poor predictors of what actually occurs in the electoral "marketplace." Why? Because the findings are also subject to the different types of nonsampling error discussed in this chapter. While these types of error can be much more dangerous than sampling error, they are hard to estimate, and many survey sponsors are either unaware of them or simply do not publicly acknowledge them.

The same is true in marketing research studies. Managers are much more aware of sampling error than the various types of nonsampling error. What they do not realize is that their own behavior can lead to a tremendous increase in total error. For example, they may require researchers to generate large sample sizes believing the error in the study will be minimized—but then insist that the study be completed within a short time period. The larger sample may decrease sampling error (assuming an appropriate probability sampling plan is employed), but racing to complete a larger study may cause an exponential increase in nonsampling error. For instance, interviewers may read questions too quickly, rush the responses of interviewees, record responses less accurately, and call new numbers rather than make callbacks when designated respondents are not available. Similarly, field editors may skim over completed surveys rather than scrutinize them for mistakes.

These are but a few examples of how nonsampling error can quickly enter a study. The main point is that managers need to allocate ample time to generate samples and provide resources for the various approaches we discuss later in this chapter for reducing nonsampling error. We urge you to have a candid discussion with your research supplier about all of the types of error that are likely to occur in a study and to offer support for all reasonable efforts to reduce each type of error.

being discovered all the time. Smart researchers try to manage total error, not just one particular kind of error.

Exhibit 17.2 attempts to summarize nonsampling errors and how they can be reduced and controlled. The table can be used as a sort of checklist for marketing managers and other users to evaluate the quality of research prior to making substantive decisions on the basis of the research results. Although not all methods for handling nonsampling errors will be applicable in every study, a systematic analysis of the research effort, using the table guidelines, should prove helpful.

Learning Objective

CALCULATING RESPONSE RATES

7. Cite the standard definition for response rate.

response rate
The number of completed interviews with responding units divided by the number of eligible responding units in the sample.

Once the data have been collected, the researcher must calculate the **response rate** for the project. The response rate—the number of completed interviews with responding units divided by the number of eligible responding units in the sample—serves two important functions. First, it allows an assessment of the potential influence of nonresponse error on the study's results. Although this assessment is qualitative in nature (because even if you were to obtain responses from 90% of those chosen for the sample, the other 10% could have been very different on the issue in question), higher response rates generally suggest fewer problems with nonresponse bias. Second, the response rate serves as an indicator of the overall quality of a data collection effort. For example, very low response rates may indicate poor questionnaire design, lack of interest among respondents, failure to gain the intended respondents' attention, and so on. Unless the client is willing to collect more data, however, it is too late to do anything about these problems. To avoid this outcome, we again strongly urge the use of thoughtful exploratory research and questionnaire pretesting.

The following general formula is used to calculate a project's response rate:

$$\text{response rate} = \frac{\text{number of completed interviews with responding units}}{\text{number of eligible responding units in the sample}}$$

How this formula is applied depends upon the data collection method used. "Completed interviews" includes completed survey forms for methods that don't include an actual interview. We address the most common approaches in the following sections.

Mail and E-Mail Surveys

With these forms of data collection, response rate calculation is usually straightforward. The first step is to determine the number of usable questionnaires completed. Not every questionnaire that is returned is usable, as we'll see in the following chapter. Common reasons for excluding a questionnaire include evidence that a respondent wasn't really paying attention to the questions, or a large percentage of items were not answered by the respondent.

Once the number of usable questionnaires is known, the number of eligible response units must be determined. With these types of data collection, it is usually assumed that all elements or people in the sampling frame meet the criteria for membership in the population and sample, which makes calculating the number of eligible response units quite simple. The researcher need only take the number of response units that she or he attempted to contact and subtract the number of addresses that turned out to be invalid. With mail surveys, the postal service will normally return surveys that are not deliverable because of a wrong address. Similarly, e-mail systems typically notify the sender when an e-mail message cannot successfully be delivered. The point is simply that contacts that could not be made should not count against the researcher in the calculation of response rates. Thus, for these methods of data collection, response rate (RR) is calculated as shown at the top of page 386:

Exhibit 17.2	Overview of Nonsampling Errors and Some Methods for Handling Them	
Type	**Definition**	**Methods for Handling**
Noncoverage	Failure to include some units or entire sections of the defined target population in the sampling frame.	1. Improve basic sampling frame using other sources. 2. Adjust the results by appropriately weighting the subsample results.
Nonresponse	Failure to obtain information from some elements of the population that were selected for the sample.	
	Not-at-homes: Designated respondent is not home when the interviewer calls.	1. Have interviewers make advance appointments. 2. Call back at another time, preferably at a different time of day. 3. Attempt to contact the designated respondent using another approach (e.g., use a modified callback).
	Refusals: Respondent refuses to cooperate in the survey.	1. Attempt to convince the respondent of the value of the research and the importance of his or her participation. 2. Provide advance notice that the survey is coming. 3. Guarantee anonymity. 4. Provide an incentive for participating. 5. Hide the identification of the sponsor by using an independent research organization. 6. Try to get a foot in the door by getting the respondent to comply with some small task before getting the survey. 7. Use personalized cover letters. 8. Use a follow-up contact at a more convenient time. 9. Avoid unnecessary questions. 10. Adjust the results to account for the nonresponse.
Response	Although the individual participates in the study, he or she provides an inaccurate response, consciously or subconsciously, to a survey item.	1. Match the background characteristics of interviewer and respondent as closely as possible. 2. Make sure interviewer instructions are clear and written down. 3. Conduct practice training sessions with interviewers. 4. Examine the interviewers' understanding of the study's purposes and procedures. 5. Have interviewers complete the questionnaire and examine their replies to see if there is any relationship between the answers they secure and their own answers. 6. Verify a sample of each interviewer's interviews.
Office[a]	Errors that arise when coding, tabulating, or analyzing the data.	1. Use a field edit to detect the most glaring omissions and inaccuracies in the data. 2. Use a second edit in the office to decide how data collection instruments containing incomplete answers, obviously wrong answers, and answers that reflect a lack of interest are to be handled. 3. Use closed-ended questions to simplify the coding, but when open-ended questions need to be used, specify the appropriate codes that will be allowed before collecting the data. 4. When open-ended questions are being coded and multiple coders are being used, divide the task by questions and not by data collection forms. 5. Have each coder code a sample of the other's work to ensure that a consistent set of coding criteria is being used. 6. Follow established conventions; for example, use numeric codes and not letters of the alphabet when coding the data for computer analysis. 7. Prepare a codebook that lists the codes for each variable and the categories included in each code. 8. Use appropriate methods to analyze the data.

[a]Steps to reduce the incidence of office errors are discussed in more detail in the analysis chapters.

$$RR = \frac{\text{number of usable questionnaires returned}}{\text{number of contacts attempted} - \text{number of bad addresses or fax numbers}}$$

In order to accurately calculate the response rate on a project, researchers must keep track of certain information. In this case, the researcher must know the number of contacts attempted, the number of wrong addresses, and, of course, the number of usable questionnaires.

Suppose that an online retailer decided to conduct a survey among its past customers. A sample of 1,000 customers was randomly selected to receive an e-mail survey. A total of 202 customers responded to the survey; 58 of the e-mail addresses were no longer valid. The response rate on the project would be correctly calculated as follows:

$$RR = \frac{202}{1,000 - 58} = 21\%$$

Telephone Surveys (No Eligibility Requirement)

Things get a little more complicated with telephone surveys—but not much. In cases where there is no eligibility requirement (that is, all response units meet the criteria for being included in the sample), we can categorize the attempted contacts into three groups: completed interviews, refusals, and not-at-homes (which includes when no one answers as well as when someone who isn't the correct respondent answers the telephone). The response rate formula looks like this:

$$RR = \frac{\text{number of completed interviews}}{\text{number of completed interviews} + \text{number of refusals} + \text{number of not-at-homes}}$$

Notice that wrong numbers or nonworking numbers are automatically excluded from the formula and thus don't lower the calculated response rate. The researcher should keep track of the number of bad telephone numbers (along with completed interviews, refusals, and not-at-homes), however, as an indication of the quality of the sampling frame.

Consider the following scenario: A researcher has designed a project using a telephone survey as the method of data collection. The respondents are current members of a health club. Using the membership roster as a sampling frame, the researcher has randomly selected 200 members. At the conclusion of the data collection phase, 112 interviews had successfully been conducted, 27 people refused to participate in the study, 57 people could not be reached after at least three tries, and 4 telephone numbers were no longer in service. What is the response rate for this project?

$$RR = \frac{112}{112 + 27 + 57} = 57\%$$

In addition, the quality of the sampling frame appeared to be very good, with only 4 nonworking numbers, or $4/200 = 2\%$.

Before moving on, a couple of other issues should be addressed. It is possible, particularly with older sampling frames, that the intended respondent has moved away from the area and the telephone number has been reassigned to someone else. These cases should be categorized as nonworking numbers for research purposes. Another concern is what counts as a "completed" interview. It is not uncommon for respondents to terminate a telephone survey prior to answering all the questions. In these cases, the researcher must use good judgment. Clearly, a response that is very nearly complete should be included in the data set and counted as a completed interview. At the other extreme, a respondent who hangs up after one or two questions should probably not be included. The troubling cases are those lying between these extremes. Our general recommendation is to count any interview on which answers are obtained for most of the survey items as a completed interview.

Telephone Surveys (With Eligibility Requirement)

Sometimes researchers are forced to work with sampling frames that include response units that are not members of the population being studied. Suppose, for example, that a department store wants to know shoppers' opinions of a new store layout. Store managers believe that at least half of the households in a test market city contain at least one adult who has visited the store since the new layout was introduced; these potential respondents should be in a position to offer an opinion on the layout. Even though the store has a well-developed customer database, it cannot keep records on those who have shopped but not purchased. As a result, to conduct a telephone survey, researchers working with the company might choose to use the local telephone directory as a sampling frame. The trouble is that some of the households won't include anyone who has shopped at the store during the relevant time frame. The members of these households are ineligible to complete the telephone survey. To identify these households, a screening question will be included ("Has any adult in this household visited Smart's Department Store in the previous three months?"); interviews with those that have not visited the store will end at that point.

A telephone survey can yield a high-quality sampling frame if the researcher has a current list of telephone numbers of the population to be studied, such as members of a health club.

Because some households are ineligible, how should you calculate response rate? The first step is to count the number of completed interviews, refusals, not-at-homes—*and* the number of ineligible response units. Now, you may be wondering why it is necessary to keep track of the number of ineligibles since they aren't supposed to count against the researcher in the calculation of response rate. That's true; we don't include them when we calculate response rate. We need them, however, for another purpose. Look back to the response rate formula for telephone surveys with no eligibility requirement. In particular, think about the refusals and not-at-homes. With no eligibility requirements, we know that each of these response units would have been qualified to complete the telephone survey had we been able to reach them and/or convince them to participate. In the current situation, *we don't know* that they would have been eligible; in fact, we're sure that many of them would not have visited the store in the previous three months. Adjusting for this requires one simple extra step when calculating response rate. The *eligibility percentage (E%)* is computed as follows:

$$E\% = \frac{\text{number of completed interviews}}{\text{number of completed interviews} + \text{number of ineligibles}}$$

The eligibility percentage is then used to adjust the number of refusals and not-at-homes to reflect the fact that many of them would not have qualified to participate in the survey even if we had successfully contacted them and gotten them to agree to participate. Response rate is calculated as follows:

$$RR = \frac{\text{number of completed interviews}}{\text{number of completed interviews} + E\% \,(\text{number of refusals} + \text{number of not-at-homes})}$$

Imagine that researchers working with the department store had randomly selected 1,000 telephone numbers from the local telephone directory and had attempted to contact each household. Here are the final results of the calls, along with the correct response rate calculation:

Completed interviews	338
Refusals	89
Not-at-homes	169
Ineligibles	292
Nonworking numbers	112
	1,000 telephone numbers

$$E\% = \frac{338}{338 + 292} = 54\%$$

$$RR = \frac{338}{338 + (0.54)(89 + 169)} = 71\%$$

Without adjusting for ineligibles, the calculated response rate would have been only 57%, so it is important to keep track of the number of response units that don't qualify for the survey.

Other Methods of Data Collection

So far, we've talked about calculating response rate for most of the major types of data collection. What about other types, such as personal interviews or the residential "drop-off" surveys common with area samples? Regardless of the type of data collection, the same logic is applied: The response rate equals the number of completed interviews with responding units divided by the number of eligible responding units in the sample. If the method used allows a distinction between refusals and not-at-homes, one of the formulas shown above for telephone surveys can likely be utilized or adapted. If not, then a variation of the formula for mail surveys is likely to apply. If there is an eligibility requirement, start with the formula for telephone surveys with an eligibility requirement. Regardless of the circumstances, the researcher can usually use common sense and the basic formulas we've discussed to arrive at the appropriate response rate.

Learning Objective

8. Discuss several ways in which response rates might be improved.

IMPROVING RESPONSE RATES

As noted, the lower the response rate, the more likely it is that nonresponse error will affect research results. Because of this potential problem, researchers have suggested and tested numerous techniques over the years for improving response rates. Most research has been conducted in the context of mail surveys, because this method of data collection has traditionally produced the lowest response rates.

In this section, we briefly discuss some of the general techniques that are thought to increase response rates. Empirical support is available for most, if not all, of these approaches in one context or another. The trick, of course, is to figure out which ones are likely to be most influential in a particular study. Because of its growing popularity, we pay special attention to improving Internet-based survey response rates in Exhibit 17.3.

Before examining these techniques, we should note one factor that probably has more effect than any other on response rates, but that is, for the most part, not under the control of the researcher. The topic of the research, and its ability to generate interest among potential respondents, will have a huge influence on whether or not respondents participate, regardless of the form of data collection. Some topics are inherently more interesting than other topics to particular respondents. Although we can't change the topic of research, we can consider different approaches for introducing and framing the issue under study. Exploratory research can be used effectively to gauge respondent interest in the topic and to give trial runs to different introductory scripts.

MANAGER'S FOCUS

Different ways of administering a data collection instrument (e.g., telephone, mail, Internet) have different normally accepted ranges for response rates. All other things being equal, total error will be reduced if you employ a *probability sampling plan* that achieves the highest possible response rate from the people in the target population. In other words, you are much more likely to obtain an accurate portrayal of the market situation if your research supplier probabilistically samples a smaller number of target population members and does whatever it can to maximize the response rate. Conversely, your assessment of the market situation will likely be less precise if your research provider generates the desired sample size by contacting a large number of prospective respondents through a low response mode of administration. The latter situation should be avoided because the risk is simply too high that those who respond will not be representative of those who do not.

"Foot-in-the-Door" Technique

Although most of the techniques in this section are most applicable to mail surveys, a couple of approaches are applicable to personal interviews and telephone surveys. The foot-in-the-door technique relies on the psychological principle that people are

---

Exhibit 17.3   **Tips for Increasing Response Rates on Online Surveys**

The E-Mail Invitation

- ☑ Use recognizable or personal "From:" name.
- ☑ Keep subject line short, but engaging.
- ☑ Avoid SPAM language (using all caps, exclamation points, money symbols, "free," "important message," etc.) in subject line or message.
- ☑ Personalize message using recipient's name.
- ☑ Include short, effective message to capture attention containing information about: (a) purpose of study, (b) benefits to respondent, (c) length/time of survey, (d) confidentiality, and (e) incentives.
- ☑ Offer meaningful incentives (if at all).
- ☑ Consider timing of e-mail—know your audience.
- ☑ Send reminder e-mails—but no more than two.
- ☑ Pretest e-mail invitation.

The Online Survey

- ☑ Keep it as short as possible.
- ☑ Minimize instructions.
- ☑ Begin with question likely to engage the respondent's attention.
- ☑ Keep questions as simple as possible.
- ☑ Use visuals/graphics if they help, but don't make survey complex or difficult to navigate.
- ☑ Remind respondents about incentives and explain how to obtain them.
- ☑ For long surveys (not a good idea), let respondents see progression through survey and how much remains.
- ☑ Pretest online survey.

Sources: "Write Survey Invitations to Increase Response Rates" and "10 Tips to Improve Your Surveys," downloaded from www.zoomerang.com, November 5, 2008; Jennifer M. Jensen, "Ten Easy Ways to Increase Response Rates for Your Online Survey," downloaded from www.questionpro.com, November 5, 2008; "Response Rates & Surveying Techniques," downloaded from http://s3.amazonaws.com/SurveyMonkeyFiles/Response_Rates.pdf, November 5, 2008; and "Customer Surveys—Improving Online Survey Response Rates," downloaded from http://www.vendorseek.com/improving-online-survey-rates.asp, November 5, 2008.

ETHICAL DILEMMA 17.2

"These new computer-voiced telephone surveys are wonderful!" your friend enthuses over lunch. "Because we don't have to pay telephone interviewers, we can afford to have target numbers automatically redialed until someone answers. Of course, the public finds the computer's voice irritating and the whole notion of being interviewed by a machine rather humiliating. Nevertheless, we can overcome most people's reluctance to participate by repeatedly calling them until they give in and complete the questionnaire."

- Is it ethical to contact respondents repeatedly until they agree to participate in a research study? How many contacts are legitimate?
- If an industry is unable to constrain its members to behave ethically, should the government step in with regulations?
- If the public reacts against this kind of telephone survey, what are the results likely to be for researchers using traditional, more considerate telephone surveys?

more likely to respond positively to a request from another person if they have previously responded positively to another, typically smaller, request. In one classic study, 74% of potential respondents agreed to complete a 20-question survey after they had already completed a brief five-question survey for the researchers. Only 58% of potential respondents agreed to complete the 20-question survey when there was no initial request.[6] One reason for this is that people simply want to maintain consistency, and "I said 'yes' before, so I'll say 'yes' again." An alternative explanation is found in social psychology: By responding positively to the initial smaller request, something of a rudimentary relationship has been established, making it harder to say "no" to the follow-up request.

Interviewer Characteristics and Training

Another approach that applies to personal interviews and telephone surveys involves the selection and training of interviewers. The evidence suggests that an interviewer is likely to get better cooperation and more information from the respondent when the two share similar backgrounds. This is particularly true for characteristics such as race, age, and gender but also applies to things such as social class and income.

Interviewers must also be trained to quickly convince potential respondents of the value of the research and the importance of their participation. Thus, the script to be used when approaching possible respondents must be carefully developed, and interviewers must be trained to follow the script. To the extent possible, the script should also communicate information about the content and purpose of the study, so that respondents may develop greater involvement and interest in the topic.

Guarantee of Confidentiality and/or Anonymity

It is routine practice to promise respondents that their answers will be held in confidence by the researcher. Such a practice is especially important when the topic or specific questions are likely to be sensitive to the respondent. With mail surveys, it is also possible to guarantee that responses will be anonymous, providing an even greater sense of security to the respondent. By the way, if you promise confidentiality or anonymity, you are ethically bound to keep the promise. Sometimes managers will want access to respondent names, addresses, or telephone numbers—particularly those who have expressed some level of interest in a proposed product or service. Even if you made no promises at all, such a practice is unacceptable because it blurs the line between research and sales.

Prenotification

One effective strategy for increasing response rates to surveys is to notify potential respondents about the survey in advance. One benefit of prenotification is that the respondent may remember the prior contact, which then serves as a sort of foot-in-the-door; at the time of data collection, the respondent may subconsciously feel something like "Well, I've heard from them before, so they're a friend, not a stranger." A second benefit is that the respondent may think a little bit in advance about the issue to be addressed, potentially raising the interest level when the actual data collection takes place. Note, however, that prenotification will likely raise the costs of the overall project.

Personalization

Anything the researcher can do to make the data collection process seem more personalized for a particular respondent should help improve response rates. For example, research has demonstrated that hand-addressed envelopes and handwritten signatures on letters can increase response. Along the same lines, data collection forms should rarely, if ever, be sent to "occupant" or by bulk mail. In addition, some respondents will be more likely to open an envelope that has been stamped rather than one that has been sent through a postage meter. It just feels more personal, as if someone has spent the time to contact them individually. Similarly, including a reply envelope that has been stamped rather than metered is normally a good idea.

An issue that the researcher must consider is whether to include a stamped reply envelope or a business-reply envelope. With business-reply postage, the researcher opens an account with the postal service and then only pays postage on the questionnaires that are actually returned. Business reply postage is more costly than regular postage, but, again, you're only paying for questionnaires actually returned. With regularly stamped reply envelopes, the researcher obviously pays postage for each questionnaire distributed, not just those returned. The stamped envelope may increase the likelihood of response a little, but if the overall rate of response isn't great enough, the use of business-reply envelopes will be less expensive. The researcher can easily determine the response rate at which it is more economical to use either business-reply or regular postage by working with the costs of regular and business-reply postage.

The foot-in-the-door technique relies on the principle that people are likely to respond to a request from someone if they have responded positively to a previous request.

Sponsor Disguise

If the identification of the organization sponsoring the research is likely to increase nonresponse, researchers can overcome this bias by concealing that information or by hiring a professional research organization to conduct the field study. This is one reason companies with established, sophisticated research departments of their own sometimes employ research firms to collect data.

Response Incentives

Considerable research has shown that offering an incentive to respondents will increase response rates on a project. Response incentives can take several forms ranging from money to lotteries to donations for charity. Monetary incentives often have the greatest influence on response rates. Be careful, though. Some research suggests that at some point the respondent begins to feel that she or he is being paid to participate rather than given a token of appreciation. In this case, a "gift" is more psychologically motivating than are "wages." How much is too much to include with a survey? The answer likely depends on the nature of the survey and the type of respondent, but for most purposes it probably isn't advisable to give more than a few dollars.

Many researchers have effectively used lotteries as a means of generating response. By participating in the survey, the respondent is typically entered into a drawing for a prize. The difficulty, if there is one, lies in the amount of trust that the respondent must place in the researcher. From the respondents' perspective, there may or may not be an actual lottery, they may or may not actually be entered in such a lottery, and their responses may not be confidential or anonymous if name, address, and telephone number are to be kept for contact purposes (in order to notify the winner). To overcome these issues, respondents to a mail survey might be allowed to send back a separate postcard along with the reply envelope; only the postcard includes contact information and is included in the actual drawing. The downside is the added cost of postcards and postage. In general, you can expect lotteries to be less effective than monetary incentives.

Some people may respond more to an offer to make a donation on their behalf to a charity. Still others may appreciate a coupon for free food and drink, or tickets to a movie. Researchers are advised to help their clients avoid the temptation to include coupons for discounts on the purchase of their own products and services. The temptation will sometimes be great, because such coupons will likely cost the client less than other sorts of incentives and because the client may view this as an opportunity to generate a little business. Remember, research is research, and selling is selling, and the two should never be confused.

Survey Length

Although there are exceptions, respondents typically do not appreciate or respond well to long surveys. Thus, all else equal, short surveys are more likely to be completed than are long surveys. This is one reason for researchers to include only questions that are truly important and that will be used in the analysis.

Follow-Up Surveys

In some cases, the circumstances surrounding a contact are responsible for a respondent's refusal to participate. Since these circumstances may be temporary or changeable, follow-up contacts are sometimes useful for generating a response. If a respondent declined participation because he or she was busy or sick, a callback at a different time or using a different approach may be enough to secure cooperation. In a mail survey, this may mean a follow-up mailing at a more convenient time.

If a respondent has refused to participate in a personal interview or a telephone survey for reasons other than circumstances, callbacks will be less successful. This isn't the case with mail surveys. Frequently, responses are obtained with the second and third mailings from those who did not respond to the initial mailing. Of course, follow-up in a mail survey requires identification of those not responding earlier, which in turn requires identification of those who did respond, and this removes the possibility of anonymity. The alternative, which is to send each new

MANAGER'S FOCUS

Marketing research studies are often expensive endeavors and managers understandably look for ways to reduce costs. Before you dismiss the idea of offering response incentives because you believe they will increase the study's cost, you should first run the numbers. In an earlier chapter, we stressed how important it is to pretest your data collection instrument. When completing this important step, we recommend testing alternative incentives (including having no incentive) and calculating the differences in response rates. If you do this, you will find that paying for incentives will often decrease the overall cost of the study by reducing the amount of interviewer time or postage expenses that would be necessary to get the study completed without an incentive.

mailing to each designated sample member without screening those who have responded previously, can be expensive for the research organization and frustrating for the respondent.

Are Some Techniques More Effective?

An obvious question at this point is which techniques are more effective at improving response rates. While dozens of studies have been conducted, most have examined the effects of one or two techniques at a time. In recent years, however, several large review studies have been conducted. The results of one of the most extensive reviews of mail-survey response inducement techniques indicated that, on average, the most successful response inducement techniques in mail surveys are the use of monetary incentives, preliminary notification that the survey is coming, and follow-ups or repeated mailings.[7]

SUMMARY

Learning Objective 1

Describe four basic types of nonsampling errors.

There are four basic types of nonsampling errors: noncoverage errors, nonresponse errors, response errors, and office errors. Noncoverage errors occur because part of the population of interest was not included in the sampling frame. Nonresponse errors are possible when some elements designated for inclusion in the sample did not respond and were systematically different from those who did respond on key characteristics. Response errors occur because inaccurate information was secured from the sample elements. Office errors occur when errors are introduced in the processing of the data or in reporting the findings.

Learning Objective 2

Discuss noncoverage error and how it can be reduced.

Noncoverage bias can be reduced, although not necessarily eliminated, by recognizing its existence and working to improve the sampling frame.

Learning Objective 3

Explain what nonresponse error is.

Error due to nonresponse represents a failure to obtain information from some elements of the population that were selected and designated for the sample. It is a problem because those who provide responses are often systematically different from those who do not provide responses.

Learning Objective 4

Identify the two main sources of nonresponse error.

The two main sources of nonresponse error are not-at-homes and refusals.

Learning Objective 5

Define response error and discuss some of its causes.

Response error reflects bias due to securing inaccurate information from a respondent. Many factors can lead to response error, including (1) respondent failure to understand, know the answer, or provide the true answer to a question; (2) the wording of questions and the situations in which the questions are asked; and (3) interviewers' failure to accurately record responses provided by respondents or fabrication of responses.

Learning Objective 6

Discuss how interviewers can contribute to response error.

There are numerous ways interviewers can increase response error during the data collection process. Some of these include the phrasing and inflection of questions, misinterpretation of respondent answers, mistakes in recording respondent answers, inconsistent follow-up questions across respondents, and the fabrication of responses.

Learning Objective 7

Cite the standard definition for response rate.

Response rate may be defined as the number of completed interviews with responding units divided by the number of eligible responding units in the sample.

Learning Objective 8

Discuss several ways in which response rates might be improved.

There are several approaches for improving response rates, including making the data collection instrument and procedure as interesting and as short as possible, carefully choosing and training interviewers, asking respondents to complete a short task before asking them to complete the longer data collection instrument (the "foot-in-the-door" technique), guaranteeing confidentiality and/or anonymity, notifying potential respondents in advance, personalizing data collection forms as much as possible, providing incentives, disguising the sponsor if necessary, and sending follow-up surveys.

KEY TERMS

nonsampling error (page 375)
noncoverage error (page 376)
nonresponse error (page 377)
refusals (page 377)

not-at-homes (page 378)
response error (page 380)
office error (page 383)
response rate (page 384)

REVIEW QUESTIONS

1. Distinguish between sampling error and nonsampling error. Why is the distinction important?

2. What are noncoverage errors? Explain how they might be a problem with personal interview, telephone interviews, mail surveys, and Internet-based surveys.

3. How can noncoverage bias be assessed? What can be done to reduce it?

4. What is nonresponse error?

5. What are the basic types of nonresponse error? Are they equally serious for the different methods of administration?

6. What can be done to reduce the incidence of not-at-homes in the final sample?

7. What are the typical reasons designated respondents refuse to participate in a study? What can be done to reduce the incidence of refusals?

8. What is response error?

9. What factors lead to response error? How might the respondent, the interviewer, and the situation lead to response error?

10. How might the different types of response error be reduced?

11. What is office error?

12. Explain the statement, "Total error is key."

13. What is the response rate?

14. How should response rates be calculated for (a) mail or e-mail surveys, (b) telephone surveys with no eligibility requirements, and (c) telephone surveys with eligibility requirements?

15. Why does increasing response rate reduce the possibility of nonresponse error?

16. Explain how the "foot-in-the-door" technique works.

17. Why might regularly stamped return envelopes sometimes be favored over business-reply envelopes, even if the cost is higher?

18. Explain several techniques for improving response rates.

DISCUSSION QUESTIONS, PROBLEMS, AND PROJECTS

1. J. Hoffman was the owner of a medium-sized supermarket located in St. Cloud, Minnesota. He was considering altering the layout of the store so that the frozen food section would be near the section with fresh fruit and vegetables. These changes were designed to better accommodate customer shopping patterns and thereby increase customer patronage. Prior to making the alterations, he decided to administer a short questionnaire in the store to a random sample of customers. For a period of two weeks, three of the store cashiers were instructed to stand at the end of selected aisles and conduct personal interviews with every fifth customer. Hoffman gave specific instructions that on no account were customers to be harassed or offended. Identify the major sources of noncoverage and nonresponse errors. Explain.

2. Tough-Grip Tires was a large manufacturer of radial tires located in New Orleans, Louisiana, and it was experiencing a problem common to tire manufacturers. The poor performance of the auto industry was having a severe negative impact on the tire industry. To try to maintain sales and competitive positions, various manufacturers were offering wholesalers additional credit and discount opportunities. Tough-Grip's management was particularly concerned about wholesaler reaction to a new discount policy it was considering. The first survey the company conducted to explore this reaction was unsatisfactory to management. Management felt it was conducted in a haphazard manner and contained numerous nonsampling errors. Tough-Grip's management decided to conduct another study, containing the following changes:

   • The sampling frame was defined as a list of 1,000 of the largest wholesalers that stocked Tough-Grip tires, and the sample elements were to be randomly selected from this list.

   • A callback technique was to be used, with the callbacks being made at different times than the original attempted contact.

   • The sample size was to be doubled, from 200 to 400 respondents.

   • The sample elements that were ineligible or refused to cooperate were to be substituted by the next element from the list.

   • An incentive of $1.00 was to be offered to respondents.

   Critically evaluate the steps that were being considered to prevent the occurrence of nonsampling errors. Do you think they were appropriate? Be specific.

3. The placement office at a university has hired you to assist it in determining the size of starting salaries and the range of salary offers received by graduating seniors. The placement office has always gathered some information in this regard in that historically some seniors have come in to report the name of the company for which they are going to work and the amount of their starting salary. The office feels that these statistics may be biased, and thus it wishes to approach the whole task more systematically. This is why it has hired your expertise to determine what the situation was with respect to last year's graduating seniors.

   a. Describe how you would select a sample of respondents to answer the question of starting salaries. Why would you use this particular sample?

   b. What types of nonsampling errors might you expect to encounter with your approach, and how would you control for them?

4. An executive recruitment firm used a lengthy mail survey to gather information on the job mobility of mid-level managers. A sample of 500 eligible middle managers was selected, using a simple random sampling procedure. The firm used three waves of mailings. Sixteen of the questionnaires were returned due to bad addresses; all but two of the returned surveys were usable. After the third mailing, each of the nonresponding (NR) sample units was contacted by phone and asked to answer only four questions regarding variables that the recruitment firm thought were particularly important, given the objective of the study. The table below gives mean values for these variables.

Wave	Number of Responses	Age	Income ($)	Years in Current Position	Total Years of Management Experience
1	125	30	22,000	1.2	5.1
2	100	37	27,000	4.0	9.4
3	75	42	32,500	5.1	15.1
NR	200	50	31,250	10.2	24.2

a. What was the response rate for the completed questionnaire?

b. Which variables, if any, seem to be most affected by potential nonresponse bias? Does this tell you anything about the sample selection procedure?

5. The local outlet of a large home and garden chain store wants to better understand the needs and perceptions of its customers. The general manager is attracted to the option of using a Web-based survey (with e-mail recruitment) because it won't cost her much to implement. She prepared a 57-item questionnaire, posted it online using one of the many online survey providers, and then had several employees stay late after work one Friday night to send the following e-mail message to 100 recent customers whose e-mail addresses were in the store's customer database:

> To: john.customer@provider.net
> Subject: Customer Survey!
> Hello. Thank you for your recent purchase at HomeStop.
> Please go to the following web site and complete our
> customer survey: www.oursurvey01.surveysmaster.net.
> Thank you!

The manager was disappointed when she found that only three surveys had been completed by the middle of the following week. Evaluate her approach to data collection and offer suggestions for how to improve the response rate the next time that she chooses to do a Web-based survey.

6. A large furniture store located in a city in the southwestern United States was interested in determining how households living in and around the city viewed the image of the store. Store managers hired a local market research company to collect data. The researchers drew a systematic sample of 2,500 names from the local telephone directory and set out to conduct telephone interviews. At the conclusion of the data collection phase of the project, the researchers recorded 1,223 completed interviews, 598 not-at-homes, 427 refusals, and 252 nonworking telephone numbers. Calculate the response rate on the project.

7. Suppose that the managers in the previous problem had decided prior to data collection to only include households that planned to make a furniture purchase in the next six months. A screening question was used to identify households that qualified to complete the survey. Further, the 2,500 elements drawn for the sample were accounted for as follows:

473 completed interviews, 612 not-at-homes, 431 refusals, 222 nonworking telephone numbers, and 762 ineligibles.

    a. What was the response rate on this project?

    b. What would the response rate have been without adjusting for ineligible households?

8. A remodeling contractor located in a small community had developed a relatively inexpensive type of storage shed and wanted to determine the likely level of demand for the sheds among local homeowners before he began producing and marketing them. Because the population of homeowners was not easily identifiable in the telephone directory, and because it would be very inefficient to screen for homeowners due to the fact that it was a college town with the associated high proportion of renters, he didn't want to use a telephone survey. Although he could purchase a mailing list of homeowners in the relevant zip code areas, the cost of mail surveys was prohibitive. Because of these constraints, the contractor decided to collect data via an area sample and residential drop-off survey. That is, for randomly selected neighborhoods, local college students working for the contractor would approach each household in the neighborhood, determine whether or not the resident was the homeowner, and if so ask him or her to complete a short written survey that the student would pick up later in the evening. If no one answered the door, the worker was to leave the survey (with instructions) at the door, and to return later to pick it up.

At the conclusion of the project, 438 homes had been approached, with the following outcomes: 212 completed surveys, 31 refusals, 78 residents that rented the residence, and 117 not-at-homes. What was the response rate on this project?

PART 6

DATA ANALYSIS

TiVo: Friend or Foe?

"Did you watch that TV show last night?"

"No, but I TiVo'ed it. That way I can watch the show without the commercials."

Since its inception in 1997, this sort of give-and-take has become more and more common-place among families, friends, and coworkers as TiVo, the company that made digital video recorders (DVRs) commercially viable, makes its way into more and more households. While consumer infatuation has helped make the TiVo brand name a verb, marketers, advertisers, and television networks have been far less favorable. Television commercials are an important source of promotion for firms and an important source of revenue for networks. According to David F. Poltrack, executive vice president for research and planning at CBS, "Advertisers don't want to count people [who watch recorded programs] in playback mode at all because they assume they are all fast-forwarding through the commercials. We say that not everybody is fast-forwarding."

The problem has been that neither Mr. Poltrack nor the advertisers had any data to support their claims—until now. TiVo sought 20,000 of its users to be volunteer consumer panelists. All these volunteers have to do is watch TV. TiVo tracks their second-by-second viewing patterns and analyzes the data in search of behavioral patterns. Because these volunteers also agreed to supply their demographics, TiVo's analyses can directly benefit the very advertisers who scorned the company initially.

For instance, TiVo found that commercials for consumer-packaged goods featuring animal characters were skipped less often when shown during animal-related programs. In another example, households with children under 12 watched commercials for schools, camps, and computer games/educational software an average of about six seconds longer than those same ads were watched in households with adults over 50. Results such as these promise to give TiVo a second chance to make a first impression with advertisers.

While TiVo's role as a measurement and data analysis service is new, the insights it is able to provide give it a second chance to make a first impression with advertisers.

Sources: "TiVo Launches Power Watch Ratings Service," downloaded from http://investor.tivo.com, Aug. 29, 2008; Maria Aspan, "TiVo Shifts to Help Companies It Once Threatened," Dec. 10, 2007, downloaded from http://www.nytimes.com, Aug. 29, 2008; Saul Hansell, "TiVo Is Watching When You Don't Watch, and It Tattles," July 26, 2006, downloaded from http://www.nytimes.com, Aug. 29, 2008.

TiVo ®

Data Analysis: Preliminary Steps

Learning Objectives

1. Explain the purpose of the field edit.
2. Define what coding is.
3. Discuss two types of open-ended questions.
4. List the basic steps in coding open-ended responses.
5. Describe the kinds of information contained in a codebook.
6. Describe common methods for cleaning the data file.
7. Discuss options for dealing with missing data in analyses.

Introduction

In a marketing research project, a number of things must take place after the data are collected, but before they can be analyzed. This chapter presents and explains a number of these preliminary steps.

EDITING

The basic purpose of editing is to impose some minimum quality standards on raw data. Editing involves the inspection and, if necessary, correction of each questionnaire or observation form. Inspection and correction are often done in two stages: the field edit and the central-office edit.

Field Edit

The **field edit** is a preliminary edit designed to detect the most glaring omissions and inaccuracies in the data. It is also useful in helping to control the behavior of the field force personnel and to clear up any misunderstandings they may have about directions, procedures, specific questions, and so on. For example, some years ago in a survey conducted in Ukraine, the field edit revealed that an employee had left the questionnaire with the respondents instead of interviewing them as instructed. The tip-off was the different ways the answers were circled.[1]

field edit
A preliminary edit, typically conducted by a field supervisor, which is designed to detect the most glaring omissions and inaccuracies in a completed data collection instrument.

Ideally, the field edit is done as soon as possible after the questionnaire or other data collection form has been administered. In that way, problems can be corrected before the interviewing or observation staff is disbanded, and while the particular contacts that were the source of trouble are still fresh in the interviewer's or observer's mind. The preliminary field edit is usually conducted by a field supervisor. Some of the items checked are described in Exhibit 18.1.

Central-Office Edit

The field edit is typically followed by a **central-office edit**, or "eyeball" edit, which involves the careful physical inspection of each data collection form and the correction of mistakes where possible. For example, suppose a researcher was surveying a

central-office edit
Thorough and exacting scrutiny and correction of completed data collection forms, including a decision about what to do with the data.

Exhibit 18.1   **Items Checked in the Field Edit**

1. **Completeness:** The check for completeness involves scrutinizing the data form to ensure that no sections or pages were omitted, and it also involves checking individual items. A blank for a specific question could mean that the respondent refused to answer; alternatively, it may simply reflect an oversight on the respondent's part or that he or she did not know the answer. It may be very important for the purposes of the study to know which reason is correct. It is hoped that by contacting the field-worker while the interview is fresh in his or her mind, the field editor can obtain the needed clarification.

2. **Legibility:** It is impossible to code a questionnaire that cannot be deciphered because of illegible handwriting or obscure abbreviations. It is a simple matter to correct this now, whereas it is often extremely time consuming later.

3. **Comprehensibility:** Sometimes a recorded response is incomprehensible to all but the field interviewer. By detecting this now, the field editor can obtain the necessary clarification.

4. **Consistency:** Marked inconsistencies within an interview or observation schedule typically indicate errors in collecting or recording the data and may indicate ambiguity in the instrument or carelessness in its administration. For instance, if a respondent indicated that he or she saw a particular commercial on television last night on one part of the questionnaire, and later indicated that he or she did not watch television last night, the analyst would be in a dilemma. Such inconsistencies can often be detected and corrected in the field edit.

5. **Uniformity:** It is very important that the responses be recorded in uniform units. For instance, if the study is aimed at determining the number of magazines read per week per individual, and the respondent indicates the number of magazines for which he or she has monthly subscriptions, the response base is not uniform, and the result could cause confusion in the later stages of analysis. If the problem is detected now, perhaps the interviewer can recontact the respondent and get the correct answer.

© BANANASTOCK/JUPITERIMAGES

After the field edit is complete, a central-office edit is performed. An experienced researcher conducts this *eyeball* edit of all questionnaires, deciding how to handle incomplete or incorrect data.

company's employees with respect to job satisfaction and an open-ended classification question asked respondents how long they had worked for the company in years. Further suppose that one of the respondents wrote "eleven months" in response to the item. The editor must convert this answer to the correct unit of time (i.e., years). To ensure consistency of treatment, it is best if one individual performs the edit on all forms. If that isn't possible because of the number of surveys, the work should be divided by parts of the data collection instruments rather than by respondents. That is, one editor would edit Part A of all questionnaires, while the other would edit Part B.

In the central-office edit, the editor must decide how data collection instruments containing incomplete answers, obviously wrong answers, and answers that reflect a lack of interest will be handled. Because such problems are more common with questionnaires than with observation forms, we'll discuss these difficulties from that perspective, although our discussion applies generally to all types of data collection forms.

It is extremely unlikely that all the respondents to a survey will have completed all the items on the survey, especially when the surveys are completed without the involvement of an interviewer (for example, mail surveys). Some surveys will have complete sections omitted. In others, responses for one or more individual items will be missing. The editor's decision on how to handle these incomplete questionnaires depends on the severity of the problem. Questionnaires that omit complete sections are obviously suspect, yet should not be thrown out automatically. It might be, for example, that the omitted section refers to the influence of the spouse in the purchase of some durable good, and the respondent is not married. This type of reply is certainly usable in spite of the incomplete section. If there is no logical justification for the large number of unanswered questions (say, half or more of the questions on the survey), the total reply will probably be thrown out, decreasing the response rate for the study. Questionnaires containing only isolated instances of item nonresponse should be kept.

Careful editing of the questionnaire sometimes shows that an answer to a question is obviously incorrect. For example, a researcher at a consumer panel research company once reviewed data that indicated that 45% of the households in the panel had purchased dog food, but only 40% of the households reported that they owned a dog.[2] Apparently, data on some of the panel questionnaires indicated a dog food purchase but not dog ownership. One explanation for this seeming inconsistency is that some of the questionnaires contained incorrect answers. (Other possible explanations include the purchase of dog food for others, or unusual personal taste preferences.) The editor may be able to determine which of the two answers (i.e., 45% purchasing dog food vs. 40% owning a dog) is correct from other information in the questionnaire.

Editors must also be on the alert to spot completed questionnaires that have failed to engage the respondent's interest. Evidence of this lack of interest may be obvious or quite subtle. Consider, for example, a respondent who checked the "5" position on a five-point scale for each of 40 items in an attitude questionnaire, even though some items were expressed negatively and some positively. This sort of response set

---

Exhibit 18.2   **Primary Tasks in the Central-Office Edit**

1. ***Convert all responses to consistent units.*** For example, if income is to be measured in thousands of dollars, convert the response "46,350" to 46.

2. ***Assess degree of nonresponse.*** If limited, keep the survey; if excessive, eliminate the survey.

3. ***Where possible, check for consistency across responses.*** For example, if the respondent indicates in one part of a survey that he has never been seen by a particular healthcare provider but later reports that he was "very satisfied" with the service provided by that healthcare provider, the editor must decide whether to correct one or the other answer or to treat both responses as if they were missing.

4. ***Look for evidence that respondent wasn't really thinking about his or her answers.*** This typically takes the form of response set bias in which the respondent provides the same answer to a series of rating scale items. Responses that are clearly due to response set should be treated as missing. If this creates an excessive degree of nonresponse, eliminate the survey.

5. ***Add any needed codes.*** For example, each completed survey must have an identification number.

---

bias occurs fairly frequently. We've also seen returned surveys on which respondents created patterns out of their responses, for example, circling the numbers 1, 2, 3, 4, 5, 6, 7, 6, 5, 4, 3, 2, 1, and so on, for successive items. When it is obvious that a respondent has not taken the study seriously, his or her answers should not be recorded, at least for that section of the survey.

Any additional codes that need to be placed on the data collection forms should be added during the central-office edit. For example, a unique identifying number of some type should be added unless one already exists on the form. This number will be coded in the data file along with the answers provided by the respondent and will be used to look up the original questionnaire if necessary. Exhibit 18.2 provides a list of the primary tasks involved in the central-office edit.

CODING

Learning Objective

2. Define what coding is.

Coding is the process of transforming raw data into symbols. Most often, the symbols are numerals, because they can be handled easily by computers. The task is to transform respondents' answers (or other information to be coded) into numbers representing the answers. Sometimes the transformation is almost automatic (e.g., when respondents have circled numbers on rating scales); sometimes, however, the coding process involves considerable effort on the part of the coder (e.g., when respondents answer certain types of open-ended questions).

coding
The technical procedure by which raw data are transformed into symbols; it involves specifying the alternative categories or classes into which the responses are to be placed and assigning code numbers to the classes.

Coding Closed-Ended Items

In descriptive research, most of the items included in a questionnaire are likely to be closed-ended. That is, most questions will provide a limited number of response categories and will ask the respondent to choose the best response or, sometimes, all responses that apply. These types of items are generally quite simple to code. When there is a single possible answer to a question (e.g., male or female), the researcher uses one variable for the question and simply assigns a character (almost always a number) to each possible response (for example, 1 = female, 2 = male). The appropriate code number is then recorded in the data file. The coding process can be facilitated in advance by "precoding" the questionnaire (i.e., printing the actual code numbers beside each possible response) or by using numerical rating scales on the questionnaire, but these techniques are by no means required. If respondents have been asked to check boxes or to provide some other form of response, it is usually a simple matter to assign a number to represent each particular response. For example, the following semantic differential item to measure attitude toward a service provider can easily be coded with the numbers 1–7, where 1 represents the box nearest "unfavorable" and 7 represents the box nearest "favorable:"

| **unfavorable** | ❑ | ❑ | ❑ | ❑ | ❑ | ❑ | ❑ | **favorable** |

For purposes of analysis, there will be a single variable representing this item with possible codes 1 through 7 representing increasing levels of favorability.

The coding process for closed-ended items becomes a bit more complex when respondents can indicate more than one answer for a given question, as with "check all that apply" types of items. For example, consider the following question:

> **How did you learn about Brown Furniture Company? (check all that apply)**
> ❑ newspaper advertising
> ❑ radio advertising
> ❑ billboard advertising
> ❑ recommended by others
> ❑ drove by the store
> ❑ other

In this situation, using a single variable coded 1–6 representing the different options will not work; how would you code responses for someone who checked both "newspaper advertising" and "billboard advertising"? A simple solution is to create six variables to represent the six possible answers and to indicate for each whether or not the option was selected. An easy coding scheme is to record a "1" if a respondent selected a response and to record a "0" if she did not select that response. For the respondent who checked "newspaper advertising" and "billboard advertising," the variables representing these two responses would be coded "1" and each remaining variable would be coded "0."

Coding Open-Ended Items

Learning Objective

3. Discuss two types of open-ended questions.

Recall that open-ended items do not provide response categories for respondents. Instead, respondents answer open-ended questions using their own words. Coding open-ended responses is typically much more difficult than coding closed-ended responses.

Coding Factual Open-Ended Items Before proceeding, we should distinguish between two general classes of open-ended questions. One type seeks factual information from a respondent. For example, consider the following open-ended questions:

> In what year were you born? _____
> How many times have you eaten at Streeter's Grill in the last month? _____

Each of these questions seeks a factual answer from the respondent. There is a correct answer to each question, and the researcher assumes that the respondent can provide that answer. This type of open-ended question is easy to code by simply coding the actual response (or, if the actual responses were not numeric, converting the responses to numbers). Numerical data should be recorded as they were reported on the data collection form, rather than be collapsed into smaller categories. For example, it is not advisable to code age as 1 = under 20 years, 2 = 20–29, 3 = 30–39, and so on, if actual ages of the people were provided. This would result in an unnecessary sacrifice of information in the original measurement and could just as easily be done at later stages in the analysis. (Remember our advice from Chapter 12: You should use the highest level of measurement possible. In this case, recording the actual age results in ratio-level measurement; recording age in categories would result in ordinal-level measurement.)

Coding Exploratory Open-Ended Items   The other type of open-ended question is often more exploratory in nature and, consequently, much more difficult and expensive to code. For many open-ended questions, there are multiple legitimate responses, some of which are likely to be unanticipated by the researcher. Suppose that a researcher were interested in determining the causes of "brain drain," the migration of college and university graduates from one state to another after graduation. In response to the question, **"In your own words, give us two or three reasons why you prefer to leave the state after graduation,"** students provided answers such as "my family lives in another state," "want to try something different," "going to graduate school in another state," and so on. Some people provided a single reason to leave, while others provided multiple reasons to leave.

Step 1

The first step in coding this type of open-ended question is to go through each questionnaire and highlight each separate response given by each individual. Some respondents can provide multiple answers in only a few words, while others can write whole paragraphs and communicate only one answer, so be careful at this stage. Normally, at least two coders should review all of the responses separately and then compare results to ensure that all responses are considered.

Step 2

The next step in coding is specifying the categories or classes into which the responses are to be placed. The goal is to reduce the great number of individual responses into a much smaller set of general categories so that insights may be drawn from the results. The categories must be mutually exclusive and exhaustive, so that every open-ended response logically falls into one and only one category. Usually, a researcher can anticipate some or most of the categories in advance—but don't become "locked in" on those categories alone. Respondents' actual answers will often reveal categories that were initially overlooked or anticipated categories that turn out to have very few responses. For example, the brain drain researcher may not have anticipated that some graduates want to leave just to try something new. To make the categories exhaustive, it is often necessary to include an "other" category for responses that simply don't fit anywhere else. However, if the number of responses in the "other" category rises to more than 5–10% of the total number of responses, the researcher should consider whether additional categories are needed.

Step 3

After an appropriate set of categories is identified, the actual coding of responses into the categories begins. Each response identified during the first step must be given the code number for one and only one of the categories developed in the second step. Unless the questions (and responses) are very straightforward (rarely the case for this type of open-ended question), at least two coders who have been trained to understand the types of responses that should be placed in each category should code the responses. Multiple coders help reduce bias in the interpretation of the different responses, a form of office error. Each coder will individually decide which category is appropriate for a response and then assign the numerical code for that category to the response.

Learning Objective

4.   List the basic steps in coding open-ended responses.

MANAGER'S FOCUS

Coding open-ended items is a time-consuming process that involves a significant amount of subjective interpretation of respondents' comments. There are several reasons why open-ended questions in descriptive surveys generally produce relatively imprecise findings. Respondents are not always capable of clearly expressing their precise thoughts, interviewers do not always probe properly to clarify what is meant, and responses do not always get recorded accurately. And different respondents may attempt to communicate the same ideas using very different language.

All of this means that it is a daunting task for a coder to produce a set of categories that captures what respondents were thinking or trying to convey. Although quite useful in exploratory research where the purpose is to obtain insights and new ideas that can be further tested, these types of open-ended questions generally should be avoided in descriptive research.

Step 4

When all responses have been coded by each coder, the coders meet to compare results, discuss differences in the codes assigned to particular responses, and assign a final code for each response. The coders must keep careful records of the number of codings for which initial disagreement existed so that a summary measure of percentage agreement (or other measure of reliability) can be computed. The lower the overall level of agreement, the greater the possibility that either the categories are not mutually exclusive or that one or more coders have not done a thorough job.

On very large projects, it is sometimes necessary to have several coders. In general, it is best to divide the work by question, not to divide up the questionnaires. That way, the same set of coders always works on the same question(s), creating efficiencies and a consistent set of standards for all responses to a given question.

Building the Data File

In order to use a computer to analyze the data, it is necessary to enter the codes from each questionnaire into a data file that can be read by the computer. With most online data collection tools, this process is automatic; data are normally stored in spreadsheet format and can be downloaded for further analysis. This is also the case for other computer-assisted forms of data collection (e.g., telephone surveys in which the interviewer enters data directly into the database as they are received from respondents). In many cases, however, it is necessary to manually enter the data.

There are numerous methods of entering data including creating text data files in word processing software, using spreadsheet software, entering data directly into statistical software packages such as SPSS, or using optical scanning. Regardless of how the data input process will be handled, it is helpful to visualize the input in terms of a multiple-column record where columns represent different variables (based on items from the questionnaire) and rows represent different respondents. Our experience suggests that entering

After the set of categories is identified, the actual coding of responses into the categories begins.

data directly in the statistical software is satisfactory when there are relatively few respondents and/or relatively few variables, but that creating a simple text file in fixed column format using a word processing package is often preferred for larger jobs.

To illustrate the process of building a data file, consider the brief questionnaire presented in Figure 18.1. Suppose that this questionnaire were sent to randomly selected members of a fitness center to determine member demographics and usage characteristics, among other things. Figure 18.2 (on pages 409–410) presents the first two completed questionnaires received back from respondents.

The Codebook   Note that during the editing and coding process, the researcher has added respondent identification numbers (upper left-hand corner), code numbers for the open-ended responses, and revenues received from the respondent (based on internal records). The codebook, presented in Figure 18.3 (on page 411), contains explicit directions about how raw data from the questionnaires are to be coded in the data file. At a minimum, the codebook must provide (a) the variable name to be used in statistical analyses for each variable included in the data file; (b) the column(s) in which each variable is located in the data file; (c) a description of how each variable is coded; and (d) an explanation of how missing data are treated in the data file. In a very real sense, the codebook is a map to help the researcher navigate from completed questionnaires to the data file. Finally, Figure 18.4 (on page 412) reproduces the first 25 rows of the raw data file (text file, fixed column format). The first two rows present data from the first two respondents (see Figure 18.2).

Although there are numerous ways to code and enter data into the data file, we suggest using the following conventions and tips:

■ Assign specific column locations (often referred to as "fields") for particular variables. That way, the same variable is recorded in the same place for each different respondent.

■ Use as many columns for the field assigned to a variable as are necessary to capture the variable. Thus, if the 10 codes from 0 to 9 can represent all the possible different responses, you need only one column for that variable. If there are more possible responses, add additional columns as needed. For example, if gender is the variable, there are only two possible responses and a single column is enough. Because the Avery Fitness Center researchers found only a few general categories for reasons that members began using the center (see question 7 on the survey in Figure 18.1), they needed only one column to code each of the possible responses. However, with many open-ended questions, it will be necessary to leave two columns for each response.

■ When a question allows multiple responses, allow separate columns in the coding for each answer. Look at question 1 on the Avery Fitness Center survey (Figure 18.1). Because this question allows multiple answers ("please check all that apply"), the researchers have assigned a column for each option in the data file (see columns 4–8 on the codebook in Figure 18.3). Similarly, if question 7 had asked for two reasons that members began using the fitness center, the coder would have provided separate columns for each of the answers.

■ Use only numeric codes, not letters of the alphabet or special characters, like @. Most computer statistical programs have trouble manipulating anything but numerals.

■ Use standard codes for "no information." Thus, all "don't know" responses might be coded as 8, "no answers" as 9, and "does not apply" as 0. It is best if the same code is used throughout the study for each of these types of "no information." If "don't know" and "does not apply" are not response options (and thus there is no distinction between different types of "no information"), it is often best to just leave the column(s) blank.

codebook
A book that contains explicit directions about how data from data collection forms are to be coded in the data file.

Learning Objective

5.   Describe the kinds of information contained in a codebook.

FIGURE 18.1 Avery Fitness Center Questionnaire

AVERY FITNESS CENTER SURVEY

Thank you for taking time to provide important feedback about **Avery Fitness Center** (AFC). Please answer the following questions. Your candid responses will help us provide better services in the future. No one at AFC will see your specific responses, so please be honest.

(1) Which of the following AFC services have you utilized at least once in the last 30 days? (Please check all that apply)

- ☐ Weight Training   ☐ Exercise Circuit   ☐ Therapy Pool
- ☐ Classes   ☐ Circulation Station

(2) Within the past 30 days, approximately how many times have you visited AFC to exercise?

_____Times in the last 30 days

(3) During what part of the day have you <u>normally</u> visited AFC? (Please check only <u>one</u>)

- ☐ morning   ☐ afternoon   ☐ evening

(4) How did you learn about AFC? (Please check all that apply)

- ☐ Recommendation from Doctor   ☐ Drove by location
- ☐ Recommendation from Friend or Acquaintance   ☐ Article in Paper
- ☐ Advertising (including Yellow Pages)   ☐ Other
- ☐ Heard AFC director speak

(5) How important to you personally is each of the following reasons for participating in AFC programs? (Circle a number on each scale)

	not at all important				very important
General Health and Fitness	1	2	3	4	5
Social Aspects	1	2	3	4	5
Physical Enjoyment	1	2	3	4	5
Specific Medical Concerns	1	2	3	4	5

(6) How likely is it that you would recommend AFC to a friend or colleague?

not at all likely					neutral					extremely likely
0	1	2	3	4	5	6	7	8	9	10

(7) What was the original event that caused you to begin using services from AFC?

_____

(8) Current Age_____

(9) Gender ☐ Male   ☐ Female

(10) Highest Level of Education Achieved:

- ☐ Less than High School   ☐ Some College   ☐ Four-year College Degree
- ☐ High School Degree   ☐ Associates Degree   ☐ Advanced Degree

(11) What is your approximate annual household income from all sources, before taxes? (Please check the appropriate category & employment status)

- ☐ $0–15,000   ☐ $60,001–75,000
- ☐ $15,001–30,000   ☐ $75,001–90,000   ☐ Employed
- ☐ $30,001–45,000   ☐ $90,001–105,000   ☐ Retired
- ☐ $45,001–60,000   ☐ $105,001–120,000
- ☐ more than $120,000

THANK YOU!

FIGURE 18.2	Initial Responses to Avery Fitness Center Questionnaire

001

AVERY FITNESS CENTER SURVEY

Thank you for taking time to provide important feedback about *Avery Fitness Center* (AFC). Please answer the following questions. Your candid responses will help us provide better services in the future. No one at AFC will see your specific responses, so please be honest.

(1) Which of the following AFC services have you utilized at least once in the last 30 days? (Please check all that apply)

[X] Weight Training   [ ] Exercise Circuit   [ ] Therapy Pool

[ ] Classes   [ ] Circulation Station

(2) Within the past 30 days, approximately how many times have you visited AFC to exercise?

___8___ Times in the last 30 days

(3) During what part of the day have you <u>normally</u> visited AFC? (Please check only <u>one</u>)

[X] morning   [ ] afternoon   [ ] evening

(4) How did you learn about AFC? (Please check all that apply)

[ ] Recommendation from Doctor   [ ] Drove by location

[X] Recommendation from Friend or Acquaintance   [ ] Article in Paper

[ ] Advertising (including Yellow Pages)   [ ] Other

[ ] Heard AFC director speak

(5) How important to you personally is each of the following reasons for participating in AFC programs? (Circle a number on each scale)

	not at all important				very important
General Health and Fitness	1	2	3	4	(5)
Social Aspects	1	2	3	(4)	5
Physical Enjoyment	1	2	3	4	(5)
Specific Medical Concerns	1	(2)	3	4	5

(6) How likely is it that you would recommend AFC to a friend or colleague?

not at all likely					neutral					extremely likely
0	1	2	3	4	5	6	7	8	9	(10)

(7) What was the original event that caused you to begin using services from AFC?

need to exercise to maintain strength 1

(8) Current Age __69__

(9) Gender   [ ] Male   [X] Female

(10) Highest Level of Education Achieved:

[ ] Less than High School   [ ] Some College   [ ] Four-year College Degree

[X] High School Degree   [ ] Associates Degree   [ ] Advanced Degree

(11) What is your approximate annual household income from all sources, before taxes? (Please check the appropriate category & employment status)

[ ] $0–15,000   [ ] $60,001–75,000   ┌─────────────────┐
[ ] $15,001–30,000   [ ] $75,001–90,000   │ [X] Employed   │
[ ] $30,001–45,000   [ ] $90,001–105,000   │ [ ] Retired   │
[ ] $45,001–60,000   [ ] $105,001–120,000   └─────────────────┘
                       [ ] more than $120,000

$1,170

THANK YOU!

002

AVERY FITNESS CENTER SURVEY

Thank you for taking time to provide important feedback about **Avery Fitness Center** (AFC). Please answer the following questions. Your candid responses will help us provide better services in the future. No one at AFC will see your specific responses, so please be honest.

(1) Which of the following AFC services have you utilized at least once in the last 30 days? (Please check all that apply)

☐ Weight Training   ☐ Exercise Circuit   ☐ Therapy Pool

☒ Classes   ☐ Circulation Station

(2) Within the past 30 days, approximately how many times have you visited AFC to exercise?

__10__ Times in the last 30 days

(3) During what part of the day have you <u>normally</u> visited AFC? (Please check only <u>one</u>)

☒ morning   ☐ afternoon   ☐ evening

(4) How did you learn about AFC? (Please check all that apply)

☐ Recommendation from Doctor   ☐ Drove by location

☐ Recommendation from Friend or Acquaintance   ☒ Article in Paper

☐ Advertising (including Yellow Pages)   ☐ Other

☐ Heard AFC director speak

(5) How important to you personally is each of the following reasons for participating in AFC programs? (Circle a number on each scale)

	not at all important				very important
General Health and Fitness	1	2	3	4	⑤
Social Aspects	1	2	3	4	⑤
Physical Enjoyment	1	2	3	4	⑤
Specific Medical Concerns	1	2	3	4	5

(6) How likely is it that you would recommend AFC to a friend or colleague?

not at all likely					neutral					extremely likely
0	1	2	3	4	5	6	7	8	9	⑩

(7) What was the original event that caused you to begin using services from AFC?

__*general need for exercise 1*__

(8) Current Age__77__

(9) Gender   ☐ Male   ☒ Female

(10) Highest Level of Education Achieved:

☐ Less than High School   ☒ Some College   ☐ Four-year College Degree

☐ High School Degree   ☐ Associates Degree   ☐ Advanced Degree

(11) What is your approximate annual household income from all sources, before taxes? (Please check the appropriate category & employment status)

☐ $0–15,000   ☐ $60,001–75,000
☐ $15,001–30,000   ☐ $75,001–90,000   ☐ Employed
☐ $30,001–45,000   ☐ $90,001–105,000   ☒ Retired
☐ $45,001–60,000   ☐ $105,001–120,000
                                   ☐ more than $120,000

$1,070

THANK YOU!

FIGURE 18.3	Codebook for Avery Fitness Center Questionnaire

Column(s)	Variable Name	Description	
1–3	ID	Questionnaire identification number	
4	WEIGHT	Utilized <u>weight training</u> in previous 30 days?	0 = no 1 = yes
5	CLASSES	Utilized <u>classes</u> in previous 30 days?	0 = no 1 = yes
6	CIRCUIT	Utilized <u>exercise circuit</u> in previous 30 days?	0 = no 1 = yes
7	STATION	Utilized <u>circulation station</u> in previous 30 days?	0 = no 1 = yes
8	POOL	Utilized <u>therapy pool</u> in previous 30 days?	0 = no 1 = yes
9–10	VISITS	Number of visits to AFC in previous 30 days?	(record number)
11	DAYPART	Normal time to visit AFC?	1 = morning 2 = afternoon 3 = evening
12	DOCTOR	How learned about AFC? <u>Doctor Rec.</u>	0 = no 1 = yes
13	WOM	How learned about AFC? <u>Friend Rec.</u>	0 = no 1 = yes
14	ADVERT	How learned about AFC? <u>Advertising</u>	0 = no 1 = yes
15	SPEAKER	How learned about AFC? <u>Heard director speak</u>	0 = no 1 = yes
16	LOCATION	How learned about AFC? <u>Drove by location</u>	0 = no 1 = yes
17	ARTICLE	How learned about AFC? <u>Article in newspaper</u>	0 = no 1 = yes
18	OTHER	How learned about AFC? <u>Other</u>	0 = no 1 = yes
19	FITNESS	Importance for participation: <u>General Health and Fitness</u>	(1–5, "not at all important – very important")
20	SOCIAL	<u>Social Aspects</u>	SAME
21	ENJOY	<u>Physical Enjoyment</u>	SAME
22	MEDICAL	<u>Specific Medical Concerns</u>	SAME
23–24	RECOM	How likely to recommend?	(1–10, "not at all likely–extremely likely")
25	EVENT	What original event caused you to begin AFC? (open ended)	1 = general health / exercise 2 = pool / facilities 3 = rehab / specific medical needs 4 = social considerations 5 = transfer from another center 6 = other
26–27	AGE	Current Age	(record number)
28	GENDER	Gender	1 = male 2 = female
29	EDUCAT	Highest level of education achieved?	1 = less than high school 2 = high school degree 3 = some college 4 = associates degree 5 = four-year college degree 6 = advanced degree
30	INCOME	Annual household income before taxes	1 = $0 – 15,000 2 = $15,001 – 30,000 3 = $30,001 – 45,000 4 = $45,001 – 60,000 5 = $60,001 – 75,000 6 = $75,001 – 90,000 7 = $90,001 – 105,000 8 = $105,001 – 120,000 9 = more than $120,000
31	STATUS	Work Status	1 = employed 2 = retired
32–35	REVENUE	Two–year Revenue from Respondent	($$$ from secondary records)
		MISSING = BLANK	

FIGURE 18.4	Partial Data File, Avery Fitness Center Study

```
001100000810100000054521016922 11170
002010001010000010555 1017723 21070
003110001410000000153341057525521095
004111111220000000533 1037425 21115
005000011410100000051441058725521115
006001011210100000053350857422121175
007011001610000000154341036626521195
008000012010000010355 1017222321065
009100001220100000534410380 421170
010001112011001000544510375233321033
01100101  110000015334101882221150
012010012010000010513310376 3421095
013000010811000000544510375234421108
014000010811000000043330817813421108
015010101210100000055551047123321115
016100000620000001113101178133 1085
017100011820001000544510470253221085
018101002010001110544107563257110 20
019001001010100 015 540936626311130
020000011211000004  51018523 21015
021010002010000001544510179 6 21095
022111101521000000053240739016521050
023001011810110010545510487234 1050
024101000510000001523410280165210 85
025000010610100000055551037926621085
```

- Code a respondent identification number on each record. This number normally won't identify the respondent by name. Instead, the number simply ties the questionnaire to the coded data. This is often useful information in data cleaning (discussed later).

- When entering data in fixed column format, use a font, such as Courier, in which all characters require equal space on the line. This practice allows easy inspection of the data file to see if all records are the same length. A record that is too long or too short indicates a mistake in the data entry process.

- Save the data file as a text-only file, so that only the data and hard returns (that is, pressing the Enter key) to start new records appear in the file. Be sure to eliminate any extra hard returns at the end of the data file before saving the file, as these will often indicate to the statistical software that more records exist, resulting in a greater number of missing cases for analyses than really exist.

blunder
An error that arises during editing, coding, or data entry.

Learning Objective

6.   Describe common methods for cleaning the data file.

CLEANING THE DATA

Before proceeding to data analysis, it is necessary to examine the data to ensure that they have been entered correctly into the data file. **Blunders** are errors that occur during editing, coding, or, especially, data entry. Of all possible sources of error in a marketing research project, blunders are among the most frustrating because they are usually caused by simple carelessness. In this section, we will talk about how to identify blunders and discuss several data entry options that might limit this source of error.

MANAGER'S FOCUS

As a manager, it is not your responsibility to "clean the data" or "handle missing data." However, you should verify that these tasks are completed in an appropriate way by your research provider. These two preanalysis steps may not seem as important as the final analyses, but if they are not handled properly, the findings produced by the final analyses will be compromised.

Prior to a study, it might be instructive to ask all of the prospective research suppliers how they generally handle these tasks. If a research firm does not give a direct and convincing response, choose a different provider. Once the data collection process is underway, you should revisit these two topics with your research provider to ensure there is an appropriate plan in place to handle each step prior to completing the final analyses.

Sometimes blunders are relatively easy to diagnose. For example, suppose that a researcher were coding a 1–5 Likert scale and accidentally entered a 7 instead of the 4 that the respondent circled on the questionnaire. The blunder can be seen by performing a simple univariate analysis known as a frequency count (which we will introduce in the next chapter). A frequency count tells us all of the different responses coded for a variable along with how many cases responded in each way. In our example, the miscoded 7 will turn up as a response in the frequency analysis, and we will immediately know that a mistake has been made (remember that only the numbers 1 through 5 are valid responses to the question). At this point, it is only a matter of identifying which questionnaire was coded 7 for that variable, pulling the actual questionnaire to find the correct response (i.e., 4), and correcting the mistake in the data file. On most projects, frequencies should initially be run on all variables to help identify blunders.

Other blunders are more difficult to detect. In the previous example, suppose that the researcher accidentally enters a 1 instead of the 4 circled by the respondent. Because a 1 is one of the possible valid responses to this item (i.e., a 1–5 scale), a frequency analysis will not uncover this blunder; more involved types of examination are required. One possibility, which is similar to quality control in manufacturing processes, is to select a sample of questionnaires that have been coded and entered and compare the data file against the original questionnaires to find discrepancies. If no blunders are found, there is less concern about data entry error. If several blunders are identified, it may be necessary to check additional records or even examine all records.

A better option, known as **double-entry** of data, requires that the data be entered by two separate people in two separate data files and then the data files be compared for discrepancies. The differences are resolved by referring to the original questionnaires. Because it is unlikely that two different people would make the same blunders during data entry, this approach is likely to produce the "cleanest" data file possible with manual data entry. Using modern word processing software packages, the file comparison process is quite straightforward. Note, however, that this technique requires greater resources (i.e., time, effort, money).

Enhanced data collection technology offers at least two important options for reducing blunders. For example, **optical scanning** of data collection forms takes information directly from the data collection form and reads it into a data file. The Gallup Organization routinely uses optical scanning for mail or other self-administered questionnaires. The company claims an extremely high accuracy rate; any responses that the scanner can't read with 100% confidence are sent for verification to company employees.[3]

double-entry
Data entry procedure in which data are entered separately by two people in two data files and the data files are compared for discrepancies.

optical scanning
The use of scanner technology to "read" responses on paper surveys and to store these responses in a data file.

We noted earlier that computer-assisted data collection will automatically create a data file, in most cases. Respondents or interviewers enter responses directly into the data file, eliminating the need for a separate data entry procedure. Note, however, that these approaches are less useful as a means of limiting blunders when working with open-ended questions, for which categories and codes must be developed by the researcher.

HANDLING MISSING DATA

Learning Objective

7. Discuss options for dealing with missing data in analyses.

item nonresponse
A source of nonsampling error that arises when a respondent agrees to an interview but refuses, or is unable, to answer specific questions.

As noted in the previous chapter, item nonresponse is often a significant problem. Some percentage of the survey instruments suffers from it in most projects. Usually, the only exceptions occur when researchers "force" respondents to complete each item before moving on in the survey. For example, with self-administered computer-assisted studies (usually involving the Internet), the system can be programmed to require a response before moving to the next item. Although such a strategy is convenient for the researcher (i.e., it eliminates missing data), we suspect that it also leads to (1) response error when respondents simply choose a response so that they can get on with the survey, or (2) nonresponse error when individuals become frustrated and simply terminate the process. Researchers planning to use this approach must ensure that all or most potential respondents know the answers to the questions and that all potential responses are represented (that is, the response categories are exhaustive). As always, we advise careful exploratory research and pretesting in order to avoid problems.

The degree of item nonresponse often serves as a useful indicator of the quality of the research. When it is excessive, it calls the whole research effort into question and suggests that the research objectives and procedures should be examined critically. Even when the amount of missing information isn't all that much, however, you still must decide what to do about it before you analyze the data. Here are several possible strategies:

- **Leave the items blank, and report the number as a separate category.** Although this procedure works well for some simple analyses (e.g., frequencies and cross tabulations), it does not work well for a number of other statistical techniques.

- **Eliminate the case with the missing item(s) from all further analyses.** This strategy results in a "pure" data set with no missing information at all. The sample size will thus be equal for all analyses. This strategy, however, excludes data that may be perfectly useful for some analyses. In the extreme, the researcher might discard a questionnaire from which only a single piece of information was missing. Given that data are so valuable and sometimes difficult to collect, we would rarely recommend this strategy. Any case with a significant amount of missing information (say, half or more as a rule of thumb) should have been eliminated during the central-office edit.

- **Eliminate the case with the missing item in analyses using the variable.** When using this approach, the analyst must continually report the number of cases on which the analysis is based, since the sample size is not constant across analyses. It also ignores the fact that a significant degree of nonresponse on a particular item might be informative in that it suggests respondents do not care very deeply about the issue being addressed by the question or that they do not know the answer to the question. The obvious advantage to this strategy is that all available data are used for each analysis.

- **Substitute values for the missing items.** Sometimes you can estimate a value for the missing item based on responses to other related items on the respondent's questionnaire, perhaps using a statistical technique known as regression

MANAGER'S FOCUS

In Chapter 2, we encouraged you to have the results of each research study entered into your organization's marketing information system (MIS). This will enable all managers to benefit from what was learned. As part of this process, we would advise you to develop a system for archiving copies of the (a) final report, (b) blank questionnaire, (c) data file, and (d) codebook. These materials will enable research personnel (or even managers) to understand the nature of the original data and will enhance their ability to conduct appropriate new analyses at future points in time. This ability will dramatically enhance the value of the research findings when managers use them as secondary data with which to address new marketing problems.

analysis, which measures the relationship between two or more variables (see Chapter 20). Alternatively, sometimes the analyst uses the values from other respondents' questionnaires to determine the mean, median, or mode for the variable and substitutes that value for the missing item. The substitution of values makes maximum use of the data, since all the reasonably good cases are used. At the same time, it requires more work from the analyst, and it contains some potential for bias, because the analyst has "created" values where none previously existed.

■ **Contact the respondent again.** If the missing information is critical to the study and responses were not anonymous, it is sometimes possible to contact the respondent again to obtain the information. This approach is especially applicable if it appears that the respondent simply missed the item altogether or if the respondent tried to answer the question but didn't follow the instructions.

There is no "right" or simple answer as to how missing items should be handled. It all depends on the purposes of the study, the incidence of missing items, and the methods that will be used to analyze the data.

SUMMARY

Learning Objective 1

Explain the purpose of the field edit.
The field edit is a preliminary edit designed to detect the most glaring omissions and inaccuracies in the data. It is also useful in helping to control the actions of the field force personnel and to clear up any misunderstanding they may have about directions, procedures, specific questions, and so on.

Learning Objective 2

Define what coding is.
Coding is the technical procedure by which data are categorized. Through coding, the raw data are transformed into symbols—usually numerals—that may be tabulated and counted. The transformation involves judgment on the part of the coder.

Learning Objective 3

Discuss two types of open-ended questions.
Some open-ended questions ask for specific information, or facts, from respondents and are usually quite easy to code. Another type of open-ended question seeks less structured information and often allows multiple responses. This type of open-ended question is usually much more difficult to code.

Learning Objective 4

List the basic steps in coding open-ended responses.

1. Identify the separate responses given by each individual.
2. Specify categories into which the responses can be placed.
3. Place each response into one and only one category using multiple coders.
4. Assess the degree of agreement between the multiple coders.

Learning Objective 5

Describe the kinds of information contained in a codebook.

The codebook contains the general instructions indicating how each item of data was coded. It contains the variable names, location of each variable in the data file, a description of how each variable is coded, and an explanation of how missing data are treated in the data file.

Learning Objective 6

Describe common methods for cleaning the data file.

Blunders may be located by examining frequency distributions for all variables to identify obviously incorrect codings, by sampling records from the data file and comparing them with the original questionnaires, or by using double-entry of data in which data are entered into two separate data files and then compared for discrepancies.

Learning Objective 7

Discuss options for dealing with missing data in analyses.

Several options exist, including (a) reporting missing information as a separate category, (b) eliminating the case with missing information from all analyses, (c) eliminating the case with missing information from only analyses using variables with missing information, (d) substituting values for the missing items, and (e) contacting the respondent again.

KEY TERMS

field edit (page 401)
central-office edit (page 401)
coding (page 403)
codebook (page 407)

blunder (page 412)
double-entry (page 413)
optical scanning (page 413)
item nonresponse (page 414)

REVIEW QUESTIONS

1. What are the differences in focus between a field edit and a central-office edit?

2. What should an editor do with incomplete answers? Obviously wrong answers? Answers that reflect a lack of interest?

3. How might a researcher best code "check all that apply" questions?

4. What are the two kinds of open-ended questions, and why is one more difficult to code than the other?

5. What are the principles that underlie the establishment of categories so that responses to open-ended questions may be properly coded?

6. Why should multiple coders be used to establish categories and code responses for open-ended questions? Does this apply to all open-ended questions?

7. Suppose that you have a large number of very long questionnaires, making it impossible for one person to handle the entire coding task. How should the work be divided?

8. What methods are available for building a data file?

9. What is the purpose of the codebook?

10. If a respondent fails to answer a question on a survey, how should the item nonresponse be coded in the data file?

11. What is a blunder?

12. What is double-entry of data?

13. What are the possible ways for dealing with missing data? Which strategy would you recommend?

DISCUSSION QUESTIONS, PROBLEMS, AND PROJECTS

1. The KIST television station was conducting research in order to help develop programs that would be well received by the viewing audience and would be considered dependable sources of information. A two-part questionnaire was administered by personal interviews to a panel of 3,000 respondents residing in the city of Houston. The field and office edits were done simultaneously, so that the deadline of May 1 could be met. A senior supervisor, Marlene Howe, was placed in charge of the editing tasks and was assisted by two junior supervisors and two field-workers. The two field-workers were instructed to discard instruments that were illegible or incomplete. Each junior supervisor was instructed to scrutinize 1,500 of the instruments for incomplete answers, wrong answers, and responses that indicated a lack of interest. They were instructed to discard instruments that had more than five incomplete or wrong answers (the questionnaire contained 30 questions). In addition, they were asked to use their judgment in assessing whether the respondent showed a lack of interest and, if so, to discard the questionnaire.

    a. Critically evaluate the above editing tasks. Please be specific.

    b. Make specific recommendations to George Brady, the owner of the KIST television station, as to how the editing should be done.

2. a. Establish response categories and codes for the question, "What do you like about this new brand of cereal?"

    b. Code the following responses using your categories and codes.

        1. "$1.50 is a reasonable price to pay for the cereal."
        2. "The raisins and nuts add a nice flavor."
        3. "The sizes of the packages are convenient."
        4. "I like the sugarcoating on the cereal."
        5. "The container does not tear and fall apart easily."
        6. "My kids like the cartoons on the back of the packet."
        7. "It is reasonably priced compared with other brands."
        8. "The packet is attractive and easy to spot in the store."
        9. "I like the price; it is not so low that I doubt the quality, and at the same time it is not so high as to be unaffordable."
        10. "The crispness and lightness of the cereal improve the taste."

3. a. Establish response categories and codes for the following question, which was asked of a sample of business executives: "In your opinion, which types of companies have not been affected by the present economic climate?"

    b. Code the following responses using your categories and codes.
        1. *Washington Post*
        2. Colgate Palmolive

3. Procter & Gamble
4. Hilton Hotels
5. Bank of America
6. Fabergé
7. Marine Midlands Banks
8. Amana
9. Holiday Inn
10. Whirlpool
11. Chili's
12. CitiBank

4.   Based on the following codebook, reconstruct the questionnaire used to gather information for a local restaurant.

	Codebook for The Pasta Shop Project	
Column(s)	**Variable Name**	**Description**
1–4	ID	Identification Number for respondent
5	RESID	Resident of Glendale at least 6 months per year?
		1 = yes
		2 = no
6	BAGES	Between ages of 18–74?
		1 = yes
		2 = no
7	AGEGROUP	What age group are you in?
		1 = 18–24
		2 = 25–44
		3 = 45–74
8	SEX	Sex of respondent
		1 = male
		2 = female
9	DINEOUT	Number of times you dine out per 2 weeks?
		1 = 1–2 times
		2 = 3–4 times
		3 = 5–6 times
		4 = more than 6
10–11	REST1	Name your favorite restaurants? (open-ended)
		01 = The Pasta Shop
		02 = Applebee's
		03 = El Chico
		04 = Carter's
		05 = Missy's Steakhouse
		06 = Glendale Inn
		07 = Hideaway
		08 = Ko's Japanese Restaurant
		09 = Pedro's
		10 = Sirloin Stockade
		11 = Doc's Seafood
		12 = Western Sizzlin
		13 = Al's Diner
		14 = Denny's

Codebook for The Pasta Shop Project (*Continued*)

Column(s)	Variable Name	Description
		15 = Pony Express
		16 = Lenny's
		17 = Red Lobster
		18 = Pizza Hut
		19 = Mom's Place
		20 = Brad's BBQ
		21 = Perkins
		22 = China Table
		23 = Bagel Shop
		24 = Pasta Palace
		25 = Dragon's Garden
12–13	REST2	Second favorite restaurant
14–15	REST3	Third favorite restaurant
16	AWARE	Have you heard of The Pasta Shop?
		1 = yes
		2 = no
17	NEWSPAPR	How did you hear of The Pasta Shop?
		By newspaper advertisement?
		1 = yes
		2 = no
18	RADIO	By radio advertisement?
		1 = yes
		2 = no
19	DRIVEBY	Did you drive by it?
		1 = yes
		2 = no
20	WORDOF	Word of mouth?
		1 = yes
		2 = no
21	DIDUEAT	Have you eaten at The Pasta Shop?
		1 = yes
		2 = no
22	SATISFY	Were you satisfied with overall service?
		(1–5, "extremely dissatisfied"–"extremely satisfied")
23	PRICE	Was the price you paid:
		1 = too low
		2 = about right
		3 = too high
		MISSING = BLANK

5. The following is a questionnaire to be completed by customers of the Hilltop Smoked Meat Co. Restaurant. Build a codebook that might be used to transfer raw answers from completed questionnaires to a data file. Be specific about locations in the data file, variable names, the codes to be used, and how missing data will be treated.

Hilltop Smoked Meat Co. Customer Survey

This survey was developed to get your opinions concerning satisfaction with your current visit to Hilltop. Please complete this survey after your meal and return it to us.

Check the boxes that most accurately reflect your candid opinion about Hilltop!
Your input and time are Greatly Appreciated!

1. Are You Currently a Customer During   Lunch ☐   Evening Meal ☐   In between ☐

2. Is this Your first visit to Hilltop?   Yes ☐   No ☐

3. If this is **not** Your first visit, approximately how many times have you eaten at Hilltop in the last 3 months? _____ times

How Would You Rate The Following:	Very Poor	Poor	Fair	Good	Very Good
4. Friendliness of the employees	☐	☐	☐	☐	☐
5. Speed of Service	☐	☐	☐	☐	☐
6. Cleanliness of the Establishment	☐	☐	☐	☐	☐
7. Price for the Quantity Received	☐	☐	☐	☐	☐
8. Price for the Quality Received	☐	☐	☐	☐	☐
9. Variety of Menu Items	☐	☐	☐	☐	☐
10. Overall Quality of the Food	☐	☐	☐	☐	☐
11. Overall Atmosphere	☐	☐	☐	☐	☐
12. How convenient is this location?	☐	☐	☐	☐	☐
13. How would you rate Hilltop overall?	☐	☐	☐	☐	☐

14. Are you aware of Hilltop's full catering menu?   Yes ☐   No ☐

15. Have you ever seen or heard an advertisement for Hilltop?   Yes ☐   No ☐

16. If you **Have, Check All that Apply:**

   Newspaper ☐   Radio ☐   Television ☐   Word of Mouth ☐

17. Do you come to Hilltop more often for:

   Dine-in Lunch ☐   Dine-in Dinner ☐   Take-out Lunch ☐   Take-out Dinner ☐

18. What, if any, items would you like to see added to the menu? _____

_____

19. What is your favorite item on the menu? _____

20. What is your zip code? _____

Thank You for your participation!

---

6. A research team is working on an important project and has decided to use double-entry to identify and eliminate blunders. The following are data from the first 12 respondents as they appear in the two data files constructed during the double-entry process. Enter each of the data sets into a separate file and use the "compare versions" (or similar command) option in a word processing software package to identify blunders.

Data Set A
0011659358458545565845568955758559
0026954582 135 65565535 55647653257
0031654885789786544255409890043434
004142323455 514925342383694458596
0051029237476456453423423423 5346457
0065847831928353745675849 5665256475
007655445455414243 544556462345456
0089485849588784858784785747272 1646
0095747313544464545751312231224 5465
0107346197845   5864 5427276469458
01173875194673854 9464 579454356475
01269787564615846764 7 9565749455365

Data Set B
0011659358458545565845568955758559
0026954582 135 65565535 55647653257
0031654884789786544255409890043434
004142323455 514925342383694458596
0051029237476456453423423423 5346457
0065847831928353745675849 5665226475
007655445455414243 544556462345456
0089485849588784858784785747272 1646
0095747313544464545751312231224 5465
0107346197845   5864 5427576469458
01173875194673854 9464 579454356475
01269787564615846764 7 9565749455365

Data Analysis: Analyzing Individual Variables and Basics of Hypothesis Testing

Learning Objectives

1. Distinguish between univariate and multi-variate analyses.
2. Describe frequency analysis.
3. Explain the various ways in which frequency analysis can be used.
4. Discuss confidence intervals for proportions.
5. Describe commonly used descriptive statistics.
6. Discuss confidence intervals for means.
7. List the steps involved in hypothesis testing.
8. Describe the chi-square goodness-of-fit test.
9. Discuss the process for comparing a proportion against a standard.
10. Describe the appropriate tests for comparing a mean against a standard for (a) small samples and (b) large samples.

Introduction

There are some aspects of marketing research that are relatively difficult. Fortunately, data analysis usually isn't one of them, despite what many people seem to believe. As we will demonstrate in the next two chapters, data analysis hinges on two key considerations about the variable(s) to be analyzed. First, will the variable be analyzed in isolation (univariate analysis) or in relationship to one or more other variables (multivariate analysis)? Second, what level of measurement (nominal, ordinal, interval, ratio) was used to measure the variable(s)? Analysis generally proceeds in a straightforward manner once these questions are answered.

In this chapter, we present a number of common types of univariate data analysis techniques and introduce the concept of hypothesis testing. A great many analyses in applied marketing research involve simple univariate analyses. For example, the publisher of a magazine might want to know the proportion of the magazine's readers who are male; a restaurant might like to know the average income of its typical diner; a service provider might need to know her customers' average level of satisfaction with the services provided. In each of these cases, a single variable is analyzed in isolation—gender, income, satisfaction.

THE AVERY FITNESS CENTER (AFC) PROJECT

1. Distinguish between univariate and multivariate analyses.

Recall the Avery Fitness Center (AFC) project that we introduced in the previous chapter. Located in a mid-size city in the southeastern United States, the company offers a variety of exercise programs to its members under the supervision of personal trainers. The company was founded 10 years ago and operates from a single location in an old shopping center near a large university. AFC primarily targets "prime-timers"—men and women ages 55 years and older, some of whom are struggling with health issues. Many customers are attracted to the large indoor therapy pool that allows exercise using water resistance which is much easier on bones and joints than traditional exercise options. Individuals become members of the fitness center by paying a monthly fee. Although business has been steady, AFC managers believe that the company could grow substantially without adding additional facilities. As a result, AFC managers are interested in better understanding the kinds of individuals that are attracted to AFC and how best to recruit more of these kinds of people. More specifically, the AFC researchers are addressing two research problems: (1) determine member demographics and usage patterns and (2) investigate how members learn about AFC.

To address these research problems, researchers decided to conduct a mail survey of AFC's customer base (see the questionnaire in Figure 18.1 in the previous chapter). "Customer" was defined as any individual in the company's member database who had visited AFC at least once in the previous 12 months. Surveys were sent to 400 members drawn using a simple random sample; respondents completed and returned 231 usable surveys for a response rate of 58%. Returned surveys were matched with total fees paid by each respondent over the most recent two-year period. After editing, coding, and cleaning the data, the researchers were ready to begin data analysis (see the codebook in Figure 18.3 in the previous chapter).

BASIC UNIVARIATE STATISTICS: CATEGORICAL MEASURES

Because both nominal and ordinal measures are easily used to group respondents or objects into groups or categories, researchers often refer to these types of measures as **categorical measures**. For example, the AFC survey included measures of (1) the gender and (2) the highest level of education achieved of the population of AFC members. The first of these measures is clearly at the nominal level of measurement: Each responding individual belongs to either the "male" or the "female" category.

categorical measures
A commonly used expression for nominal and ordinal measures.

MANAGER'S FOCUS

Managers depend upon researchers to perform data analysis. Why, then, should they know something about data analysis techniques? Technology has developed to the point where data analysis software is very user-friendly, even for nonresearchers. You may find yourself in a position of wanting or needing to quickly analyze data for yourself. Being able to easily run software is not the same thing, though, as running and understanding the analyses properly. You need to be able to determine which analyses are appropriate given such considerations as the level of measurement (i.e., nominal, ordinal, interval, or ratio) and the nature of the research objectives. Additionally, you need to know how to properly interpret the results of each test. Even when researchers do the data analysis, you will be less reliant on the judgment of others and better able to independently interpret the marketing relevance of the findings if you understand the nature of the statistical tests performed for you.

Exhibit 19.1 reveals that 80% of the respondents in the AFC sample were women. Although this statistic is interesting, AFC managers should be more interested in what would be true for the entire population of AFC customers.

The second measure was assessed at the ordinal level of measurement. Respondents indicated the highest level of education they had achieved by choosing one of six categories ordered from low ("less than high school") to high ("advanced degree"). Sample statistics for both items are easily obtained via frequency analysis.

Frequency Analysis

A **frequency analysis** consists of counting the number of cases that fall into the various response categories. This is a very simple analytic tool, yet it is incredibly important and commonly used to report the overall results of marketing research studies. Frequencies may be produced for each of the variables in a study, but the tabulation for each variable is independent of the tabulation for the other variables.

Any packaged statistical program such as SPSS and even spreadsheet programs such as Excel can perform frequency analysis. Some programs will calculate summary statistics and plot a histogram of the values (discussed later) in addition to reporting the number of cases in each category.

Exhibit 19.1 presents the frequency analysis for the gender of the AFC study respondents. The standard computer output for a frequency analysis includes the raw count of cases falling into each category, the percentage of total cases falling into each category, the percentage of valid (nonmissing) cases falling into each category, and the cumulative valid percentage for each category. As indicated, 177 of the 222 individuals who responded to the gender item (9 respondents did not answer the question) were women. The second column in Exhibit 19.1 includes percentages calculated using all respondents, including those who didn't answer the question. The third column presents "valid" percentages (the missing cases are excluded). Although the number of missing cases in a frequency analysis should be indicated, valid percentages are normally reported along with the count. The final column in Exhibit 19.1 reports the cumulative valid percent associated with each level of the variable. This is the percentage of observations with a value less than or equal to the level indicated.

frequency analysis
A count of the number of cases that fall into each category when the categories are based on one variable.

Exhibit 19.1	Avery Fitness Center: Gender			
Gender	**Number**	**Percent**	**Valid Percent**	**Cumulative Valid Percent**
Male	45	19%	20%	20%
Female	177	77	80	100
Total	222	96	100	
Missing	9	4		
Overall total	231	100		

Exhibit 19.2	**Avery Fitness Center: Level of Education**		
Level of Education Achieved	**Number**	**Valid Percent**	**Cumulative Percent**
Less than high school	4	2%	2%
High school degree	34	15	17
Some college	46	20	37
Associates degree	7	3	40
Four-year college degree	52	23	64
Advanced degree	82	36	100
Total	225	100	

(number of missing cases = 6)

Exhibit 19.2 presents frequency results for the highest level of education reported by the AFC members. As indicated, 15% of respondents reported a high school degree as the highest level of education achieved. Working with the cumulative percentages, however, it is probably more informative to report that 81% of respondents indicated having taken courses beyond the high school level. The results in Exhibit 19.2 indicate that AFC members tend to be well educated (60% have at least a four-year college degree).

About Percentages Before going further, let's think about using percentages for reporting results. First, it's always smart to include percentages along with the raw count for frequency analyses because percentages help readers interpret results. For example, it is much more informative to learn that "80% of respondents were women" than that "177 of 222 respondents were women." Second, percentages should be rounded off to whole numbers (i.e., no decimals), because whole numbers are easier to read and because decimals might make the results look more accurate or "scientific" than they really are, especially in a small sample. In some cases, it might be reasonable to report percentages to one decimal place (rarely two decimal places), but the general rule is to use whole numbers.[1]

Other Uses for Frequencies

In addition to communicating the results of a study, frequency analysis is useful for several other purposes. For example, frequencies are useful for determining the degree of item nonresponse for a variable and for locating blunders, as we discussed in Chapter 18. Frequencies should be produced for all variables included in a study before any additional data analysis is attempted.

Another use of frequency analysis is to locate outliers, valid observations that are so different from the rest of the observations that they ought to be treated as special cases. This may mean eliminating the observation from the analysis or determining the specific factors that generated this unique observation. For instance, consider the histogram of AFC respondents' ages presented in Figure 19.1. A histogram is a form of bar chart that is based on information from a frequency count. Successive values of a variable (ages, in this example) are placed along the x-axis, and the raw count or proportion of cases that occur at each level is plotted on the y-axis. A quick look at the histogram in Figure 19.1 reveals that one respondent reported an age that is considerably younger than all the other cases. A look at the actual SPSS frequency analysis output (see Exhibit 19.3 on page 427) shows that this particular customer is 18 years old; the next youngest customer among the respondents was 35 years old. This case is clearly out of line with the rest of the sample—it should be considered an

Learning Objective

3. Explain the various ways in which frequency analysis can be used.

outlier
An observation so different in magnitude from the rest of the observations that the analyst chooses to treat it as a special case.

histogram
A form of bar chart on which the values of the variable are placed along the x-axis and the absolute frequency or relative frequency of occurrence of the values is indicated along the y-axis.

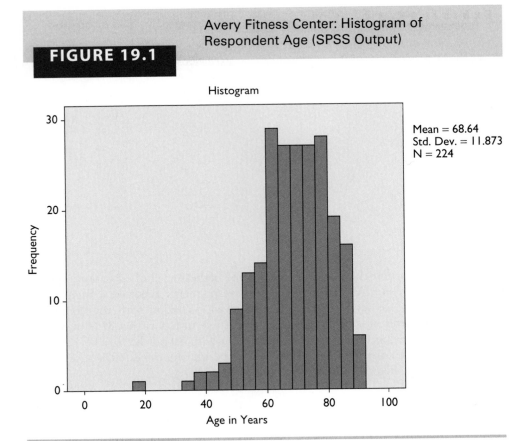

FIGURE 19.1

Avery Fitness Center: Histogram of Respondent Age (SPSS Output)

Histogram

Mean = 68.64
Std. Dev. = 11.873
N = 224

outlier. What you choose to do with this observation depends on the objectives of the study. In this case, it is not unreasonable for a respondent to be 18 years old (although unusual), so we'll keep it in the data file for now.

The frequency count for age presented in Exhibit 19.3 also allows us to point out one final use of frequency analysis. With ordinal-, interval-, or ratio-level measures, it is often useful to identify the median point as a measure of "average" for the distribution. It is a simple matter to locate the value of age at which the 50th percentile (the observation in the middle of the distribution when ordered from low to high) lands; in this case, the median age is 70. (And, if it matters, the first quartile falls at age 61 and the third quartile at age 77.)

So, what have we learned so far about AFC members from frequency analysis? They are mostly female, well educated, and older. Additional analyses on customer demographics (try these on your own using the data file located at www.cengage.com/marketing/churchill) reveal that most are retired (77%) and have household incomes above $45,000 (70%). In addition, Exhibit 19.4 (on page 428) presents information about AFC service usage behavior—all of these results were obtained using simple frequency analysis.

Confidence Intervals for Proportions

Learning Objective

4. Discuss confidence intervals for proportions.

We learned from the results presented in Exhibit 19.1 that 80% of the respondents in the sample were women. Although this statistic is interesting, AFC managers should be less interested in what happened for a particular sample than in what would be true for the entire population of AFC customers. Recall that we draw a sample to represent the population. In this case, our best guess is that 80% of the members in

Exhibit 19.3   **Avery Fitness Center: Age (SPSS Output)**

Age in Years

		Frequency	Percent	Valid Percent	Cumulative Percent
Valid	18	1	.4	.4	.4
	35	1	.4	.4	.9
	36	1	.4	.4	1.3
	38	1	.4	.4	1.8
	40	1	.4	.4	2.2
	43	1	.4	.4	2.7
	45	1	.4	.4	3.1
	46	1	.4	.4	3.6
	47	1	.4	.4	4.0
	48	2	.9	.9	4.9
	49	2	.9	.9	5.8
	50	3	1.3	1.3	7.1
	51	2	.9	.9	8.0
	52	1	.4	.4	8.5
	53	4	1.7	1.8	10.3
	54	4	1.7	1.8	12.1
	55	4	1.7	1.8	13.8
	56	1	.4	.4	14.3
	57	3	1.3	1.3	15.6
	58	3	1.3	1.3	17.0
	59	7	3.0	3.1	20.1
	60	6	2.6	2.7	22.8
	61	7	3.0	3.1	25.9
	62	3	1.3	1.3	27.2
	63	13	5.6	5.8	33.0
	64	6	2.6	2.7	35.7
	65	5	2.2	2.2	37.9
	66	8	3.5	3.6	41.5
	67	8	3.5	3.6	45.1
	68	4	1.7	1.8	46.9
	69	6	2.6	2.7	49.6
	70	6	2.6	2.7	52.2
	71	11	4.8	4.9	57.1
	72	4	1.7	1.8	58.9
	73	6	2.6	2.7	61.6
	74	9	3.9	4.0	65.6
	75	8	3.5	3.6	69.2
	76	6	2.6	2.7	71.9
	77	7	3.0	3.1	75.0
	78	7	3.0	3.1	78.1
	79	8	3.5	3.6	81.7
	80	5	2.2	2.2	83.9
	81	2	.9	.9	84.8
	82	11	4.8	4.9	89.7
	83	1	.4	.4	90.2
	84	3	1.3	1.3	91.5

(Continued)

Exhibit 19.3

Avery Fitness Center: Age (SPSS Output) (Continued)

Age in Years				
	Frequency	**Percent**	**Valid Percent**	**Cumulative Percent**
85	4	1.7	1.8	93.3
86	4	1.7	1.8	95.1
87	5	2.2	2.2	97.3
88	2	.9	.9	98.2
89	3	1.3	1.3	99.6
90	1	.4	.4	100.0
Total	224	97.0	100.0	
Missing System	7	3.0		
Total	231	100.0		

the population are female, but because of sampling error (as well as nonsampling error) we cannot be confident that this estimate is precisely true for the population.

Fortunately, because the researchers drew a sample using a probabilistic sampling plan, we can account for sampling error and make inferences about the population as a whole based on the results from the sample. A **confidence interval** is a projection of the range within which a population parameter will lie at a given level of confidence based on a statistic obtained from an appropriately drawn sample.[2] To produce a confidence interval, all we need to do is calculate the degree of sampling error for the particular statistic. To calculate sampling error for a proportion, we need three pieces of information: (1) z, the z score representing the desired degree of confidence (usually 95% confidence, where $z = 1.96$); (2) n, the number of valid cases overall for the proportion; and (3) p, the relevant proportion obtained from the sample. These pieces of information are entered into the following formula for sampling error for a proportion:

confidence interval
A projection of the range within which a population parameter will lie at a given level of confidence based on a statistic obtained from a probabilistic sample.

$$\text{sampling error for proportion} = z\sqrt{\frac{p(1-p)}{n}}$$

The resulting value is also frequently called the *margin of sampling error*. Drawing from the information presented in Exhibit 19.1, the margin of sampling error for the proportion of women in the AFC customer population is calculated as follows:

$$\text{sampling error} = 1.96\sqrt{\frac{0.80(1-0.80)}{222}} = 0.05$$

Exhibit 19.4

Avery Fitness Center: Services Utilized within Past 30 Days

Service	Number	Percent Respondents Utilizing
Weight training	80	35%
Classes	63	27
Exercise circuit	59	26
Circulation station	28	12
Therapy pool	109	47

(n = 231; no missing cases)

The confidence interval itself is constructed around the sample statistic in the following manner:

$$(p - \text{sampling error} \leq \pi \leq p + \text{sampling error})$$
$$(0.80 - 0.05 \leq \pi \leq 0.80 + 0.05)$$
$$\text{or } (0.75, 0.85)$$

Accordingly, we can be 95% confident that the actual proportion of women in the population (π) lies between 0.75 and 0.85, inclusive. This is a strong statement that highlights the beauty of probabilistic sampling. Even though the researchers had responses from only 222 individuals, they have a strong notion of what the answer would have been had they taken measures from all AFC customers within the population. As we discussed at length with respect to sample size calculation, if the analyst wants a narrower confidence interval (i.e., greater precision), she can decrease the degree of confidence desired (e.g., at 90% confidence, $z = 1.65$) or increase sample size.

A Word of Caution Before we start letting the numbers do the thinking for us, recognize that the confidence interval only takes sampling error into account. To the extent that nonsampling error has entered the study (see Chapter 17)—and you can be sure that it has to some degree—the confidence interval is less likely to have "captured" the population parameter within its bounds. Unfortunately, there is no quantitative way of adjusting the confidence interval to reflect these types of errors.

Suppose that an organization promoting the lowering of taxes reported survey results indicating that 90% of U.S. citizens were in favor of lowering federal income taxes, with +/− 3% margin of sampling error at 95% confidence. Further suppose that the organization obtained this result through the use of a leading question and that the proportion representing the true sentiment of citizens is somewhat lower. The resulting confidence interval itself is probably accurate in the sense that we can be 95% confident that if all U.S. citizens were asked the same leading question, the proportion in favor of lowering income taxes would fall in the range 0.87 to 0.93. Obviously, however, the error introduced by the leading question makes it entirely unlikely that the actual proportion of citizens who want to lower taxes falls within this interval. As we have noted elsewhere, reducing total error is the key, and researchers must resist the temptation to focus too closely on sampling error simply because it can be readily assessed.

BASIC UNIVARIATE STATISTICS: CONTINUOUS MEASURES

Because interval- and ratio-level measures are similar when it comes to analysis (the mean is the most commonly calculated statistic for both types), many researchers refer to both types as **continuous measures**, even though the label is not technically correct, especially for interval measures such as rating scales. For example, consider the age reported by the AFC study respondents, who were asked to report their actual age (a ratio-level measure). Earlier, we treated this variable as if it were a categorical variable (see Exhibit 19.3) in order to demonstrate some useful functions of frequency analysis. In this section, we'll take advantage of its higher-level measurement properties and demonstrate a more powerful analysis.

Descriptive Statistics

For continuous measures, numerous types of descriptive statistics can be calculated. **Descriptive statistics** describe the distribution of responses on a variable, including measures of central tendency (mean, median, and mode), measures of the spread, or variation, in the distribution (range, variance, standard deviation), and various measures of the shape of the distribution (e.g., skewness, kurtosis). In this section, we discuss the calculation and interpretation of two commonly used descriptive statistics, the mean and standard deviation.

continuous measures
A commonly used expression for interval and ratio measures.

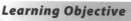
Learning Objective

5. Describe commonly used descriptive statistics.

descriptive statistics
Statistics that describe the distribution of responses on a variable. The most commonly used descriptive statistics are the mean and standard deviation.

sample mean
The arithmetic average value of the responses on a variable.

The **sample mean** ($\overline{x}$) is simply the arithmetic mean value across all responses for a variable and is found using the following formula:

$$\overline{x} = \frac{\sum\limits_{i=1}^{n} X_i}{n}$$

where X_i is the value of the variable for the ith respondent and n is the total number of responses. In the AFC customer study, mean age is found by summing the age values across respondents and dividing by 224, the total number of valid cases. Fortunately, all statistics packages will easily calculate variable means. In this example, the computed mean age turns out to be 68.6 years.

Although means are easy to calculate or obtain from computer output, there are several issues to keep in mind. First, while mean values can be calculated for any variable in a data set, they are only meaningful for continuous (i.e., interval, ratio) measures. Thus, knowing that the mean level of education is 4.4 is of little value at best—and misleading at worst—because this variable is at the ordinal level of measurement. The mean is only useful with equal-interval scales, one of the common characteristics of interval and ratio measures.

A second issue with respect to interpreting mean values concerns spurious precision. Just as we advised against the use of decimals with percentages, you'll need to be careful about just how precise a mean value can be. Consider the original values of respondent age shown in Exhibit 19.3. Each respondent provided his or her age in years, as a whole number. Knowing this, would it be reasonable to report that mean age for the sample was 68.6437261 years? No. Round the result off to a whole number (69 years) or use a single decimal (68.6 years) at the most. Anything more suggests a level of precision that simply isn't justified or necessary.

The third issue about mean values concerns their use with variables with one or more extreme cases, or outliers. As noted earlier, one AFC customer reported being only 18 years old, while most members were 60 years or older. In this case, leaving the respondent in the data set has only a slight effect on the mean age calculated for the sample, so it really isn't much of an issue. There are situations, however, where outliers can have a very strong influence on the sample mean. Suppose that an automobile manufacturer was basing an important decision on whether or not the average income in a target market is at least $50,000. The choice of which "average" income value to consider (i.e., mean vs. median) can affect the manager's decision if there are even just a few large outliers, as often seems to be the case with income. As a rule, the appropriate univariate measure of central tendency for variables with extreme responses is the median because it more accurately portrays the vast majority of cases. Alternatively, the extreme cases can be temporarily ignored and the mean calculated across the remaining cases.[3]

sample standard deviation
A measure of the variation of responses on a variable. The standard deviation is the square root of the calculated variance on a variable.

The **sample standard deviation** (s) provides a convenient measure of the variation in responses for continuous measures. If there is little difference in a particular response across the sample, that is, everyone was basically the same on some characteristic or felt the same way about some topic or object, then the standard deviation will be very small. If, on the other hand, responses are different—some high, some low—then the standard deviation for the variable will be larger. Failing to take the variation of responses into account can lead to poor decisions. Consider the classic case of a new sauce product:

> On the average, consumers wanted it neither really hot nor really mild. The mean rating of the test participants was quite close to the middle of the scale, which had "very mild" and "very hot" as its bipolar adjectives. This happened to fit the client's preconceived notion.
>
> However, examination of the distribution of the ratings revealed the existence of a large proportion of consumers who wanted the sauce to be mild and an equally large proportion who wanted it to be hot. Relatively few wanted the

in-between product, which would have been suggested by looking at the mean rating alone.[4]

The following formula is used to calculate the sample standard deviation:

$$s = \sqrt{\frac{\sum_{i=1}^{n} (X_i - \bar{x})^2}{n - 1}}$$

where X_i is the value of the variable for the ith respondent, $\bar{x}$ is the mean value of the variable, and n is the total number of responses. Again, statistical software packages easily calculate descriptive statistics including the standard deviation. For the age of the AFC members, the sample standard deviation turns out to be 11.9 years, providing evidence of considerable spread in ages around the sample mean. As demonstrated by the hot sauce example above, this could have important implications for AFC managers if different marketing mix elements are found to be more or less effective among different age groups, for example.

Because of the important information about variation held by the standard deviation, analysts reporting descriptive statistics for continuous measures should almost always report standard deviations along with mean values. A word of caution, however: Issues related to spurious precision and the presence of outlier cases apply to standard deviations as well as to means. And remember, the standard deviation is meaningful only for interval- and ratio-level measures.

In response to a taste test of a new hot sauce, a large proportion of consumers wanted the sauce to be mild and an equally large proportion wanted it to be hot. Relatively few desired a medium heat, which would have been suggested by looking at the mean rating alone.

Converting Continuous Measures to Categorical Measures

Sometimes analysts find it useful to convert interval- or ratio-level measures to categorical measures. Because higher levels of measurement have all the properties of measures lower in the hierarchy, this conversion is perfectly acceptable and in many cases advisable for aiding in interpretation of research study results. Figure 19.1 was created by converting open-ended responses to the age question (ratio-level measure) into a number of age categories (ordinal-level measure) and plotting the results on the graph. Was this conversion necessary for describing the sample with respect to age? No. The researchers could simply have reported descriptive statistics for the original measure ($\bar{x} = 68.6$ years, $s = 11.9$ years, median = 70 years). On the other hand, Figure 19.1 allows a condensed picture of the distribution that should be easy for managers or other readers to grasp, particularly when presented in combination with the descriptive statistics.

There are few rules for the actual conversion process. Normally, analysts use their own judgment to determine relevant categories. Occasionally, a client will have a predetermined structure for categories. In other cases, the data themselves determine category divisions. For example, researchers who want to convert a continuous measure into two approximately equal-sized groups often will create categories based on a **median split**. That is, the cumulative percent column of the frequency analysis output will identify a value at the 50th percentile, and values up to and including this value will form one group (typically the "low" group for ratio measures) and values above the median value will form the second group (the "high" group). The median split is actually just one case of the **cumulative percentage breakdown**, a technique

median split
A technique for converting a continuous measure into a categorical measure with two approximately equal-sized groups. The groups are formed by "splitting" the continuous measure at its median value.

cumulative percent breakdown
A technique for converting a continuous measure into a categorical measure. The categories are formed based on the cumulative percentages obtained in a frequency analysis.

© ROB BELKNAP/ISTOCKPHOTO

in which groups are created using cumulative percentages. For example, look again at the age data in Exhibit 19.3. If we wanted to convert these data into three approximately equal-sized groups, which categories would be combined? Based on the cumulative percent breakdown, the three groups would be as follows:

Less than 64 years
64 to 74 years
More than 74 years

When using statistical software for analyses—which is almost always—the recommended approach for recasting a continuous variable into categories is to create a new variable whose values are initially identical to the original continuous variable and then to recode the new variable into the desired categories using data manipulation commands. This way, both the original variable and the new categorical variable are available for analyses.

The example presented thus far involved converting a ratio-level measure to a categorical measure. It is also common to recast interval-level measures, such as rating scales, into categorical measures to aid readers in interpreting results of analyses. The **two-box technique** is sometimes used in industry to present rating scale results. A "two-box" is simply the percentage of respondents who rated some object or attribute as either of the top two positions on a rating scale. As an example, look at the response frequencies (and percentages) presented in Exhibit 19.5. The AFC researchers wanted to understand the importance of various reasons for participating in AFC programs. The researchers could correctly report that the mean rating score for the importance of physical enjoyment was 3.9 on a five-point importance scale. To make this result easier to grasp, they might also report that 70% of respondents selected one of the top two levels of importance on the five-point scale. Responses for the other reasons for participation are interpreted in the same way. The next table, Exhibit 19.6, presents two-box results and descriptive statistics as they might appear in the research report.

It is important to note that converting from continuous to categorical measures inevitably results in the loss of information about a variable. Most of the time, conclusions drawn using categorical approaches will roughly parallel those drawn using the full information from the continuous measure, but this is not necessarily so. Analyses should be performed using the highest level of measurement possible for a particular variable, but if converting the variable to a lower level of measurement makes it easier for the reader to interpret and understand the result, then we encourage the practice. A simple solution for many univariate analyses is to provide both types of results (see Exhibit 19.6).

two-box technique
A technique for converting an interval-level rating scale into a categorical measure usually used for presentation purposes. The percentage of respondents choosing one of the top two positions on a rating scale is reported.

Exhibit 19.5	**Avery Fitness Center: Reasons for Participation**				
	"How important to you personally is each of the following reasons for participating in AFC programs?"				
	Not at All Important				**Very Important**
General health and fitness	5 (2)[a]	2 (1)	4 (2)	26 (11)	192 (84)
Social aspects	27 (13)	34 (17)	59 (29)	48 (24)	35 (17)
Physical enjoyment	8 (4)	10 (5)	43 (21)	67 (33)	74 (37)
Specific medical concerns	17 (8)	8 (4)	22 (11)	62 (30)	100 (48)

[a]Percentages in parentheses

Exhibit 19.6	**Avery Fitness Center: Two-Box Results, with Descriptive Statistics**			
	Two-Box	**Mean**	**(s.d.)**	**_n_**
General health and fitness	95%	4.7	(0.7)	229
Social aspects	41%	3.2	(1.3)	203
Physical enjoyment	70%	3.9	(1.1)	202
Specific medical concerns	78%	4.1	(1.2)	209

Confidence Intervals for Means

Learning Objective

6. Discuss confidence intervals for means.

The sample mean ($\bar{x}$) is an important piece of information about a variable, but as we noted earlier, managers must be more concerned with the mean of the variable for the entire population (μ) than with the results for only a sample from the population. One important piece of information that the fitness center researchers gathered with respect to usage was the number of times that the respondents had visited AFC over the previous 30 days. Note that the number of visits is a ratio-level measure, with the mean number of visits equal to 10.0, and standard deviation of 7.3, based on the responses of the 198 AFC members who answered the question on the survey. So, 10 visits per month on average per individual is our best point estimate about the mean value of the population parameter (μ), but we have so little confidence that this point estimate is correct that we need to construct an interval that will allow us greater confidence that we have actually "captured" the parameter within its bounds. As with proportions, to establish the confidence interval we must estimate the degree of sampling error for the sample mean. The following formula is used:

$$\text{sampling error} = z \, \frac{s}{\sqrt{n}}$$

where z = z score associated with confidence level (for 95% confidence, $z = 1.96$), s = sample standard deviation, and n = total number of cases. Thus, at the 95% confidence level,

$$\text{sampling error} = 1.96 \, \frac{7.3}{\sqrt{198}} = 1.0$$

Thus, the margin of sampling error for this estimate is approximately 1.0. Substituting this value and the sample mean ($\bar{x} = 10.0$) into the following formula

$$(\bar{x} - \text{sampling error} \leq \mu \leq \bar{x} + \text{sampling error})$$

$$(10.0 - 1.0 \leq \mu \leq 10.0 + 1.0)$$

$$\text{or } (9.0, 11.0)$$

results in a 95% confidence interval ranging from 9 to 11. We can therefore be 95% confident that the mean number of visits to the fitness center in the past 30 days in the population lies somewhere between 9 and 11, inclusive.

Think about what we've accomplished. On the basis of only 198 observations, we can say with 95% confidence that had we taken measures on number of visits to AFC from every individual in the population the mean number of visits would fall in the range 9 to 11. We note again, however, that the confidence interval takes only sampling error into account. To the degree that other types of error are present, our estimates may be off target.

Now let's set aside the AFC study until the next chapter and focus on testing hypotheses for the remainder of this chapter.

HYPOTHESIS TESTING

The fact that marketing researchers are almost always working with a sample rather than full information from all population members creates something of a dilemma for managers who must make decisions based on research results. *How can we tell if a particular result obtained from a sample would be true for the population as a whole and not just for the particular sample?* In truth, we can never know with complete certainty that a sample result is true for the population. However, through hypothesis testing, researchers can establish standards for making decisions about whether or not to accept sample results as valid for the overall population. We introduce hypothesis testing at this point because it applies to both univariate analyses (the remainder of this chapter) and multivariate analyses (the next chapter).

When marketers prepare to launch a research study, they generally begin with a hypothesis. "I'll bet," the advertising manager might say to the marketing director, "that if we hired an attractive actress to promote our shampoo, sales would increase." Or the sales manager might say to the company's financial officer, "If my department had more money to spend on training, our people would be more productive." Or a product development team might predict that "At least 10% of the target market will be interested in our new product."

hypotheses
Unproven propositions about some phenomenon of interest.

Through the use of statistical techniques, we are often able to determine whether there is empirical evidence from a sample to confirm that such **hypotheses** may be true for the population. In this section, we review some basic concepts that underlie hypothesis testing in classical statistical theory, such as framing the null hypothesis, setting the risk of error in making a wrong decision, and the general steps involved in testing the hypothesis.

Null and Alternative Hypotheses

Marketing research studies are unable to prove results. At best, we can indicate which of two mutually exclusive hypotheses are more likely to be true, based on the results of the study. The general forms of these two hypotheses and the symbols attached to them are as follows:

- H_0, the hypothesis that a proposed result is not true for the population.

- H_a, the alternate hypothesis that a proposed result is true for the population.

null hypothesis
The hypothesis that a proposed result is not true for the population. Researchers typically attempt to reject the null hypothesis in favor of some alternative hypothesis.

alternative hypothesis
The hypothesis that a proposed result is true for the population.

The first of these hypotheses, H_0, is known as the **null hypothesis**. The typical goal is to reject the null hypothesis in favor of the **alternative hypothesis**. Note, however, that we can't "prove" that the alternative hypothesis is true even if we can reject the null. A hypothesis may be rejected but it can never be accepted completely, because further evidence may prove it wrong. In other words, we either reject a hypothesis or we do not reject the hypothesis (as opposed to proving the hypothesis) on the basis of the evidence at hand.

Unless you have perfect information about the population of interest—which rarely happens—the best you can do is form hypotheses about what is true. Your conclusions about these hypotheses can be wrong, and thus there is always some probability of error in accepting any hypothesis. In statistical terms, researchers commit a *Type I error* when they reject a true null hypothesis and tentatively accept (note that this is not the same as "proving") the alternative hypothesis. They commit a *Type II error* when they do not reject a false null hypothesis, which they should, given that it is false. The null hypothesis is assumed to be true for the purpose of the test.

The null hypothesis should be framed in such a way that its rejection leads to the tentative acceptance of the desired conclusion, which is stated in the alternative hypothesis. For example, suppose a firm was considering introducing a new product if 20% of the population (members of a specific target market) could be expected to prefer it to the competing products. Thus, the researchers are comparing a sample proportion against a standard. Here is the way to frame this sort of hypothesis.

$$H_0: \pi \leq 0.20$$
$$H_a: \pi > 0.20$$

If the results of our study led us to reject H_0, we would then be able to tentatively accept the alternative hypothesis that the product would be preferred by more than 20% of the market, and the product would be introduced, because such a result would have been unlikely to occur if the null was indeed true. If H_0 could not be rejected, however, the product would not be introduced.

This is an example of a directional hypothesis; that is, the question is whether or not the population parameter is greater than or less than a certain value. In this case, we wanted to know if the percentage of the population preferring the new product to competing products would be greater than 20%. To test directional hypotheses, we use one-tailed statistical tests. Some research problems, however, call for a two-tailed test. For example, suppose we wanted to test the hypothesis that the market share achieved by the new formulation of a particular product is no different from that achieved by the old formulation, which was 20%. A two-tailed test would be expressed as follows:

$$H_0: \pi = 0.20$$
$$H_a: \pi \neq 0.20$$

There is no direction implied with the alternate hypothesis; the proportion is simply expressed as not being equal to 0.20.

One-tailed tests are more commonly used than two-tailed tests in marketing research. There are two basic reasons for this. First, there is typically some hypothesized or preferred direction to the outcome; for example, the greater the market share, the higher the product quality, or the lower the expenses, the better. Two-tailed tests are used when there is no preferred direction in the outcome or when the research is meant to demonstrate the existence of a difference, but not its direction. Second, the one-tailed test, when it is appropriate, is more powerful statistically than the two-tailed alternative.

Hypothesis Testing Procedure

Learning Objective

7. List the steps involved in hypothesis testing.

Research Window 19.1 shows the typical sequence of steps that researchers follow in testing hypotheses. In this section, we'll walk through a simple example of how these steps would be applied. Even though researchers rarely are required to go through these steps—most of the time, statistical analysis software produces the appropriate statistical tests—it is important that you have a basic understanding of the process.

Suppose that we wanted to test the potential for a new product, as we discussed above. We have conducted a study testing consumer preferences toward our proposed new product and several competing products. Brand managers have decided that the product should not be introduced unless over 20% of the population could be expected to prefer it to the competing products. We have collected data from a random sample of 625 respondents using telephone interviews.

research window 19.1

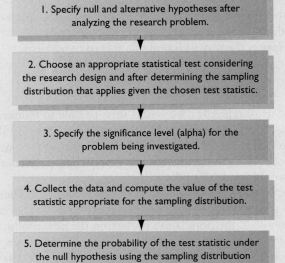

Typical Hypothesis-Testing Procedure

1. Specify null and alternative hypotheses after analyzing the research problem.

2. Choose an appropriate statistical test considering the research design and after determining the sampling distribution that applies given the chosen test statistic.

3. Specify the significance level (alpha) for the problem being investigated.

4. Collect the data and compute the value of the test statistic appropriate for the sampling distribution.

5. Determine the probability of the test statistic under the null hypothesis using the sampling distribution specified in Step 2.

6. Compare the obtained probability with the specified significance level and then reject or do not reject the null hypothesis on the basis of the comparison.

Step 1

The null and alternate hypotheses would be as follows:

$$H_0: \pi \leq 0.20$$
$$H_a: \pi > 0.20$$

The hypotheses are framed so that if the null hypothesis is rejected, the product should be introduced.

Step 2

The appropriate sample statistic is the sample proportion, and the distribution of all possible sample proportions under the sampling plan is based on the assumption that the null hypothesis is true. Although the distribution of sample proportions is theoretically binomially distributed, the large sample size permits the use of the normal approximation.[5] The z-test therefore applies. The z statistic in this case equals

$$z = \frac{p - \pi}{\sigma_p}$$

where p is the sample proportion preferring the product, σ_p is the standard error of the proportion, or the standard deviation of the distribution of sample p's. And σ_p in turn equals

$$\sigma_p = \sqrt{\frac{\pi(1 - \pi)}{n}} = \sqrt{\frac{0.20(1 - 0.20)}{625}} = 0.016$$

where n is the sample size.

Step 3

At this point, the researcher selects an appropriate level of Type I error, the probability of rejecting the null hypothesis (H_0) when it is actually true for the population. The acceptable level of Type I error is usually referred to as the **significance level** or alpha level of the test and is symbolized by alpha (α). In this situation, α error is the probability of rejecting H_0 and concluding that $\pi > 0.2$, when in reality $\pi \leq 0.2$. This conclusion will lead the company to market the new product. However, since the venture will be profitable only if $\pi > 0.2$, a wrong decision would be financially unprofitable, possibly disastrous. As a result, we would prefer the probability of Type I error to be as small as possible.

significance level (α)
The acceptable level of Type I error selected by the researcher, usually set at 0.05. Type I error is the probability of rejecting the null hypothesis when it is actually true for the population.

You must recognize, however, that the probability of a Type II error (symbolized as β) increases as α is decreased, other things being equal. In this situation, we would make a Type II error if we decided not to introduce the new product when in fact $\pi > 0.2$ and the new product would be profitable. The opportunity lost from making such an error could be quite serious. Because α and β are related to one another, setting an extremely low value of α, say 0.01 or 0.001, will make it very unlikely that we'll make a Type I error (rejecting the null hypothesis when we should accept it) but much more likely that we'll make a Type II error (accepting the null hypothesis when we should reject it).

How do we decide the "right" significance level for the test? By convention, most social scientists have decided on an α level of 0.05 as an acceptable compromise, which means that we'll end up rejecting a true null hypothesis 5% of the time. If the consequences of a Type I error (in this case, to introduce the product when we shouldn't) are much worse than the consequences of a Type II error (fail to introduce the new product when we should), then it is appropriate to lower the α level, perhaps to 0.01 or 0.001.

Step 4

Because Step 4 involves the computation of the test statistic, it can be completed only after the sample is drawn and the information collected. Suppose 140 of the 625 sample respondents preferred the product. The sample proportion is thus $p = 140/625 = 0.224$. The basic question that needs to be answered is straightforward: Is this value of p too large to have occurred by chance from a population with π assumed to be less than or equal to 0.2? Or, in other words, what is the probability of getting $p = 0.224$ when $\pi \leq 0.20$? The appropriate test statistic differs depending upon the type of test being performed. In this case, we calculate the test statistic z as follows:

$$z = \frac{p - \pi}{\sigma_p} = \frac{0.224 - 0.200}{0.016} = 1.500$$

Step 5

The probability of occurrence of a z value of 1.500 can be found from standard tabled values of areas under the normal curve. (See Table 1 in the appendix at the end of the book.) Figure 19.2 shows the procedure. The shaded area between $-\infty$ and 1.500 equals 0.9332; this means the area to the right of $z = 1.500$ is $1.000 - 0.9332$, or 0.0668. This is the probability of securing a z value of 1.500 under a true situation of

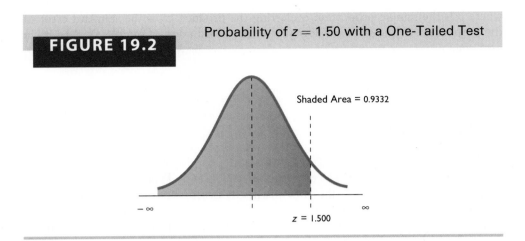

FIGURE 19.2 Probability of $z = 1.50$ with a One-Tailed Test

Shaded Area = 0.9332

$-\infty$ $z = 1.500$ ∞

p-value

The probability of obtaining a given result if in fact the null hypothesis were true in the population. A result is regarded as statistically significant if the p-value is less than the chosen significance level of the test.

$\pi \leq 0.2$. This probability is often referred to as the **p-value**. (Some statistical software packages place p-values in a column labeled "significance.") The p-value represents the likelihood of obtaining the particular value of a test statistic if the null hypothesis were true.

Step 6

Because the calculated probability (p-value $= 0.0668$) of obtaining a sample proportion of 0.224 when the null hypothesis is assumed to be true is higher than the specified significance level of $\alpha = 0.05$, the acceptable level of Type I error, we cannot reject the null hypothesis. The product would not be introduced because, while the evidence is in the right direction, it is not sufficient to conclude beyond any reasonable doubt that $\pi > 0.20$. If we could tolerate a 10% chance of committing a Type I error, the null hypothesis would have been rejected and the product marketed, since the probability of getting a sample $p = 0.224$ when the true $\pi \leq 0.20$ is, as we have seen, 0.0668.

Issues in Interpreting Statistical Significance

When the p-value associated with a test statistic is lower than the level of α (probability of Type I error) set by the researcher, we refer to the result as a statistically significant result. However, there are several common misinterpretations of p-values and the associated phrase "statistically significant."[6] One of the most frequent is to view a p-value as representing the probability that the null hypothesis is true. Thus, a p-value of 0.04 might be mistakenly interpreted to mean that there is a probability of only 0.04 that the results were caused by chance. Instead, a p-value of 0.04 means that if—and this is a big if—the null hypothesis is true, the odds are only 1 in 25 of getting a sample result of the magnitude that was observed. Unfortunately, there is no way in classical statistical significance testing to determine whether the null hypothesis is true.

Another very frequent misinterpretation is the belief that the α level set by the researcher or the p-value obtained in the analysis is related to the probability that the alternative hypothesis is true. For example, some people might incorrectly interpret a p-value of 0.07 to mean that the probability that the alternative hypothesis is true is $1 - 0.07$, or 0.93. This interpretation is wrong. The p-value simply represents the probability that the result from the sample could have been obtained if the null hypothesis is true.

Marketing researchers, then, need to be careful when interpreting the results of their hypothesis testing procedures so that they do not mislead themselves and others. You must constantly keep in mind both types of errors that it is possible to make. And you need to make sure that you do not misinterpret what a test of significance reveals. It represents no more than a test against the null hypothesis.

MANAGER'S FOCUS

During presentations, researchers frequently stress the findings that are *statistically* significant, and when they do not, managers commonly inquire "are those differences significant?" (meaning *statistically* significant). The emphasis placed on statistical significance by both managers and researchers would appear to suggest that it is the primary consideration when interpreting the results of a study. However, other factors should be given equal—if not more—attention.

Throughout this book, we have been highlighting the role that you as a manager can play in helping a research project generate *actionable* findings. That is, the goal is to generate information that is relevant to the marketing decisions you face and gives you clear guidance on how to respond to your market situation. Therefore, it is crucial that you understand that statistical significance is not the same thing as managerial relevance or actionability.

We do not mean to suggest that knowing whether or not specific findings are statistically significant is unimportant. What we are saying, though, is that your search for the meaning of findings must go beyond this one consideration. Why? One reason is that data patterns can be of practical importance and yet not be statistically significant. This commonly occurs when sample sizes are small. If sample sizes are not sufficiently large, the power of a statistical test is lower, and the chances of finding statistically significant results (i.e., rejecting a false null hypothesis) are lower. In such a situation, a marketing researcher might find that average attitude scores (measured on a seven-point favorability scale) are much higher for men (mean = 6.2) than for women (mean = 4.4), but the differences are not statistically significant. This pattern of findings, nonetheless, may be suggestive of the need for different marketing actions for men versus women (or, perhaps, a larger sample size to determine whether or not this apparent difference is real).

Conversely, results can be statistically significant and yet have little managerial relevance. This can occur when sample sizes are very large, resulting in a high level of statistical power (i.e., a much greater chance of rejecting a false null hypothesis). In such situations, very small differences in proportions or means can be statistically significant. For example, a marketing researcher might find that attitude scores (using the same seven-point favorability scale) are higher for men (mean = 6.2) than for women (mean = 6.1) and that the difference is statistically significant. Do these "statistically significant" results suggest that the company should forget about marketing the product to women, or develop separate marketing strategies for men versus women? Your managerial sensibilities should be telling you that such a conclusion would be ill-founded given both genders had very similar and relatively high mean ratings. You should employ these same managerial sensibilities whenever you are forming conclusions about how to respond to a set of research findings.

TESTING HYPOTHESES ABOUT INDIVIDUAL VARIABLES

There are numerous occasions when marketing researchers are called upon to compare univariate sample statistics against preconceived standards. In our hypothesis testing example in the previous section, the analyst was asked to determine if the sample results provided sufficient evidence that more than 20% of the population (i.e., the standard) would prefer a certain product. In other situations, an analyst might need to compare the mean customer satisfaction score for a particular department store against the overall mean satisfaction score for all department stores in the chain, or to determine if the characteristics of sample respondents match those of the overall population from which the sample was drawn. Each of these examples calls for a researcher to test a hypothesis about a univariate measure.

Chi-Square Goodness-of-Fit Test for Frequencies

A breakfast food manufacturer has recently developed a new cereal. Through single source scanner data for its existing cereals, the manufacturer found that for every package of cereal sold to a household with no children, three packages were sold to households with children and two packages were sold to retirement households (households with at least one spouse of retirement age). The researchers were careful that each household was categorized into only one category. The manufacturer wants to know if this same tendency will hold with this new cereal, because a change in consumption patterns could have significant marketing communication implications. The manufacturer therefore decides to conduct a market test to determine the relative frequencies with which different household categories purchase the new cereal.

Suppose that, in an appropriate test market, over a one-week period, 1,200 boxes of the new cereal are sold and that the distribution of sales by household category is as follows:

Number Bought per Household Category			
No children	**Children**	**Retirement**	**Total**
240	575	385	1,200

As some quick analysis would show, these figures do not match the pattern established earlier with other cereal brands. Does this preliminary evidence indicate that the firm should expect a change in the purchase patterns of different types of households for the new cereal?

chi-square goodness-of-fit test
A statistical test to determine whether some observed pattern of frequencies corresponds to an expected pattern.

This is the type of problem for which the **chi-square goodness-of-fit test** is ideally suited. (Note that chi, χ, is a Greek letter that rhymes with *sky*.) The variable of interest has been broken into k mutually exclusive categories ($k = 3$ in the example), and each observation logically falls into one of the k classes or cells. In short, this is simply a frequency analysis for a variable representing type of household. The trials (purchases) are independent, and the sample size is large.

All that is necessary to use the test is to calculate the expected number of cases that would fall in each category and to compare the expected number with the observed number actually falling in the category, using the equation

$$\chi^2 = \sum_{i=1}^{k} \frac{[O_i - E_i]^2}{E_i}$$

where

- O_i is the observed number of cases falling in the ith category

- E_i is the expected number of cases falling in the ith category

- k is the number of categories

The expected number falling into a category is generated from the null hypothesis, which in this case is that the composition of sales for the cereal by household type will follow the manufacturer's normal sales pattern (that is, for every package purchased by a household with no children, three packages will be purchased by households with children, and two packages will be purchased by retirement households). In terms of the proportion of all sales, that means that one-sixth of the sales could be expected to be to households with no children, one-half to households with children, and one-third to retirement households if sales of the new cereal follow traditional patterns. If the 1,200 boxes sold in the test market followed the normal or expected pattern, then 200 (1/6 × 1,200) would have been sold to households with no children, 600 (1/2 × 1,200) to households with children, and 400 (1/3 × 1,200) to retirement households. How does the observed pattern compare with the expected pattern? The appropriate χ^2 statistic is computed as follows:

$$\chi^2 = \frac{(240 - 200)^2}{200} + \frac{(575 - 600)^2}{600} + \frac{(385 - 400)^2}{400} = 9.60$$

The chi-square distribution is completely determined by its degrees of freedom, μ. The term *degrees of freedom* refers to the number of things that can vary independently, and for the chi-square test, degrees of freedom is one less than the number of categories ($\mu = k - 1$), or $\mu = 3 - 1 = 2$ in the breakfast cereal example.[7]

Suppose the researcher has chosen a significance level of $\alpha = 0.05$ for this test. The tabled value of χ^2 for two degrees of freedom and $\alpha = 0.05$ is 5.99 (see Table 2 in the appendix at the end of the book). Since the calculated value ($\chi^2 = 9.60$) is larger, the conclusion is that the probability that we could obtain differences this large—if the null hypothesis were true—is less than 0.05. Rather, the preliminary market-test results suggest that sales of the new cereal will follow a different pattern than is typical. In particular, sales to families with no children are higher than expected. The null hypothesis of sales in the ratio of 1:3:2 is rejected.

The chi-square goodness-of-fit test is quite useful for gauging the possibility of nonresponse error in a research project (see Method 2 in Exhibit 17.1). For example, researchers working with a sample of customers from an automobile dealership determined that the likelihood of nonresponse error was low by comparing respondent gender and age against known population demographics using chi-square good-of-fit tests.[8]

Adult cereal or children's cereal? Researchers can conduct a market test to determine the relative frequencies with which different household categories purchase a new cereal.

Z-Test for Comparing Sample Proportion against a Standard

Learning Objective

9. Discuss the process for comparing a proportion against a standard.

In our earlier discussion of hypothesis testing, we used an example in which a company planned to introduce a new product only if more than 20% of consumers could be expected to prefer it. Recall that we calculated a z statistic to test the hypothesis using the following formulas:

$$z = \frac{p - \pi}{\sigma_p} \qquad \sigma_p = \sqrt{\frac{\pi(1 - \pi)}{n}}$$

where p = proportion of consumers who preferred the new product in the sample, π = the proportion standard to be achieved, σ_p = the standard error of the proportion, and n = number of respondents in the sample. We then found the probability of obtaining the z statistic if the null hypothesis were true and compared that probability to the significance level of the test (often, $\alpha = 0.05$) to determine whether or not to reject the null hypothesis.

Suppose that the company was particularly concerned about the strength of the leading competing product in the category and added a second constraint on the decision to introduce the new product. That is, even if the new product achieved the threshold level of preference among consumers, the company decided not to introduce the product if more than 50% of consumers still preferred the competing product. In this case, the null hypothesis (that is, more than 50% of consumers prefer the competing product) and alternative hypothesis (50% or less prefers the competing product) are stated in symbols as follows:

$$H_0: \pi > 0.50$$
$$H_a: \pi \leq 0.50$$

The results of the study indicated that 290 of the 625 sample respondents preferred the competing product, so $p = 290/625 = 0.46$. Thus, it appears that less than 50% of consumers will prefer the competing product after introduction of the new product, but we must determine whether or not the sample proportion (0.46) is statistically distinct from the standard (0.50). Accordingly,

$$\sigma_p = \sqrt{\frac{0.50(1 - 0.50)}{625}} = 0.02$$

and

$$z = \frac{0.46 - 0.50}{0.02} = -2.00$$

The probability of occurrence of a z value of -2.00 is found from standard tabled values of areas under the normal curve in Table 1 in the appendix at the end of the book. Figure 19.3 indicates the probability of the occurrence of a z value as low as -2.00, given that the null hypothesis is true. This probability turns out to be 0.0228, the area to the left of the shaded area. Because this probability is lower than the significance level of the test established by the researchers ($\alpha = 0.05$), the researchers would reject the null hypothesis and tentatively accept the alternative hypothesis that after introduction of the new product, the proportion of consumers preferring the competing product would be 50% or less. As a result, the company would move forward with the introduction of the new product.

Learning Objective

10. Describe the appropriate tests for comparing a mean against a standard for (a) small samples and (b) large samples.

Z-Test for Comparing Sample Mean against a Standard

When the variable to be compared against a standard is a continuous measure, the analyst can take advantage of greater statistical power by working with the mean of the variable and comparing it against a standard just as we did with categorical measures in the previous sections. The appropriate statistical tests differ depending upon whether the sample size is small ($n \leq 30$) or large ($n > 30$).[9]

To illustrate the comparison of a sample mean to a standard when the sample size is small, consider a supermarket chain that is thinking about adding a new product to the shelves of its stores. Since many products must compete for limited shelf space, managers have determined that the chain must sell 100 units per week in each store in order for the item to be sufficiently profitable to warrant handling it. Suppose that the research department decides to investigate the item's turnover by putting it in a random sample of 10 stores for a limited period of time. Suppose further that the average sales per store per week were as shown in Exhibit 19.7.

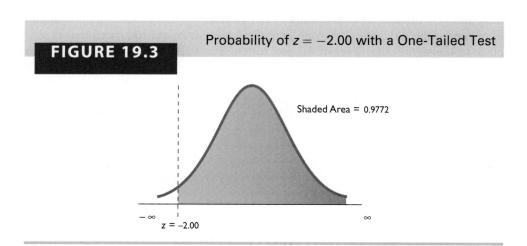

FIGURE 19.3   Probability of $z = -2.00$ with a One-Tailed Test

Shaded Area = 0.9772

$-\infty$ $z = -2.00$ ∞

Exhibit 19.7		**Store Sales of Trial Product per Week**	
Store i	**Sales** X_i	**Store** i	**Sales** X_i
1	86	6	93
2	97	7	132
3	114	8	116
4	108	9	105
5	123	10	120

In this situation, the t test is the correct statistical test. Further, a one-tailed test is appropriate, because it is only when the sales per store per week reach at least 100 units that the product will be introduced on a national scale. The null and alternate hypotheses are

$$H_0: \mu < 100$$
$$H_a: \mu \geq 100$$

and suppose the significance level is set at $\alpha = 0.05$. From the data in Exhibit 19.7, we can calculate that mean sales in units of the product across the 10 test stores is 109.4 and that the sample standard deviation is 14.4. The t statistic is calculated using the following formula:

$$t = \frac{\bar{x} - \mu}{s_{\bar{x}}}$$

where $\bar{x}$ is the sample mean, μ is the population standard, and $s_{\bar{x}}$ is the standard error of the mean, which is estimated as follows:

$$s_{\bar{x}} = \frac{s}{\sqrt{n}}$$

where s is the sample standard deviation and n is the sample size. Thus, the standard error of the mean is calculated to be $14.4/\sqrt{10} = 4.55$. Further calculations yield:

$$t = \frac{109.4 - 100}{4.55} = 2.07$$

Critical t as read from the t table with $\mu = n - 1 = 9$ degrees of freedom is 1.833 ($\alpha = .05$). (See Table 3 in the appendix at the end of the book.) Thus, the obtained t value exceeds the critical value and we can reject the null hypothesis. It is unlikely that the stores in the sample would have averaged sales of 109.4 units if the sales per store in the overall population were less than 100 units per week.

Suppose that company management was still nervous about the product and decided to conduct a larger scale test. The product was placed in 50 stores this time, with a resulting sample mean and sample standard deviation of 108.7 and 14.2, respectively. With large n, the z distribution becomes appropriate; the test statistic is calculated as follows:

$$z = \frac{\bar{x} - \mu}{s_{\bar{x}}}$$

ETHICAL DILEMMA 19.1

A manufacturer of aspirin had its marketing research department conduct a national survey among doctors to investigate what common household remedies doctors would most likely recommend when treating a patient with a cold. The question asked doctors to pick the one product they would most likely prescribe for their patients from among the choices: Advil, Tylenol, aspirin, or none of the above. The distribution of responses was as follows:

Advil	100
Tylenol	100
Aspirin	200
None of the above	600
Total	1,000

The firm used the results of the survey as a basis for an extensive ad campaign that claimed, "In a national survey, doctors recommended aspirin two to one over Advil and Tylenol as the medicine they would most likely recommend to their patients suffering from colds."

- Was the firm's claim legitimate?
- Was it ethical for the firm to omit reporting the number of doctors that expressed "none of the above"?
- What would be the fairest way to state the ad claim? Do you think stating the claim in this way would be as effective as stating it in the way the firm did?

The estimated standard error of the mean is $s_{\bar{x}} = 14.2/\sqrt{50} = 2.01$, and the test statistic is

$$z = \frac{108.7 - 100}{2.01}$$

and is referred to a normal table. Calculated z is greater than critical $z = 1.645$ for $\alpha = 0.05$ (remember that this is a one-tailed test), and we reach the same conclusion that we did in the initial test. The product could be expected to sell at the rate of 100 units or more per store per week.

SUMMARY

Learning Objective 1

Distinguish between univariate and multivariate analyses.
Univariate analyses are conducted on individual variables; multivariate analyses involve multiple variables.

Learning Objective 2

Describe frequency analysis.
A frequency analysis, or one-way tabulation, is a univariate technique that involves counting the number of responses that fall into various response categories.

Learning Objective 3

Explain the various ways in which frequency analysis can be used.
Frequency analysis can be used (1) to communicate the results of a study, (2) to determine the degree of item nonresponse, (3) to locate blunders, (4) to locate outliers, and (5) to determine the empirical distribution of the variable in question.

Learning Objective 4

Discuss confidence intervals for proportions.
The confidence interval is the range within which the true proportion in the population (π) will fall, with a given level of confidence (usually 95% confidence). The confidence interval is equal to the sample proportion (p) plus or minus estimated sampling error.

Learning Objective 5

Describe commonly used descriptive statistics.

The most commonly used descriptive statistics for continuous measures (interval- or ratio-level measures) are the mean, or arithmetic average, and the standard deviation. The mean is a measure of central tendency; the standard deviation provides a convenient measure of the dispersion of responses.

Learning Objective 6

Discuss confidence intervals for means.
The confidence interval is the range within which the true mean value for the population (μ) will fall, with a given level of confidence (usually 95%). The confidence interval is equal to the sample mean ($\bar{x}$) plus or minus estimated sampling error.

Learning Objective 7

List the steps involved in hypothesis testing.
The steps in hypothesis testing are as follows:
1. Specify null and alternative hypotheses.
2. Choose the appropriate test statistic.
3. Specify significance (α) level for the test.
4. Compute value of test statistic based on sample data.
5. Determine probability of test statistic given true null hypothesis.
6. Compare obtained probability with specified significance level.

Learning Objective 8

Describe the chi-square goodness-of-fit test.
The chi-square goodness-of-fit test is a univariate analysis in which the frequency distribution obtained on a categorical variable is compared against a standard to determine if

the obtained frequency is statistically different from the standard.

Learning Objective 9

Discuss the process for comparing a proportion against a standard.

A sample proportion is compared against a standard by calculating a z statistic, finding the probability of obtaining this level of z given a true null hypothesis, and comparing the obtained probability with the significance level of the test.

Learning Objective 10

Describe the appropriate tests for comparing a mean against a standard for (a) small samples and (b) large samples.

For small samples ($n < 30$), a sample mean is compared against a standard by calculating a t statistic, finding the probability of the obtained t statistic given a true null hypothesis, and comparing the obtained probability with the significance level of the test. For large samples, the process is similar, except that a z statistic is calculated instead of the t statistic.

KEY TERMS

categorical measures (page 423)
frequency analysis (page 424)
outlier (page 425)
histogram (page 425)
confidence interval (page 428)
continuous measures (page 429)
descriptive statistics (page 429)
sample mean (page 430)
sample standard deviation (page 430)

median split (page 431)
cumulative percent breakdown (page 431)
two-box technique (page 432)
hypotheses (page 434)
null hypothesis (page 434)
alternative hypothesis (page 434)
significance level (α) (page 437)
p-value (page 438)
chi-square goodness-of-fit test (page 440)

REVIEW QUESTIONS

1. What types of variables might be analyzed with frequency analysis?

2. What is an outlier?

3. With how many digits should percentages be reported?

4. What is a histogram? What information does it provide?

5. Why do analysts often construct confidence intervals? What is their purpose?

6. What type of error do confidence intervals take into account?

7. How do continuous measures differ from categorical measures? Which type offers analysts more statistical power in analyses?

8. What are the most commonly used descriptive statistics?

9. Why must the distribution of responses be taken into account when deciding which type of "average" to present?

10. Why might an analyst choose to convert a continuous measure to a categorical measure?

11. What is a two-box? A median split? A cumulative percentage breakdown?

12. What is the difference between the null and alternative hypotheses?

13. Why can a hypothesis be rejected, but never fully accepted?

14. What is the difference between a one-tailed test and a two-tailed test of statistical significance? When would each be appropriate?

15. What is a p-value? Do researchers typically want to obtain higher or lower p-values?

16. Is a statistically significant result necessarily managerially significant? Why or why not?

17. What is the basic use of a chi-square goodness-of-fit test? How is the value of the test statistic calculated? How are the expected frequencies determined?

18. What is the appropriate test statistic for making inferences about a population proportion?

19. What is the appropriate test statistic for making inferences about a population mean when the sample is small? Suppose that the sample is large. What is the appropriate procedure then?

DISCUSSION QUESTIONS, PROBLEMS, AND PROJECTS

1. A large manufacturer of electronic components for automobiles once conducted a study to determine the average value of electronic components per automobile. Personal interviews were conducted with a random sample of 400 respondents. The following information was secured with respect to each subject's "main" vehicle when he or she had more than one.

Average Dollar Value of Electronic Equipment per Automobile

Dollar Value of Electronic Equipment	Number of Automobiles
Less than or equal to $50	35
$51 to $100	40
$101 to $150	55
$151 to $200	65
$201 to $250	65
$251 to $300	75
$301 to $350	40
$351 to $400	20
More than $400	5
Total number of automobiles	400

  a. Convert the above information into percentages.

  b. Compute the cumulative percentages.

  c. Prepare a histogram with the average value of electronic equipment on the x-axis and the absolute frequency on the y-axis.

2. Compute the 95% confidence interval for the percentage of automobiles with more than $250 worth of electronics in them using the information in the previous question.

3. Suppose that the researchers had originally asked an open-ended question about the dollar value of the electronics in the automobile, and that respondents had provided these values. If the mean value in the sample were $234 with standard deviation of $76, construct the 95% confidence interval for the mean value in the population.

4. A large publishing house recently conducted a survey to assess the reading habits of senior citizens. The company published four magazines specifically tailored to suit the needs of senior citizens. Management hypothesized that there were no differences in the preferences for the magazines. A sample of 1,600 senior citizens interviewed in the city of Albuquerque, New Mexico, indicated the following preferences for the four magazines:

Publication	Frequency of Preference
1. *Golden Years*	350
2. *Maturation*	500
3. *High Serenity*	450
4. *Time of Living*	300
Total	1,600

Management needs your expertise to determine whether there are differences in senior citizens' preferences for the magazines.

a. State the null and alternate hypotheses.

b. How many degrees of freedom are there?

c. What is the chi-square critical table value at the 5% significance level?

d. What is the calculated χ^2 value? Show all your calculations.

e. Should the null hypothesis be rejected? Explain.

5. Management of the publishing house was particularly concerned about *Time of Living*. This magazine had been introduced almost 20 years earlier, but had begun slipping in circulation about five years ago. A "facelift" for the magazine had helped a little a year ago, but rising costs were threatening the remaining profits in the magazine. A recent analysis indicated that at current circulation rates, the title was barely breaking even. Knowing that it sometimes takes time for changes and improvements to be noticed by the market, management decided prior to the survey that if at least 20% of the market preferred the magazine to its three siblings in the publishing house, they would continue the title for another year.

a. State the null and alternative hypotheses.

b. What is the calculated z statistic? Show all your calculations.

c. Should the null hypothesis be rejected with a significance level of 0.05? Explain.

6. Silken-Shine Company is a medium-sized manufacturer of shampoo. In recent years, the company has increased the number of variations of its shampoo from three to five to increase its market share. Management conducted a survey to compare sales of Silken-Shine shampoo with sales of Rapunzel and So-Soft, its two major competitors. A sample of 1,800 consumers indicated the following frequencies with respect to the most recent shampoo purchased:

Shampoo	Number Buying
1. Silken-Shine	425
2. Rapunzel	1,175
3. So-Soft	200
Total	1,800

Experience had indicated that three times as many households preferred Rapunzel to Silken-Shine and that, in turn, twice as many households preferred Silken-Shine to So-Soft. Management wants to determine if the historic tendency still holds, given that Silken-Shine Company has increased the range of shampoos available.

a. State the null and alternative hypotheses.

b. How many degrees of freedom are there?

c. What is the chi-square critical table value at the 5% significance level?

d. What is the calculated χ^2 value? Show all your calculations.

e. Should the null hypothesis be rejected? Explain.

7. Liberty Foods markets vegetables in six different sized cans: A, B, C, D, E, and F. Through the years, the company has observed that sales of all its vegetables in the six can sizes are in the proportion 6;4;2;1.5;1.5;1, respectively. In other words, for every 1 case of size F that is sold, 6 cases of size A, 4 of size B, 2 of size C, 1.5 of size D, and 1.5 of size E are also sold.

    The marketing manager would like the sales data for a new canned vegetable—pureed carrots—compared with the pattern for the rest of Liberty's product line to see if there is any difference. Based on a representative sample of 600 cases of pureed carrots, he observes that 30% were Size A, 20% B, 10% C, 10% D, 15% E, and 15% F. Use the chi-square goodness-of-fit test to determine whether the pureed carrots' sales pattern is similar to the pattern for other vegetables. Show all your calculations clearly.

8. The manager of the Budget Department Store recently increased the store's use of in-store promotions in an attempt to increase the proportion of entering customers who made a purchase. The effort was prompted by a study made a year ago that showed 65% of a sample of 1,000 parties entering the store made no purchase. A recent sample of 900 parties contained 635 who made no purchases. Management is wondering whether there has been a change in the proportion of entering parties who make a purchase.

    a. State the null and alternate hypotheses.

    b. What is the calculated value? Show your calculations clearly.

    c. Based on your results, would you reject the null hypothesis? Explain.

9. A medium-sized manufacturer of paper products was planning to introduce a new line of tissues, hand towels, and toilet paper. However, management had stipulated that the new products should be introduced only if average monthly purchases per household would be $2.50 or more. The product was market tested, and the diaries of the 100 panel households living in the test market area were checked. They indicated that average monthly purchases were $3.10 per household with a standard deviation of $0.50. Management is wondering what decision it should make and has asked for your recommendation.

    a. State the null and alternate hypotheses.

    b. Is the sample size considered large or small?

    c. Which test should be used? Why?

    d. At the 5% level of significance, would you reject the null hypothesis? Support your answer with the necessary calculations.

10. The president of a chain of department stores had promised the managers of the various stores a bonus of 8% if the average monthly sales per store increased $300,000 or more. A random sample of 12 stores yielded the following sales increases:

Store	Sales	Store	Sales
1	$320,000	7	$380,000
2	230,000	8	280,000
3	400,000	9	420,000
4	450,000	10	360,000
5	280,000	11	440,000
6	320,000	12	320,000

    The president is wondering whether this random sample of stores indicates that the population of stores has reached the goal.

    a. State the null and alternate hypotheses.

    b. Is the sample size considered small or large?

c. Which test should be used? Why?

d. Would you reject the null hypothesis at the 5% level of significance? Support your conclusion with the necessary calculations.

Use the AFC member survey (Figure 18.1), codebook (Figure 18.3), and data to perform the analyses in Problems 11 through 15. The data are available in raw form ("AFC.txt") or as an SPSS data file ("AFC.sav") at www.cengage.com/marketing/churchill.

11. One of the research problems in the AFC study was to investigate how members learn about AFC. Question 4 on the survey deals directly with this issue. Using frequency analysis, build a table that communicates how members learned about AFC.

12. For the last several years, the company has been sending gift cards for meals in local restaurants to doctors who regularly refer their patients to the fitness center for therapy. Managers have noticed that most of the people who join AFC are *not* referred by physicians and they are considering whether or not the doctor referral incentives are worth the added expense. They have decided to discontinue the program unless there is evidence that at least 25% of members learn about AFC from their doctors. Use a *z*-test for comparing the sample proportion of members who reported learning about AFC from their doctors against the standard proposed by AFC managers (that is, 25%). Should the referral incentive program be discontinued?

13. Five years ago, AFC conducted a survey of its members. At that time, the reported education levels of respondents were as follows:

Less than high school	15	5%
High school degree	65	22
Some college	74	25
Associates degree	12	4
Four-year college degree	50	17
Advanced degree	80	27
Total	296	100

Using the current results reported in Exhibit 19.2 and the χ^2 goodness-of-fit test, is there evidence that AFC is attracting more educated members than in the past?

14. The company's budget calls for average revenues of $40 per month (or $960 over a two-year period) per member. Is AFC currently meeting this target? Assume for a moment that the only information AFC holds about revenues comes from the sample. Calculate mean revenues per member, construct the 95% confidence interval around this mean value, and determine if calculated mean revenues likely reach the stated standard for the population.

15. A popular business consultant has suggested that a company's success can be predicted by the degree to which customers are willing to recommend the company to others. Take a look at item 6 on the AFC questionnaire (see Exhibit 18.1). A score of 0–6 places a respondent in the "detractor" category; those with scores of 7 or 8 are considered "passively satisfied;" and those with scores of 9 or 10 are "promoters." Furthermore, for any company, a net promoter score (NPS) can be calculated by subtracting the percentage of detractors from the percentage of promoters.[10]

   a. Recode the responses to item 6 into three categories (i.e., detractors, passively satisfied, promoters).

   b. Compute the NPS for the company.

Data Analysis: Analyzing Multiple Variables Simultaneously

Introduction

The previous chapter demonstrated various approaches for analyzing individual variables. While such univariate analyses are sometimes sufficient for providing the information necessary for a research problem, analysts often encounter situations in which multiple variables must be taken into account in the same analysis. In many ways, multivariate analyses allow researchers a closer look at their data than is possible with univariate analyses.

For instance, suppose that in an awareness test for a new ice cream shop, 58% of survey respondents could name the shop in a recall task. Closer analysis revealed several insights, however. Only 45% of male respondents could name the shop, compared with 71% of female respondents. Further, age also seemed to be related to awareness: 69% of respondents 20 years old and younger could name the shop, while only 54% of those who were 21 to 40 years old, and 39% of those over 40 years old could do so. The researcher who stopped with the univariate analysis result (i.e., 58% correct in recall task) would miss potentially important managerial insights about the relationships between gender and awareness and age and awareness. Figure 20.1 presents the information graphically; note how conclusions change when we consider the additional variables.

In this chapter, we present a number of commonly used multivariate analysis

FIGURE 20.1   Univariate versus Multivariate Analysis

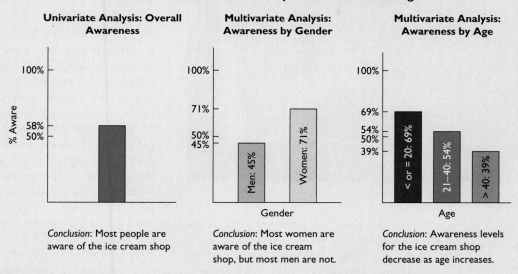

Univariate vs. Multivariate Analysis: Enhanced Meaning

Univariate Analysis: Overall Awareness

Conclusion: Most people are aware of the ice cream shop

Multivariate Analysis: Awareness by Gender

Conclusion: Most women are aware of the ice cream shop, but most men are not.

Multivariate Analysis: Awareness by Age

Conclusion: Awareness levels for the ice cream shop decrease as age increases.

techniques. As with all types of analysis, the level of measurement used with the variables to be analyzed largely determines the analyses that are appropriate. The chapter includes three general categories of analyses: those involving categorical measures, those involving both categorical and continuous measures, and those involving continuous measures. For more information about these or other multivariate techniques, we encourage you to consult one of the many multivariate statistics texts that are available.

Regardless of the particular type of analysis, when the analysis is based on a sample appropriately drawn from a population, it is possible to test the statistical significance of the result. That is, we can use the hypothesis testing procedure outlined in the previous chapter to determine the probability of obtaining the given result in the sample if, in fact, there was no relationship between the variables in the population. Rather than focus on the calculation of the test statistics, however, in most cases we prefer to demonstrate how they are applied in practice. Any good statistical software package can compute the test values for the inferential statistics we discuss.

ANALYSES INVOLVING CATEGORICAL MEASURES

Two-Way Cross Tabulations

Cross tabulation is an important tool for studying the relationships between two (or more) categorical variables. It is clearly the most used multivariate data-analysis technique in applied marketing research. Many marketing research studies go no further than simple cross tabulations between two variables at a time (i.e., "two-way" cross tabs). Because they are so commonly used, both researchers and managers need to understand how cross tabulations are developed and interpreted.

Learning Objective

1. Explain the purpose and importance of cross tabulation.

cross tabulation
A multivariate technique used for studying the relationship between two or more categorical variables. The technique considers the joint distribution of sample elements across variables.

In cross tabulation, we usually seek to investigate the influence of one variable (the independent variable) on another variable (the dependent variable). In effect, the respondents are divided into subgroups based on the independent variable in order to see how the dependent variable varies from group to group. For example, consider again the Avery Fitness Center project discussed in previous chapters. AFC researchers wanted to know if being referred by a doctor to the fitness center led to greater usage of the therapy pool. A quick look back at Exhibit 19.4 reveals that the therapy pool was the service used by the highest percentage (47%) of respondents in the 30 days prior to the survey. Does this percentage differ for people who were recommended by a doctor compared with people who were not?

AFC researchers wanted to know if being referred by a doctor to the fitness center led to greater usage of the therapy pool.

This is an ideal problem for a cross-tab analysis. Both pool usage (yes or no) and learning about AFC from a doctor (yes or no) are measured on categorical scales, and there is a reasonable possibility that one of the variables may have led to the other variable (that is, a doctor's recommendation may have caused someone to utilize the therapy pool). Is it necessary that the two variables have the possibility of being causally related in order to use cross-tab analysis? No, but managers are looking for actionable results. Showing that two variables may be related is interesting; showing

MANAGER'S FOCUS

This chapter will help you become familiar with some analytical techniques that are a bit more sophisticated than the basic analyses discussed in Chapter 19. Your primary role in this process is to accurately and comprehensively describe your information needs to your research provider. It is then the researcher's responsibility to develop an analysis plan that will fill those needs. As the client, though, you will ultimately have to approve the proposed plan. If you select highly competent and trustworthy research suppliers, you will likely rely heavily on their judgment.

One benefit of having a basic understanding of the various analyses presented in this chapter, however, is

that when your provider believes techniques other than conventional cross tabulations will better meet your information needs, you may be more understanding and receptive of more advanced or innovative methods. Like everyone else, managers tend to fear what they do not understand. The objective of data analysis is not to simply do what is conventional or comfortable. The goal is to employ the techniques that will most directly address your marketing problem. In other words, the material in this chapter will help you become an informed consumer of research services and make you less likely to block the path that will best answer the questions you have about your market situation.

that two variables may be related in a situation where one could have led to the other usually provides better direction for managers.

Exhibit 20.1 presents SPSS output for the two-way classification of the sample respondents by pool usage and whether or not they learned about AFC from a doctor. There's a lot going on in this table, so take some time to look it over carefully. First, note the *marginal totals* for each variable: 109 (47%) respondents had used the therapy pool (122, or 53%, had not), and 54 (23%) respondents had learned about AFC from a doctor (177, or 77%, did not). The marginal totals represent the frequency counts for each of the variables independently.

With a cross-tab analysis, however, we can examine the joint distribution of the two variables. This will allow us to see if the outcome (% of people using the pool) is different for those who learned about AFC from a doctor vs. those who did not. Because there are two levels for each of the variables being considered, there are four possible combinations when both variables are considered together ($2 \times 2 = 4$). These combinations are represented by four *cells* in the cross tabulation. For example, of the 54 respondents who had learned about AFC from a doctor, 35 of them had used the therapy pool in the past 30 days and 19 of them had not. Of 177 who did not learn about AFC from a doctor, 74 had used the pool and 103 had not. But what does this mean for AFC managers? Does it appear that there is some connection between doctors' recommendations and therapy pool usage?

We've noted before that percentages are incredibly useful for interpreting results. Each of the cells in Exhibit 20.1 contains three different percentages that differ depending upon what number is used as the denominator in the calculation of the percentage. The first percentage in each cell, sometimes called the "row percentage" is calculated using the row total as the denominator. For example, consider the cell representing respondents who neither used the pool nor learned about AFC from a doctor. The row percentage is 58% (that is, 103/177 = 0.582). The next percentage in each cell is the "column percentage" and is calculated using the column total as the denominator. Thus, for those who neither used the pool nor learned about AFC

Exhibit 20.1			Avery Fitness Center: Therapy Pool Usage by Doctor's Recommendation (SPSS Output)		

Cross tab

			Utilized therapy pool?		
			no	**yes**	**Total**
Doctor recommendation?	no	Count	103	74	177
		% within Doctor recommendation?	58.2%	41.8%	100.0%
		% within Utilized therapy pool?	84.4%	67.9%	76.6%
		% of Total	44.6%	32.0%	76.6%
	yes	Count	19	35	54
		% within Doctor recommendation?	35.2%	64.8%	100.0%
		% within Utilized therapy pool?	15.6%	32.1%	23.4%
		% of Total	8.2%	15.2%	23.4%
	Total	Count	122	109	231
		% within Doctor recommendation?	52.8%	47.2%	100.0%
		% within Utilized therapy pool?	100.0%	100.0%	100.0%
		% of Total	52.8%	47.2%	100.0%

from a doctor, the column percentage is 84% (i.e., 103/122 = 0.844). The final percentage shown in each cell is the "total percentage;" it uses the total number of respondents as the denominator. So, for the same cell, the total percentage is 45% (i.e., 103/231 = 0.446).

The obvious question is "Which percentage should I use?" To answer this question, think about which of the variables being studied is likely to be the independent variable (cause) and which is likely to be the dependent variable (effect). *Percentages are always calculated in the direction of the causal variable.* That is, the marginal totals for the causal variable are always used as the denominator when calculating percentages in cross tabulations. We've already decided that a doctor's recommendation might have caused respondents to utilize the therapy pool; because the different levels of the causal variable are represented by the rows in the cross tabulation (see Exhibit 20.1), the row percentages should be used. Exhibit 20.2 demonstrates one method of presenting these results in a research report.

Now back to the original question: Does it appear that people who are recommended by doctors are more or less likely to use the therapy pool? Looking only at the row percentages in Exhibit 20.1, can you detect a different pattern of responses for the two groups (i.e., those who learned about AFC from doctors and those who did not)? For this sample, it looks as though people who learn about AFC from doctors are more likely to use the therapy pool than people who don't learn about it from a doctor (65% vs. 42%, respectively, had utilized the pool). Thus, from a manager's perspective, it appears that if the proportion of AFC customers who come because of a doctor's recommendation increases (perhaps through increased promotion to doctors), utilization of the therapy pool may go up significantly. We will address how to determine whether or not this relationship is likely to be true for the population (as opposed to the sample) in the following section.

And what about the least used service at AFC (only 12% of respondents reported having used the circulation station in the prior 30 days)? Is it likely that increased promotion with doctors would yield a larger share of users compared with promoting in other ways? From the results presented in Exhibit 20.3, we learn that 17% of respondents who learned about AFC from a doctor used the circulation station as opposed to 11% who didn't learn about AFC from a doctor. It appears that there might be a small difference, but how do we know that this is a real difference and didn't just occur by chance? That's the subject of the next section.

Learning Objective

2. Describe how percentages should be calculated for a two-way cross tab.

Exhibit 20.2	**Avery Fitness Center: Therapy Pool Usage by Doctor's Recommendation**		
	Did Respondent Learn about AFC from Doctor?		
Used Therapy Pool?	**No**	**Yes**	**Total**
No	103 (58%)	19 (35%)	122
Yes	74 (42%)	35 (65%)	109
Total	177 (100%)	54 (100%)	231

Exhibit 20.3	**Avery Fitness Center: Circulation Station Usage by Doctor's Recommendation (SPSS Output)**

Cross tab

			Utilized circulation station?		
			no	**yes**	**Total**
Doctor recommendation?	no	Count	158	19	177
		% within Doctor recommendation?	89.3%	10.7%	100.0%
		% within Utilized circulation station?	77.8%	67.9%	76.6%
		% of Total	68.4%	8.2%	76.6%
	yes	Count	45	9	54
		% within Doctor recommendation?	83.3%	16.7%	100.0%
		% within Utilized circulation station?	22.2%	32.1%	23.4%
		% of Total	19.5%	3.9%	23.4%
	Total	Count	203	28	231
		% within Doctor recommendation?	87.9%	12.1%	100.0%
		% within Utilized circulation station?	100.0%	100.0%	100.0%
		% of Total	87.9%	12.1%	100.0%

Testing for Statistical Significance

The hypothesis testing procedure outlined in the previous chapter applies to multivariate analyses as well as to univariate analyses: Hypotheses are specified, an inferential test statistic is computed, and the test statistic is compared to a critical value to determine if the result is statistically significant. Numerous statistical tests can be applied to cross-tabulation results to test for statistical significance. Two of the more commonly used tests are the Pearson chi-square test of independence and Cramer's V.

The **Pearson chi-square (χ^2) test of independence** assesses the degree to which the two variables in a cross-tabulation analysis are independent of one another. Note that the Pearson chi-square test does not measure the degree of association between variables but instead is used to test the null hypothesis that the variables are independent. Though we omit the details, the chi-square test is conceptually similar to the chi-square goodness-of-fit test described in Chapter 19, except that expected frequencies are determined jointly using the marginal totals for both variables in the cross tabulation. The Pearson chi-square value can range from zero to some upper value limited by sample size and the distribution of cases across the cells. The chi-square value, degrees of freedom for the chi-square test, and the p-value are provided in the output for standard statistical analysis software packages.

For the analysis presented in Exhibit 20.1, which was the cross tab of learning about AFC from a doctor (yes or no) and use of the therapy pool (yes or no), the Pearson chi-square value is 8.788, on 1 degree of freedom (df), and the associated p-value is 0.003. Thus, if these variables are truly independent of one another in the population, the probability that we could have obtained a chi-square value of this magnitude is less than 1%, and we can reject the null hypothesis that the variables are independent. The chi-square value for the analysis in Exhibit 20.3, which exams the combination of learning about AFC from a doctor and use of the circulation station, is 1.367 on 1 degree of freedom, and the p-value equals 0.242. Therefore, if use of the circulation station and learning about AFC from a doctor are unrelated in the population, the likelihood that we could have obtained results of this magnitude is 0.242, and we cannot reject the null hypothesis of independence. (Recall that for most

Learning Objective

3. Describe how one determines if there is a statistically significant relationship between two categorical variables in a cross-tabulation table.

Pearson chi-square test of independence
A commonly used statistic for testing the null hypothesis that categorical variables are independent of one another.

MANAGER'S FOCUS

Sometimes managers request that every question on a questionnaire be cross tabulated against every other question. What is wrong with that? First, seldom do all of the questions pertain to the same marketing issues. Conducting every conceivable analysis represents little more than an aimless fishing expedition. The primary purpose of a descriptive (or causal) study is not to explore the data for unanticipated relationships, but to test hypothesized relationships that were suggested by previous exploratory research.

The second reason this approach might be problematic is statistical in nature. The more analyses that are performed, particularly those that are not guided by a set of meaningful hypotheses, the greater the likelihood of obtaining results that are "statistically significant" due to chance rather than real relationships between the variables in the target population(s). Remember, when you set the significance level (α) at 0.05, there is 1 chance in 20 of drawing the wrong conclusion about the null hypothesis. Accordingly, as more and more analyses are

performed, roughly 5% of the statistically significant findings you obtain will suggest relationships or differences that really do not exist. This, in turn, can lead you to take unwarranted marketing actions.

Having extended this caution, we should note that there are times when managers or researchers identify legitimate unplanned new tests to run. In other words, if guided by the original purpose of the study and logic, rather than mere availability of data, there is nothing wrong with searching for additional insights that your data may offer. However, when exploring your data beyond the primary purpose of your study, it would be best to treat any "interesting" or "surprising" findings as tentative in nature. In other words, you should avoid automatically concluding that these findings represent something meaningful about your market situation. Instead, you should view these findings as representing new hypotheses that should be confirmed or disconfirmed through additional research designed for that specific purpose.

Cramer's V
A statistic used to measure the strength of relationship between categorical variables.

purposes p-values need to be under 0.05 in order for a result to be "statistically significant;" this is the case for the analysis in Exhibit 20.1, but not for the analysis in Exhibit 20.3.)

While the chi-square test indicates whether two variables are independent, it does not measure the strength of association when they are dependent. Numerous approaches have been developed to measure the strength of the relationship between two categorical variables. One of the more popular measures is **Cramer's V**, which is scaled to range between 0 and 1, with higher values representing a stronger relationship between the variables. For example, consider again the possible relationship between learning about AFC from a doctor and using the therapy pool (Exhibit 20.1). The chi-square test indicated that the two variables are not independent; Cramer's V for the analysis is equal to 0.195, an indication of a modest degree of association between the variables. Technically Speaking 20.1 includes a chi-square test and Cramer's V for a cross-tab analysis that includes a variable that has been converted to a categorical measure from a continuous measure.

Presenting Cross-Tab Results: Banner Tables

banner
A series of cross tabulations between an outcome, or dependent variable, and several (sometimes many) explanatory variables in a single table.

Cross-tab results for commercial marketing research studies are often presented using banners. A **banner** is a series of cross tabulations between an outcome (dependent) variable and several possible causal variables in a single table on a single page. The outcome variable usually serves as the row variable, which is also known as the stub. The causal variables serve as the column variables, with each category of these variables serving as a banner point. Exhibit 20.4 (on page 458) shows what the banner format might look like for part of the fitness center analysis. In this example, three variables

technically speaking 20.1

Converting Continuous Measures into Categorical Measures for Use in Cross Tabulations

Cross tabulations work equally well with continuous measures that have been recast as categorical measures. Although converting continuous measures into categories results in the loss of information and lowered statistical power, managers will often find it easy to interpret and use results from a cross-tabulation analysis. Suppose, for example, the managers of the fitness center wanted to better understand what motivates members to use the therapy pool. We saw earlier that people who learn about AFC from their doctors tend to use the pool more than do people who learn about it in other ways. This might suggest that people with specific medical issues—the ones more likely to be referred by doctors—may be especially likely to use the therapy pool.

To check out this possibility, we can see if there is a connection between pool usage and the importance of specific medical concerns to AFC members (see question 5 on the survey presented in Figure 18.1). For this item, respondents indicated how important "specific medical concerns" were to their participation at AFC on a 1–5, "not at all important – very important" scale. Notice that this is measured at the interval level of measurement and, as a result, is not appropriate in a cross-tab analysis. It is a simple matter, however, to convert this interval measure into an ordinal (and, thus, categorical) measure that can be used effectively in a cross-tab analysis. A quick frequency analysis reveals that about half of the respondents (48%) circled a "5" in response to this item.

If we combine everyone who circled a number other than 5, we'll have two groups, one that represents those for whom the issue is very important, and one that includes those for whom the issue was less important. Using the converted measure to predict therapy pool usage produces the following cross tabulation:

Used Therapy Pool?	Importance of "Specific Medical Concerns"		
	Less Important	Very Important	Total
No	71	39	110
	(65%)	(39%)	0
Yes	38	61	99
	(35%)	(61%)	
Total	109	100	209
	(100%)	(100%)	

Does usage of the therapy pool seem to depend upon the importance of specific medical concerns? It certainly seems so, because 61% of the respondents for whom this issue was very important reported using the therapy pool, compared with only 35% for whom the issue was less important. Because we are working with a sample, however, we must consider whether or not this result could have been due to chance. The χ^2 value was equal to 14.291 (1 df) and p < 0.000, so it does not appear that these variables are independent of one another. In addition, the value of Cramer's V was 0.261, an indication of a modest degree of association between the variables.

that are statistically significantly related to whether or not respondents use the therapy pool are included. The top line in each row of the table indicates the absolute number possessing the characteristic; the second line indicates the percentage. All percentages are presented as whole numbers as we recommended in the previous chapter.

There are a couple of big advantages of using banner tables. First, they allow a lot of information to be presented using very little space. Second, the display format

Exhibit 20.4	Avery Fitness Center: Banner Table					
	Gender		Did Respondent Learn about AFC from Doctor?		Importance of "Specific Medical Concerns"	
Used Therapy Pool?	**Male**	**Female**	**No**	**Yes**	**Less**	**Very**
No	36	81	103	19	71	39
	(80)[a]	(46)	(58)	(35)	(65)	(39)
Yes	9	96	74	35	38	61
	(20)	(54)	(42)	(65)	(35)	(61)
	(n = 222)		(n = 231)		(n = 209)	

[a]Percentages shown in parentheses

makes it easy for managers to understand. Because banner tables can sometimes hide more complex relationships that involve several variables (see Technically Speaking 20.2), however, they should not be considered as a substitute for careful cross-tabulation analysis, but more as an efficient form of data presentation.

ANALYSES INVOLVING CATEGORICAL AND CONTINUOUS MEASURES

Learning Objective

4. Explain two techniques for comparing groups on dependent variables assessed on continuous measures.

Researchers commonly encounter situations in which a continuous outcome measure must be compared across levels of one or more categorical independent variables. For instance, imagine that a brand manager wanted to know whether men and women held different attitudes toward her brand. Or maybe a manager for a small hospital chain wanted to compare patient perceptions of service quality across the three different hospitals in the chain. In these and many other cases, the task is to test for differences across groups (i.e., men vs. women; hospital A patients vs. hospital B patients vs. hospital C patients) on some important variable assessed using a continuous measure (i.e., attitude toward the brand; perceptions of service quality). In this section, we present two related techniques for examining differences of these types: the independent samples *t*-test for means and the analysis of variance. It is important to note that these techniques apply only to situations in which there is at least the potential for a causal relationship between one or more categorical independent variables and a continuous dependent variable. More sophisticated techniques are required to analyze the reverse situation [i.e., continuous independent variable(s) and categorical dependent variable].

In this section, we also consider the situation in which a researcher wants to compare mean scores for variables provided by the same group of respondents. For example, suppose that a department store had a sample of its customers rate the quality of its merchandise in two general categories, clothing and accessories, using the same "very poor" to "very good" rating scale, and that everyone evaluated both categories. Department store managers were interested in determining whether the quality of its clothing was superior to the judged quality of the accessories that they offered. The appropriate analysis, the paired sample *t*-test for means, is presented in this section.

technically speaking 20.2

Adding Variables to an Analysis

Most of the examples in this chapter examine relationships between only two variables at a time. Unfortunately, life is usually a bit more complicated than that. A particular dependent variable will almost always be influenced by more than one independent variable, and the effect of one independent variable on the dependent variable may well be influenced, or modified, by some third variable. Recall from Chapter 6 that one of the requirements for establishing causality is the elimination of other possible causes. For this reason alone, you need to consider how a particular bivariate relationship might change with the introduction of a third variable. The bivariate analysis may initially indicate the existence or nonexistence of a relationship between the variables. The introduction of a third variable may result in no change in the initial conclusion, or it may produce a completely different result.

For example, suppose that a lender wanted to understand the characteristics of individuals who financed the purchase of their automobiles. She hired a research company to conduct a study of consumers in the bank's trade area. Initially, she was interested in determining whether or not education (high school or less vs. attended college) had any effect on whether or not the individual had financed the most recent car purchase.

Based on the two-way cross-tab analysis shown in Exhibit A, it appears that there is no relationship between education and financing the purchase; the percentage of individuals with outstanding car debt is 30% in each case. Look at what happens, though, when annual income (divided into two categories, less than $37,500 vs. $37,500 or more) is also considered in the analysis (see Exhibit B). A clear picture of the relationship among the three variables considered simultaneously emerges by reporting the percentage of people who

Exhibit A	Financed Car Purchase by Education Level		
	Financed Car Purchase?		
Education	**Yes**	**No**	**Total**
High school or less	24 (30%)	56 (70%)	80 (100%)
At least some college	6 (30%)	14 (70%)	20 (100%)

Exhibit B	Financed Car Purchase by Education Level and Income		
	Income		
Education	**Less than $37,500**	**$37,500 or More**	**Total**
High school or less	12%	58%	30%
At least some college	40%	27%	30%

(continued)

financed the car purchase in each of the categories.

For lower incomes, the presence of debt increases with education. For higher incomes, automobile debt decreases with education. The effect of education was hidden in the original bivariate analysis because the effects canceled each other. When income is also considered, the relationship of installment debt to education is quite pronounced. This is an example of *spurious non-correlation*; that is, we would have concluded that there was no relationship between two variables when in fact a strong relationship existed—but was hidden until the third variable was included in the analysis. It is also possible that a bivariate analysis can suggest that a relationship exists between two variables when in fact there is none. Instead, one or both variables may simply be related to a third variable and the relationship will disappear when that variable is taken into account.

This situation represents *spurious correlation* between the two original variables.

Thus, a conclusion can change dramatically when a third variable is added to an analysis. This is true for any type of analysis, not just bivariate cross tabs. Can conclusions change again with the addition of a fourth variable? How about a fifth? Sure they can. The problem is that we never really know for sure when to stop introducing variables. The conclusion is always susceptible to change with the introduction of the "right" variable or variables. Later research may demonstrate that our earlier conclusions were incorrect. This is why the accumulation of studies, rather than a single study, supporting a particular relationship is so vital to the advancement of knowledge. The development of sound theory is also critical to determining which variables should be related to other variables and when to stop putting more variables into an analysis.

Independent Samples *T*-Test for Means

independent samples *t*-test
A technique commonly used to determine whether two groups differ on some characteristic assessed on a continuous measure.

The manager in charge of the therapy pool at Avery Fitness Center noticed that the members who used the therapy pool tended to come to the center more regularly than most other members. Believing that regular customers probably led to a stronger revenue stream, he wanted to make the case that investing in a second therapy pool was a good idea.

Do the data obtained from AFC members verify that pool users tend to visit the fitness center more regularly than those who don't? Given that the outcome variable is continuous (number of visits; see question 2 on the survey presented in Figure 18.1) and the independent variable is categorical (use of therapy pool; see question 1), this is an ideal situation to use the **independent samples *t*-test** to determine if the two groups (that is, those who used the pool vs. those who did not) truly differ with respect to how frequently they visit the fitness center.

Just about any statistical software package can be used to easily perform the analysis. Exhibit 20.5 presents the output from an SPSS analysis. First, notice that the mean number of visits over the 30-day period does appear to be different for members who used the therapy pool (mean = 12.4 visits) compared with those who did not (mean = 7.5 visits). Can we conclude, however, that this is the case? Not yet. As usual, we must test to determine how likely it is that we could have obtained these *sample* results (a difference of about 5 visits per month) if there really were no difference in the overall *population* from which the samples were drawn.

The test statistic, t, is found in the SPSS output in Exhibit 20.5. In this case, the calculated t-value is -5.07 with 196 degrees of freedom (df = total sample size for analysis $- 2 = 198 - 2 = 196$). The associated p-value, using a two-tailed test, is less than 0.001. Thus, if there really were no difference in number of visits for those who use the therapy pool vs. those who don't use the pool in the population, the probability that we could have obtained the results we did in our sample is less than 1 in 1,000, which is considerably less than conventional standards for achieving statistical

Exhibit 20.5	**Avery Fitness Center: Number of Visits by Therapy Pool Usage (SPSS Output)**

Group Statistics

	Utilized therapy pool?	N	Mean	Std. Deviation	Std. Error Mean
number of visits	no	99	7.51	6.780	.681
	yes	99	12.43	6.899	.693

Independent Samples Test

		Levene's Test for Equality of Variances		t-test for Equality of Means					95% Confidence Interval of the Difference	
		F	Sig.	t	df	Sig. (2-tailed)	Mean Difference	Std. Error Difference	Lower	Upper
number of visits	Equal variances assumed	.160	.689	−5.071	196	.000	−4.929	.972	−6.847	−3.012
	Equal variances not assumed			−5.071	195.941	.000	−4.929	.972	−6.847	−3.012

significance ($p < 0.05$). As a result, we can conclude that members who use the therapy pool do, in fact, visit the fitness center more frequently than those who do not use the pool.

Because the space required for a second therapy pool would require remodeling one part of the fitness center, managers thought it might be necessary to consider adding an additional changing room and restroom facilities for their female members. They already knew from basic univariate analysis that about four times as many women as men were AFC members, but they were concerned that if women also visited the center more frequently per month than men, the existing facilities might not be sufficient. Researchers performed a quick independent samples (that is, men vs. women) t-test analysis and discovered that men visited the center an average of 9.2 times per month, while women visited an average of 10.0 times per month. The associated t-value, with 187 degrees of freedom, is −0.644 and the p-value is 0.520; the difference is not statistically significant. As a result, managers decided not to add the proposed facilities.

Paired Sample *T*-Test for Means

The independent samples t-test for means always compares mean scores for the same variable measured in two separate groups. What happens when a researcher needs to compare two means when both measures are provided by the same sample? The analyst will use the **paired sample t-test** for means. For instance, advertising researchers might be interested in determining whether attitude toward a brand increases after consumers watch a 30-second ad for the brand. The researchers would measure attitude toward the brand *both before and after* showing the 30-second ad and then compare mean scores across the consumers in the study. In this situation, the continuous

Learning Objective

5. Explain the difference between an independent sample t-test for means and a paired sample t-test for means.

paired sample t-test
A technique for comparing two means when scores for both variables are provided by the same sample.

dependent variable is the measure of brand attitude, and the categorical independent variable is time of measurement (i.e., before vs. after).

Another common situation that calls for the use of the paired sample *t*-test arises when researchers take the same measure and apply it to different objects. For example, suppose that a local grocery store wanted to compare consumers' overall perceptions of its prices versus overall perceptions of prices for a nearby competitor. Researchers might prepare a questionnaire that includes measures designed to assess perception of prices on a 1–10 rating scale for each of the two stores and then collect data from a sample of community residents. The continuous dependent variable is perception of price, and the categorical independent variable is the store (i.e., local store vs. competitor).

As with the independent samples *t*-test, the paired sample *t*-test is common in marketing research. For example, take a quick look back at question 5 on the Avery Fitness Center survey presented in Figure 18.1. The researchers wanted to understand what motivates people to participate in AFC programs so that they could further customize the services offered to better meet member needs. If the results indicated that the social benefits of meeting with other people were especially important, managers planned to develop additional social activities for members and were even considering rearranging the layout of the center to encourage greater interaction among members while they exercise.

Figure 20.2 presents the mean importance scores for four possible reasons for participating in AFC programs in graphic format. Based on these results, it seems that social aspects may not be all that important to AFC members. In fact, social aspects would appear to be the least important of all the possible reasons for participating in AFC programs that were included in the survey. Managers wanted to be sure, however, before giving up their plans. Is there evidence in the sample data to support the conclusion that social aspects are least important to population members?

The *t*-value is the appropriate test statistic and can be obtained using any statistical software package. Exhibit 20.6 presents SPSS output for three different paired sample *t*-tests, one each for comparing the importance of social aspects with the importance of the other three possible reasons for participating in AFC programs. As an example, the paired sample *t*-value comparing the importance of social aspects with the importance of physical enjoyment is $t = -10.12$, on 198 degrees of freedom, and

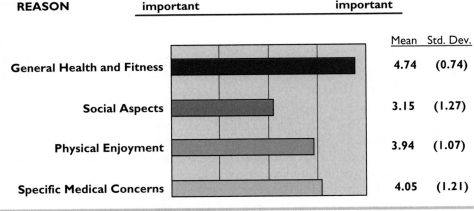

FIGURE 20.2   Avery Fitness Center: Importance of Various Reasons for Participating

Exhibit 20.6	Avery Fitness Center: Paired Sample *T*-Tests (SPSS Output)

Paired Samples Test

		Paired Differences							
					95% Confidence Interval of the Difference				
		Mean	Std. Deviation	Std. Error Mean	Lower	Upper	t	df	Sig. (2-tailed)
Pair 1	Importance: Social Aspects − Importance: General Health and Fitness	−1.631	1.315	.092	−1.813	−1.449	−17.667	202	.000
Pair 2	Importance: Social Aspects − Importance: Physical Enjoyment	−.794	1.107	.078	−.949	−.639	−10.120	198	.000
Pair 3	Importance: Social Aspects − Importance: Specific Medical Concerns	−.917	1.546	.112	−1.137	−.697	−8.214	191	.000

the associated p-value is well under 0.05, so we can conclude that AFC members place greater importance on physical enjoyment than social considerations when it comes to program participation.

Analysis of Variance (ANOVA)

The *t*-test is a useful tool for comparing means between two groups. What happens, though, when there are more than two groups to be compared, or when there is more than one categorical independent variable to be considered? In these situations, you can resort to a series of *t*-tests, taking two groups at a time for one independent variable at a time, but such a strategy would be inefficient, would increase the likelihood of rejecting a true null hypothesis, and wouldn't allow for the joint effects of the independent variables. Fortunately, there is a better way.

The analysis of variance (ANOVA) has the distinct advantage of being applicable when there are more than two means being compared. The basic idea underlying the analysis of variance is that the parent-population variance can be estimated from the sample in several ways, and comparisons among these estimates tell us a great deal about the population. If the null hypothesis of no differences across groups is true (i.e., scores on the dependent variable are unaffected by which category the member of the sample belongs to), the following three estimates of the population variance should be equal:

1. The total variation, computed by comparing each of the individual scores on the continuous dependent variable (across all groups) with the overall mean score.

2. The between-group variation, computed by comparing each of the group means with the overall mean score.

3. The within-group variation, computed by comparing each of the individual scores with the mean of its own group.

If, however, the null hypothesis is not true, and there is a difference in the mean scores across the groups, then the between-group variation should produce a higher

Learning Objective

6. List three advantages of using analysis of variance versus conducting a series of *t*-tests to examine differences across groups.

analysis of variance (ANOVA)
A statistical technique used with a continuous dependent variable and one or more categorical independent variables.

estimate than the within-group variation, which considers only the variation within groups and is independent of differences between groups.

As an example, managers at the fitness center wanted to increase the frequency at which members visited the center. This would be good for the health of the participants—and it would be good for AFC, because analyses had shown that the more frequently someone visits the center, the healthier the revenue stream. As a result, the managers were developing a promotional campaign that could be targeted at one or more subgroups of AFC members to encourage them to participate more frequently. We learned earlier that AFC members who use the therapy pool visited the center more often than did people who don't use the pool, so one possibility was to target those who don't use the pool for the promotions. Managers had also noticed, however, that members who utilized the facility's weight training equipment tended to visit the center regularly as well. In fact, a quick analysis indicated that those who used the facility for weight training visited the facility more frequently (mean visits = 11.4) than those who did not (mean visits = 9.1), and an independent samples t-test confirmed that this difference was statistically significant (t, 196 degrees of freedom, = −2.27, p < 0.05). As a result, managers were concerned that sending promotional incentives to all members who don't use the pool would be inefficient if some of these members were already coming regularly for weight training.

To shed more light on the situation, we can perform an ANOVA. This statistical technique allows us to determine, in a single analysis, if utilizing the therapy pool and weight training are each associated with more visits to the center. We can also determine if the effects of using the therapy pool and weight training produce effects on visit frequency independently of one another or should be considered simultaneously. This last consideration carries important implications for the managers' promotional strategies (that is, whether to include all members who don't use the pool or to also consider whether or not the members use the weight training offered by AFC). In our analysis, we have a continuous dependent variable (number of visits to AFC in the last 30 days) and two categorical independent variables each measured on two levels (use of therapy pool, yes or no; use of weight training, yes or no). In ANOVA, the independent variables are typically called *factors*, and the different levels of the independent variables are referred to as *treatment levels*.

Exhibit 20.7 presents the mean number of visits for each of the four groups formed by considering the two independent variables simultaneously. (Figure 20.3 presents the same information in graphic form.) As you probably expected, people who utilized both the therapy pool and weight training reported going to the fitness center more frequently (mean visits = 13.60) than the other groups and people who utilized neither service offering attended less frequently than the other groups (mean visits = 4.46). What is more interesting is that the influence of either factor seems to depend upon the level of the other factor. That is, use of the therapy pool has a big effect on number of visits to the center when people don't use weight training (an increase of about 7.5 trips per month); the effect is not as large when the members use AFC for weight training (an increase of 3.2 trips per month). And we can easily

Exhibit 20.7

Avery Fitness Center: Mean Number of AFC Visits in Last 30 Days for Four Groups

Utilized Therapy Pool?	Utilized Weight Training?			
	No	(n)	Yes	(n)
No	4.46	(48)	10.37	(51)
Yes	12.04	(74)	13.60	(25)

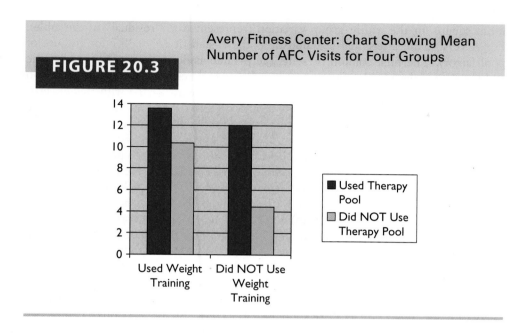

FIGURE 20.3   Avery Fitness Center: Chart Showing Mean Number of AFC Visits for Four Groups

rearrange Figure 20.3 to show that use of weight training has a much larger effect on frequency of visits to the center for AFC members who don't use the pool than for members who do use the pool.

Based on the sample results, it appears that both use of the pool and use of weight training influence number of monthly visits to AFC and that these effects are not independent; the effects of each factor vary depending upon the level of the other factor. Can we safely conclude, however, that these results are likely to be true for all AFC members?

Using SPSS to analyze the data, we obtained the ANOVA table presented in Exhibit 20.8. Looking at the Mean Square column allows an insight into the size of the between-group variation relative to the within-group variation for each of the effects we are considering (i.e., use of the therapy pool, use of weight training, and the joint effect, known as an *interaction* term). The mean square for the between-group variation for use of the pool is 1646.7 and is nearly 40 times larger than the

Exhibit 20.8   **Avery Fitness Center: ANOVA Table (SPSS Output)**

ANOVA[a]

					Experimental Method		
			Sum of Squares	df	Mean Square	F	Sig.
number of visits	Main Effects	(Combined)	1911.261	2	955.630	22.448	.000
		Utilized therapy pool?	1646.712	1	1646.712	38.682	.000
		Utilized weight training?	708.513	1	708.513	16.643	.000
	2-Way Interactions	Utilized therapy pool?* Utilized weight training?	201.841	1	201.841	4.741	.031
	Model		2113.102	3	704.367	16.546	.000
	Residual		8258.717	194	42.571		
	Total		10371.818	197	52.649		

[a]number of visits by Utilized therapy pool?, Utilized weight training?

mean square for the within-group variation (represented as "residual" in the table). For ANOVA, the inferential test statistic is the F-statistic ($F = 38.7$ for the use of pool factor). The final column presents the p-value associated with the test statistic and represents the likelihood of obtaining the sample results if there were truly no difference in the parent-population scores. The p-value associated with this effect is less than 0.05 so the result is statistically significant and represents a real effect in the population. Notice that similar *main effect* results are obtained for use of weight training ($F = 16.6$; p < 0.05).

As we have already shown, it would have been a simple matter to perform independent samples t-tests to arrive at the same conclusions because there were only two groups associated with each of the two factors. However, the ANOVA allowed us to examine both factors in a single analysis (technically, this is known as a *factorial design*), plus it can handle the common situation in which one or more factors have more than two levels. Just as importantly, the ANOVA lets us test for the effect of the interaction, or joint effect, of both factors. As we have seen, it looks as though use of the therapy pool has a much stronger effect on AFC visit frequency for members who don't use weight training. As evidenced in Exhibit 20.8, the interaction term is statistically significant ($F = 4.7$; p < 0.05), so we can conclude that these effects are real in the population.

Before we move on, let's back up just a second. In the previous chapter, we reported that the overall mean number of visits to AFC in the past 30 days across respondents was 10.0. While this univariate result is interesting, can we learn more about frequency of visiting by adding additional variables to the analysis? Yes! We have demonstrated that people who use the therapy pool attend the center more often. We've seen that people who come for weight training show up more often as well. Through the use of the ANOVA technique, we have also confirmed that use of the pool and use of weight training have interactive effects on the number of visits to the center. What have the AFC managers learned from all this analysis? It would likely be inefficient to focus their promotions on all members who don't use the therapy pool or on all members who don't use the center for weight training. Using just one of these services already results in visit frequencies that are above the overall mean (see Exhibit 20.7). Instead, the biggest payoff is likely to come from promotions aimed at members who currently don't use the center for either service (these members currently visit the center only 4.5 times per month). The monetary efficiencies of targeting a smaller group can be taken as cost savings that affect the center's bottom line or can be used to offer greater incentives to get these members engaged and attending more regularly.

ANALYSES INVOLVING CONTINUOUS MEASURES

Learning Objective

7. Discuss two techniques for determining the degree of association between two continuous measures.

The earlier sections of this chapter have examined relationships in which at least one of the variables involved in the analysis was a categorical measure. What happens when both variables in a bivariate analysis are measured on continuous scales? Suppose a researcher wanted to determine if there was a relationship between salespeople's years of experience and annual sales per salesperson. Similarly, a company might be interested in knowing whether or not there is a relationship between household income and units purchased per household for its product within a certain market segment. In this section, we discuss two closely related analyses involving continuous measures: the correlation coefficient and simple regression analysis. We also overview multiple regression analysis, a technique used to investigate the nature of the relationship between two or more predictor variables and a continuous outcome variable.

Pearson Product-Moment Correlation Coefficient

The correlation coefficient is a fundamental building block of data analysis. Most people have a basic understanding of what it means when someone says that two things are "correlated." Though they may not understand the technical details, there is an implicit understanding that the two concepts, events, or ideas somehow "go to-gether," that there is some sort of association between them. As one thing changes, so does the other. People intuitively understand the basic concept because life is full of examples. For example, as temperatures rise, the average amount of clothing worn decreases; as family incomes rise, the size of the family house increases; as study time increases, so should exam scores.

We've done a lot of analyses using the fitness center, so let's look at a different company for the remainder of the chapter. Consider the manufacturer of Click pens, which is interested in investigating the effectiveness of the firm's marketing efforts. The company uses wholesalers to distribute Click, along with company sales repre-sentatives and spot television advertising. The company has divided its market area into sales territories and tracks the following information for each territory: (1) the mean number of TV spots per month, (2) the number of sales representatives, (3) the wholesaler efficiency index, and (4) annual sales revenue. The data for a simple ran-dom sample of 40 territories are contained in Exhibit 20.9.

The company plans to use annual territory sales as its measure of effectiveness. Sales data and information on the number of sales representatives serving a territory are readily available in company records. The other variables—television spot adver-tising and wholesaler efficiency—are a little more difficult to get. To obtain informa-tion on television spot advertising in a territory, researchers analyze advertising schedules and study area coverage by television channel to determine what areas each broadcast might reach. Wholesaler efficiency requires rating the wholesalers on a number of criteria and aggregating the ratings into an overall measure of wholesaler efficiency, where 4 is outstanding, 3 is good, 2 is average, and 1 is poor. Because of the time and expense required to generate these advertising and distribution charac-teristics, the company has decided to analyze only a sample of sales territories.

Initially, the company simply wants to determine if there is any relationship between TV spot advertising and annual sales. This relationship might be investigated in several ways. One simple way is to plot sales and number of TV spots on a graph known as a **scatter diagram**, or scatter plot. Figure 20.4 (on page 469) contains the plot. An "eyeball" analysis suggests that sales increase as the number of television spots per month increases. While the scatter plot gives us an idea about the potential rela-tionship between two variables, a much more precise measure of association is provided by the **Pearson product-moment correlation coefficient** which provides a means of quantifying the degree of association between two continuous variables. Essentially, the Pearson product-moment correlation coefficient assesses the degree to which two con-tinuous variables change consistently across cases. That is, are higher or lower scores on one variable associated with higher or lower scores on the second variable as we go across cases? The correlation coefficient can range from -1 (representing perfect nega-tive linear correlation) to $+1$ (representing perfect positive linear correlation). In prac-tice, it is rare for correlations to approach -1 or $+1$.

Exhibit 20.10 (on page 469) presents SPSS output for the correlation between sales (SALES) and mean number of TV spots per month (NUMSPOTS). Notice that the output provides the correlation coefficient, the corresponding p-value (Sig.), and the number of cases in the analysis (N). By default, the SPSS program assumes a two-tailed test, which is appropriate for testing the null hypothesis that the correla-tion does not differ from 0 in either direction (positive or negative). One-tailed tests are readily available if you have proposed a directional hypothesis. In this case, the Pearson product-moment correlation coefficient equals 0.88, which is evidence of a strong, linear relationship between the number of TV spots and annual sales per ter-ritory in the sample data. The larger question is whether or not there is an association between the variables in the population of sales territories, not just within the sample territories. The p-value for the analysis in Exhibit 20.10 shows up as "0.000" indicat-ing that the probability that we could have obtained a correlation value this high if there really were no relationship between these variables in the population is some-thing less than 1 in 1,000. Thus, the relationship is taken to be statistically significant.

scatter diagram
A graphic technique in which a sample element's scores on two variables are used to position the ele-ment on a graph so that the nature of the relationship between the variables can be observed.

Pearson product-moment correlation coefficient
A statistic that indicates the degree of linear association between two continuous variables. The correlation coefficient can range from -1 to $+1$.

| Exhibit 20.9 | | Click Pens: Data from a Sample of 40 Territories | | |

Territory	Sales (in thousands) Y	Advertising (TV spots per month) X_1	Number of Sales Representatives X_2	Wholesaler Efficiency Index X_3
005	260.3	5	3	4
019	286.1	7	5	2
033	279.4	6	3	3
039	410.8	9	4	4
061	438.2	12	6	1
082	315.3	8	3	4
091	565.1	11	7	3
101	570.0	16	8	2
115	426.1	13	4	3
118	315.0	7	3	4
133	403.6	10	6	1
149	220.5	4	4	1
162	343.6	9	4	3
164	644.6	17	8	4
178	520.4	19	7	2
187	329.5	9	3	2
189	426.0	11	6	4
205	343.2	8	3	3
222	450.4	13	5	4
237	421.8	14	5	2
242	245.6	7	4	4
251	503.3	16	6	3
260	375.7	9	5	3
266	265.5	5	3	3
279	620.6	18	6	4
298	450.5	18	5	3
306	270.1	5	3	2
332	368.0	7	6	2
347	556.1	12	7	1
358	570.0	13	6	4
362	318.5	8	4	3
370	260.2	6	3	2
391	667.0	16	8	2
408	618.3	19	8	2
412	525.3	17	7	4
430	332.2	10	4	3
442	393.2	12	5	3
467	283.5	8	3	3
471	376.2	10	5	4
488	481.8	12	5	2

Cautions in the Interpretation of Correlations Before going further, it is important that we offer some words of caution about the correlational techniques (including regression) presented in this chapter. First, the correlation coefficient only assesses the strength of the *linear relationship* between two variables. Look again at the scatter diagram for the relationship between number of TV spots and sales for the different sales territories (Figure 20.4). The relationship between the variables seems to be

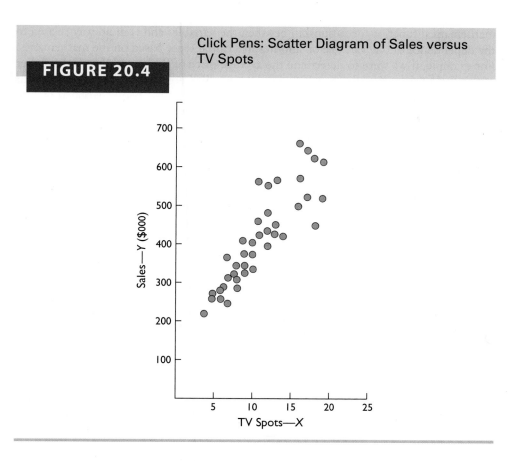

FIGURE 20.4

Click Pens: Scatter Diagram of Sales versus TV Spots

relatively steady; that is, equal increases in number of TV spots (say, from 5 to 10 and from 10 to 15) are associated with about equal changes in sales for the entire diagram. A straight line drawn through the points could provide a good summary of the relationship between TV spots and sales. When two variables are related to one another, there is usually a linear component to their relationship, and the correlation coefficient will usually provide a reasonable summary of the relationship. There are situations, however, in which there can be a very strong nonlinear relationship between variables that cannot be reflected in the correlation coefficient.

The second caution concerns the distinction between correlation and causation. Sometimes researchers assume a causal relationship between two variables when calculating correlation or regression coefficients. Researchers often use the terms *dependent* (criterion) and *independent* (predictor) *variables* to describe the different variables in a correlation or regression analysis. The use of these terms, however, stems from the

Exhibit 20.10   **Click Pens: Correlation of Sales and TV Spots (SPSS Output)**

CORRELATIONS		Numspots	Sales
Pearson Correlation	NUMSPOTS	1.000	.880[a]
	SALES	.880[a]	1.000
Sig. (2-tailed)	NUMSPOTS	.	.000
	SALES	.000	.
N	NUMSPOTS	40	40
	SALES	40	40

[a]Correlation is significant at the 0.01 level (2-tailed).

mathematical functional relationship between the variables and is in no way related to the dependence of one variable on another in a causal sense based on the mathematics. For example, if we were to determine the average price of Bibles and the total number of people in prison over the past 100 years, we would almost certainly find a significant positive correlation. Would we be able to conclude, then, that people stopped buying (and reading) Bibles as prices increased and as a result were more likely to embark on lives of crime? Maybe that partially explains the relationship, but the association between these variables more likely represents spurious correlation rather than a causal relationship (see Technically Speaking 20.2). Two rising trends will be positively correlated regardless of whether or not they have anything to do with one another.

There is nothing in correlation analysis, or any other mathematical procedure, that can be used to establish causality. All these procedures can do is measure the nature and degree of association between variables. Statements of causality must come from underlying knowledge and theories about the phenomena under investigation. They do not come from the mathematics.

Simple Regression

simple regression
A statistical technique used to derive an equation that relates a single continuous dependent variable to a single independent variable.

Simple regression provides a means for getting at the nature of the relationship between two variables, an independent or predictor variable and a dependent or criterion variable. Usually, the researcher has reason to believe that the predictor variable somehow influences the dependent variable (keeping in mind that the mathematics alone cannot prove causation), although this does not have to be the case. For example, the goal might simply be to predict the value of the dependent variable, given the level of the predictor value, with no concern about the issue of causation.

Consider again the manufacturer of Click pens. If the company wanted to determine if there is a relationship between number of sales representatives assigned per territory and annual sales in a territory, researchers might simply develop a scatter diagram and look at the relationship (Figure 20.5) or they might calculate the correlation coefficient between the variables. Researchers might also use simple regression analysis, in which a line is mathematically fit to the data. Figure 20.5 suggests that it would be possible to summarize the relationship between sales and number of sales representatives by drawing a straight line through the data points to represent the "average" relationship between the variables. We could then enter the graph with the number of sales representatives and then read off the average level of sales expected for that number of representatives. Naturally, different researchers would likely draw different lines through the scatter diagram. The issue, then, is determining how to find the best fitting line for the data.

The most common mathematical procedure for determining the best line is known as the *ordinary least-squares (OLS)* approach. Unless there is a perfect linear relationship between two variables (virtually impossible in practice), the data points will not all lie along a single line, resulting in deviations between the actual data points and the line itself (which, in effect, represents predicted values of the dependent variable for different levels of the independent variable). The OLS approach identifies the line that minimizes the sum of the squared deviations about the line. This best fitting line is symbolized as

$$Y_i = \alpha + \beta X_i + \varepsilon_i$$

where Y_i is the level of sales in the ith territory, X_i is the number of sales reps in the ith territory, ε_i is the error associated with the ith observation, α is the intercept, and β is the slope coefficient. The best fitting line for the data determined through the OLS procedure is known as the regression line. Note that the error term is part of the model. It represents a failure to include all factors related to the dependent variable in the model, the fact that there is an unpredictable element in human behavior, and the condition that there are errors of measurement. This probabilistic model allows for the fact that the Y value is not uniquely determined for a given X_i value.

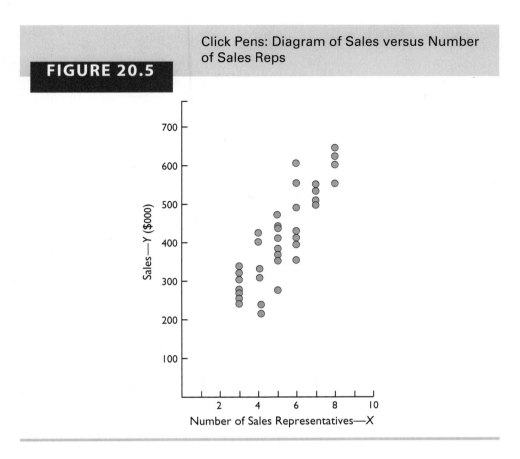

FIGURE 20.5

Click Pens: Diagram of Sales versus Number of Sales Reps

Instead, all that is determined for a given X_i value is the "average value" of Y. Individual values can be expected to fluctuate above and below this average.

Although estimates for α and β can be calculated by hand, it is much more common to conduct regression analyses using a computer. Using the data in Exhibit 20.9 for sales (Y) and number of sales reps per territory (X), it turns out that the intercept term (α) is 80.1 and the slope (β) is 66.2, based on the information contained in the "Coefficients" section of the SPSS output for the analysis (Exhibit 20.11). The equation is plotted in Figure 20.6. The slope of the line (β) indicates how much we can expect Y (sales) to change for every 1 unit change in X (number of sales representatives). So, for each additional sales rep in a territory, we can expect an increase in sales of $66,200. Keep in mind, however, that this is only an estimate of what is going on in the population based on our particular sample of 40 territories. We still must determine if this result is statistically significant or whether it is likely to have occurred by chance. To do this, we simply look at the final two columns in the "Coefficients" section of the SPSS output to see that the t-value associated with the independent variable NUMREPS is equal to 11.6 and that the likelihood of obtaining a β coefficient of 66.2 if there were truly no relationship between number of representatives and sales is less than 0.001. Thus, we conclude that the number of sales representatives in a territory is related to total sales in that territory.

We should note one other important statistic in the regression analysis output at this point. Analysts typically want to gauge how well a particular predictor variable (or set of predictor variables, as we will see in the following section) does at predicting the outcome variable. A commonly used measure for this purpose is R^2, the **coefficient of determination**, which represents the relative proportion of the total variation in the outcome variable (sales in this case) that can be accounted for by the predictor variable in the regression. This value is presented in the "Model Summary" section of the SPSS output. In this case, with a single predictor variable (number of representatives), we are able to explain about 78% of the variation in sales per territory.

coefficient of determination
A measure representing the relative proportion of the total variation in the dependent variable that can be explained or accounted for by the fitted regression equation.

Exhibit 20.11

Click Pens: Simple Regression Analysis (SPSS Output)

MODEL SUMMARY

Model	R	R Square	Adjusted R Square	Std. Error of the Estimate
1	.882[a]	.778	.773	59.016

[a]Predictors: (Constant), NUMREPS.

ANOVA[b]

Model		Sum of Squares	df	Mean Square	F	Sig.
1	Regression	465161.13	1	465161.13	133.556	.000[a]
	Residual	132349.55	38	3482.883		
	Total	597510.67	39			

[a]Predictors: (Constant), NUMREPS.
[b]Dependent Variable: SALES.

COEFFICIENTS[a]

Model		Unstandardized Coefficients		Standardized Coefficients		
		B	Std. Error	Beta	t	Sig.
1	(Constant)	80.141	30.141		2.659	.011
	NUMREPS	66.244	5.732	.882	11.557	.000

[a]Dependent Variable: SALES.

Click Pens: Plot of Equation Relating Sales to Number of Sales Reps

FIGURE 20.6

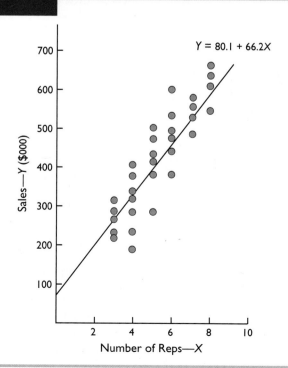

$Y = 80.1 + 66.2X$

Multiple Regression

With simple regression, we examined the relationship between a single predictor variable and an outcome variable. **Multiple regression** analysis allows the introduction of additional variables, so that the regression equation reflects the values of several rather than one predictor variable. Why add additional variables? The goal is to improve our ability to predict, or explain, the outcome variable.

multiple regression
A statistical technique used to derive an equation that relates a single continuous dependent variable to two or more independent variables.

We have seen that the number of sales representatives in a territory is strongly related to the level of sales for the territory. Can we improve our ability to predict sales by including additional variables? The researcher would decide if there were any other pieces of information available that might help predict sales for the territories. Earlier, we saw that there is a significant positive correlation between advertising level (number of TV spots) and sales and—importantly—it seems reasonable to expect that increases in the level of advertising might lead to increases in sales, so advertising is one variable that might be added. We also have information about the efficiency of the wholesalers who also sell and distribute Click pens in each territory. Presumably, more efficient wholesalers should produce higher levels of sales than less efficient ones. The regression equation including all three predictor variables is

$$Y_i = \alpha + \beta_1 X_{1i} + \beta_2 X_{2i} + \beta_3 X_{3i} + \varepsilon_i$$

where X_{1i}, X_{2i}, and X_{3i} are the values for number of reps, number of TV ads, and wholesaler efficiency index for the ith territory, respectively; and β_1, β_2, and β_3 are the regression coefficients corresponding to the three variables. Each of the regression coefficients is called a coefficient of partial regression and represents the average change in the outcome or criterion variable per unit change in the associated predictor variable, holding all other predictor variables constant.

Before running the multiple regression analysis, we need to look at the bivariate scatterplot for the relationship between wholesaler efficiency index (WEI) and sales (the bivariate plots for number of TV spots and number of sales reps were presented earlier). Judging from Figure 20.7, it is not clear what relationship may exist between WEI and sales, if any exists at all. There does not appear to be any particular pattern to the placement of observations.

With statistical software packages, it is quite easy to perform the multiple regression analysis. The SPSS analysis output is presented in Exhibit 20.12 (on page 475). The resulting regression equation is

$$Y = 31.4 + 41.3 X_1 + 12.9 X_2 + 11.5 X_3$$

but before attempting to interpret it we must determine whether or not the overall model is statistically significant (because we are working with a sample). With simple regression, it was only necessary to test the significance of the single beta coefficient to determine whether or not the model was significant. With multiple regression, we need to consider all predictors simultaneously to establish the statistical significance of the overall model. The model is tested via the F-statistic found in the ANOVA section of the computer output. The overall model is tested on the basis of the amount of variance in the dependent variable that can be explained by the regression relative to the variation in the dependent variable that cannot be explained. In this case, the F-statistic equals 89.471 and the corresponding p-value is less than 0.001, so we are safe in concluding that there is a statistically significant linear relationship between sales and the predictor variables (number of television spots, number of sales representatives, and wholesaler efficiency index).

ETHICAL DILEMMA 20.1

The newly appointed analyst in the firm's marketing research department was given the responsibility of developing a method by which market potential for the firm's products could be estimated by small geographic areas. The analyst went about the task by gathering as much secondary data as he could. He then ran a series of regression analyses using the firm's sales as the criterion and the demographic factors as predictors. He realized that several of the predictors were highly correlated (e.g., average income in the area and average educational level), but he chose to ignore this fact when presenting the results to management.

- What is the consequence when the predictors in a regression equation are highly correlated?
- Is a research analyst ethically obliged to learn all he or she can about a particular technique before applying it to a problem in order to avoid incorrectly interpreting the results?
- Is a research analyst ethically obliged to advise those involved to be cautious in interpreting results because of violations of the assumptions in the method used to produce the results?
- What are the researcher's responsibilities if management has no interest in the technical details by which the results are achieved?

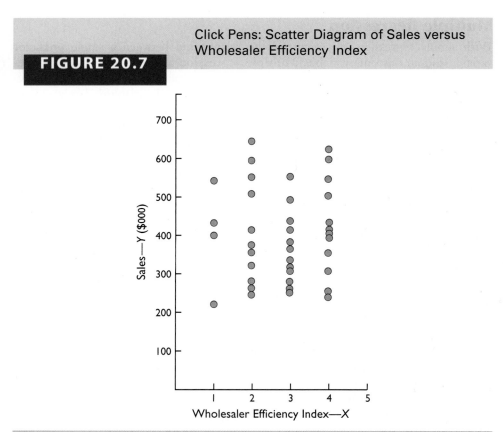

Click Pens: Scatter Diagram of Sales versus Wholesaler Efficiency Index

FIGURE 20.7

One additional consideration is necessary before interpreting the individual components of the regression equation. A key assumption of multiple regression is that the independent variables are independent of one another; there must not be high levels of correlation between predictors. Multicollinearity is said to be present in a multiple regression problem when the predictor variables are correlated among themselves. The higher the level of intercorrelation among the predictor variables, the worse the problem becomes. At higher degrees of multicollinearity, the coefficients for individual predictors become unstable—and as a result they cannot be interpreted effectively.

Let's assume that the predictor variables are not too highly correlated with one another. Looking at the t-values associated with the three predictors (see Exhibit 20.12), we see that number of sales reps and number of TV spots are statistically significant predictors of sales in a territory, but that WEI is not (the p-value, the probability that we could have seen an effect of this magnitude if there truly were no relationship between WEI and sales, is greater than 0.05). This result for WEI is consistent with what we observed in the scatter diagram shown in Figure 20.7 and, unless there is a compelling theoretical reason for further consideration of WEI, we would be about as well off to eliminate this variable from further analyses.

Just as we used the coefficient of determination as a measure of closeness of the relationship between the predictor variable and outcome variable in simple regression, we can calculate the **coefficient of multiple determination** in multiple regression analyses. Also symbolized by R^2, the coefficient of multiple determination represents the proportion of variation in the outcome variable that is accounted for by the covariation in the predictor variables. As presented in Exhibit 20.12, R^2 for the current example is 0.882. This means that 88% of the variation in sales is associated with variation in television spots, number of sales reps, and WEI (though we suspect that WEI adds very little to improving the fit of the regression line).

As a final note to our discussion of regression, we should point out that regression is a robust analytic tool that can also be used when one or more independent variables

multicollinearity
A condition said to be present in a multiple regression analysis when the independent variables are correlated among themselves.

coefficient of multiple determination
In multiple regression analysis, the proportion of variation in the dependent variable that is explained or accounted for by the covariation in the independent variables.

Exhibit 20.12	Click Pens: Multiple Regression Analysis (SPSS Output)

MODEL SUMMARY

Model	R	R Square	Adjusted R Square	Std. Error of the Estimate
1	.939[a]	.882	.872	44.304

[a]Predictors: (Constant), WEI, NUMSPOTS, NUMREPS.

ANOVA[b]

Model		Sum of Squares	df	Mean Square	F	Sig.
1	Regression	526849.11	3	175616.37	89.471	.000[a]
	Residual	70661.569	36	1962.821		
	Total	597510.67	39			

[a]Predictors: (Constant), WEI, NUMSPOTS, NUMREPS.
[b]Dependent Variable: SALES.

COEFFICIENTS[a]

Model		Unstandardized Coefficients		Standardized Coefficients		
		B	Std. Error	Beta	t	Sig.
1	(Constant)	31.382	34.083		.921	.363
	NUMREPS	41.316	7.260	.550	5.691	.000
	NUMSPOTS	12.931	2.730	.450	4.737	.000
	WEI	11.486	7.670	.091	1.497	.143

[a]Dependent Variable: SALES.

are categorical as opposed to continuous variables. In fact, the analysis of variance discussed earlier in the chapter is actually just a special case of regression analysis in which all of the predictor variables are categorical. The analysis, including the testing of interaction effects, could easily be performed in multiple regression analysis. Such analysis, however, goes beyond the scope of this book. Interested students can learn more about these or other techniques by reading a good multivariate statistics text.

SUMMARY

Learning Objective 1

Explain the purpose and importance of cross tabulation.
Cross tabulation is the most commonly used multivariate technique. Its purpose is to study the relationships among and between categorical variables.

Learning Objective 2

Describe how percentages should be calculated for a two-way cross tab.
In a two-way cross-tab analysis, percentages should be calculated using the marginal totals

for the causal variable as the denominator. Thus, percentages are calculated in the direction of the causal variable.

Learning Objective 3

Describe how one determines if there is a statistically significant relationship between two categorical variables in a cross-tabulation table.
The Pearson chi-square test of independence is used to determine whether or not two categorical variables are independent of one

another. Cramer's *V* is used to obtain an indication of the strength of the relationship between the categorical variables.

Learning Objective 4

Explain two techniques for comparing groups on dependent variables assessed on continuous measures.
When there are only two groups, the independent samples *t*-test is used to determine if the mean score on the dependent variable for one group is significantly different than the mean score for the second group. If there are more than two groups, the analysis of variance technique, which compares the variance in dependent variable scores within groups with the variance in dependent variable scores between groups, is appropriate.

Learning Objective 5

Explain the difference between an independent sample *t*-test for means and a paired sample *t*-test for means.
In the independent samples *t*-test, mean scores on the dependent variable are compared for different groups of respondents. In a paired sample *t*-test, mean scores on two different variables (measured on similar scales) are compared across a single group (i.e., all respondents provide scores on both variables).

Learning Objective 6

List three advantages of using analysis of variance versus conducting a series of *t*-tests to examine differences across groups.
The ANOVA technique (a) would be more efficient, requiring fewer computations; (b) would decrease the likelihood of rejecting a true null hypothesis; and (c) would consider the joint effects of different independent variables.

Learning Objective 7

Discuss two techniques for determining the degree of association between two continuous measures.
One approach is to calculate the Pearson product-moment correlation coefficient, which assesses the degree of linear association between the variables. Another approach is to use simple regression, a technique in which a mathematical equation is derived that relates a dependent variable to an independent variable.

Learning Objective 8

Describe how multiple regression differs from simple regression.
Simple regression and multiple regression differ in that only one independent variable is used to predict the dependent variable in simple regression, whereas more than one independent variable is included in multiple regression.

KEY TERMS

cross tabulation (page 451)
Pearson chi-square test of independence
  (page 455)
Cramer's *V* (page 456)
banner (page 456)
independent samples *t*-test (page 460)
paired sample *t*-test (page 461)
analysis of variance (ANOVA) (page 463)

scatter diagram (page 467)
Pearson product-moment correlation
coefficient (page 467)
simple regression (page 470)
coefficient of determination (page 471)
multiple regression (page 473)
multicollinearity (page 474)
coefficient of multiple determination (page 474)

REVIEW QUESTIONS

1. What is the proper procedure for investigating the following hypotheses using cross-tabulation analysis?

    a. Consumption of Product X depends on a person's income.

    b. Consumption of Product X depends on a person's education.

2. Illustrate the procedure from Question 1 with data of your own choosing; that is, develop the tables, fill in the assumed numbers, and indicate the conclusions to be drawn from each table.

3. How do you explain the condition in which a two-way cross tabulation of variables X and Y revealed no relationship between X and Y, but the introduction of Z revealed a definite relationship between X and Y?

4. How do you test for differences between two groups on a continuous outcome measure? Explain.

5. How do you test for differences between scores on two continuous measures when each respondent provides both measures? Explain.

6. How do you test for differences between scores on the same measure provided by the same people at two different points in time? Explain.

7. What is the proper procedure for testing the influences of two different categorical independent variables on a single continuous dependent variable simultaneously?

8. What is the difference between regression analysis and correlation analysis?

9. Suppose that an analyst wished to make an inference about the slope coefficient in a regression model. What is the appropriate procedure? What does it mean if the null hypothesis is rejected? If it is not rejected?

10. What is the correlation coefficient, and what does it measure? What is the coefficient of determination, and what does it measure?

11. What is the coefficient of multiple determination?

DISCUSSION QUESTIONS, PROBLEMS, AND PROJECTS

1. A social organization was interested in determining if there were various demographic characteristics that might be related to people's propensity to contribute to charities. The organization was particularly interested in determining if individuals 40 years of age or over were more likely to contribute larger amounts than individuals under 40. The average contribution in the population was $1,500, and this figure was used to form two groups based on a median-split. The following table presents a two-way classification of the number of individuals by contributions and age.

Personal Contributions by Age			
	AGE		
Personal Contribution	**39 or Less**	**40 or More**	**Total**
Less than or equal to $1,500	79	50	129
More than $1,500	11	60	71
Total	90	110	200

    Does the amount of personal contributions depend on age? Generate a table for a report that communicates the relevant information.

2. A large toy manufacturer wants to determine the characteristics of families who have purchased a new electronic game that is designed and marketed for all age groups. Management needs your assistance in interpreting the cross-tab tables in Exhibits 1 and 2.

Exhibit 1	Purchased Electronic Games versus Number of Children		

	PURCHASED ELECTRONIC GAMES		
Number of Children	**Yes**	**No**	**Total**
Less than or equal to 1	63	87	150
More than 1	21	29	50

Exhibit 2	Purchased Electronic Games versus Number of Children and Age of Head of Household		

	AGE OF HEAD OF HOUSEHOLD		
Number of Children	**Less than or Equal to 45**	**More than 45**	**Total**
Less than or equal to 1	14%	46%	42%
More than 1	38%	19%	42%

a. What does Exhibit 1 indicate? Explain and show calculations where necessary.

b. What does Exhibit 2 indicate? Have your conclusions changed or remained the same? Explain.

3. Plaza AutoMall is a medium-sized automobile dealership located in a small city in the southeastern United States. The dealership sells and services new and pre-owned automobiles. In recent months, revenues from the automotive servicing side of the business have been flat, while revenues from new car sales have been rising. The owner suspects that part of the service and repair business may have shifted to a new auto repair shop that opened about a year ago on the other side of town. The new repair shop is much more conveniently located for consumers who live on that side of town. To better understand the perceptions and behaviors of the dealership's customer base (i.e., those who had purchased a car from the dealership) regarding auto servicing, the owner brought in a team of researchers. The researchers developed a mail questionnaire that asked respondents the percentage of times they use Plaza AutoMall for auto repairs (assessed on a 0% to 100% scale). The researchers also coded the return envelopes so that they could determine in which section of town the respondent resides (the city can easily be divided into three well-defined areas, which the researchers coded A, B, and C). The questionnaire was sent to a random sample of the dealership's customer base. Mean scores on the dependent variable were as follows: region A (where the dealership is located) = 93; region B = 82; and region C (where the competing auto repair shop is located) = 70. The researchers utilized the analysis of variance technique to determine if the difference in these means is statistically significant, producing the following ANOVA table:

	ANOVA Table				
Source	**Sum of Squares**	**df**	**Mean Square**	**F**	**Sig.**
Between Groups	3934.103	2	1967.051	2.057	.136
Within Groups	59290.513	62	956.299		
Total	63224.615	64			

a. Assuming $\alpha = 0.05$, can the researchers reject the null hypothesis of no difference across groups? Why or why not?

b. Suppose that the researchers were willing to change the level of significance to $\alpha = 0.15$; would your answer to part (a) change? What would be the consequences for Type I error? Explain.

4. The researchers working with Plaza AutoMall decided to take a closer look at the data. In addition to information about the region where the respondent was located (see Problem 3), they also knew whether or not the respondent had purchased a new or pre-owned car from Plaza. Mean scores (representing the percentage of times the respondent uses the dealership for auto repairs, assessed on a 0% to 100% scale) broken down by region and type of car are as follows:

	TYPE OF CAR	
Region	New Car	Pre-Owned Car
A	92	96
B	90	63
C	95	50

Note: ($n = 65$)

An analysis of variance produced the following ANOVA table:

ANOVA Table

Source	Sum of Squares	df	Mean Square	F	Sig.
MAIN EFFECTS					
Region	2555.532	2	1277.766	1.505	.230
Type of Car	4676.456	1	4676.456	5.509	.022
INTERACTION					
Region by Type of Car	4531.600	2	2265.800	2.669	.078
Within Groups	50082.456	59	848.855		
Total	63224.615	64			

a. Examine closely the mean scores reported above for the six combinations of region and type of car. Based on these results, does it appear that there is a relationship between region and the proportion of times owners take their cars to Plaza for repair? If so, what is the nature of this relationship?

b. Explain the ANOVA table. What can you conclude about the effects of region and type of car on the proportion of times owners take their cars to Plaza for repair?

5. The chancellor of Enormous State University (ESU) has decided that ESU needs to develop a new marketing plan in order to attract the best students. The objective is to attract students who will have the best chance of graduating within four years of their matriculation. The administration has assigned you, the associate vice chancellor, the responsibility for carrying out this project. You have decided that, as part of the research to be performed in designing the new marketing plan, it would be helpful to know what, if any, characteristics possessed by high school seniors are associated with success in college. You decide that a multiple regression approach seems to be the way to proceed. Your task is simplified by the existence of a large, comprehensive database that contains

the results of several broad-based surveys of high school seniors, many of whom later attended ESU. However, you know that simply mining the database is not likely to be much help. Accordingly, your first task is to develop a theory of why students succeed in college. After explaining your theory, specify the dependent variable and predictor variables that you will use in the regression equation. How serious a problem is multicollinearity in the data likely to be, given your objective?

6. Crystallo Bottling Company, which provides plastic bottles to various soft drink manufacturers, has the following information pertaining to the number of cases per shipment and the corresponding transportation costs:

Number of Cases per Shipment	Transportation Costs in Dollars
1,500	$200
2,200	260
3,500	310
4,300	360
5,800	420
6,500	480
7,300	540
8,200	630
8,500	710
9,800	730

The marketing manager is interested in studying the relationship between the number of cases per shipment and the transportation costs. Your assistance is needed.

a. Plot the transportation costs as a function of the number of cases per shipment.

b. Interpret the scatter diagram.

c. Using a statistical software package, enter the data and calculate the Pearson product-moment correlation coefficient.

d. Does it appear that there is a relationship between number of cases and transportation costs? Explain.

7. The marketing manager at Crystallo Bottling Company is studying the relationship between number of cases per shipment and transportation costs. An analysis of the data from the previous problem produced the following simple regression output:

COEFFICIENTS[a]

Model		Unstandardized Coefficients		Standardized Coefficients		
		B	Std. Error	Beta	t	Sig.
1	(Constant)	87.000	25.984		3.348	.010
	CASES	6.545E-02	.004	.985	15.981	.000

[a]Dependent Variable: TRANCOST

$$R^2 = 0.970$$

Thus, the regression equation is
$$Y = 0.065X + 87.000.$$

a. What is the interpretation of the slope coefficient?

b. Does it appear that number of cases per shipment influences transportation cost?

c. If so, how strong is the relationship between the variables?

8. The marketing manager of Crystallo Bottling Company is considering multiple regression analysis with the number of cartons per shipment and the size of cartons as predictor variables and transportation costs as the dependent variable (refer to the previous two problems). He has devised the following regression equation:

$$Y = 23.95 X_1 + 24.44 X_2 - 41.44$$

where X_1 is the number of cartons per shipment and X_2 is the size of the cartons.

   a. Interpret each of the values in the regression equation.

   b. Is multiple regression appropriate in this situation? If yes, why? If no, why not?

Use the AFC member survey (Figure 18.1), codebook (Figure 18.3), and data to perform the analyses in Problems 9 through 15. The data are available in raw form ("AFC.txt") or as an SPSS data file ("AFC.sav") at www.cengage.com/marketing/churchill.

9. Managers at AFC were interested in learning more about members and their usage patterns. Use cross-tabulation analysis to investigate the following relationships. In each case, tell whether or not it appears that the variables may be related to one another, present the results in an appropriate table, and provide Cramer's V (if the results are statistically significant).

   a. Does use of the pool influence the time of day that a member normally visits AFC?

   b. Is gender related to the use of the facility for weight training?

   c. If someone learns about AFC from a friend, is she or he more likely to utilize classes at AFC?

10. Managers noticed that over time AFC members who used the therapy pool tended to develop social relationships with other members, probably because of the time spent together in the pool. They also hypothesized that social aspects were more important for people who were retired and needed greater social interaction.

   a. Perform an ANOVA with the importance of social aspects as the dependent variable and use of the therapy pool and employment status as the independent variables. Does either variable appear to be related to increasing levels of importance for social aspects?

   b. Do the two variables interact with one another in prediction of the importance of social aspects?

11. Which is the more important reason for attending AFC according to members, physical enjoyment or specific medical concerns? Justify your answer.

12. Managers at the fitness center believed that word-of-mouth recommendations from friends bring in new members who spend more money at AFC than those who don't join the center because of a friend's recommendation.

   a. Using the independent samples *t*-test, determine whether or not managers' assumptions are correct. (*Note:* Revenue data for each member in the sample are included in the data file; see the codebook.)

   b. Would your answer to part (a) change if the level of significance for determining whether or not a result is statistically significant were changed from 0.05 to 0.10? Explain.

13. The AFC managers have been assuming that there is a correlation between the number of visits per month that a member makes to the center and the revenues provided by that member. Is there evidence in the data that this might be true for the population of all members?

14. If analysts believed that there was a dependence relationship between number of visits per month and revenues (that is, visiting the center more frequently at least partially caused revenues to be higher), what would be the appropriate analysis to establish this relationship? Perform this analysis. Is the influence of number of visits on revenues statistically significant? How much of the variation in revenues is accounted for by considering only the number of visits per month?

15. AFC managers asked the researchers to extend the analysis in the previous question to include several additional variables that they thought might be related to revenues. In particular, they thought that increasing member age might be associated with increasing revenues per member. They also were interested in determining if any of the four reasons for attending AFC mentioned in question 5 of the survey lead to greater revenues.

a. Conduct a multiple regression analysis with number of visits, member age, and importance scores for the four reasons for participating in AFC programs as predictors and revenues as the dependent variable. Is the overall model statistically significant?

b. Which predictors are statistically significant?

c. Interpret the unstandardized coefficient associated with age. What does this value mean?

d. What is the coefficient of multiple determination for the analysis? Has adding additional predictors to the model (beyond visit frequency only) improved the ability to explain variation in revenues?

e. Does it appear that multicollinearity might have been a problem in this analysis? Why or why not?

PART 7

RESEARCH REPORTS

CHAPTER 21   The Research Report

© ZICPLAY/PRNEWSFOTO/ASSOCIATED PRESS

Is iTunes in trouble? No, not at all. But share prices for Apple Computer, Inc., dropped 3% during a period in December 2006 after reports started surfacing in the media about a sharp drop in revenues from the iTunes music download service offered by the company. An article in Britain's *The Register*, for example, described iTunes monthly revenues as "collapsing" by 65% since January of that year, citing a marketing research report prepared by Forrester Research.

Fortunately for Apple, media reports of the demise of its iTunes music download business were a bit premature. It turns out that media members had misunderstood data in the report released by Forrester Research. What the study actually revealed was a leveling off of iTunes downloads, certainly nothing coming close to a collapse in sales. Not surprisingly, with its market value on the line, Forrester received a call from a "clearly upset" Apple, and analysts quickly set the record straight. Since that time, iTunes has gone on to become the top music retailer in the United States, surpassing Wal-Mart and Best Buy in the spring of 2008, and boasting over 4 billion song downloads to over 50 million customers.

So what's the moral of this story? We're not really sure who deserves more blame in this situation—the reporters who ran with a story before they fully understood the facts, or the company who released information that could be easily misunderstood. Having accurate marketing research information is important, but the job isn't finished until the results are communicated effectively to the people who need to act on the information.

Sources: Andrew Orlowski, "iTunes Sales 'Collapsing,'" *The Register*, downloaded from www.theregister.co.uk/2006/12/11/digital_downloads_flatline/, December 4, 2008; Antone Gonsalves, "Research Firm Clarifies: iTunes Sales Are Not Collapsing," *InformationWeek*, downloaded from www.informationweek.com, August 29, 2008; and "iTunes Store Top Music Retailer in the US," downloaded from www.apple.com/pr/library/2008/04/03itunes.html, December 4, 2008.

The Research Report

Introduction

It doesn't help much to conduct a near-flawless research project if you can't communicate the research results. Creating an effective report, whether written or oral, is a challenging process that takes considerably more time than many researchers seem to budget for the process. Much knowledge, skill, and attention to detail are required. Regardless of the sophistication displayed in other portions of the research process, the project is a failure if the research results are not communicated effectively.

In virtually every case, researchers will be expected to prepare a written report. Much of the time, they also get to present an oral report as well. These reports have a huge impact on whether or not the information generated by the research is actually used. This makes sense when you consider that the reports are all that most executives—the people who needed answers in the first place and who can make decisions based on the results—will see of the project. A solid written report or presentation sends an important signal about the likely quality of the overall project.

As we discuss research reports in the following pages, please keep in mind that the whole point of the marketing research process is to provide solid, usable information for making important decisions. As critics have noted (see Research Window 21.1), researchers have often failed to deliver information that is useful at the strategic level in the organization. As a result, the marketing research function in many companies has taken on a secondary role with little influence. Part of the problem often lies in the inability to communicate the results of marketing research projects and what those results mean for a company.

In this chapter, we will offer some simple guidelines for developing successful research reports. In the first part of the chapter, we will focus on written research reports; in the second part, we discuss oral reports and some graphic means of presenting the results.

research window 21.1

The Role of Marketing Research within the Organization: An Interview with Don Schultz

Don E. Schultz is professor emeritus-in-service, Integrated Marketing Communications, Northwestern University, and president of Agora Inc., an integrated marketing company with clients located around the globe. He has received numerous teaching awards, worked with countless corporate clients, and was named by Sales and Marketing Management *magazine as one of the most influential people in America. Through his interactions with managers at the highest levels in companies, he's had the chance to observe the role of marketing research within many companies, agencies, and media firms. Here's what he has to say about the current practice of marketing research in organizations.*

Q: What should be the role of marketing research within the organization?

That's interesting. What I keep seeing in the real world is that the large amounts of data inside organizations are being managed by the technology (IT) people, rather than by marketing researchers. The kinds of things that the IT people do are useful, primarily tumbling the numbers, but they can't really help you get much customer insight. Marketing research needs to become much more managerially focused and less technology and technique focused. Marketing research people have gotten too tangled up in the techniques and statistics and not focused enough on consumer insights that help drive the business.

I'll give you an example. I was in a meeting recently where the research director came into the room, threw a report down on the chief marketing officer's desk, and said "Here's the report . . . I don't have time to explain it to you; I've got to go get another report out." That's where research has failed. Researchers have become vendors or data suppliers, not information managers. Research has now been pushed down to the level of "you gather the data, you give it to me, and I'll make the analysis . . . you bring nothing to me other than a bunch of cross-tabs and maybe a little managerial report at the top . . . and I'm going to make my own decisions, right or wrong." The research guy really adds nothing to the process. Anyone could have gathered and assembled the data. The value of the research comes from the insights generated, not the cross-tabs created.

I think the role of the researcher lies in helping managers—most of whom never see the customers—gain an understanding of what the research means, what insights can be gleaned from the data, what alternative decisions are possible with the data that has been gathered. That's the important part, not so much the ability to gather the data or put it into neat piles. In a sense, marketing research has become a commodity: The research people within the organization have become order-takers, rather than managers, and marketing research companies have become vendors to, rather than partners with, their client companies. Research must rise above the marketing department in companies where marketing is treated like just another functional area. Customer understanding and knowledge of the marketplace is too important to be isolated that way because it impacts the entire organization. I think that research has to be something that senior management looks to and relies on for understanding. To know what's happening to the business, what's happening to customers, what's happening to the industry, where the competitors are coming from, and so on.

Unfortunately, the marketing people within too many organizations often don't have a managerial view. Instead, they have a tactical view of how things operate, how research is done. For research to play the kind of role that's essential to the health of an organization, it's going to have to rise above the marketing functional area. To be effective, marketing researchers will need to have input into a higher level in the organization, i.e., the corporate suite level, rather than the product manager.

Q: It doesn't sound as if marketing research is faring very well within the organizations with which you work.

In my consulting practice, we're dealing primarily with chief financial officers, chief operating officers, chief marketing officers, corporate communications people, and strategic planners . . . people who are responsible for the future of the business. We seldom see market research people at this level. They're out doing consumer studies, focus groups, conjoint analysis, and that sort of stuff. They're not considered terribly relevant in

(Continued)

a managerial system . . . they've turned into runners who go get information needed by others in the organization. And often decision makers can't relate to the information that they do bring. When they bring intent-to-purchase data, the managers ask "can we use this information to make a forecast?" and the researchers often say: "well . . . no, not really . . . but isn't it nice to know?" So, a lot of the money is being spent on things that are "nice to know" but not terribly critical to the success of the business. I think that's really where the challenge is.

We need to get to a point where research, particularly research about customers, prospects, influencers, and the like, is driving the organization, where it contributes to everything—it's not just something that we go off and do on an "as-needed" basis. Right now, most research isn't being used to drive the business . . . it's being used by managers to either support decisions they've already made or to serve as a handy scapegoat if things don't work out the way they want. That's the box that researchers have gotten themselves into. And, that's the box from which they must extricate themselves if they hope to have an impact on the firm and the business.

Q: What advice do you have for aspiring marketing researchers?
It is critical that future marketing researchers develop the managerial skills that can gain them access to the people who are actually running the company. Usually, that means the chief financial officer. The CFO and the research people generally make a great combination, because the CFO only has hard numbers and the research people can and should be the ones that say "here's why that's happening or here's what might likely happen next." Unfortunately, most marketing researchers don't have the skill set that will allow them to go toe to toe with a company's CFO. Most researchers have practically no management experience; they are tool-driven, and they often don't really understand how businesses are run. As a result, they tend to translate everything into research talk, when what they need to do is to translate everything into management talk.

This has happened because researchers have basically isolated their attention on end-users, when in reality there are many stakeholder groups who influence the business . . . the financial community, suppliers, employees, media, the labor market, etc. There are a whole group of audiences out there the research people should be dealing with, because that's what's driving the business. Just take a look at the impact and effect of social networks. Consumers talking to other consumers. And, in too many cases, the marketing firm doesn't even know it's going on. That's what researchers should be doing. Identifying the networks that drive the marketplace, not the relevant statistics for a chi-square analysis. Right now, companies get bits and pieces of information about the various audiences from different sources, but there's no central resource that brings all of it together and says "here is some knowledge that will help us run this business better." Some will argue that that's the role of the strategic planners, but they're not currently doing it, and they certainly don't bring the skill sets that marketing researchers can provide.

THE WRITTEN RESEARCH REPORT: WRITING STANDARDS

Only one thing really matters with written research reports—how well they communicate with the reader. The report must be tailor-made for its readers, paying attention to their technical sophistication, their interest in the subject area, the circumstances under which they will read the report, and the use they will make of it.

Some readers understand technical issues such as experimental design, measurement issues, sampling plan, analysis technique, and so on. Others don't. As a general rule, it is *not* a good idea to try to impress the boss with big, scientific-sounding words in the written report. That strategy can backfire because the use of technical language will often make managers suspicious of the report writer. Be careful about this,

MANAGER'S FOCUS

In case you're thinking "I can coast a little bit here and let the researchers be responsible for this final stage of the research process" — hold on a minute. Researchers begin the process of disseminating research findings by writing reports and giving oral presentations, but ultimately it is marketing managers that are responsible for transmitting relevant market research findings to key decision makers throughout the organization. There will likely be times when you create abbreviated reports that are passed along to others on the management team, and you will probably need to tailor the report differently for the different types of managers who will receive it. You might even need to give oral presentations to managers higher in the chain of command about what has been learned from research studies. For these reasons, the material in this chapter is just as relevant to you as it is to researchers.

---

because researchers often don't even realize that they are using technical language. Take the time and put forth the effort to make the report understandable to the reader.

Sometimes managers prefer having less information than more information. They only want the results, not a discussion of how the results were obtained nor any conclusions or recommendations. Other executives prefer just the opposite. They not only want a discussion of the results, but also detailed information on how the results were obtained as well as the researcher's conclusions, reasoning, and recommendations. In a nutshell, the audience determines the type of report, and researchers need to learn the specific preferences of their audiences.

To achieve the goal of communicating effectively, a written report must be complete, accurate, clear, and concise.[1] These writing standards are closely related.

Learning Objective

1. Identify and discuss four writing standards that a report should meet if it is to communicate effectively with readers.

Completeness

A report is **complete** when it provides all the information readers need in language they understand. This means that you must continually ask whether every question in the original assignment has been addressed. What alternatives were examined? What was found? An incomplete report probably means that you'll soon be writing supplementary reports, which are annoying and potentially deadly to your credibility as a researcher. Waiting for additional reports also means delaying managerial action, which can be harmful to the business.

When it comes to completeness, there's a bit of a paradox. A written report must be complete, without being *too* complete. All relevant information must be included, but including too much information will quickly detract from the usability of the report (see the sections on clarity and conciseness that follow). You certainly don't want to force the reader to sift through page after page of nonimportant results looking for the things that really matter. The trick is in determining what really matters and what ought to be included in appendices to the report or left out entirely. This isn't always easy, particularly when multiple managers with differing levels of technical sophistication will be reading the report. Readers are thus the key to determining completeness.

completeness
The degree to which the report provides all the information readers need in language they understand.

Accuracy

Imagine that you've done an amazing job of collecting and analyzing data that are perfectly appropriate for making a key decision ... but due to carelessness of report preparation, poor thinking, or poor writing the answer never gets communicated to

accuracy
The degree to which the reasoning in the report is logical and the information correct.

managers. Accuracy in report development is another important consideration. Exhibit 21.1 illustrates some examples of sources of inaccuracy in report writing.

These sorts of problems are terribly difficult to resolve once the written report has been distributed. As a result, it's a really, *really* good idea to have multiple people review the report for accuracy before it is delivered to managers. And, much like a pretest of a survey, it wouldn't hurt to have a manager review a preliminary version of the written report.

Clarity

clarity
The degree to which the phrasing in the report is precise.

Clarity of writing is one of the most difficult standards to achieve. Clarity is produced by clear and logical thinking and precision of expression. When the underlying logic is fuzzy or the presentation imprecise, readers experience difficulty in understanding what they read. They may be forced to guess, in which case bad things may happen. Achieving clarity, however, requires effort.

The first, and most important, rule is that the report be well organized. For this to happen, you must first clarify for yourself the purpose of your report and how you intend to accomplish writing it. Make an outline of your major points. Put the points in logical order and place the supporting details in their proper position. Tell the reader what you are going to cover in the report and then do what you said you were going to do.

When it comes to the actual writing of the report, you should use short paragraphs and short sentences. Do not be evasive or ambiguous; once you have decided what you want to say, come right out and say it. Choose your words carefully, making them as precise and understandable as possible. Research Window 21.2 shows how one corporate vice president sank into the quicksand of his own words. Research Window 21.3 (on page 490) offers some specific suggestions when choosing words.

Exhibit 21.1   **Some Examples of Sources of Inaccuracy in Report Writing**

A. Simple Errors in Addition or Subtraction
"In the United States, 14% of the population has an elementary school education or less, 51% has attended or graduated from high school, and 16% has attended college."

An oversight such as this (14 + 51 + 16 does not equal 100%) can easily be corrected by the author, but not so easily by the reader, because he or she may not know if one or more of the percentage values is incorrect or if a category might have been left out of the tally.

B. Confusion between Percentages and Percentage Points
The company's profits as a percentage of sales were 6.0% in 2000 and 8.0% in 2005. Therefore, they increased only 2.0% in five years.

In this example, the increase is 2.0 percentage points, or 33%.

C. Inaccuracy Caused by Grammatical Errors
The reduction in the government's price supports for dairy products has reduced farm income $600 million to $800 million per year.

To express a range of reduction, the author should have written, "The reduction in the government's price supports for dairy products has reduced farm income $600–800 million per year."

D. Confused Terminology Resulting in Faulty Conclusions
The Jones' household annual income increased from $15,000 in 1979 to $45,000 in 2009, thereby tripling the family's purchasing power.

While the Jones' household income annual may have tripled in 30 years, the family's purchasing power certainly did not, as the cost of living, as measured by the consumer price index, more than tripled in the same period.

research window 21.2

How to Write Your Way out of a Job

Jock Elliott, a former executive with the Ogilvy & Mather advertising agency, offered this example of the importance of clear writing:

"Last month I got a letter from a vice president of a major management consulting firm. Let me read you two paragraphs. The first:

> Recently, the companies of our Marketing Services Group were purchased by one of the largest consumer research firms in the United States. While this move well fits the basic business purpose and focus of the acquired MSG units, it is personally restrictive. I will rather choose to expand my management opportunities with a career move into industry.

"What he meant was: The deal works fine for my company, but not so fine for me. I'm looking for another job." Second paragraph:

> The base of managerial and technical accomplishment reflected in my enclosed resumé may suggest an

opportunity to meet a management need for one of your clients. Certainly my experience promises a most productive pace to understand the demands and details of any new situation I would choose.

"What he meant was: As you can see in my resumé, I've had a lot of good experience. I am a quick study. Do you think any of your clients might be interested in me?"

"At least, that's what I think he meant."

"This fellow's letter reveals him as pompous. He may not be pompous. He may only be a terrible writer. But I haven't the interest or time to find out which . . . Bad writing done him in—with me, at any rate."

Source: Jock Elliott, "How Hard It Is to Write Easily," *Viewpoint: By, For, and About Ogilvy & Mather,* 2, 1980, p. 18. The use of jargon and imprecise expression have become so commonplace that computer programs that analyze grammar, readability, and sentence structure and suggest alternative wordings have been developed to deal with it.

Don't expect your first draft to be satisfactory. First drafts are *never* satisfactory. Expect to rewrite—or at least severely edit—the written research report several times. When rewriting, attempt to reduce the length by half. That forces you to simplify and remove the clutter. It also forces you to think about every word and its purpose, to evaluate whether each word is helping you say what you want to say.

Having a college degree won't protect you from the hazards of unclear writing. In fact, the more educated a person is, the more likely he or she may be to get it wrong. Consider the president of a major university who, in the late 1960s, wrote a letter to soothe anxious alumni after a spell of campus unrest. "You are probably aware," he began, "that we have been experiencing very considerable potentially explosive expressions of dissatisfaction on issues only partially related." He meant that the students had been hassling the university about different things.[2]

conciseness
The degree to which the writing in the report is crisp and direct.

Conciseness

Although the report must be complete, it must also be **concise**. This means that you must be selective in what is included. Don't try to impress the reader with

"WE GOT THE ASPIRIN ACCOUNT! A STUDY SHOWED OUR ADS GIVE PEOPLE HEADACHES."

© HARLEY SCHWADRON

research window 21.3

Some Suggestions When Choosing Words for Marketing Research Reports

1. **Use short words.** Always use short words in preference to long words that mean the same thing.

Use this	Not this
Now	Currently
Start	Initiate
Show	Indicate
Finish	Finalize
Use	Utilize
Place	Position

2. **Avoid vague modifiers.** Avoid lazy adjectives and adverbs and use vigorous ones. Lazy modifiers are so overused in some contexts that they have become clichés. Select only those adjectives and adverbs that make your meaning precise.

Lazy modifiers	Vigorous modifiers
Very good	Short meeting
Awfully nice	Crisp presentation
Basically accurate	Baffling instructions
Great success	Tiny raise
Richly deserved	Moist handshake
Vitally important	Lucid recommendation

3. **Use specific, concrete language.** Avoid technical jargon. There is always a simple, down-to-earth word that says the same thing as the show-off fad word or the vague abstraction.

Jargon	Down-to-Earth English
Implement	Carry out
Viable	Practical, workable
Suboptimal	Less than ideal
Proactive	Active
Bottom line	Outcome

4. **Write simply and naturally—the way you talk.** Use only those words, phrases, and sentences that you might actually say to your reader if you were face to face. If you wouldn't say it, if it doesn't sound like you, don't write it.

Stiff	Natural
The reasons are fourfold	There are four reasons
Importantly	The important point is
Visitation	Visit

5. **Strike out words you don't need.** Certain commonly used expressions contain redundant phrasing. Cut out the extra words.

Don't write	Write
Advance plan	Plan
Take action	Act
Study in depth	Study
Consensus of opinion	Consensus
Until such time as	Until

Source: Table adapted from Chapter 2 of *Writing That Works* by Kenneth Roman and Joel Raphaelson. Copyright © 1981 by Kenneth Roman and Joel Raphaelson, HarperCollins Publishers Inc.

---

everything that you found, every analysis that you ran. If something doesn't pertain directly to the subject, don't try to include it. You should also avoid lengthy discussions of commonly known methods.

Even when the content is appropriate, conciseness can still be violated by writing style. This commonly occurs when the writer is groping for the phrases and words that capture an idea. Instead of finally coming to terms with the idea, the writer writes around it, restating it several times, in different ways, hoping that repetition will overcome poor expression. Concise writing, on the other hand, is effective because it forces the writer to know what she wants to say and then to say it directly. Concise reports say everything that needs to be said, but do so with the minimum number of words.

One helpful technique for accomplishing conciseness is to read the draft aloud. Hearing yourself read the report often helps identify sections that need to be shortened, rewritten, or eliminated.

THE WRITTEN RESEARCH REPORT: OUTLINE

Learning Objective

2. Outline the main elements that make up a standard research report.

Research reports can be organized in a variety of ways. In this section, we'll offer some advice about the key components that need to be in the report, regardless of the specific way that you choose to organize them. Using a good outline can help you achieve clarity, conciseness, accuracy, and completeness in your report. Don't forget that the report format should be guided by the nature and needs of your audience. As a result, the following format should be considered flexible:

1. Title page
2. Table of contents
3. Executive summary
4. Introduction
5. Data collection and results
   a. Methodology
   b. Results
   c. Limitations
6. Conclusions and recommendations
7. Appendices
   a. Copies of data collection forms
   b. Codebook
   c. Technical appendix
   d. Exhibits not included in the body
   e. Data file for archival storage
   f. Bibliography

Title Page

The title page shows the subject/title of the report; the name of the organization, department, or individual for whom the report was written; the name of the organization, department, or individual submitting it; and the date. It is especially important to include the name and contact information of the researcher responsible for the project. If a report is confidential, the names of the individuals authorized to see it must be listed on the title page.

Table of Contents

The table of contents lists the headings and subheadings of the report with page references. The table of contents will also typically include tables and figures and the pages on which they may be found. For most reports, exhibits will be labeled as either tables or figures, with maps, diagrams, and graphs falling into the latter category.

ETHICAL DILEMMA 21.1

As a member of an independent research team, it is your job to write the final report for a client. One of your colleagues whispers to you in passing, "Make it sound very technical. Lots of long words and jargon—you know the sort of thing. We want to make it clear that we earned our money on this one."

- Is it ethical to obscure the substance of a report beneath complex language?
- Will some clients be impressed by words that they do not fully understand?

Executive Summary

Learning Objective

3. Explain the kind of information contained in the executive summary.

The executive summary is the most important part of the report, because many executives will read only the summary. So, it must contain the most essential information in the report. A good strategy when writing the executive summary is to think about what you would most want to communicate about the project if you only had 60 seconds to do so. A good executive summary is no more than one page long.

A good summary contains the necessary background information as well as the important results and conclusions. Whether it contains recommendations is determined to an extent by the reader. Some managers prefer that the writer suggest appropriate action, while others prefer to draw their own conclusions on the basis of the evidence contained in the study.

The summary begins with a statement of who authorized the research and the specific research problems or hypotheses that guided it. Next comes a brief statement about how the data were collected, including the response rate. The most important results obtained in the study are included next, often in "bullet" format. Note that there will be several important results in any project but that only the most important results—typically the ones that directly tie back to the research problems—are highlighted in the executive summary. The key results are followed by conclusions (and maybe recommendations, depending upon what managers want to see).

Introduction

The introduction provides the background information readers need to appreciate the discussion in the remainder of the report. Some form of introduction is almost always necessary. Its length and detail, however, depend upon the audience.

The introduction often serves to define unfamiliar terms or terms that are used in a specific way in the report. For instance, in a study of market penetration of a new product, the introduction might define the market and name the products and companies considered "competitors" in calculating the new product's market share.

The introduction may provide some pertinent history, answering such questions as the following: What similar studies have been conducted? What findings did they produce? What circumstances led to the present study? If readers are familiar with the history of this project and related research or the circumstances that inspired the current research, these items can be omitted. A report going to executives with little background in the particular product or service dealt with would probably have to include them.

The introduction should state the specific research problems being addressed by the research. If the project was part of a larger, overall project, this should be mentioned. Each of the research problems (and hypotheses where appropriate) should be explicitly stated.

Data Collection and Results

The details of the research—its method, results, and limitations—are contained in the next section of the report.

Method The methods section is one of the most difficult sections of the report to write. The writer faces a real dilemma here. She must give enough information so that readers can appreciate the research design, data collection methods, sampling procedures, and analysis techniques that were used without boring or overwhelming her reader. Technical jargon should *not* be used, because many in the audience will not understand it.

Readers must be told whether the design was exploratory, descriptive, or causal (or some combination). They should also be told why the particular design was chosen and what its merits are in terms of the problem at hand. If your project involved multiple stages, say both exploratory and descriptive research, you should present the method, results, and limitations of the stages sequentially (that is, discuss the exploratory stage and its results first, followed by the descriptive stage). In some ways, your methods section is a summary—enough detail, but not too much—of the research proposal we discussed in Chapter 4. Readers should also be told whether the results are based on secondary or primary data. If primary, are they based on observation or questionnaires? And, if the latter, were the questionnaires administered in person, or by mail, e-mail, fax, or telephone? Once again, it is important to mention why the particular method was chosen. What were its perceived advantages over alternative schemes? This may mean discussing briefly the perceived weaknesses of the other data collection schemes that were considered.

Sampling is a technical subject, and the writer cannot usually hope to convey all the nuances of the sampling plan in the body of the report but must be somewhat selective in this regard. At the very minimum, the researcher should answer the following questions:

1. How was the population defined? What were the geographical, age, sex, or other bounds?

2. What sampling units were used? Were they business organizations or business executives? Were they dwelling units, households, or individuals within a household? Why were these particular sampling units chosen?

3. How was the list of sampling units generated? Did this produce any weaknesses? Why was this method used?

4. Were any difficulties experienced in contacting designated sample elements? How were these difficulties overcome, and was bias introduced in the process?

5. Was a probability or nonprobability sampling plan used? Why? How was the sample actually selected? How large a sample was selected? Why was this size chosen?

In essence, the readers need to understand at least three things with respect to the sample: What was done? How was it done? Why was it done?

Results   The results section of the body of the report presents the findings of the study in some detail, often including supporting tables and figures. This section should make up the bulk of the report. The results need to address the specific problems posed and must be presented with some logical structure. Results that are interesting but irrelevant in terms of the specific problems that guided the research should be omitted. By "logical structure," we simply mean that the results section should be organized in some logical way that makes sense to the readers. A word of advice: Very few managers have any interest in seeing computer output or long lists showing frequencies for every variable in the study. It is crucial that you think about how to best organize and present your research findings.

One effective approach is to organize the results section around the questions to be answered by the research. There are typically one or two key issues that are central to the manager's decision problem. Organize the results to provide information and answers to these issues. If a central issue was one of awareness of a particular company, then present the results for the three or four questions used to assess awareness (for example, overall recall, recognition, location recall). If you have useful breakdowns on these variables (for example, perhaps by gender or zip code), present these results in the same section. If another issue driving the research was target market perceptions of the company, organize these results in a subsequent section.

When they are appropriate, tables and figures are usually more effective than plain text for communicating results. Note something, though. Tables, figures, and exhibits of other kinds can not replace text completely. You'll need to explain what the tables and figures are illustrating, including a summary of the results. Still, clients will expect to see keys points illustrated clearly. Tables and figures that appear in this section of the report should each be easy to understand and focused around a single issue. More complex exhibits should appear in the technical appendix. A couple of words of caution: Not every result requires a table or figure. And tables are often the better choice for presenting results, compared with figures. It might be wise to reserve the use of figures for those really important findings that need extra emphasis, because having too many figures can quickly become a distraction.

Limitations It is impossible to conduct a "perfect" study, because every study has limitations. As the researcher, you know what the limitations are, and it is in your better interest to point them out to the reader. Researchers sometimes fear that pointing out a study's limitations will lower the reader's opinion of the quality of the research—or the researcher. Just the opposite is often true. If you don't state the limitations and readers discover them on their own, they may begin to question the whole report. Stating the limitations also allows the researcher to discuss whether, and by how much, the limitations might bias the results. This is important; do you want your research to be held accountable for many sources of error that are beyond your control? Make the limitations of the research clear to everyone.

When discussing the limitations, you'll want to provide some idea of the accuracy with which the work was done. Specifically, discuss the sources of nonsampling error and the suspected direction of their biases. This often means that the researcher provides some limits by which the results are distorted due to these inaccuracies. Readers should be informed specifically as to how far the results can be generalized. To what populations can they be expected to apply? If the study was done in Miami, Florida, readers should be warned not to generalize the results to all U.S. markets. The writer should provide the proper caveats for readers and not make them discover the weaknesses themselves. However, you don't need to overstate the limitations either. Try to take a balanced perspective.

Conclusions and Recommendations

Learning Objective

4. Distinguish between a conclusion and a recommendation.

The results lead to the conclusions and recommendations. Conclusions and recommendations are not the same thing. Conclusions are opinions based on the results; recommendations are suggestions as to appropriate future action. In this section, the writer shows the step-by-step development of the conclusions and states them in greater detail than in the summary. There should be a conclusion for each study research problem. One good strategy is to link research problems and conclusions so closely that the reader—after reviewing the research problems—can turn directly to the conclusions to find a specific conclusion for each objective. If the study does not provide enough evidence to draw a conclusion about a research problem, this should be explicitly stated.

Researchers' recommendations should follow the conclusions. With strategy-oriented research, recommendations should be straightforward; after all, the whole point of the project was to make a decision. Recommendations are less straightforward—and probably more important—with discovery-oriented research. You've collected information and now have some answers; how should the manager use this information? Note, however, that some managers simply prefer to determine the appropriate courses of action themselves and do not want the writer to offer recommendations. Others want the researcher, who is closest to the research, to suggest a course of action. Increasingly, marketing researchers are being asked to interpret the findings in terms of what they mean to the business and to make recommendations as to appropriate courses of action.

Appendices

Learning Objective

5. Describe the kind of information that should be contained in the appendices.

The appendices to the report contain material that is too complex, too detailed, too specialized, or not absolutely necessary for the text. The appendices will typically include as an exhibit a copy of the questionnaire or observation form used to collect the data. They will also contain any maps used to draw the sample. If there are more detailed calculations for such things as sample size justification or test statistics, these will often appear in a technical appendix. It's also a good idea to append a copy of the data collection form that includes the basic univariate results. That way, if all else fails, a manager can at least get an overall look at how respondents answered the questions.

MANAGER'S FOCUS

As we emphasized in the early parts of this book, marketing managers are responsible for evaluating the quality of marketing research studies before using the information they provide. Written research reports are the primary and most comprehensive sources of evidence for this purpose and should, therefore, be carefully scrutinized.

Things to think about: Were the research objectives made explicit, and does the report demonstrate they were actually attained? Is the communication throughout the report clear, concise, complete, and correct? Was a sound research design employed, and were all of the procedures employed equally sound? Are all of the insights offered in the conclusions and recommendations based directly on the research information (or data)? Is the report openly honest about what was done, and was the research conducted in an objective manner? Are the numerical data (or qualitative findings) reliable and trustworthy?

As you assess the degree to which these criteria were met, you must finally answer the big question: Does the report provide clear suggestions for appropriate **action** given my marketing situation, and am I willing to risk my reputation and career by acting on this information? Thus, the ACTION acronym presented below.

- **A**ttained research objectives
- **C**ommunication is clear, concise, complete, and correct
- **T**echnically sound design and procedures
- **I**nformation-based insights in conclusions and recommendations
- **O**bjective and open
- **N**umerically (or qualitatively) reliable and trustworthy

---

There will also often be detailed tables from which the summary tables in the body of the report were generated. The writer should recognize that the appendices typically will be read by only the most technically competent and interested reader.

The research report will probably be the only document that eventually remains of the research project. As a result, it serves an important archival function. In addition to the copy of the data collection form, we suggest that you also include a copy of the codebook along with the actual data file containing the raw data of the project. This usually means including the electronic data file in some form. Some researchers also like to include a printout of the raw data. With the data collection form, the codebook, and the data file, any competent researcher ought to be able to re-create your results—or conduct additional analyses—if necessary, many years into the future. Remember that your current project might become a useful piece of secondary data for some later project.

THE ORAL REPORT

Learning Objective

6. Specify three things to keep in mind when preparing an oral report.

In addition to the written report, most marketing research investigations require one or more oral reports. Often, clients or managers want progress reports during the course of the project. Almost always, they require a formal oral report at the conclusion of the study. The principles surrounding the preparation and delivery of the oral report parallel those for the written report.

This means that those who prepare and present the report need to realize that many listeners will not truly understand the technical ramifications involved in research and certainly will not be able to judge the quality of the research. They can, however, judge whether the research was presented in a professional, confidence-inspiring manner or in a disorganized, uninformed one. A quality presentation can

research window 21.4

OPEN UP! Exceptional Presentation Skills

OPEN UP! is an acronym representing the six characteristics shared by exceptional presenters. The secret is not just knowing the characteristics, but understanding how to incorporate them into your presentation style.

The Exceptional Presenter Is:

Organized Exceptional presenters take charge! They look poised and polished. They sound prepared. You get the sense that they are not there to waste time. Their goal is not to overwhelm, but to inform, persuade, influence, entertain, or enlighten. Their message is well structured and clearly defined.

Passionate Exceptional presenters exude enthusiasm and conviction. If the presenter doesn't look and sound passionate about his or her topic, why would anyone else be passionate about it? Exceptional presenters speak from the heart and leave no doubt as to where they stand. Their energy is persuasive and contagious.

Engaging Exceptional presenters do everything in their power to engage each audience member. They build rapport quickly and involve the audience early and often. If you want their respect, you must first connect.

Natural An exceptional presenter's style is natural. Their delivery has a conversational feel. Natural presenters make it look easy. They appear comfortable with any audience. A presenter who appears natural appears confident.

As an Exceptional Presenter, You Must:

Understand Your Audience Exceptional presenters learn as much as they can about their audience before presenting to them. The more they know about the audience, the easier it will be to connect and engage.

Practice Those who practice improve. Those who don't, don't. Exceptional skills must become second nature. Practice is the most important part of the improvement process. If your delivery skills are second nature, they will not fail under pressure.

Source: Excerpted from Timothy J. Koegel, *The Exceptional Presenter* (Austin, TX: Greenleaf Book Group Press, 2007), pp. 4–5.

---

disguise poor research to some extent, but quality research cannot improve a poor presentation. Research Window 21.4 contains some excellent ideas about becoming an effective presenter.

Preparing the Oral Report

Preparing a successful oral report requires advance knowledge of the audience. What is their technical level of sophistication? What is their involvement in the project? Their interest? Once again, researchers may want to present more detailed reports to those who are deeply involved in the project or who have a high level of technical sophistication than to those who are only slightly involved or interested. In general, it is better to have too little technical detail rather than too much. Executives want to hear and see what the information means to them as managers of marketing activities. What do the data suggest with respect to marketing actions? They can ask for the necessary clarification with respect to the technical details if they want it.

Researchers must also decide in advance how the presentation will be organized. There are two popular forms of organization. Both begin by stating the general purpose of the study and the specific objectives that were addressed. They differ, however, with respect to when the conclusions are introduced. In the more common structure, the conclusions are introduced after all of the evidence supporting a particular course of action is presented. This allows the presenter to build a logical case in sequential fashion.

An alternative approach is to present conclusions immediately after the purpose and main objectives. This is an immediate attention-grabber, especially if the conclusions are surprising. It not only gets managers to think about what actions the results suggest but also causes them to pay close attention to the evidence supporting the conclusions.

A third important aspect of preparing the oral report is the development of effective visual aids. Even if you can avoid the technical aspects of the research in your presentation, it is all but impossible to communicate results without the use of tables and figures. Most oral presentations make use of computer presentation software, such as Microsoft's PowerPoint or Apple's Keynote. Presentation software allows the relatively easy preparation of many different, high-quality kinds of exhibits ranging from definitions, to bulleted lists, to maps, to various types of graphs. Presentation software also allows the presenter to go forward or backward during the presentation or to focus on a particular point. It allows the use of various font sizes, font styles, and colors to create emphasis. It also allows the use of special effects such as the addition of sound or video in the presentation or the use of animation, fading, dissolving, progressively adding or deleting items in an exhibit, all of which can also create some desired emphasis.

Another advantage of preparing the report using computer presentation software is that it can easily be distributed electronically to the appropriate managers. By not being stuck in a file drawer, the research report is more likely to contribute to the company's key learnings or accumulated knowledge about some product or issue.

Regardless of how the visuals are prepared or which types are used, it is important to make sure they can be read by everyone in the room. We have endured far too many presentations in which the words are too small or are so close in color to the slide background that they can't be read. It is also important that visuals be kept simple so that they can be understood at a glance. In addition, obey the other principles of effective visual aid design listed in Research Window 21.5.

> ## ETHICAL DILEMMA 21.2
>
> The results of a research study you supervised are disappointing. Only one of the four basic questions motivating the study has been clearly answered. The answers to the other three questions are rather equivocal in spite of careful planning of the study and a sizable expenditure of money to carry it out. Unanticipated difficulties in contacting people by telephone raised the cost of each contact, which meant the obtained sample was smaller than the planned sample, which in turn made the evidence less clear cut. You are concerned that you and your research team will be evaluated unfavorably because of this. Members of your research team are arguing that when you deliver the oral report to management, you should attempt to somewhat hide the fact that only one of the four basic questions has been answered satisfactorily. The team members propose a multimedia presentation with lots of glitz, with maximum time devoted to the formal presentation and minimum time allowed for questions.
>
> - Is it ethical to hide disappointing results in this way?
> - What are the consequences of doing so?
> - Is it okay to use so much glitz to generate interest in the topic being presented that the glitz overwhelms the substance of the findings? Should you not use glitz at all?

Delivering the Oral Report

You probably already know that speaking in front of people is one of the most frightening, stressful events in life for most people. We've experienced that fear, too, whether teaching a new group of students for the first time, speaking at church, giving speeches, making research presentations, or on other occasions. Delivering an oral marketing research report is no different; it can be an anxious process, especially for researchers with little experience. It turns out, however, that most of the fear can be eliminated with a little preparation prior to the presentation. You're still likely to experience a little anxiety, but that's OK. The complete lack of apprehension would mean that you aren't taking it seriously and may be about to embarrass yourself.

There are two fundamental rules for delivering good oral presentations. Carefully following these rules will also alleviate the fear of speaking in front of people for most people. Here's the first rule: ***Know your stuff.*** It's amazing how much fear is caused by uncertainty. In an oral presentation of a marketing research project, there are many potential sources of uncertainty: the nature of the problem, the processes involved with data collection, what the results really mean, whether decision makers want recommendations in addition to conclusions, what objectives need to be

Learning Objective

7. Discuss two fundamental rules for making good oral presentations.

research window 21.5

Ten Tips for Preparing Effective Presentation Slides

- **Keep them simple.** Present one point per slide, with as few words and lines as possible.

- **Use lots of slides as you talk,** rather than lots of talk per slide. Less is more when you are speaking.

- **Aim for one minute per slide,** then move on. Visuals should make their impact quickly.

- **Highlight and emphasize significant points** using bullets, font sizes or styles, color, or by some other means.

- **Make the slides easy to read.** Use large, legible fonts. Limit fonts to one or two different ones and no more than three sizes. Make certain that the color of the text or exhibits shows up well against the background color.

- **Be careful with the use of color.** Color can add interest and emphasis; it can also distract the audience if not used carefully. Plan your color scheme and use it faithfully throughout.

- **Be careful with the use of slide backgrounds.** A consistent background (figure, logo, etc.) can help the visual display, but not if it gets in the way of communicating the content of the slide.

- **Build complex thoughts sequentially.** If you have a complicated concept to communicate, start with the ground level and use three or four slides to complete the picture.

- **Prepare copies of slides.** Hand them to the audience before or after your presentation. If people have to take notes, they won't be watching or listening closely.

- **Number the slides or pages in the handout.** You will have a better reference for discussion or a question-and-answer period.

ETHICAL DILEMMA 21.3

A colleague confides in you: "I've just run a survey for a restaurant owner who is planning to open a catering service for parties, weddings, and the like. He wanted to know the best way to advertise the new service. In the questionnaire, I asked respondents where they would expect to see advertisements for catering facilities, and the most common source was the newspaper. I now realize that my question only established where people are usually exposed to relevant ads, not where they would like to see relevant ads or where they could most productively be exposed to an ad. All we know is where other caterers advertise! Yet I'm sure my client will interpret my findings as meaning that the newspaper is the most effective media vehicle. Should I make the limitations of the research explicit?"

- What are the costs of making the limitations of the research explicit?
- What are the costs of not doing so?
- Isn't promoting the correct use of the research one of the researcher's prime obligations?

accomplished in the oral report, and so on. If you know what you're talking about, it's much easier to stand up and tell your audience what they need to know. And don't forget to practice. Presenting an oral report without practicing it, perhaps multiple times, is foolhardy; you're asking for trouble.

It's OK to use notes during a presentation; just know how to use them effectively. Sue Hershkowitz-Coore, a communications expert known for her work with salespeople, offers some terrific advice about how to prepare and use notes during a presentation in Research Window 21.6. Knowing your stuff also means knowing how the presentation room will be organized, how the presentation software works, and who will be in your audience.

That brings us back around to the other fundamental rule for making good presentations, one we've already mentioned: **Know your audience.** The audience is likely to be composed of marketing managers, other executives, or others. You need to know your audience at the group and individual levels. If possible, find out in advance who will be attending the oral presentation. Always keep in mind the purpose of the research and the general answers that your overall audience is interested in learning. And you'll also need to understand the level of technical sophistication of the overall audience. For example, if most people listening to you would understand the notions of sampling error or statistical significance, then feel free to talk about these issues if needed.

There are a few other things to keep in mind about the oral presentation. Honor the time limit set for the meeting. Use no more than half of the time for the formal presentation. But be careful not

research window 21.6

Tips for Creating and Using Notes for a Presentation

- **Use key words only.** Don't write full sentences, no matter how good the statement may sound while you're creating it. Notes are helpful only when you can glance at them to know where you are and where you're going. Full sentences can't be absorbed in one glance. Also, if you use full sentences for speaking points, you'll have a greater tendency to want to read from your notes. No one wants to hear you read!

- **As you rehearse, determine which key words remind you of your entire thought.** If you can't reduce them to one to three words, keep working and practicing until you can.

- **Write your notes in a font large enough to see!** Remember, you want to be able to look quickly to find the information you need. That doesn't happen with 12-point Times New Roman font!

- **Icons or other graphic representations can be used in place of words in your notes.** Colors can help, too. Let's say you have three supporting points, but realize that with discussion, you may have time to address only one. Circle that point in a bright color, highlight it, or type it in a different color. That way, when you look at the clock, and your notes, you'll quickly know which point is most important.

- **Almost all presentations have time limits.** To stay on target, add notes that remind you when you're a quarter of the way through, halfway, and three-quarters complete. That way, if you see that you're at your halfway mark, but you've spoken for only five minutes out of a 30-minute presentation, you'll be aware that you should slow down, take questions, or let your audience know you'll be done a bit early! You can add notes to remind yourself to "ask for question" or other cues you're concerned you may forget.

- **Practice with your notes and with everything else you'll use during the presentation.** Consider where you'll place them when you speak. Will they be on a lectern, on a table in front of you, on a desk next to you? Practice with them from that position.

- **If your hand shakes and your notes are in your hand, your [audience] will lose confidence in what you're saying.** Place your notes on a table or desk in a place where you can see them. If there is no table, put them into a small binder or note pad that you can hold as you speak so your shaking is not visible.

- **Don't play with your notes!** Don't roll them up like a scroll and bang them into the palm of your other hand, on the table, or any place else! In fact, it's best to place your notes on something instead of in your hand.

Source: Excerpted from Sue Hershkowitz-Coore, *How to Say It® to Sell It* (New York: Prentice Hall Press, 2008), pp. 147–150.

to rush the presentation of the information contained in the visuals. Remember, the audience is seeing them for the first time. Order your presentation in such a way that there is enough time to both present and discuss the most critical findings. Reserve the remaining time for questions and further discussion.

One of the unique benefits of the oral presentation is that it allows interaction. A question-and-answer period may be the most important part of your presentation. It allows you to clear up any confusion that may have arisen during your talk, to emphasize points that deserve special attention, and to get a feeling for the issues that are of particular concern to your audience.

When delivering the message, use the time-honored principles of public speaking: Keep the presentation simple and uncluttered so that the audience does not have to backtrack mentally to think about what was said, and choose words and sentences that are appropriate for you and your audience.

Learning Objective

8. Explain how the time allotted for an oral presentation should be organized.

MANAGER'S FOCUS

As the client, there are essentially two routes you can take. You can follow the conventional path and passively wait to see if your research supplier's written report and oral presentation meet your expectations and needs. Or, you can be proactive and provide concrete guidelines in advance that your research provider can follow when writing the report and developing the oral presentation.

To illustrate this proactive approach, when a researcher we know was beginning a relationship with a particular client, a manager from the marketing department came to the researcher's office for a one-day orientation/training session. He had developed a standards manual that outlined the company's expectations and standards for each phase of a marketing research project (not simply the report and presentation). Because the client took this initiative, the researcher did not have

to assume what his company expected and desired—he knew with certainty. It provided a sound start to what proved to be a long-term, mutually beneficial relationship.

We highly recommend that you follow a similar approach. By developing a standards manual, you and your colleagues will become clearer in your own minds as to what your specific expectations are. When you develop a clear understanding of your own expectations and needs (which would be very difficult without the knowledge of marketing research you have acquired from this book, research providers, or your own experience), you will be able to communicate them more clearly to your research suppliers, and this will dramatically increase the likelihood you will be satisfied with the services they provide to you.

GRAPHIC PRESENTATION OF THE RESULTS

The old adage that a picture is worth a thousand words is equally true for business reports. A picture, called a *graphic illustration* in the case of the research report, can indeed be worth a thousand words when it is appropriate to the presentation and well designed. When inappropriate or poorly designed, such an illustration may actually detract from the value of the written or oral research report. In this section, we will review briefly some of the most popular forms of graphics and when each is best used.

In a research report, graphic illustration usually involves the presentation of quantities (percentages, mean values, etc.) in graph form. To be effective, it must be more than simply converting a set of numbers into a drawing; the picture must give the readers an accurate understanding of the comparisons or relationships that they would otherwise have to search for in the numbers in the report. If well done, the graphic illustration will give the readers this understanding more quickly, more forcefully, more completely, and more accurately than could be done in any other way.

The use of tables, graphs, and figures is important in an oral presentation, as long as there is time to both present and discuss.

Graphic presentation is not the only way to present quantitative information, nor is it always the best. Sometimes text and tables are better used. Graphics should be used only when they serve the purpose better than other approaches. Written textual material is generally the most useful in explaining, interpreting, and evaluating results; tables are particularly good for providing emphasis and for vivid demonstrations of important findings. Given the ease with which graphs, charts, and other visual displays can be prepared using presentation software, there is no good excuse for not using graphics when appropriate.

Because charts are generally the most useful—and most often used—kinds of graphics in marketing research, the following discussion focuses on some of the more common chart types.

Pie Chart

A **pie chart** is simply a circle divided into sections, with each of the sections representing a portion of the total. Since the sections are presented as part of a whole, or total, the pie chart is particularly effective for depicting relative size or emphasizing static comparisons. Figure 21.1 (resulting from the data of Exhibit 21.2), for instance, shows the breakdown of personal consumption expenditures by major category for a particular year (Year 12). The conclusion is obvious. Expenditures for services account for the largest proportion of total consumption expenditures. Furthermore, expenditures for services and nondurable goods completely dwarf expenditures for durable goods.

Figure 21.1 has three slices, and it is easy to interpret. Had the information been broken into finer categories (for example, if the separate components of durable and nondurable goods had been depicted), a greater number of sections would have been required. Although more information would have been conveyed, emphasis would have been lost. As a rule of thumb, no more than six slices should be generated; the division of the pie should start at the 12 o'clock position; the sections should be organized clockwise in decreasing order of size; and the exact percentages (but remember, no decimal places) should be provided on the graph.

pie chart
A circle representing a total quantity and divided into sectors, with each sector showing the size of the segment in relation to that total.

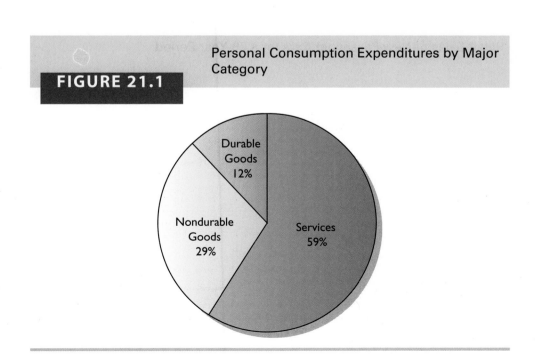

FIGURE 21.1

Personal Consumption Expenditures by Major Category

Durable Goods 12%

Nondurable Goods 29%

Services 59%

| Exhibit 21.2 | Personal Consumption Expenditures for a Recent 12-Year Period (billions of dollars) |

Year	Total Personal Consumption Expenditures	Durable Goods	Nondurable Goods	Services
Year 1	$3,659.3	$480.3	$1,193.7	$1,983.3
Year 2	3,887.7	446.1	1,251.5	2,190.1
Year 3	4,095.8	480.4	1,290.7	2,324.7
Year 4	4,378.2	538.0	1,339.2	2,501.0
Year 5	4,628.4	591.5	1,394.3	2,642.7
Year 6	4,957.7	608.5	1,475.8	2,873.4
Year 7	5,207.6	634.5	1,534.7	3,038.4
Year 8	5,433.7	657.4	1,619.9	3,156.7
Year 9	5,856.0	693.2	1,708.5	3,454.3
Year 10	6,246.5	755.9	1,830.1	3,660.5
Year 11	6,683.7	803.9	1,972.9	3,906.9
Year 12	6,987.0	835.9	2,041.3	4,109.9

Line Chart

line chart
A two-dimensional chart constructed on graph paper with the *x*-axis representing one variable (typically time) and the *y*-axis representing another variable.

The pie chart is a one-dimensional chart, which is why it is best used for static comparisons of a phenomenon at a point in time. The line chart is a two-dimensional chart that is particularly useful in depicting relationships that change over time. For example, Figure 21.2 (produced from the data of Exhibit 21.3) shows that over a 25-year period new car sales of imports were subject to less fluctuation than were sales of domestic autos.

| FIGURE 21.2 | Retail Sales of New Passenger Cars for a 25-Year Period |

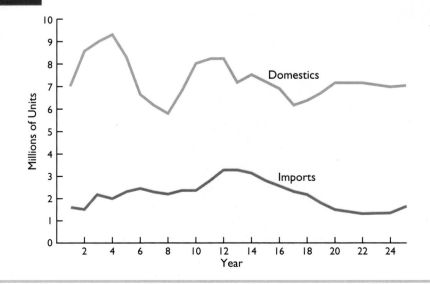

Exhibit 21.3	Retail Sales of New Passenger Cars (millions of units)		
Year	**Domestics**	**Imports**	**Total**
Year 1	7.0	1.6	8.6
Year 2	8.5	1.5	10.0
Year 3	9.0	2.1	11.1
Year 4	9.2	2.0	11.2
Year 5	8.2	2.3	10.5
Year 6	6.6	2.4	9.0
Year 7	6.2	2.3	8.5
Year 8	5.8	2.2	8.0
Year 9	6.8	2.4	9.2
Year 10	8.0	2.4	10.4
Year 11	8.2	2.8	11.0
Year 12	8.2	3.2	11.4
Year 13	7.1	3.2	10.3
Year 14	7.5	3.1	10.6
Year 15	7.1	2.8	9.9
Year 16	6.9	2.6	9.5
Year 17	6.1	2.3	8.4
Year 18	6.3	2.1	8.4
Year 19	6.7	1.8	8.5
Year 20	7.3	1.7	9.0
Year 21	7.1	1.5	8.6
Year 22	7.2	1.3	8.5
Year 23	6.9	1.4	8.3
Year 24	6.7	1.4	8.1
Year 25	7.0	1.7	8.7

The line chart is probably used even more often than the pie chart. The *x*-axis normally represents time, and the *y*-axis represents values of the variable or variables. When more than one variable is presented, use different colors or types of lines (dots and dashes in various combinations) to represent the different variables. And be sure to identify the different variables using a key, or legend.

Stratum Chart

The stratum chart serves in some ways as a dynamic pie chart, in that it can be used to show relative emphasis by sector (for example, quantity consumed by user class) and change in relative emphasis over time. The stratum chart consists of a set of line charts whose quantities are grouped together (or a total that is broken into its components). It is also called a *stacked line chart*. For example, Figure 21.3 (resulting from the data of Exhibit 21.2) shows personal consumption expenditures by major category for the 12-year period. The lowest line shows the expenditures just for services; the second lowest line shows the total expenditures for services plus nondurable goods. Personal consumption expenditures for nondurable goods are thus shown by the area between the two lines. So it is with the remaining area. We would need multiple pie charts (one for each year) to capture the same information, and the message would not be as obvious.

The *x*-axis typically represents time in the stratum chart, and the *y*-axis again captures the value of the variables. The use of color or distinctive cross-hatching is

stratum chart
A set of line charts in which quantities are aggregated or a total is disaggregated so that the distance between two lines represents the amount of some variable.

FIGURE 21.3 Stratum Chart Showing Personal Consumption Expenditures by Major Category

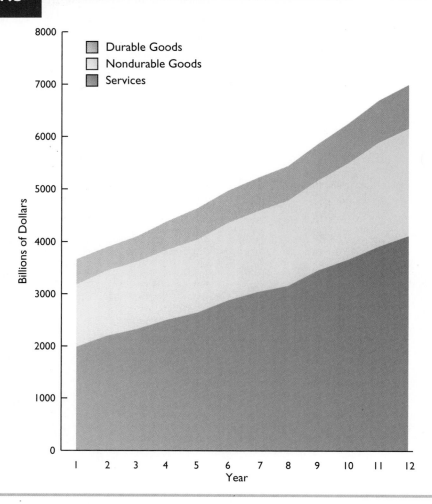

strongly recommended to distinguish the various components in the stratum chart. As was true for the pie chart, no more than six components should be depicted in a stratum chart.

Bar Chart

The **bar chart** can be either a one-scale or a two-scale chart. This feature, plus the many other variations it permits, probably accounts for its wide use. Figure 21.4, for example, is a one-scale chart. It also shows personal consumption expenditures by major category at a single point in time. Figure 21.4 presents the same information as Figure 21.1 but is, in at least one respect, more revealing; it not only offers some appreciation of the relative expenditures by major category but also indicates the magnitude of the expenditures by category.

Figure 21.5, on the other hand, is a two-scale bar chart. It uses the data contained in Exhibit 21.3 and shows total automobile sales for the 25-year period. The *y*-axis represents quantity, and the *x*-axis, time.

Figures 21.4 and 21.5 show that the bar chart can be drawn either vertically or horizontally. When emphasis is on the change in the variable through time, the vertical form is preferred, with the *x*-axis as the time axis. When time is not a variable, either the vertical or the horizontal form is used.

FIGURE 21.4

Bar Chart Showing Personal Consumption Expenditures by Major Category for Year 12

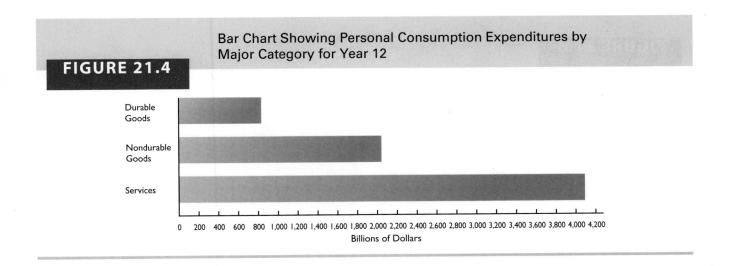

FIGURE 21.5

Bar Chart Showing Total Automobile Sales

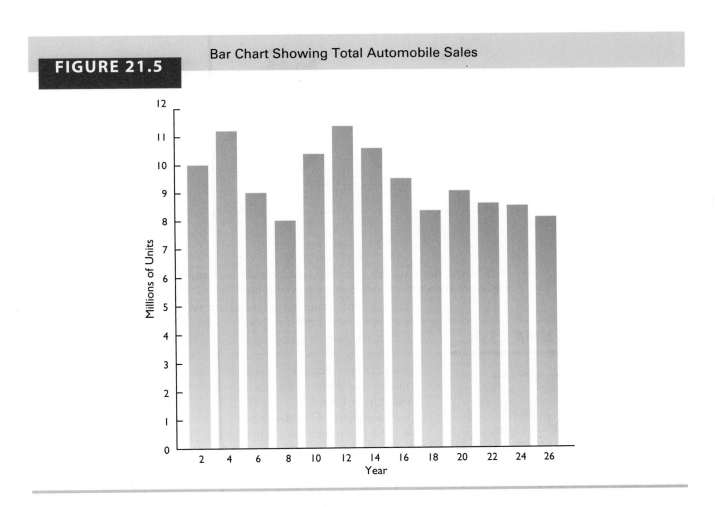

Bar Chart Variations

As you can tell, bar charts are flexible and can be used in many ways. One variation is to convert them to pictograms. Instead of using the length of the bar to capture quantity, amounts are shown by piles of dollars for income, pictures of cars for automobile production, people in a row for population, and so on. This can be a welcome change of pace for the reader if there are a number of graphs in the report. Be careful with

pictogram
A bar chart in which pictures represent amounts—for example, piles of dollars for income, pictures of cars for automobile production, people in a row for population.

FIGURE 21.6   Two Versions of a Pictogram

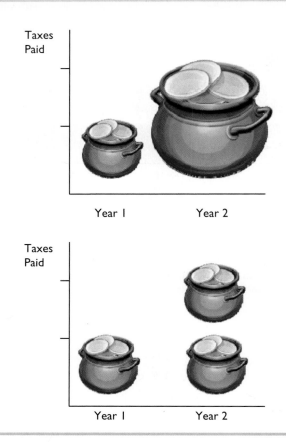

pictograms, however, because they are especially susceptible to perceptual distortions. Figure 21.6 shows two different pictograms, both of which are supposed to communicate the same doubling of corporate taxes paid by a company from one year to the next. For some reason, the top chart makes the tax burden seem much greater, don't you think? The proper form for the pictogram is the bottom version. You need to be especially careful when reading pictograms because it's easy to be led to incorrect conclusions (which may be exactly what those who practice advocacy research are hoping).

A variation of the basic bar chart—the grouped-bar chart—can be used to capture the change in two or more series through time. Figure 21.7, for example, shows the change in consumption expenditures by the three major categories in Exhibit 21.2 across the 12-year period. Just as distinctive symbols are effective in distinguishing the separate series in a line chart, distinctive coloring and/or cross-hatching is equally helpful in a grouped-bar chart.

There is also a bar chart equivalent to the stratum chart—the divided-bar chart or, as it is sometimes called, the stacked-bar chart. Its construction and interpretation are similar to those for the stratum chart. Figure 21.8, for example, is a divided-bar chart of personal consumption expenditures by major category. It shows both total and relative expenditures through time, and it makes use of distinctive color for each component.

ETHICAL DILEMMA 21.4

You are preparing to deliver the final report to top management to make the case that your new advertising campaign has increased sales dramatically in trial areas. Your conceptual arguments on behalf of the new campaign are very convincing, but although there has been a consistent rise in sales in trial areas, the bar charts look rather disappointing: 61,500 units the first month, 61,670 units the next, 61,820 the next. Why, the increase is barely visible! Then you realize how much more exciting your results would look if the *y*-axis were broken above the origin so that the plots started at 50,000 units.

- Where does salesmanship stop and deception start?

FIGURE 21.7

Grouped-Bar Chart Showing Personal Consumption Expenditures by Major Category

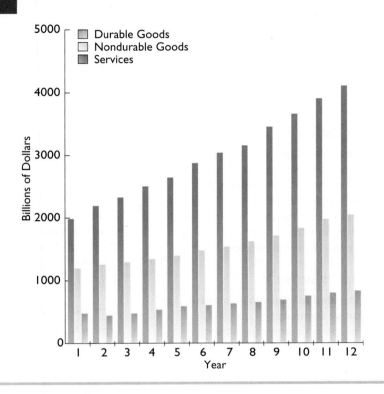

FIGURE 21.8

Divided-Bar Chart Showing Personal Consumption Expenditures by Major Category

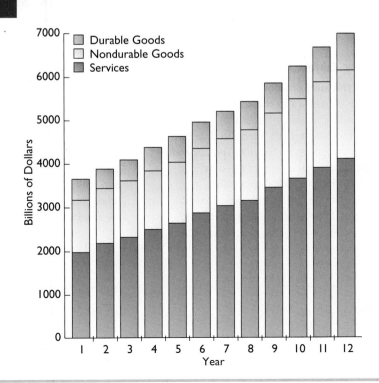

SUMMARY

Learning Objective 1

Identify and discuss four writing standards that a report should meet if it is to communicate effectively with readers.
A report that achieves the goal of communicating effectively with readers is generally one that meets the standards of completeness, accuracy, clarity, and conciseness.

Learning Objective 2

Outline the main elements that make up a standard research report.
A standard report generally contains the following elements: title page, table of contents, executive summary, introduction, data collection and results, conclusions and recommendations, and appendices.

Learning Objective 3

Explain the kind of information contained in the executive summary.
A good executive summary gives the most important points of the report, especially focusing on key results, conclusions, and recommendations.

Learning Objective 4

Distinguish between a conclusion and a recommendation.
A conclusion is an opinion based on the results. A recommendation is a suggestion as to appropriate future action.

Learning Objective 5

Describe the kind of information that should be contained in the appendices.
The appendix contains material that is too complex, too detailed, too specialized, or not absolutely necessary for the text. The appendix will typically contain a copy of the data collection form, a technical appendix containing detailed calculations and exhibits too complicated for the text, the codebook,

a copy of the data file for archival purposes, and a copy of the data collection form with basic univariate results for the items on the form.

Learning Objective 6

Specify three things to keep in mind when preparing an oral report.
Three important things to keep in mind when preparing an oral report are (1) know your audience, (2) organize the presentation carefully, and (3) use visual aids in your presentation.

Learning Objective 7

Discuss two fundamental rules for making good oral presentations.
When presenting oral reports the two fundamental rules are (1) know your stuff and (2) know your audience.

Learning Objective 8

Explain how the time allotted for an oral presentation should be organized.
Honor the time limit set for the meeting. Use no more than half of the time for the formal presentation. Reserve the remaining time for questions and discussion.

Learning Objective 9

List some of the different kinds of charts that can be used in presenting study results.
A number of different charts can be used. Some of these include (1) pie charts, (2) line charts, (3) stratum charts, (4) bar charts, (5) pictograms, (6) grouped-bar charts, and (7) divided-bar charts.

Learning Objective 10

Cite the reason bar charts are so widely used.
The bar chart can be either a one-scale or a two-scale chart. This feature, plus the many other variations it permits, probably accounts for its wide use.

KEY TERMS

completeness (page 487)
accuracy (page 488)
clarity (page 488)
conciseness (page 489)
pie chart (page 501)

line chart (page 502)
stratum chart (page 503)
bar chart (page 504)
pictogram (page 505)

REVIEW QUESTIONS

1. What is the most important goal of a research report? Explain.

2. What is meant by the written report standards of completeness, accuracy, clarity, and conciseness?

3. On the one hand, it is argued that the research report must be complete and, on the other, that it must be concise. Are these two objectives incompatible? If so, how do you reconcile them?

4. What is the essential content of each of the following parts of the research report?

   a. Title page

   b. Table of contents

   c. Executive summary

   d. Introduction

   e. Data collection and results

   f. Conclusions and recommendations

   g. Appendices

5. What are the key considerations in preparing an oral report?

6. What are the two rules for presenting the oral report?

7. What is a pie chart? For what kinds of information is it particularly effective?

8. What is a line chart? For what kinds of information is it generally used?

9. What is a stratum chart? For what kinds of information is it particularly appropriate?

10. What is a bar chart? For what kinds of problems is it effective?

11. What is a pictogram?

12. What is a grouped-bar chart? When is it used?

DISCUSSION QUESTIONS, PROBLEMS, AND PROJECTS

1. It should be clear from your reading of this chapter that a professional marketing researcher must possess a well-developed ability to write effectively. Many colleges and universities offer a variety of programs designed to help students develop their writing skills. These programs may take a variety of forms, such as writing labs, special seminars, word-processing tutorials, one-on-one writing tutors, and regular written communication classes. Prepare a research report of the resources available at your school that can be used to enhance written communication skills. Assume that your report will be furnished to incoming first-year students as part of their orientation materials.

2. The owner of a medium-sized home-building center specializing in custom-designed and do-it-yourself bathroom supplies requested the Liska and Leigh Consulting Firm to prepare a report on the customer profile of the bathroom design segment of the home-improvement market. Evaluate the following excerpts from the report:

   Research report excerpts
   The customer market for the company can be defined as the do-it-yourself and bathroom design segments. A brief profile of each follows.

   The do-it-yourself (DIY) market consists of individuals in the 25–45 age group living in a single dwelling. DIY customers are predominantly male, although an increasing number of females are becoming active DIY customers. The typical DIY customer has an income in excess of $20,000, and the median income is $29,100 with a standard deviation of 86. The DIY customer has an increasing amount of leisure time, is strongly value- and convenience-conscious, and displays an increasing desire for self-gratification.

The mean age of the custom bathroom design segment is 41.26, and the annual income is in the range of $55,000 to $65,000. The median income is $59,000 with a standard deviation of 73. The custom bathroom design customers usually live in a single dwelling. The wife is more influential and is the prime decision maker about bathroom designs.

3. Discuss the difference between conclusions and recommendations in research reports.

4. Assume that Wendy's International, Inc., wants to diversify into another fast-food area. You are required to prepare a brief report for the company executives outlining an attractive opportunity. In preparing the report, go through the following steps:

    a. Decide on the particular fast-food area you think is most appropriate.

    b. Collect secondary data relating to the area and analyze consumption trends over the past five years.

    c. Decide on the outline of the report and its various sections.

    d. Develop the appropriate tables and charts to support your analysis.

    e. Write the report.

5. Describe the information that should be contained in the executive summary, and discuss why this is the most important part of the research report.

6. In presenting a report to a group of grocery store managers, a researcher stated the following: "The data from the judgment sample of 10 grocery stores were analyzed and the results show that the 95% confidence interval for average annual sales in the population of grocery stores is $1,000,000 +/− $150,000."

    a. As far as the audience is concerned, what is wrong with this statement?

    b. Rewrite the statement. Be sure to include all the relevant information while correcting the problem.

7. Your marketing research firm is preparing the final written report on a research project commissioned by a major manufacturer of lawn mowers. One objective of the project was to investigate seasonal variations in sales, both on an aggregate basis and by each of the company's sales regions individually. Your client is particularly interested in the width of the range between maximum and minimum seasonal sales. The following table was submitted by one of your junior analysts. Critique the table and prepare a revision suitable for inclusion in your report.

Seasonal Sales Variation				
	SALES IN THOUSANDS OF DOLLARS			
Sales Region	**Spring**	**Summer**	**Fall**	**Winter**
Northeast	$120.10	$140.59	$ 50.90	$ 30.00
East-central	118.80	142.70	61.70	25.20
Southeast	142.00	151.80	134.20	100.10
Midwest	100.20	139.42	42.90	20.00
South-central	80.77	101.00	90.42	78.20
Plains	95.60	120.60	38.50	19.90
Southwest	105.40	110.50	101.60	92.10
Pacific	180.70	202.41	171.54	145.60

8. The management of Seal-Tight Company, a manufacturer of metal cans, has presented you with the following information:

Seal-Tight Company: A Comparative Statement of Profit and Loss for the Fiscal Years 2004–2008					
	2004	**2005**	**2006**	**2007**	**2008**
Net sales	$40,000,000	$45,000,000	$48,000,000	$53,000,000	$55,000,000
Cost and expenses Cost of goods sold	$28,000,000	$32,850,000	$33,600,000	$39,750,000	$40,150,000
Selling and admin. expenses	4,000,000	4,500,000	4,800,000	5,300,000	5,500,000
Depreciation	1,200,000	1,350,000	1,440,000	1,590,000	1,650,000
Interest	800,000	900,000	960,000	1,060,000	1,100,000
	$34,000,000	$39,600,000	$40,800,000	$47,700,000	$48,400,000
Profits from operations	$ 6,000,000	$ 5,400,000	$ 7,200,000	$ 5,300,000	$ 6,600,000
Estimated taxes	2,400,000	2,160,000	2,880,000	2,120,000	2,640,000
Net profits	$ 3,600,000	$ 3,240,000	$ 4,320,000	$ 3,180,000	$ 3,960,000

a. Develop a visual aid to present the company's distribution of sales revenues in 2004.

b. Develop a visual aid that would compare the change in the net profit level with the change in the net sales level.

c. Develop a visual aid that will present the following expenses (excluding cost of goods sold) over the five-year period: selling and administration expenses and depreciation and interest expenses.

d. The management of Seal-Tight has the following sales data relating to its two major competitors:

	2004	**2005**	**2006**	**2007**	**2008**
Metalmax Co.	$35,000,000	$40,000,000	$42,000,000	$45,000,000	$48,000,000
Superior Can Co.	$41,000,000	$43,000,000	$45,000,000	$46,000,000	$48,000,000

You are required to prepare a visual aid to facilitate the comparison of the sales performance of Seal-Tight Company with its major competitors.

9. Most universities and colleges offer a variety of computer graphics software for student use in campus microcomputer labs. Investigate the availability of graphics software on your campus. Prepare a report outlining your findings. Be sure to include the following information for each available package:

a. Name of package and basic capabilities

b. Location(s) of access point(s)

c. Times available for use

d. Name of contact person(s) for further information

e. Any special skills required for use and availability of training if needed

f. Access fees, if any

g. Hard-copy formats available (e.g., laser printers, color printers, transparencies)

10. Visit a local library and find examples of each of the graphic illustrations described in this chapter. Look for these in such publications as *Business Week, Fortune, Newsweek,* and *The Wall Street Journal.* Make a copy of each chart and critique it, using the criteria noted in the text. For example, does the pie chart you found exceed the recommended maximum number of divisions? Are the exact percentages displayed? In each case, is the chart appropriate for its intended purpose, or would another type of chart be more informative? Are there any changes you might recommend if the chart were to be used in an oral presentation?

case 1

Barbecue Blues Sauce Company[1]

Background Information

Shamara Williams was an accountant in Peoria, Illinois, and had two hobbies about which she was very passionate, collecting blues music and perfecting her homemade barbecue sauce recipe. She regularly entertained guests by playing her music and feeding them dishes prepared with her barbecue sauce. Four years ago, at the urging of her friends, she abruptly quit her job to pursue a life-long dream of owning her own business. Using her savings and money borrowed from family members, she purchased a small food processing facility and began bottling her sauce. Because her two hobbies had always been inseparable, Ms. Williams decided to employ the name *Barbecue Blues* as her brand. Thus, Barbecue Blues Sauce Company was born.

The initial strategy was to sell the sauce through retail grocery stores and specialty food markets within a three-state region. Indeed, the strategy was so effective that after three years, *Barbecue Blues* had captured an 18% share of the retail barbecue sauce market in the region. The third and fourth years of operation were stable, but there was virtually no growth in unit sales, and increases in revenue were largely attributable to inflation. To assist her in devising a strategy for sales growth, Ms. Williams hired a marketing director, Heather Cohen.

Ms. Cohen advocated extending the line of barbecue sauces, so Ms. Williams created a new "Chicago style" barbecue sauce. She gathered together the group of friends who had originally encouraged her to enter the barbecue sauce business. After sampling the new sauce, all of them thought it was very different from the original sauce in terms of flavor, but of the same level of quality. This positive initial response led Ms. Cohen to commission a marketing research study to be conducted by InfoGather to determine consumer reactions to the new sauce.

Shortly before the marketing research report was completed, Ms. Cohen resigned from Barbecue Blues Sauce Company to take a position at a larger food processing company, so Ms. Williams needs your assistance in interpreting the study's findings. The Executive Summary of the report is presented in Exhibit 1.

Exhibit 1   **InfoGather: Barbecue Blues Restaurants Study**

Executive Summary

Marketing Problem

    To determine whether the new barbecue sauce formula should be marketed, in addition to the original **Barbecue Blues** sauce, through retail grocery and specialty stores; and if so, which of the following two brand names should be used: **Barbecue Blues–Chicago Style Sauce** or **Barbecue Blues–Spicy Blend Sauce**?

Summary of Findings

Of the 728 study participants:

    Approximately 83% claimed to use barbecue sauce at home (i.e., 56% use it frequently and 27% use it occasionally). Of these 604 barbecue sauce users . . .

- Approximately 41% use barbecue sauce exclusively when cooking outdoors, 24% use barbecue sauce exclusively when cooking indoors, and 35% use barbecue sauce for both indoor and outdoor cooking.

The average number of times in the last month barbecue sauce was used while cooking at home was 2.67.

Approximately 52% reacted favorably to the new barbecue sauce (i.e., 21% liked it and 31% liked it very much).

- Approximately 49% reacted favorably when "Chicago Style" was the subbrand name (i.e., 12% liked it and 37% liked it very much).
- Approximately 53% reacted favorably when "Spicy Blend" was the subbrand name (i.e., 29% liked it and 24% liked it very much).

Approximately 43% indicated they would be likely to purchase the new barbecue sauce (i.e., 25% were likely and 19% were very likely).

- Approximately 45% indicated they would be likely to purchase the new barbecue sauce when "Chicago Style" was the subbrand name (i.e., 27% were likely and 18% were very likely).

---

[1]This case was prepared by Jon R. Austin, Ph.D., Associate Professor of Marketing, Cedarville University, 251 North Main Street, Cedarville, OH 45314.

Questions

1. Based on the information provided in the Executive Summary, would you recommend the new formulation of barbecue sauce be marketed, in addition to the original sauce, through retail grocery and specialty foods markets? Why or why not?

2. If you are recommending marketing the new barbecue sauce, use information from the Executive Summary to develop a strong justification for which of the two subbrand names, *"Chicago Style"* or *"Spicy Blend,"* should be employed.

case 2

Kinshasa Abroad—African Cuisine and Culture (A)[1]

Youlou Kabasella owned and operated a restaurant and nightclub in Kinshasa, Zaire, for nearly 14 years. The restaurant's menu was filled with popular dishes and drinks from the region. In addition to his food and beverage services, Mr. Kabasella provided a dance floor and live Zairian/Congolese rumba and soukous music. While the popularity of most musical styles in Africa were largely confined to specific countries or regions, rumba and soukous were popular throughout the African continent.

Anticipating increased political turmoil, Mr. Kabasella and his family left Zaire in 1995 and ended up living with relatives in Dayton, Ohio. Soon thereafter, they moved to Columbus, Ohio, where he worked odd jobs to make ends meet. A Columbus businessperson befriended him and offered to loan him the capital necessary to establish a new restaurant. In 2003, Mr. Kabasella opened Kinshasa Abroad in the downtown area of Columbus. Like his former restaurant, it has a dance floor and features Zairian/Congolese rumba and soukous music. On most nights, recorded music from the top artists of the genre is played. There are, however, a few Congolese bands, such as Tabu Ley Rochereau & Orchestra Afrisa International and Les Quatre Etoiles (The Four Stars), that occasionally tour the United States and as a favor to their fellow countryman (Mr. Kabasella) play at Kinshasa Abroad whenever they are in the area. A cover of $10 is charged when there are live acts, but there is otherwise no cover charge. The restaurant has 20 quads (tables for four), 15 deuces (tables for two), and larger parties can be accommodated by pushing tables together.

Mr. Kabasella and his wife prepare and serve a variety of African entrees. Some of their specialties include Peanut Stew, Beef and Greens in Peanut Sauce, Muamba Nsusu (Congo chicken soup), Malay Curry (stewed lamb in a curry sauce), Samaki wa Kupaka (grilled fish in a coconut-tamarind sauce), Nyama Choma (roasted spare ribs seasoned with curry), and Liboke de Poisson (fish in banana leaf). The entrees are accompanied by various African side dishes such as Plantains in Coconut Milk, Baton de Manioc and Chikwangue (made from cassava tubers), Irio (peas, potatoes, corn, and greens), Maharagwe (red beans), and Mbaazi wa Nazi (pigeon peas in coconut milk). The Kabasellas also serve a variety of soft drinks imported from Africa along with the usual American beverages found in casual dining restaurants.

When contemplating opening the restaurant, Mr. Kabasella had predicted it would generate immediate interest due to the cultural diversity in the Columbus area. Moreover, because of the restaurant's proximity to Ohio State University, he thought there would be a high level of awareness and interest in African cuisine and music. Despite his optimism, and the ads he regularly places in local and school newspapers, Mr. Kabasella has been discouraged by the fact that customer turnout and revenue have been far short of what had been projected.

Questions

1. If you were to serve as a research consultant for Mr. Kabasella, what information would you need to enable you to help him diagnose his marketing problem(s)?
2. Create a list of probing questions you would ask Mr. Kabasella if you were going to meet with him to help him specify (a) the manager's decision problem and (b) research problems.

---

[1]This case was prepared by Jon R. Austin, Ph.D., Associate Professor of Marketing, Cedarville University, 251 North Main Street, Cedarville, OH 45314.

case 3
E-Food and the Online Grocery Competition

When everybody's busy, something's got to give. The online grocery industry (that is, grocery shopping online and home delivery of purchased items) has developed slowly over the past 20 years to address today's consumer demands of convenience and time savings. Perhaps the best known provider in the industry is Peapod.com, an operation that began outside Chicago. Since its founding in 1989, it has expanded to 18 U.S. markets, making over 10 million deliveries to over 270,000 customers. Other national competitors have entered the market, but only a few have had any staying power. One of these is netgrocer .com which delivers groceries and an assortment of other merchandise as well across the country using FedEx. In addition to larger multi-market online grocers, there have been many local providers.

Online grocery services typically provide virtual stores through which the electronic visitor navigates, as if pushing a shopping cart in a traditional grocer. The user clicks on items to purchase, which are placed in the user's cart. When complete, the user is "checked out," specifying a delivery date and time. Users pay delivery costs proportionate to each shopping bill.

The software allows the user to store his or her preferences in a personal shopping list that can be altered, adding or deleting items as necessary with each e-visit. Across the various providers, the software also usually allows easy consumer comparison. For example, the SKUs in a particular category may be sorted by brand name, by price, by value (price per ounce, for example), by what is on "feature" (sale and point-of-purchase promotions), by various dietetic goals (such as "healthy," "low fat"), and so on. The user may write in "notes," to specify in more detail, for example, "Please pick up green (unripe) bananas, not yellow ones," or "If Fancy Feast is out of beef, please get turkey instead," which

instruct the professional shopper as to the user's particular preferences. Categories of items that can be purchased are continually expanding, from foods to drugstore items and other merchandise.

Online grocery providers tend to conduct the online business very well, if customer satisfaction, repeat visits, and word-of-mouth advertising are any indicators. That is, the software provided, the merchandise selected, the delivery reliability, and so on, are valued by the customer, with few complaints. Most users are women, employed full-time, and married, with well-above-average household incomes.

Ashley Sims is an M.B.A. student, taking her last term of classes, and thinking about starting up a local online grocer. She's certain that by learning from the templates of the current providers in other markets, she, too, can run the logistics of the business. However, she hopes that, given her contacts with computer experts, she can create a competitive advantage in the software setup, if she understands the consumers' mindset as they travel through the e-grocery stores. She wants to know just what a user is thinking from the first click onto the Web site to the last "Done Shopping" click off the site. This knowledge would allow her to offer better advice to her software developers in terms of what features would facilitate the visitors' navigation through the grocery store. Data like these would help improve the system, and it would also lend great insight to the consumers' decision processes.

Questions

1. What is the decision problem?
2. What is (are) the research problem(s)?
3. Prepare a research proposal to submit to an online grocer on behalf of your research team.

case 4

Kinshasa Abroad—African Cuisine and Culture (B)[1]

Youlou Kabasella and his wife opened a restaurant in Columbus, Ohio, called Kinshasa Abroad. The underlying concept is to provide a unique African cultural experience in terms of cuisine, music, and atmosphere. Mr. Kabasella had expected immediate success due to the cultural diversity in the area and proximity to Ohio State University. However, customer turnout and revenue have fallen well short of his projections. He is seeking guidance from a consultant as to how marketing research might help him understand why performance has been below expectations and identify some possible ways to turn around performance.

Bill Christianson returned to his office after his initial meeting with Mr. Kabasella at Kinshasa Abroad. He felt confident that Mr. Kabasella had answered his questions honestly and comprehensively. However, he was less confident that the client's perspective alone was a sufficient basis for formulating the marketing problem. As he reflected on the meeting, he began to create a list of questions he had about what might account for the lackluster performance of Kinshasa Abroad.

It is clear that Mr. Kabasella is not pursuing a well-defined market segment, but that is probably true of most restaurants in the area, perhaps even of some that are highly successful. But what segments would be most inclined to frequent Kinshasa Abroad? What groups would be most interested in African food and beverages? Would these same groups be the ones most interested in African music? Are there groups interested in dancing in a restaurant environment?

The absence of a target market might account for why the advertising messages Mr. Kabasella places in local newspapers are so general in nature. What have consumers thought when they have seen these ads? Specifically, what comes to mind when they think of African food, African beverages, or African music? Are their thoughts at all consistent with what the food, beverages, and music are really like? Among consumers who have not tried Kinshasa Abroad, what would their reactions be if they sampled African food, beverages, or music? Are there more effective ways to communicate the nature of an African restaurant to people in Ohio? Are there some "hot button" advertising themes that could be employed if Mr. Kabasella better understood certain consumer groups?

Apart from the above questions, there is the issue of the perceived quality of the menu items at Kinshasa Abroad. In particular, have previous patrons been satisfied with their dining experiences? Also, how satisfied were they with the atmosphere? What has motivated previous patrons to try Kinshasa Abroad? Have they been motivated by cultural curiosity, a more basic search for novelty, or something else? Was this a one-time-only experience, or do they see Kinshasa Abroad as a viable dining alternative in the future?

At a broader level, what are people in the area seeking when they dine out on different occasions? What types of food and entertainment are they seeking when they go to restaurants on these occasions? Does Kinshasa Abroad provide an experience that is consistent with what is being sought on any of these occasions? What changes might Kinshasa Abroad consider in its concept to make itself more attractive to consumer groups in Columbus, Ohio?

These questions and more kept swirling around in Bill's mind as he tried to identify Kinshasa Abroad's underlying marketing problem(s). Because you were also at the meeting with Mr. Kabasella, Bill shared his thoughts with you and asked you to help him attack these issues.

Questions

1. What consumer groups (possible target markets) should be studied using exploratory research methods?
2. What secondary sources are available that might provide useful information for this project?
3. Sort through the issues Bill Christianson identified above and any others you think may be relevant. Which ones would be best addressed using depth interviews, and which ones would be more appropriately investigated with focus group interviews?
4. Create a list of open-ended questions you would propose using in the depth interviews to capture the insights necessary to more precisely define Kinshasa Abroad's marketing problem(s).
5. Create a list of open-ended questions a focus group moderator could use to guide participants through a discussion of issues that might generate insights concerning Kinshasa Abroad's marketing problem(s).

[1]This case was prepared by Jon R. Austin, Ph.D., Associate Professor of Marketing, Cedarville University, 251 North Main Street, Cedarville, OH 45314.

case 5

Student Computer Lab[1]

A major university served over 2,000 undergraduate and graduate students majoring in business administration. The large number of students enrolled in the Business School coupled with increasing use of computer technology by faculty and students created overwhelming demands on the Business School's computer center. In order to respond, the Business School decided to upgrade its computer facilities.

Rod Stevenson, director of the Student Computer Center (SCC), opened a new computer lab in the fall of 2007. The new lab offered specialized software required by student courses and the latest technology in hardware and software.

Computer Lab Project

After operating for six months, Stevenson recognized some potential problems with the new computer lab. Although the number of computers had doubled, student suggestions and complaints indicated that the demand for computers at times exceeded the available resources. To address this problem, Stevenson established a task force to investigate the level of student satisfaction with the computer lab. The task force was made up of four graduate students and was established in January 2008. The task force aimed to help the computer lab identify student needs and provide suggestions on how those needs could be most effectively met.

The first activity of the task force was to examine available information on the lab and its functions and resources. Services offered by the computer lab included network and printer access. The lab usually had three to four lab monitors to collect money for printouts and answer any of the student's questions. Lab hours were 8:00 a.m. to 9:30 p.m. on weekdays and 8:00 a.m. to 5:00 p.m. on Saturdays and Sundays.

After reviewing available information on the lab, the task force decided it needed to conduct some research before making recommendations on the services offered. Exhibit 1 displays a proposal written by the task force outlining the information to be obtained and the time frame for the research.

Focus Group Study

Stevenson received the proposal and approved it. He agreed with the task force's use of focus groups to gain a preliminary understanding of the students' attitudes. The focus groups would identify existing problems better than secondary research, although the process of collecting and analyzing the data would be more time consuming. After receiving approval, the task force posted information around the Business School to alert students that focus groups were being conducted. Free laser copies were offered as an incentive for participation. Students were selected based on their interest. The student focus group was held on March 10, 2008. Seven students participated, five graduate and two undergraduate. Transcripts are provided in Exhibit 2.

Because one of the responsibilities of the lab monitors is to assist students with questions and problems, separate focus groups were also conducted on March 9, 2008, and March 11, 2008, with eight lab monitors. Information from both the student and lab monitor focus groups was used as a guide to develop questions for the second phase, a student survey. Information from the focus groups was reduced to a list of key issues, which were then categorized. An exhaustive list of statements was devised to address potential user attitudes with respect to each issue. When the list was complete, statements were revised, combined, or eliminated to a set that succinctly covered the original key issue categories. The questionnaire was then pretested and finally administered to a sample of students attending class in the Business School.

Questions

1. Did the moderator do an adequate job of getting the information needed by the SCC?
2. Do you think it was wise to have a group with both graduate and undergraduate students included?
3. Analyze the focus group transcript very thoroughly. Make a list of problems and ideas generated for the student computer lab.
4. What do you see as the benefits and limitations of the focus group findings? Do you think the task force plan for utilizing the focus groups is appropriate?

---

[1]The contributions of Monika E. Wingate to the development of this case are gratefully acknowledged.

Exhibit 1   **Task Force Proposal**

DATE: February 1, 2008
TO: Rod Stevenson
FROM: Computer Center Improvement Task Force
RE: Computer Lab Research Proposal

Background: In 2007, the Business School opened a new student computer lab. Through suggestions and complaints, the SCC realizes that there is a service delivery problem in that student demand for computers at times exceeds available resources. The aim of this research is to help the SCC identify student needs and provide suggestions on how those needs can be most effectively met. The results of this research will be limited to the student computer lab. Other Business School computer facilities, such as the computer classrooms and the multimedia lab, are outside the scope of this project.

Objectives: The research objectives are as follows:

- Determine overall student satisfaction with the lab
- Identify current problem areas
- Collect student recommendations for improvements

Methodology: The research design is divided into two parts, exploratory research followed by descriptive research. The exploratory research would attempt to gain a better understanding of students' perceptions of the computer lab and to identify the issues that concern them. The student survey would aim to quantify the magnitude of these problems and to develop recommendations.

Focus Groups: The task force feels that focus groups would be the most appropriate method for exploratory research. Two sets of focus groups are recommended. One set will focus on students who use the computer lab, while the other will address the lab monitors who deal with student problems on a daily basis.

Student Survey: The focus group information would be used to develop questions for a subsequent survey. Since the population of interest is students enrolled in the Business School, this survey would be administered to students attending classes within the Business School, both graduates and undergraduates.

Time Schedule	Completed By
Focus Groups	March 11
Questionnaire Design	April 2
Pretest Questionnaire	April 9
Survey	April 23
Data Analysis	May 10

Exhibit 2   **Student Focus Group Transcript**

Moderator: I'm Robert from Professional Interviewing. I really appreciate your participation in this group session. As you can see, I am taping this session so I can review all of your comments. We are here tonight to talk about the computer lab at the Business School. As business students, you all have access to the lab for your class assignments. How do you think the computer lab is meeting your needs?

Lisa: I think there is a problem with the lab because the folks who are using computers don't know about computers. That's been reflected in the fact that you go to one computer and you pick up a virus. These people don't know anything about viruses, they're transmitting them all over the place, nobody is scanning for viruses, and there's something that could easily be put on the systems.

Oliver: I think there has to be training for the people who are watching the computers. They are ignorant. You ask them any question and they can't answer it. It's a computer lab and this computer doesn't seem to be doing the thing that it should be doing, why? Why is this network different from the rest? How are we supposed to handle this network? They don't know.

Lisa: Not only that, they don't know any of the software.

Oliver: Absolutely!

Lisa: This is like I have Word at home and this is WordPerfect, "How do I do XYZ in WordPerfect?" They don't know. They say, let me go check with John and it takes three of them to try to answer the question.

(Continued)

Exhibit 2   **Student Focus Group Transcript (Continued)**

Marion: And there are three of them!

Lisa: I know!

Oliver: There is always a big queue so you cannot get onto a Windows machine; you have to go to Pagemaker Plus if you need to make a presentation. You cannot go to these WordPerfect machines that have just keyboard entries. But there are very few computers and a lot of lines in the peak times and they are just not equipped to handle it. They have so many staff over there, five people, all of these people, but not one of them will help anyone.

Moderator: How about you, Jennifer, have you experienced this?

Jennifer: Yeah, I even had it today. I just don't have time to wait in line to get a computer. It's a half hour sometimes to go in and get one.

Lisa: And that's now. At the end of the semester it's worse.

Jennifer: Yeah, it gets worse.

Lisa: It takes an hour and there's no sign-up. There's no regular sign-up.

Mike: They truncated the hours the last two weeks of the semester.

Jennifer: You could take these four people and turn that into one educated person, or take the four people and have one uneducated person there 24 hours a day. That would be nice. If all they're going to do is take your card and give you your copy, why do you have to have four of them? That's all they're doing. And studying.

Moderator: How about you, I didn't get your name?

Tammy: Tammy.

Moderator: Welcome, Tammy, how about you. What kind of things have you come across?

Tammy: What I'm hearing are a lot of the problems I've seen, too. I just think there needs to be more computers in the lab and the hours need to be longer.

Mike: I don't think they need more computers. They just need to expand the hours and the computing labs.

Oliver: I had an idea where they don't need more computers. One suggestion I already put in the suggestion box is to have people bring their own computers. Why doesn't a grad student who is going to be here for two years, going to interface with technology when he leaves here, spend a thousand dollars and go buy his own system? They should do that. Have your own computer here, I'm saying it's a requirement. It's a requirement at a lot of universities that you come with your own system. Then you don't have to worry, you don't need access to our labs. Now for undergraduates we still have similar problems, but it would put less stress on the system.

Moderator: What would you suggest for people who would say, okay I can get this computer system, but I have to get this software for this class, and this software for this class, and this software. That is a lot of money.

Oliver: Yeah, we can already jump into the network from home. All you need is the software.

Lisa: I don't think so.

Oliver: You can get in. I can check my mail and stuff.

Lisa: But not software.

Oliver: Oh, software. I haven't tried, so I don't know.

Tammy: Getting back to the machine. I'd love to have my own machine but I don't want to have it if I don't have to. As long as we have all these other computers, why not use what we've got?

Mike: I can't afford it. If you want to buy a good computer, a decent printer, a decent monitor, you are still going to spend between $1,600 and $2,000.

Oliver: I think while we're in school the school should support us with computers.

Mike: I think one of the reasons there aren't enough computers is that people who aren't enrolled in the Business School have access to the lab. In the old building, they always checked your ID.

Tammy: Yeah. Why don't we use the card machines? They were working, weren't they? They had the doors closed and you used a key card.

Oliver: I think the old lab was better because they controlled people coming and going.

Exhibit 2   **Student Focus Group Transcript** (*Continued*)

Mike: Yeah. Gatekeeping.

Tammy: They had hours when only graduate students could come in. I think that's something that should be started again because they have a lot more papers to type up.

Mike: I don't see why this lab isn't open 24 hours. I really don't. Why aren't the labs open 24 hours?

Lisa: Monitor problem, they need someone to monitor them, to work with them.

Jennifer: Three people, three eight-hour shifts.

Mike: They don't have a budget to increase their hours. They need to double the hours, like not having four monitors at one time.

Moderator: There are peak hours and there are hours that there are a lot of open computers, where people don't generally come in. If there was a way to monitor those times and put a schedule up, people could come in and indicate a time when we could go there. Continually monitor that, what do you think about that?

Mike: Every hour is a peak hour, particularly at the end of the semester.

Oliver: I think it would be a good way of trying to smooth it out, because that's what you are trying to do. Have people go there when it's not so busy. But then what about times like today? I happened to get out of class one-half hour early and went downstairs and used it. But if I hadn't signed up early, there were a million folks in there. There are some trade-offs, but I think it's a great idea to try and smooth it out. This morning there were four of us in there at 8:00 or 8:15 when it opened, and I don't think anybody else showed up until 10:00.

Mike: Another problem in the lab right now is that there are a lot of computers that are broken at one time.

Oliver: Oh yeah!

Mike: There are six of them right now that aren't working.

Oliver: That's from people not knowing what they are doing. I was sitting down there on one of the old machines and there was a gentleman sitting next to me who couldn't figure out why it wouldn't work. He took his disk out and shut the computer off. When it came back on it got a boot error. Then he got scared and he just left. He didn't go tell anyone. The monitors are looking from the other side, so they don't know there is anything wrong. Someone comes in, they just look around, and see that the computer is broken, or it's not booted up, and so on. That's why I am saying, it's the students themselves. People need to know how to use the system.

Ira: I think there should be a small note pasted next to the computers with instructions as to how to use each computer.

Marion: Even a template for the word processing.

Ira: Even a small hint for troubleshooting, please don't do this and do this.

Tammy: I think an excellent model for this are the computer labs in the dorms. The first time you use them, they scan your ID to be sure you are a dorm resident, they know if it's the first time you are using it, they ask you to make sure you know how to use the software. They have a rack with every different kind of title and anything you need to use the software. They tell you exactly what's going to come up on the machine and what you have to do. I'm sure the Business School can get copies of it all and then just copy it.

Marion: We have no reference guides for the software.

Tammy: And then they have the guides there. The little orange books.

Moderator: Are there any other concerns we haven't talked about?

Ira: Is there any way the cost for a laser print can be reduced?

Tammy: It kills me.

Ira: It should be 7 cents. It is 6 cents in the library.

Tammy: You used to have the option to go to a dot matrix printer. They changed that this semester. The only way to go to the dot matrix was to go to an AT&T machine. Don't tell me someone is looking at cost.

Ira: I think the initial cost is pretty high, that is why they're keeping it at 10 cents.

Jennifer: If they are planning on getting more printers, I think they should have at least one or two individual print stations where you can grab your stuff. If you're working on your resume and you want to print on bond paper or do envelopes, the people behind the desk won't let you do it because they don't know if other people are going to send before you do, they don't know what is going to come out.

(Continued)

Exhibit 2   **Student Focus Group Transcript** (*Continued*)

Oliver: Or they waste your paper because they can't coordinate it.

Jennifer: So I think there should be some individual workstations.

Oliver: I have something to say and maybe I'm the only one with this problem. I always find that when I go there and I am working alone, other groups are creating a racket, so it's really frustrating. I'm working on a project, I need to think. I don't need this kind of heavy distraction, this loud talk. I go and work in groups too, we try to whisper. There should be some kind of discipline in the computer lab. I think I may be the only one being that sensitive, but I think silence has to be maintained. It is a computer lab, it is a place for people working, if you're having a fun time go have it outside.

Moderator: How effective do you think their waiting lists system is?

Tammy: It stinks.

Ira: I didn't even know they had one.

Tammy: It would be better to set up a physical waiting list where there would be chairs or a bench or something like that.

Ira: Or like a number.

Tammy: Or six chairs in a row and you sit down next to the computers and that means you are next to get on; then if you leave the next person can move down and then you can see that no one is getting in front of you.

Oliver: It worked pretty well for me. Every time I used the waiting list I had to wait for maybe a half hour and my name was called and I could get a computer. I have no complaints. This happened every time. There was no problem. I had no problems at all.

Mike: Until now I didn't even know there was a waiting list. If there was an open computer, I would just sit down.

Tammy: I found out the hard way, I went down and sat down and someone told me.

Jennifer: It's not very consistent. It's kind of whenever they feel like.

Moderator: Anything else?

Jennifer: I have one comment about the resources, since we are able to use the resources like e-mail and the Internet. The Internet's great, but if you don't know any of the numbers to call out, it's kind of a useless thing. But there are books out there with the numbers that cost about $30 and if you keep one of the books as a reference copy at the desk for people to look at, I think it would be a great resource. I looked at the bookstore once, and it's incredible the different things you can search for on the Internet.

Tammy: Good point. I think they could put it down there with all the reference items.

Jennifer: I think they need more computers and longer hours. They're not meeting the demands.

Ira: At least the building hours.

Tammy: Match the library's hours. They're open 100 plus hours a week. Sunday night. They could close earlier on Friday and Saturday night (like 8:00 a.m. to 11:00 p.m.).

Jennifer: And do it during exams, too—all of a sudden it's close to 5:00 and even Memorial Library is open later than that.

Moderator: We're close to wrapping up. Is there anything else?

Tammy: Oh, can I get templates? For the word processing, I don't know how to use them. You have to use control that, shift that.

Ira: They used to have them. Just photocopy them.

Moderator: Is there anything else? I want to thank all of you. Your concerns will definitely be evaluated and considered. I have some printout cards for all of you. I knew I would give you $5.00 for each copy, but as it turned out there's $9.75 on each card.

case 6

Chestnut Ridge Country Club[1]

The Chestnut Ridge Country Club has long maintained a distinguished reputation as one of the outstanding country clubs in the Elma, Tennessee, area. The club's golf facilities are said by some to be the finest in the state, and its dining and banquet facilities are highly regarded as well. This reputation is due in part to the commitment by the board of directors of Chestnut Ridge to offer the finest facilities of any club in the area. For example, several negative comments by club members regarding the dining facilities prompted the board to survey members to get their feelings and perceptions of the dining facilities and food offerings at the club. Based on the survey findings, the board of directors established a quality control committee to oversee the dining room, and a new club manager was hired.

Most recently, the board became concerned about the number of people seeking membership to Chestnut Ridge. Although no records are kept on the number of membership applications received each year, the board sensed that this figure was declining. They also believed that membership applications at the three competing country clubs in the area—namely, Alden, Chalet, and Lancaster—were not experiencing similar declines. Because Chestnut Ridge had other facilities, such as tennis courts and a pool, that were comparable to the facilities at these other clubs, the board was perplexed as to why membership applications would be falling at Chestnut Ridge.

To gain insight into the matter, the board of directors hired an outside research firm to conduct a study of the country clubs in Elma, Tennessee. The goals of the research were (1) to outline areas in which Chestnut Ridge fared poorly in relation to other clubs in the area; (2) to determine people's overall perception of Chestnut Ridge; and (3) to provide recommendations for ways to increase membership applications at the club.

Research Method

The researchers met with the board of directors and key personnel at Chestnut Ridge to gain a better understanding of the goals of the research and the types of services and facilities offered at a country club. A literature search of published research relating to country clubs uncovered no studies. Based solely on their contact with individuals at Chestnut Ridge, therefore, the research team developed the survey contained in Exhibit 1. Because personal information regarding demographics and attitudes would be asked of those contacted, the researchers decided to use a mail questionnaire.

The researchers thought it would be useful to survey members from Alden, Chalet, and Lancaster country clubs in addition to those from Chestnut Ridge for two reasons: (1) Members of these other clubs would be knowledgeable about the levels and types of services and facilities desired from a country club and (2) They had at one time represented potential members of Chestnut Ridge. Hence, their perceptions of Chestnut Ridge might reveal why they chose to belong to a different country club.

No public documents were available that contained a listing of each club's members. Consequently, the researchers decided to contact each of the clubs personally to try to obtain a mailing list. Identifying themselves as being affiliated with an independent research firm conducting a study on country clubs in the Elma area, the researchers first spoke to the chairman of the board at Alden Country Club. The researchers told the chairman that they could not reveal the organization sponsoring the study but that the results of their study would not be made public. The chairman was not willing to provide the researchers with the mailing list. The chairman cited an obligation to respect the privacy of the club's members as his primary reason for turning down the research team's request.

The researchers then made the following proposal to the board chairman: In return for the mailing list, the researchers would provide the chairman a report on Alden members' perceptions of Alden Country Club. In addition, the mailing list would be destroyed as soon as the surveys were sent. The proposal seemed to please the chairman, for he agreed to give the researchers a listing of the members and their addresses in exchange for the report. The researchers told the chairman they had to check with their sponsoring organization for approval of this arrangement.

The research team made similar proposals to the chairmen of the boards of directors of both the Chalet and Lancaster country clubs. In return for a mailing list of the club's members, they promised each chairman a report outlining their members' perceptions of their clubs, contingent on approval from the research team's sponsoring organization. Both chairmen agreed to supply the requested list of members. The researchers subsequently met with the Chestnut Ridge board of directors. In their meeting, the researchers outlined the situation and asked for the board's approval to provide each of the clubs with a report in return for the mailing lists. The researchers emphasized that the report would

[1]The contributions of David M. Szymanski to the development of this case are gratefully acknowledged.

1. Of which club are you currently a member? _____
2. How long have you been a member of this club? _____
3. How familiar are you with each of the following country clubs?

   Alden Country Club
   _____ very familiar (I am a member or I have visited the club as a guest)
   _____ somewhat familiar (I have heard of the club from others)
   _____ unfamiliar

   Chalet Country Club
   _____ very familiar (I am a member or I have visited the club as a guest)
   _____ somewhat familiar (I have heard of the club from others)
   _____ unfamiliar

   Chestnut Ridge Country Club
   _____ very familiar (I am a member or I have visited the club as a guest)
   _____ somewhat familiar (I have heard of the club from others)
   _____ unfamiliar

   Lancaster Country Club
   _____ very familiar (I am a member or I have visited the club as a guest)
   _____ somewhat familiar (I have heard of the club from others)
   _____ unfamiliar

4. The following is a list of factors that may be influential in the decision to join a country club. Please rate the factors according to their importance to you in joining your country club. Circle the appropriate response, where 1 = not at all important and 5 = extremely important.

Golf facilities	1	2	3	4	5
Tennis facilities	1	2	3	4	5
Pool facilities	1	2	3	4	5
Dining facilities	1	2	3	4	5
Social events	1	2	3	4	5
Family activities	1	2	3	4	5
Number of friends who are members	1	2	3	4	5
Cordiality of members	1	2	3	4	5
Prestige	1	2	3	4	5
Location	1	2	3	4	5

5. The following is a list of phrases pertaining to Alden Country Club. Please place an X in the space that best describes your impressions of Alden. The ends represent extremes; the center position is neutral. Do so even if you are only vaguely familiar with Alden.

Club landscape is attractive.	:__:__:__:__:__:__:	Club landscape is unattractive.
Clubhouse facilities are poor.	:__:__:__:__:__:__:	Clubhouse facilities are excellent.
Locker room facilities are excellent.	:__:__:__:__:__:__:	Locker room facilities are poor.
Club management is ineffective.	:__:__:__:__:__:__:	Club management is effective.
Dining room atmosphere is pleasant.	:__:__:__:__:__:__:	Dining room atmosphere is unpleasant.
Food prices are unreasonable.	:__:__:__:__:__:__:	Food prices are reasonable.
Golf course is poorly maintained.	:__:__:__:__:__:__:	Golf course is well maintained.
Golf course is challenging.	:__:__:__:__:__:__:	Golf course is not challenging.
Membership rates are too high.	:__:__:__:__:__:__:	Membership rates are too low.

6. The following is a list of phrases pertaining to Chalet Country Club. Please place an X in the space that best describes your impressions of Chalet. Do so even if you are only vaguely familiar with Chalet.

Club landscape is attractive.	:__:__:__:__:__:__:	Club landscape is unattractive.
Clubhouse facilities are poor.	:__:__:__:__:__:__:	Clubhouse facilities are excellent.
Locker room facilities are excellent.	:__:__:__:__:__:__:	Locker room facilities are poor.

Club management is effective.   :__:__:__:__:__:__: Club management is ineffective.
Dining room atmosphere is pleasant.   :__:__:__:__:__:__: Dining room atmosphere is unpleasant.
Food prices are unreasonable.   :__:__:__:__:__:__: Food prices are reasonable.
Food quality is excellent.   :__:__:__:__:__:__: Food quality is poor.
Golf course is poorly maintained.   :__:__:__:__:__:__: Golf course is well maintained.
Golf course is challenging.   :__:__:__:__:__:__: Golf course is not challenging.
Tennis courts are in excellent condition.   :__:__:__:__:__:__: Tennis courts are in poor condition.
There are too many tennis courts.   :__:__:__:__:__:__: There are too few tennis courts.
Membership rates are too high.   :__:__:__:__:__:__: Membership rates are too low.

7. The following is a list of phrases pertaining to Chestnut Ridge Country Club. Please place an X in the space that best describes your impressions of Chestnut Ridge. Do so even if you are only vaguely familiar with Chestnut Ridge.

Club landscape is attractive.   :__:__:__:__:__:__: Club landscape is unattractive.
Clubhouse facilities are poor.   :__:__:__:__:__:__: Clubhouse facilities are excellent.
Locker room facilities are excellent.   :__:__:__:__:__:__: Locker room facilities are poor.
Club management is ineffective.   :__:__:__:__:__:__: Club management is effective.
Dining room atmosphere is pleasant.   :__:__:__:__:__:__: Dining room atmosphere is unpleasant.
Food prices are unreasonable.   :__:__:__:__:__:__: Food prices are reasonable.
Food quality is excellent.   :__:__:__:__:__:__: Food quality is poor.
Golf course is poorly maintained.   :__:__:__:__:__:__: Golf course is well maintained.
Tennis courts are in poor condition.   :__:__:__:__:__:__: Tennis courts are in excellent condition.
There are too many tennis courts.   :__:__:__:__:__:__: There are too few tennis courts.
Swimming pool is in poor condition.   :__:__:__:__:__:__: Swimming pool is in excellent condition.
Membership rates are too high.   :__:__:__:__:__:__: Membership rates are too low.

8. The following is a list of phrases pertaining to Lancaster Country Club. Please place an X in the space that best describes your impressions of Lancaster. Do so even if you are only vaguely familiar with Lancaster.

Club landscape is attractive.   :__:__:__:__:__:__: Club landscape is unattractive.
Clubhouse facilities are poor.   :__:__:__:__:__:__: Clubhouse facilities are excellent.
Locker room facilities are excellent.   :__:__:__:__:__:__: Locker room facilities are poor.
Club management is ineffective.   :__:__:__:__:__:__: Club management is effective.
Dining room atmosphere is pleasant.   :__:__:__:__:__:__: Dining room atmosphere is unpleasant.
Food prices are unreasonable.   :__:__:__:__:__:__: Food prices are reasonable.
Food quality is excellent.   :__:__:__:__:__:__: Food quality is poor.
Golf course is poorly maintained.   :__:__:__:__:__:__: Golf course is well maintained.
Tennis courts are in poor condition.   :__:__:__:__:__:__: Tennis courts are in excellent condition.
There are too many tennis courts.   :__:__:__:__:__:__: There are too few tennis courts.
Swimming pool is in poor condition.   :__:__:__:__:__:__: Swimming pool is in excellent condition.
Membership rates are too high.   :__:__:__:__:__:__: Membership rates are too low.

9. Overall, how would you rate each of the country clubs? Circle the appropriate response, where 1 = poor and 5 = excellent.

Alden	1	2	3	4	5
Chalet	1	2	3	4	5
Chestnut Ridge	1	2	3	4	5
Lancaster	1	2	3	4	5

10. The following questions are designed to give a better understanding of the members of country clubs.

Have you ever been a member of another club in the Elma area?

_____yes   _____no

Approximately what is the distance of your residence from your club in miles?

_____0–2 miles   _____3–5 miles   _____6–10 miles   _____10+ miles

Age: _____21–30   _____31–40   _____41–50   _____51–60   _____61 or over
Sex: _____male   _____female
Marital status: _____married   _____single   _____widowed   _____divorced

Number of dependents including yourself:

_____2 or less   _____3–4   _____5 or more

(Continued)

Total family income:

_____ Less than $20,000
_____ $20,000–$29,999
_____ $30,000–$49,999
_____ $50,000–$99,999
_____ $100,000 or more
_____ Do not know/Refuse to answer

Thank you for your cooperation!

contain no information regarding Chestnut Ridge nor information by which each of the other clubs could compare itself to any of the other clubs in the area, in contrast to the information to be provided to the Chestnut Ridge board of directors. The report would only contain a small portion of the overall study's results. After carefully considering the research team's arguments, the board of directors agreed to the proposal.

Membership Surveys

A review of the lists subsequently provided by each club showed that Alden had 114 members, Chalet had 98 members, and Lancaster had 132 members. The researchers believed that 69 to 70 responses from each membership group would be adequate. Anticipating a 70 to 75% response rate because of the unusually high involvement and familiarity of each group with the subject matter, the research team decided to mail 85 to 90 surveys to each group; a simple random sample of members was chosen from each list. In all, 87 members from each country club were mailed a questionnaire (348 surveys in total). Sixty-three usable surveys were returned from each group (252 in total) for a response rate of 72%.

Summary results of the survey are presented in the exhibits. Exhibit 2 gives members' overall ratings of the

country clubs, and Exhibit 3 shows their ratings of the various clubs on an array of dimensions. Exhibit 4 is a breakdown of attitudes toward Chestnut Ridge by the three different membership groups: Alden, Chalet, and Lancaster. The data are average ratings of respondents. Exhibit 2 scores are based on a five-point scale, where "1" is poor and "5" is excellent. The last two are based on seven-point scales in which "1" represents an extremely negative rating and "7" an extremely positive rating.

Questions

1. What kind of research design is being used? Is it a good choice?
2. Do you think it was ethical for the researchers not to disclose the identity of the sponsoring organization? Do you think it was ethical for the boards of directors to release the names of their members in return for a report that analyzes their members' perceptions toward their own club?
3. Overall, how does Chestnut Ridge compare to the other three country clubs (Alden, Chalet, and Lancaster)?
4. In what areas might Chestnut Ridge consider making improvements to attract additional members?

Exhibit 2

Average Overall Ratings of Each Club by Club Membership of the Respondent

Club Rated	Membership			Composite Ratings Across All Members
	Alden	Chalet	Lancaster	
Alden	4.57	3.64	3.34	3.85
Chalet	2.87	3.63	2.67	3.07
Chestnut Ridge	4.40	4.44	4.20	4.35
Lancaster	3.60	3.91	4.36	3.95

Exhibit 3

Average Ratings of the Respective Country Clubs across Dimensions

| | Country Club | | | |
Dimension	Alden	Chalet	Chestnut Ridge	Lancaster
Club landscape	6.28	4.65	6.48	5.97
Clubhouse facilities	5.37	4.67	6.03	5.51
Locker room facilities	4.99	4.79	5.36	4.14
Club management	5.38	4.35	5.00	5.23
Dining room atmosphere	5.91	4.10	5.66	5.48
Food prices	5.42	4.78	4.46	4.79
Food quality	a	4.12	5.48	4.79
Golf course maintenance	6.17	5.01	6.43	5.89
Golf course challenge	5.14	5.01	a	4.77
Condition of tennis courts	b	5.10	4.52	5.08
Number of tennis courts	b	4.14	4.00	3.89
Swimming pool	b	b	4.66	5.35
Membership rates	4.49	3.97	5.00	4.91

[a]Question not asked
[b]Not applicable

Exhibit 4

Attitudes toward Chestnut Ridge by Members of the Other Country Clubs

Dimension	Alden	Chalet	Lancaster
Club landscape	6.54	6.54	6.36
Clubhouse facilities	6.08	6.03	5.98
Locker room facilities	5.66	5.35	5.07
Club management	4.97	5.15	4.78
Dining room atmosphere	5.86	5.70	5.41
Food prices	4.26	4.48	4.63
Food quality	5.52	5.75	5.18
Golf course maintenance	6.47	6.59	6.22
Condition of tennis courts	4.55	4.46	4.55
Number of tennis courts	4.00	4.02	3.98
Swimming pool	5.08	4.69	4.26
Membership rates	5.09	5.64	4.24

case 7

Suchomel Chemical Company

Suchomel Chemical Company was an old-line chemical company that was still managed and directed by its founder, Jeff Suchomel, and his wife, Carol. Jeff served as president and Carol as chief research chemist. The company, which was located in Savannah, Georgia, manufactured a number of products that were used by consumers in and around their homes. The products included waxes, polishes, tile grout, tile cement, spray cleaners for windows and other surfaces, aerosol room sprays, and insecticides. The company distributed its products regionally. It had a particularly strong consumer following in the northern Florida and southern Georgia areas.

The company had not only managed to maintain but had also increased its market share in several of its key lines in the past half dozen years in spite of increased competition from the national brands. Suchomel Chemical had done this largely through product innovation, particularly innovation that emphasized modest product alterations rather than new technologies or dramatically new products. Jeff and Carol both believed that the company should stick to the things it knew best rather than try to be all things to all people and in the process spread the company's resources too thin, particularly given its regional nature. One innovation the company was now considering was a new scent for its insect spray, which was rubbed or sprayed onto a person's body. The new scent had undergone extensive testing both in the laboratory and in the field. The tests indicated that it repelled insects, particularly mosquitoes, as well as or even better than the two leading national brands. One thing that the company was particularly concerned about as it considered the introduction of the new brand was what to call it.

The Insecticide Market

The insecticide market had become a somewhat tricky one to figure out over the past several years. Although there had been growth in the purchase of insecticides in general, much of this growth had occurred in the tank liquid market. The household spray market had decreased slightly during the same time span. Suchomel Chemical had not suffered from the general sales decline, however, but had managed to increase its sales of spray insecticides slightly over the past three years. The company was hoping that the new scent formulation might allow it to make even greater market share gains.

The company's past experience in the industry led it to believe that the name that was given to the new product would be a very important element in the product's success, because there seemed to be some complex interactions between purchase and usage characteristics among repellent users. Most purchases were made by married women for their families. Yet repeat purchase was dependent on support by the husband that the product worked well. Therefore, the name must appeal to both the buyer and the end user, but the two people are not typically together at the time of purchase. To complicate matters further, past research indicated that a product with a name that appeals to both purchaser and end user would be rejected if the product's name and scent do not match. In sum, naming a product that is used on a person's body is a complex task.

Research Alternatives

The company followed its typical procedures in developing possible names for the new product. First, it asked those who had been involved in the product's development to suggest names. It also scheduled some informal brainstorming sessions among potential customers. Subjects in the brainstorming sessions were simply asked to throw out all the names they could possibly think of with respect to what a spray insecticide could or should be called. A panel of executives, mostly those from the product group but a few from corporate management as well, then went through the names and reduced the large list down to a more manageable subset based on their personal reactions to the names and subsequent discussion about what the names connoted to them. The subset of names was then submitted to the corporate legal staff, who checked them for possible copyright infringement. Those that survived this check were discussed again by the panel, and a list of 20 possibilities was generated. Those in the product group were charged with the responsibility of developing a research design by which the final name could be chosen.

The people charged with the name test were considering two different alternatives for finding out which name was preferred. Both alternatives involved personal interviews at shopping malls. More specifically, the group was planning to conduct a set of interviews at one randomly determined mall in Atlanta, Savannah, Tallahassee, and Orlando. Each set of interviews would involve 100 respondents. The target respondents were married females, ages 21 to 54, who had purchased the product category during the past year. Likely looking respondents would be approached at random and asked if they had used any insect spray at all over the past year and then asked their age. Those who qualified would be asked to complete the insecticide-naming exercise using one of the two alternatives being considered.

Alternative 1 involved a sort of the 20 tentative names by the respondents. The sort would be conducted in the following way. First, respondents would be asked to sort the 20 names into two groups based on their appropriateness for an insect repellent. Group 1 was to consist of the 10 best names and Group 2 the 10 worst. Next, respondents would be asked to select the four best from Group 1 and the four worst from Group 2. Then they would be asked to pick the one best from the subset of the four best and the one worst from the subset of the four worst. Finally, all respondents would be asked why they picked the specific names they did as the best and the worst.

Alternative 2 also had several stages. All respondents would first be asked to rate each of the 20 names on a seven-point semantic differential scale with end anchors "Extremely inappropriate name for an insect repellent" and "Extremely appropriate name for an insect repellent." After completing this rating task, they would be asked to spray the back of their hands or arm with the product. They would then be asked to repeat the rating task using a similar scale, but this time it was one in which the polar descriptors referred to the appropriateness of the name with respect to the specific scent. Next they would be asked to indicate their interest in buying the product by again checking one of the seven positions on a scale that ranged from "Definitely would not buy it" to "Definitely would buy it." Finally, each respondent would be asked why she selected each of the names she did as being most appropriate for insect repellents in general and the specific scent in particular.

Questions

1. Evaluate each of the two methods being considered for collecting the data. Which would you recommend and why?
2. How would you use the data from each method to decide what the brand name should be?
3. Do you think that personal interviews in shopping malls are a useful way to collect these data? If not, what would you recommend as an alternative?

case 8

Premium Pizza Inc.[1]

The past several decades have shown an increase in the use of promotions (coupons, cents-off deals marked on the package, free gifts, etc.), primarily because of their success at increasing short-term purchase behavior. In fact, sales promotion has been estimated to account for over one-half of the typical promotion budget, while advertising accounts for less than half. In many industries, however, the initial benefit of increased sales has resulted in long-term escalation of competition. As firms are forced to "fight fire with fire," special offer follows special offer in a never-ending spiral of promotional deals.

The fast-food industry has been one of the most strongly affected by this trend. Pizzas come two for the price of one; burgers are promoted in the context of a double-deal involving cuddly toys for the kids; tacos are reduced in price on some days, but not on others. It is within this fiercely competitive, erratic environment that Premium Pizza Corporation has grown from a small local chain into an extensive Midwestern network with national aspirations. Over the past few years, Jim Battaglia, vice president of marketing, has introduced a number of promotional offers, and Premium Pizza parlors have continued to flourish. Nevertheless, as the company contemplates further expansion, Jim is concerned that he knows very little about how his customers respond to his promotional deals. He believes that he needs a long-term strategy aimed at maximizing the effectiveness of dollars spent on promotions. And, as a first step, he thinks it is important to assess the effectiveness of his existing offers.

Specific Objectives

In the past, Jim has favored the use of five types of coupons, and he now wants to determine their independent appeal, together with their relation to several identifiable characteristics of fast-food consumers. The five promotional concepts are listed in Exhibit 1. The consumer characteristics that Jim's experience tells him warrant investigation include number of children living at home, age of youngest child, propensity to eat fast food, propensity to eat Premium Pizza in particular, preference for slices over pies, propensity to use coupons, and occupation.

The specific research problems of the study can be summarized as follows:

- Evaluate the independent appeal of the five promotional deals to determine which deals are most preferred;
- Determine why certain deals are preferred; and
- Examine the relationships between the appeal of each promotional concept and various consumer characteristics.

Proposed Methodology

After much discussion, Jim's research team finally decided that the desired information could best be gathered by means of personal interviews, using a combination of open- and closed-ended questions. A medium-sized shopping mall on the outskirts of a metropolitan area in the Midwest was selected as the research site. Shoppers were intercepted by professional interviewers while walking in the mall and asked to participate in a survey requiring five minutes of their time.

The sampling procedure used a convenience sample in which interviewers were instructed to approach anyone passing by, provided that they met certain criteria (see Exhibit 2). In sum, the sample of respondents was restricted to adult men and women between the ages of 18 and 49 who had both purchased lunch, dinner, or carryout food at a fast-food restaurant in the past seven

Exhibit 1	**Five Promotional Concepts**

Coupon A: Get a medium soft drink for 5 cents with the purchase of any slice.

Coupon B: Buy a slice and get a second slice of comparable value free.

Coupon C: Save 50 cents on the purchase of any slice and receive one free trip to the salad bar.

Coupon D: Buy a slice and a large soft drink and get a second slice free.

Coupon E: Get a single-topping slice for only 99 cents.

[1]The contributions of Jacqueline C. Hitchon to this case are gratefully acknowledged.

days and had eaten restaurant pizza within the last 30 days, either at a restaurant or delivered to the home. In addition, interviewers were warned not to exercise any bias during the selection process, as they would do, for example, if they approached only those people who looked particularly agreeable or attractive. Finally, interviewers were asked to obtain as close as possible a 50–50 split of male and female participants.

The questionnaire was organized into three sections (Exhibit 3). The first section contained the screening questions aimed at ensuring that respondents qualified for the sample. In the second section, respondents were asked to evaluate on 10-point scales the appeal of each of the five promotional concepts based on two factors:

perceived value and likelihood of use. After they had evaluated a concept, interviewees were asked to give reasons for their likelihood-of-use rating. The third and final section consisted of the questions on consumer characteristics that Jim believed to be pertinent.

The questionnaire was to be completed by the interviewer based on the respondent's comments. In other words, the interviewer read the questions aloud and wrote down the answer given in each case by the interviewee. It was decided to show respondents an example of each coupon before they rated it. For this purpose, enlarged photographs of each coupon were produced. It was also thought necessary to depict the 10-point scales that consumers would use to evaluate the promotional

---

Exhibit 2 — Interviewer Instructions

Below are suggestions for addressing each question. Please read all of the instructions before you begin questioning people.

Interviewer Instructions
Approach shoppers who appear to be between 18 and 49 years of age. Since we would like equal numbers of respondents in each age category and a 50% male-female ratio, please do not select respondents based on their appeal to you. The interview should take approximately five minutes. When reading questions, read answer choices *if indicated.*

Question 1: Terminate any respondent who has not eaten lunch or dinner from any fast-food restaurant in the last seven days.

Question 2: Terminate any respondent who has not eaten pizza within the last 30 days. This includes carry-out, drive-thru, or dining in.

Question 3: Terminate respondent if not between 18 and 49 years of age. If between 18 and 49, circle the appropriate number answer. For this question, please read the question and the answer choices.

After completing questions 1 through 3, hand respondent the coupon booklet. *Make sure that the booklet and the response sheets are the same color.* Also check to see that the coupon booklet number indicated on the upper right-hand corner of the response sheet matches the coupon book number.

Question 4: Ask the respondent to open the coupon booklet and read the first coupon concept. Read the first section of Question 4 showing the respondent that the scales are provided on the page above the coupon concept. Enter his or her answer in the box provided.
　　Read the second section of the question and enter respondent's answer in the second box provided.
　　When asking the respondent, "Why did you respond as you did for use," please record the first reason mentioned and use the lines provided to probe and clarify the reasons.

This set of instructions applies to Questions 5 through 8. Periodically remind the respondent to look at the scales provided on the page above the coupon concept that he or she is looking at.

Question 9: Enter number of children living at home. If none, enter the number zero and proceed to Question 11.
Question 10: Enter age of *youngest* child living at home in the box provided.
Question 11: Read the question and each answer slowly. Circle the number corresponding to the appropriate answer.
Question 12: Read the question and each answer slowly. Circle the number corresponding to the appropriate answer. If answer is never, proceed to Question 14. Otherwise, continue to Question 13.
Question 13: Circle the number corresponding to the appropriate answer. Do not read answer choices.
Question 14: Circle the number corresponding to the appropriate answer. Do not read answer choices.
Question 15: Read the question and each answer slowly. Circle the number corresponding to the appropriate answer.
Question 16: Read the question and each answer slowly. Circle the number corresponding to the appropriate answer.
Question 17: If an explanation is requested for occupation, please tell respondent that we are looking for a broad category or title. "No occupation" is not an acceptable answer. If this should happen, please probe to see if the person is a student, homemaker, retired, unemployed, etc.

At the end of the questionnaire, you are asked to indicate whether the respondent was male or female. Please circle the appropriate answer. This is not a question for the respondent.

Response Number _____
Coupon Book   _____

(Approach shoppers who appear to be between the ages of 18 and 49 and say . . .)

Hi, I'm _____ from Midwest Research Services. Many companies like to know your preferences and opinions about new products and promotions. If you have about 5 minutes, I'd like to have your opinions in this marketing research study.

(If refused, terminate)

1. *Have you eaten lunch or dinner in, or carried food away from, a fast-food restaurant in the last seven days? . . .* (must answer yes to continue)

2. *Have you eaten restaurant pizza within the last thirty days, either at the restaurant or by having it delivered? . . .* (must answer yes to continue)

3. *Which age group are you in? (read answers, circle number)*

   1 18–24   2 25–34   3 35–49   4 Other—Terminate interview

I am now going to show you five different coupon concepts and ask you three questions for each. Please respond to each coupon independently of the others. Look at the next coupon only when I ask you to.

4. *Please read the first coupon concept. Using a ten-point scale, how would you rate this concept if one represents very poor value and ten represents very good value?* _____

   Looking at the second scale, how would you rate this concept if one represents definitely would not use and ten represents definitely would use? _____

   Why did you respond as you did for use? _____
   _____
   _____

5. *Please turn the page and read the next coupon concept. Ignoring the last coupon and using the same scale, how would you rate this concept in terms of value?*

   Referring to the second scale, how would you rate this concept in terms of your likeliness to use? _____

   Why did you respond as you did for use? _____
   _____
   _____

6. *Please turn the page and read the next coupon concept. Ignoring the last coupon and using the same scale, how would you rate this concept in terms of value?*

   Referring to the second scale, how would you rate this concept in terms of your likeliness to use? _____

   Why did you respond as you did for use? _____
   _____
   _____

7. *Please turn the page and read the next coupon concept. Ignoring the last coupon and using the same scale, how would you rate this concept in terms of value?*

   *Referring to the second scale, how would you rate this concept in terms of your likeliness to use?*_____

   Why did you respond as you did for use? _____
   _____
   _____

Exhibit 3   **Questionnaire (*Continued*)**

8. Please turn the page and read the next coupon concept. Ignoring the last coupon and using the same scale, how would you rate this concept in terms of value?

   Referring to the second scale, how would you rate this concept in terms of your likeliness to use? _____

   Why did you respond as you did for use? _____
   _____
   _____

Thank you. The following questions will help us classify the preceding information.

9. How many children do you have living at home? _____
   If answer is none, proceed to question 11.

10. What is the age of your youngest child? _____

11. How often do you eat fast food for lunch or dinner? _____
    (read answers, circle number) 1 Once per month or less
                                   2 Two to three times per month
                                   3 Once or twice a week
                                   4 More than twice a week

12. How often do you eat at Premium Pizza? _____
    (read answers, circle number) 1 Never visited Premium Pizza
                                   2 Once per month or less
                                   3 Two to three times per month
                                   4 Once a week or more
    If answer is never, proceed to question 14.

13. Do you yourself usually buy whole pies or slices at Premium Pizza?
                                   1 whole pies
                                   2 slices
                                   (circle one)

14. Have you used fast-food or restaurant coupons in the last 30 days?
                                   1 yes
                                   2 no
                                   (circle one)

15. Have you ever used coupons for Premium Pizza?
    (read answers, circle number) 1 Never
                                   2 I sometimes use them when I have them.
                                   3 I always use them when I have them.

16. What is your marital status:
    (read answers, circle number) 1 Single
                                   2 Married
                                   3 Divorced, separated, widowed

17. What is your occupation? _____

    This is *not* a question for the respondent.
    Please circle appropriate answer—respondent was: 1 male
                                                      2 female
                                                      (circle number)

Thank you for your participation—Terminate interview at this time.

Exhibit 4   Stimuli

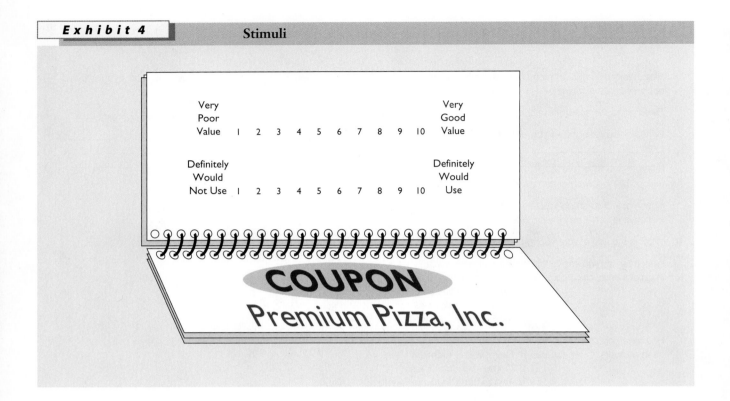

offer. Coupons and scales were therefore assembled in a booklet so that, as the interviewer showed each double-page spread, the respondent would see the scales on the top page and the coupon in question on the bottom page (see Exhibit 4).

Because the researcher wished to counterbalance the order in which the coupons were viewed and rated, the five coupons were organized into booklets of six different sequences. Each sequence was subsequently bound in one of six distinctly colored binders. A total of 96 questionnaires were then printed in six different colors to match the binder. In this way, there were 16 questionnaires of each color, and the color of the respondent's questionnaire indicated the sequence that he or she had seen.

The questionnaire and procedure were pretested at a mall similar to the target mall and were found to be satisfactory.

Questions

1. Is the choice of mall intercept interviews an appropriate data collection method given the research objectives?
2. Do you think that there are any specific criteria that the choice of shopping mall should satisfy?
3. Evaluate the instructions to interviewers.
4. Evaluate the questionnaire.
5. Do you think that it is worthwhile to present the coupons in a binder, separate from the questionnaire? Why or why not?
6. Do you consider it advisable to rotate the order of presentation of coupons? Why or why not?

case 9

First Federal Bank of Bakersfield

The Equal Credit Opportunity Act, which was passed in 1974, was partially designed to protect women from discriminatory banking practices. It forbade, for example, the use of credit evaluations based on gender or marital status. Although adherence to the law has changed the way many bankers do business, women's perception that there is a bias against them by a particular financial institution often remains unless some specific steps are taken by the institution to counter that perception.

Close to a dozen "women's banks"—that is, banks owned and operated by and for women—opened their doors during the 1980s with the specific purpose of targeting and promoting their services to this otherwise underdeveloped market. Although women's banks currently are evolving into full-service banks serving a wide range of clients, a number of traditional banks are moving in the other direction by attempting to develop services that are targeted specifically toward women. Many of these institutions see such a strategy as a viable way to attract valuable customers and to increase their market share in the short term while gaining a competitive advantage by which they can compete in the long term as the roles of women in the labor force gain in importance. One can find, with even the most cursory examination of the trade press, examples of credit-card advertising that depicts single, affluent, and head-of-the-household female card holders; financial seminar programs for wives of affluent professional men; informational literature that details how newly divorced and separated women can obtain credit; and entire packages of counseling, educational opportunities, and special services for women.

The First Federal Bank of Bakersfield was interested in developing its own program of this kind. The executives were curious about a number of issues. Were women's financial needs being adequately met in the Bakersfield area? What additional financial services would women especially like to have? How do Bakersfield's women feel about banks and bankers? Was First Federal in a good position to take advantage of the needs of women? What channels of communication might be best to reach women who might be interested in the services that First Federal had to offer?

The executives believed that First Federal might have some special advantages if it did try to appeal to women. For one thing, the Bakersfield community seemed to be quite sensitive to the issues being raised by the feminist movement. For another, First Federal was a small, personal bank. The executives thought that women might be more comfortable in dealing with a smaller, more personalized institution and that the bank might not have the traditional "image problem" among women that larger banks might have.

Research Objectives

One program the bank executives were considering that they believed might be particularly attractive to women was a series of financial seminars. The seminars could cover a number of topics, including money management, wills, trusts, estate planning, taxes, insurance, investments, financial services, and establishing a credit rating. The executives were interested in determining women's reactions to each of these potential topics. They were also interested in knowing what the best format might be in terms of location, frequency, length of each program, and so on, if there was a high level of interest. Consequently, they decided that the bank should conduct a research study that had the assessment of the financial seminar series as its main objective but that also shed some light on the other issues they had been debating. More specifically, the objectives of the research were as follows:

1. Determine the interest that exists among women in the Bakersfield area for seminars on financial matters.

2. Identify the reasons why Bakersfield women would change, or have changed, their banking affiliations.

3. Examine the attitudes of Bakersfield women toward financial institutions and the people who run them.

4. Determine if there was any correlation between the demographic characteristics of women in the Bakersfield area and the services they might like to have.

5. Analyze the media usage habits of Bakersfield-area women.

Method

The assignment to develop a research strategy by which these objectives could be assessed was given to the bank's internal marketing research department. The department consisted of only five members—Beth Anchurch, the research director, and four project analysts. As Anchurch pondered the assignment, she was concerned about the best way to proceed. She was particularly concerned with the relatively short amount of time she was given for the project. Top executives thought that there was promise in the seminar idea. If they were right, they wanted to get on with designing and offering the seminars before any of their competitors came up with a similar idea. Thus, they specified that they would like the results of the research department's investigation to be available within 45 to 50 days.

As Anchurch began to contemplate the data collection, she became particularly concerned with whether the study should use mail questionnaires or telephone interviews. She had tentatively ruled out personal interviews because of the short deadline that had been imposed. After several days of contemplating the alternatives, she finally decided that it would be best to collect the information by telephone. Further, she decided that it would be better to hire out the telephone interviewing than to use her four project analysts to make the calls.

Anchurch believed that the multiple objectives of the project required a reasonably large sample of women so that the various characteristics of interest would be sufficiently represented to enable some conclusions to be drawn about the population of Bakersfield as a whole. After pondering the various cross tabulations in which the bank executives would be interested, she finally decided that a sample of 500 to 600 adult women would be sufficient. The sample was to be drawn from the white pages of the Bakersfield telephone directory by the Bakersfield Interviewing Service, the firm that First Federal had hired to complete the interviews.

The sample was to be drawn using a scheme in which two names were selected from each page of the directory, first by selecting two of the four columns on the page at random and then by selecting the fifteenth name in each of the selected columns. The decision to sample names from each page was made so that each interviewer could operate with certain designated pages of the directory, since each was operating independently out of her home.

The decision to sample every fifteenth name in the selected columns was determined in the following way. First, there were 328 pages in the directory with four columns of names per page. There were 80 entries per column on average, or approximately 26,240 listings. Using Bureau of the Census data on household composition, it was estimated that 20% of all households would be ineligible for the study because they did not contain an adult female resident. This meant that only 20,992 (0.80 × 26,240) of the listings would probably qualify. Since 500 to 600 names were needed, it seemed easiest to select two columns on each page at random and to take the same numbered entry from each column. The interviewer could then simply count or measure down from the top of the column. The number 15 was determined randomly; thus, the fifteenth listing in the

randomly selected columns on each page was called. If the household did not answer or if the women of the house refused to participate, the interviewers were instructed to select another number from that column through the use of an abbreviated table of random numbers that each was given. They were to use a similar procedure if the household that was called did not have an adult woman living there.

First Federal decided to operate without callbacks because the interviewing service charged heavily for them. Anchurch did think it would be useful to follow up with a sample of those interviewed to make sure that they indeed had been called, since the interviewers for Bakersfield Interviewing Service operated out of their own homes and it was impossible to supervise them more directly. She did this by selecting at random a handful of the surveys completed by each interviewer. She then had one of her project assistants call that respondent, verify that the interview had taken place, and check the accuracy of the responses of a few of the most important questions. This audit revealed absolutely no instances of interviewer cheating.

The completed interview forms were turned over to First Federal for its own internal analysis. As part of this analysis, the project analyst compared the demographic characteristics of those contacted to the demographic characteristics of the population in the Bakersfield area as reported in the 2000 census. The comparison is shown in Exhibit 1. The analyst also prepared a summary of the nonresponses and refusals by interviewer. This comparison is shown in Exhibit 2.

Questions

1. Compare the advantages and disadvantages of using telephone interviews rather than personal interviews or mail questionnaires to collect the needed data.
2. The short deadline moved Anchurch to forgo personal interviews and mail questionnaires, but there were other options besides telephone interviews. Could you make a case for another communication method that might be appropriate here?
3. Given the large number of not-at-home attempts, was First Federal wise to skip callbacks? Why or why not?
4. If you were Anchurch, would you be happy with the performance of the Bakersfield Interviewing Service? Why or why not?

Exhibit 1

Selected Demographic Comparison of Survey Respondents with Bureau of Census Data

Characteristic/Category	PERCENTAGE OF WOMEN	
	Survey	Census
Marital Status		
Married	53	42
Single	30	40
Separated	1	2
Widowed	9	9
Divorced	7	7
Age		
18–24	23	23
25–34	30	28
35–44	16	14
45–64	18	21
65+	13	14
Income		
Less than $10,000	9	29
$10,000–$19,999	19	29
$20,000–$50,000	58	36
More than $50,000	2	6
Refused	12	

Exhibit 2

Results of Calls by Interviewer

Interviewer	NUMBER OF NOT-AT-HOMES		INELIGIBLES[a]	NUMBER OF REFUSALS		NUMBER OF COMPLETIONS
	Line Busy	No Answer		Initial	After Partial Completion	
1	7	101	36	15	0	30
2	2	45	13	16	0	30
3	11	71	23	17	7	30
4	14	56	47	35	6	39
5	9	93	10	23	13	30
6	5	102	28	63	14	35
7	6	36	17	16	0	18
8	7	107	23	13	0	30
9	11	106	36	47	0	30
10	10	55	6	35	9	30
11	38	83	48	92	0	30
12	5	22	3	8	0	9
13	23	453	102	65	7	99
14	12	102	27	31	0	19
15	7	173	29	66	0	34
16	2	65	9	33	0	22
Total	169	1,670	457	575	56	515
	1,839			631		

[a]No adult female resident.

case 10

Caldera Industries[1]

Chris Totten has just begun a summer internship at Caldera Industries, a national supplier of electronics components. Caldera's clients include OEM (original equipment manufacturers) firms that market televisions, home stereo and audio, and computer products to the general public. Returning from lunch, Chris finds a memo and questionnaire in her mailbox (see Exhibits 1 and 2).

Questions

1. Evaluate the questionnaire in relation to the issues raised by Manuel Ortega.
2. How would you recommend the instrument be pretested?

Exhibit 1   **Caldera Industries**

Serving our Customers' Electronics Needs for over 22 Years

CI

Internal Memorandum

TO: Chris Totten
Marketing Analyst Intern

cc: Caren Menlo
Marketing Manager

From: Manuel Ortega
Vice President for Sales and Marketing

Date: May 23, 2003

Regarding: Evaluation of Market Research Questionnaire

In three weeks, I will be meeting with executives from a number of our client companies. One of the items on the agenda is the research project our company has agreed to undertake on their behalf. At that meeting, the final version of our questionnaire will be distributed and approved.

On the attached pages is an initial draft of the Consumer Electronics Questionnaire we plan on using for the study. As the newly hired marketing intern, and because of your marketing research coursework experience, I suggested to our marketing manager, Caren Menlo, that reviewing the questionnaire would make an ideal first assignment for you. She agreed.

Please examine the attached questionnaire and provide me with a written memo of your analysis, comments, and suggestions for improvement (if you believe any are warranted) within two (2) weeks. More specifically, I am interested in your comments on the following issues:

- The type and amount of information being sought
- Appropriateness of the type of questionnaire designed and its method of administration
- The content of questions in the draft document
- Response formats used for the various questions
- Question wording
- Question sequencing
- Physical characteristics and layout of the instrument

I am also interested in any comments or suggestions you have on pretesting the questionnaire. I look forward to reading your memo.

---

[1]This case was prepared by Michael R. Luthy, Ph.D., Professor of Marketing, W. Fielding Rubel School of Business, Bellarmine University, 2001 Newburg Road, Louisville, KY 40205. Reprinted with permission.

Exhibit 2   **Consumer Electronics Research Questionnaire**

Directions: This questionnaire has been developed for a consortium of computer and home entertainment companies (who wish to remain anonymous). Complete all questions and mail this questionnaire to us today.

Quality Research Associates
5716 N. Woodlawn Court
Champaign, IL 61820

1. Name: _____   ____ Mr.   ____ Mrs.
2. Sex: _____
3. How old are you: _____
4. Intelligence: ____ Only completed college degree (Bachelor's)
____ Completed some graduate work
____ Completed graduate degree
____ Completed graduate degree beyond masters
5. Ethnic Status: ____ White ____ Asian
____ Black ____ Indian
____ Asian ____ Other What? _____
6. Political Party Support: ____ Democrat
____ Republican
____ Independent
____ Other
7. Your Occupation: _____
8. Spouse's Name and Age: _____
9. Number of Children: _____ (if children, go to question 61)
10. Your Company: _____
11. Your Work Fax Number: (__ __ __) __ __ __ - __ __ __ __
12. How Long Have You Been Married: ____ Never married
____ Less than a year
____ Between 1 and 5 years
____ Over 5 but less than 10 years
____ Over 15 years but less than 20 years
____ More than 20 years
13. Your Annual Income: $ _____
14. Social Security Number: __ __ __ - __ __ - __ __ __ __
15. The sponsors of this research are constantly introducing new products that they believe you (and your loved one, if any) will be interested in. In order to better make you aware of these offerings, please provide your telephone number below.
(__ __ __) __ __ __ - __ __ __ __
16. Do you own a computer at home or at work?
____ Yes ____ No
17. During an average week, how much time do you spend on it?
_____ Hours _____ Minutes
18. Doing what mostly?

_____

For each of the products listed below, please indicate the extent of your satisfaction with it, ceteris paribus, by either circling or placing an "X" on the line to the right of each statement.

	Mild Satisfaction	**Extremely Satisfied**
19. Apple Computers and Peripherals.	←	→
20. Gateway Computers and Peripherals.	←	→
21. Dell Computers and Peripherals.	←	→
22. IBM Computers and Peripherals.	←	→
23. Samsung Computers and Peripherals.	←	→
24. Hewlett-Packard Computers and Peripherals.	←	→
25. MacIntosh Computers and Peripherals.	←	→
26. Hitachi, Ltd. Computers and Peripherals.	←	→
27. Unisys Computers and Peripherals.	←	→
28. Tandy Computers and Peripherals.	←	→

(Continued)

29. Without being too loquacious, what emerging trends or technologies do you see as important to you that computer manufacturers (both hardware and software) should consider in developing new products?

_____

_____

30. How many different computer chatrooms have you visited in the last month?

____ 1–2
____ 2–3
____ 3–4
____ more than four

Below is a listing of ways in which people interact with consumer electronics on a quasi regular basis. What percentage of your time do you typically spend with each?

Check Below If You Do Not Use	Do Use		On Average, Number of "Others" Present During Your Usage
31. ____	____ %	Work related computer activities	____
32. ____	____ %	Entertainment related computer activities	____
33. ____	____ %	Watching Network Television	____
34. ____	____ %	Watching Cable Television	____
35. ____	____ %	Watching Premium Cable Services	____
36. ____	____ %	Watching Rented Movies on VCR	____
37. ____	____ %	Watching Rented Movies on DVD	____
38. ____	____ %	Listening to Music on Radio or on CD's	____
39. ____	____ %	Other (specify)	____

Referencing the music you listen to, vis à vis your response to question 38 above (see question 38 if needed), which are your favorite musical periods or types? Please indicate your first 10 choices in numerical order.

40. Earlier than Renaissance ____
41. Renaissance ____
42. Baroque ____
43. Classical ____
44. Romantic ____
45. Impressionistic ____
46. Neo-Classical ____
47. Contemporary ____
48. Contemporary Christian ____
49. Rock ____
50. Hard Rock ____
51. Grunge Rock ____
52. Jazz ____
53. Easy Listening ____
54. Jazz/Rock Fusion ____
55. Bluegrass ____
56. Contemporary ____
57. Folk Music ____
58. Country ____
59. Western ____
60. Other ____

Exhibit 2 **Consumer Electronics Research Questionnaire (*Continued*)**

61. Chart your child's usage of the following computer-related activities in 2002: (A = never, B = once to twice a per month, C = once to twice a week, D = every week, E = twice or more per week, F = daily, G = multiple times a day). If you have more than one child, use the computer usage of the oldest.

	Word Processing	EXCEL	Database Programs	E-Mail	Internet "Surfing"	Internet Chatrooms	Games
Jan 1–Jan 15	_____	_____	_____	_____	_____	_____	_____
Jan 16–Jan 31	_____	_____	_____	_____	_____	_____	_____
Feb 1–Feb 15	_____	_____	_____	_____	_____	_____	_____
Feb 16–Feb 28	_____	_____	_____	_____	_____	_____	_____
Mar 1–Mar 15	_____	_____	_____	_____	_____	_____	_____
Mar 16–Mar 31	_____	_____	_____	_____	_____	_____	_____
Apr 1–Apr 15	_____	_____	_____	_____	_____	_____	_____
Apr 16–Apr 30	_____	_____	_____	_____	_____	_____	_____
May 1–May 15	_____	_____	_____	_____	_____	_____	_____
May 16–May 31	_____	_____	_____	_____	_____	_____	_____
Jun 1–Jun 15	_____	_____	_____	_____	_____	_____	_____
Jun 16–Jun 30	_____	_____	_____	_____	_____	_____	_____
Jul 1–Jul 15	_____	_____	_____	_____	_____	_____	_____
Jul 16–Jul 31	_____	_____	_____	_____	_____	_____	_____
Aug 1–Aug 15	_____	_____	_____	_____	_____	_____	_____
Aug 16–Aug 31	_____	_____	_____	_____	_____	_____	_____
Sep 1–Sep 15	_____	_____	_____	_____	_____	_____	_____
Sep 16–Sep 30	_____	_____	_____	_____	_____	_____	_____
Oct 1–Oct 15	_____	_____	_____	_____	_____	_____	_____
Oct 16–Oct 31	_____	_____	_____	_____	_____	_____	_____
Nov 1–Nov 15	_____	_____	_____	_____	_____	_____	_____
Nov 16–Nov 30	_____	_____	_____	_____	_____	_____	_____

After completing, return to question 23

What is the *most* you would be willing to spend to purchase the following consumer electronic products if you were going to purchase them within the next year? and why?

Why?

62. $ _____ DVD player
63. $ _____ External Zip drive
64. $ _____ Big Screen Television
65. $ _____ Portable Stereo or Television
66. $ _____ Digital Camera

67. To what degree do you believe that access to the Internet is important to your family's entertainment needs?

A ←————————————→ E

68. What emerging trends or technologies do you see as important to you that computer manufacturers (both hardware and software) should consider in developing new products?

_____

_____

69. On a separate sheet of paper, please provide the names and addresses of at least three (3) friends or relatives that have recently (within the last two years) purchased an advanced consumer electronics product so that we may contact them.

Mail your completed questionnaire in a standard business size envelope to:

Quality Research Associates
4518 North Trails End
Cleveland, OH 34454
(a first-class stamp will be needed)

case 11

School of Business[1]

The School of Business, one unit in a public university enrolling over 40,000 students, has approximately 2,100 students in its bachelor's, master's, and doctorate programs emphasizing such areas of business as accounting, finance, information and operations management, marketing, management, and others. Because the School of Business must serve a diverse student population on limited resources, it feels it is important to accurately measure students' satisfaction with the school's programs and services.

Accurate measurement of student satisfaction will enable the school to target improvement efforts to those areas of greatest concern to students, whether that be by major, support services, or some other aspect of their educational experience. The school feels that improving its service to its customers (students) will result in more satisfied alumni, better community relations, additional applicants, and increased corporate involvement. Because graduate and undergraduate students are believed to have different expectations and needs, the school plans to investigate the satisfaction of these two groups separately.

In a previous survey of graduating seniors using open-ended questions, three primary areas of concern were identified: the faculty, classes/curriculum, and resources. Resources consisted of five specific areas: Undergraduate Advising Services, the Learning Center, Computer Facilities, the Library, and the Career Services Office. The research team for this project developed five-point Likert scale questions to measure students' satisfaction in each of these areas. In addition, demographic questions were included to determine whether satisfaction with the school was a function of a student's grade point average, major, job status upon graduation, or gender. Previous surveys used by the

School of Business and other published satisfaction scales provided examples of questions and question formats. Exhibit 1 shows the questionnaire that was used.

Although the survey contained primarily Likert scale questions, a few open-ended questions were also asked. Specifically, respondents were asked to list the Business School's strengths and weaknesses as well as their reasons for not using the various resource areas. The responses obtained to the question seeking the school's strengths and weaknesses were classified into four major subgroups: classes, reputation, resources, and professors. A sample of the actual verbatims are provided in Exhibit 2.

Questions

1. Considering customer satisfaction as it applies to a university setting, what are some other areas in addition to those identified for the project that may contribute to students' satisfaction/dissatisfaction with their education experience?

2. Does the current questionnaire provide information on students' overall satisfaction with their undergraduate degree program? Explain. What revisions are necessary to this questionnaire to obtain an overall satisfaction rating?

3. Can the School of Business use the results of this study to target the most important areas for improvement? Explain. Identify changes to the questionnaire that would allow the school to target areas based on importance.

4. What are the advantages and disadvantages of using open-ended questions to identify the school's strengths and weaknesses? Taking the responses in Exhibit 2, what system would you use for coding these responses?

---

[1]The contributions of Sara Pitterle to the development of this case are gratefully acknowledged.

Exhibit 1

In your opinion, what are the greatest strengths and weaknesses of the Business School?

Strengths

_____
_____
_____
_____

Weaknesses

_____
_____
_____
_____

CLASSES/CURRICULUM

Please indicate the extent to which you agree with the following statements.

Strongly Agree	Agree	Neither Agree/Disagree	Disagree	Strongly Disagree

I was satisfied with the quality of classes I took within my major.

(1) ____ (2) ____ (3) ____ (4) ____ (5) ____

I was able to take enough electives within my major.

(1) ____ (2) ____ (3) ____ (4) ____ (5) ____

"Lecture-Driven" vs. "Project" or "Group" class formats are most useful for learning.

(1) ____ (2) ____ (3) ____ (4) ____ (5) ____

The business school taught too much theory and not enough about real-life applications.

(1) ____ (2) ____ (3) ____ (4) ____ (5) ____

Creative problem solving was encouraged in my classes.

(1) ____ (2) ____ (3) ____ (4) ____ (5) ____

My classes were too large.

(1) ____ (2) ____ (3) ____ (4) ____ (5) ____

I was challenged by my coursework.

(1) ____ (2) ____ (3) ____ (4) ____ (5) ____

There were not enough group projects in my classes.

(1) ____ (2) ____ (3) ____ (4) ____ (5) ____

More night courses should be offered.

(1) ____ (2) ____ (3) ____ (4) ____ (5) ____

Overall, the material presented in my classes was current.

(1) ____ (2) ____ (3) ____ (4) ____ (5) ____

FACULTY

Strongly Agree	Agree	Neither Agree/Disagree	Disagree	Strongly Disagree

My professors are concerned about my future success.

(1) ____ (2) ____ (3) ____ (4) ____ (5) ____

Overall, the Business School professors are good teachers.

(1) ____ (2) ____ (3) ____ (4) ____ (5) ____

The Business School places too much emphasis on research and not enough on teaching.

(1) ____ (2) ____ (3) ____ (4) ____ (5) ____

Overall, my professors were accessible outside of class.

(1) ____ (2) ____ (3) ____ (4) ____ (5) ____

The Business School takes my comments on professor evaluation forms seriously.

(1) ____ (2) ____ (3) ____ (4) ____ (5) ____

Overall, my professors provided adequate office hours during the semester.

(1) ____ (2) ____ (3) ____ (4) ____ (5) ____

(Continued)

Exhibit 1   **Survey of Graduating Business Students (*Continued*)**

Overall, my professors encouraged students to raise relevant questions during class.

(1) ____   (2) ____   (3) ____   (4) ____   (5) ____

My professors tested memorization skills on exams more than my ability to apply concepts.

(1) ____   (2) ____   (3) ____   (4) ____   (5) ____

Overall, the Business School professors interacted well with students.

(1) ____   (2) ____   (3) ____   (4) ____   (5) ____

My professors showed creativity in their teaching methods.

(1) ____   (2) ____   (3) ____   (4) ____   (5) ____

My professors are at the leading edge of knowledge in their fields.

(1) ____   (2) ____   (3) ____   (4) ____   (5) ____

I approve of TA's teaching foundation courses.

(1) ____   (2) ____   (3) ____   (4) ____   (5) ____

My professors were stimulating.

(1) ____   (2) ____   (3) ____   (4) ____   (5) ____

RESOURCES
Advising

Did you ever use the undergraduate advising office?

(1) ____ Yes   (2) ____ No

If not, why not?

_____
_____
_____
_____

If you answered yes to the question above, please complete the remainder of the questions regarding Advising. If you answered no, please proceed to the following section—Learning Center.

Strongly Agree	Agree	Neither Agree/Disagree	Disagree	Strongly Disagree

The undergraduate advising office played a big role in helping me plan my business curriculum.

(1) ____   (2) ____   (3) ____   (4) ____   (5) ____

The undergraduate advising office should have more advisors.

(1) ____   (2) ____   (3) ____   (4) ____   (5) ____

The advisor(s) in the undergraduate advising office was (were) helpful.

(1) ____   (2) ____   (3) ____   (4) ____   (5) ____

The staff in the advising office was helpful.

(1) ____   (2) ____   (3) ____   (4) ____   (5) ____

I felt like I was bothering the advisor(s) in the undergraduate advising office if I asked him/her a question.

(1) ____   (2) ____   (3) ____   (4) ____   (5) ____

The advisor(s) in the undergraduate advising office was (were) concerned about my needs.

(1) ____   (2) ____   (3) ____   (4) ____   (5) ____

If there were more undergraduate advisors, I would have utilized the advising services more often.

(1) ____   (2) ____   (3) ____   (4) ____   (5) ____

Advice offered by the advising office was not helpful to me.

(1) ____   (2) ____   (3) ____   (4) ____   (5) ____

Exhibit 1   **Survey of Graduating Business Students (*Continued*)**

Learning Center

Did you ever use The Learning Center?

(1) _____ Yes   (2) _____ No

If not, why not?

_____
_____
_____
_____

If you answered yes to the question above, please complete the remainder of the questions regarding The Learning Center. If you answered no, please proceed to the following section—Career-Services Facilities/Staff.

Strongly Agree	Agree	Neither Agree/Disagree	Disagree	Strongly Disagree
The Learning Center was useful to me.				
(1) _____	(2) _____	(3) _____	(4) _____	(5) _____
The staff at the Learning Center are helpful.				
(1) _____	(2) _____	(3) _____	(4) _____	(5) _____
The Learning Center needs to extend its hours.				
(1) _____	(2) _____	(3) _____	(4) _____	(5) _____

Career-Services Facilities/Staff

Did you ever use the Career-Services office as a resource in your search for full- or part-time employment?

(1) _____ Yes   (2) _____ No

If not, why not?

_____
_____
_____
_____

If you answered yes to the question above, please complete the remainder of the questions regarding Career-Services Facilities/Staff. If you answered no, please proceed to the following section—Computer Facilities/Staff.

Strongly Agree	Agree	Neither Agree/Disagree	Disagree	Strongly Disagree
Overall, the Career-Services office has been a valuable resource in my job search.				
(1) _____	(2) _____	(3) _____	(4) _____	(5) _____
The staff in the Career-Services office are helpful.				
(1) _____	(2) _____	(3) _____	(4) _____	(5) _____
The Career-Services office is/was my main resource used in my search for my job.				
(1) _____	(2) _____	(3) _____	(4) _____	(5) _____
In my opinion, the Career-Services office is understaffed.				
(1) _____	(2) _____	(3) _____	(4) _____	(5) _____
I was pleased with the number of companies interviewing at the Career-Services office within my major.				
(1) _____	(2) _____	(3) _____	(4) _____	(5) _____
The Career-Services office is successful at attracting desirable employers to interview on campus.				
(1) _____	(2) _____	(3) _____	(4) _____	(5) _____
The sign-up process for interviews at the Career-Services office is fair.				
(1) _____	(2) _____	(3) _____	(4) _____	(5) _____
The Career-Services office provides enough information on how to use the Resume Expert software.				
(1) _____	(2) _____	(3) _____	(4) _____	(5) _____
The Career-Services office offers adequate interview training.				
(1) _____	(2) _____	(3) _____	(4) _____	(5) _____

(Continued)

Exhibit 1   **Survey of Graduating Business Students (*Continued*)**

Computer Facilities/Staff

Did you ever use the Business School's computer facilities?

(1) _____ Yes   (2) _____ No

If not, why not?

_____

_____

_____

_____

If you answered yes to the question above, please complete the remainder of the questions regarding Computer Facilities/Staff. If you answered no, please proceed to the following section—Library Facilities/Staff.

Strongly Agree	Agree	Neither Agree/Disagree	Disagree	Strongly Disagree
The computer room needs to extend its weekend hours.				
(1) _____	(2) _____	(3) _____	(4) _____	(5) _____
The computer room needs to extend its night hours.				
(1) _____	(2) _____	(3) _____	(4) _____	(5) _____
More computers are needed in the computer room.				
(1) _____	(2) _____	(3) _____	(4) _____	(5) _____
More printers are needed in the computer facilities.				
(1) _____	(2) _____	(3) _____	(4) _____	(5) _____
The computer-room staff is helpful.				
(1) _____	(2) _____	(3) _____	(4) _____	(5) _____
A computer was available when I needed to use one.				
(1) _____	(2) _____	(3) _____	(4) _____	(5) _____

Library Facilities/Staff

Did you use the Business School's library facilities?

(1) _____ Yes   (2) _____ No

If not, why not?

_____

_____

_____

_____

If you answered yes to the question above, please complete the remainder of the questions regarding Library Facilities/Staff. If you answered no, please proceed to the following section—Student Organizations.

Strongly Agree	Agree	Neither Agree/Disagree	Disagree	Strongly Disagree
The Library staff is helpful.				
(1) _____	(2) _____	(3) _____	(4) _____	(5) _____
The Library has adequate study space.				
(1) _____	(2) _____	(3) _____	(4) _____	(5) _____

Exhibit 1   Survey of Graduating Business Students (*Continued*)

Student Organizations

Were you a member of any Business School student organizations?

    (1) ____ Yes   (2) ____ No

If not, why not?

_____
_____
_____
_____

If you answered yes to the question above, please complete the remainder of the questions regarding Student Organizations. If you answered no, please proceed to the following section—GENERAL.

How many organizations were you a member of?

    (1) ____ 1
    (2) ____ 2
    (3) ____ 3
    (4) ____ 4

Did you hold an office?   (1) ____ Yes   (2) ____ No

Do you believe the faculty and staff were supportive of the student organizations?

    (1) ____ Yes   (2) ____ No   (3) ____ Don't know

What were your reasons for joining?

_____
_____
_____
_____

GENERAL

	Strongly Agree	Agree	Neither Agree/Disagree	Disagree	Strongly Disagree
My Business School education has given me a sense of accomplishment.	(1) ____	(2) ____	(3) ____	(4) ____	(5) ____
The Business School is well respected nationally.	(1) ____	(2) ____	(3) ____	(4) ____	(5) ____
My undergraduate degree has prepared me well for a successful career in business.	(1) ____	(2) ____	(3) ____	(4) ____	(5) ____
The caliber of my classmates enhanced my learning.	(1) ____	(2) ____	(3) ____	(4) ____	(5) ____
The Business School should require more computer courses.	(1) ____	(2) ____	(3) ____	(4) ____	(5) ____
The copying facilities at the Business School are inadequate.	(1) ____	(2) ____	(3) ____	(4) ____	(5) ____
My undergraduate experience was disappointing.	(1) ____	(2) ____	(3) ____	(4) ____	(5) ____
The Business School placed too much emphasis on a high GPA and not enough on learning.	(1) ____	(2) ____	(3) ____	(4) ____	(5) ____
I felt like a number here at the Business School.	(1) ____	(2) ____	(3) ____	(4) ____	(5) ____
The Business School should have a mandatory class on ethics for undergraduates.	(1) ____	(2) ____	(3) ____	(4) ____	(5) ____

(Continued)

Exhibit 1   **Survey of Graduating Business Students (*Continued*)**

Please indicate the extent to which you agree that each of the following factors POSITIVELY CONTRIBUTED to the quality of your overall undergraduate business education:

Strongly Agree	Agree	Neither Agree/Disagree	Disagree	Strongly Disagree

Class size in major classes:
(1) ____   (2) ____   (3) ____   (4) ____   (5) ____

Class size in required courses:
(1) ____   (2) ____   (3) ____   (4) ____   (5) ____

Group projects:
(1) ____   (2) ____   (3) ____   (4) ____   (5) ____

Case studies:
(1) ____   (2) ____   (3) ____   (4) ____   (5) ____

Multiple-choice exams:
(1) ____   (2) ____   (3) ____   (4) ____   (5) ____

Use of creative thought:
(1) ____   (2) ____   (3) ____   (4) ____   (5) ____

Guest lecturers:
(1) ____   (2) ____   (3) ____   (4) ____   (5) ____

Required classes:
(1) ____   (2) ____   (3) ____   (4) ____   (5) ____

Number of electives you can take:
(1) ____   (2) ____   (3) ____   (4) ____   (5) ____

Number of required computer courses:
(1) ____   (2) ____   (3) ____   (4) ____   (5) ____

Please indicate the extent to which you agree that each of the following core classes POSITIVELY CONTRIBUTED to the quality of your overall undergraduate business education:

	Strongly Agree	Agree	Neither Agree/Disagree	Disagree	Strongly Disagree
Comp Sci	(1) ____	(2) ____	(3) ____	(4) ____	(5) ____
Managerial Acctg 302	(1) ____	(2) ____	(3) ____	(4) ____	(5) ____
Financial Acctg 200	(1) ____	(2) ____	(3) ____	(4) ____	(5) ____
Communications 320	(1) ____	(2) ____	(3) ____	(4) ____	(5) ____
Business Law 330	(1) ____	(2) ____	(3) ____	(4) ____	(5) ____
Corporate Finance 510	(1) ____	(2) ____	(3) ____	(4) ____	(5) ____
Marketing 520	(1) ____	(2) ____	(3) ____	(4) ____	(5) ____
Org. Behavior 530	(1) ____	(2) ____	(3) ____	(4) ____	(5) ____
Business Statistics 570	(1) ____	(2) ____	(3) ____	(4) ____	(5) ____
Mgt of Serv-Mfg Op 574	(1) ____	(2) ____	(3) ____	(4) ____	(5) ____
OVERALL	(1) ____	(2) ____	(3) ____	(4) ____	(5) ____

GENERAL INFORMATION

Please mark the number corresponding to your gender:
(1) ____ Female   (2) ____ Male

Are you a state resident?
(1) ____ Yes   (2) ____ No

Please mark the number(s) corresponding to your major(s).

(1) ____ Accounting
(2) ____ Actuarial Science
(3) ____ Diversified
(4) ____ Finance
(5) ____ Information Systems
(6) ____ Management and Human Resources

(7) ____ Marketing
(8) ____ Quantitative Analysis
(9) ____ Real Estate
(10) ____ Risk Management
(11) ____ Transportation and Public Utilities

Survey of Graduating Business Students (*Continued*)

Please mark the number corresponding to your GPA.
(1) ____3.5–4.0   (2) ____3.0–3.49   (3) ____2.5–2.99   (4) ____2.0–2.49

Please mark the number of years it will take you to graduate.
(1) ____3½   (2) ____4   (3) ____4½   (4) ____5   (5) ____>5½

During the program (excluding summers), have you been employed?
(1) ____Employed full time   (2) ____Employed part time   (3) ____Not employed

What do you plan to do upon graduation?
(1) ____full-time employment
(2) ____part-time employment
(3) ____graduate school
(4) ____other, please specify

If you intend to work full time, please specify if you:
(1) ____have already accepted a position
(2) ____are still in the process of interviewing
(3) ____other, please specify

THANK YOU FOR COMPLETING THE SURVEY OF GRADUATING BUSINESS STUDENTS

A Sample of the Survey Responses to Question 1 Regarding Strengths and Weaknesses

Strengths
Breadth of courses and disciplines.
The increase in group projects was also helpful.
Classes in your major are relatively small.
Excellent faculty advising (not undergrad advising).
Good faculty. Excellent profs.
Has a good reputation.
Required some thought-provoking classes (literature, philosophy).
Free laser printing in the computer lab.
The resources for information gathering are great.
The options of resources available are great.
The competitiveness, quality of students.
Nice that classes aren't greatly dependent on Fridays (open to work or volunteering).
Clear curriculum of what classes are needed if in Pre-Business or Business—although there are a lot of them, the core classes allow you to touch all majors.
A well-respected and less costly route to a business undergrad degree than other alternatives available.
National reputation.
A few good professors that make up for all the bad ones.
Some of the professors are terrific and really care about the students.

Weaknesses
Not enough real-life applications.
Core classes tedious.
Too much emphasis on GPA.
Lack of advisors.
Lack of support facilities.
Awful undergraduate advising.
Classes are too much on theory.
The computer classes are a waste of time.
Too many unnecessary core requirements that could be used for another class or elective.
Too many exams scheduled in the 6th and 12th weeks.
Too many required group projects.
Can't get classes when needed.
Too few resources for the number of students.
Students not treated as individuals.
Not enough computers.
Makes students take core classes in each function of business.
Need more case studies and seminar-type classes with fewer students.
There is too much memorization and not enough practical application of knowledge.
Making appointments to see advisors.
Professors expect too much.
Computer courses are too technical.

case 12

Young Ideas Publishing Company

How does a company go about marketing products to a specific niche of the teenage market? That is the question confronting Bev Halley, co-owner of Young Ideas Publishing Company. Halley is convinced that her unconventional novels for young people would be very attractive to at least a segment of the teenaged market. She is unsure, however, about how to reach this "nonconformist" segment of the market.

Background

Three years ago, Halley wrote her first novel, a youth-oriented book (ages 15–18) entitled *Illusions of Summer*. None of the major publishers would publish the book, however, primarily because it dealt with several controversial social and political concerns. Most publishers simply felt that such topics would not be of interest to enough high school teenagers to justify publication, although many agreed that the novel was of publication quality in other respects.

Frustrated in her efforts to publish her novel, Halley and a business partner, Teresa Martinez, decided to form their own publishing company and publish the book themselves. Both believed that teenagers would be interested in social and political topics and would buy the book. Thus, Young Ideas Publishing Company was born. Halley hoped that effective marketing of the book on a local basis by the company might encourage national distributors to alter their positions toward the novel.

When *Illusions of Summer* was released, it was very well received by several literary critics, winning promising reviews and awards. Despite its critical success, however, commercial acceptance has been much harder to find. During the first 24 months after publication, only about 1,500 copies of the book have been sold, mostly through local bookstores, mail orders, and the company's Web site. Most distributors were unwilling to handle the book because it was not from an established publisher. With few channels through which to market the product, it remains virtually unknown outside of a limited local market.

Even with this poor showing from a commercial standpoint, Halley continued to believe that so-called "nonconformist" teenagers would be willing to buy books of this nature. Accordingly, she wrote and published a second novel, *Ultimate Choices*. Once again, the novel dealt with several controversial issues for teens and social and political concerns; once again, the critics reacted favorably. Initial sales for *Ultimate Choices* have been better than they were for *Illusions of Summer*;

currently (two months after publication), about 250 copies have been sold. By talking to clerks in local bookstores, Halley has learned that most of the books are being sold to teenagers.

Nature of the Problem

Although encouraged by the good reviews and increased sales of the second book, Halley and Martinez are concerned about the future of Young Ideas Publishing Company. The company has struggled to break even so far, and Martinez has indicated that the survival of the company may well depend on the success of the new novel.

Both partners are still convinced that a market exists for the novels. They now recognize, however, that they may not know enough about the teenage market to effectively market the novels. For example, they believe that insights are needed in the following areas:

- Will high school teenagers specifically select young adult novels, or do they think that these are written for younger teens?
- Are teenagers interested in social and political issues?
- Where do high school teenagers usually obtain books for pleasure reading?
- Do teens purchase books for themselves, or do parents purchase books for them?
- What types of promotional items do high school teens enjoy most?
- What advertising media are most effective in reaching teens?
- How do "nonconformist" teens differ on these issues from other teens?

You have been hired by Young Ideas Publishing Company to develop and implement a research project to investigate these ideas. Resources are limited; Halley would like the results of the research within 60 days.

Questions

1. Based on the information provided and your knowledge of marketing and marketing research, define the research problem.
2. How would you propose to measure the degree of nonconformity? Develop a set of items intended to assess this construct.
3. What is the target population for your study?
4. Discuss your proposed sampling plan, including the implications for the implementation of the project.

case 13
Newt vs. Toade[1]

Shortly after assuming his position as majority leader of the U.S. Senate four years ago, Republican Senator James Newton began receiving overwhelmingly negative coverage in the news media. A year later, he was reprimanded by his colleagues for an admitted breach of Senate ethics that had occurred prior to his becoming majority leader. Although his infraction was not serious enough to force him to resign, he was nicknamed "Newt" by his detractors, and his job approval ratings plummeted. While it seems implausible to most observers now, he would like to make a political recovery and become a viable candidate for the presidency in the next election.

Nearly two years ago, Senator Newton's aides hired a public relations firm to help boost his approval ratings among all registered voters. Between January and December of that year, however, nothing this firm tried had any impact. At that point Salvadore Toade, principal owner of Toade & Associates, a relatively new public relations firm, approached Newton's top aides with the following bold proposal. "If the Senator will turn the account over to my firm, my associates and I will develop and implement a new public relations campaign and will initially bill him only for out-of-pocket expenses. If after six months the senator's overall approval rating among all registered voters remains at 18%, the current level in virtually every media poll, or if it moves lower, no additional payment will be required. But, if his approval rating increases in that time period from the baseline level of 18%, the senator must pay $10,000 for every percentage point it has gone up."

Senator Newton agreed to the deal. In July, he received a letter from Toade & Associates claiming his approval rating among registered voters had increased 15 points and requesting payment in the amount of $150,000. Toade & Associates indicated it had conducted its own poll because, unlike six months ago when all of the media-sponsored polls reported similar approval ratings (i.e., approximately 18%), recent polls reported approval ratings ranging from as low as 13% to as high as 27%. Because none of the media-sponsored polls indicated an increase as large as 15 points (using 18% as the baseline), Newton asked his lawyers to investigate the sampling plan used by Toade to measure his approval rating. The investigation produced the following deposition from Mr. Toade himself:

> We exercised great care to do things very scientifically. To ensure that people from every

socioeconomic group were represented, we defined five different groups based on household income: (1) Under $20,000, (2) $20,000–$34,999, (3) $35,000–$59,999, (4) $60,000–$99,999, and (5) $100,000 and above. We then obtained comprehensive national lists of people in each income category. Within each list, our software numbered the names from 1 to n and used a random-number generator to select 1,000 names. We then called each of the 5,000 names generated and interviewed everybody willing to participate. The overall refusal rate was 9%, and none of the income groups had refusal rates any larger than 12%. Our participation rate was so high because we asked only two questions: (1) "Are you familiar with James Newton, majority leader of the U.S. Senate?" and (2) "Do you approve or disapprove of Senator Newton's performance as majority leader?"

Being dissatisfied with Toade's study, Senator Newton asked his staff to commission a study with an independent research firm using the same questions employed in the Toade study. For political and financial reasons, a firm from the senator's home state was employed rather than one of the larger Washington-based polling agencies. This survey found the senator's approval rating had improved by only 5 points. Therefore, Newton sent a letter to Toade summarizing the findings and enclosed a check for $50,000.

Angry that Newton had not paid the full $150,000, Mr. Toade dispatched his lawyers to look into the matter. The transcript of an interrogation of the research director who managed Newton's study included the following statement:

> We felt it to be very important to ensure that every region of the country was fairly represented. Therefore, we identified all of the major newspapers in each of the 50 states. Within each state, we selected the newspaper with the largest number of subscribers. With the assistance of Republican members of Congress in each state, we obtained a random list of 250 subscribers for each selected newspaper. I want to emphasize, each newspaper randomly selected the names for our list. Our interviewers then called as many names on each list as were necessary to get 100 people to complete the survey. Using this approach, we obtained a total sample size of 5,000. As you know, our survey found that Senator Newton's approval rating had not increased nearly as much as indicated in your client's study.

[1]This case was prepared by Jon R. Austin, Ph.D., Associate Professor of Marketing, Cedarville University, 251 North Main Street, Cedarville, OH 45314.

Questions

1. What is the target population?
2. What population parameter is being estimated, and what statistic is being calculated?
3. What sampling frames were used in each of the two studies?
4. What type of sampling procedure was employed in the study conducted by Toade & Associates? Explain the basis of your determination.
5. Do you believe the sampling procedure employed in the Toade study was appropriate given the objective of measuring the senator's overall job approval rating? Describe your reasoning in detail.
6. What type of sampling procedure was employed in the study conducted by the research firm on behalf of Senator Newton? Explain the basis of your determination.
7. Do you believe the sampling procedure employed in the study conducted for Senator Newton was appropriate given the objective of measuring the senator's overall job approval rating? Describe your reasoning in detail.
8. Which of the two studies do you believe produced the numbers that are most trustworthy? Explain why you have drawn this conclusion.
9. Design a sampling plan that could be used in a new study that you believe would provide the fairest way to resolve this case. Describe in detail your reasoning for proposing this method of sampling.

case 14

Rockway Publishing Company, Inc.[1]

The Problem

Rockway Publishing Company publishes telephone directories for suburban and rural communities. Headquartered in a large Midwestern metropolitan area, Rockway publishes directories for over 80 markets, mostly in the Midwestern and southern parts of the United States. The telephone directories are published as an alternative to, and in competition with, directories published by the local telephone companies serving these markets. Rockway has been very successful in offering yellow-page advertisers a quality product at competitive rates. However, there have been some problems with distribution.

The distribution of the directories is handled in one of two ways. Winston Delivery Company has been under contract for the past two years to hand deliver directories in suburban areas and small cities. Winston hires college students, at minimum wage plus car expenses, to make the deliveries. Each student is given an assigned area of streets and rural routes to cover. For some locations, particularly where the households are heavily rural, the directories are sent through the mail. Recently, Rockway's salespeople have been receiving complaints from advertisers that some of their customers have not received a directory. It is believed by some of the salespeople that as many as 10 to 15% of households, in any given market, are not receiving a directory.

Survey Method

Faced with the prospect that not all of the directories intended for households are being delivered, Ron Combs, president of Rockway, instituted a plan for measuring the discrepancy. Approximately three weeks after a directory is delivered in an area, a sample of households is telephoned, and respondents are asked if the directory has been received. The results are tabulated according to whether the household has a city or rural address. To be counted, the respondent must be sure that the book has been received or has not been received. Respondents who are uncertain or don't know are given more information about the time of delivery, what the face of the book looks like, and how it was delivered (by mail or by hand). If they are still uncertain, they are replaced in the sample and not included in the tally. The respondent may be anyone in the household who answers the phone or is available at the time of the call. Combs wants to ensure that sampling error is not greater than +/− 2 percentage points.

The Sampling Plan

The sampling frame is an internally produced cross directory of white-page listings by street. The interviewer goes through the pages, arbitrarily pulling names from the listings. If a respondent says a directory has not been received, additional calls are made on that street to determine if the entire street was missed. However, these additional calls are not included in the survey results.

Exhibit 1 shows the results of the survey for areas distributed to in the most recent months.

Exhibit 1	Survey Results				
	HAND DELIVERED			**MAIL DELIVERED**	
	Area 1	Area 2	Area 3	Area 4	Area 5
Total area population	35,000	50,000	69,000	85,000	155,000
City	24,000	45,700	52,000	43,000	100,000
Rural	11,000	4,300	17,000	42,000	55,000
Total sample	525	750	1,035	1,275	2,325
City	325	650	775	685	1,325
Rural	200	100	260	590	1,000
Overall percentage receiving directory	88%	90%	95%	85%	92%

[1]This case was prepared by Paul D. Boughton, Ph.D., Associate Professor of Marketing, Saint Louis University, 3674 Lindell Blvd., St. Louis, MO 63108.

The total sample size for each area was determined by taking 1.5% of the area population. The breakdown between city and rural sample is arbitrary and the result of actual calls completed.

Combs wants to determine three things: (1) the overall soundness of the sampling plan; (2) the amount of sampling error in the results; and (3) the amount of response error by respondents.

Questions

1. What type of sample is being taken? Are city and rural residents being represented adequately? What other approach would you recommend and why?

2. What is the range of sampling error experienced from Area 1 to Area 5? (Assume 95% level of confidence.) How can Combs's error goal of $+/-$ 2 percentage points be achieved?

3. What would you recommend as a sample size for each of the five areas?

4. Does Combs have enough information to determine respondent error? What would you recommend he do to obtain this information?

case 15
Fancher Golf Center[1]

As a boy growing up in Harrisonburg, Virginia, Brian Fancher dreamed of being a professional golfer. His remarkable talent prompted his teammates to select him as captain of the high school golf team during both his junior and senior years, and he led the team to many tournament championships. This success did not go unnoticed by college coaches, and he was offered scholarships by the University of Texas at Austin, UCLA, Stanford, and Pepperdine University. He initially planned to accept Stanford's offer because the school has an impeccable academic reputation and is the alma mater of his idol Tiger Woods. However, when visiting Pepperdine's mountain-side campus, with its breathtaking view of the Pacific Ocean, Brian knew he was destined to spend his college days in Malibu, California.

Brian's freshman year at Pepperdine was unremarkable, but he emerged as the team's star during his sophomore year. During his last two seasons, he experienced enough success to begin believing his dream of a professional career might actually come to fruition. After graduation, he pursued his goal by entering the PGA Qualifying Tournament ("Q-school") but failed to qualify. Dejected, he returned home to Virginia and worked for a year as an assistant teaching professional at a local country club. The following year, his fortunes changed when he qualified at the PGA Q-school and received his PGA tour card. In his first season on the tour, he missed the cut at several tournaments but managed to earn enough money to keep his playing card. His financial situation changed the next season when in the first tournament he lost a sudden death playoff, came in second place, and earned $631,700. He had six more top-10 finishes, earning him a total of $2,243,500, before tragedy struck. While playing the first round of a tournament, Brian's club caught a tree root during his downswing, resulting in serious wrist and shoulder injuries. Surgeons were able to repair the damage but informed Brian that his professional playing days had come to an end.

Feeling confused by what had transpired, Brian returned home to seek solace and counsel from his family. Shortly thereafter, his mother experienced serious health problems; this made him decide to remain in his hometown. Despite his bitter disappointment, Brian still loved golf and wanted to earn his living by being involved in the game in some way. Several friends urged him to begin offering golf lessons, but his year at the country club made him realize he wanted more independence than that job offered. Based on discussions with people in the community, he began to believe there might be an opportunity to invest what remained of his PGA Tour earnings to create a "Golf Center" in Harrisonburg. The concept was to have state-of-the-art indoor and outdoor training facilities. Initially, he would provide all of the golf instruction, but more instructors would be hired as finances permitted. The Fancher Golf Center would also offer high-end golf equipment along with custom club-fitting services. Brian felt confident he could create excitement and interest by periodically inviting friends from the PGA tour to come to the center for playing exhibitions, question-and-answer forums, and autograph sessions.

Harrisonburg, Virginia, is a quiet, unassuming community of approximately 41,000 people located in the heart of the Shenandoah Valley. A central fixture in town is James Madison University (JMU), which enrolls over 16,000 students. There are a few smaller communities in the immediate vicinity, but Brian and his associates were hopeful the city of Staunton, because its population of roughly 24,000 has a similar demographic profile as Harrisonburg, might be a viable secondary market even though it is located 25 miles to the south. To obtain assistance in testing the viability of his business idea, Brian contacted the Shenandoah Valley Small Business Development Center which is housed at JMU. The center arranged for JMU students in a marketing research course to conduct some research on his behalf. Discussions between Brian, the marketing research professor, and students produced the following list of research problems:

Among the populations of (1) permanent Harrisonburg residents 18–70 years of age, (2) JMU students, and (3) Staunton residents 18–70 years of age:

A. Determine the percentage of consumers who classify themselves as serious golfers.

B. Determine the frequency of playing golf during the spring (March through May), summer (June through August), and fall (September through November) seasons.

C. Measure the level of satisfaction with current playing abilities.

D. Measure the level of satisfaction with current (a) golf instruction opportunities, (b) high-end golf equipment sources, and (c) club-fitting services in the area.

E. Measure evaluations of the proposed golf center concept.

[1]This case was prepared by Jon R. Austin, Ph.D., Associate Professor of Marketing, Cedarville University, 251 North Main Street, Cedarville, OH 45314.

F. Measure intentions to utilize (a) the golf instruction services or (b) club-fitting services if the proposed golf center were opened.

The marketing research professor divided the class into three teams. Each team conducted a study that addressed all of the research objectives for one of the three target populations. Presented next are brief descriptions of how the teams collected the data for their studies.

Team 1

This team focused on the "permanent Harrisonburg residents 18–70 years of age" population. Using the intercept method, they administered a survey at Valley Mall. Of the 613 shoppers they approached, 227 were within the designated age range, and 143 of these shoppers agreed to complete the survey.

Team 2

This team conducted a study of the JMU student population. Because two members had extensive experience building Web pages, the group decided to take an innovative approach. They obtained the e-mail distribution lists for 12 campus organizations and sent an e-mail message to every fourth person on each list (a total of 2,219 messages) asking the person to visit the team's Web site and complete an online survey. Using this approach, the team obtained 392 completed questionnaires.

Team 3

This team examined the "Staunton residents 18–70 years of age" population. Because Staunton is 25 miles away, the team decided to conduct telephone interviews. Moreover, the Small Business Development Center agreed to pay for the long-distance calls as long as they were made from the center's telephone bank. The team members worked at the center during normal hours of operation (8:00 a.m. to 5:00 p.m.). Using systematic sampling, and the Staunton telephone directory as a sampling frame, they made 472 calls and obtained 96 completed surveys.

Questions

1. For each team, identify *all* of the types of error that were likely introduced by the data collection process. Discuss why you believe particular procedures produced each type of error you identify.
2. What could have been done to prevent/minimize each type of error by conducting the study differently?
3. What might be done to deal with each type of error now that it has occurred?

case 16

Fabhus, Inc.

Fabhus, Inc., a manufacturer of prefabricated homes located in Atlanta, Georgia, had experienced steady, sometimes spectacular, growth since its founding in the early 1950s. In recent years, however, things have not been so rosy, with sales dropping about 20% from their high point three years earlier, in spite of a very attractive interest-rate environment for home building.

In an attempt to offset the decline in sales, company management decided to use marketing research to get a better perspective on their customers so that they could better target their marketing efforts. After much discussion, the members of the executive committee finally determined that the following questions would be important to address in this research effort:

1. What is the demographic profile of the typical Fabhus customer?

2. What initially attracts these customers to a Fabhus home?

3. Do Fabhus home customers consider other factory-built homes when making their purchase decision?

4. Are Fabhus customers satisfied with their homes? If they are not, what particular features are unsatisfactory?

Method

The research firm that was called in on the project suggested conducting a mail survey to past buyers. Preliminary discussions with management revealed that Fabhus had the greatest market penetration near its factory. As one moved farther from the factory, the share of the total new housing business that went to Fabhus declined. The company suspected that this might result from the higher prices of the units due to shipping charges. Fabhus relied on a zone-price system in which prices were based on the product delivered at the construction site.

Local dealers actually supervised construction. Each dealer had pricing latitude and could charge more or less than Fabhus's suggested list price. Individual dealers were responsible for seeing that customers were satisfied with their Fabhus home, although Fabhus also had a toll-free number that customers could call if they were not satisfied with the way their dealer handled the construction or if they had problems moving in.

Considering the potential impact distance and dealers might have, the research team thought it was important to sample purchasers in the various zones as well as customers of the various dealers. Since Fabhus's records of houses sold were kept by zone and by date sold within zone, sample respondents were selected in the following way: First, the registration cards per zone were counted. Second, the sample size per zone was determined so that the number of respondents per zone was proportionate to the number of homes sold in the zones. Third, a sample interval, k, was chosen for each zone, a random start between 1 and k was generated, and every kth record was selected. The mail questionnaire shown in Exhibit 1 was sent to the 423 households selected.

A cover letter informing Fabhus's customers of the general purpose of the survey accompanied the questionnaire, and a new $1 bill was included with each survey as an incentive to respond. Furthermore, the anonymity of the respondents was guaranteed by enclosing a self-addressed postage-paid postcard in the survey. Respondents were asked to mail the postcard when they mailed their survey. All those who had not returned their postcards in two weeks were sent a notice reminding them that their survey had not been returned. The combination of incentives, guaranteed anonymity, and follow-up prompted the return of 342 questionnaires for an overall response rate of 81%.

Questions

1. Using the data in the file "FABHUS" and analytic techniques of your own choosing, address as best you can the objectives that prompted the research effort in the first place.

2. Do you think the research design was adequate for the problems posed? Why or why not?

Exhibit 1   **Factory-Built Home Owners Survey**

1. How did you first learn of the factory-built home that you bought? (check one, please)

   ☐ Friend or relative   ☐ Direct mail
   ☐ Another customer   ☐ Newspaper
   ☐ Realtor   ☐ Radio
   ☐ Model home   ☐ TV
   ☐ Yellow pages   ☐ Don't remember
   ☐ National magazine   ☐ Other _____
                                                  (please specify)

2. Did you own the land your home is on before you first visited your home builder?

   ☐ Yes   ☐ No

3. How long have you lived in your home? _____ years

4. Where did you live before purchasing your factory-built home? (please check one)

   ☐ Rented a house, apartment, or mobile home
   ☐ Owned a mobile home
   ☐ Owned a conventionally built home
   ☐ Owned another factory-built home
   ☐ Other _____
                          (please specify)

5. Please rate your overall level of satisfaction with your home. (please check one)

   ☐ Very satisfied
   ☐ Somewhat satisfied
   ☐ Somewhat dissatisfied
   ☐ Very dissatisfied

6. How important to you were each of the following considerations in purchasing your factory-built home?
   (please check one space for each item)

Considerations	Extremely Important	Important	Slightly Important	Not Important
Investment value	___	___	___	___
Quality	___	___	___	___
Price	___	___	___	___
Energy features	___	___	___	___
Dealer	___	___	___	___
Exterior style	___	___	___	___
Floor plan	___	___	___	___
Interior features	___	___	___	___
Delivery schedule	___	___	___	___

7. Below, please list any other homes you looked at before purchasing the home you chose. Please state the reason you did not purchase the other home.

Name of Home	Factory-Built?	Reason for Not Purchasing
_____	☐ Yes ☐ No	_____
_____	☐ Yes ☐ No	_____
_____	☐ Yes ☐ No	_____
_____	☐ Yes ☐ No	_____

Now we would like you to please tell us about yourself and your family.

8. How many children do you have living at home? _____ children

9. What is the age of the head of your household? (check one, please)

   ☐ Under 20   ☐ 35–44   ☐ 55–64
   ☐ 20–24   ☐ 45–54   ☐ 65 or over
   ☐ 25–34

Exhibit 1   **Factory-Built Home Owners Survey (*Continued*)**

10. What is the occupation of the head of the household? (check one, please)
   ☐ Professional or official   ☐ Labor or machine operator
   ☐ Technical or manager   ☐ Foreman
   ☐ Proprietor   ☐ Service worker
   ☐ Farmer   ☐ Retired
   ☐ Craftsperson   ☐ Other _____
   ☐ Clerical or sales   (please specify)

11. Which of the following categories includes your family's total annual income? (check one, please)
   ☐ Less than $20,000   ☐ $50,000-$59,999
   ☐ $20,000-$29,999   ☐ $60,000-$69,999
   ☐ $30,000-$39,999   ☐ $70,000-$79,999
   ☐ $40,000-$49,999   ☐ $80,000 or over

12. Is the spouse of the head of the household employed? (check one, please)
   ☐ Spouse employed full-time   ☐ Spouse not employed
   ☐ Spouse employed part-time   ☐ Not married

One final question:

13. Would you recommend your particular factory-built home to someone interested in building a new home?
   ☐ Yes   ☐ No

Thank you very much for completing this survey.
Your help in this study is greatly appreciated.

case 17

Marty's Department Store

Bethany Tate was nervous. As the general manager of the local Marty's, a regional department store chain based in the southwest United States, she was apprehensive about lackluster sales growth at her store over the most recent quarter. The problem, she believed, was the nearby presence of Naples Clothing Co., a nationally known specialty retailer of clothing that had opened about six months ago. She had expected sales to be flat while the new Naples store went through its honeymoon period with shoppers, but she didn't expect it to last this long.

Marty's Department Store

The Marty's chain was founded in 1967 in Scottsdale, Arizona. The company currently operates 113 stores across a dozen southwestern states. In general, the company's strategy is to locate stores in strip malls in small to medium-sized cities in an attempt to avoid direct competition with larger retailers in regional shopping centers. Compared with similarly sized regional department store chains, Marty's typically performs rather poorly, with lower than average revenue growth and much higher than average cost structure.

The local store had been a bright spot for the company. Located in a small university city (population 43,000, including 15,000 students), the store had enjoyed steady sales growth since its opening four years earlier. The store offers most types of goods usually found in department stores, with the bulk of sales revenues coming from clothing. The store prides itself on offering the most complete range of clothing for the whole family available locally. Like all Marty's stores, the local store sells several national brands as well as its own private label brand. The store normally runs at least one price promotion per month in an attempt to emphasize its attractive prices. Until recently, the store's primary local competitors included a nationally known department store, a locally owned department store, and several small specialty clothing stores.

Bethany Tate had managed the store for the past two years. She had been a management trainee with the company for only two months when the local store's original manager left the company to work for a competitor. Although company policy is for all general managers to have been with the company at least a year before being placed in their own stores, the district manager liked Bethany a lot and believed she had the qualities necessary to be successful in the retailing industry. Although she was young and relatively inexperienced (this was her first job after graduating from college with a marketing degree), she was bright, worked very hard, and people seemed to enjoy working with her, even employees twice her age. For the first 18 months, everything had gone smoothly, despite Bethany's unspoken fears of getting in over her head. Things began to change when Naples came to town.

Naples Clothing Co.

The Naples Clothing Co. chain has been in existence barely 10 years, yet routinely outperforms virtually all other specialty clothing chains. The company sells only its own brand of casual clothes, which it manufactures in various locations around the world. The clothing line is extremely popular at the present time; the Naples Clothing Co. name and logo appear on millions of articles of clothing in current use. In many cases, wearers become walking advertisements for the company. The company emphasizes reasonable everyday prices, with occasional price promotions, particularly on overstocked or out-of-season merchandise.

Initially, the company's strategy was to locate in newer strip malls in cities of 400,000 and above. The company often opened two to four stores (or more) in these cities. With increasing success, however, the company has begun to locate in selected smaller communities. The stores are uniform in design, appearance, and merchandise selection (with some small regional differences). The stores feature an open, no-frills layout, which helps keep costs low. There are currently 524 Naples Clothing Co. outlets in the United States, with the company opening about 80 new stores per year.

Marketing Research

Bethany Tate was convinced that her revenues were suffering due to the popularity of Naples Clothing Co., particularly among college students. Worse, she realized that she had no real idea what college students thought about her store. Recognizing the need for more information, she convinced her district manager to allow her to hire a local research company to determine consumer perceptions of both Marty's Department Store and Naples Clothing Co. among younger consumers. The company was interested in the results, because they expected to be competing with Naples Clothing Co. in more and more markets.

The research company and Bethany agreed to focus on three key areas in their research with young consumers: (1) identifying the attributes of retail stores deemed most important, (2) determining perceptions of Marty's, and (3) determining perceptions of Naples Clothing Co. for comparison purposes. After some preliminary exploratory research, the research company developed a one-page (front and back) survey to be administered to local residents between the ages of 18 and 25 (Exhibit 1; the codebook is presented in Exhibit 2). An area sample was used, and surveys were dropped off at each residence within randomly selected clusters. A total of 208 usable questionnaires were received from eligible respondents.

Questions

1. Did this research result from planned or unplanned change? Is the research discovery or strategy oriented? Explain.
2. Suppose that the mean score for "good service" is 4.1 on the five-point "definitely no–definitely yes" scale (see survey). What can you conclude from this information? How might this score be given more meaning? Explain.
3. How important are the various attributes of retail stores to young consumers in this market? Present your answer using (a) mean scores and standard deviations and (b) two-boxes. Technically speaking, can Bethany conclude that service is more important than atmosphere to these consumers?
4. In terms of service quality and employee helpfulness, do perceptions of Marty's Department Store differ for those who have visited the store versus those who have not? What would your results mean to Bethany Tate, if anything?
5. Overall, how does Marty's Department Store compare with Naples Clothing Co. on key attributes? Are any differences statistically significant? If so, what do they mean?

Exhibit 1	**Marty's Questionnaire**

PART I

1. Please rate how important each of the following items are to you for retail stores on a scale of 1 to 5, where "1" is "not important" and "5" is "very important":

	Not Important				Very Important
Service	1	2	3	4	5
Merchandise quality	1	2	3	4	5
Merchandise variety	1	2	3	4	5
Price	1	2	3	4	5
Atmosphere	1	2	3	4	5
Convenience	1	2	3	4	5
Value of brand name	1	2	3	4	5
Merchandise style	1	2	3	4	5

2. Please rate Naples Clothing Co. on each of the following characteristics on a scale of 1 to 5, where "1" is "definitely NO" and "5" is "definitely YES":

	Definitely NO				Definitely YES
Good service	1	2	3	4	5
Good quality	1	2	3	4	5
Good variety	1	2	3	4	5
Low price	1	2	3	4	5
Appealing atmosphere	1	2	3	4	5
Convenient location	1	2	3	4	5
Brand name is appealing	1	2	3	4	5
Stylish products	1	2	3	4	5
Good value	1	2	3	4	5
Good reputation	1	2	3	4	5
Fun to shop	1	2	3	4	5
Helpful employees	1	2	3	4	5

Have you visited the local Naples Clothing Co.? ☐ Yes ☐ No

(Continued)

Exhibit 1   **Marty's Questionnaire (*Continued*)**

3. Please rate Marty's Department Store on each of the following characteristics on a scale of 1 to 5, "1" being "definitely NO" and "5" being "definitely YES."

	Definitely NO				Definitely YES
Good service	1	2	3	4	5
Good quality	1	2	3	4	5
Good variety	1	2	3	4	5
Low price	1	2	3	4	5
Appealing atmosphere	1	2	3	4	5
Convenient location	1	2	3	4	5
Brand name is appealing	1	2	3	4	5
Stylish products	1	2	3	4	5
Good value	1	2	3	4	5
Good reputation	1	2	3	4	5
Fun to shop	1	2	3	4	5
Helpful employees	1	2	3	4	5

Have you visited the local Marty's Department Store?   ☐ Yes   ☐ No

PART II

1. What do you perceive as the average age of a typical person who shops at the local Naples Clothing Co.?
         _____ years old

2. What do you perceive as the average age of a typical person who shops at the local Marty's Department Store?
         _____ years old

3. Approximately how many times in the past month have you shopped at the following:
         a. local Marty's Department Store
         _____ times
         b. local Naples Clothing Co.
         _____ times

4. Approximately how many times in the past month have you seen an advertisement for Naples Clothing Co. on the following forms of media?
         Television: _____ times
         Print (newspaper and magazine): _____ times
         Radio: _____ times

5. Approximately how many times in the past month have you seen an advertisement for Marty's Department Store on the following forms of media?
         Television: _____ times
         Print (newspaper and magazine): _____ times
         Radio: _____ times

6. Approximately how much money do you spend on clothing each month?
         $_____

Thank you for your time.

Exhibit 2   Marty's Codebook

Columns		Variable Name/Description	
1–4		ID	SURVEY ID#
5	GEN	Gender	1 = male 2 = female
6	IMP1	Retail Store Attribute Importance - item 1	1–5; Not Important, Very Important
7	IMP2	Retail Store Attribute Importance - item 2	1–5; Not Important, Very Important
8	IMP3	Retail Store Attribute Importance - item 3	1–5; Not Important, Very Important
9	IMP4	Retail Store Attribute Importance - item 4	1–5; Not Important, Very Important
10	IMP5	Retail Store Attribute Importance - item 5	1–5; Not Important, Very Important
11	IMP6	Retail Store Attribute Importance - item 6	1–5; Not Important, Very Important
12	IMP7	Retail Store Attribute Importance - item 7	1–5; Not Important, Very Important
13	IMP8	Retail Store Attribute Importance - item 8	1–5; Not Important, Very Important
14	NAPLES1	Perceptions of Naples Clothing Co., item 1	1–5; Definitely NO, Definitely YES
15	NAPLES2	Perceptions of Naples Clothing Co., item 2	1–5; Definitely NO, Definitely YES
16	NAPLES3	Perceptions of Naples Clothing Co., item 3	1–5; Definitely NO, Definitely YES
17	NAPLES4	Perceptions of Naples Clothing Co., item 4	1–5; Definitely NO, Definitely YES
18	NAPLES5	Perceptions of Naples Clothing Co., item 5	1–5; Definitely NO, Definitely YES
19	NAPLES6	Perceptions of Naples Clothing Co., item 6	1–5; Definitely NO, Definitely YES
20	NAPLES7	Perceptions of Naples Clothing Co., item 7	1–5; Definitely NO, Definitely YES
21	NAPLES8	Perceptions of Naples Clothing Co., item 8	1–5; Definitely NO, Definitely YES
22	NAPLES9	Perceptions of Naples Clothing Co., item 9	1–5; Definitely NO, Definitely YES
23	NAPLES10	Perceptions of Naples Clothing Co., item 10	1–5; Definitely NO, Definitely YES
24	NAPLES11	Perceptions of Naples Clothing Co., item 11	1–5; Definitely NO, Definitely YES
25	NAPLES12	Perceptions of Naples Clothing Co., item 12	1–5; Definitely NO, Definitely YES
26	VISNAT	Visited Naples Clothing Co.?	1 = yes, 2 = no
27	MARTYS1	Perceptions of Marty's Department Store, item 1	1–5; Definitely NO, Definitely YES
28	MARTYS2	Perceptions of Marty's Department Store, item 2	1–5; Definitely NO, Definitely YES
29	MARTYS3	Perceptions of Marty's Department Store, item 3	1–5; Definitely NO, Definitely YES
30	MARTYS4	Perceptions of Marty's Department Store, item 4	1–5; Definitely NO, Definitely YES
31	MARTYS5	Perceptions of Marty's Department Store, item 5	1–5; Definitely NO, Definitely YES
32	MARTYS6	Perceptions of Marty's Department Store, item 6	1–5; Definitely NO, Definitely YES
33	MARTYS7	Perceptions of Marty's Codepartment Store, item 7	1–5; Definitely NO, Definitely YES
34	MARTYS8	Perceptions of Marty's Department Store, item 8	1–5; Definitely NO, Definitely YES
35	MARTYS9	Perceptions of Marty's Department Store item 9	1–5; Definitely NO, Definitely YES
36	MARTYS10	Perceptions of Marty's Department Store, item 10	1–5; Definitely NO, Definitely YES
37	MARTYS11	Perceptions of Marty's Department Store, item 11	1–5; Definitely NO, Definitely YES
38	MARTYS12	Perceptions of Marty's Department Store, item 12	1–5; Definitely NO, Definitely YES
39	VISMARTY	Visited Marty's Department Store?	1 = yes, 2 = no
40–41	AGENAP	Naples average perceived age of customers	
42–43	AGEMART	Marty's average perceived age of customers	
44–45	SHOPMART	Marty's times shopped in last month	
46–47	SHOPNAP	Naples times shopped in last month	
48–49	NAPTV	Number of Naples advertisements seen on TV last month	
50–51	NAPPRINT	Number of Naples advertisements seen in print last month	
52–53	NAPRADIO	Number of Naples advertisements heard on radio last month	
54–55	MARTV	Number of Marty's advertisements seen on TV last month	
56–57	MARPRINT	Number of Marty's advertisements seen in print last month	
58–59	MARRADIO	Number of Marty's advertisements heard on radio last month	
60–62	MONEY	Average money spent on clothing each month	

Missing Data: Blank

case 18

Wisconsin Power & Light[1]

In response to the current consumer trend toward increased environmental sensitivity, Wisconsin Power & Light (WP&L) adopted several high-visibility environmental initiatives. These environmental programs fell under the BuySmart umbrella of WP&L's Demand-Side Management Programs and were intended to foster the conservation of energy among WP&L's residential, commercial, and industrial customers. Examples of specific programs include Appliance Rebates, Energy Analysis, Weatherization Help, and the Home Energy Improvement Loan (HEIL) program. All previous marketing research and information gathering focused primarily on issues from the customers' perspective, such as an evaluation of net program impacts in terms of energy and demand savings and an estimation of the levels of free ridership (individuals who would have undertaken the conservation actions promoted by the program, even if there was no program in place). In addition, a study has been designed and is currently being conducted to evaluate and identify customer attitudes and opinions concerning the design, implementation, features, and delivery of the residential programs. Having examined the consumer perspective, WP&L's next objective is to focus on obtaining information from other participants in the programs, namely employees and lenders.

WP&L's immediate research focus is to undertake a study of the Home Energy Improvement Loan (HEIL) program of the BuySmart umbrella. The HEIL program was introduced in 1987 and was designed to make low-interest-rate financing available to residential gas and electric WP&L customers for conservation and weatherization measures. The low-interest guaranteed loans are delivered through WP&L account representatives in conjunction with participating financial institutions and trade allies. The procedures for obtaining a loan begin with an energy "audit" of the interested customer's residence to determine the appropriate conservation measures. Once the customer decides on which measures to have installed, the WP&L representative assists in arranging low-interest-rate financing through one of the participating local banking institutions. At the completion of the projects, WP&L representatives conduct an inspection of the work by checking a random sample of participants. Conservation measures eligible under the HEIL program include the installation of natural gas furnaces/boilers, automatic vent dampers, intermittent ignition devices, heat pumps, and heat pump water heaters. Eligible structural improvements include the addition of attic/wall/basement insulation, storm windows and doors, sillbox insulation, window weatherstripping, and caulking.

Purpose

The primary goal of the current study is to identify ways of improving the HEIL program from the lenders' point of view. Specifically, the following issues need to be addressed:

- Identify the lenders' motivation for participating in the program.
- Determine how lenders get their information regarding various changes/updates in the program.
- Identify how lenders promote the program.
- Assess the current program with respect to administrative and program features.
- Determine the type of credit analysis conducted by the lenders.
- Identify ways of minimizing the default rate from the lenders' point of view.
- Assess the lenders' commitment to the program.
- Identify lenders' opinions of the overall program.
- Identify if the reason for loan inactivity in some lending institutions is due to lack of a customer base.

Methodology

WP&L decided to use a telephone survey of participating lending institutions to collect the data for its study. WP&L referenced two lists of lending institutions, which were supplied by its residential marketing staff, in order to select the sample for the survey. A total of 124 participating lending institutions were identified. However, one of the lists was shorter than the other by 15 names. Specifically, the names of some of the branches of major banks were not enumerated on one of the lists. Nevertheless, all 124 institutions, including the 15 discrepant ones, were included in the pool of names from which the sample was drawn.

The sample pool was stratified into three groups based on loan activity in the previous calendar year, as follows:

Group	Number of Lenders	Loan Activity
1	44	0 loans
2	40	1 to 7 loans
3	40	8 to 54 loans

The final sample for the survey consisted of 20 systematically chosen lenders from Groups 2 and 3, and

[1]The contributions of Kavita Maini and Paul Metz to the development of this case are gratefully acknowledged as is the permission of Wisconsin Power & Light to use the material included.

10 randomly chosen institutions from Group 1. The 40 institutions selected from among Groups 2 and 3 formed the sample base in which WP&L was most interested (each of these 40 institutions demonstrated loan activity in the past year). Consequently, WP&L used a systematic selection procedure for this key group in order to ensure that the sample was representative of the population and to improve the statistical efficiency of the sample. The sample size ($n = 40$) was based on judgment. The 10 randomly selected institutions from Group 1 were chosen primarily to explore the hypothesized reasons for zero-loan activity. These 10 zero-loan lenders received a shortened version of the telephone survey that focused only on their lack of activity.

All the districts within WP&L's service territory were notified two weeks in advance that a survey was going to be conducted. A survey was designed to address the research objectives and included both closed- and open-ended questions. The survey was pretested and modified prior to final administration. All interviewing was conducted over a one-week period by a project manager and research assistant, both employees of WP&L's marketing department.

One of the open-ended questions in the survey asked lenders to identify the benefits gained by participating in the HEIL program. The actual wording of the question follows:

Q.6 Does your bank benefit in any way by participating in this program?

1 Yes

2 No

Q.7 Would you please explain your answer?

Data from this question, it was hypothesized, could be used to address several of the aforementioned research objectives. First, the responses would provide qualitative insights into the lenders' motivation for participating in the program. Second, they would help explain lenders' level of commitment to the program as well as help identify reasons why banks promote (or fail to promote) the HEIL program. Finally, the benefits cited could provide WP&L with an understanding of the lenders' overall opinion of the program. Exhibit 1 contains a list of the verbatim responses to this open-ended question.

Questions

1. Synthesize the verbatim responses by developing a set of codes and then grouping them into categories that would help WP&L understand the perceived benefits of the HEIL program.
2. What advantages does the researcher gain by coding open-ended data?
3. What recommendations would you make to WP&L about the HEIL program based on what the open-ended data suggest?

Exhibit 1

Verbatim Responses Regarding the Benefits Conveyed to Lenders by Participation in the HEIL Program

1. We acquire a new loan customer. The customer likes the fact that the loan is guaranteed.
2. It's good public relations to be associated with WP&L. Also, we have nothing to lose on it. It is a risk-free program.
3. It fulfills the CRA (Credit Reinvestment Act) requirement.
4. We got some new customers. People from other towns cannot get into the HEIL program from their bank.
5. We make some money through the buydown.
6. We have access to more customers and can therefore cross-sell other services. We stay competitive this way. It's also good PR to be associated with WP&L.
7. We provide another service to the customer. It helps us to stay competitive.
8. We improve on customer service by providing an additional service. It helps us stay competitive.
9. We can provide another service. We have also built customer contact a lot more.
10. We earn interest income. Customers look on us more favorably because this program is really good.
11. We got some new customers. In addition, the HEIL program helps us make more loans, which is helping us to make revenue.
12. We get money out of the interest buydowns.
13. Another service to provide our customers.
14. It is an added service that enriches our offerings. People come back for other loans.
15. If fulfills CRA. Also, good public relations to be associated with WP&L.
16. It fulfills CRA. Also, more loans implies more income for the bank and a higher proportion can be reinvested back into the community.
17. Another service to provide our customers.
18. It fulfills CRA.
19. Another service to provide for our customers.
20. Good public relations.

(Continued)

21. We can provide another service to our customers.
22. We got some new customers.
23. It's good for our customers.
24. No benefits anymore. There are so many restrictions. There should be more types of options.
25. We are in it for the CRA.
26. We can provide another service to our customers.
27. No benefits because too many good options are excluded.
28. It fulfills the CRA requirement. We are providing the customers a service that has very good rates.
29. We got some new customers.
30. Financially, we get more money by lending without the program.
31. We provide another service to our customers.
32. We are in it for the CRA.
33. We get money through the buydowns.
34. We gain new customers.
35. Good public relations.
36. We provide another service and it allows us to help people who really need the loan.
37. We provide another service to our clients and community.
38. It helps us provide another service to our clients and community.
39. We don't have a high enough volume to be able to say that there has been a benefit.
40. We provide another service to our customers.

| Table 1 | Cumulative Standard Unit Normal Distribution |

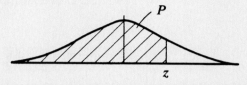

Values of P corresponding to Z for the normal curve. Z is the standard normal variable. The value of P for $-Z$ equals one minus the value of P for $+Z$, (e.g., the P for -1.62 equals $1 - .9474 = .0526$).

Z	.00	.01	.02	.03	.04	.05	.06	.07	.08	.09
.0	.5000	.5040	.5080	.5120	.5160	.5199	.5239	.5279	.5319	.5359
.1	.5398	.5438	.5478	.5517	.5557	.5596	.5636	.5675	.5714	.5753
.2	.5793	.5832	.5871	.5910	.5948	.5987	.6026	.6064	.6103	.6141
.3	.6179	.6217	.6255	.6293	.6331	.6368	.6406	.6443	.6480	.6517
.4	.6554	.6591	.6628	.6664	.6700	.6736	.6772	.6808	.6844	.6879
.5	.6915	.6950	.6985	.7019	.7054	.7088	.7123	.7157	.7190	.7224
.6	.7257	.7291	.7324	.7357	.7389	.7422	.7454	.7486	.7517	.7549
.7	.7580	.7611	.7642	.7673	.7704	.7734	.7764	.7794	.7823	.7852
.8	.7881	.7910	.7939	.7967	.7995	.8023	.8051	.8078	.8106	.8133
.9	.8159	.8186	.8212	.8238	.8264	.8289	.8315	.8340	.8365	.8389
1.0	.8413	.8438	.8461	.8485	.8508	.8531	.8554	.8577	.8599	.8621
1.1	.8643	.8665	.8686	.8708	.8729	.8749	.8770	.8790	.8810	.8830
1.2	.8849	.8869	.8888	.8907	.8925	.8944	.8962	.8980	.8997	.9015
1.3	.9032	.9049	.9066	.9082	.9099	.9115	.9131	.9147	.9162	.9177
1.4	.9192	.9207	.9222	.9236	.9251	.9265	.9279	.9292	.9306	.9319
1.5	.9332	.9345	.9357	.9370	.9382	.9394	.9406	.9418	.9429	.9441
1.6	.9452	.9463	.9474	.9484	.9495	.9505	.9515	.9525	.9535	.9545
1.7	.9554	.9564	.9573	.9582	.9591	.9599	.9608	.9616	.9625	.9633
1.8	.9641	.9649	.9656	.9664	.9671	.9678	.9686	.9693	.9699	.9706
1.9	.9713	.9719	.9726	.9732	.9738	.9744	.9750	.9756	.9761	.9767
2.0	.9772	.9778	.9783	.9788	.9793	.9798	.9803	.9808	.9812	.9817
2.1	.9821	.9826	.9830	.9834	.9838	.9842	.9846	.9850	.9854	.9857
2.2	.9861	.9864	.9868	.9871	.9875	.9878	.9881	.9884	.9887	.9890
2.3	.9893	.9896	.9898	.9901	.9904	.9906	.9909	.9911	.9913	.9916
2.4	.9918	.9920	.9922	.9925	.9927	.9929	.9931	.9932	.9934	.9936
2.5	.9938	.9940	.9941	.9943	.9945	.9946	.9948	.9949	.9951	.9952
2.6	.9953	.9955	.9956	.9957	.9959	.9960	.9961	.9962	.9963	.9964
2.7	.9965	.9966	.9967	.9968	.9969	.9970	.9971	.9972	.9973	.9974
2.8	.9974	.9975	.9976	.9977	.9977	.9978	.9979	.9979	.9980	.9981
2.9	.9981	.9982	.9982	.9983	.9984	.9984	.9985	.9985	.9986	.9986
3.0	.9987	.9987	.9987	.9988	.9988	.9989	.9989	.9989	.9990	.9990
3.1	.9990	.9991	.9991	.9991	.9992	.9992	.9992	.9992	.9993	.9993
3.2	.9993	.9993	.9994	.9994	.9994	.9994	.9994	.9995	.9995	.9995
3.3	.9995	.9995	.9995	.9996	.9996	.9996	.9996	.9996	.9996	.9997
3.4	.9997	.9997	.9997	.9997	.9997	.9997	.9997	.9997	.9997	.9998

Source: Paul E. Green, *Analyzing Multivariate Data* (Chicago: Dryden Press, 1978).

Table 2

Selected Percentiles of the χ^2 Distribution

Values of χ^2 corresponding to P

ν	$\chi^2_{.005}$	$\chi^2_{.01}$	$\chi^2_{.025}$	$\chi^2_{.05}$	$\chi^2_{.10}$	$\chi^2_{.90}$	$\chi^2_{.95}$	$\chi^2_{.975}$	$\chi^2_{.99}$	$\chi^2_{.995}$
1	.000039	.00016	.00098	.0039	.0158	2.71	3.84	5.02	6.63	7.88
2	.0100	.0201	.0506	.1026	.2107	4.61	5.99	7.38	9.21	10.60
3	.0717	.115	.216	.352	.584	6.25	7.81	9.35	11.34	12.84
4	.207	.297	.484	.711	1.064	7.78	9.49	11.14	13.28	14.86
5	.412	.554	.831	1.15	1.61	9.24	11.07	12.83	15.09	16.75
6	.676	.872	1.24	1.64	2.20	10.64	12.59	14.45	16.81	18.55
7	.989	1.24	1.69	2.17	2.83	12.02	14.07	16.01	18.48	20.28
8	1.34	1.65	2.18	2.73	3.49	13.36	15.51	17.53	20.09	21.96
9	1.73	2.09	2.70	3.33	4.17	14.68	16.92	19.02	21.67	23.59
10	2.16	2.56	3.25	3.94	4.87	15.99	18.31	20.48	23.21	25.19
11	2.60	3.05	3.82	4.57	5.58	17.28	19.68	21.92	24.73	26.76
12	3.07	3.57	4.40	5.23	6.30	18.55	21.03	23.34	26.22	28.30
13	3.57	4.11	5.01	5.89	7.04	19.81	22.36	24.74	27.69	29.82
14	4.07	4.66	5.63	6.57	7.79	21.06	23.68	26.12	29.14	31.32
15	4.60	5.23	6.26	7.26	8.55	22.31	25.00	27.49	30.58	32.80
16	5.14	5.81	6.91	7.96	9.31	23.54	26.30	28.85	32.00	34.27
18	6.26	7.01	8.23	9.39	10.86	25.99	28.87	31.53	34.81	37.16
20	7.43	8.26	9.59	10.85	12.44	28.41	31.41	34.17	37.57	40.00
24	9.89	10.86	12.40	13.85	15.66	33.20	36.42	39.36	42.98	45.56
30	13.79	14.95	16.79	18.49	20.60	40.26	43.77	46.98	50.89	53.67
40	20.71	22.16	24.43	26.51	29.05	51.81	55.76	59.34	63.69	66.77
60	35.53	37.48	40.48	43.19	46.46	74.40	79.08	83.30	88.38	91.95
120	83.85	86.92	91.58	95.70	100.62	140.23	146.57	152.21	158.95	163.64

Source: Adapted with permission from W. J. Dixon and F. J. Massey, Jr., *Introduction to Statistical Analysis*, 2nd ed. © 1957 McGraw-Hill.

Table 3

Upper Percentiles of the t Distribution

ν	$1-\alpha$ .75	.90	.95	.975	.99	.995	.9995
1	1.000	3.078	6.314	12.706	31.821	63.657	636.619
2	.816	1.886	2.920	4.303	6.965	9.925	31.598
3	.765	1.638	2.353	3.182	4.541	5.841	12.941
4	.741	1.533	2.132	2.776	3.747	4.604	8.610
5	.727	1.476	2.015	2.571	3.365	4.032	6.859
6	.718	1.440	1.943	2.447	3.143	3.707	5.959
7	.711	1.415	1.895	2.365	2.998	3.499	5.405
8	.706	1.397	1.860	2.306	2.896	3.355	5.041
9	.703	1.383	1.833	2.262	2.821	3.250	4.781
10	.700	1.372	1.812	2.228	2.764	3.169	4.587
11	.697	1.363	1.796	2.201	2.718	3.106	4.437
12	.695	1.356	1.782	2.179	2.681	3.055	4.318
13	.694	1.350	1.771	2.160	2.650	3.012	4.221
14	.692	1.345	1.761	2.145	2.624	2.977	4.140
15	.691	1.341	1.753	2.131	2.602	2.947	4.073
16	.690	1.337	1.746	2.120	2.583	2.921	4.015
17	.689	1.333	1.740	2.110	2.567	2.898	3.965
18	.688	1.330	1.734	2.101	2.552	2.878	3.922
19	.688	1.328	1.729	2.093	2.339	2.861	3.883
20	.687	1.325	1.725	2.086	2.528	2.845	3.850
21	.686	1.323	1.721	2.080	2.518	2.831	3.819
22	.686	1.321	1.717	2.074	2.508	2.819	3.792
23	.685	1.319	1.714	2.069	2.500	2.807	3.767
24	.685	1.318	1.711	2.064	2.492	2.797	3.745
25	.684	1.316	1.708	2.060	2.485	2.787	3.725
26	.684	1.315	1.706	2.056	2.479	2.779	3.707
27	.684	1.314	1.703	2.052	2.473	2.771	3.690
28	.683	1.313	1.701	2.048	2.467	2.763	3.674
29	.683	1.311	1.699	2.045	2.462	2.756	3.659
30	.683	1.310	1.697	2.042	2.457	2.750	3.646
40	.681	1.303	1.684	2.021	2.423	2.704	3.551
60	.679	1.296	1.671	2.000	2.390	2.660	3.460
120	.677	1.289	1.658	1.980	2.358	2.617	3.373
∞	.674	1.282	1.645	1.960	2.326	2.576	3.291

ν = degrees of freedom

Source: Taken from Table III of R. A. Fisher and F. Yates, *Statistical Tables for Biological, Agricultural, and Medical Research* (London: Longman Group UK, Ltd., 1974).

Selected Percentiles of the F Distribution

$$F_{.90(\nu_1, \nu_2)} \quad \alpha = 0.1$$

ν_1 = degrees of freedom for numerator

ν_2 = degrees of freedom for denominator

$\nu_2 \backslash \nu_1$	1	2	3	4	5	6	7	8	9	10	12	15	20	24	30	40	60	120	∞
1	39.86	49.50	53.59	55.83	57.24	58.20	58.91	59.44	59.86	60.19	60.71	61.22	61.74	62.00	62.26	62.53	62.79	63.06	63.33
2	8.53	9.00	9.16	9.24	9.29	9.33	9.35	9.37	9.38	9.39	9.41	9.42	9.44	9.45	9.46	9.47	9.47	9.48	9.49
3	5.54	5.46	5.39	5.34	5.31	5.28	5.27	5.25	5.24	5.23	5.22	5.20	5.18	5.18	5.17	5.16	5.15	5.14	5.13
4	4.54	4.32	4.19	4.11	4.05	4.01	3.98	3.95	3.94	3.92	3.90	3.87	3.84	3.83	3.82	3.80	3.79	3.78	3.76
5	4.06	3.78	3.62	3.52	3.45	3.40	3.37	3.34	3.32	3.30	3.27	3.24	3.21	3.19	3.17	3.16	3.14	3.12	3.10
6	3.78	3.46	3.29	3.18	3.11	3.05	3.01	2.98	2.96	2.94	2.90	2.87	2.84	2.82	2.80	2.78	2.76	2.74	2.72
7	3.59	3.26	3.07	2.96	2.88	2.83	2.78	2.75	2.72	2.70	2.67	2.63	2.59	2.58	2.56	2.54	2.51	2.49	2.47
8	3.46	3.11	2.92	2.81	2.73	2.67	2.62	2.59	2.56	2.54	2.50	2.46	2.42	2.40	2.38	2.36	2.34	2.32	2.29
9	3.36	3.01	2.81	2.69	2.61	2.55	2.51	2.47	2.44	2.42	2.38	2.34	2.30	2.28	2.25	2.23	2.21	2.18	2.16
10	3.29	2.92	2.73	2.61	2.52	2.46	2.41	2.38	2.35	2.32	2.28	2.24	2.20	2.18	2.16	2.13	2.11	2.08	2.06
11	3.23	2.86	2.66	2.54	2.45	2.39	2.34	2.30	2.27	2.25	2.21	2.17	2.12	2.10	2.08	2.05	2.03	2.00	1.97
12	3.18	2.81	2.61	2.48	2.39	2.33	2.28	2.24	2.21	2.19	2.15	2.10	2.06	2.04	2.01	1.99	1.96	1.93	1.90
13	3.14	2.76	2.56	2.43	2.35	2.28	2.23	2.20	2.16	2.14	2.10	2.05	2.01	1.98	1.96	1.93	1.90	1.88	1.85
14	3.10	2.73	2.52	2.39	2.31	2.24	2.19	2.15	2.12	2.10	2.05	2.01	1.96	1.94	1.91	1.89	1.86	1.83	1.80
15	3.07	2.70	2.49	2.36	2.27	2.21	2.16	2.12	2.09	2.06	2.02	1.97	1.92	1.90	1.87	1.85	1.82	1.79	1.76
16	3.05	2.67	2.46	2.33	2.24	2.18	2.13	2.09	2.06	2.03	1.99	1.94	1.89	1.87	1.84	1.81	1.78	1.75	1.72
17	3.03	2.64	2.44	2.31	2.22	2.15	2.10	2.06	2.03	2.00	1.96	1.91	1.86	1.84	1.81	1.78	1.75	1.72	1.69
18	3.01	2.62	2.42	2.29	2.20	2.13	2.08	2.04	2.00	1.98	1.93	1.89	1.84	1.81	1.78	1.75	1.72	1.69	1.66
19	2.99	2.61	2.40	2.27	2.18	2.11	2.06	2.02	1.98	1.96	1.91	1.86	1.81	1.79	1.76	1.73	1.70	1.67	1.63
20	2.97	2.59	2.38	2.25	2.16	2.09	2.04	2.00	1.96	1.94	1.89	1.84	1.79	1.77	1.74	1.71	1.68	1.64	1.61
21	2.96	2.57	2.36	2.23	2.14	2.08	2.02	1.98	1.95	1.92	1.87	1.83	1.78	1.75	1.72	1.69	1.66	1.62	1.59
22	2.95	2.56	2.35	2.22	2.13	2.06	2.01	1.97	1.93	1.90	1.86	1.81	1.76	1.73	1.70	1.67	1.64	1.60	1.57
23	2.94	2.55	2.34	2.21	2.11	2.05	1.99	1.95	1.92	1.89	1.84	1.80	1.74	1.72	1.69	1.66	1.62	1.59	1.55
24	2.93	2.54	2.33	2.19	2.10	2.04	1.98	1.94	1.91	1.88	1.83	1.78	1.73	1.70	1.67	1.64	1.61	1.57	1.53
25	2.92	2.53	2.32	2.18	2.09	2.02	1.97	1.93	1.89	1.87	1.82	1.77	1.72	1.69	1.66	1.63	1.59	1.56	1.52
26	2.91	2.52	2.31	2.17	2.08	2.01	1.96	1.92	1.88	1.86	1.81	1.76	1.71	1.68	1.65	1.61	1.58	1.54	1.50
27	2.90	2.51	2.30	2.17	2.07	2.00	1.95	1.91	1.87	1.85	1.80	1.75	1.70	1.67	1.64	1.60	1.57	1.53	1.49
28	2.89	2.50	2.29	2.16	2.06	2.00	1.94	1.90	1.87	1.84	1.79	1.74	1.69	1.66	1.63	1.59	1.56	1.52	1.48
29	2.89	2.50	2.28	2.15	2.06	1.99	1.93	1.89	1.86	1.83	1.78	1.73	1.68	1.65	1.62	1.58	1.55	1.51	1.47
30	2.88	2.49	2.28	2.14	2.05	1.98	1.93	1.88	1.85	1.82	1.77	1.72	1.67	1.64	1.61	1.57	1.54	1.50	1.46
40	2.84	2.44	2.23	2.09	2.00	1.93	1.87	1.83	1.79	1.76	1.71	1.66	1.61	1.57	1.54	1.51	1.47	1.42	1.38
60	2.79	2.39	2.18	2.04	1.95	1.87	1.82	1.77	1.74	1.71	1.66	1.60	1.54	1.51	1.48	1.44	1.40	1.35	1.29
120	2.75	2.35	2.13	1.99	1.90	1.82	1.77	1.72	1.68	1.65	1.60	1.55	1.48	1.45	1.41	1.37	1.32	1.26	1.19
∞	2.71	2.30	2.08	1.94	1.85	1.77	1.72	1.67	1.63	1.60	1.55	1.49	1.42	1.38	1.34	1.30	1.24	1.17	1.00

Source: From *Biometrika Tables for Statisticians*, Vol. 1, 2nd Ed., ed. E. S. Pearson and H. O. Hartley, (Cambridge University Press, 1958).

Table 4 — Selected Percentiles of the F Distribution (Continued)

$$F_{.95}(\nu_1, \nu_2) \qquad \alpha = 0.05$$

ν_1 = degrees of freedom for numerator

ν_2 = degrees of freedom for denominator

$\nu_2 \backslash \nu_1$	1	2	3	4	5	6	7	8	9	10	12	15	20	24	30	40	60	120	∞
1	161.4	199.5	215.7	224.6	230.2	234.0	236.8	238.9	240.5	241.9	243.9	245.9	248.0	249.1	250.1	251.1	252.2	253.3	254.3
2	18.51	19.00	19.16	19.25	19.30	19.33	19.35	19.37	19.38	19.40	19.41	19.43	19.45	19.45	19.46	19.47	19.48	19.49	19.50
3	10.13	9.55	9.28	9.12	9.01	8.94	8.89	8.85	8.81	8.79	8.74	8.70	8.66	8.64	8.62	8.59	8.57	8.55	8.53
4	7.71	6.94	6.59	6.39	6.26	6.16	6.09	6.04	6.00	5.96	5.91	5.86	5.80	5.77	5.75	5.72	5.69	5.66	5.63
5	6.61	5.79	5.41	5.19	5.05	4.95	4.88	4.82	4.77	4.74	4.68	4.62	4.56	4.53	4.50	4.46	4.43	4.40	4.36
6	5.99	5.14	4.76	4.53	4.39	4.28	4.21	4.15	4.10	4.06	4.00	3.94	3.87	3.84	3.81	3.77	3.74	3.70	3.67
7	5.59	4.74	4.35	4.12	3.97	3.87	3.79	3.73	3.68	3.64	3.57	3.51	3.44	3.41	3.38	3.34	3.30	3.27	3.23
8	5.32	4.46	4.07	3.84	3.69	3.58	3.50	3.44	3.39	3.35	3.28	3.22	3.15	3.12	3.08	3.04	3.01	2.97	2.93
9	5.12	4.26	3.86	3.63	3.48	3.37	3.29	3.23	3.18	3.14	3.07	3.01	2.94	2.90	2.86	2.83	2.79	2.75	2.71
10	4.96	4.10	3.71	3.48	3.33	3.22	3.14	3.07	3.02	2.98	2.91	2.85	2.77	2.74	2.70	2.66	2.62	2.58	2.54
11	4.84	3.98	3.59	3.36	3.20	3.09	3.01	2.95	2.90	2.85	2.79	2.72	2.65	2.61	2.57	2.53	2.49	2.45	2.40
12	4.75	3.89	3.49	3.26	3.11	3.00	2.91	2.85	2.80	2.75	2.69	2.62	2.54	2.51	2.47	2.43	2.38	2.34	2.30
13	4.67	3.81	3.41	3.18	3.03	2.92	2.83	2.77	2.71	2.67	2.60	2.53	2.46	2.42	2.38	2.34	2.30	2.25	2.21
14	4.60	3.74	3.34	3.11	2.96	2.85	2.76	2.70	2.65	2.60	2.53	2.46	2.39	2.35	2.31	2.27	2.22	2.18	2.13
15	4.54	3.68	3.29	3.06	2.90	2.79	2.71	2.64	2.59	2.54	2.48	2.40	2.33	2.29	2.25	2.20	2.16	2.11	2.07
16	4.49	3.63	3.24	3.01	2.85	2.74	2.66	2.59	2.54	2.49	2.42	2.35	2.28	2.24	2.19	2.15	2.11	2.06	2.01
17	4.45	3.59	3.20	2.96	2.81	2.70	2.61	2.55	2.49	2.45	2.38	2.31	2.23	2.19	2.15	2.10	2.06	2.01	1.96
18	4.41	3.55	3.16	2.93	2.77	2.66	2.58	2.51	2.46	2.41	2.34	2.27	2.19	2.15	2.11	2.06	2.02	1.97	1.92
19	4.38	3.52	3.13	2.90	2.74	2.63	2.54	2.48	2.42	2.38	2.31	2.23	2.16	2.11	2.07	2.03	1.98	1.93	1.88
20	4.35	3.49	3.10	2.87	2.71	2.60	2.51	2.45	2.39	2.35	2.28	2.20	2.12	2.08	2.04	1.99	1.95	1.90	1.84
21	4.32	3.47	3.07	2.84	2.68	2.57	2.49	2.42	2.37	2.32	2.25	2.18	2.10	2.05	2.01	1.96	1.92	1.87	1.81
22	4.30	3.44	3.05	2.82	2.66	2.55	2.46	2.40	2.34	2.30	2.23	2.15	2.07	2.03	1.98	1.94	1.89	1.84	1.78
23	4.28	3.42	3.03	2.80	2.64	2.53	2.44	2.37	2.32	2.27	2.20	2.13	2.05	2.01	1.96	1.91	1.86	1.81	1.76
24	4.26	3.40	3.01	2.78	2.62	2.51	2.42	2.36	2.30	2.25	2.18	2.11	2.03	1.98	1.94	1.89	1.84	1.79	1.73
25	4.24	3.39	2.99	2.76	2.60	2.49	2.40	2.34	2.28	2.24	2.16	2.09	2.01	1.96	1.92	1.87	1.82	1.77	1.71
26	4.23	3.37	2.98	2.74	2.59	2.47	2.39	2.32	2.27	2.22	2.15	2.07	1.99	1.95	1.90	1.85	1.80	1.75	1.69
27	4.21	3.35	2.96	2.73	2.57	2.46	2.37	2.31	2.25	2.20	2.13	2.06	1.97	1.93	1.88	1.84	1.79	1.73	1.67
28	4.20	3.34	2.95	2.71	2.56	2.45	2.36	2.29	2.24	2.19	2.12	2.04	1.96	1.91	1.87	1.82	1.77	1.71	1.65
29	4.18	3.33	2.93	2.70	2.55	2.43	2.35	2.28	2.22	2.18	2.10	2.03	1.94	1.90	1.85	1.81	1.75	1.70	1.64
30	4.17	3.32	2.92	2.69	2.53	2.42	2.33	2.27	2.21	2.16	2.09	2.01	1.93	1.89	1.84	1.79	1.74	1.68	1.62
40	4.08	3.23	2.84	2.61	2.45	2.34	2.25	2.18	2.12	2.08	2.00	1.92	1.84	1.79	1.74	1.69	1.64	1.58	1.51
60	4.00	3.15	2.76	2.53	2.37	2.25	2.17	2.10	2.04	1.99	1.92	1.84	1.75	1.70	1.65	1.59	1.53	1.47	1.39
120	3.92	3.07	2.68	2.45	2.29	2.17	2.09	2.02	1.96	1.91	1.83	1.75	1.66	1.61	1.55	1.50	1.43	1.35	1.25
∞	3.84	3.00	2.60	2.37	2.21	2.10	2.01	1.94	1.88	1.83	1.75	1.67	1.57	1.52	1.46	1.39	1.32	1.22	1.00

(Continued)

Table 4 Selected Percentiles of the F Distribution (Continued)

$$F_{.975}(\nu_1, \nu_2) \qquad \alpha = 0.025$$

ν_1 = degrees of freedom for numerator

ν_2 = degrees of freedom for denominator

$\nu_2 \backslash \nu_1$	1	2	3	4	5	6	7	8	9	10	12	15	20	24	30	40	60	120	∞
1	647.8	799.5	864.2	899.6	921.8	937.1	948.2	956.7	963.3	968.6	976.7	984.9	993.1	997.2	1001	1006	1010	1014	1018
2	38.51	39.00	39.17	39.25	39.30	39.33	39.36	39.37	39.39	39.40	39.41	39.43	39.45	39.46	39.46	39.47	39.48	39.49	39.50
3	17.44	16.04	15.44	15.10	14.88	14.73	14.62	14.54	14.47	14.42	14.34	14.25	14.17	14.12	14.08	14.04	13.99	13.95	13.90
4	12.22	10.65	9.98	9.60	9.36	9.20	9.07	8.98	8.90	8.84	8.75	8.66	8.56	8.51	8.46	8.41	8.36	8.31	8.26
5	10.01	8.43	7.76	7.39	7.15	6.98	6.85	6.76	6.68	6.62	6.52	6.43	6.33	6.28	6.23	6.18	6.12	6.07	6.02
6	8.81	7.26	6.60	6.23	5.99	5.82	5.70	5.60	5.52	5.46	5.37	5.27	5.17	5.12	5.07	5.01	4.96	4.90	4.85
7	8.07	6.54	5.89	5.52	5.29	5.12	4.99	4.90	4.82	4.76	4.67	4.57	4.47	4.42	4.36	4.31	4.25	4.20	4.14
8	7.57	6.06	5.42	5.05	4.82	4.65	4.53	4.43	4.36	4.30	4.20	4.10	4.00	3.95	3.89	3.84	3.78	3.73	3.67
9	7.21	5.71	5.08	4.72	4.48	4.32	4.20	4.10	4.03	3.96	3.87	3.77	3.67	3.61	3.56	3.51	3.45	3.39	3.33
10	6.94	5.46	4.83	4.47	4.24	4.07	3.95	3.85	3.78	3.72	3.62	3.52	3.42	3.37	3.31	3.26	3.20	3.14	3.08
11	6.72	5.26	4.63	4.28	4.04	3.88	3.76	3.66	3.59	3.53	3.43	3.33	3.23	3.17	3.12	3.06	3.00	2.94	2.88
12	6.55	5.10	4.47	4.12	3.89	3.73	3.61	3.51	3.44	3.37	3.28	3.18	3.07	3.02	2.96	2.91	2.85	2.79	2.72
13	6.41	4.97	4.35	4.00	3.77	3.60	3.48	3.39	3.31	3.25	3.15	3.05	2.95	2.89	2.84	2.78	2.72	2.66	2.60
14	6.30	4.86	4.24	3.89	3.66	3.50	3.38	3.29	3.21	3.15	3.05	2.95	2.84	2.79	2.73	2.67	2.61	2.55	2.49
15	6.20	4.77	4.15	3.80	3.58	3.41	3.29	3.20	3.12	3.06	2.96	2.86	2.76	2.70	2.64	2.59	2.52	2.46	2.40
16	6.12	4.69	4.08	3.73	3.50	3.34	3.22	3.12	3.05	2.99	2.89	2.79	2.68	2.63	2.57	2.51	2.45	2.38	2.32
17	6.04	4.62	4.01	3.66	3.44	3.28	3.16	3.06	2.98	2.92	2.82	2.72	2.62	2.56	2.50	2.44	2.38	2.32	2.25
18	5.98	4.56	3.95	3.61	3.38	3.22	3.10	3.01	2.93	2.87	2.77	2.67	2.56	2.50	2.44	2.38	2.32	2.26	2.19
19	5.92	4.51	3.90	3.56	3.33	3.17	3.05	2.96	2.88	2.82	2.72	2.62	2.51	2.45	2.39	2.33	2.27	2.20	2.13
20	5.87	4.46	3.86	3.51	3.29	3.13	3.01	2.91	2.84	2.77	2.68	2.57	2.46	2.41	2.35	2.29	2.22	2.16	2.09
21	5.83	4.42	3.82	3.48	3.25	3.09	2.97	2.87	2.80	2.73	2.64	2.53	2.42	2.37	2.31	2.25	2.18	2.11	2.04
22	5.79	4.38	3.78	3.44	3.22	3.05	2.93	2.84	2.76	2.70	2.60	2.50	2.39	2.33	2.27	2.21	2.14	2.08	2.00
23	5.75	4.35	3.75	3.41	3.18	3.02	2.90	2.81	2.73	2.67	2.57	2.47	2.36	2.30	2.24	2.18	2.11	2.04	1.97
24	5.72	4.32	3.72	3.38	3.15	2.99	2.87	2.78	2.70	2.64	2.54	2.44	2.33	2.27	2.21	2.15	2.08	2.01	1.94
25	5.69	4.29	3.69	3.35	3.13	2.97	2.85	2.75	2.68	2.61	2.51	2.41	2.30	2.24	2.18	2.12	2.05	1.98	1.91
26	5.66	4.27	3.67	3.33	3.10	2.94	2.82	2.73	2.65	2.59	2.49	2.39	2.28	2.22	2.16	2.09	2.03	1.95	1.88
27	5.63	4.24	3.65	3.31	3.08	2.92	2.80	2.71	2.63	2.57	2.47	2.36	2.25	2.19	2.13	2.07	2.00	1.93	1.85
28	5.61	4.22	3.63	3.29	3.06	2.90	2.78	2.69	2.61	2.55	2.45	2.34	2.23	2.17	2.11	2.05	1.98	1.91	1.83
29	5.59	4.20	3.61	3.27	3.04	2.88	2.76	2.67	2.59	2.53	2.43	2.32	2.21	2.15	2.09	2.03	1.96	1.89	1.81
30	5.57	4.18	3.59	3.25	3.03	2.87	2.75	2.65	2.57	2.51	2.41	2.31	2.20	2.14	2.07	2.01	1.94	1.87	1.79
40	5.42	4.05	3.46	3.13	2.90	2.74	2.62	2.53	2.45	2.39	2.29	2.18	2.07	2.01	1.94	1.88	1.80	1.72	1.64
60	5.29	3.93	3.34	3.01	2.79	2.63	2.51	2.41	2.33	2.27	2.17	2.06	1.94	1.88	1.82	1.74	1.67	1.58	1.48
120	5.15	3.80	3.23	2.89	2.67	2.52	2.39	2.30	2.22	2.16	2.05	1.94	1.82	1.76	1.69	1.61	1.53	1.43	1.31
∞	5.02	3.69	3.12	2.79	2.57	2.41	2.29	2.19	2.11	2.05	1.94	1.83	1.71	1.64	1.57	1.48	1.39	1.27	1.00

Table 4

Selected Percentiles of the F Distribution (Continued)

$F_{.99}(\nu_1, \nu_2)$ $\alpha = 0.01$

ν_1 = degrees of freedom for numerator

ν_2 = degrees of freedom for denominator

ν_2 \\ ν_1	1	2	3	4	5	6	7	8	9	10	12	15	20	24	30	40	60	120	∞
1	4052	4999.5	5403	5625	5764	5859	5928	5982	6022	6056	6106	6157	6209	6235	6261	6287	6313	6339	6366
2	98.50	99.00	99.17	99.25	99.30	99.33	99.36	99.37	99.39	99.40	99.42	99.43	99.45	99.46	99.47	99.47	99.48	99.49	99.50
3	34.12	30.82	29.46	28.71	28.24	27.91	27.67	27.49	27.35	27.23	27.05	26.87	26.69	26.60	26.50	26.41	26.32	26.22	26.13
4	21.20	18.00	16.69	15.98	15.52	15.21	14.98	14.80	14.66	14.55	14.37	14.20	14.02	13.93	13.84	13.75	13.65	13.56	13.46
5	16.26	13.27	12.06	11.39	10.97	10.67	10.46	10.29	10.16	10.05	9.89	9.72	9.55	9.47	9.38	9.29	9.20	9.11	9.02
6	13.75	10.92	9.78	9.15	8.75	8.47	8.26	8.10	7.98	7.87	7.72	7.56	7.40	7.31	7.23	7.14	7.06	6.97	6.88
7	12.25	9.55	8.45	7.85	7.46	7.19	6.99	6.84	6.72	6.62	6.47	6.31	6.16	6.07	5.99	5.91	5.82	5.74	5.65
8	11.26	8.65	7.59	7.01	6.63	6.37	6.18	6.03	5.91	5.81	5.67	5.52	5.36	5.28	5.20	5.12	5.03	4.95	4.86
9	10.56	8.02	6.99	6.42	6.06	5.80	5.61	5.47	5.35	5.26	5.11	4.96	4.81	4.73	4.65	4.57	4.48	4.40	4.31
10	10.04	7.56	6.55	5.99	5.64	5.39	5.20	5.06	4.94	4.85	4.71	4.56	4.41	4.33	4.25	4.17	4.08	4.00	3.91
11	9.65	7.21	6.22	5.67	5.32	5.07	4.89	4.74	4.63	4.54	4.40	4.25	4.10	4.02	3.94	3.86	3.78	3.69	3.60
12	9.33	6.93	5.95	5.41	5.06	4.82	4.64	4.50	4.39	4.30	4.16	4.01	3.86	3.78	3.70	3.62	3.54	3.45	3.36
13	9.07	6.70	5.74	5.21	4.86	4.62	4.44	4.30	4.19	4.10	3.96	3.82	3.66	3.59	3.51	3.43	3.34	3.25	3.17
14	8.86	6.51	5.56	5.04	4.69	4.46	4.28	4.14	4.03	3.94	3.80	3.66	3.51	3.43	3.35	3.27	3.18	3.09	3.00
15	8.68	6.36	5.42	4.89	4.56	4.32	4.14	4.00	3.89	3.80	3.67	3.52	3.37	3.29	3.21	3.13	3.05	2.96	2.87
16	8.53	6.23	5.29	4.77	4.44	4.20	4.03	3.89	3.78	3.69	3.55	3.41	3.26	3.18	3.10	3.02	2.93	2.84	2.75
17	8.40	6.11	5.18	4.67	4.34	4.10	3.93	3.79	3.68	3.59	3.46	3.31	3.16	3.08	3.00	2.92	2.83	2.75	2.65
18	8.29	6.01	5.09	4.58	4.25	4.01	3.84	3.71	3.60	3.51	3.37	3.23	3.08	3.00	2.92	2.84	2.75	2.66	2.57
19	8.18	5.93	5.01	4.50	4.17	3.94	3.77	3.63	3.52	3.43	3.30	3.15	3.00	2.92	2.84	2.76	2.67	2.58	2.49
20	8.10	5.85	4.94	4.43	4.10	3.87	3.70	3.56	3.46	3.37	3.23	3.09	2.94	2.86	2.78	2.69	2.61	2.52	2.42
21	8.02	5.78	4.87	4.37	4.04	3.81	3.64	3.51	3.40	3.31	3.17	3.03	2.88	2.80	2.72	2.64	2.55	2.46	2.36
22	7.95	5.72	4.82	4.31	3.99	3.76	3.59	3.45	3.35	3.26	3.12	2.98	2.83	2.75	2.67	2.58	2.50	2.40	2.31
23	7.88	5.66	4.76	4.26	3.94	3.71	3.54	3.41	3.30	3.21	3.07	2.93	2.78	2.70	2.62	2.54	2.45	2.35	2.26
24	7.82	5.61	4.72	4.22	3.90	3.67	3.50	3.36	3.26	3.17	3.03	2.89	2.74	2.66	2.58	2.49	2.40	2.31	2.21
25	7.77	5.57	4.68	4.18	3.85	3.63	3.46	3.32	3.22	3.13	2.99	2.85	2.70	2.62	2.54	2.45	2.36	2.27	2.17
26	7.72	5.53	4.64	4.14	3.82	3.59	3.42	3.29	3.18	3.09	2.96	2.81	2.66	2.58	2.50	2.42	2.33	2.23	2.13
27	7.68	5.49	4.60	4.11	3.78	3.56	3.39	3.26	3.15	3.06	2.93	2.78	2.63	2.55	2.47	2.38	2.29	2.20	2.10
28	7.64	5.45	4.57	4.07	3.75	3.53	3.36	3.23	3.12	3.03	2.90	2.75	2.60	2.52	2.44	2.35	2.26	2.17	2.06
29	7.60	5.42	4.54	4.04	3.73	3.50	3.33	3.20	3.09	3.00	2.87	2.73	2.57	2.49	2.41	2.33	2.23	2.14	2.03
30	7.56	5.39	4.51	4.02	3.70	3.47	3.30	3.17	3.07	2.98	2.84	2.70	2.55	2.47	2.39	2.30	2.21	2.11	2.01
40	7.31	5.18	4.31	3.83	3.51	3.29	3.12	2.99	2.89	2.80	2.66	2.52	2.37	2.29	2.20	2.11	2.02	1.92	1.80
60	7.08	4.98	4.13	3.65	3.34	3.12	2.95	2.82	2.72	2.63	2.50	2.35	2.20	2.12	2.03	1.94	1.84	1.73	1.60
120	6.85	4.79	3.95	3.48	3.17	2.96	2.79	2.66	2.56	2.47	2.34	2.19	2.03	1.95	1.86	1.76	1.66	1.53	1.38
∞	6.63	4.61	3.78	3.32	3.02	2.80	2.64	2.51	2.41	2.32	2.18	2.04	1.88	1.79	1.70	1.59	1.47	1.32	1.00

Source: Adapted with permission from *Biometrika Tables for Statisticians*, Vol. 1, 2nd ed., ed. E. S. Pearson and H. O. Hartley (Cambridge University Press, 1958).

ENDNOTES

CHAPTER 1

1. For more information about the relationship between market orientation and business performance, see Ahmet H. Kirca, Satish Jayachandran, and William O. Bearden, "Market Orientation: A Meta-Analytic Review and Assessment of Its Antecedents and Impact on Performance," *Journal of Marketing*, April 2005, pp. 24–41.

2. For more information on these examples, see Bruce Horovitz, "Marketers Take a Close Look at Your Daily Routines," *USA Today* (April 30, 2007); Jack Neff, "P&G Kisses Up to the Boss: Consumers," *Advertising Age* (May 2, 2005), downloaded via ProQuest, July 25, 2008; Patricia Sellers, "Birth of a Rib Joint," *Fortune* (April 29, 2002), Matthew Swibel, "Where Money Doesn't Talk," *Forbes* (May 24, 2004), Judy Schoenburg, Kimberlee Salmond, Paula Fleshman, "Change It Up! What Girls Say About Redefining Leadership," GirlScouts.org; Brian O'Keefe, "Meet Your New Neighborhood Grocer," *Fortune* (May 13, 2002).

3. Downloaded from the American Marketing Association Web site, http://www.marketingpower.com, July 24, 2008.

4. Downloaded from the McDonald's U.K. Corporate Web site, http://www.mcdonalds.co.uk/?f=y, July 24, 2008; "How McDonald's Conquered the UK," *Marketing*, downloaded from http://www.brandrepublic.com/, July 24, 2008.

5. Lawrence C. Lockley, "History and Development of Marketing Research," Section 1, p. 4, in Robert Ferber, ed., *Handbook of Marketing Research*, Copyright © 1974 by McGraw-Hill, 1974. Used with permission of McGraw-Hill Book Company.

6. "Keio University and Dentsu Announce the Commencement of Second Life Joint Research" (July 31, 2007), http://www.keio.ac.jp/.

7. Downloaded from the McCann-Erickson WorldGroup Web site, http://www.mccann.com, July 2, 2002.

8. Jack Honomichl, "Strong Progress," *Marketing News*, August 2008, p. H3.

9. Jack Honomichl, "Acquisitions Up, Growth Rate Varies," *Marketing News*, August 2008, p. H3.

10. "Economists and Market and Survey Researchers," *Occupational Outlook Handbook*, 2002–2003 edition (Washington, D.C.: Bureau of Labor Statistics), pp. 239–241, downloaded from http://www.bls.gov/oco/pdf/ocos013.pdf, July 29, 2008.

CHAPTER 2

1. Robert J. Williams, "Marketing Intelligence Systems: A DEW Line for Marketing Men," *Business Management*, January 1966, p. 32.

2. Peter D. Bennett, ed., *Dictionary of Marketing Terms*, 2nd ed. (Chicago: American Marketing Association, 1995), p. 167. American Marketing Association, downloaded from www.marketingpower.com, August 2, 2008.

3. Ibid., p. 77.

4. Eldon Y. Li, Raymond McLeod, Jr., and John C. Rogers, "Marketing Information Systems in *Fortune* 500 Companies: A Longitudinal Analysis of 1980, 1990, and 2000," *Information & Management* 38, 2001, pp. 307–322.

5. Evan Schuman, "At Wal-Mart, World's Largest Retail Data Warehouse Gets Even Larger," October 13, 2004, downloaded from http://www.eweek.com, August 2, 2008; downloaded from http://walmartstores/FactsNews/, August 2, 2008; Jeremy Kahn, "Wal-Mart Goes Shopping in Europe," *Fortune*, June 7, 1999, pp. 105–106.

6. "Protecting Customers' Personal Information: The Safeguards Rule," downloaded from http://www.ftc.gov/bcp/edu/microsites/idtheft/business/safeguards.html, July 31, 2008.

7. James Studnicki, Frank V. Murphy, Donna Malvey, Robert A. Costello, Stephen L. Luther, and Dennis C. Werner, "Toward a Population Health Delivery System: First Steps in Performance Measurement," *Health Care Management Review*, Winter 2002, pp. 76–95.

8. For more information, see Berend Wierenga and Gerrit H. Van Bruggen, "Developing a Customized Decision-Support System for Brand Managers," *Interfaces*, May–June 2001, pp. S128–S145; S. Kanungo, S. Sharma, and P. K. Jain, "Evaluation of a Decision Support System for Credit Management Decisions," *Decision Support Systems* 30, 2001, pp. 419–436; R. Jeffrey Thieme, Michael Song, and Roger J. Calantone, "Artificial Neural Network Decision Support Systems for New Product Development Project Selection," *Journal of Marketing Research*, November 2000, pp. 499–507; and Jehoshua Eliashberg, Jedid-Jah Jonker, Mohanbir S. Sawhney, and Berend Wierenga, "MOVIEMOD: An Implementable Decision-Support System for Prerelease Market Evaluation of Motion Pictures," *Marketing Science*, Summer 2000, pp. 226–243.

9. For a general discussion of the history of expert systems, see David Brown, "'Intelligent' Systems?" *Information World Review*, November 2001, downloaded via ProQuest Direct, August 2, 2008.

10. *Next Generation of Data-Mining Applications*, ed. Mehmed M. Kantardzic and Jozef Zurada (Hoboken, N.J.: 2005 John Wiley & Sons, Inc.), p. 1.

11. Miriam Wasserman, "Regional Review: Mining Data," Federal Reserve Bank of Boston, Quarter 3, 2000, downloaded from Federal Reserve Bank of Boston Web site, http://www.bos.frb.org, July 31, 2008.

12. Laurie Hays "Using Computers to Decide Who Might Buy a Gas Grill," *The Wall Street Journal*, August 16, 1994, pp. B1 and B6.

13. Lauren Gibbons Paul, "Why Three Heads Are Better Than One (How to Create a Know-it-all

Company)," *CIO Magazine*, December 1, 2003, downloaded from the CIO Web site, http://www.cio.com, July 31, 2008.

14. Megan Santosus "Underwriting Knowledge," June 12, 2007, downloaded from www.cio.com, August 2, 2008.

15. Paul, "Why Three Heads Are Better Than One."

CHAPTER 3

1. Much of the discussion in this section is based on Anne T. Lawrence and James Weber, *Business and Society: Stakeholders, Ethics, Public Policy*, 12th ed. (New York: McGraw-Hill Irwin, 2008), pp. 103–107.

CHAPTER 4

1. Frederick Allen, *Secret Formula* (New York: HarperColling Publishers, Inc., 1994).
2. Ibid. p. 401.
3. Jeff Ousborne, "The 25 Dumbest Business Decisions of All Time," *MBA Jungle* 1, May 2001, pp. 64–70.
4. Alex Taylor III, "Survival on Dealer's Row," *Fortune*, March 31, 2008, p. 24.
5. Kevin J. Clancy and Peter C. Krieg, "Surviving Death Wish Research," *Marketing Research: A Magazine of Management & Applications* 13, Winter 2001, p. 9.
6. William I. Zangwill, "When Customer Research Is a Lousy Idea," *The Wall Street Journal*, March 8, 1993, p. A12. See also Justin Martin, "Ignore Your Customer," *Fortune*, May 1, 1995, pp. 121–126.

CHAPTER 5

1. Claire Selltiz, Lawrence S. Wrightsman, and Stuart W. Cook, *Research Methods in Social Relations*, 3rd ed. (New York: Holt, Rinehart and Winston, 1976), pp. 90–91. See also Fred N. Kerlinger, *Foundations of Behavioral Research*, 4th ed. (New York: Holt, Rinehart and Winston, 1999). David A. deVaus, *Research Design in Social Research* (Thousand Oaks, Calif: Sage Publications, 2000).
2. Steven P. Galante, "More Firms Quiz Customers for Clues About Competition," *The Wall Street Journal*, March 3, 1986, p. 17. See also Thomas L'egare, "Acting on Customer Feedback," *Marketing Research: A Magazine of Management*

& *Applications* 8, Spring 1996, pp. 46–51.
3. Bob Deierlein, "A New Louisville Slugger," *Beverage World* 114, June 1995, pp. 116–117.
4. Noah Schachtman, "Web Enhances Market Research," *Advertising Age*, June 18, 2001, downloaded via Proquest, August 10, 2008.
5. Tom Greenbaum, "The Case Against Internet Focus Groups," *MRA Alert Newsletter*, April 2002, downloaded from http://www.groupsplus.com, August 10, 2008.
6. Daniel Gross, "Lies, Damn Lies, and Focus Groups," *Slate*, posted October 10, 2003, downloaded from http://slate.msn.com, August 10, 2008.
7. This quotation is credited to Dev Patnaik. See Philip Hodgson, "Focus Groups: Is Consumer Research Losing Its Focus?" *Userfocus*, June 1, 2004, downloaded from http://www.userfocus.co.uk, August 10, 2008.
8. Ko de Ruyter, "Focus versus Nominal Group Interviews: A Comparative Analysis," *Marketing Intelligence and Planning*, Vol. 14, No. 6, January 1996, pp. 44–50; downloaded via www.proquest.com, August 1, 2008.
9. "Online Extra: Targeting the Universal American Kid," *BusinessWeek online*, June 7, 2004, downloaded from http://www.businessweek.com, August 10, 2008.
10. Robert K. Yin, *Case Study Research: Design and Methods* (Thousand Oaks, Calif.: Sage Publications, 1994); Robert E. Stake, *The Art of Case Study Research* (Thousand Oaks, Calif.: Sage Publications, 1993).
11. Jennifer Chang Coupland, "Invisible Brands: An Ethnography of Households and the Brands in Their Kitchen Pantries," *Journal of Consumer Research*, June 2005, pp. 106–118, downloaded using the Business Source Elite database, August 10, 2008.
12. Kathleen Kerwin, "How to Market a Groundbreaking SUV," *BusinessWeek online*, October 18, 2004, downloaded from http://www.businessweek.com, August 10, 2008.
13. Teresa Fagulha, "The Once-Upon-A Time Test", in Richard Henry Dana, ed., *Handbook of Cross-Cultural and Multicultural*

Personality Assessment (Mahwah, N.J.: Lawrence Earlbaum Associates, 2000), pp. 515–536; Sidney J. Levy, "Interpreting Consumer Methodology: Structural Approach to Consumer Behavior Focuses on Story Telling," *Marketing Management* 2, 1994, pp. 4–14.

CHAPTER 6

1. Charles M. Brooks, Patrick J. Kaufmann, and Donald R. Lichtenstein, "Trip Chaining Behavior in Multi-Destination Shopping Trips: A Field Experiment and Laboratory Replication," *Journal of Retailing* 84, No. 1, 2008, pp. 29–38.
2. "Test and Learn," *Marketing Management*, May/June 2002, p. 22.
3. "McDonalds Rolls out Coffee Bar Buildout Concept at Select Restaurants in Southwest," *Financial Wire*, July 9, 2008, downloaded via ProQuest (www.proquest.com), July 11, 2008; Dana Flavelle, "Competitor Brouhaha Brewing, Starbucks Tests Buck-a-Cup Java," *Toronto Star*, January 24, 2008, downloaded via EBSCO Host (www.ebscohost.com), July 11, 2008.
4. Robert Walker, "Working with Marketing Research: A Message to Marketers," *Quirk's*, October 2001, downloaded from www.quirks.com, July 11, 2008; "Test Marketing: What's in Store," *Sales and Marketing Management* 128, March 15, 1982, pp. 57–85. See also Richard Gibson, "Pinning Down Costs of Product Introductions," *The Wall Street Journal*, November 26, 1990, p. B1.
5. Gabriele Stern, "GM Expands Its Experiment to Improve Cadillac's Distribution, Cut Inefficiency," *The Wall Street Journal*, February 8, 1995, p. A12.
6. Annetta Miller and Karen Springen, "Egg Rolls for Peoria," *Newsweek*, October 12, 1992, pp. 59–60.
7. Vanessa O'Connell, "Altria Drops New Filter Cigarettes in Strategic Setback," *The Wall Street Journal*, June 23, 2008, downloaded via ProQuest (www.proquest.com), July 11, 2008.
8. Natalie Zmuda and Emily Bryson York, "McD's Tries to Slake Consumer Thirst for Wider Choice of Drinks," *Advertising Age*, June 9, 2008, downloaded via EbscoHost

(www.ebscohost.com), July 11, 2008; "Rite Aid Caters to Spanish-Language Customers," *DSN Retailing Today*, March 28, 2005, downloaded via ProQuest, June 23, 2005; Ellen Florian, "100 Fastest-Growing Companies," *Fortune*, September 6, 2004, downloaded from http://www.fortune.com, June 23, 2005.

9. Don A. Wright, "The Perfect Place for a Test Market," *The Business Journal*, May 21, 2001, p. 12.

10. "GfK Group: Annual Report 2006," downloaded from http://www.gfk.com/imperia/md/content/gb_2006/gfk_ar_2006_complete.pdf, July 2, 2008.

11. Peter S. Fader, Bruce G. S. Hardie, Robert Stevens, and Jim Findley, "Forecasting New Product Sales in a Controlled Test Market Environment," downloaded from the Wharton College of Business's Marketing Web site, http://www.marketing.wharton.upenn.edu, June 23, 2005. See also the 10-K SEC filing by Information Resources, Inc., March 27, 2003, downloaded from http://sec.edgar-online.com, July 2, 2008.

12. "BASES Validations," August 2002, downloaded from www.bases.com, July 24, 2008.

13. Julie S. Wherry "Simulated Test Marketing: Its Evolution and Current State in the Industry," June 2006, MBA Thesis, MIT Sloan School of Management, downloaded from http://dspace.mit.edu/bitstream/1721.1/37225/1/85813336.pdf, July 23, 2008.; Jim Miller and Sheila Lundy, "Test Marketing Plugs into the Internet," *Consumer Insight*, Spring 2002, pp. 20–23.

CHAPTER 7

1. Phaedra Hise, "Grandma Got Run Over by Bad Research," *Inc.*, January 1998, downloaded September 13, 2008.

2. "You May Not Care but 'Nappie' La-joie Batted .422 in 1901," *The Wall Street Journal*, September 13, 1974, p. 1.

3. David Goetzl, "Second Magazine Study Touts Value of DTC Drug Ads," *Advertising Age*, June 28, 1999, p. 22.

4. Wally Wood, "Targeting: It's in the Cards," *Marketing & Media Decisions*, September 1988, pp. 121–122.

5. The figure and surrounding discussion are adapted from David W. Stewart and Michael A. Kamins, *Secondary Research: Information Sources and Methods*, 2nd ed. (Thousand Oaks, Calif.: Sage Publications, 1993).

6. Enid Burns, "Top 10 U.S. Search Providers, September 2007," October 26, 2007, downloaded from searchenginewatch.com, September 13, 2008.

CHAPTER 8

1. "GIS for Business: Chase Manhattan Bank," downloaded from http://www.gis.com, June 24, 2002.

2. Downloaded from the NPD Food-world Web site, http://npdfoodworld.com, July 5, 2005.

3. Downloaded from the NPD Group Web site, http://www.npd.com, October 6, 2008.

4. See "Convenience Store Measurement at the Local Level," downloaded from the Nielsen Web site, http://us.nielsen.com, October 6, 2008.

5. In 2005, North American companies were to begin implementing systems that would allow compatibility with the 13-digit EAN symbols used throughout the rest of the world. For more information, see http://www.officialeancode.com/faq.html, downloaded December 20, 2008.

6. "BSkyB Hangs Marketing Hat on Interactive Ads," *Satellite News*, November 1, 2004, p. 1, downloaded via ProQuest, October 6, 2008.

7. "Intended User Survey," downloaded from the Nielsen Web site, http://us.nielsen.com, December 20, 2008; Ken Greenberg, "Using Panels to Understand the Consumer," *Consumer Insight*, Spring 2002, pp. 16–18, 28, downloaded from the Nielsen Web site, http://www.acnielsen.com, June 12, 2002; *Nielsen Household Panel* (Northbrook, Ill.: A. C. Nielsen Company, undated).

8. Information downloaded from the Arbitron Web site, http://www.arbitron.com, October 6, 2008.

9. Information downloaded from the NOP World Web site, http://www.nopworld.com, July 8, 2005. See also *Starch Readership Report: Scope, Method, and Use* (Mamaroneck, N.Y.: Starch INRA Hooper, undated).

10. Information downloaded in part from the Experian Simmons Web site, http://www.smrb.com, October 6, 2008.

11. "About MRI," downloaded from the company's Web site, http://www.mediamark.com, December 20, 2008.

CHAPTER 9

1. "Frito-Lay Profiles Salty Snack Consumers," *Supermarket News*, March 18, 1996, p. 39.

2. For a general discussion of the role of attitude in consumer behavior, see J. Paul Peter and Jerry C. Olson, *Consumer Behavior & Marketing Strategy*, 7th ed. (Burr Ridge, Ill.: Irwin/McGraw-Hill, 2004).

3. Tonita Perea Monsuwe, Benedict G. C. Dellaert, and Ko de Ruyter, "What Drives Consumers to Shop Online? A Literature Review," *International Journal of Service Industry Management*, Issue 1, 2004, downloaded via ProQuest, October 8, 2008.

4. Albert C. Bemmaor, "Predicting Behavior from Intention-to-Buy Measures: The Parametric Case," *Journal of Marketing Research* 32, May 1995, pp. 176–191; William J. Infosino, "Forecasting New Product Sales from Likelihood of Purchase Ratings," *Marketing Science* 5, Fall 1986, p. 375.

CHAPTER 10

1. Justus J. Randolph, Marjo Virnes, Ilkka Jormanainen, and Pasi J. Eronen, "The Effects of a Computer-Assisted Interview Tool on Data Quality," *Educational Technology & Society*, Vol. 9, No. 3, 2006, pp. 195–205.

2. David H. Wilson, Gary J. Starr, Anne W. Taylor, and Eleonora Dal Grande, "Random Digit Dialing and Electronic White Pages Samples Compared," *Australian and New Zealand Journal of Public Health* 23, December 1999, pp. 627–633.

3. Michael W. Link and Robert W. Oldendick, "Call Screening: Is It Really a Problem for Survey Research?" *Public Opinion Quarterly* 63, Winter 1999, pp. 577–589.

4. Rob Farbman, "Edison Media Research: Has the Do Not Call Registry Turned out to Be a Survey Researcher's Best Friend?" July 1,

2005, downloaded from the Edison Media Research Web site, http://www.edisonresearch.com, October 28, 2008.

CHAPTER 11

1. Paco Underhill, *Why We Buy: The Science of Shopping* (New York: Touchstone, 2000), p. 18.
2. Bob Becker, "Take Direct Route When Data-Gathering," *Marketing News* 33, September 27, 1999, pp. 29 and 31.
3. Jeffrey Kluger, "Oh, Rubbish— A Study of Garbage in Tucson, Arizona Is Used to Collect Dental Hygiene Statistics," *Discover*, August 1994, downloaded from BNET Web site at http://findarticles.com, December 20, 2008.
4. Tony Case, "Getting Personal," *Brandweek* 41, March 6, 2000, pp. M52–M54.
5. Krispy Kreme example (dated December 2002), downloaded from the Williams Inference Center Web site, http://www.williamsinference.com, July 21, 2005; Barbara Whitaker, "Yes, There Is a Job That Pays You to Shop," *The New York Times*, March 13, 2005, downloaded via ProQuest, November 17, 2008.
6. "Undercover Shoppers Find It Increasingly Difficult for Children to Buy M-Rated Games," May 8, 2008, downloaded from http://www.ftc.gov/opa/2008/05/secretshop.shtm, August 20, 2008.
7. Information downloaded from the VirTra Systems Web site, http://www.virtrasystems.com, July 25, 2005; Betsy Stewart, "Multimedia Market Research," *Marketing Research* 11, Fall 1999, pp. 14–18; Glen L. Urban et al., "Information Acceleration: Validation and Lessons from the Field," *Journal of Marketing Research* 34, February 1997, pp. 143–153; Fareena Sultan and Gloria Barczak, "Turning Marketing Research High-Tech," *Marketing Management* 8, Winter 1999, pp. 25–29.
8. Nicholas Varchaver, "Scanning the Globe," *Fortune*, May 31, 2004, pp. 144–156.
9. Xavier Dreze and Francois-Xavier Hussherr, "Internet Advertising: Is Anybody Watching?" *Journal of Interactive Marketing*, Autumn 2003, downloaded from ABI/INFORM Global, June 30, 2005.

CHAPTER 12

1. Peter D. Bennett, ed., *Dictionary of Marketing Terms*, 2nd ed. (Chicago: American Marketing Association, 1995), p. 173.
2. Our classification follows that of Stanley S. Stevens, "Mathematics, Measurement and Psychophysics," in Stanley S. Stevens, ed., *Handbook of Experimental Psychology* (New York: John Wiley, 1951), the most accepted classification in the social sciences.
3. Elia Kacapyr, "Money Isn't Everything," *American Demographics* 18, July 1996, pp. 10–11; Elia Kacapyr, "The Well-Being Index," *American Demographics* 18, February 1996, pp. 32–35, 43.
4. Tom J. Brown, John C. Mowen, D. Todd Donavan, and Jane W. Licata, "The Customer Orientation of Service Workers: Personality Trait Effects on Self- and Supervisor Performance Ratings," *Journal of Marketing Research* 39, February 2002, pp. 110–119.
5. Eunkyu Lee, Michael Y. Hu, and Rex S. Toh, "Are Consumer Survey Results Distorted? Systematic Impact of Behavioral Frequency and Duration on Survey Response Errors," *Journal of Marketing Research* 37, February 2000, pp. 125–133.
6. See Gilbert A. Churchill, Jr., "A Paradigm for Developing Better Measures of Marketing Constructs," *Journal of Marketing Research* 16, February 1979, pp. 64–73, for a procedure that can be used to construct scales having construct validity. See J. Paul Peter, "Construct Validity: A Review of Basic Issues and Marketing Practices," *Journal of Marketing Research* 18, May 1981, pp. 133–145, for an in-depth discussion of the notion of construct validity. See also Robert DeVellis, *Scale Development: Theory and Applications* (Thousand Oaks, Calif.: Sage Publications, 1991).

CHAPTER 13

1. The scale was first proposed by Rensis Likert, "A Technique for the Measurement of Attitudes," *Archives of Psychology* 140, 1932.
2. Charles E. Osgood, George J. Suci, and Percy H. Tannenbaum, *The Measurement of Meaning* (Champaign: University of Illinois Press, 1957).
3. Joel Herche and Brian Engelland, "Reversed-Polarity Items and Scale

Unidimensionality," *Journal of the Academy of Marketing Science* 24, Fall 1996, pp. 366–374.
4. Gilbert A. Churchill, Jr. and J. Paul Peter, "Research Design Effects on the Reliability of Rating Scales: A Meta-Analysis," *Journal of Marketing Research* 21, November 1984, pp. 360–375.
5. Irvine Clarke III, "Global Marketing Research: Is Extreme Response Style Influencing Your Results?" *Journal of International Consumer Marketing* 12, 4, 2000, pp. 91–110; Churchill and Peter, "Research Design Effects on the Reliability of Rating Scales."
6. Jon A. Krosnick et al., "The Impact of 'No Opinion' Response Options on Data Quality: Nonattitude Reduction or an Invitation to Satisfice?" *Public Opinion Quarterly* 66, Fall 2002, pp. 371–403, downloaded via ProQuest, July 15, 2004.
7. National Public Radio, "All Things Considered," September 7, 1999, summary and audio downloaded from the NPR Web site, http://www.npr.org, September 9, 1999; National Public Radio, "Americans Willing to Pay for Improving Schools," downloaded from the NPR Web site, http://www.npr.org, September 9, 1999; "NPR/Kaiser/Kennedy School Education Survey," downloaded from the NPR Web site, http://www.npr.org, September 9, 1999.
8. See Tom J. Brown, "Using Norms to Improve the Interpretation of Service Quality Measures," *Journal of Services Marketing* 11, 1, 1997, pp. 66–80.
9. Customer satisfaction scores downloaded from The American Customer Satisfaction Index at http://www.theacsi.org/ as listed as "Scores by Company" and "Scores by Industry" on December 2, 2008.

CHAPTER 14

1. This procedure is adapted from one suggested by Arthur Kornhauser and Paul B. Sheatsley, "Questionnaire Construction and Interview Procedure," in Claire Selltiz, Lawrence S. Wrightsman, and Stuart W. Cook, *Research Methods in Social Relations*, 3rd ed. (New York: Holt, Rinehart and Winston, 1976), pp. 541–573.
2. Chris Grecco and Hal King, "Of Browsers and Plug-Ins: Researching

Web Surfers' Technological Capabilities," *Quirk's Marketing Research Review*, July 1999, pp. 58–62.

3. These questions were suggested by Kornhauser and Sheatsley, "Questionnaire Construction and Interview Procedure." See also Norman Bradburn, Seymour Sudman, and Brian Wansink, *Asking Questions*, rev. ed. (San Francisco: Jossey-Bass, 2004).

4. Sam Gill, "How Do You Stand on Sin?" *Tide* 21, March 14, 1947, p. 72.

5. Bradburn, Sudman, and Wansink, *Asking Questions*, p. 66.

6. Ibid.

7. Lee Valeriano Lourdes, "Marketing: Western Firms Poll Eastern Europeans to Discern Tastes of Nascent Consumers," *The Wall Street Journal*, April 27, 1992, p. B1.

8. Jeffrey Pope, *How Cultural Differences Affect Multi-Country Research* (Minneapolis, Minn.: GfK Custom Research Inc., 1991).

9. E. Noelle-Neumann, "Wanted: Rules for Wording Structural Questionnaires," *Public Opinion Quarterly* 34, Summer 1970, p. 200; Philip Gendall and Janet Hoek, "A Question of Wording," *Marketing Bulletin* 1, May 1990, pp. 25–36.

10. Linda Kirby, "Bloopers," *Newspaper Research Council*, January/February 1989, p. 1.

CHAPTER 15

1. Joseph R. Hochstim, "Practical Uses of Sampling Surveys in the Field of Labor Relations," *Proceedings of the Conference on Business Application of Statistical Sampling Methods* (Monticello, Ill.: The Bureau of Business Management, University of Illinois, 1950), pp. 181–182.

2. Jack Neff, "P&G Enlists 13-Year-Olds in Summer Intern Jobs," *Advertising Age*, June 28, 1999, p. 20.

CHAPTER 16

1. For a more thorough discussion of the estimation of sample size for different types of samples and characteristics other than the mean and proportion, see Paul S. Levy and Stanley Lemeshow, *Sampling of Populations: Methods and Applications*, 4th ed. (New York: John Wiley, 2008); Morris H. Hansen, William

N. Hurwitz, and William G. Madow, *Sample Survey Methods and Theory*, Vol. I, *Methods and Applications* (New York: John Wiley, 1993); and Leslie Kish, *Survey Sampling* (New York: John Wiley, 1995).

2. "Number of 'Cyberchondriacs'—Adults Going Online for Health Information—Has Plateaued or Declined," July 29, 2008, downloaded from the Harris Interactive Web site, http://www.harrisinteractive.com, August 26, 2008.

3. Seymour Sudman, *Applied Sampling* (San Francisco: Academic Press, 1976), p. 30. See also Patrick Dattalo, *Determining Sample Size: Balancing Power, Precision, and Practicality* (New York: Oxford University Press, 2008).

CHAPTER 17

1. W. H. Williams, "How Bad Can 'Good' Data Really Be?" *The American Statistician* 32, May 1978, p. 61. See also Judith T. Lessler and William D. Kalsbeek, *Nonsampling Errors in Surveys* (New York: John Wiley, 1992).

2. Leslie Kish, *Survey Sampling* (New York: John Wiley, 1995). Chapter 13, "Biases and Nonsampling Errors," is particularly recommended for discussion of the biases arising from nonobservation.

3. W. Edwards Deming, "On a Probability Mechanism to Attain an Economic Balance between the Resultant Error of Response and the Bias of Nonresponse," *Journal of the American Statistical Association* 48, December 1953, pp. 766–767. See also Benjamin Lipstein, "In Defense of Small Samples," *Journal of Advertising Research* 15, February 1975, pp. 33–40; William C. Dunkelburg and George S. Day, "Nonresponse Bias and Callbacks in Sample Surveys," *Journal of Marketing Research* 10, May 1973, pp. 160–168; Lorna Opatow, "Some Thoughts about How Interview Attempts Affect Survey Results," *Journal of Advertising Research* 31, February/March 1991, pp. RC6–RC9.

4. Ronald M. Weiers, *Marketing Research*, 2nd ed. (Englewood Cliffs, N.J.: Prentice Hall, 1988), pp. 213–217.

5. Beth Clarkson, "Research and the Internet: A Winning Combination,"

Quirk's Marketing Research Review, July 1999, pp. 46, 48–51.

6. Peter H. Reingen and Jerome B. Kernan, "Compliance with an Interview Request: A Foot-in-the-Door, Self-Perception Interpretation," *Journal of Marketing Research* 14, 1977, pp. 365–369.

7. Frances J. Yammarino, Steven J. Skinner, and Terry L. Childers, "Understanding Mail Survey Response Behavior: A Meta-Analysis," *Public Opinion Quarterly* 55, Winter 1991, pp. 613–639.

CHAPTER 18

1. Lourdes Lee Valeriano, "Marketing: Western Firms Poll Eastern Europeans to Discern Tastes of Nascent Consumers," *The Wall Street Journal*, April 27, 1992, p. B1.

2. Art Shulman, "War Stories: True-Life Tales in Marketing Research," *Quirk's Marketing Research Review*, December 1998, p. 16.

3. "The Gallup Panel," downloaded from www.gallup.com, June 27, 2008.

CHAPTER 19

1. See the classic book by Hans Zeisel, *Say It with Figures*, 5th ed. (New York: Harper and Row, 1968), pp. 16–17, for conditions that would support reporting percentages with decimal-place accuracy.

2. In Chapter 16, we referred to this range as the precision range. After data have been collected and analyzed, it is more appropriate to refer to this range as a confidence interval, because the range itself, which represents the margin of sampling error, is established for a given level of confidence. If we change the level of confidence, the confidence interval itself will also change.

3. See the classic book by Darrell Huff, *How to Lie with Statistics* (New York: Norton, 1954).

4. Robert J. Lavidge, "How to Keep Well-Intentioned Research from Misleading New-Product Planners," *Marketing News* 18, January 6, 1984, p. 8.

5. The binomial distribution tends toward the normal distribution for a fixed π as sample size increases. The tendency is most rapid when $\pi = 0.5$. With sufficiently large samples, normal probabilities may

be used to approximate binomial probabilities with π's in this range. As π departs from 0.5 in either direction, the normal approximation becomes less adequate, although it is generally held that the normal approximation may be used safely if the smaller of $n\pi$ or $n(1 - \pi)$ is 10 or more. If this condition is not satisfied, binomial probabilities can either be calculated directly or found in tables that are readily available. In the example, $n\pi = 625(0.2) = 125$, and $n(1 - \pi) = 500$, and thus there is little question about the adequacy of the normal approximation to binomial probabilities.

6. For an excellent discussion of some of the most common misinterpretations of classical significance tests and some recommendations on how to surmount the problems, see Alan G. Sawyer and J. Paul Peter, "The Significance of Statistical Significance Tests in Marketing Research," *Journal of Marketing Research* 20, May 1983, pp. 122–133. See also Jacob Cohen, "Things I Have Learned (So Far)," *American Psychologist* 45, December 1990, pp. 1304–1312; Jacob Cohen, "The

Earth Is Round (π,.05)," *American Psychologist* 49, December 1994, pp. 997–1003.

7. If we know the total number of packages sold and the number of packages sold for two of the three categories, the number of packages sold in the third category is fixed and cannot vary independently.

8. See Tom J. Brown, Thomas E. Barry, Peter A. Dacin, and Richard F. Gunst, "Spreading the Word: Investigating Antecedents of Consumers' Positive Word-of-Mouth Intentions and Behaviors in a Retailing Context," *Journal of the Academy of Marketing Science* 33, Spring 2005, pp. 123–138.

9. The appropriate test statistics and how they are calculated also differ (1) if population variance is known or unknown and (2) if the distribution of the variable in the population is normal (or at least symmetric) or asymmetric. We consider only the common case in which population variance is unknown and the distribution can be assumed to be symmetric.

10. For more on the net promoter score, see Frederick F. Reichheld,

"The One Number You Need to Grow," *Harvard Business Review* 81, December 2003, pp. 46–54. For a different perspective, see Timothy L. Keiningham, Bruce Cooil, Tor Wallin Andreassen, and Lerzan Aksoy, "A Longitudinal Examination of Net Promoter and Firm Revenue Growth," *Journal of Marketing* 71, July 2007, pp. 39–51; and Gina Pingitore, Neil A. Morgan, Lopo L. Rego, Adriana Gigliotti, and Jay Meyers, "The Single-Question Trap," *Marketing Research* 19, Summer 2007, pp. 9–13.

CHAPTER 21

1. William J. Gallagher, *Report Writing for Management* (Reading, Mass.: Addison-Wesley, 1969), p. 78. Much of this introductory section is also taken from this excellent book. See also Pnenna Sageev, *Helping Researchers Write, So Managers Can Understand* (Columbus, Ohio: Batelle Press, 1995).

2. Taken from William Zinsser, *On Writing Well*, 6th ed. (New York: Harper and Row, 1998), pp. 7–8, a modern classic for writers that is as helpful as it is fun to read.

GLOSSARY

A

Accuracy The degree to which the reasoning in the report is logical and the information correct.

Advocacy research Research conducted to support a position rather than to find the truth about an issue.

Alternative hypothesis The hypothesis that a proposed result is true for the population.

Analysis of variance (ANOVA) A statistical technique used with a continuous dependent variable and one or more categorical independent variables.

Area sample A form of cluster sampling in which areas (for example, census tracts, blocks) serve as the primary sampling units. The population is divided into mutually exclusive and exhaustive areas using maps, and a random sample of areas is selected.

Assumed consequences A problem that occurs when a question is not framed so as to clearly state the consequences, and thus it generates different responses from individuals who assume different consequences.

Attitude An individual's overall evaluation of something.

Awareness/knowledge Insight into, or understanding of facts about, some object or phenomenon.

B

Banner A series of cross tabulations between an outcome, or dependent variable, and several (sometimes many) explanatory variables in a single table.

Bar chart A chart in which the relative lengths of the bars show relative amounts of variables or objects.

Behavior What subjects have done or are doing.

Benchmarking Using organizations that excel at some function as sources of ideas for improvement.

Blunder An error that arises during editing, coding, or data entry.

Branching question A technique used to direct respondents to different places in a questionnaire, based on their response to the question at hand.

C

Case analysis Intensive study of selected examples of the phenomenon of interest.

Categorical measures A commonly used expression for nominal and ordinal measures.

Causal research Research design in which the major emphasis is on determining cause-and-effect relationships.

Census A type of sampling plan in which data are collected from or about each member of a population.

Central-office edit Thorough and exacting scrutiny and correction of completed data collection forms, including a decision about what to do with the data.

Chi-square goodness-of-fit test A statistical test to determine whether some observed pattern of frequencies corresponds to an expected pattern.

Clarity The degree to which the phrasing in the report is precise.

Cluster sample A probability sampling plan in which (1) the parent population is divided into mutually exclusive and exhaustive subsets and (2) a random sample of one or more subsets (clusters) is selected.

Codebook A book that contains explicit directions about how data from data collection forms are to be coded in the data file.

Coding The technical procedure by which raw data are transformed into symbols; it involves specifying the alternative categories or classes into which the responses are to be placed and assigning code numbers to the classes.

Coefficient of determination A measure representing the relative proportion of the total variation in the dependent variable that can be explained or accounted for by the fitted regression equation.

Coefficient of multiple determination In multiple regression analysis, the proportion of variation in the dependent variable that is explained or accounted for by the covariation in the independent variables.

Communication A method of data collection involving questioning of respondents to secure the desired information, using a data collection instrument called a questionnaire.

Comparative-ratings scale A scale requiring subjects to make their ratings as a series of relative judgments or comparisons rather than as independent assessments.

Completeness The degree to which the report provides all the information readers need in language they understand.

Composite measure A measure designed to provide a comprehensive assessment of an object or phenomenon, with items to assess all relevant aspects or dimensions.

Computer-assisted interviewing (CAI) Using computers to manage the sequence of questions and to record the answers electronically through the use of a keyboard.

Conceptual definition A definition in which a given construct is defined in terms of other constructs in the set, sometimes in the form of an equation that expresses the relationship among them.

Conciseness The degree to which the writing in the report is crisp and direct.

Confidence The degree to which one can feel confident that an estimate approximates the true value.

Confidence interval A projection of the range within which a population parameter will lie at a given level of confidence based on a statistic obtained from a probabilistic sample.

Constant-sum method A comparative-ratings scale in which an individual divides some given sum among two or more attributes on a basis such as importance or favorability.

Construct validity Assessment of how well the instrument captures the construct, concept, or trait it is supposed to be measuring.

Content validity The adequacy with which the important aspects of the characteristic are captured by the measure; it is sometimes called *face validity*.

Continuous measures A commonly used expression for interval and ratio measures.

Continuous panel A fixed sample of respondents who are measured repeatedly over time with respect to the same variables.

Contrived setting Subjects are observed in an environment that has been specially designed for recording their behavior.

Controlled test market An entire test program conducted by an outside service in a market in which it can guarantee distribution.

Convenience sample A nonprobability sample in which population elements are included in the sample because they were readily available.

Cramer's *V* A statistic used to measure the strength of relationship between categorical variables.

Cross tabulation A multivariate technique used for studying the relationship between two or more categorical variables. The technique considers the joint distribution of sample elements across variables.

Cross-sectional study Investigation involving a sample of elements selected from the population of interest that are measured at a single point in time.

Cumulative percent breakdown A technique for converting a continuous measure into a categorical measure. The categories are formed based on the cumulative percentages obtained in a frequency analysis.

D

Data mining The use of powerful analytic technologies to quickly and thoroughly explore mountains of data to obtain useful information.

Data-driven decision support system The part of a decision support system that includes the processes used to capture and the methods used to store data coming from a number of external and internal sources. It is the creation of a database.

Debriefing The process of providing appropriate information to respondents after data have been collected using disguise.

Decision problem The problem facing the decision maker for which the research is intended to provide answers.

Decision support system (DSS) A coordinated collection of data, systems, tools, and techniques with supporting software and hardware, by which an organization gathers and interprets relevant information from business and the environment and turns it into a basis for marketing decisions.

Depth interview Interviews with people knowledgeable about the general subject being investigated.

Descriptive research Research design in which the major emphasis is on determining the frequency with which something occurs or the extent to which two variables covary.

Descriptive statistics Statistics that describe the distribution of responses on a variable. The most commonly used descriptive statistics are the mean and standard deviation.

Dialog-driven decision support system The part of a decision support system that permits users to explore the databases by employing the system models to produce reports that satisfy their particular information needs. It is the user interface of the decision support system, which is also called a language system.

Discontinuous panel A fixed sample of respondents who are measured repeatedly over time but on variables that change from measurement to measurement.

Discovery-oriented decision problem A decision problem that typically seeks to answer "what" or "why" questions about a problem/ opportunity. The focus is generally on generating useful information.

Disguise The amount of knowledge about the purpose or sponsor of a study communicated to the respondent. An undisguised questionnaire, for example, is one in which the purpose of the research is obvious.

Disguised observation The subjects are not aware that they are being observed.

Double-barreled question A question that calls for two responses and creates confusion for the respondent.

Double-entry Data entry procedure in which data are entered separately by two people in two data files and the data files are compared for discrepancies.

Dummy table A table (or figure) with no entries used to show how the results of the analysis will be presented.

E

Electrical or mechanical observation An electrical or mechanical device observes a phenomenon and records the events that take place.

Ethics Moral principles and values that govern the way an individual or a group conducts its activities.

Ethnography The detailed observation of consumers during their ordinary daily lives using direct observations, interviews, and video and audio recordings.

Experiment Scientific investigation in which an investigator manipulates and controls one or more independent variables and observes the degree to which the dependent variables change.

Expert system A computer-based, artificial intelligence system that attempts to model how experts in the area process information to solve the problem at hand.

Exploratory research Research design in which the major emphasis is on gaining ideas and insights; it is particularly helpful in breaking broad, vague problem statements into smaller, more precise subproblem statements.

External data Data that originate outside the organization for which the research is being done.

External validity The degree to which the results of an experiment can be generalized, or extended, to other situations.

Eye camera A device used by researchers to study a subject's eye movements while he or she is reading advertising copy.

F

Field edit A preliminary edit, typically conducted by a field supervisor, which is designed to detect the most glaring omissions and inaccuracies in a completed data collection instrument.

Field experiment Research study in a realistic situation in which one or more independent variables are manipulated by the experimenter under as carefully controlled conditions as the situation will permit.

Filter question A question used to determine if a respondent is likely to possess the knowledge being sought; also used to determine if an individual qualifies as a member of the defined population.

Fixed sample A sample for which size is determined in advance and needed information is collected from the designated elements.

Fixed-alternative questions Questions in which the responses are limited to stated alternatives.

Focus group An interview conducted among a small number of individuals simultaneously; the interview relies more on group discussion than on directed questions to generate data.

Frequency analysis A count of the number of cases that fall into each category when the categories are based on one variable.

Funnel approach An approach to question sequencing that gets its name from its shape, starting with broad questions and progressively narrowing down the scope.

G

Galvanometer A device used to measure the emotion induced by exposure to a particular stimulus by recording changes in the electrical resistance of the skin associated with the minute degree of sweating that accompanies emotional arousal; in marketing research, the stimulus is often specific advertising copy.

Geodemography The availability of demographic, consumer-behavior, and lifestyle data by arbitrary geographic boundaries that are typically quite small.

Global measure A measure designed to provide an overall assessment of an object or phenomenon, typically using one or two items.

Graphic-ratings scale A scale in which individuals indicate their ratings of an attribute typically by placing a check at the appropriate point on a line that runs from one extreme of the attribute to the other.

H

Halo effect A problem that arises in data collection when there is carryover from one judgment to another.

Histogram A form of bar chart on which the values of the variable are placed along the x-axis and the absolute frequency or relative frequency of occurrence of the values is indicated along the y-axis.

Human observation Individuals are trained to systematically observe a phenomenon and to record on the observational form the specific events that take place.

Hypotheses Unproven propositions about some phenomenon of interest.

Hypothesis A statement that specifies how two or more measurable variables are related.

Hypothetical construct A concept used in theoretical models to explain how things work. Hypothetical constructs include such things as attitudes, personality, and

intentions—things that cannot be seen but that are useful in theoretical explanations.

I

In-bound telephone surveys A method of data collection in which respondents place a telephone call at their convenience to a research firm and answer questions, typically by pressing buttons on the telephone.

Incidence The percent of a general population or group that qualifies for inclusion in the population.

Independent samples *t*-test A technique commonly used to determine whether two groups differ on some characteristic assessed on a continuous measure.

Intentions Anticipated or planned future behavior.

Internal data Data that originate within the organization for which the research is being done.

Internal validity The degree to which an outcome can be attributed to an experimental variable and not to other factors.

Internet-based questionnaire A questionnaire that relies on the Internet for recruitment and/or completion; two forms include e-mail surveys and questionnaires completed on the Web.

Interval scale Measurement in which the assigned numbers legitimately allow the comparison of the size of the differences among and between members.

Item nonresponse A source of nonsampling error that arises when a respondent agrees to an interview but refuses, or is unable, to answer specific questions.

Itemized-ratings scale A scale on which individuals must indicate their ratings of an attribute or object by selecting the response category that best describes their position on the attribute or object.

J

Judgment sample A nonprobability sample in which the sample elements are handpicked because they are expected to serve the research purpose.

Justice approach A method of ethical or moral reasoning that focuses on the degree to which benefits and costs are fairly distributed across individuals and groups. If the benefits and costs of a proposed action are fairly distributed, an action is considered to be ethical.

K

Knowledge management The systematic collection of employee knowledge about customers, products, and the marketplace.

L

Laboratory experiment Research investigation in which investigators create a situation with exact conditions in order to control some variables and manipulate others.

Leading question A question framed so as to give the respondent a clue as to how he or she should answer.

Line chart A two-dimensional chart constructed on graph paper with the x-axis representing one variable (typically time) and the y-axis representing another variable.

Literature search A search of statistics, trade journal articles, other articles, magazines, newspapers, and books for data or insight into the problem at hand.

Longitudinal study Investigation involving a fixed sample of elements that is measured repeatedly through time.

M

Mail questionnaire A questionnaire administered by mail to designated respondents with an accompanying cover letter. The respondents return the questionnaire by mail to the research organization.

Mall intercept A method of data collection in which interviewers in a shopping mall stop or interrupt a sample of those passing by to ask them if they would be willing to participate in a research study.

Market testing (test marketing) A controlled experiment done in a limited but carefully selected sector of the marketplace.

Marketing ethics The principles, values, and standards of conduct followed by marketers.

Marketing information system (MIS) A set of procedures and methods for the regular, planned collection, analysis, and presentation of information for use in making marketing decisions.

Marketing research The function that links the consumer to the marketer through information—information used to identify and define marketing problems; generate, refine, and evaluate marketing actions; monitor marketing performance; and improve understanding of marketing as a process.

Measurement Rules for assigning numbers to objects to represent quantities of attributes.

Median split A technique for converting a continuous measure into a categorical measure with two approximately equal-sized groups. The groups are formed by "splitting" the continuous measure at its median value.

Model-driven decision support system The part of a decision support system that includes all the routines that allow the user to manipulate the data so as to conduct the kind of analysis the individual desires. It is the collection of analytical tools to interpret the database.

Moderator The individual that meets with focus group participants and guides the session.

Moderator's guidebook An ordered list of the general (and specific) issues to be addressed during a focus group; the issues normally should move from general to specific.

Motive A need, a want, a drive, a wish, a desire, an impulse, or any inner state that energizes, activates, or moves and that directs or channels behavior toward goals.

Multichotomous question A fixed-alternative question in which respondents are asked to choose the alternative that most closely corresponds to their position on the subject.

Multicollinearity A condition said to be present in a multiple regression analysis when the independent variables are correlated among themselves.

Multiple regression A statistical technique used to derive an equation that relates a single continuous dependent variable to two or more independent variables.

N

Natural setting Subjects are observed in the environment where the behavior normally takes place.

Nominal group A group interview technique which initially limits respondent interaction to a minimum while attempting to maximize input from individual group members.

Nominal scale Measurement in which numbers are assigned to objects or classes of objects solely for the purpose of identification.

Noncoverage error Nonsampling error that arises because of a failure to include some units, or entire sections, of the defined target population in the sampling frame.

Nonprobability sample A sample that relies on personal judgment in the element selection process.

Nonresponse error Nonsampling error that represents a failure to obtain information from some elements of the population that were selected and designated for the sample.

Nonsampling error Error that arises in research that is not due to sampling; nonsampling error can occur because of errors in conception, logic, interpretation of questions and replies, statistics, arithmetic, analyzing, coding, or reporting.

Normative standard A comparative standard used to provide meaning to raw scale scores.

Not-at-homes Nonsampling error that arises when replies are not secured from some designated sampling units because the respondents are not at home when the interviewer calls.

Null hypothesis The hypothesis that a proposed result is not true for the population. Researchers typically

researcher, usually set at 0.05. Type I error is the probability of rejecting the null hypothesis when it is actually true for the population.

Simple random sample A probability sampling plan in which each unit included in the population has a known and equal chance of being selected for the sample.

Simple regression A statistical technique used to derive an equation that relates a single continuous dependent variable to a single independent variable.

Simulated test market (STM) A study in which consumer ratings are obtained along with likely or actual purchase data often obtained in a simulated store environment; the data are fed into computer models to produce sales and market share predictions.

Single-source data Data that allow researchers to link together purchase behavior, household characteristics, and advertising exposure at the household level.

Snake diagram A diagram that connects the average responses to a series of semantic-differential statements, thereby depicting the profile of the object or objects being evaluated.

Snowball sample A judgment sample that relies on the researcher's ability to locate an initial set of respondents with the desired characteristics.

Split-ballot technique A technique used to combat response bias in which one phrasing is used for a question in one-half of the questionnaires while an alternative phrasing is used in the other one-half of the questionnaires.

Standard test market A test market in which the company sells the product through its normal distribution channels.

Stapel scale A self-report technique for attitude measurement in which respondents are asked to indicate how accurately each of a number of statements describes the object of interest.

Statistic A characteristic or measure of a sample.

Storytelling A projective method of data collection relying on a picture

stimulus such as a cartoon, photograph, or drawing, about which the subject is asked to tell a story.

Strategy-oriented decision problem A decision problem that typically seeks to answer "how" questions about a problem/opportunity. The focus is generally on selecting alternative courses of action.

Stratified sample A probability sample in which (1) the population is divided into mutually exclusive and exhaustive subsets, and (2) a simple random sample of elements is chosen independently from each group or subset.

Stratum chart A set of line charts in which quantities are aggregated or a total is disaggregated so that the distance between two lines represents the amount of some variable.

Structure The degree of standardization used with the data collection instrument.

Structured observation The problem has been defined precisely enough so that the behaviors that will be observed can be specified beforehand, as can the categories that will be used to record and analyze the situation.

Summated-ratings scale A self-report technique for attitude measurement in which respondents indicate their degree of agreement or disagreement with each of a number of statements.

Systematic error Error in measurement that is also known as constant error since it affects the measurement in a constant way.

Systematic sample A probability sampling plan in which every kth element in the population is selected for the sample pool after a random start.

T

Telephone interview Telephone conversation between a representative of the research organization, the interviewer, and a respondent, or interviewee.

Telescoping error A type of error resulting from the fact that most people remember an event as having occurred more recently than it did.

Total sampling elements (TSE) The number of population elements that must be drawn from the population and included in the initial sample pool in order to end up with the desired sample size.

Two-box technique A technique for converting an interval-level rating scale into a categorical measure usually used for presentation purposes. The percentage of respondents choosing one of the top two positions on a rating scale is reported.

U

Undisguised observation The subjects are aware that they are being observed.

Unstated alternative An alternative answer that is not expressed in a question's options.

Unstructured observation The problem has not been specifically defined, so a great deal of flexibility is allowed the observers in terms of what they note and record.

Utility approach A method of ethical or moral reasoning that focuses on society and the net consequences that an action may have. If the net result of benefits minus costs is positive, the act is considered ethical; if the net result is negative, the act is considered unethical.

V

Validity The extent to which differences in scores on a measuring instrument reflect true differences among individuals, groups, or situations in the characteristic that it seeks to measure, or true differences in the same individual, group, or situation from one occasion to another, rather than systematic or random errors.

Voice-pitch analysis Analysis that examines changes in the relative frequency of the human voice that accompany emotional arousal.

W

Word association A projective method in which respondents are asked to respond to a list of words with the first word that comes to mind.

INDEX